P9-BJB-768

SONATA FOR JUKEBOX

Also by Geoffrey O'Brien

PROSE

Hardboiled America:
Lurid Paperbacks and the Masters of Noir

Dream Time: Chapters from the Sixties

The Phantom Empire

The Times Square Story

Bardic Deadlines: Reviewing Poetry, 1984–1995

The Browser's Ecstasy: A Meditation on Reading

Castaways of the Image Planet:
Movies, Show Business, Public Spectacle

POETRY

A Book of Maps

The Hudson Mystery

Floating City: Selected Poems, 1978–1995

A View of Buildings and Water

SONATA
FOR
JUKEBOX

Pop Music,

Memory,

and the

Imagined Life

GEOFFREY O'BRIEN

COUNTERPOINT

A MEMBER OF THE PERSEUS BOOKS GROUP

NEW YORK

Counterpoint books are available at special discounts for bulk
purchases in the United States by corporations, institutions, and
other organizations. For more information, please contact the Special
Markets Department at the Perseus Books Group, 11 Cambridge Center,
Cambridge, MA 02142, or call (617) 252-5298, (800) 255-1514
or e-mail special.markets@perseusbooks.com.

Designed by Brent Wilcox

Library of Congress Cataloging-in-Publication Data
O'Brien, Geoffrey, 1948–
    Sonata for jukebox : pop music, memory, and the imagined life /
by Geoffrey O'Brien.
        p.   cm.
    ISBN 1-58243-192-2 (alk. paper)
    1. Popular music—Psychological aspects.   2. Popular music—
Analysis, appreciation.   I. Title.
ML3470.O27   2004
781.64'0973—dc22

                                              2003019024

04 05 06 / 10 9 8 7 6 5 4 3 2 1

Expression has never been an inherent property of music. That is by no means the purpose of its existence. If, as is nearly always the case, music appears to express something, this is only an illusion and not a reality.

IGOR STRAVINSKY

HE PLANNED A GREAT BRIDGE . . . FOR HER IT WAS TWI-LIGHT BY A LITTLE LAKE . . . Even above the special pleasure of sharing music with others are the things that music does for you alone as it reaches into your private world of memories, ambitions, hopes. Sometimes it's loneliness made into a song by a cowboy under the stars . . . or primitive sadness that's worked its way into a dance tune . . . a love song centuries old, or one published yesterday . . . Whatever kind of music means most to you will mean even more when you hear it at its best—on a Stromberg-Carlson.

SOUND SYSTEM ADVERTISEMENT, *LIFE*, 1945

It's Make-Believe Ballroom time . . .
OLD RADIO THEME (SUNG TO THE
TUNE OF "JERSEY BOUNCE")

Music, that mysterious form of time
JORGE LUIS BORGES

CONTENTS

Introduction

THIS IS A BOOK WRITTEN IN THE PRESENCE OF MUSIC, AND ITS intent is to describe some aspects of how lives are lived in the presence—and the memory of the presence—of music. The soloist—a virtual jukebox containing the archive of twentieth-century pop music, or as much of it as might filter over a lifetime into the consciousness of a fairly curious listener—remains necessarily inaudible. It must be imagined, however, as pervading, influencing, and in turn responding to the activities of an accompanying string trio constituting the book proper and deploying those resources of language, memory, historical information, and sheer make-believe that the listener deploys in an attempt to make sense of what he hears. To make sense of it—or perhaps merely to make it his own, since to appropriate music (for purposes often far from musical) can at times be almost a matter of survival.

This is not a history of popular music, although fragments of that history find their way into its pages. It considers different ways of describing how one listener (this listener, for convenient example) hears, or imagines he hears, and how he connects that listening to the rest of life. I've avoided crowd scenes. The emphasis is more on solitary listening, or the listening among lovers or a pair of friends or a small family group, than on that ecstatic experience of group listening—whether rolling down the highway with the radio on or vibrating in a club's crowded darkness—in which music declares its powers most openly and overwhelmingly. But any occasion of listening is partly defined by the memory of other occasions and of the means by which those occasions were made possible. Since most of the music I talk about is prerecorded, this becomes in part a story about how our machines continue to change how we experience what we might nonetheless continue to think of as timeless.

To attempt to describe how music pervades and flavors a life feels a little like an invasion of privacy, even if the privacy is my own. Listening to music, which can be the very embodiment of public life (whether at Woodstock or marching down Fifth Avenue on the Fourth of July), is finally the most inward of acts—so inward that even language, even the language of thought, can come to seem intrusive. It is necessary to proceed by analogy, by fable, by parody; by memoir that takes the form of fiction or fiction that takes the form of memoir.

After all these procedures the unbreachable mysteriousness of music remains intact. The book can never be more than an interruption. Afterward, the listening begins again, to generate, in turn, other and completely different books.

EXPOSITION

1

The Return of Burt Bacharach

I T WAS THE END OF THE TWENTIETH CENTURY AND THIS WAS what a cultural resurrection looked like. Here's how it could be when the system was really working: the machinery oiled and the gears properly lined up, as a body of once-discarded material was inserted again and permitted to work its way—at first randomly (as a test) and then with increasing calculation—through the layers of the marketing universe, issuing ultimately as a collection of shrink-wrapped products ready to be catalogued and appraised in a range of magazines and television shows. The material could be anything at all, whatever served. When did they get this good at it? Was it while I was sleeping that the system achieved this almost seamless level of synchronization? The case in question happened to be that of the music of Burt Bacharach, songwriter, arranger, producer, and sometime performer. I was paying attention because it was a considerable chunk of my own memory that was being recycled. As they dug up old recordings, they were digging up parts of my experience that I hadn't realized were buried.

How could I have forgotten Burt Bacharach? Pretty much the way everyone else did. Bacharach had enjoyed a remarkable run of hit records throughout the 1960s but largely disappeared from view during the decades following a disastrous 1973 musical version of

Lost Horizon and the breakup of his long collaboration with the lyricist Hal David. In the truncated short-term memory of the music business, it was easy to forget the twelve years or so of unbroken success that preceded the Shangri-La debacle. In those heady years he had come to be viewed not only as a last bastion of the Tin Pan Alley tradition of the well-crafted song—hitting the Top 40 again and again with songs even Tony Bennett could love—but as an involuntary emblem of whatever notion of luxurious glamor that beleaguered epoch could cling to. When things turn out differently than expected, nothing is harder than to remember how they once seemed.

If serious discussions of his music—in the rather specialized precincts where they occurred—tended to revolve around the complexity of its meters or the novelty of its instrumentation, discussions of Bacharach himself in those days focused on things like his marriage (one of four) in 1965 to Angie Dickinson, his long professional association with Marlene Dietrich, the casual elegance of his clothes, the relaxed, almost bashful grace with which he appeared to enjoy the comfortable trappings of his life, and his movie star looks (Sammy Cahn called him "the only songwriter who doesn't look like a dentist"). The brilliance of his music seemed to bestow on him the rare fate of being able to savor his good fortune without the slightest twinge of guilt. He was simply the luckiest of guys.

Having achieved this apotheosis, he proceeded to fade slowly into a Southern Californian haze. Not that he ever stopped working, or altogether stopped having hits. He won an Oscar for the main title theme from the 1981 movie *Arthur*; he married the songwriter Carole Bayer Sager and collaborated with her extensively; with Sager and a number of others he wrote the 1985 "That's What Friends Are For," a song whose profits were donated to help fund AIDS research. These however were mere afterechoes of the stream of songs he wrote for Dionne Warwick and other singers during the period that generated eventual standards such as "Wives and Lovers," "Walk on By," "What the World Needs Now Is Love," "Alfie," and "I Say a Little Prayer": to cite only some of those most hackneyed through repetition.

Perhaps the worst enemy of Bacharach's reputation was the numbing effect of hearing his five or six most familiar songs trotted out on oldies stations or transmuted into background music for the waiting room at the clinic or the lull before the in-flight movie. After a decade or so of "Do You Know the Way to San Jose," its once-novel melody offered no more adventurous a prospect than a promenade on a treadmill. It became difficult to hear the orchestral textures and structural intricacies that had once made Bacharach's music seem an exploration of interesting and unknown territory. Far from being an emblem of what was most exciting about popular music in the 1960s, Bacharach was on his way to becoming a symbol of the sort of scientifically crafted, antiseptically perfect romantic balladry that ends up being sold as fodder for nostalgia to insomniacs—"this collection is not available in stores"—on late-night television.

Bacharach's reemergence became noticeable when younger musicians such as Elvis Costello, Eric Matthews, the Cranberries, Oasis, Yo La Tengo, Stereolab, and the Pizzicato Five began to pay tribute through cover versions, imitations, and allusions or gave interviews in which they made much of Bacharach's influence on their work. The revamping, or more precisely reversal, of Bacharach's reputation evolved further under the guidance of the eclectic experimental composer John Zorn—a man perfectly at home in a fusion of Ornette Coleman, Serge Gainsbourg, spaghetti western soundtracks, bop, klezmer, and random electronic noise—who oversaw performances of Bacharach's music (newly arranged or disarranged) at the Knitting Factory and elsewhere by a variety of downtown New York avant-gardists inspired by what Zorn described as "advanced harmonies and chord changes with unexpected turnarounds and modulations, unusual changing time signatures and rhythmic twists, often in uneven numbers of bars." This project culminated in the release (under the deliberately provocative rubric *Great Jewish Music*) of a double-CD set of Bacharach songs interpreted by such prophets of eclecticism as Marc Ribot, Dave Douglas, Erik Friedlander, Medeski, Martin, Wood, and Joey Baron (with a drums-only version of "Alfie").

While such approval bestowed hipness by association, a more mainstream recycling was achieved through the interpolation of

Bacharach's old songs into the soundtracks of movies such as *The First Wives Club, My Best Friend's Wedding,* and *Romy and Michele's High School Reunion.* Since movie soundtracks had by now evolved away from the symphonic elaboration associated with Miklos Rozsa or Alex North, soundtrack albums increasingly were simply compilations of pre-existing recordings. These served to introduce younger audiences to the hits of previous generations, a role once played by television variety shows of a sort that no longer exists.

The expanding Internet, in the meantime, revealed an international corps of Bacharach aficionados: Nils of Sweden, Roberto of Italy, Ian of Australia, and the fan who declared "I am Japanese Bacharachmania," tirelessly swapping factoids and lists of favorite songs. The revival had gathered sufficient steam by 1997 to prompt a campy guest appearance in the retro-60s comedy *Austin Powers,* in which Bacharach came dangerously close to figuring as a sort of Liberace of the Pop Art era.

Bacharach naturally participated enthusiastically in the revival process, staging a successful tour with the singer of his greatest hits, Dionne Warwick, with whom he also appeared on a luxurious New Year's Eve special calculated to suggest the return of an elegance eclipsed since, say, Guy Lombardo and His Royal Canadians. He collaborated felicitously with Elvis Costello on the song "God Give Me Strength" (from the movie *Grace of My Heart*) and followed it up with *Painted from Memory,* a heavily promoted album of new songs co-written with Costello. Another television special, *One Amazing Night,* featured Bacharach in company with contemporary stars like Sheryl Crow, All Saints, and Barenaked Ladies and was subsequently released in CD and video form. In the meantime, a flood of CD reissues of earlier recordings culminated in an ambitious box set from the industrious repackager Rhino *(The Look of Love: The Burt Bacharach Collection)* surveying Bacharach's progress in the years since his first hit, the 1957 Marty Robbins record "The Story of My Life."

In such a process, the myth of the original career is amplified by the myth of the return. Each step of the comeback is charted as part of a legendary progression: years of glory, years in limbo, years of triumphant rebirth. The past is symbolically brought into the present, so that through the contemplation of Bacharach and his music—not as museum exhibit but as living presence—latter-day devotees can gain access to a realm of lost bliss. By a back derivation typical of pop revivals, the fantasy glamor of the original songs is translated into a description of the era in which they originated, as if life in the early '60s had been a live-action Dionne Warwick song, with deft periodic accentuation by oboe, xylophone, or celeste. For those who had been there the first time around—including those precocious Bacharach enthusiasts for whom, before *Pet Sounds* or *Revolver,* the 1964 Kapp release *Burt Bacharach—Hitmaker!* was the cult album of choice. It all had the predictable eeriness of seeing experience transmuted into its movie-of-the-week version, as one moment's dawning sensibility becomes another's irresistible marketing opportunity.

Bacharach of course always had as many detractors as admirers. That Rhino's box set was received with contempt in some quarters—Robert Christgau in the *Village Voice* spoke of "fancy hackwork," while Neil Strauss of the *New York Times* announced that "the Burt Bacharach revival stops here"—may have reflected an ancient antipathy among those who preferred their rock and roll untainted by association with string sections, nightclubs, television specials, or the likes of Tony Orlando, Tom Jones, or the Carpenters. On the other hand, Bacharach was often enough invoked in the '60s as a rejoinder to the musically illiterate, virtually as a remnant of higher culture holding his own against the onslaught of untutored garage bands. The singer Anthony Newley (whose "What Kind of Fool Am I?" had itself struck exactly the right note of heartfelt midlife regret to please the middle-aged ears of 1961) was quoted to that effect on the back of *Hit Maker!*: "Burt Bacharach has revolutionized the world of commercial recording in the most unlikely way—he has replaced noise with creative music."

In the event, Bacharach's revolution was to be drowned out by layers of noise that would have been inconceivable for Newley, who presumably was reacting against nothing more threatening to his sense of musical decorum than "I Wanna Be Your Man," or perhaps "The Mashed Potatoes," rather than anticipating further decades of psychedelic jams, heavy metal three-chord anthems, dub echo chambers, punk abrasions, gangsta imprecations, and rumbling chasms of trance-inducing amplified bass patterns.

Even at the moment of his triumphant return to eminence, the question remained how much the renewed appeal of Bacharach's work owed to the fortuitous kitschiness of the associations it aroused. To what extent had he been brought back to serve as an artifact of the martini-and-cigar subculture, a mere strand, however glittering, in the gaudy tapestry of Lounge: the music track for a lost dream of adulthood set in an alternative Kennedy era, in which the man who reads *Playboy* meets that *Cosmopolitan* girl on a spring evening outside the Plaza and discovers that romance really exists?

The lounge music revival, which provided the wider backdrop to Bacharach's comeback, was a phenomenon of the '90s involving the recycling of Hawaiian exotica and spy movie soundtracks, surf instrumentals, bachelor pad classics of the stereophonic revolution crafted by easy-listening maestros such as Juan Garcia Esquivel and Ferrante & Teicher, bouncy main title themes from Italian sex comedies, "smooth jazz" (a code name for the gently swinging flute-and-guitar-inflected music backdrop favored by the Weather Channel) performed by the likes of Cal Tjader and Vince Guaraldi, big band adaptations of pop tunes and TV detective themes, the back catalogues of forgotten torch singers and second-tier Vegas regulars. Perhaps at the outer limit Dean Martin was singing Christmas favorites: a permissive range extending almost (but not quite) as far as garage-sale standbys like Mitch Miller and Mantovani.

Permissiveness is of the essence here. The listener is encouraged to surrender to music that not so long ago he might have defined as the Other, the enemy, the counter-counterculture. At the same time, however, he is left free to distort or reimagine it any way he pleases. History in this context amounts to little more than a crowded closet from which, with a bit of scrounging, useable bits of fabric or costume jewelry can be salvaged for an extended game of dress-up. "Lounge music" is a deliberately unhistorical term designed to assert power over history, the power to remake what happened into whatever world the customers are asking for this month. A capacious reference book, *MusicHound Lounge: The Essential Album Guide to Martini Music and Easy Listening,* proposes a category encompassing Coleman Hawkins, Gordon Lightfoot, Nino Rota, the Four Preps, the Carpenters, Jimmy Durante, Tito Puente, Serge Gainsbourg, Carmen McRae, the 101 Strings, the Swingle Singers, Erik Satie, Kurt Weill, and Rodgers and Hart, not to mention the good-for-a-laugh albums released by such "singers" as Leonard Nimoy and Robert Mitchum. (No one, as the millennium dawned, had yet reissued the late '60s album on which Yvette Mimieux read the poetry of Baudelaire accompanied by Ali Akhbar Khan on sarod, but the moment could not be too distant.)

It is a definition intended to undermine the notion of definition as such, appropriately for a mix 'n' match music cobbled out of any elements that grab you: Marimba? Theremin? Bossa nova beat? Cheesy echo effects? Hammond organ? Surf guitar? Mariachi trumpet? Cowbells? Tuned bongos? Wind chimes? Close harmony backup singers mimicking the style of classic cigarette commercials? Press the buttons for the fantasy combo of your choice and a mix tape will be generated on demand.

Make of anything what you will. In the definitive Kennedy-era jazz crossover, Vince Guaraldi's "Cast Your Fate to the Winds" (1962), accept a belated invitation to lose your mind in the most cool and sophisticated way, preferably in a tastefully avant-garde apartment overlooking the San Francisco Bay. You can keep some reefer in the drawer—"I like to blow a little pot now and then, it makes the music so interesting, you can really hear what they're getting at"—and on the wall a Bernard Buffet still life of coffeepot with fruit like the Ella Fitzgerald album covers, or the inevitable bullfight poster. With any luck the apartment will also be home at least part of the time to a girl in espadrilles and toreador pants, the sort who might decorate an album by Art Pepper or George Shearing, draping herself over the divan against a soft-focus hint of summer dusk. It's time to light the candles and uncork the chianti.

So mellow, and this is to be enjoyed in the confidence that the straight world from which you are taking a vacation—you advertising man, journalist, budding market research executive—will still be there waiting for you when you are ready to make some serious money. At this distance you can even feel a mild affection for its reassuringly gray and boring presence. You almost need the world of briefcases and neckties for contrast with the swing and color of the fate you have cast to the winds, with the help of some freelance bread coming in from the occasional layout or arrangement or magazine piece so you can afford the Johnny Walker Black Label and the Italian jackets. No problem there, unless you have the bad luck to end up like Jack Lemmon and Lee Remick in that motel room on the edge of the highway in the alcoholic nether reaches of *Days of Wine and Roses*. More likely you'll just spend the rest of your days listening to Henry Mancini's theme song from *Days of Wine and Roses*. You'll hear it played by Cal Tjader, by Dizzy Gillespie, by Toots Thielmans, by Phil Woods, by Eumir Deodato, by the Boston Pops, the Quartette Tres Bien, and the Bossa Nova Orchestra, by Vince Guaraldi, by Mancini himself, and will indeed—just as the lyrics suggested—find at the core of it a residuum of pain, the pain of discovering a window on a world that went away recently enough for you to sense its presence but before you had a chance to inhabit it.

Partly, the lounge phenomenon represents a generational shift conspiring to admit a range of musical effects that rock had excluded so as to preserve the purity of its identity. If one posits (as a worst-case scenario) a consciousness restricted to heavy metal, punk, and grunge, and then imagines the sudden infusion of, say, the "exotica" of Martin Denny, it becomes possible to grasp the revolutionary possibilities of tracks like "Stone God" or "Jungle River Boat." A new sensuous universe opens. Glissandos, bird calls, the undulation of waves and steel guitars: the massage music works its way into pressure points that garage rock failed to reach, an ethereal but efficiently lubricant patchouli oil.

Irony quickly becomes a dead issue. Finally you are left alone with your ears; either you get pleasure from listening to Martin Denny or the Hollyridge Strings, or you don't. The only variations are on the order of how much pleasure, to be repeated how many times. Irony meets its double: flat-out banality. The alienated contemplation of schmaltz merges with the unrepentant enjoyment of it. Or else it doesn't quite merge, as the mind clings to a detachment in which unironic enjoyment is almost successfully simulated. You get the pleasurable abandon of sincerity with none of the heartbreak.

There was a certain appropriateness in the soundtrack of *fin de siècle* America shaping up as a potpourri of decades-old mood music, movie music, elevator-and-supermarket music. Since you had long since gotten used to hearing canned versions of Bob Marley and Talking Heads en route to the yogurt or the breakfast links, it was not so hard to accept the ersatz as ultimate authenticity. The point is not roots but connections, the more far-fetched the better. How far from its point of origin can an artifact wash up? How wildly can its original intent be distorted while remaining tantalizingly recognizable?

It becomes part of listening to chart the migration of materials. Note, for instance, how the Bacharach-David number "Me Japanese Boy I Love You," a sleekly efficient Orientalist confection originally sung by Bobby Goldsboro in 1964, is eventually woven by the Japanese group the Pizzicato Five into their methodically hip pop-art collages of an imaginary 1960s in which James Bond and Twiggy serve as benign, lighter-than-air demigods. In the world of lounge music, collage is indispensable, if only because there is so much music to be listened to—a whole world of buried recordings—that only by mixing it up as rapidly and heterogeneously as possible can one even begin to sample all the subgenres.

It was sampling (the extrapolation of fragments of preexisting recordings into repeated figures, or their insertion as isolated sound effects, a practice that rapidly transformed pop music) that was doubtless responsible for the dredging up of much of this material in the first place. That aura of fragmentation—the sense that music can be appreciated just as well out of order, in pieces, juxtaposed inappropriately with other fragments—is perhaps the only atmosphere in which to sanely approach a potentially infinite canon. Yet the manifest need for editing is balanced against a simmering desire to hear everything, to accept the late-night television offer (featured in one of Robert Klein's comic monologues) of "every record ever made since recording began." Listening to all the records substitutes for leading all the lives, being in all the places. The deliberately all-encompassing category of Lounge signals a relaxation that permits an inexhaustible series of brightly lit dream sequences set in imaginary epochs: no identity, no history, no reason to regret anything ever again.

The catch is that even for someone who was there at the time, the original experience has by now become almost as much a fantasy. The question of what exactly we remember when we listen to old recordings, or whether it can be called remembering at all, becomes less and less answerable over a lifetime. In that commonest of fetishistic practices—listening to the same song repeatedly, year after year and decade after decade—do you reenact an original experience or shut out memory by substituting a fixed pattern of sounds tied to an equally fixed pattern of associations? Can you hope to hear new and different things over the course of time, or would that interfere with the need to be reassured by an unvarying response?

Every listener's personal history can be stitched together from recollections of first encounters, recollections that in due course become private legends. There is some piece of vinyl that will forever be (for random instance) March 23, 1962. It is the peculiar faculty of music to make each such first meeting, in retrospect, a snapshot of what the world was at that moment. Sound is the most absorbent medium of all, soaking up histories and philosophical systems and physical surroundings and encoding them in something so slight as a single vocal quaver or icy harpsichord interjection. The listener wants not merely to hear the beloved record again but to hear it always for the first time. The shock of coming up against music that truly sounds like nothing ever heard before—whether the encounter is with a Caruso 78 of "Santa Lucia," or the Basie band broadcasting live from the Famous Door, or the flip side of the new Zombies single—involves the apprehension, or the invention, of an unsuspected reality, an emotional shade not defined until then, the revelation (tenuous or overpowering) of a possible future. If music promised anything less than entry into a new world, how account for its hold on the many for whom it can stand in, if need be, for a belief system or a way of life? Every first hearing that is remembered constitutes a creation myth. What is created is a self irrevocably transformed by a particular piece of music, a particular phrase, a particular catch in the throat.

In pursuit of an archaeology of memory, it is sometimes possible to reconstruct the encounter. I enter a room just as an unknown song is beginning to play and have an impression that the room changes. I remember where I was standing, as if it were an assassination or a first kiss. The weather of the day is imprinted for future recollection. I had been warned, perhaps—"You've got to hear this one"—as my brother slipped the 45 onto the turntable. The song is, for instance, "What the World Needs Now Is Love," a newly released Imperial single by Jackie De Shannon, with words by Hal David and music by Burt Bacharach. It is an April afternoon in 1965, and this year, in the world beyond high school, the usual urgencies of the season seem to converge with a broader impatience in the whole culture, as if things were going to have to move a little faster to get on with the impending changes.

The song's impact has a great deal to do with its emphatic deployment of the word "now." It's like a political program, an urgent placard. "What the world needs now"—everybody has been weighing in on that question for a while now: anxious diplomats and somber population experts, nuclear physicists and sex educators, think-tank sociologists and pacifist chaplains, an earnest chorus emanating from podium and pulpit, from *Meet the Press* and the evening news. And now it is Jackie De Shannon's turn tremulously and unignorably to overrule them all, to sing beyond their world into the next. A program of worldwide empathy is being set in motion under the ad hoc leadership of a singer whose stunning promotional photograph amounts to a poster for youth itself as imagined in 1965, radiating sincerity and spontaneity and the dissolution of hidebound social forms into a universal and sweetly unproblematic sexual availability.

Yet the defiantly fragile sentiment embodied in her singing exists at the center of the most sophisticated imaginable orchestral setting, in a harmonious wedding of feeling and production machinery. No question of counterculture: the culture itself appears to be changing at its core. In the space of under three minutes I construct a story about the way the world is going, even if my outward registration of this experience may be only to venture the knowing opinion that "this record is going to be huge." It is satisfying—somehow an omen of emerging positive transformation—that what is perfectly beautiful and undeniable should succeed ubiquitously, beaming into the world from every available outlet. Every subsequent playback plays back as well a compressed version of that original cloud of nuance; and that was only one such record out of thousands.

The age of recording is necessarily an age of nostalgia—when was the past so hauntingly accessible?—but its bitterest insight is the incapacity of even the most perfectly captured sound to restore the moment of its first inscribing. That world is no longer there. On closer listening, it probably never was, for longer than the instant during which unfamiliar music ripped open spaces equally and drastically unfamiliar. The listener will go on to more such encounters. It could become something like his life's work. He may resort to wide-ranging searches for the never-before-heard, anything from Uzbeki wedding music to unreleased garage bands of southern Wisconsin, whatever might spring the life-changing surprise. Yet the laboriously sought musical epiphany rarely compares to the unsought, even unwanted tune whose ambush is violent and sudden: the song the cab driver was tuned to, the song rumbling from the speaker wedged against the fire-escape railing, the song tingling from the transistor on the beach blanket. To locate those songs again can become, with age, something like a religious quest, as suggested by the frequent use of the phrase "Holy Grail" to describe hard-to-find tracks. The collector is haunted by the knowledge that somewhere on the planet an intact chunk of his past still exists, uncorrupted by time or circumstance.

It was a devotional impulse of sorts that from the outset gave that music—pop music, jukebox music, radio music—such power over its listeners. Where some lit candles to saints, others listened to the Shirelles. To fully reconstruct how I came to be haunted by the memory of constantly playing both sides of Lou Johnson's 45 of "Kentucky

Bluebird" b/w "The Last One To Be Loved" in the fall of 1964, or, a few months earlier (it was the moment when Burt Bacharach's name first started to mean something), becoming voluntarily submerged in Dionne Warwick's record of "Walk On By," it is necessary to recollect the way the 45 rpm record once provided the basis for something like a religion, or at any rate a religion of art. For a youth culture that had not yet discovered its destiny to change the world, cultural life was often a matter of keeping up with the Top 40 countdown when it was released each Sunday, to culminate in the apotheosis of "And this week's Hot 100 *Billboard* number one record is . . . 'Game of Love' by Wayne Fontana and the Mindbenders!" The transistor radio at minimal volume, listened to well after midnight, could seem like a direct line to the godhead. In the heart of emptiness and darkness, music continued to pour out.

Functionally, the 45 was something of a detour from the forward sweep of technological progress by which the long-playing record had liberated popular music from the temporal constraints of the 78. The LP allowed a symphony to be heard straight through without messing around with three or four fragile shellac disks, and permitted Duke Ellington, for example, to create extended suites. Listeners could go about their housework or their homework or their lovemaking for as long as half an hour without having to change the music. The 45, by contrast, perpetuated the time limits of the 78, although in an admittedly greatly improved form. Miniaturized, lightweight, and unbreakable, it could be held in the palm of the hand yet contained immeasurable depths and reaches, a perfect mystical object made of cheap plastic.

Its virtues were not limited to cheapness. Pop LPs tended to be diffuse affairs in which one or two hits were surrounded by filler of varying quality. The 45 by contrast focused attention unwaveringly on a solitary object of desire. If the B side turned out to be worthy of attention that was merely a gratuitous extra fillip. (In the faith defined by 45s, the cultivation of brilliant and obscure B sides represented the occult or esoteric branch.) Listening to a 45 was a separate act, preceded by careful selection and attended by reverently close attention. Each was judged by how completely and unpredictably it mapped a reality in its allotted playing time. The best carved vast stretches out of that limited duration, while the worst felt interminable even at a minute and a half.

The density of pop music in the '60s was such that any week might yield two or three or more of these life-changing experiences, whether emanating from Detroit or London or Memphis or Los Angeles. The impact of the Beatles and the Beach Boys, Motown and Stax-Volt, Curtis Mayfield and James Brown and Aretha Franklin and Bob Dylan did not register successively but more or less simultaneously. Many scores of secondary figures contributed records equally unexpected: Billy Stewart ("Sitting in the Park") or the Castaways ("Liar Liar"); the Left Banke ("Walk Away Renee") or Barbara Lewis ("Hello Stranger") or Fontella Bass ("Rescue Me") would crop up with the brusqueness of a prophetic visitation, explosions of feeling amid a ground bass provided by reliable rhythm machines ranging from "Louie, Louie" to "Boogaloo Down Broadway."

The songs that Burt Bacharach and Hal David were writing in those years were not marginal but central to all that, and when the revival hit it was disconcerting to find Bacharach treated after so many years as a quaint anachronism in whom, nonetheless, some unique qualities could be found. Bacharach's music became a victim of the Balkanizing tendency of a latter-day pop music industry happiest when "niche marketing" one subdivision or another of a pop universe that in the mid-1960s was briefly convergent, no matter how ludicrous were some of the forms that convergence took. For a time it made perfect sense for Sam Cooke to sing Bob Dylan's "Blowin' in the Wind" on his *Live at the Copa* album, for Marvin Gaye to record an album-length tribute to Nat King Cole, for Otis Redding to adapt the Rolling Stones' "Satisfaction," for the Who to record the theme from the TV series *Batman,* for both Bobby Darin and Jim Morrison to sing Kurt Weill, or for the Beatles to record material by the Shirelles, Buck Owens and His Buckaroos, and Buddy Holly, not to mention a song from *The Music Man*. Genre-bending and marketing crossovers were the norm, and the Top 40 sound of any given moment was likely to be a curious amalgam of disparate elements, "Stranger in the Night" followed immediately by "Papa's

Got a Brand New Bag," the Troggs in regular rotation with Herb Alpert and the Tijuana Brass. A hit was a hit.

And what of the man himself, and how much did the listener really care to know? In biographical notes Bacharach tended to sound like the sum of his training and influences: a songwriter who cited both Ravel's *Daphnis and Chloe* and the late '40s work of Charlie Parker and Miles Davis as pivotal in his musical development; who studied with Henry Cowell, Bohuslav Martinů, and Darius Milhaud; and who then took his skills into the heart of what was then still a thriving "adult popular" market, as accompanist-arranger for Vic Damone, Polly Bergen, and Steve Lawrence, and as musical director for Marlene Dietrich's international tours. Yet none of that would have counted for anything had he not collided with the songwriting culture symbolized by the Brill Building at 1619 Broadway, where in the early 1960s hit songs were being concocted with something approaching industrial precision by teams like Carole King and Gerry Goffin, Barry Mann and Cynthia Weill, and Jerry Leiber and Mike Stoller.

Bacharach's earliest hits were very much part of that wider musical scene; indeed for melodic invention he could scarcely surpass early songs like "Any Day Now" or "Make It Easy on Yourself" or "It's Love That Really Counts." Bacharach never evolved into a rock and roller (his song for Manfred Mann, "My Little Red Book," is a fascinatingly stylized approximation of rock and roll, or perhaps a veiled commentary on its limitations), but pop music as defined in the Brill Building (and its Southern California equivalents) still had plenty of room for records that were neither dance music nor exclusively youth music. It is impossible to imagine how Bacharach's art might have evolved had he not had the good fortune to encounter songs like Leiber and Stoller's "Spanish Harlem" and King and Goffin's "Oh No, Not My Baby." In his later songs he seems torn between an almost disdainfully virtuosic elaborateness (the relatively unpopular masterpiece "Looking with My Eyes") and a knowing command of the simplistic (the hugely successful jingle "Raindrops Keep Fallin' on My Head"); the earlier compositions suggest no such conflict.

The Rhino box set turned out to be something of a eulogy for an era that can be characterized simply by citing some of the artists, familiar or mostly forgotten, for whom Bacharach and David tailored their songs: Chuck Jackson, Gene Pitney, the Shirelles, Jerry Butler, Bobby Vinton, Brook Benton, Jack Jones, and of course Dionne Warwick, who first showed up as part of a trio of backup singers and went on to record over sixty Bacharach-David songs. (The box set would have been a significant event, for this fan at least, if only for making available four of Lou Johnson's great if sadly unsuccessful first recordings of some of Bacharach's best songs, most notably "The Last One To Be Loved.") Later would come the British contingent—Tom Jones, Cilla Black, the Walker Brothers, and the sublime Dusty Springfield— to fill out the picture of a music industry still functioning something like the old Hollywood, obeying notions of classic songwriting form and respecting a sharp division of labor between singers and songwriters, with the indispensable "A&R men" working out the mystical equations to determine who should sing what. It was a world that became more intensely interesting just as it was being hit with the external convulsions that would compel it to ditch much of the old-timers' wisdom and radically regroup. In the final stages you might come upon inadvertent grotesqueries like Dusty Springfield being assigned to sing a romantic ballad called "The Corrupt Ones," from the international co-production of the same name. Imagine the plight of the songwriter coerced to incorporate the title phrase into a pop lyric, with the assurance, "Don't worry, Dusty can sing anything!"

What finally had to be jettisoned was the idea of music made, by definition, by studio guys, real pros with not a trace of amateurism, even if they had to put up with the sometimes clearly amateurish front-liners that the kids went for. The music's identifying mark was a combination of perfectionism and commercialism, both unquestioned: not just slick sounds and the finest engineering, but the real poetic antennae to detect the underlying current that meant the difference between Top 40 and nothing. The studio wizards could create, wherever necessary, any effect on demand: cowboys and Indians, dawn in the tropics, sea chantey, snake charmer oboe solo, doo-wop under the overpass. A single chord, a single smear or deftly warped echo could put you at the county fair or in lovers' lane or on the fringes of the Outer Limits. The idea was to make the perfect record—perfection being certified by grosses—and admiration for the calculation and control that went into it was part of the listener's response as well. The ultimate miracles of expression could not be planned, of course, but they sounded a lot better when that backup was in place.

Fans listened to the new releases as if they were assessing new machines, checking out how smoothly the gears worked and what effect they produced from different angles, in different settings. Every element was up for examination: how the singing compared with the competition, the lyrics of the second verse, the peculiar organ break, the breathless spoken interjection toward the end. There was no assumption—as there would be in the wake of hits like the Kingsmen's "Louie Louie"—that the listeners could produce such a record themselves. It really was like the movies, with a wide screen and a cast of thousands: a superb technical feat created solely to make the fans happy, as they could verify if they cared to by reading the copy in magazines like *Hit Parader* and *Song Hits,* or by sampling liner notes that tended to posit a relentlessly productive show business, driven by nothing more than the optimistic energies of seasoned veterans and youthful go-getters.

What no one who cared ever doubted was that they were in the presence, often enough, of deliberate beauty. There were no accidents here—least of all in the Bacharach records (not originally billed as such, but increasingly recognizable), which had no need for echo effects or other electronic distortion to make their point. The musical elements were clearly exposed, so that even the most casual listener would notice how every note contributed. These were total compositions, to be appreciated like a series of paintings: "Baby It's You" (its spareness allowing abysses to open between its lines, the "sha la la" chorus washing mournfully like chill surf over rock) or "Any Day Now" (the limits of its landscape of feeling laid out almost sternly by strings, organ, and drums, leaving the words—"then the blue shadows will fall all over town"—free to go about their work of suggestion).

If many pop records (Phil Spector's, for instance) sought to recede into a curtain of indeterminate sound, the Bacharach songs were placed against a backdrop of silence: everything of which the record consisted was audible and distinguishable. The miniature cowboy symphony "The Man Who Shot Liberty Valance" (with Gene Pitney singing Hal David's deft synopsis of the John Ford movie) seemed, right from its annunciatory fiddle line, a synthesis of songs that were already synthetic, even farther from any conceivable prairie than the Hollywood themes of Dimitri Tiomkin and Elmer Bernstein and Jerome Moross: a pocket West, scrimshawed into two and a half minutes.

When people talk about Bacharach they generally have in mind the profuse body of work that resulted from his intersection with the lyrics of Hal David and the singing of Dionne Warwick. Warwick's early albums consist of almost nothing but Bacharach-David songs, all of them interesting to listen to and many of the best never to become widely known. What the three apparently shared, aside from anything else, was a relishing of difficulty, whether of pitch or meter or rhyme or narrative compression. Their records make no appeal to special effects or topical allusions. Bacharach would come to be identified almost exclusively with the products of this three-way collaboration, whose dissolution brought to an end his long run of extraordinary productivity.

By the same token, the associations called up by Bacharach's music become inextricably entangled with David's peculiar blend of sophisticated versification and heartfelt emotional statement, a blend in which the encroachments of the maudlin are generally kept at bay by the wit of his rhymes and the elliptical elegance of his storytelling. It is impossible to measure how much Warwick adds to the tone of the songs, since so many of them were written for the benefit of her interpretation. The persona created by her vocal art reveals her to be as much actor as singer. Around her laconic pleadings, interrupted gasps, and almost successfully suppressed cries of anger, an implied dramatic universe forms.

The listener might fill in the implications of these arias without operas with stray elements borrowed from the surrounding air. What is pop music for, if not to be embroidered upon, converted into wholly idiosyncratic, sometimes grotesquely idiosyncratic, cues for a private soundtrack? Here was adult romance, born under the same astrological signs that presided over *Sex and the Single Girl* (book and movie), the Pill, and the perfume ads that instructed "Want him to be more of a man? Try being more of a woman." In Jacqueline Susann's *Once Is Not Enough,* the potential connection became explicit as a female protagonist mused, between love bouts, on the music she loved best. (By 2000 Bacharach would be writing the soundtrack for a movie about Susann's brief life, a movie made in the first place because her novels, charting the lusts and horrors of the '60s entertainment industry with the enthusiasm for detail of a bubblegum Balzac, were swept up in the same nostalgic wave responsible for the lounge revival.) The romantic dream-world of Manhattan rain covering up tears on mascara cohabited uneasily with the leering ambience of '60s sex comedies—old men's movies, born antiquated—like *Who's Been Sleeping in My Bed* and *Sunday in New York* and *Not With My Wife You Don't!*, movies that seemed to emanate from the *Esquire* cartoon world of goggle-eyed overweight execs chasing voluptuously stacked secretaries around the desk in private offices; movies like *Made in Paris* and *Promise Her Anything* and *Wives and Lovers,* remembered now mostly because Burt Bacharach wrote tie-in songs for them.

Hal David's lyrics lightly sketched in a world of rainy days and breakups and telephones, airports and doorbells, makeup and taxis, "an empty tube of toothpaste and a half-filled cup of coffee": and, unmentioned, booze and Valium and cigarettes, therapists and exercise programs, broken glass, hours of silence and immobility, crowded bars and dates gone sour: a woman's world, most of the time, the world as it might be imagined by the one who didn't go to the disco with her roommate, who stayed home watching some old Olivia de Havilland movie—perhaps the one about the nice girl undermined and nearly destroyed by her murderous schizophrenic twin—and who would despite everything be obliged to show up Monday morning and somehow shuffle through the monthly billing. Billy Wilder's movie *The Apartment,* with its themes of wage slavery and sexual harassment, was the perfect source material for Bacharach and David's only Broadway musical, *Promises, Promises.*

In the heart of the song was a cry from inside a box. "In Between the Heartaches," for instance, evokes a hidden universe of pain; it's a love ballad for a distant or abusive lover sometimes kind enough to make things nice for a while. But the crack-ups are private, under control as long as anyone is watching. This is a well-bred melancholia, the hidden side of a Kennedy-era effervescence personified outwardly by Burt himself, casual in knit turtleneck and loafers, flanked by his glamorous wife Angie Dickinson and his close associates Marlene Dietrich and Dionne Warwick, the inhabitants of a world where nothing is likely to go seriously wrong.

Kennedy died in November 1963, but songs like "A House Is Not a Home" and "Wives and Lovers" and "Land of Make Believe" just kept on coming: future souvenirs of the awareness that once upon a time one was fooled by appearances, got conned for a moment by the delusions of glamour and celebrity, actually believed that the people in those photographs were having fun. The disco scene in *What's New Pussycat?*—with Peter O'Toole and Romy Schneider frugging insouciantly under red lights to the music of Manfred Mann—incarnated with appropriate randomness the frothy evanescence of a scene already over by the time any public ever caught its afterglimmer. The Kennedy '60s could be like that, were like that for most of the audience: a succession of parties that one hadn't attended, leaving in their wake, through the medium of film clips and candid shots and songs, a detritus of feathers and glitter.

As the decade moved forward or downward, these ballads inevitably became emblems of the part of the '60s that was not about youth culture, the part where listeners still aspired toward some kind of sleek adulthood, up-to-date and liberated but never sloppy; who coveted nice suits, hairdos with architectonic grace rather than the free flow of the "natural," the artifices of comfort, the rituals of air travel, whatever evoked the big dream of the modern, as if the twentieth century were a reverie best indulged "while you're lounging in your leather chair." (The words are from a song, "Paper Mâché," whose satirical commentary on the materialism of consumer culture was far too gracefully muted even to register in the confrontational atmosphere of 1970.)

It might have been an unreal world, but the cravings that defined it kept coming back, like one of those hooks to which Bacharach's songs were finally reduced in memory, the fragments of tunes that rise to the surface at three in the morning, the hour when melodic progression can become a torture implement. Somehow the tunes began to pall; the mood was perhaps too upbeat to be believed, the charts too anxiously busy. The '70s had arrived, and it no longer seemed likely that the music business would change the world. The Bacharach songs would melt into that larger repertoire of sweetened, self-pitying ballads to which, for the better part of a decade, office workers were condemned to listen for eight hours at a stretch. They appeared to be songs for a world that had turned out not to exist.

It was hard not to wonder what sort of songs Bacharach might have written with a collaborator other than Hal David. (Bertolt Brecht, perhaps; think what *Promises, Promises* could have been with its full cynical potential realized.) But in some sense the lyrics hardly mattered to Bacharach's music; he could adapt to anything. Those love scenarios, were they anything more than an occasion to let him play with shapes, textures, pauses, intervals, varieties of harmonic space? The tension that singled out Bacharach's songs from the goop in which they sometimes threatened to dissolve came from the sense of a detached intelligence working not against the mood of the songs but outside it.

These intricate fetish-objects are about their own virtuosity, a virtuosity that delights in difficulty and intricacy, and delights even more in disguising them as just another pop tune. At his most characteristic Bacharach exudes a dry constructivist energy. A given song might evoke Stravinsky's *Agon* gone pop, or a fragment of Schoenberg deftly sweetened and cajoled, in extremis, back into conventional harmonic resolution. The drama—or the game—of a Bacharach melody is the risk that it might not circle back acceptably, might simply extend outward in a series of increasingly far-flung spirals. How far can he swim from shore before losing any hope of getting back? The melody branches at angles so abrupt that it threatens unbridgeable gaps, unacceptable dissonances: until, with the aplomb of Douglas Fairbanks as Zorro, Bacharach abruptly brings it home by one deft shortcut or another. One can imagine him as a connoisseur of emotional precision, whose own feelings would be irrelevant, the embodiment of a dandyism capable nonetheless of appreciating the expression of true feeling. In that light the music would be all surface, but the most beautiful surface imaginable.

There was always a temptation to remove the words from the songs, remove any layers of the arrangement that were mere ornamentation, the sonic furniture enabling them to "pass" as acceptable AM product. Set free from their context and commercial purpose—no longer in the business of selling a particular three-minute emotional drama— those changes and textures could then be reassembled as parts of some symphonic suite, the sort of extended composition that Bacharach evidently had no interest in pursuing. The nostalgia that is so often the theme of Hal David's lyrics might suggest by extension the listener's inchoate yearning for another song hidden within the actual song, a wild kernel of shape-making.

In the early movie soundtracks, *What's New Pussycat?*, *After the Fox*, and *Casino Royale,* a more secret aspect of Bacharach's talent emerged: not the romantic wholeheartedness one might have expected from a composer known for his love songs, but rather a parodistic collage of styles, the Charleston rearranged for harpsichord, Neapolitan street song metamorphosing into strip-joint fanfare and again into a pastiche of *L'Histoire du Soldat*. "Here I Am" and "The Look of Love" were employed in comic contexts calculated to undermine the effect of two of Bacharach's most beautiful ballads. Nobody will notice—it's only a silly movie—so he can play games with structure and instrumentation and mood, games that predict a good many more solemn exercises in postmodern patchwork.

By reinterpretation, musicians sometimes tried to tease out those unsounded implications, yet Bacharach's songs proved curiously recalcitrant to improvisers. They were designed to work roughly the same way no matter who sang or played them. Whether by Cilla

Black, Dionne Warwick, the Delfonics, or Stevie Wonder, "Alfie" stubbornly remains "Alfie." The televised tribute *One Amazing Night* ended up sounding more like Karaoke Night, so little did the younger performers add to earlier versions of Bacharach-David standards. As a vehicle for jazz musicians, Bacharach's music seems too tightly constructed to permit much fruitful alteration; the jazz component tends to be more or less tacked on to songs that determinedly resist being bent out of shape.

When the concept worked, as on Stan Getz's 1968 album *What the World Needs Now,* it was because Getz contented himself with virtually singing the songs on sax, while McCoy Tyner's elaborations on the similarly titled 1996 outing *What the World Needs Now: The Music of Burt Bacharach* seemed superfluous ornamentations of tunes that come pre-ornamented. Sonny Rollins chose wisely to play "A House Is Not a Home" pretty much note for note. Of later variations, John Zorn's *Great Jewish Music* collection was finally the most satisfying and, oddly, the most faithful. It gave credence to the notion that the way to recapture the past is to tear it apart. At its best it was something like the Burt Bacharach album of one's dreams: not adding further decoration to the tunes, but stripping away superfluous textures and trappings to find the song's skeleton.

Bacharach lent himself to austere treatments because what counted in his music was fundamentally austere. The hard core of that music had always been curiously at odds with his image as diffident aristocrat given to breeding race horses, or strolling along that pristine stretch of Southern Californian beachfront that one imagined as his natural habitat. The period colorings, the mythology that would make him a walking advertisement for The Good Life, seemed finally irrelevant. The real Bacharach—the Bacharach one could not, finally, actually hear except obliquely and by implication—was Out There, totally gone into form. He was a maker of patterns whose stark durable structures could give continuing pleasure without having to be *about* something, as if to confirm Stravinsky's dictum that "music itself does not signify anything."

But was there any such music finally, that abstract *Bacharach-Musik* orbiting in a space of Pure Idea, disdaining the ambient detritus that had clung to its self-sufficient forms? Did it not recede into a black hole of imperceptibility, to be guessed at only as mediated through the inadequate hints offered by mere fleshly performance and fleshly perception, and further distorted through the prism of historical happenstance, personal memory, wilful misunderstanding and misappropriation? Such pure music, raked free of the casual junk of human accident that strictly speaking had nothing to do with it, could be conceived only as a music without listeners: and that was as impossible as to imagine a listener without music.

2

House Music

HEARING, AFTER ALL, IS IN THE FIRST PLACE INVOLUNTARY. The baby on the rug (the listener I once was) soaks up ambient sounds. As he absorbs them he changes them. Kitchen murmur of adults, wind raking trees, radio jingle buzz, noon siren, rumble of car rounding a bend: it is a river of sound he does not so much hear as inhabit. Its bumps and rapids, as they wash over him, warp and smash apart. The cantatas of deep hums, the baby operas made of plaintive tweets too rapid and various to be held for long in the mind, disappear unnoticed into the upholstery pattern at which he has been staring in apparent stupor.

It takes so long even for such a simple thing as a nursery rhyme to acquire fixed limits, a beginning and an end. Everything has to begin somewhere, but that somewhere is always the tangled middle. A space is crisscrossed by sound patterns that emanate from as yet undetectable sources. Before they can be properly identified they've already blended. It takes years to learn to think of sounds as distinct entities that can be fenced off into enclosures, and by the time you get that far, you're already being overwhelmed by the realization that no such fences can keep out the sounds that leak in from neighboring enclosures. Whatever was once separated out will eventually find its way back into the mix. Born into infinite complexity, we almost find a way to simplify things before being overwhelmed by the impossibility of the task. Ripple effects disturbed by other ripple effects: the inevitable condition of music in a world without adequate soundproofing.

As with sounds, so with images. The house where that baby was to spend his first years survives in memory only as a shimmering floor plan of the first world. A tremulous blueprint is glimpsed in stolen flashes and odd gusts of recall. What seemed in childhood a timeless homestead was a relatively brief way station in lives that were to shift dozens of times from one space to another. Contemplated in a black-and-white snapshot taken in 1948 when the family first moved in, it seems a handsome enough structure. It was said to have been built in ancient times—the early '20s—designed according to family legend by the architect of the Lincoln Memorial. The slate roof and steep gables, the hints of Tudor making the façade just slightly spectral, suggested a storybook manor condensed and dropped into place like an oversized toy. The past to which it belonged was being rapidly outstripped by the structures around it, whose sleeker, glassier, perkier look predicted a future already on display in magazines and television commercials. The house commanded the upper end of a tree-lined suburban street, where the land crested just before an unexpected stretch of dirt road sloped down toward the highway whose police sirens and roadside taverns, on a quiet enough night, were just audible through an open bedroom window.

Years later the grown-up infant can map out, through concentrated recollection, the inner and outer pathways of the place, its long narrow flower garden and cement patio, its winding gravel driveway and enclosing hedges. Here was the fort concealed in the tree; here was the observation post for awaiting interstellar visitations; here, in the space behind the garage, was refuge from imagined privateers or cattle rustlers. Memory can do almost anything with such a house—make inventory of its broom closets and fireplaces and kitchen utensils—anything but make its parts sit still. Porous, shifting, never altogether unobscured, they slide and glimmer in phosphorescent unreliability.

The spaces open widest on those nights when the involuntary re-memberer (myself, stripped of everything but a past not recoverable by other means) has the impression of swimming through the rooms of a shipwrecked house. In deep sleep every detail of the house can be savored, its two stories and eleven rooms, its earthy basement steeped in the residues of bleaches and chemicals, its attic cluttered with dis-carded toys and stage props, its central staircase winding in such hair-pin fashion that from its head the bottom steps cannot be seen, a staircase that doubled so often in imagination as well or tunnel or pathway to another world. Wrapped in the silence of a diver, the re-turning ghost floats from room to room, touching the surfaces of the furniture, negotiating the abrupt left turn into the kitchen, the car-peted escarpment of the steps where they begin their spiral toward the upper bedrooms.

Only silence permits this operation. Sound would restore time, and with the resurgence of time these relics would crumble. At the slight-est sound the walls of the sunken hulk would fall inward and its stores disperse. Like a burglar he pries out objects one by one: the souvenir ashtray from a Caribbean vacation, the pack of Viceroys left nearby next to the folded newspaper with the crossword puzzle fac-ing out, the after-dinner wine glass bearing an imprint of lipstick on the rim, the four-leaf clover preserved in clear plastic in a drawer next to the rabbit's-foot keychain, the abandoned chemistry set whose ele-ments and poisons have begun to congeal in their glass jars, the piles of cards saved from a previous Christmas, with their geography of small towns nestled among glistening snowbanks and dark sheltering forests, the rack of pipes, the scores of match packs from liquor stores, night clubs, diners, Bohack's, the A&P. Slide back the clothes in the closets to get to the formal dresses, veils, shawls, tuxedos, high hats, broad silk neckties with images of palm trees and saxophones, a lac-quered walking stick left over from an old play.

But there are other and more densely packed hiding places, the archives that hold the wire recorder, the antique camera, the stamp collection preserving the names of countries that no longer exist, Bosnia-Herzegovina, Cochin China, Anglo-Egyptian Sudan, the post-cards stamped Printed in Occupied Japan, and from occupied Germany the box of hand-carved wooden puppets, fairy tale crones and wizards whose aura of menace is almost too authentic. Finally the albums that might hold the key to these disparate relics, filled with photographs of people in wedding gowns, people in uniforms, people in bathing suits, people with baby carriages, people on lawns and in driveways, on stage and in broadcasting studios, holding microphones, playing pianos, delivering monologues, leaning forward for a kiss. Each photograph is separate and solemn, with hardly ever a caption to name or explain, a piece of a self-sufficient story that began long ago and is somehow still going on, unresolved, in silence.

Scattered among these things are reminders that sound once existed: a metronome, a drumming pad, a guitar pick, a trumpet mouthpiece, a music stand, a tuning fork, a block of rosin. There can never be enough storage space to hold the awkward shapes of the instruments—maracas, kazoo, bugle left over from the war, Haitian bongos, pennywhistle, accordion, harmonica, mandolin, plastic ukulele, ocarina, bird whistle, jew's harp, saxophone, tambourine, and the immense piano filling one side of the sunporch, surrounded by piles of sheet music and volumes of vocal scores—an accumulation of mute objects begging to be plucked or pounded or blown. The older instruments bear the marks of those who have already played them, the scuffs and bites and dents that are the mysterious scars of sound. In their midst the house hangs, tenuous and enveloping, a sounding board waiting to be struck.

Only music could bring those spaces to life. There is always music all over the house. It starts with the radio, a dark squat plastic box about the size of a toaster, with big white knobs for locating sound and attempting to hold it fast. The box gets turned on first thing in the morning.

The spot where it sits—on a table wedged altar-like in the innermost corner of the dining room—seems, from the moment the knob turns and the hum begins, the headquarters of the house. Here come the voices: the weather man, the news man, the man in the uproarious beer commercial. And here in the midst of them is my father's voice, announcing songs or telling jokes or selling hair tonic. He is the Morning Man, on the air every day from six to ten throughout the tri-state area. That I should hear my father first thing in the morning without seeing him (he had driven into the city many hours earlier, while everyone slept) and only hours later—in an entirely different and (from the perspective of the long childhood morning) remote phase of the day—see him, hear his non-radio voice, is just an aspect of the way life in the house goes, part of its obscure system of cues and exits and convergences.

From the outset there are two spheres: the unseen place from which the sounds emanate (a remote studio, fascinating to imagine as the sort of interplanetary control center from which a Buck Rogers or Captain Video would coordinate stellar explorations and ward off the incursions of alien fleets) and the place where they are listened to, this homestead, with its familiar ponderous lamps and fringed curtains and soft generous armchairs and sofas, this sitting room transformed into an auditorium where people attend to transmitted messages over whose timing and content they have no control. At most they can choose to sit there, or to leave the room.

Once it has been set into action, the radio pretty much stays on throughout the day. Ruth—the young woman from Pennsylvania to whom the house and my care have been entrusted during those hours when my parents are both away, and who for so long I took to be simply another member of the family—turned it on before I woke, as one of the small actions by which she gets the house moving each morning. It establishes the ground bass against which she advances through the complicated paces of her day, overhauling furniture, shaking out cloth, and generally creating order as she proceeds from room to room. It stays on as other women from time to time drift downstairs or through the front door—aunts, grandmothers, the women of the neighborhood—and a low-voiced animated conversation is sustained, an open-ended chronicle of war and sickness, the shifts and fortunes, calamitous or otherwise, of families and strangers, the temper of the man at the drugstore, the trip to California, the cousin's marriage, the uncle's disaster, the brother's expectations.

The talk withdraws to the kitchen where Ruth prepares miracles of casserole and soup and pudding, the sizzling and chopping interspersed with dialogue that itself becomes a kind of music. Her catch-phrases come back like refrains, shards of call-and-response structures that got broken up somewhere between the back country and the suburbs: "Everything is shipshape." "Give them an inch and they'll take a yard." "He's slow as molasses in January." "I declare I thought I'd die, I was fit to be tied." "They're nothing but a bunch of hooligans over there." "You can have the whole kit and caboodle of them as far as I'm concerned." "You're darn tootin'!" "I'm all tuckered out." "That's me, the chief cook and bottlewasher." "Give it a lick and a promise." "Don't sit there like a lump on a log." "Hold your horses." "Rome wasn't built in a day." "I don't know what this world is coming to." Whatever it is coming to, it doesn't seem to be getting any nearer to it from one day to the next. The rhythms of the days are cyclical and more or less reliable.

Ruth undertakes her meticulous work of arranging and folding and dusting accompanied by Perry Como and the McGuire Sisters and the Mills Brothers arranging and folding sound as if to keep the whole enterprise moving forward. It seems that the music has been made for her, and if whenever one song happens to suit her even better than the rest of them it's an occasion for gratitude: a song like that is a token of mutual assistance. As smoothly and with as little apparent effort as pillow slides into pillow slip—part of her labor is to conceal the fact of labor—the voices of the Four Lads slide into the final harmonic resolutions of "Stranger in Paradise." For me it is not really a question of liking or disliking the records on the radio. They are part of the air. Their turns of phrase and instrumental bridges and catches in the throat are presences as absolute as the squirrels in the branches and the milk bottles deposited twice weekly on the back stoop.

"Love and Marriage," "Cry Me a River," "Sentimental Journey," "Three Coins in the Fountain," "Rags to Riches," "Music, Music, Music": these are pieces of an unending cycle of story-poems, an opera without boundaries or fixed roles that has been unfolding since before I was born and will keep playing until I figure out what they are singing about. Understanding is gradual and always partial. Now and then an isolated phrase stands out. The turning of Kay Starr's "Wheel of Fortune" mesmerizes even while its function remains unknown.

When Doris Day sings "the future's not ours to see," it's as if she's dropping a disturbing hint into an atmosphere of confident sweetness.

The songs take place in a world complete in itself yet with tantalizing connections to the one in which the music pours out. In that world one degree removed, the singers invite each other for dinner and sleigh rides, travel by boat to tropical islands, wake up with notes on their pillows, walk home angry because of what happened at the dance, see birds on the grass announcing a change in the weather, hear bells and weep, stay up all night and become lonely. It is a sphere defined by candles and kisses, tears and letters and eyelashes, parties and jukeboxes and lipstick and doorsteps. South of the border down Mexico way it happened in Monterey in a little Spanish town, lady of Spain I adore you on the isle of Capri and on Santa Catalina the isle of romance and when the swallows come back to Capistrano. I wish I didn't love you so, I love you so much it hurts, I'm alone because I love you, I'm the king of broken hearts, I'm nobody's baby till I waltz again with you.

The singers confide, flirt, choke up as their feelings uncontrollably spill out despite their brave efforts to smile through the tears. They cheer themselves (with help from some energetic backup singers) into gusty declarations of faith in sunshine and rhythm. They work very hard at their happiness. Or else—and here it no longer sounds like work, it's effortless flotation—they simply buoy up beyond loneliness and heartbreak into the paradise of harmony whose secrets have been handed on from the Yacht Club Boys to the Modernaires to the Pied Pipers, from the Mills Brothers to the Ink Spots to the Platters, from the Boswell Sisters to the Andrews Sisters to the McGuire Sisters to the King Sisters, from the Mel-Tones to the Hi-Lo's to the Four Freshmen, the Four Lads, the Four Aces. It is the Church of Sound: an ethereal cathedral made of breaths that intermesh to form "Laura" and "Poinciana" and "Perfidia" and "Stella by Starlight." In that realm there is mist on the lagoon, the moon shines alone, and the meadow is made of chimes.

If I can't tell how sad a song is—never having been jilted or had my heart broken, never having attended a dance or experienced the agonies that apparently take place there—other people let me know.

Sometimes it is sad for reasons I can only begin to guess. A reprise of Dick Haymes singing "It Might As Well Be Spring" brings back the war that ended just a few years earlier even if hardly anyone talks about it, coming out as it had done just as that war was ending. What a spring that was, when everyone wanted to be happy but couldn't quite manage to put that catastrophe behind them. Ruth sometimes starts to cry when one of the wartime songs comes on: "That was on the radio all the time just when your uncle was in the war. I can't help thinking about it every time I hear it, you're lucky you'll never know what an awful time that was." She wants to forget, as all of them want to forget, yet the war has become part of her speech, the phrases of its songs—"praise the lord and pass the ammunition" or "coming in on a wing and a prayer"—reduced by long use to comic catchphrases. The war is a consuming blackness impossible to imagine from within the solidity of that house. Bombs fell, soldiers were trapped. And people sang songs, these same songs about apple blossoms and polka dots?

Beneath the songs are further layers of sound, less freighted with emotion but penetrating deeper than the listener even suspects. Before any appreciation of sorrow or disaster has had time to form, a child is defenseless against the incursions of the pre-recorded jingles that will become the earliest remembered artifacts of human civilization. Even before speech or the least glimmer of understanding they have already taken up residence. Years later—at the most inappropriate moments—they will rise unbidden to consciousness, those little songs that were the delight of infancy:

> *Buy a Castro convertible sofa,*
> *It has comfort and beauty and style;*
> *So wake up to a Castro convertible,*
> *For Castro makes sleeping worthwhile*

or

> *Where the values go up, up, up*
> *And the prices go down down down!*

Robert Hall this season
Will show you the reason:
Low overhead, low overhead!

"I like Bosco," or the Wildroot Cream Oil song: these get their hooks in deeper than any subsequent hymn or love ballad, working their way into the circuitry while it is still forming. Here is substructure that will always be there, underneath the flights of fancy and cries of passion, like the oil burner in the basement that rumbles loud enough to seem at times on the verge of exploding.

Closely linked with the jingles—linked like chain mail—is the incidental clatter that delineates radio's structures and thereby the divisions of the day, the fanfares and signature themes that mark the ends and beginning of shows, the station identifications, the emergency teletype signaling news flashes, the melting organ warble underscoring the narration at the beginning of a soap opera ("In our last episode, Rosemary learned that as a result of his amnesia her husband Jim has married another woman"), the emphatic cues that give the radio world the air of a railroad station where trains forever arrive and depart amid swarming crowds and billowing smoke.

Over the course of sweltering afternoons the radio transmits the roar of baseball games, horse races, prize fights. The ball games are an abstract drama whose story line—a pattern of chance incursions and concerted flankings—becomes absorbing primarily through the energies of the commentators. They never take their eyes off the invisible spectacle whose reality is attested by the surging murmur of the spectators responding to each abrupt turning. The game consists, finally, of a concerto for crowd noise and solo narrator, the narrator maintaining a steady oscillation between jabs and drones, gasps and clucks, and ready at any instant to translate climactic action into soaring extended outbursts, articulate shouts. He is just as ready to introduce a further structural variation by weaving in the inevitable jingles:

Hey, getcha cold beer,
Hey getcha Ballantine beer!

and do some pitching himself: "Yes, folks, on a hot summer afternoon there's nothing like the cold, refreshing taste of Ballantine beer . . ." The world makes a great noise as it goes about its business. My older brothers, Bob and Joel, are glued to its moment-by-moment shifts of gravity. Baffled, I only half listen.

All this pours in before there has been a chance to get a real sense of chronology. How did we end up here? What happened before what, who met who first, in what other world? Such knowledge—the history of the house and those who live in it, where it belongs in that global geography I only begin to grasp, block by block, station by station—is not acquired in orderly fashion. A past is constructed, haphazardly, from stray documents and neglected trinkets, bits of rec- ollection and interrupted dialogues, the story about the night on the roof or the old apartment before the war, or the car door that swung open on the highway. Bootleggers steered boats somewhere near Pearl Harbor, either before or after the blizzard of '48. The piano player got drunk at the wedding, a different wedding, not the one where grand- father's dance band played. That was years before the famous boating galas on the lake in summer, and the riot on amateur night.

The stitching together of the fragments takes place in the midst of a present that never stops. Hard to find time to sort out the past while caught up in a circus full of noisy and imposing attractions. The peo- ple in the family are forever on their way to or from meetings, recep- tions, rehearsals, music lessons, concerts, opening nights, taping ses- sions. They transform themselves with Cub Scout uniforms, satiny gowns, brilliant ties and caps. Trousers are ironed into knife-edge creases. Hair is made to gleam. They arrange for walls to be painted or a hammock set up in the garden in time for the first party of summer; they string lights up and take them down in season; learn lines, learn scales, block scenes, work out playlists, always with enough commo- tion to make it seem that the rehearsal itself is a play, the house a the- ater periodically resounding with monologues and bursts of small- group jamming.

In scattered pieces the story comes out. The puppets came from Germany, the wooden ones in the shapes of Crone and Maiden, Jester and Wizard. Dad bought them there after the war. What war? The war with Germany and Japan. Cities were burned in air raids. Dad would have been shipped to Japan except for the atom bomb. Joel was born during the war. Bob too; he came before him, just after Pearl Harbor. It was a long war. Your uncle suffered terribly. No, Ruth wasn't in the house then, she was in Pennsylvania helping Mom's parents. Mom had left the country already to go to the city to be an actress. She went on the road with *Stage Door* and afterward she met Dad in an acting class. He worked in radio, so she showed up at the station with her sister, trying to sell an idea for a new kind of quiz show. No, they didn't buy it. And then one New Year's Eve—it was the year Germany invaded Poland—while the World's Fair was on—he was doing a live broadcast from a rooftop, right in the middle of the city, and looked down into the crowd and there she was, and that time they got married.

The war went on and he kept working in radio—doing all sorts of things at the station back then, sports, music, interviews, commercials, jokes—because radio was important for morale. Besides, he had two children at home. But toward the end of it they started calling up everybody. And then the bomb dropped on Hiroshima and Dad went to Frankfurt and did a radio show for the troops, and bought the puppets. After he got home from the war and the youngest child was born, the apartment in the city near the bridge really was too small. Dad was doing very well now; he had the morning show and the cigar spots for the Friday night fights and on top of that his picture in *Life*. So they packed up everything and moved into the house in the town just outside the city limits, the pleasant town that Mom remembered from when she had acted in a play there once, before the war. It was almost like the country except that it was full of houses. And here we are.

Music seeps from every enclave in the house, as if each room were a separate village with its own traditions and rhythm patterns. As a child wandering from room to room—or crawling, in some play of soldiers or explorers—I detect the characteristic sound of each enclosure, the signature music of its inhabitant. They are such large beings that they have soundtracks attached to them, like characters in movies. They choose the beats and harmonies by which they wish to live. The shortwave radio by Ruth's bed, for example, can reel in the Grand Ole Opry live on a Saturday night, and Ernest Tubb and Kitty Wells might be followed by, say, an hour of hymns presented by the Billy Graham Crusade, "Rock of Ages" and "Abide with Me" and "Jesus Loves Me, This I Know."

It is only a thin wall that separates those sounds from the music on the other side, in Joel's room where the hours are marked by nonstop bebop, what Ruth calls "that terrible noisy music, it gives me a headache to listen to it!" They play for hours: Art Blakey, Art Pepper, Art Farmer, Art Taylor, Babs Gonzales, Harold Land, Johnny Griffin, Horace Silver, Horace Parlan, Shelley Manne, Russ Freeman, Gerry Mulligan, live from the Black Hawk, the Lighthouse, Birdland, the Five Spot, the Newport Jazz Festival. The rests between blowing sessions are interspersed with the voices of Lord Buckley doing the New Testament in hip talk or Lenny Bruce playing all the parts in a Warner Brothers prison picture or Kenneth Patchen reading his poem "The Murder of Two Men by a Young Man Wearing Lemon-Colored Gloves" to jazz accompaniment.

Here the music goes on all night, even at dawn. It's turned down so low it sounds like the scratching of a squirrel trapped in the walls. Sometimes Joel accompanies it on his drums, otherwise on the drum pad that must substitute for them in the still hours. "A Night in Tunisia," "Jordu," "Ah-Leu-Cha," "Airegin," "Manteca": these exotic stopovers (are those places? people? foreign words?) full of trumpets and saxophones and vibraphones move back in space and time, as far as the prehistoric world sketched by Charles Mingus in the whirlwind of *Pithecanthropus Erectus*. It takes me a long time, years, to hear the music as tune or pattern, as anything but the sonic overflow of the people playing it—those monosyllabic beings Bud, Chet, Prez, Getz, Miles, Hawk, Newk, Monk—the people photographed on the covers of the albums, at dawn and midnight, haunted and exhausted, slumped over a music stand or alone on a city street, arms flung out exuberantly or wrapped in impenetrable meditation. They are driven by an energy that apparently can never be satisfied, that wants only to keep going all night. A landscape of smoke and smeared lighting is required—suitable for tunes called "Blue Haze" or "When Lights Are

Low"—with enough areas blurred or blotted out to permit those cries and rumbles, those urgent bursts of dialogue couched in a secret alphabet of noise, the dark space they need to expand in.

At the bottom of the stairs leading to the attic room that Bob has by now carved out for himself, to get away from the room he used to share with Joel—he was in junior high school and needed more room for his records and scores, his French horn and conductor's baton—there echoes the not so distant booming of Wagner, Mahler, Bruckner, Orff, Hindemith, Prokofiev, Stravinsky, played if possible at the highest volume. These sounds suggest an entirely different kind of story. This gigantic audible architecture, which has room inside it for deafening chorales and brass fanfares, the sarcasm of courtiers and the pain of prisoners, tumultuous second-act finales and protracted deaths, is a music of event. At the top of the stairs, filtering down into the lower reaches of the house from its mountain home, it describes a landscape of peaks and crevasses. The horns are perhaps hewn from rock. Violins shriek among crags. Piccolos and bassoons consort like maddened goblins. It's the Walpurgisnacht scene, the Fantastic Symphony, the Ritual of the Ancients. After death comes transfiguration, whatever that might be: something that can be described only in music, never in words.

Operas go on for hours. Saturday afternoons he's taping them. They are not merely sung stories but worlds constructed entirely of music. They are furnished by kettle drums, costumed by clarinets, illuminated by flutes, watered by streams of violas. A dream stage—whether Catfish Row or the gardens of the palace of Turandot or the foredeck of the *Pinafore*—rises in the middle of blackness. The artifice is made more artificial by being merely imagined from album covers or the photographs in *Opera News,* far from any actual opera house. Only think what it must be like! He has murdered his daughter. He has been tricked into executing his brother. They have stabbed her son. She is losing her mind right on stage.

Once the process has been set in motion it can no longer be stopped. The innocents will not be rescued. The concentrated emotional force of the finale of Act Two cannot be evaded. The earliest hints of oboe or glockenspiel build inexorably toward the final orchestral debacles: the smashing of the anvil, the enacting of the curse. Is this something like what history might be, these crashes that people cannot duck even as they see them coming? These overarching and colliding shapes beneath and among which their lives try to continue, almost as if there had been no war, no murders, no ruined palaces?

At other times the mood of the music in Bob's room changes, because even history must have a rest. A different kind of immensity takes its place, the blare of Broadway—*yes, it has to be that loud*—and the pulsing big-band arrangements of Quincy Jones or Luther Henderson, festivals of precise blare and timed explosion. This begins to be a story about power deliberately and rationally wielded, about how the machinery of sound elicits involuntary responses, makes the listener want to dance, join the army, surrender to prayer, lose himself in sheer exactness of pitch and cadence. There are musicians dedicated to constructing a world devoid of mistakes, where things click always neatly into their appointed slots. It will be another stretch of time before I grasp that what I'm hearing is embedded in the ruled sheets covered with black ink dots and vertical strokes and inexplicable bits of Italian terminology that are maps of sound. The secret can be made explicit through the deciphering of diagrams and codes.

These are august mysteries, distant glimpses of a cathedral to be explored on some later day, only just not yet. What childish relief to turn to music on a scale whose implications my ears can encompass, like the theme songs streaming from the bulky black-and-white television installed in the upstairs den that overlooks the driveway. They are ready-to-eat folk tunes off a cereal box, toys for the ear. When one of these plays it drowns out every other possibility of sound, whether it is

> *Wyatt Earp, Wyatt Earp,*
> *Courageous and daring and bold:*
> *Long live his fame and long live his glory*
> *And long may his story be told*

or

Robin Hood, Robin Hood,
Riding through the glen,
Robin Hood, Robin Hood,
With his band of men:
Feared by the bad,
Loved by the good,
Robin Hood, Robin Hood.

These are the songs it is actually incumbent on me to master—my proper repertoire, the anthems of my world. Everything else is overheard and only half understood. These, by contrast, were clearly brought into being for my particular benefit. They must have been, since no one else in the house even finds them tolerable.

That there is music that cannot be tolerated I've learned from hearing my father and brothers, as they sit around a table at the latter end of a suburban afternoon, arguing the merits of Crosby versus Sinatra, written music versus improvised, Lester Young versus Benny Goodman, opera versus rhythm and blues, Johann Strauss versus Mahler, bop versus Dixieland. "I need the machine, I'm taping *Parsifal*." "As punishment for what?" There are sounds that some people cannot bear to hear: "That's not music, that's Chinese water torture." There are sounds in whose defense people will shout passionately even if it disturbs what was to have been a quiet Sunday.

Lives and all the significance and effort attached to them are at stake, hence the shouting: the lives it takes to learn the scales, develop the embouchure, become effortlessly adept at sight-reading and transposing and improvising, and on top of that to learn the ropes of the business, meet the right people, keep up with changes in fashion and technique. It's still not enough; you also need luck. Each recording is a convergence of lives. You can't imagine how those people fought, beat their brains out, just to get near a mike, and just to get the record played on the radio.

The turmoil is happening in another room, while I sprawl out on the porch where the climate is free of argument. From down the block I hear the music most native to me, the ultimate suburban melody of summer dusk, as the circular tootling of the Mister Softee theme beyond the hedges signals the approaching ice cream truck. (I will forget about it until the day when, inevitably, the Beach Boys work it into a song.) Sundown is at hand. I am killing time waiting for my favorite show to go on.

It is happy music that the television sets loose in the house: peppy, chirpy, never quite rollicking or out of control, punctuated by ticktocks. The themes from shows like *December Bride* and *I Married Joan* know only how to bounce; other themes, the ones for game and quiz and sing-along, know only how to announce show time—get ready folks—curtain going up—everything's ready to roll—here it comes, it's here. Television music acquires urgency from the fact that it can be heard only once a week, when the program is actually on. Often, since there is only that one shot, I tune in mainly to hear the theme. A fixture like the "request" theme on the Perry Como show—

> *Letters, we get letters*
> *We get stacks and stacks of letters*
> *Dear Perry, would you be so kind*
> *As to fill a request*
> *And sing the song I like best—*

has the comfort of liturgy. Saturday has come again, as it always ought to.

The curtain goes up on frills and gleaming backdrops. There is an ongoing televised music festival presided over by Dinah Shore, Bing Crosby, Pearl Bailey, Polly Bergen, Louis Armstrong, Fred Astaire, Jo Stafford, Vic Damone, Gisele MacKenzie. They all know each other, and smile at each other as at some perpetual family reunion. They exchange anecdotes about burlesque, vaudeville, the movie business; they engage perpetually in "tributes" to one aspect or another of an apparently familiar past that bears no resemblance to any known reality, a past that comprises soft-shoe numbers, music hall patter, Gay Nineties balladry and barbershop quartets, the Sophie Tucker medley, the Al Jolson medley, the George M. Cohan medley, the hayride bit, the country auction bit, the circus bit, the Dutch ice skaters bit, the polka party bit, the Mississippi steamboat bit (the girls wear hoop skirts, the boys have top hats and walking sticks) set to the tune of "Waiting for the Robert E. Lee." After the variety shows are over, the late movies come on, where some of the same singers show up twenty or thirty years younger doing the original versions of the same songs. How could those faces once have been so smooth? "They were a lot younger then." It is the first lesson in aging.

Soon will come the epoch of the violence-tinged jazz of the cops-and-robbers shows, the age of *Dragnet* and *Perry Mason,* of combos wailing from the nightclubs that line the neon boulevards of *77 Sunset Strip* or *Peter Gunn.* Finally—but by then it will already be clear that the world is changing in such unforeseeable ways that it will become something quite different, fascinating and terrifying—the oscillating and encircling themes of *The Twilight Zone* and *The Outer Limits* will invite me to let my mind be taken over by aliens, or by alien thoughts.

Late at night, every now and again, Mom and Dad might end up communing with some old favorite, the Benny Goodman Quartet or Artie Shaw and the Gramercy Five, sounding just as it did when first heard at the Famous Door or at Carnegie Hall, or broadcast live at midnight back when the "sweet" bands began to give way to swing. On her own, though, my mother is the least likely of anyone in the house to play a record or turn on radio or television. Maggie alone suggests, by her own restraint, that it might be preferable to savor an occasional moment of silence, and finds it in kitchen or garden or in the living room when everyone else has gone away for a moment. Only then—thinking perhaps that no one is listening—might she lift the piano lid and idly run through a half-remembered fragment of a Chopin nocturne, a sound unearthly in its stillness by contrast with the bands who battle by day and night from one machine to another.

There are times when she has a door closed and I can catch through the wooden divide an isolated music of unaccompanied language, the actual words not quite audible, as she runs over lines for a play. The tremor of a sustained monologue by Shakespeare or O'Neill or Tennessee Williams—variants of grief, madness, breakdown—is unmistakably a kind of singing, a matter of rises and falls and rests and dynamic shifts. The prosier percussion of the dialogue from *Dial M for*

Murder or *Witness for the Prosecution* or *Separate Tables,* the clipped interjections of courtroom drama and drawing-room comedy. Every specimen of theatrical discourse has its place along the spectrum that leads from throwaway chitchat to full-blown *arioso.*

At other times she creates spaces that need no sound to ornament them, centers of decorative calm marked out by flowers and vases, shawls and painted landscapes. If each person in the house carries around a certain musical environment, a repertoire implicit in tone and bearing and speech patterns, she has elected the domain of meditative silence. It is almost as if she reproached the ultimate inadequacies of even the most splendid and overpowering music. Silence is what is left to savor after even the finest harmonies become tiresome.

Without the music being funneled into the house, carried on wires or transmitted by television from some remote pylon, or dredged by a needle out of the spiraling grooves, what would the world sound like? Even the silence when everyone is asleep can be broken down into the rattling of insects or sonar of night birds, distant ground-bass of nighttime traffic on Northern Boulevard, clack of branch against window as if a burglar hidden under the ledge were tapping to test perimeter defenses, the slurred howl of the wind. Whatever unidentifiable sound is left over might be cosmic interference whistling all the way from the cold bright stars above the tree tops. In its passage it is translated—bounced by what Einsteinian peculiarity of spatial curvature?—into a faint falsetto chorale broadcasting from deep in the inner ear. The distant choir beckons to come closer, go deeper inside, lose yourself in the music.

At the year-end festival of Christmas, the inevitable symbolic center of life, the house reaches its annual crescendo. Crowded with relatives as none of our future residences ever will be, it is converted for a few nights into a bustling hotel. Overlapping conversations weave together a dozen different lives. Room is somehow found in closets for overcoats and overnight cases, jars for spare toothbrushes, a corner to put a bugle or a photo album in, sofas and spare cots for those aunts and uncles, cousins and grandparents who have made a far journey, from Scranton or Yonkers or a military base on the other side of the world, to be there. The house is transformed as its ordinary functions are redesigned to accommodate the guests, unexpected surfaces strewn with peculiar razors and scarves and packets of breath mints. On the great morning itself, others nearer at hand will drive over to stay for the whole nearly interminable day. Music is the only proper culmination of such disorderly stirring.

After sunset, when the uproar of the long dinner table has subsided, the family starts to gather near the piano. Pop—my mother's father, a piano teacher whose home is filled with 78s by Art Tatum and Pete Johnson and Mary Lou Williams, and who years ago, I have heard, led a dance band in Pennsylvania's Wyoming Valley—takes his traditional place at the keyboard. The song books are laid out and the succession of tunes begins, a bouncing start with "Jingle Bells" leading by easy steps into the more serious challenges of "Joy to the World" and "Hark, the Herald Angels Sing."

If the process remains at all orderly, it's only because the younger participants care that things be done in the ordained sequence and without leaving out any essential steps. The value of such order, however, is in the raucous disorderliness it keeps only slightly at bay. Christmas is the marriage of chaos and design. The real sound of life, for once, can burst out because a formal place has been set for it. At the moment when things have gotten sufficiently loose, the secret selves that these familiar persons hold inside them shake the room. Ten or twelve hoarse and booming voices full of ale and Christmas wine join in on the fa-la-la's of "Deck the Halls," or, with unexpectedly sweet and heartfelt chanting, fill out the lines of "Silent Night" or "What Child Is This?" As always somebody tries and fails to hit the high C in "O Holy Night." An aunt from the Catholic side of the family makes, once again, a well-worn joke about the difficulties of singing "Away in a Manger": "What do you expect from a song written by Martin Luther?" An undercurrent of clowning and jostling is part of the process by which we succeed finally in making our necessary noise: despite the difficulty of getting the words right, of getting the singers on the same page, of keeping the ritual from falling apart into the anarchy of separate impulses. From such clatter—extended and punctuated by whatever instrument is handy, a triangle, a tambourine, a Chinese gong—beauty is born. By this standard of high emotion and exuberant total participation all other music will be measured.

Christmas, as event, is too turbulent really to be perceived. It can only be anticipated or recollected. Only in the contemplation of imaginary Christmases can its mournful side emerge. When I watch the British movie of *A Christmas Carol*, shown regularly on television every December, the tears well up on cue as the choristers launch into "Barbara Allen":

> *In Scarlet Town where I was born*
> *There was a fair maid dwelling . . .*

In the melancholy of minor-key melodies like "God Rest Ye Merry Gentlemen" or "Oranges and Lemons" or "Greensleeves" can be heard, as through a half-opened door, intimations of a boy-soprano universe of lovely grief. It is a universal folk music that dares to propose unhappy endings not only for individual lives but for life itself. In its unearthly prettiness it is sadder than Teresa Brewer nursing a broken heart or Vic Damone having a lonely time on Saturday night. This is a sorrow that no big band flourish, with its brassy cheer, can quite put right: the sorrow that is our native condition, the one that advertised remedies can't reach. It will come back, even after everybody else is dead, to clarify what the world finally is. The sweetness—the keening frequencies that will return in "Scarlet Ribbons" and "In the Pines" and "The Springhill Mining Disaster"—camouflages a message of doom.

Beyond the family there are further communities, of church and school and summer camp, under whose tutelage children acquire a repertoire of hymns, marches, rounds, humorous ballads, lullabies, dance tunes. The elementary school standbys—"Comin' Round the Mountain," "Oh! Susanna," "Reuben, Reuben," "A Bicycle Built for Two"—are supplemented in summer by the songs of campfire and trail, "The Happy Wanderer," "Hey, Ho! Nobody Home," or "Marching to Pretoria." The group sing winds up, as darkness gathers on the mountain top, in a final chorus of "Day Is Done."

Singing in church can seem like Christmas without the fun; but the dreariness of the service and the discomfort of the benches accentuate the thrill of the musical component. If I choose to attend Sunday services that the rest of the family takes little or no interest in, it is finally only because there is nowhere else I can go to get lost in "O Come, O Come Emanuel," "We Gather Together," "A Mighty Fortress Is Our God," or "Holy, Holy, Holy." It's a voluntary self-abandonment—almost a secret vice—to the sorrow the songs hold as if in safekeeping.

The hymns proclaim what depths they sound. They speak of "soul" and "eternity"; merely to sing them is to enter a domain of solemnity. Other songs—the silliest, sung to amuse the very young—sting where least expected:

> *Row, row, row your boat*
> *Gently down the stream*
> *Merrily, merrily, merrily, merrily*
> *Life is but a dream*

Mother sings to baby, her sister joining in: two women still young enough to be silly, dissolving in giggles that in recollection make a music of ultimate indulgent delight. When, in the mind's silence, the song plays back, it soothes less than intended. In that dream what can become of you, or your boat? Here we go down the stream vanishing.

A certain tradition still stands to the side, part of the implicit architecture of all that we inhabit: the world of "real music" shored up on the one hand by piano lessons and the other by gigantic institutions like the Metropolitan Opera and the New York Philharmonic. RCA Victor runs full-page ads in *Life* to plug Toscanini's "transcendent" performance of an all-Wagner program and comparing the tone of the Minneapolis Symphony under Dimitri Mitropoulos to "clear, rich wine." Saturday afternoons there is opera on the radio: Texaco presents *La Forza del Destino*. Who more appropriately than an oil company could present the force of destiny or the twilight of the gods? Opera is reassuring like the ball game, and like the ball game accompanied by its own characteristic narration, delivered in a suave and sonorous baritone: "And so, as Leonora weeps in shame and Baltazar thunders the terrible words of the Papal curse, the curtain falls on Act Two of Donizetti's *La Favorita* . . . " In the cities there are said to be neighborhoods where you can still set your watch by "Caro nome" or "Vissi d'arte," Tebaldi beaming outward from the radio perched on a fire escape. But a hundred little signs proclaim that the splendor has begun to fade. The movie of Toscanini conducting the Hymn of the Nations, screened regularly for schoolchildren, is splotchy, the soundtrack scarcely audible. The ear is cocked toward the past, to catch the strains of the departed masters.

In the schools there are still music appreciation classes in which immortal melodies are set to appropriate mnemonic lyrics so effective that no one need ever again be stumped in this lifetime:

Beethoven's Fifth
Starts out like this

or

This is the symphony
That Schubert wrote
But never finished . . .

The children are encouraged to close their eyes to envision the woodland characters of *Peter and the Wolf,* the snows of Russia destroying Napoleon's army while the Moscow bells ring out in the last bars of the *1812 Overture,* the strangled death-rattle of Tyl Eulenspiegel in Strauss's tone poem. A mimeographed lyric sheet for Carmen's song—

Love is like a wood bird wild
Whose nature never never can be tamed—

proves obscurely suggestive for sixth-graders already excited by the xylophones and flutes of Kabalaevsky's Saber Dance and de Falla's Ritual Fire Dance, exotic creations loosely classed in the same category as the Mexican Hat Dance or the hypnotic theme to *Alfred Hitchcock Presents*. Tricky music, *misterioso* music.

When the soundtrack album of *My Fair Lady* comes out, it's as if normal household business were suspended so that it can be played again and again, until each rhyme and inflection and melodic twist has been internalized; as if a new holiday had been born, fit to rank with Christmas and the Fourth of July. Broadway musicals are a tradition still alive, still offering up astonishing surprises, as latecomers like *My Fair Lady* and *West Side Story* and *Gypsy* join *South Pacific, Finian's Rainbow, Guys and Dolls, Kiss Me Kate, The Pajama Game, Damn Yankees.* Each brings not just new songs but new situations: musicals about underwear factories, about baseball players seduced by demons in black tights, about strippers, about street gangs. There is nothing that can't be made into a musical! People can even die in the end.

Each of the original cast albums is a world in itself, with its own emotional range and peculiarities of tone. Musicals are like what Verdi was, what Wagner was: only they're American, meaning they're also fun. People look forward to them, sensing that they will go on becoming more complex, more real, while never denying us a continuing supply of those legendary showstoppers in which the form finds ecstatic fulfillment, "There Is Nothing Like a Dame" or "This Is My Once a Year Day" or "You Gotta Have a Gimmick." Surely their hit songs will continue to be covered simultaneously by every major pop singer, they will continue to be transformed into widescreen musicals, and small children will continue to replicate their patter songs and dance numbers. Hardly any of us find any significance in the fact that in December 1954—the same year that the score of *The Pajama Game* provides Top 20 hits for Archie Bleyer, Patti Page, Rosemary Clooney, and Sammy Davis, Jr.—Bill Haley and His Comets also hit the Top 20 with "Shake, Rattle, and Roll."

The sound of all these disparate sounds bouncing off each other makes a higher music of clashing styles, unintended comic collisions, the honking traffic jams of a vigorous multiplicity. Yet as if all that were still not quite enough—even with the new and raucous intrusions of "See You Later Alligator" and "Be Bop a Lula" factored in—the ear fantasizes about other music that isn't even there. I listen for a music capable of summoning spirits or transporting me to alternate planes of being, music to charm snakes with or unleash the passions of harems: the music of pagan dances, lost civilizations, ancient secretly transmitted traditions. There have already been hints from sources whose authenticity is not yet in question: the muezzin in an episode of *Assignment Foreign Legion*; jungle drums in the movies, or even a bit of real African music surfacing in John Ford's *Mogambo;* Apache drums heard in terror at the Saturday matinee and then imitated in an ecstasy of imitative savagery on a souvenir authentic Indian-style tom-tom brought back from somebody's Colorado vacation: not least, from *South Pacific's* "Bali Hai," with its suggestion that the most haunting sound would come from afar, from an island hidden in mist. The song frustrates because, no matter how soothing it is, it alludes to something more beautiful and more potent, an inaudible song hidden beyond the song that can be heard. What Juanita Hall sings is not the actual call of Bali Hai, merely the promise that Bali Hai "will call" when you're ready and if you're lucky.

The real sound of the call of Bali Hai might of course turn out to be quite different in its sonorities from what the Rodgers and Hammerstein song suggests. That savagery has something important to do with that imagined call is becoming apparent no matter what direction you look in, whether toward Charles Mingus's *Pithecanthropus Erectus* or Stravinsky's *The Rite of Spring* or Les Baxter's *Ritual of the Savage*. In one form or another there is the promise of a return to an oddly familiar land of terror and beauty, nakedness and feathers, altars and waterfalls. In such a country the grammar of music is permitted to break down so it can be reassembled into new forms, new languages, new histories, new beings. Nothing here can ever be too discordant or too impassioned. Swirls and crashes are as at home as moans and ululations. Unearthly notes are chanted by an ancient princess: is it Yma Sumac? This is no mere chaos. It offers up brilliant unsuspected patterns, zigzag xylophone lines cut with a shark's tooth, blues songs played by cave priests, a percussive thunder made by naked feet on sacred ground, chants echoing from hollow trees.

The sound swells into annihilating blare, a siren alarm that swallows that whole primitive world and then—and this is where my dream becomes a nightmare—flips without warning into its opposite, Stan Kenton's *City of Glass*. The cover illustration of that most dissonant of big band creations, with its landscape of neon glimmer and convergent steel megaliths, has already prepared the ears for armies of horns and a monstrous clash of tonalities. I seem to hear the terrifying dissonant weight of the "modern," the Big Machine that everyone will within this lifetime be forced to inhabit, as it rumbles ever closer.

Start poking around and authentic strangeness pops up in the most ordinary places, like the record rack at the local library, where I borrow volumes from the Folkways international series. One of these, picked at random, brings Mom downstairs early one Sunday morning, woken by the startlingly abrasive work song of a Japanese woodcutter. "It's not really very musical, is it, dear?" she asks politely but pleadingly. Microtones can cause strange disturbance, as if they threatened the otherwise stable coordinates of daily life. More tempting yet, among my parents' 78s, is a collection of Haitian music, souvenir of a trip to Port au Prince. Voodoo rites secretly recorded! Such a thing not only exists but is in the room: here, inside this weathered brown sleeve. What might it sound like? What unforeseeable effects might it not produce in the unwary listener? One of these songs—a pentatonic chant repeated over and over, apparently translatable as "Innocent, I am innocent"—sinks in instantly and for years will mark the limits of the knowable.

In any event the knowledge that any music imparts is not necessarily of the world, or at least of this world. It is into other spaces, absent, imagined, seemingly infinite, that the hearer is initiated. The unknown melody secretes histories without names, voyages undertaken without a body, love affairs of mysterious intimacy in which the beloved remains unknowable. Here is generosity without motive—embodied in, say, a low tone sustained by Bing Crosby as if he were as startled by the timbre of it as anyone else—or grief without bottom, a lament for the loss of what one has never, or not yet, known.

On the abandoned old record player in the play room—the one still equipped with a needle for playing 78s—I dip into the library of sounds. The record albums are the most arcane books of all, the ones that can best be read with eyes closed. I subject myself to them as to exotic experiments: Michel Legrand's *Bonjour Paris,* the overture from *The Gypsy Baron,* Germaine Montero's tribute to French music hall, José Marais and Miranda in a program of traditional Afrikaaner melodies. The 78s, by the time I get around to them, have become obsolete. It happened only a few years ago, but they already seem part of an irretrievable world. That's what happens to industrial products when they suddenly stop being manufactured.

A small pile of these acquire magical status as testimony of a past that can never seem as recent as it in fact is: Paul Robeson's rendition of "The Song of the Peat Bog Soldiers," an already haunting song made doubly so in light of its origins among concentration camp prisoners; Billie Holiday's "I Cover the Waterfront," containing the essence of romantic fatality and star-shot darkness, a sorrow that becomes comprehensible because translated into a tangible geography of lights glimmering through damp fog; Fats Waller's "Mister Christopher Columbus," bottling the essence of a humor able to withstand any tempest, a bounce heavy enough to repel unfriendly boarders; the raucous imitation revival meeting on an old Stinson record featuring Woody Guthrie, Cisco Houston, and Sonny Terry: "I'm gonna walk the streets of glory, I'm gonna walk the streets of glory one of these days." Woody Guthrie's anomalous fiddle solo "900 Miles"—it may have been the only fiddle tune he knew—is a spiral modal sawing that generates space, miles and miles of it, a flat prairie seen from the rear car of a departing freight train. No time for farewells, no possibility of return: the abandoned past eternally wailing, beyond change, beyond hope.

Each of these records could stand by itself for a climate, a history, a state of being. Each is so big, so isolated, like Greenland or Australia. Later there will be sixty songs, six hundred, six thousand. But for the moment imagine that there are only six records in the world: "900 Miles" and "I Cover the Waterfront" and "Streets of Glory" and "The Peat Bog Soldiers" and "Mr. Christopher Columbus" and the Haitian voodoo song. They have to substitute for everything else, and they can, because each is immense. The disks themselves—at once heavy and fragile, and freighted with an extra layer of surface noise—suggest a past surviving against heavy odds. It must be given special attention because its traces—carved into those thick grooves and extracted from them with a thick obsolete needle as crude as a barnyard nail—are so easily smashed. The past is retrieved, but just barely, and it is forever in danger of being smashed beyond recapturing: I learned that the day "The Viper's Drag" slipped from between my fingers. But whatever might be lost or broken or forgotten is nothing compared to the miraculous rebirth that occurs every time the needle hits the groove. Here is Fats Waller himself, not dead but present, so present that he overwhelms the well-ordered precincts of the living room. The sound sprawls. What vibrates here has more life than any room. In ecstasy Fats slams the keys to lay down the unending groove of "Lulu's Back in Town."

3

From a Family Album
Wyoming Valley's Most Famous Band

T HE RAINBOW CLUB ORCHESTRA CONSTITUTED A BRIGHT EPISODE in the entertainment world of eastern Pennsylvania during the early '30s. To local pageants and festivals, to campuses and music halls and newly opened dance palaces, they brought the excitement and gaiety of the most modern musical sounds, making them favorites of young people from Hazleton in the southeast to Carbondale in the north, from the Ideal Ballroom in Luzerne to the Tempo Club in Carmel. The local airwaves vibrated to live broadcasts of their concerts, and no celebration was complete without their full-bodied sound and their dapper, unfailingly professional stage presence. Wherever they went they spread an aura of magic and romantic possibility, as their sweet and sometimes swinging sounds took audiences away from a world of cares and chores into the realm of music.

Or, try it another way: The Rainbow Club Orchestra was a ten-piece dance band made up largely of untrained musicians scuffling to survive in a region suffering from the worst effects of the Depression. Eking out a living as mine workers or door-to-door salesmen or factory hands, barely finding time to rehearse, lugging instruments, cumbersome music stands, the metal trumpet hats for that "burnished brass sound," and stacks of arrangements from one small town to another along narrow and dilapidated mountain roads, they were lucky if they could make five bucks a man for many hours of continuous playing. They managed to keep it together for five or six years. They never recorded or even had an offer. Their arranger eventually committed suicide. They disappeared into that limbo where unrecorded dance bands play without interruption for the ghosts of the unremembered.

Behind the recorded music from that era that I heard as a child, their absent music hovered. Ignorant of nearly everything about music except for the fact that recordings existed, I was unduly disturbed by the idea of music drifting off into the ether without leaving a trace behind. Did that mean it was for nothing?

Roughly from 1930 to 1935 my grandfather, Bob Owens, was the leader of the Rainbow Club Orchestra. There was of course no Rainbow Club; it was simply the imaginary club at the end of the rainbow, neither too rowdy nor too buttoned-down, a hall of ordered delights, airy, floral, luminous. It was the place where you might well want to end up, especially if the alternative was a nearly played-out industrial landscape of mines and iron works, whose gouged mountainsides marked the limits of a history consisting mostly of a famous Indian massacre. Right there—somewhere in back of the rudimentary motor lodges and roadside eateries—was where the redcoats and the Iroquois slaughtered two hundred American militiamen. The scene's elaborate horror still seemed to hang around, as if the ages that followed had been a more or less subdued aftermath to that primordial burst of violence.

In a framed photograph of the Rainbow Club Orchestra, taken somewhere in Pennsylvania around 1932, my grandfather—already in his mid-forties—extends his baton toward the ten uniformed members of his band, the very figure of metronomic precision. The music can only be imagined. A little like Paul Whiteman, perhaps, but with modern touches suggested by those other Pennsylvania bandleaders, the Dorsey Brothers, who had done so well for themselves with "Dixie Dawn" and "Fine and Dandy"? The locals wanted polkas too, but Pop wanted something more like jazz, when they'd let him; something that would let him feel the self-respect of a real musician, not just a hired hand.

Pop was a man who carried the nineteenth century around with him. He existed in his own self-contained sphere, balancing rigidity and ease in a manner he seemed to have invented for himself. In the measured cadence with which he would cross a room, rise from a table, or make the rounds of his small backyard, some remnant of the bandleader setting tempos could still be discerned. His speech was as laconic as his jacket was unwrinkled, and his morals as strict as his sartorial decorum. The sight of a woman smoking on the street was enough to spoil his morning walk: "If they want to smoke at home I don't mind, but on the street it just doesn't look right." He remembered the advent of electric light and the gradual disappearance of horse-drawn wagons from dark villages where nothing like a boogie woogie record had yet been imagined.

Hidden away in a drawer was a group photo taken in 1913, in which he stood among his hundreds of co-workers at the Vulcan Iron Works in Wilkes-Barre, the bare walls of that immense workspace decorated with a huge American flag. The occasion, to judge from the inscription posted on the other wall, was Mother's Day, although there was not a mother in sight: only a mass of unsmiling men, some who look as if they could no longer remember ever having smiled, some (the younger ones) barely keeping themselves from cracking up in the middle of the solemn occasion. Some have taken the trouble to wear a vest and bow tie, others are dressed in something close to rags, arms folded or hands placed awkwardly on knees. In the corner sits one man with a trombone, a promise of music to come, to enliven the bareness of the scene. My grandfather wears a simple dark shirt and stares directly into the camera with an expression of indecipherable seriousness.

In a few years he would migrate to Bethlehem to work in the steel mills, and at the boarding house he would catch the eye of the beautiful Hungarian girl staying there with her aunt; in what seemed like no time at all they would find themselves married, and he would be looking for something better than factory work. Anna wouldn't settle for him not doing something to better himself, so as not to end up like the old men in that group shot, the life drained out of them by years of work without hope. Her younger sister's husband became foreman over at the cigar factory; Bob ought to be able to do at least as well as that.

In later years he wore a pressed white suit even in the absence of an audience, a suit conserving an ideal of tranquility and effortless good form under any circumstances. He trimmed his moustache carefully each morning, affecting in sunny weather a straw hat suitable for the most elegant boating party, and punctuated his presence in the world with a cigar that he savored as if the sweetness of life were concentrated there, smiling as he smoked. A relative took me by the hand and emphasized, "Your grandfather is a fine-looking man, a really fine-looking man. Just take a good look at him."

With unobtrusive ceremony he shut the French doors of the antechamber where he smoked cigars and played piano. (The doors were kept sealed tight at Anna's insistence, to keep the cigar fumes from "stinking up the whole house.") Removed from the rest of the household, he could re-enter the music that was his private domain. It had been decades since the end of the Rainbow Club Orchestra, which survived only in that publicity photograph faded to a dark brown, remnant of a time when backs were straighter and faces more suavely masklike. Now he did his music-making on his own, and it was at the keyboard that he appeared most fully engaged, woken from the reverie in which he seemed to pass many of his hours, watching the rest of us amiably but at a certain remove, as if his deepest concerns lay elsewhere.

He smiled, laid into the rhythm of "Sweet Sue"—it was always "Sweet Sue"—his eyes brightening with a subdued merriment as the chords and bridges intersected in their pattern. Boogie woogie was the most delicate flower in the universe, and his job was to coax it into bloom. Watching him poised over the keys like a lynx preparing to pounce, and then observing the grace that seemed to descend on him as he eased into the propulsion of the phrase was to form preliminary notions of what such words as "shuffle" or "ramble" might mean, to sense just how meticulously and rigorously a person might cast off constraint. It was unthinkable that he would scream, or shout, or discernibly gyrate: the extreme mark of his abandonment was a tiny sustained smile of private delight.

His relaxed air notwithstanding, it was discipline he admired: "Only way to keep a band together." By then the band he observed most often was Lawrence Welk's, the inevitable Saturday night entertainment once he and Anna had settled in front of the television: "They're a good band . . . Nice clean-looking boys, and they really know how to play their instruments, not like some these days. It's not as easy as it looks!" Watching him watch the Welk show you could find, again, a trace of the bandleader, inspecting his men for grooming and on-stage manners, assessing their playing, appreciating above all the tight discipline that came off looking like a bunch of amiable fellows having a relaxed good time.

Later in the evening would come *Perry Mason,* and perhaps *Alfred Hitchcock Presents* or *77 Sunset Strip,* each with its distinctive theme never heard so distinctly as up here in the mountains. This was why people didn't go out dancing on Saturday night anymore, why bands couldn't make it like they used to. The power of television to fully occupy the human attention span had never been so evident to me as against this backdrop of a silence broken only by moths banging into the screen door. This was what culture consisted of now, and it felt too easy to surrender to it. There was nothing to do finally except sit on the sofa—thinking, "This is how it will be from now on, here and everywhere else, nobody will ever get up from the sofa again"—and watch the shows roll by, waiting for the moment when the horns blared out the monumental *Perry Mason* theme or swung into the irresistible invitation to *77 Sunset Strip*. Only when the last show had finished (they finished early in eastern Pennsylvania) was it necessary to confront again the mountaintop silence broken occasionally by a car rattling along the worn-down road just outside, its edges scattered with chunks of anthracite.

Everybody had become old. The village itself—the lakeside settlement, population 700, where Bob and Anna had established themselves after the kids grew up and moved out, in a snug simple house at the top of a hill—seemed to contain only memories of a life that had been, festivals fallen mysteriously into disuse, extended families that had withered and lost sight of their own branches. "It used to be": this was the phrase that opened vistas of candlelight revelry, the legendary excursion to Harvey's Lake, islands where they built fires once, the sound of young voices among the trees in the forest, on the path that led down to the water. There was a summer theater that finally closed, a dimly lit general store that seemed to have fewer and fewer items for sale each year during the fewer and fewer hours it stayed open, and where the advertising posters tacked to the wall were still in the '40s: Buy War Bonds Here.

They tore down the amusement park to make way for a meatpacking plant and then that closed too. Songs—on radio, on TV, or drifting into someone's consciousness by random association while sitting down to breakfast or dusting off the bookcase with its antique Bible and early issues of *National Geographic*—were often enough the cue to one or another lightning-brief recollection. "I can remember exactly how he looked that day." Nobody had written anything down, and from the early years there were hardly any photographs, so that only the songs could bring back some portion of what had been swept away each morning, until a lifetime of decades had drifted off while no one was noticing.

How easy could it have been, in those days when the Rainbow Club Orchestra was at its peak of activity, to play week after week for miners and factory workers and shop clerks, Polish, Czech, Hungarian, Welsh, Irish, at bandstands or dance halls scattered over the eastern half of the state? Half a century later the music and the people were all gone. There was only a heap of clippings to tell of "that master of rhythm" playing in the early '30s at Roseland Hall in Nanticoke, with a fox-trot contest on Saturday at which "a spot dance will be enjoyed," or of the Battle of Music that pitched the Rainbow Entertainers against Jimmy Knizer's Po-Amo Dance Band. There was a lot of dancing going on. It was that or the pictures. At the Orondo Ballroom in Wilkes-Barre—"the coolest spot in town," kept cool by bags of ice suspended from the ceiling, with fans blowing on them to spread the cold air around—admission was 35 cents for gents and 25 cents for ladies, and the dances were even broadcast live over local radio. At

Hazle Park, every Tuesday and Friday, there wasn't even a gate charge for dancers, if they could thread their way through the park's "continuous round of pleasure" featuring penny arcade, merry-go-round, horseshoe games, waffles for a nickel, and Timbu the Human Ape "on the midway to make you laugh."

But it was something to know that anyone's life, a neighbor's or a stranger's, might hinge on one of their encores: the one who cut in and walked off with the other one's girl, the one who changed her mind suddenly, the one who ran out in tears when the other two got up to dance, the one who just by coming in halfway through the set changed the whole atmosphere of the room, the ones who got into a fistfight eight bars into "Rhythm on the Range," the pair from different towns who found each other by chance and turned out to share a fondness for "Love in Bloom," the one who stared at the drummer all night and went home determined to save up for a kit himself, take lessons so he could make his fortune on a bandstand, the loyalists who showed up night after night, drove from one town to the next to keep up with the band, and for at least one long summer shaped their world around that personnel and repertoire, talking like experts about the skills and habits of the first clarinetist or what that hot trumpeter did to the third chorus of "Way Down Yonder in New Orleans." To feel, from just a few feet away, how ready each of them was to be changed by music was to sense that the Rainbow Club Orchestra was at least in spirit part of the same world as all the other bands out there, Bennie Moten's band in Kansas City and Milton Brown's in Fort Worth and Benny Goodman's in New York. They made things happen in the here and now. They established the center of the world every time they stepped up to play.

Did he tell himself he was coming up in the world? There was no telling what might happen in the music business. Every band leader had a rags to riches story. No silver spoons, they all made it the hard way. The Rainbow Club Orchestra had come to be billed as "Wyoming Valley's Most Famous Band," even if the local papers couldn't seem to keep the leader's name straight, billing him variously as Bob Owen, Bobby Owen, Bob Evans. Or were these his own attempts at the perfect name for a marquee, a name to resonate like George Olsen or Ted

Lewis or Larry Clinton? At times the Rainbow Club Orchestra mutated into "Bud" Owen's 42nd Street Rhythm and Bobby Owens and
His Ambassadors, swank names appropriate to the kind of jobs they
were starting to get. Moving up from the Masonic Temple, the Elks,
the Policemen's Ball, the St. Patrick's Dance, here they were playing at
Lake Silkworth following their successful tour of the Schuylkill Valley or celebrating Laurel Blossom Time at the famous Penn-Stroud
Hotel in Stroudsburg: "Here one may travel for many miles over
paved mountain trails, along murmuring streams and by picturesque
waterfalls where Mountain Laurel, in its natural setting, blooms for
the delight of countless thousands . . . The Poconos put on their best
dress during Laurel Blossom Time and beckon the city dweller to
come and share the season's glories." The Poconos came into their own
as a cut-rate vacation paradise appropriate for hard times.

At the Legion Home in Glen Lyon they backed up a personal appearance by Miss Anthracite, winner of the Scrantonian-Newton
Lake Beauty Pageant: that is to say, Mary Mahon, a local girl "known
in theatricals as Dolores Kay." A year later—it was 1934 by now—
Miss Anthracite ("she is 17 years old, five feet four inches high,
weighs 115 pounds and has red hair") took off for Hollywood, supposedly for a screen test at Paramount. The local paper captured her,
as if by chance, just as she was getting on the train, chaperoned by
Mrs. Paul Stenson of Carbondale. Another year passes. She surfaces
again, performing at yet another local dance. She is said to have recently returned from a trip to Hollywood, with no further comment.

At Roseland (eastern Pennsylvania's Roseland, not New York's) the
Rainbow Club Orchestra plays on Christmas Eve, with Carolina's Colored Dancing Sensation, Charles Jackson. At Jake's Tavern in Shick-
shinny they share the stage with Polly and Her Polly Anns Dance
Revue—"10 Beautiful Girls." Things seem to be loosening up in the
Wyoming Valley. A little of that New York sophistication is leaking
through. The Broadway Sunshine Revue, with its bevy of Beautiful
Girls, advertises its opening engagement in Wilkes-Barre with a line
drawing of a high-stepping chorine in short-short culottes, fancy
boots, and a pirate's hat tilted at a devilish angle: and beer is now
legally served. At the Plymouth High School Alumni Ball the band

prompts a local reporter to a small flight of eloquence: "Heard were the blaring of trumpets, the wailing of the slide trombone, the sweet high tones of the clarinet and the rhythm of the piano." They are now "considered the choice of leading colleges," playing at Bucknell and Colgate, and through local radio broadcasts they have been "instrumental in entertaining thousands over the ether waves."

But this was as far as it would go. The broadcasts never got beyond the line of mountains between the mills and the mines on one side and the world of opportunities on the other. Money had been getting tight in the valley for years as the mines emptied out, and it got tighter after the crash; the whole band had never gotten more than fifty bucks a night. What would it have taken? A little more economic leverage, a little more training, or just a little more drive, that elusive but indispensable quality, otherwise known as pep or gusto? Nobody ever called Pop a go-getter. To push himself forward he would have had to push other people out of the way, and that was not his bent.

They had the three kids now, and there never seemed to be quite enough money to support a family, until Anna, having studied the beautician's art in night school, opened a beauty salon in Nanticoke. The salon would thrive by catering to the girls from the silk mill. They'd get their hair bobbed as they flipped through *Photoplay* to study the plotline of the new Warren William picture—"He takes his secretary as his kept woman!"—or pondered their futures in the pages of *Modern Astrology*. Pop tried different things. He set up a piano studio and advertised in the local papers: "Play Your Way to Profits and Popularity . . . Now you can learn to play Piano in the style of famous Radio, Recording and Player Roll Artists." Some of his students, he claimed, were "now in professional fields," but there weren't enough of them. He opened a furniture store with a Polish partner; it folded in six months. He sold suits from door to door. The payoff was paltry; he lacked the requisite glibness.

He'd sworn he'd never work down in the mines, but by 1934 he no longer had a choice. The indignity was compounded by the fact that his younger brother was the manager of the mine, a job that didn't involve getting his hands dirty. The brother had a bigger house too, and a cottage up by Lake Nuangola, where the more successful local people were beginning to invest in weekend homes. The leader of the Rainbow Club Orchestra got up at dawn and rode the elevator down into the mineshaft to work as a topping inspector, supervising the loading of coal into cars. In his relatively brief career in those depths he acquired a profound discomfort in confined crowded spaces that would never leave him, just as the coal dust that got into his lungs would leave its permanent debilitating mark.

My earliest memories of him are from the early '50s. Pop was giving piano lessons in his home, teaching local children their Czerny exercises before initiating them into the rudiments of Tschaikovsky and Grieg and presenting them in lengthy recitals of such numbers as "A Spanish Fiesta," "On a Summer Sea," and "The Spinning Song." The house in Nuangola where he and Anna had settled wasn't lakefront property, but it was only a ten-minute walk down through the woods to get to the water. Pop's students didn't seem to come around very often for lessons. How many of them could there be, in this place of long unbroken silences where the big mystery to an outsider was what the inhabitants did with their time?

Most of time was already in the past. For the people of those parts it seemed that the notable events that had broken in upon them—the brawl at the dance, the strike at the cigar factory, the boys lined up at the recruiting station in the snow that December, the day the mine shut down for keeps, the head-on collision at the bend now marked by a giant luminous death's-head painted there in warning—were shadowy punctuation for the cyclically recurring picnics and floral arrangements and table settings, the pants that needed to be altered, the repair job on the roof, the new icebox. The darker interruptions survived as fragments of talk sinking back into silence: this was where they ran out of things to say, or out of the desire to say them. They preferred to dwell if possible on the afterimage of a fine and satisfying Veterans' Day parade—the gleam of the buttons—the perfect timing of the drummer, drunk as he was, a small miracle. Nobody would ever know what it cost for everything to come out okay.

It seemed important that nothing happen, even if there was a storm and the bus had trouble arriving, even if a bat got in and put the house in an uproar for a while. People had problems: they developed headaches, they worried, they had trouble sleeping. They cried, didn't want to hear the story, couldn't bear to look at the picture: "the poor man, the poor man." It was some kind of burden simply to pack things, to untie them, untangle them. What a mess everything had gotten into, and what unexpected pieces of what had happened years ago were still clinging to them, inconveniently. It was hard enough to keep records of payments and deposits, deeds, renewal forms, to care for teeth and hair, check off gifts sent, cards received, loans and orders for which one would be held responsible. On top of that to keep the neck from stiffening, the foot from falling asleep, and the finger joints supple, and then—if everything had been taken care of, the leftovers wrapped and refrigerated, the tablecloth folded—there might be time for a chorus or two of some already ancient radio song: "Don't Sit Under the Apple Tree" or "The Merry-Go-Round Broke Down" or "Rum and Coca Cola" or "It's Only a Paper Moon." It was at a moment like that—hearing the song for the first time in someone's half-remembered version—that the shock of the possibility came across: Was it, indeed, only a paper moon? How could this solidity be so unsolid as to disappear and leave hardly a mark?

Now and then there were shopping excursions to Nanticoke or even Hazleton; bingo night came once a week; in the interim, in summer, the card table might get occasional use for a round of Pokeno at home with Aunt Sue and Cousin Margaret. But the era of excitement, of concerted effort, seemed to have rolled by. Fragments of what was going on elsewhere or what had happened in the past drifted through the murmur of after-dinner talk: the floods and mine disasters, the retail emporiums gone bust, the hideous war and the battles their son had fought in it, the wife he had brought home from Japan, the work their daughters had found in theater and radio and the movie business, with the irregular habits and late hours that implied ("getting up past ten in the morning is no way to live"), the rumors of crime and social decline in a New York City that had always been remote to them and that now they hardly visited anymore.

By an invisible process it had become the '60s, and Pop had reached the point where just taking it easy on a summer day seemed sufficiently ambitious. On a July afternoon, looking out the window of the little room with the piano, he watched the fire brigade assemble next door for its annual outdoor party. The kegs were lined up. Now the battered record player would belt out a succession of festive favorites, "Pennsylvania Polka," "Beer Barrel Polka," "Roll out the barrel and we'll have a barrel of fun." He would join them in a moment, exchange those strangely formal and understated greetings exchanged among people who had lived adjacent to one another for decades. There were cuff links to adjust, a jacket to brush off. On the radio it was the year of "Get Off of My Cloud" and "Positively 4th Street"—he was himself an enthusiastic admirer of the Supremes, whom he had seen on television, and couldn't speak too highly of "Stop! In the Name of Love"—but for that moment it was the Andrews Sisters who continued to emanate, as if for eternity, to the surrounding neighborhood.

So many eras coexisted in him. He was born less than two years after the night when Thomas Edison captured sound for the first time on a strip of paraffin. Around the time he turned twenty-one the most exciting development in recording was Ada Jones singing "By the Light of the Silvery Moon," a female voice adequately rendered at last. The month he died the charts were topped by Rufus, Abba, Bachman-Turner Overdrive, and Eric Clapton's version of Bob Marley's "I Shot the Sheriff."

The same summer of the firehouse party, his two daughters, now in their fifties, walk through the woods along the path to the lake. They are remembering songs from the Busby Berkeley musicals they watched in high school at the Rex: *Forty-Second Street, Footlight Parade, Gold Diggers of 1933*. Their girlish rendition of "Lullaby of Broadway" spreads among the birches and toadstools and carpeted leaves, the startling noise of humans shaking up the forest. If this were a Disney picture the chipmunks and songbirds would cluster around in wonderment. For a moment they have become one of those sister acts once so essential to the music business.

Part of what people wanted to hear in music in those days was the sound of family, the exquisite tuning of voices that could only come from lifelong immersion in one another's unspoken signals. I'm walking with my mother and my aunt but hardly speak. I don't want to interrupt the sound I'm hearing, with its hint of latent frequencies that so rarely become audible. They sing what they can almost never say.

The whole spectrum of what had entertained them—the movies, the records, the radio—had once been something like a familial experience. Even though Miss Anthracite didn't, as it turned out, make it onto the Paramount payroll, the movies could hardly have seemed any closer to home even if one of their own relations was up there on the screen. Fred Astaire danced in his hotel room as if no one was looking—as if he was still Freddie Austerlitz from Omaha, only spruced up to beat the band—and Ruby Keeler was so downright clunky as she went into her dance that it was hard to believe she was really a trained movie star: "You could have done that number just as well, I declare!" The radio performers you heard every day were on the screen too, making movie appearances designed to look like some kind of relaxing break from the real grind of radio. You were supposed to believe they had just happened to drop by the Paramount studio and grabbed an unexpected chance to wave to the fans. Except for the tropical vegetation and the native girls, that could be your music parlor in *Only Angels Have Wings,* where Jean Arthur and Cary Grant teamed up at the piano and took off into a roughly exuberant run-through of "The Peanut Vendor."

But now the movie theater is about to close. They can't bring in enough people anymore. Everybody moved away. The talk is of turning its shell into a supermarket. Ruby Keeler and Joan Blondell have left the scene too, and the only trace of their passage is this duet in the woods. The two women—who ended up going to New York City and making lives there—can still recreate the New York known only to small-town girls, are still tuned to the way the New York of Busby Berkeley looks when you have nothing to compare it with, can only know that it sure beats Scranton, and can half believe that lines of dancers on Times Square really do slide into kaleidoscopic formations to celebrate the mere passage of time. For a moment they have themselves become the gum-chewing, cigarette-smoking backstage girls who trade wisecracks and practice tap routines while waiting for the director to call the next number:

Broadway baby goes to bed
Early in the morning . . .
She never rests her head
Till comes the dawn . . .
Good night, baby,
Sleep tight . . .
The milkman's on his way!

It echoes among the trees like a folk song.

There lingers the whiff of a ten-cent cigar, the configuration of a smile, the recognizable silhouette of a man advancing across a small lawn, with its solitary apple tree, on a mountain top itself hemmed in by mountains. He walked around and looked at things. As for the rest, is there anything but the fading remnants of anecdotes that had themselves long since become fading remnants? There was the one about the night he went to the dance with a new overcoat, stowed it in a corner near the drummer, and at the end of the dance discovered it was full of holes from the smoldering cigarette butts the drummer had tossed in that direction all night. From the number of times he told it it must have been an economic catastrophe, transmuted over time into a rueful joke: "I'll never forget that. It was a beautiful coat."

It's as much of a past as I have, except of course that I don't have it. I make it up by imagining connections between fragments. The fragments are small and irregularly shaped. Whole lifetimes could fit into the spaces between them—spaces in which my ancestors blur with other people's ancestors, with the people in the newspaper photographs and the people who weren't even photographed, with the unreal people in books and movies, and with the people imagined altogether. A remoter past that is entirely imagined (the Gay Nineties, men in top hats with walrus mustaches, Thomas Edison inventing phonography) blends bit by bit with the primordially recollected: the interior of a Trailways bus, the smell of soap from a country "notions" shop, the topography of a lakeside resort visited once only, the tone and rhythm (but not the exact words) of the repartee of bingo players on Saturday night. The inhabitants of that world have become figures in the dream of the past that in weak moments I might mistake for History. The retrievable sensations of the long hot bus ride from Scranton to Nanticoke is a transit between imaginary cities.

Only music travels unchanged between those worlds, as if it were immune to such distinctions. Imaginary? It was imaginary even when it was happening, an audible pipe dream. But the imaginary jukebox has real songs on it. In place of the music that is well and truly lost— the sound of the Rainbow Club Orchestra providing the means for those hours of continuous dancing—there exists other music that I can listen to right now. In hundreds and hundreds of songs pressed between, say, 1930 and 1936 resides the closest thing to a sonic family album. I can listen to the same sounds those others heard. It's June 1932 and my grandfather is straightening his bow tie as he prepares to set out for the Orondo Ballroom. Running through his head might be Hoagy Carmichael singing "Lazy River" or Bing Crosby and the Mills Brothers doing "Dinah" or Joe Venuti and Jack Teagarden's version of "Beale Street Blues."

Memory cedes its place to analogy: it is no longer a question of what happened but of what could well have happened. In the same way that pieces of their possible lives are depicted in old photographs and postcards—the town, the street, the cars, the entrance to the mine, the bridge under construction, Armistice Day at the local school—the rhythm and lyrics of their lives are incised on vinyl, waiting to be revived in the imagination of their descendants. It is the parallel world of song. There is a reality of sound that survives in the form of artifacts, that can be reconstructed week by week, session by session. Teddy Wilson, Benny Goodman, Eddie Lang, Lester Young, Ivie Anderson, Fred Astaire: they're still there. You can track the movement of musicians from town to town, radio station to radio station, and lose yourself in sounds captured in 1933, 1934, 1935. Stretch just those three years to a lifetime if you like. You won't find your lost family there but you'll find something connected to it, a space you can share with ghosts.

4

From a Family Album
Early Experiences of a Radio Announcer

*[C*UE: FIELD RECORDING, VOCAL DUET ACCOMPANIED BY *mandolin and accordion, Yonkers, New York, c. 1922]*

The Italians are always there. As he boards the ferry, hanging on to his mother's hand as she wades into the crowd of passengers, the two men are already in place, one with the mandolin and the other with the accordion. It's the holiday boat, the Nasconetcong line, taking them across the Hudson for a nickel from Yonkers to the picnic grounds in Alpine, New Jersey. The Italians move among the crowd to loosen them up for their outing, playing "Santa Lucia" or "O Sole Mio." This is how the passengers get in the mood for whatever celebration awaits them on the far shore. Just before the boat reaches the other side the musicians pass the hat around. Later the memories of the picnics will erode until all that remains is the moment of embarkation, the burst of preparatory song.

The ferry to the picnic grounds is the cheap boat, with no music but what itinerants can provide. On luxury cruises, like the night boat upriver to Albany, there is a full band, snappily dressed with gleaming buttons and almost military precision. It is indeed with a soldierly discipline that they keep the waltzes and fox-trots coming for the couples on the foredeck. The river at night is intoxicating: the occasional gleaming lights from shore, the music, not to mention the bootleg flasks. One by one the couples slip off to their staterooms, the politicians and actresses, traveling salesmen and their floozies. But Joe never saw that: it is only a story told at second hand, an alluring rumor. Like so many other things that promise a brighter and more exuberant life, the night boat is not for children.

In an apartment with six children there is plenty of noise but not much music, nor much music in the neighborhood. The hurdy-gurdy men—with or without comical monkeys—are rare enough to be almost legendary. They flourished in another time, or a time that had perhaps never quite existed, in a city adjacent but out of reach. The city, for instance, where people sing for their own amusement at exuberant private parties. It happens, of course; whole families do it, inviting their friends in and gathering around the piano if they are lucky enough to have one. His isn't, though. The songs sung at home are fragmentary and unaccompanied, most of the words forgotten, snatches of ballad, hints of heartbreaking tragedy remembered because of the refrain (his mother's favorite) about a bird in a gilded cage or a girl more to be pitied than censured. The funny ones are easier to remember, easier to sing, too:

> *Mother takes in washing,*
> *So does Sister Ann,*
> *Everybody works in our house,*
> *But my old man—*

Happy-go-lucky reminders of some grown-up's music hall outing or beer garden afternoon. The memory of such occasions is to be savored as a way of alleviating the more predictable rounds of illness and unpaid bills, the nights of winter chill driving the family into the kitchen to stay warm around the stove, drying off the wet shoes by that heat until the leather cracked. Everyone seemed to be going to or coming from something they didn't much care for. They did their best. His father came home exhausted from long hours clerking at the post office, or from the weekend job moonlighting as purser on the

Hudson River Day Line. Joe and his brothers coped as well as they could with the casual bullying of street and schoolyard and—in some ways worse—the unsmiling discipline of the nuns and, later, the Christian Brothers.

[CUE: "Libera me, Domine, de morte aeterna," from Gabriel Fauré, Requiem, *recorded St. Mary's Church, Yonkers, c. 1927]*

If there is respite at St. Mary's it is in the music he sings every Sunday in the choir, the Mozart or Gounod or Fauré for High Mass. In the heart of liturgy and prohibition and hairsplitting argument there yet resides this secret thrill. There's some glory in it (he's a soprano soloist), a good deal of enjoyment (the music, learned entirely by ear, is a steady stream of gratification), and even some profit: he gets a dime a Mass, and fifteen cents per Solemn High Mass when somebody dies. This privileged haven persists for years. It ends abruptly when his voice breaks and he is summarily ejected. That the choirmaster could dismiss him without a word of thanks for years of service, with no acknowledgment that his feelings might be hurt, is a humiliation he can't forget. It's like learning that he had been a replaceable cog all along.

They never gave a damn, for all the reverential awe attached to the music and the ritual. Over the years he'll come to terms with the callousness implicit in a phrase never far from his lips—"That's show biz"—but it's under the auspices of St. Mary's that he first learns about what every producer, every agent, every theater manager and programming director and record company executive cultivates as a necessary part of his job. Anyway, it certainly opens his eyes. The church, in all its ceremonies, turns out to be just another form of show business. Only it's starting to have some trouble holding on to its audience. Why else do so many parishioners bypass Father McCune's long and reverently drawn-out liturgy and go instead to hear Mass from Father McGrath, McGrath being a priest of no perceptible intelligence whose only distinction is that by long practice he's gotten the ritual down to a cool ten minutes?

In later years he will have many opportunities to contemplate just how resistlessly the business of music prevails over questions of artistry or even pleasure. (Whose pleasure? And who's paying for it?) In the beginning, in Yonkers, it is hard to think of music as anything but a ticket to a more amusing world, one of the certifiably good things of life. It is practically the only thing, in fact, that makes people step outside their own lives for a moment or two, forget their complaints about sickness and weather and money, the unacknowledged tedium of card games and gossip. Music might even give you the idea that your time might possibly be devoted to something other than getting ready for work or school, and then getting ready for dinner, and then getting ready to get to sleep because you have to get up so soon in the morning.

Music that's fun, that is, music that someone might actually want to listen to—not liturgical drone and not (except in small doses) the military stuff played on parade days. Around Joe's thirteenth birthday, with brass band thumping, they unveil a monument by the train station, dedicated to the soldiers, sailors, and marines of Yonkers for their heroism in the Spanish-American War, the Philippine Islands Insurrection, and the Boxer Uprising. Something tells him that it has nothing to do with any kind of life that he will ever want to lead.

The day his father brings the Victrola home, the five-foot job, begins a new epoch for the family. Along with the Victrola comes a stack of twelve-inch acoustic recordings: Joseph C. Smith's Orchestra playing a three-minute condensation of "Tales from the Vienna Woods"; Ernest Hare and Billy Jones—the Happiness Boys of vaudeville legend—harmonizing on "Barney Google," "That Old Gang of Mine," and a cleaned-up version of "Hinky Dinky Parley Voo" (the dirty version still circulates on the street, taught directly by guys that were over there when the war was on, nine or ten years ago); Ada Jones and Billy Murray clowning it up on "When Frances Dances with Me." Every record will be played a thousand times. The apartment expands. Music is like having an extra room.

[CUE: Steve Porter, "She's More to Be Pitied Than Censured," recorded August 1898.]

Strange how quickly the music starts to sound old-fashioned. Many of the songs echo the era before recording began, the gaslight years when (it is said) lovers serenaded their intended under a balcony and gypsy violinists played at private champagne receptions for cabals of bankers and industrialists. Before too long—so fast do things move once recording starts—it becomes possible to imagine a time when those shiny new 78s will end up in a cardboard box in the attic, a dusty heap of forgotten favorites: comic turns and novelty numbers from Broadway's hits, the immortal operas and vaudeville routines, arias from *Faust* and *Lakmé,* Weber and Fields doing the drinking scene from *Whirl-i-gig,* "Two Black Crows," "Cohen on the Telephone," the Floradora Girls and Lillian Russell, rousing choruses by Romberg and Friml and Victor Herbert. "Give me some men who are stout-hearted men": but what they got, due to the limitations of the sound spectrum available to acoustic recording, were the curiously pinched, bodiless voices of Broadway tenors singing coyly of the first blossoms of spring.

Barely a moment ago—it must have been just before the world war—music was still a matter of sheet music to be played on the piano in the parlor, an immense boon for publishers, copyists, rack-jobbers, song pluggers, piano players, piano teachers, and piano tuners. Now, in place of that, came the modern convenience—you didn't need to know how to play or sing anymore—of recorded barbershop quartets harmonizing on "Oh, You Beautiful Doll" and "Come, Josephine, in My Flying Machine" and "Chinatown, My Chinatown," "After the Ball" and "My Wild Irish Rose," and "When It's Moonlight on the Prairie" and "The Lights of My Home Town"; thousands of blackface songs, some even sung by black performers; and the uproarious "Oriental" gibberish of James T. Powers in his 1898 recording of "Chin Chin Chinaman." Recordings do help to fill the quiet hours at home, the after-dinner lulls when no one can think of anything to say that hasn't been said too many times already. Why not, indeed, play "Chin Chin Chinaman" again? It always makes them laugh. Didn't you ever hear that one, Tom? Well, we'll play it for you right now, that's what we'll do.

It is music that somehow never goes away. Fragments cling stubbornly to people even when all they can remember is a refrain or a catchphrase that surges up unexpectedly late in the evening, the sudden memory of a chorus of "The Man Who Broke the Bank at Monte

Carlo" or "School Days." Already the echoes of the Gay Nineties—the songs that his mother sang in her courting days, "Ta Ra Ra Boom De Ay" or "The Strawberry Blonde" or "The Daring Young Man on the Flying Trapeze"—have a remarkably silly air. That outmoded world was evidently a childish place, its inhabitants easily amused by nonsense words and simple anecdotes, absurd attitudes, absurd postures: "Oh, Promise Me," the big hit from Reginald De Koven's 1903 operetta *Robin Hood*, evoked the suitor with the waxed moustache, on his knees before the crinolined beloved. People needed their music but they didn't demand much from it: simple tunes with simple words that let them roar with laughter, or weep for the jilted lovers, drunken fathers, and penniless children. Joe already feels more modern than what he's listening to.

At night, reading before bedtime, there's another music, of language that practically demands to be recited. The sonorous descriptive passages in *The Horsemen of the Plains* and the other adventure novels of Joseph Altsheler thunder as if from an inner radio: "That night the storm became terrible in its strength and intensity . . . The screaming of the wind from the peaks and among the great clefts and canyons was almost like that of a human voice, although infinitely more powerful." A human voice: his own voice, made powerful by its command of cadence and dynamics and phrasing, and by the all-important pauses in between. He has already understood the importance of not rushing, which will enable him, when he so wishes, to go very fast.

One day everything changes. Joe's brother, one of the twins, the youngest of the family, comes home sick from school. He dies the same day. Nobody will ever understand what happened. A few months later his father dies, suddenly, of pneumonia. He'd never been the same after Frankie's death. Joe, at twelve, has to work to help support the family and keep up with school at the same time. It doesn't leave much time for listening to music or going to the pictures. He looks around and thinks about what might be coming up for him. On his break at the pharmacy, or about to pitch into some geometry homework, he runs through the list of possibilities, the opportunities that exist as far as he can see. What does everyone do? What *can* they do?

He could work in the post office like his father did, diligently wearing himself out, scraping together enough to keep a wife and five kids going: come home dead tired, eyes worn from sorting, or edgy from the effort of being polite to supervisors. Or work at one of the hundred other jobs that turn men into the tired shadows that emerge from behind desks, from behind cashiers' windows, punching their time cards and slipping out the employees' entrance.

He could work as a pharmacist like his boss Joe Kerr (real name Kerensky, no relation to that Russian politician the Reds kicked out) and look forward to having himself a tidy shop by the time he's through, spend his days spieling in English or Yiddish or Italian with the old-timers who drift in to pass the time. Working at the pharmacy is educational in the company of a guy like Mr. Kerr, whose head is full of Engels and Kropotkin and the dangerous state of world affairs. "There's another war coming, just a matter of time, never mind what Hoover says." But Kerr himself has advised him: "Joe, whatever you do, don't be a wage slave, not a bright guy like you!" It would be all too easy to end with nothing to show beyond a petty mastery of prescription Latin and an intimate acquaintance with every last joke and neighborhood scandal, with the prospect of finally becoming one of those customers whose various ailments and frailties he has come to know so intimately. "McManus is home with piles again, and Mrs. Valenti will be stopping by for her liver pills." It is the horror of the local.

He has the intelligence it would have taken to be a priest, but none of the inclination and, finally, none of the belief. Certainly he could out-argue them. He was doing that in the privacy of his thoughts even back in the study halls of St. Mary's. Nothing was more frustrating than not being able to talk back when they were laying out their line of reasoning, even when he could see the holes in it a mile off. It's all politics, anyway. All organizations want to perpetuate themselves.

He had a cousin who became an FBI agent. That was a pretty big deal, in the age when you couldn't pick up the paper without reading about racketeers and public enemies. But that wouldn't be Joe's kind of thing at all. He doesn't want to work in secret; he isn't the type to enjoy working for such a regimented organization; he doesn't want to snoop on people; and carrying a gun just doesn't interest him at all.

So why not follow his gift of gab where it takes him and be a politician like the genially corrupt ward heelers who have had Yonkers to themselves for as long as anyone can remember? Be one of the top-hatted dignitaries who lined the podium on that last Memorial Day in high school while he recited the Gettysburg Address, directly following the mayor's remarks and preceding three volleys from the American Legion post. They certainly managed to look like they were feeling no need to tighten their belts, no matter what shape the markets were in. The lean times that had arrived in earnest—it was 1933—didn't seem to have shaken up the politicos in the least. To do them justice, they had been quick to find employment for his mother—got her a steady job working for the party—after she lost her husband. Say that for the Democrats, they knew what they had to do to earn votes. As much as they stole, they knew how to look after people, and forged that knowledge into something that looked enough like compassion to squeak by.

Finally the behind-the-scenes pressures and underhanded dealings of Tammany are too much of a headache to seriously think about. It takes a certain kind of person, a certain kind of nervous system, to get accustomed to those scurrilous melodramas of power and then gloss them over with hypocritical and self-congratulatory patter. But all the available roles have their limits. How about a traveling salesman, always ready with a smile and a story, and ulcers and a red nose and too many nights on bedbug-ridden pallets in Utica or Schenectady? A bartender whose sleight of hand would win the undying admiration of several generations of loyal boozehounds? And night after night of the same circular stories, the same brawls, the same low jokes and two-in-the-morning breakdowns? A tap dancer at Proctor's, a song and dance man on the Loew's circuit? He was never light enough on his feet. A warm-up act before the chorus line? Too many tough customers, and no guarantees he'll ever end up anywhere but the far reaches of the dying burlesque circuit, another broken-down comic.

The roads look narrower the farther down them he looks. They converge in what starts to resemble a mechanical maze, a factory with sealed exits. So few manage to avoid being trapped. The real achievement of the greatest individuals is that they were able to escape the rounds of boredom that everyone else is forced to put up with. The genuine heroes—the ones who managed some kind of personal freedom—had to invent their own world. Later, in compensation, their names would be carved above the entrances of university libraries, their writings bound in leather, their sayings and the titles of their books taught to children by rote, but that was after the fact and had almost nothing to do with the point. They had left the pack behind.

It is possible to imagine—nothing is more exhilarating in fact—going for broke and becoming a Mill or a Schopenhauer or a Bergson, invent a universal system, discern the secret clockwork that regulates human events, uncover the lost languages and buried palaces of the ancients, write lyrics to put alongside Keats and Burns and the other contributors to Palgrave's *Golden Treasury,* or aphorisms worthy of being collected in the Modern Library. Is there one individual who embodies the highest ideal? George Bernard Shaw perhaps, someone who with nothing but verbal brilliance can focus attention on a stage to the exclusion of everything else. To make a place for yourself in the world with nothing but words: there was a triumph that meant something.

He goes to Fordham for a year, then has to drop out when the family budget gets too tight. Grand literary goals start to seem remote. Theater still seems like a real way to make a living, though, even if it isn't necessarily George Bernard Shaw's kind of theater. There's enough of it around, from burlesque skits to Shakespeare revivals, from Expressionist dream plays to bubbly farces, from stirring revolutionary tracts to the Ziegfeld Follies. Nothing else has quite that kind of excitement. If not a famous playwright, he might at least be the stage director seeing that the process comes off as it must or the actor who speaks the lines to the audience: anything to participate in some aspect of that transmission. To be an actor seems finally the most logical and desirable choice, the one that's plausibly within grasp.

It's no pipe dream. He has an expressive and tireless voice, a flair for timing and mimicry. That effortlessly exact articulation had always dazzled friends and family. By the age of eight they were already slipping him nickels for his recitation of "Casey at the Bat." It was the first time he got the idea you could actually get paid for that kind of thing. It's a noble pursuit, after all: to go on stage, to be part of a lineage, whether as matinee idol or character comedian or classical tragedian or anything he can. From a newspaper he clips an Arthur Guiterman poem, "To All Actors":

> *In our frail dreams you clothe your protean selves,*
> *And see, those dreams are flesh and blood! They walk,*
> *They do great deeds, they talk—*

with its reminder that theatricality is to be admired at every level:

> *Robson and Crane, Bellew, Rosina Vokes,*
> *Dockstader's gang with all their rowdy jokes*
> *And Harrigan and Hart with their shillalies,*
> *And all that golden company at Daly's.*

Perfection is perfection, no matter what form it takes. It's exciting, when he can scrape some quarters together, to go to the Palladium and hear genuine opera when the Salmaggi Opera Company comes to town, complete with real elephants and horses to enhance the grandeur of *Aida* and *Carmen*. But there's more to the stage than that. There is nothing comparable, for instance, to Jimmy Durante at the Hippodrome in Billy Rose's *Jumbo*: "They say an elephant never forgets." (Pause.) "What's he got to remember?" At a moment like that—an unanticipated peak moment induced by sheer timing—the audience puts itself completely in the hands of the performer. What could be more intense than that exchange? In the meantime, he looks around to see what's on offer.

[CUE: Bing Crosby, "Brother, Can You Spare a Dime?" recorded October 1932]

He takes a whack at the movies. Everybody tells him he's a natural, with the brash confidence and the impeccable diction. The scout for Paramount takes one look and tells him his ears are too big. "What about Clark Gable?" "Get outa here!" End of interview. So he shoots for the radio amateur hours, a humbler arena but a lot more accessible, where anybody can show up with a bit of original, or not so original, material and, with luck, compete on the air for prizes. He writes a two-page play about a soldier going mad with terror in the trenches of World War I, and doesn't win. Next time he recites the lyrics of "Brother, Can You Spare a Dime?" in high oratorical style and makes five bucks. That encourages him to try out for the *Feenamint Amateur Hour* on CBS, featuring George Burns's future TV sidekick Harry Von Zell. On *Feenamint* they have a gimmick where amateurs compete to do commercials. Five hundred people stand on line to audition for a chance to work for nothing. He comes in second out of twenty-six finalists and figures it's a good omen.

He starts taking acting classes at the acting division of the state university, getting some solid experience in plays like *Tombstone Days* and *My Mother-in-Law,* making the most of dialogue that gives full scope to his vocal powers: "She was good enough for you before you came here, wasn't she? She was a good girl of good parentage, esteemed and loved by everyone . . . Have you forgotten when she was fifteen years old, just beginning to bloom? You took her love, her everything that is good!" The school's principal, a guy named McLain Gates, produces a weekly radio show sponsored by the New York Police Department, called *Spring 3–100,* after the emergency police number. Every show features a story about how crime doesn't pay, and at the end a cop delivers a public service message along the lines of: "Always remember, a policeman is your friend . . . If you're in trouble or need assistance, just walk up to a policeman on the beat and he will help you." In the five or six weeks before the program folds, Joe and the other students get more than one shot at appearing in these fifteen-minute plays. A follow-up series called *The McCarthys Step Out*—produced under the supervision of the commanding officer of the Traffic Safety Bureau and endorsed by the police commissioner—offers dramatized tips on how to cross the street, obey traffic signals, and the like, and even rates some enthusiastic reviews in the local papers.

In a few more years he'll marry one of those students at the drama division—the girl from Pennsylvania who reads Shakespeare, plays piano, and gave up the Latin scholarship to come to New York for acting classes—but first they have to lose track of each other a couple times. It will take a reunion out of a movie to seal the connection. He's broadcasting from a low rooftop in Times Square on New Year's Eve and she hails him from the crowd, so that they become engaged, in effect, right in the middle of a performance. But that won't be for another five years. Right now he can scarcely imagine where he'll be in five years.

He's given up the night job at the pharmacy in Yonkers by this time. For the moment he's still living at home, listening to the radio when he gets home at night. It isn't even a proper radio, just enough of the core of a discarded Sylvania to let him hear—if he puts his ear close enough to it—a faint signal sending him Benny Goodman, Tommy Dorsey, Xaviar Cugat. He puts it under the pillow so it doesn't wake his mother. By day he is to be found among the young actors hanging out at Hector's Cafeteria on 50th Street, scanning the trades and handbills for news of casting calls. In the *New York Times* on a September morning in 1935 he finds what he's looking for in the want ads: "Radio announcers sought, no experience necessary."

[CUE: Jimmie Lunceford and His Orchestra, "Rhythm Is Our Business," recorded May 1935]

The Annenberg family's Tele-Flash Loudspeaker Corporation isn't exactly a radio station, but it adopts many characteristics of a radio station as part of its camouflage. A wire service for horse players, designed to skirt the laws against off-track betting, it is part of the Annenberg gambling empire that also includes the *Morning Telegraph* and the *Racing Form*. Tele-Flash's New York office operates out of the same dismal West 23rd Street building as the racing papers, a warren of dank corridors and ragged smoky offices. The ad is on the level, though: it may not be real radio but it's a real job. For $25 a week Joe broadcasts for seven or eight hours a day, a little news, a little weather, some records, anything they have lying around. Restaurants that provide live music for broadcast get free Tele-Flash service, and it's a popular service: every Irish saloon lined up in the shadow of the El on Third Avenue, from 59th up to 96th, has it installed.

In a small way it's like being famous. The bartenders don't know his face but when he orders a drink they recognize the voice. He does remotes from all over town, presenting saloon singers, Irish ballads, a Hawaiian trio at the Chelsea Hotel. He emcees amateur contests, a staple of low-budget entertainment, intoning with new-found gravity (he who was not so long ago an amateur himself): "Our aim is twofold, to entertain and to give aspiring talented people an opportunity to be heard . . . It is entirely up to you folks out there listening, *who* will be the lucky winners tonight!" When he isn't doing live events he sits in a bare office with two turntables and a news ticker, playing records—anonymous orchestrations of "Wagon Wheels" and "The Very Thought of You" and "Cocktails for Two"—and reading news items about the assassination of Dollfuss and Carole Lombard's divorce from William Powell and the outlook for the playoffs, exactly as if he really was a radio announcer. On the eve of Bruno Hauptmann's execution, on April 2, 1936, reading the teletype means delivering a dramatic monologue that might have come out of one of the plays he used to put on at the drama school: "The sands of time are sinking for Bruno Richard Hauptmann. In a few hours the man who was convicted of kidnapping baby Charles Lindbergh on the night of March 1st, 1932, will be strapped into the New Jersey electric chair. A few seconds later gaunt-faced Richard Elliott will throw a switch, and the writhing form of the condemned man will strain and bulge at the unrelenting straps. How will he take it? Will his iron nerve break? These are some of the questions being discussed today in hotel lobbies, in barrooms, and at many street corners in this exciting city . . . "

Meanwhile—in a scene out of a mystery serial, or one of those neat Warner Brothers pictures with James Cagney as a fast-talking confidence trickster or Lee Tracy as a cynical Broadway agent—Tele-Flash's secret informant at the racetrack with his hidden wireless device is transmitting race reports to another agent planted in a hotel room across the street. The agent in the hotel in turn phones the results to the central Tele-Flash office in Chicago, whose operatives in minutes spread the word to subcenters nationwide. As soon as the info comes in, Joe's program is interrupted from the room next to his: "Here are the prices for the third race at Hialeah!" That's not all subscribers get for their Tele-Flash hook-up: they also get to listen in on bootlegged baseball games and title bouts. Georgie Curtis, one of the founders of the outfit, wears the bug to the arena himself.

In the only surviving photograph of Joe and his Tele-Flash colleagues, he looks like a fresh-faced kid, eager to please, who has fallen among amiable racketeers or the kind of wisecracking reporters who inhabit movies like *Five Star Final* and *The Front Page,* sharp dressers, sprawling confidently in their chairs with their hands in their pockets or flourishing cigars just like movie actors. The three young ones grin with a boyish imitation of cosmopolitan ease, especially young Jim Winchester, with his tight-waisted coat and jaunty hat, a perfect con man in the making but still young enough to enjoy it. They look as if they were one up on all the rest of the population. Only the older guy on the right—the heavyset white-haired telegraphist with his hat in his hands—looks more uneasily at the camera with not even an attempt at a grin, as if he alone knows what the score really is.

The New York wing of the Annenberg racing empire is as cozily corrupt as much of the world around it, the realm of bars and racetracks and burlesque houses and political clubs. Tele-Flash runs only for a year or two in Manhattan before Mayor La Guardia shuts it down as an illegal gambling operation. By the late '30s Moe Annenberg will sell out his racing interests as he faces a prison sentence for tax fraud; and in due time the wire service will come into the hands of businessmen who later turn out to have close ties to Cleveland mobsters. In 1951 the Kefauver Commission on organized crime will still be trying to figure out just what went on before, during, and after that transfer of ownership: "In view of its limited time and facilities, this committee was unable to study exhaustively the various subcenters that constituted the provincial capitals of the old Annenberg empire."

In the meantime the Tele-Flash broadcasting team, blissfully unaware of the outermost ramifications of their little beehive, is scattered. Most of them scurry to one corner of the radio world or another, except for the one who ends up owning the store north of 42nd Street where you can record anything on acctate for fifty cents. As for that smiling young confidence man, who knows where he will have gotten to?

By this time Joe has already been hired away to an authentic radio job. Bob Carter, the chief announcer at WMCA, is also a serious horse player who drops in at the Tele-Flash office with some frequency. It's from Tele-Flash, after all, that WMCA gets its notably accurate race results, broadcast after the delay demanded by law. On one of Carter's visits he gets a chance to watch Joe do his show and promptly offers him a job. The station has been unionized and the forty-hour week has been imposed, so they need more announcers. In the spring of 1937 Joe is hired by WMCA as an announcer, with sports the main order of business, any kind of sports, to be reported on with a minimum of prep time or background information.

[CUE: Duke Ellington and His Orchestra, "Caravan," recorded July 1937]

A retired Yankee pitcher named Waite Hoyt does baseball, Carter naturally does racing, and Joe, for $32 a week, does everything else: station breaks, fifteen- or thirty-minute music shows, and "man on the street" broadcasts, with the wires fed from a window while he walks on the sidewalk in front of the station, polling passersby: "Where do you come from?" "How do you like New York?" "Who do you figure for the pennant?" "How did you meet your wife?" "What's your favorite movie?" Entertainment never came simpler or cheaper. He does commentary on prize fights from St. Nick's Arena every week, at first more or less making it up as he goes along. He hangs in there for the six-day bicycle races at Madison Square Garden. He cooks up fifteen-minute condensations of nine-inning ball games, complete with sound effects like the sound man whacking a two-by-four to signal a homer.

There isn't much they don't hand him, except for the slots reserved for specialists: the Morning Cheer sermonette from Reverend G. A. Palmer, Hollywood Chatter by Powell Clark, the Beauty Tips inserts from the gracious Mae Murray (still a well-preserved tomato twenty years after co-starring with Wallace Reid in *To Have and To Hold*), the psychology advice from Dr. Lawrence Gould, the late-night revival meetings with Elder Rosa Horn, the Broadway gossip handled by Jack Eigen ("Remember, you heard it here") with his mannerisms stolen from Walter Winchell along with his never-once-removed hat. (It hardly seems to matter that on radio nobody can see the hat.) The fifteen-minute news broadcasts are handled by deep-voiced "broadcast journalists"—they want no taint of radio in their title—who try hard to live up to the myth of the heroic hard-nosed correspondent. Even if they are only improvising on headlines off the news ticker, they enjoy more prestige than the other announcers: "This is Garnett Marks and it's thirty here."

Nevertheless Joe is the one, on an otherwise quiet Sunday afternoon in November 1938, who has the privilege, not to mention the pleasure, of breaking the news to the public that Father Coughlin's regular broadcast from the Shrine of the Little Flower in Royal Oak, Michigan, will not be heard on WMCA today—or any future day—because of the increasingly offensive nature of his remarks. Coughlin quickly finds refuge with a Newark station where he remains free to air his charges that Soviet Russia is dominated by Jews, that the Russian Revolution was financed by Kuhn-Loeb, that Germany has no choice but to take "stern anti-Jewish measures" to rid the country of subversion. What a relief not to have to listen to that stuff anymore: "Is America going to go war for the sake of 600,000 Jews of German citizenship?" Not to mention the arguments afterward: "You've got to admit he has a point, Joe. Anyway, what business is it of ours what they want to do over there? Everybody's crazy in Europe." Hitler is still a figure of fun, a German vaudevillian screeching and gesturing to comical effect, just as Neville Chamberlain will be typed as a stand-in for Edward Everett Horton or some other Hollywood butler type. Or else Hitler is the kind of strong manager we could use over here too, according to the one of the station guys who's been to a few Bund meetings out in Jersey. For now, however, the WMCA listeners will have to settle, in lieu of the message from the Shrine of the Little Flower, for a half hour of dance music transcriptions.

That's what recorded music is for at this stage: it's a last resort, a time-filler, a form of insurance. You play it when nothing else is available. The bandleader took a powder, the singer's too drunk to go on the air, the priest turned out to be a Nazi propagandist? Grab an acetate. Most of what gets played is packaged, pre-cleared stuff from a company called Thesaurus. Think of it as wallpaper for the ears: "Welcome to Magic Melodies . . . and let's open our show with 'Tea for Two,' performed for you by the Three Suns." The Thesaurus sequences are entirely prerecorded; put it on and go for a smoke. The concept of the disc jockey, intervening between recorded songs, commenting on them, interrupting them, scarcely exists yet.

Recorded music is held in check by ASCAP and the musicians' union, eager to protect both record sales and revenue from live music. Somebody plays a Bing Crosby record and Decca threatens to sue the station. There are deals that still need to be cut. Only gradually do things start to change, as the performers realize how much exposure they can get out of radio and lobby to turn the medium into a vehicle for plugging records. For now most of the music is live, performed by the studio orchestra or broadcast from hotels and nightclubs. The tenor of it can be gauged from a WMCA music clearance sheet for a Saturday night in August 1937: the Olympian Orchestra playing a sequence of ten songs including "Dance Away the Night," "Darktown Strutters Ball," "We'll Ride the Tide Together," and "Our Penthouse on Third Avenue."

Who wants canned goods? The thrill of what is happening right now is what makes radio seem worth listening to despite the static and sound dropouts, even despite the commercials that sometimes drive people crazy the way they stick in their head. The station has a full-time orchestra and organist, and for *Grandstand and Bandstand* (sponsored by Wheaties from two to five every afternoon), the orchestra is there for the full three hours, playing twenty minutes at a stretch, their songs introduced by the genial host, "Broadway's own" Smiling Jerry Baker. Baker—who has a black eye in a surviving publicity shot—eventually gets into trouble when the station finds out that a good many of the girls to whom he's always dedicating songs work at Polly Adler's brothel. (The legendary madam has relocated from Chicago to New York, maintaining her reputation for running the most high-toned bordello around. Decades later, when Hollywood gets around to filming her best-selling memoir *A House Is Not a*

Home—starring Polly Bergen!—the tone will get even higher through the suggestive power of Burt Bacharach's tie-in song.)

At night everything is live: *Five Star Final* (a news roundup paving the way for *The March of Time*), followed by comedy and variety shows. They are a mixed bag: *The Three Little Sachs,* a fifteen-minute music and comedy show featuring three male singers, one of them Jim Brennan, known for such songs as "Rose of No Man's Land." The great Jones and Hare, the Happiness Boys of the '20s, whose records Joe had heard over and over at home on that five-foot Victrola, eventually wash up, when their career has played itself out, as two-thirds of the Three Little Sachs; and when Jones dies his daughter Marilyn takes his place, at least until Republic Pictures signs her to a long-term contract not long afterward. That's show biz: flux and uncertainty but with everybody having as much fun as possible in the meantime, for the greater glory of Sachs Quality Furniture, with its unforgettable jingle (sung to the tune of "Reuben, Reuben"): "Melrose five, five three hundred!" People walk the streets of New York with the jingle circulating in their head until they could scream.

Something for everyone: there's Barnacle Bill the Sailor singing sea chanteys with ukulele accompaniment to set the blood racing from 7 to 7:30 in the morning. There is even a fifteen-minute program featuring an alcoholic announcer reading his own sentimental and inspirational verse to organ accompaniment; he's homosexual and likes to bring rough trade into the studio to impress them with his readings. If the folks out there in radioland only knew! If, that is, anybody out there is really listening to the poems. Nobody has much of an idea how many people are tuning in. When they send in mail, that's when you know you've got something.

[*CUE: Chick Webb and His Orchestra, "T'aint What You Do (It's the Way That 'Cha Do It)," recorded March 1939*]

In 1939 Joe is already getting press attention for his *Swing Appreciation Concerts* featuring "some of the hottest swing arrangements on radio today." A year later he's hosting *For Dancers Only,* getting six thousand ticket requests a week—or so he assures Jack Shafer in an interview for his column "Radio View"—to join the "anything-goes" studio audience moving to Chick Webb and Andy Kirk. "We're cooking with gas!"

He's doing pretty much anything that comes to hand these days, like emceeing a music and comedy special on behalf of the Rodney Benson Plymouth and Dodge auto dealership, featuring that "blonde package of dynamite" Lorraine Barnett singing "Mama, I Want to Make Rhythm" and getting praise from *Variety* for his "geniality" and "lively pace," or punching away at the occasions constantly offered by sports—blow-by-blows at the Coliseum (under the sponsorship of Gem Clog-Pruf Razors), football with Mel Allen, and the recap *Today's Sports,* brought to you by Natural Bloom Cigars: "Good evening, fight fans . . . Learn how you can win a seven-tube pushbutton Farnsworth radio!" *The Referee* calls his description of the Toma-Corchado eight-round bantamweight bout at the Rockland Palace (otherwise known as "the colored palace of punch") a "masterpiece" and adds that "handsome Joe is a ringer for Phil Regan, the cinema, stage, and radio singing star." On *Cavalcade of Champions* he recreates the Sullivan-Corbett fight in up-to-date blow-by-blow style.

He starts doing the Brooklyn Fox Amateur Hour, with musical backup by Al Curtis and His Forty Fingers of Rhythm. Backed by Curtis's contingent of four pianos and drums—one of the musicians has as his claim to fame that he is one of what seem to be about a dozen co-writers of the 1923 hit "Yes We Have No Bananas"—he oversees a succession of reciters, harmonica players, tap dancers, whistlers, and singers. The singers either do "Come Back to Sorrento" or "Giannina Mia," and whoever has the loudest voice wins. The crowds are tough; they start yelling "Drop dead!" or "Get lost!" sometimes even before the contestant can get his glockenspiel to the mike. A miniature ambulance races on stage to take the losers away before the crowd can pelt them too badly. The show's fan mail pours in. This goes on for years, a weekly mob scene that over a seven-year period is attended, according to the publicity handout, by a million and a half people. "Contestants have received over 365 wristwatches!" Between screenings of *Espionage Agent* and *Pride of the Bluegrass* and *Nancy Drew and the Hidden Staircase,* the singers and jugglers and xylophonists roll along.

When the World's Fair opens in April 1939 he goes out to Flushing Meadows most days for the duration. It's almost like taking up residence in an amusement park. He strolls with mike in hand between the General Motors Futurama exhibit and the Hall of Pharmacy, through the demonstrations of broadcast television and long-distance telephone service and FM radio, as theme music by George Gershwin and Kurt Weill plays in the background. Into his listeners' homes he brings a stream of Visitors from Other Lands and comes up with a Typical American Family from central casting, the father a Guy Kibbee look-alike, the daughter ready to audition for the next Andy Hardy movie. The fair itself is Hollywood: it is the movie in which history has a happy ending and Poland will not be invaded at the end of the summer. Then Poland is invaded and the fair continues anyway, as if it was not going to make such a big difference. Joe and Maggie get married just after the fair ends, around the same time he becomes, officially, the station's chief announcer.

[CUE: Count Basie and His Orchestra, "The World Is Mad," recorded August 1940]

That next summer—with the war going on in Europe as if in another world, and Basie enjoying a hit with "The World Is Mad"—is the summer he spends reading H. G. Wells's *Outline of History,* soaking up the sun in the backyard at Maggie's parents' place in Pennsylvania. He can't put it down, can't stop thinking about the inexorable way those patterns of invasion and invention and sheer power-lust, of religious fanaticism and commercial exploitation, have been at their mischief right from the start. As he reads he thinks of how they are now converging to make the world even less livable than it already was. There is so much that people don't want to hear, so much that you can't say on the radio. They want Sonja Henie singing "I Poured My Heart into a Song," not a reminder of the Albigensian crusade or the Spanish Inquisition or the Spanish Civil War. Most of the time they don't even want to listen to the news.

You can still have fun on radio, despite everything. In fact you need to; it's impossible to stay focused on the foreign news without getting depressed. Joe's feeling loose enough to pull an April Fool stunt that gets him some ink in *Newsweek;* the personal publicity makes up for the station director's mild reprimands. After announcing a fifteen-minute program of Guy Lombardo records, he starts playing "a torrid boogie-woogie number called 'White Heat'" performed by "the notorious hot-jazz specialists" the Jimmie Lunceford orchestra. The music continues until near the end of the program he blandly announces, "And now a few words from Guy Lombardo," at which point the recorded voice of Dinah Shore emerges, plugging defense bonds. Lombardo, the real Lombardo, meanwhile has gotten in the habit of calling him up to complain about the weather reports. "Joe, why are you telling people it's going to rain?" "Because that's the forecast." "Don't tell them that! I'm playing Jones Beach tonight!"

The war moves stealthily from being something that no one could ever have imagined to being something that has always been going on. When the *New Yorker* writer A. J. Liebling comes back to New York from Paris after the Germans take over, he's shocked to see that there are still ice skaters at Rockefeller Center. New York exists in a state of marvelous invulnerability, as if those cocktail lounges and those dine-and-dance joints offered a buffer against the insane Europeans, still lost in the age of murderous dynasties, gangsters with uniforms. But France falls, and Russia is invaded, and the day of Pearl Harbor comes, and the necessary adjustments are made while radio simply continues.

That there's a war going on doesn't hurt the radio business in the least: it's booming. Radio announcers are still favored for exemption because of their importance to morale; besides, Joe has a wife and two kids at home. Things are going strangely well for him just as they're going horribly badly everywhere else. It's a boost to see his name given equal billing among the other august participants in a random day's broadcasting in November 1943: Vera Lynn, Dick Powell, Harry Emerson Fosdick, Jean Hersholt, Fiorello LaGuardia, J. Edgar Hoover, and Major A. de Seversky, author of *Victory Through Air Power.* The Sunday *New York Times* includes him in a photo feature about "the leading 'm.c.s' now to be heard on the air," alongside Clifton Fadiman, Deems Taylor, and the top-hatted, moustached, zanily grinning Ray Johnson of *Inner Sanctum.*

It's in the war years that the fortunes of WMCA—until then a scruffy but undernourished contender with a signal too weak to compete with the big boys—start to go up. The station is purchased in 1944 by Nathan Strauss, a wealthy relative of the Strausses who own Macy's and the Strauss who went down with the Titanic. Strauss moves the station to new premises on Madison Avenue, equipped with nine studios, seventeen engineers, an organ studio, an orchestra studio, a theater that holds 300 people. He loses money on the overhead until they bring in an old-time radio guy named Ralph Atlas from Chicago to straighten out the finances. The station rents the theater to Capitol Records, and Nat Cole ends up cutting most of his records there.

All this time Joe has been enjoying the music on 52nd Street, often enough as announcer: "This program is brought to you from Swing Alley in New York," night after night soaking up Louis Prima, Stuff Smith, John Kirby, Maxine Sullivan, Joe Marsala, Bobby Hackett, at the Famous Door or the Hickory House. It's part of the permanent unquestioned landscape of New York, those doors through which he walks to find bands and singers in full flight: no special occasion, just the normal course of things. This is the real soundtrack of the heart of the city, the one he could only imagine through its faint transmission when he would listen to the Basie band on his Sylvania receiver. The musicians live in their own time frame, almost oblivious to the influence they exert on what's around them. Bobby Hackett talks about the time he was out touring with Pee Wee Russell somewhere in Illinois, and he woke up in an alcoholic fog in their car in the middle of the night to register the fact that Pee Wee was at the wheel: "Wait a minute, Pee Wee doesn't know how to drive!" One night down at Nick's in the Village, Tommy Dorsey and Fats Waller walk in during Pee Wee's set, just like that. Nick had recently installed a Hammond organ in the club, so they hand Fats a bottle of gin and just let him go. And he goes for hours.

[CUE: Adolph Deutsch, main title theme, Action in the North Atlantic, released 1943]

The war is inescapable even in New York. In June 1943 Joe's emceeing a Bendix Marine–sponsored broadcast of the Brooklyn Fox amateur hour, standing on the sidelines as the audience roars for Carpenter Mate Third Class Howard Roth of the *Icarus,* who tells how he and his fellow crewmen sank a U-boat with Bendix Marine equipment. (To complete the media tie-in, the Fox is showing the Humphrey Bogart picture *Action in the North Atlantic.*) When *Life* reporter Carl Mydans and his wife Shelley arrive in New York harbor the following December aboard the Swedish liner *Gripsholm,* after their long journey home from Japanese captivity in the Philippines, Joe is there with press card in hat and microphone in hand to greet them at dockside.

In April 1945 he is finally drafted. The *Fort Dix Post* does a quickie profile of him—"Now, instead of reporting the news, he is going to make it"—in which he manages a bit of rueful doubletalk: "You never know whether you're inside looking out or outside looking in." Or is that a way of defining what show business amounts to, a way of being in the world and outside it at the same time, the detached center that everyone else sees as a vortex of activity? He does basic training at Camp Blanding in Florida. He's never been in the South before. What really drives him nuts are the repeated playings of Ernest Tubb's "Walking the Floor Over You" on the jukebox at the local roadhouse. It's a long way from Jimmie Lunceford.

He assumes he'll be shipped out with the rest of the outfit to take part in the invasion of Japan. One morning in August the D.I., visibly shaken, lines them up to inform them that a new kind of weapon—some kind of a very destructive kind of weapon called an atomic bomb—has been deployed. The war is going to be over, just like that. Joe goes into another training program and ends up getting sent to Germany in the infantry, traveling by train from Le Havre to the Marburg "repple depple" in November 1945. In a disorienting moment he finds himself, the morning after his arrival, surrounded by thousands of empty bunks with straw mattresses. Dead silence. Everybody has cleared out except for him and one other guy.

He's been earmarked for radio by the Armed Forces Network. They send him to Frankfurt—miles and miles of ruins except for the I. G. Farben complex, spared by bombers so that Eisenhower can make it his headquarters—and on to nearby Hoechst, a Farben company town, which will be the site of AFN's key station. The Von Bruening castle, a Gothic monument with moats and ramparts and spiral staircases, becomes headquarters for a state-of-the-art broadcasting setup developed out of a network already established by the Nazis, complete with portable transmitters, high-frequency circuitry, and long-distance telephone hookups. The AFN guys find two enormous German tape machines housed in a truck, and so the announcers in Hoechst have the privilege of being among the first Americans to use tape. The sophisticated studio taking shape in an ambience of medieval gargoyles will be for the Americans a kind of paradise.

Joe serves as chief announcer and head of production, developing his own show, hammering out scripts in his nearby attic room on a German typewriter: *The Joe O'Brien Show,* half an hour daily from 4:30 to 5, later broadcast weekly from the 500-seat theater in the local Farben headquarters. It is modeled on the shows of Bob Hope, Jack Benny, and Danny Kaye, with a fourteen-piece swing band and a singer: "And here he is, that star of stage, radio, and courts-martial everywhere . . . Private Joe O'Brien!" For the show's purposes he is to be billed as a private, although he's actually a sergeant; a military bureaucrat becomes aware of the discrepancy and tries to make trouble until the show business aspect of it is explained to him. ("It seems the men prefer privates to sergeants, sir.") Sample material:

Joe: Our program is broadcast from the Prevue Theater in Hoechst.
Bob: Joe, I wish I could say the name of this town like that.
Joe: It's easy. To pronounce Hoechst correctly, fill your mouth with marshmallows—and belch.

or:

Joe: What's that lovely perfume you're wearing?
Doris: Chanel's Crap Game Number Five.
Joe: Chanel's Crap Game Number Five?
Doris: Yeah . . . One whiff of it and men fall to their knees and start shaking!

or:

Bob: What's the matter with that lieutenant?
Joe: After two years with nothing but field manuals, somebody
  slipped him a copy of *Esquire*. He's harmless, though.

He lucks out with temporary duty in Paris for three weeks in the
spring of 1946 and decides that really he was intended all along to be
French. Photographed in front of a cold beer at a sidewalk café, with
his sergeant's stripes and his American cigarette, surrounded by
French people who seem to be looking down or away or inward, he
flashes at the camera the grin of someone perfectly at ease, comfortable with the person he has become and finding, in April in Paris, a
world that feels like his natural element. By August he's shipped back
to the U.S., after a military career lasting fourteen months.

[CUE: Edith Piaf, "La Vie en Rose," recorded 1946]
Back home everybody's trying to make up for lost time. Radio,
records, clubs, jukeboxes, and now television: the machinery of show
business seems to be moving into new regions of slickness, sleekness,
and controlled dynamics, just like the new cars and the new appli-
ances. Soon after coming home, Joe is announcing the Harlem Amateur Hour at the Apollo for emcee Willie Bryant and at the same time
picks up where he left off with the Fox Amateur Hour out in Brooklyn, emceeing it every Monday night from 9 to 10 just as he'd been
doing for the six previous years. In 1947 the show moves off the stage
and into a studio in the theater. It seemed like a good idea not to do it
from the stage anymore after the audience got in the habit of hurling
light bulbs at the amateurs. One night somebody winged him with a
steel crate-opener.

He fills in on a dozen different shows, announcing *Glamour Manor*
for Cliff Arquette; doing a half-hour show with Joe Franklin playing
old records; hosting *The Music Box* every morning from 9:30 to
11:30—"the master of the turntables, Joe O'Brien, brings you platter
upon platter of top tunes every morning"—and playing the best of
Broadway musicals on *Show Time;* serving as quiz master on the well-

publicized *Quiz-Down,* where high school students compete to answer questions like "What boroughs does the Triborough Bridge connect?" and "Who spread his cloak on the ground for a queen to walk on?" and "What famous man went on a hunger strike to bring peace to his country?"

On *It's in the Family,* a quiz show sponsored by the CIO, the questions are of a different order: "What do the letters ERP stand for?" "What government jobs has Henry Wallace held?" "What is the Taft-Ellender-Wagner bill?" The show is designed, under the FCC equal-time rule, to counter another show sponsored by the American Manufacturers Association: what *Variety* describes as their "look-what-a-good-boy-I-am spiel." The AMA's program is known for its oratorical heavy breathing: "Taxes must be lowered in all brackets or—[voice of doom]—there will be no venture capital left in this country by 1950!" On the CIO quiz show, by contrast, the tone is intended to be democratic and relaxed, or at least as relaxed as it can be while fielding questions about minimum wage requirements, civil rights, food prices, and union policy. Joe is not only allowed but expected to inject as much unheralded editorializing as possible into his ad libs, no problem at all for a longtime union man like himself.

In radio's marginal corners an air of hectic improvisation can still be found. For the moment there are still odd time slots to fill, unscheduled vacuums that allow space for him to recite poetry over organ and viola accompaniment (this is the 11:30 to midnight slot); to sing "I've Got a Lovely Bunch of Coconuts," and "Valentine" and "Pigalle" in French with accompaniment by the WMCA house band, Lee Grant and the Orchestra; to play claves on Latin numbers; to improvise comic intros for straight renditions of classical pieces. Six months, eight months: none of these filler programs lasts long.

In 1950 he finally gets his own show, with a partner named Roger Gallegher, the *Gallegher and O'Brien Show.* It's a hit, and for the next eight years the two of them do their own programming and write their own comedy sketches, trading jokes and insults like old companions. There is a widespread assumption among fans, neighbors, and even family that the two must be close friends, although they scarcely see each other off the air except to work out details for the show. Joe's getting outside work too: live spots on Dumont for El Producto cigars ("Brother, you never had it so mild") and Powerhouse candy bars, Wednesday night fights from the Coliseum, commercials on WPIX for Arnold Cookies in a cowboy uniform, commercials for Gulf Gasoline in a gas jockey's uniform and cap, voice-overs for Schlitz Beer, "informational programs" that are actually fifteen-minute commercials for pre-fab houses or basement repair kits or weight-loss plans.

Between times he announces the soap opera *Rosemary,* synopsizing a decade's worth of disappearances and cases of mistaken identity, terrible but not fatal accidents, and reunions in the face of heartbreaking odds. That decade turns out to be the end of the road for radio soaps, along with radio mysteries, radio children's stories. There's no reprieve even for those supposedly beloved comedy shows. In the future there will not be even fifteen minutes available for anything but top advertising dollar. No more goofing around. Time— something that could once be filled or killed insouciantly, catch as catch can—is becoming more expensive than anyone ever predicted. As the value of a minute goes up, so does the value of the two- and three-minute songs that are coming to dominate the air.

[CUE: Beryl Davis, "The Best Things in Life Are Free," recorded 1947]

For the longest time, wide stretches of show business seemed part of a world where people sat around making things up. Hastily they threw together their gimmicks and skits and, if they didn't let the pressure get them, actually managed to have fun. Only from certain angles, and on certain ceremonious occasions, did the entertainment world project the imperious pretension evident in a photo session for *Life,* published in the issue of September 29, 1947. The two-page spread offers a graph of the music and publicity business. It's a group photo designed to show just how many behind-the-scenes professionals are needed to make an American star out of a twenty-three-year-old British singer named Beryl Davis.

Davis, who started as winner of the All-Britain Tap Dancing Championship in 1934 and went on to score British hits with her versions of "I Believe" and "A Nightingale Sang in Berkeley Square," is big enough to have her own American fan club, except that on closer examination the fan club turns out to consist mostly of English war brides. As *Life*'s voice-over explains, it will take more than that: "disc jockeys who play her records on the air, press agents who plant stories about her in the newspapers, members of the press who run the stories, arrangers who drape her songs in sensuous harmonies, a dressmaker who drapes her torso in sexy but sensible costumes, managers who pick her songs, managers who pick her radio, nightclub and theater dates, and managers to manage the managers."

The point of the photograph is to illustrate the proposition that "to become a sudden singing sensation in the U.S., far more is needed than the mere ability to sing." It is not clear whether this widescreen display of product-launching is meant as a covert criticism of the kind of corporate manipulation satirized in a novel (and later movie) like *The Hucksters* and eventually subjected to alarmist analysis in books like Vance Packard's *The Hidden Persuaders*. More likely the point is a gee-whiz acknowledgment of just how complex even the simplest social phenomena are getting to be in this modern world of ours.

Life manages to squeeze all of them into a group shot that looks like the show-biz equivalent of a graduation ceremony, although it takes the whole day to work out the staging. Beryl and her personal manager, Willard Alexander, are down front on the left, flanked by two press agents seated at their typewriters. To the right, on the other side of a velvet rope, looking like a squad of well-dressed assassins, clusters a contingent of columnists, the not-so-secret eminences of this order. Danton Walker of the *Daily News*—"Mr. Two-Million Circulation," as some publicist has dubbed him—with his trim moustache and blade-like lapels, looks like a stand-in for Clifton Webb or George Sanders. "His beat," according to another publicist, "is primarily the theatres, cafés, and all the brilliant night life for which New York is famous." Dorothy Kilgallen of the Hearst papers is as tight as a bullet. Her cute little hat sits atop her head like the tiara of some vengeful queen while her eyes stare at the camera in blank tedium metamorphosing into silent rage. The pin-striped Paul Denis of the *Post* glances offstage as if to gauge how much longer he can be expected to waste his time on this charade before getting down to some really serious business, like a martini in that pleasant bar around the corner.

Elsewhere, arranged in hierarchical patterns, are representatives of CBS, NBC, and ABC, 20th Century-Fox and RCA Victor, *Cash Box* and *Radio Daily* and *Metronome* and *Music Business,* dozens of programming directors, publicity directors, repertoire directors, casting directors, agency promoters, advertising managers, account executives, and sales supervisors. Joe is lined up, in the back row, with Barry Gray, Leonard Feather, and the other disc jockeys. An impressive display, whose net effect, in retrospect, is to underscore the utter unreliability of show-biz promotions. The concerted efforts of that mob of people, it turns out, are not able to make much of a dent in the American market as far as Beryl Davis is concerned. On the other hand, she does end up working as a featured singer on Frank Sinatra's TV show, and at the end of the twentieth century she is still on the road, touring with a tribute to Glenn Miller.

[CUE: Field recording, vocal medley with various instrumental accompaniment, children's party, Long Island, c. 1954]

From the point of view of the people in the business the moment-to-moment specifics of the passing show hardly matter. It's always changing; it will always be something. No matter who's up or down, the people who work in the infrastructure can with any luck ride the current. It has by now taken Joe and his family—there are three kids now—into a suburban house out on Long Island with more space than they've ever had to play with, with a grand piano, a state-of-the-art record player, and a reel-to-reel tape recorder for pre-recording material for his shows. (The technology that a few years earlier was available only to German broadcasters is now on the market, one more item in what will be an unending parade of gizmos.) Suburban life has components undreamed of in the city: PTAs, boy scout troops, public library fund drives, the community theater in which Joe and Maggie somehow find time to immerse themselves.

What was business in the city becomes fun in the suburbs, although the fun can get quite elaborate. When Joe undertakes to help organize the entertainment for the Senior Frolic at Manhasset High

School in June 1948, the impressive roster includes Estelle and LeRoy ("international famous dancers and directors of the newest Fred Astaire Dance Studio"), Vic Damone ("singing star of Mercury Records and CBS Saturday Night Serenade"), Johnny and Penny Olsen ("stars of ABC Rumpus Room and Mutual Movies Matinee"), and Jimmy Smith and His Orchestra and Entertainers, served up with Swedish meatballs, potato salad, deviled eggs, pickles, olives, and nuts, followed by ice cream, cake, and fruit punch.

A provincial display like that is just overflow, skimmed off the top of what's churning in the city. The business—the business of performing, of singing, of speaking words in public, of playing records on the air, of greeting audiences from a stage, of thinking up jokes to tell in a hurry—is the center where novelty is born. It never stops moving, and from the outside it looks like the most fun there is. They even give away free samples: cigar boxes, hats, candy bars. The aspects and artifacts of his job that Joe brings home are commandeered quickly by his sons. Records are talismans, exotic trade goods from beyond the mountains, messages from unknown cities whose sounds have been "captured" as the liner notes always put it: secret knowledge.

Pretty soon it's as if the kids had started a cottage industry of entertainment. Barely out of the cradle it seems they're playing drums and trumpets, thinking about orchestration and repertoire, experimenting with costuming, writing scripts for plays and comedy hours, blocking out show-stopping specialty numbers for the end of the first half. The objects associated with the late war (binoculars, walkie-talkies, bugles, a German pilot's helmet with attached throat mike) blur indistinguishably with the objects associated with show business (music stands, microphones, acetates). Play and performance are one. Somebody comes down the stairs like an entrance at the Copa, or picks up a chopstick and makes like Toscanini, grabs the portable mike and goes into a Johnnie Ray imitation or gets dizzy with a speeded-up tap routine copied from Ray Bolger's guest appearance on the Kraft Music Hall. Life might amount to a kind of special guest appearance. The studio orchestra is just tuning up.

All anybody needs is a way in, and the landscape is full of points of entry. By the middle of the '50s the two older boys are far along in their knowledge of what makes the industry tick. The oldest, Bob, in junior high school already has a business leading a small band that plays local parties and dances and bar mitzvahs; they take care of their own arrangements too. He and Joel are hired to go out to the VA hospital and play music for shell-shocked veterans, standards out of combo books: "I'm in the Mood for Love," "Cherry Pink and Apple Blossom White." Soon Bob—who's been reading music almost before he could read words, and at age twelve already has some conducting experience behind him—gets a shot on *Ted Mack's Original Amateur Hour:* big excitement. Everybody tunes in to watch his five-piece combo play their own arrangement of "Manteca." He doesn't win; a cautionary note creeps in. Show business offers no guarantees even to the most highly qualified. But there's still plenty of time for them to wait in the wings, however impatiently, before the real show starts.

The youngest of the household, I attempt to track the bewildering imports and exports that flow through and to construct as best I can a model of the world to which these parts belong, their possible points of origin, the uses to which they may be put. Half of me is peering toward the imagined city where my father works, the places of nightclubs and recording studios and radio stations. But the other half is looking in another direction: with coonskin cap firmly on my head and an ear cocked to the radio to catch Bill Hayes's recording of "The Ballad of Davy Crockett," I stare into the middle distance of a backyard transformed by reverie into an unending forest. With its alphabet of trails and glades, swirling rapids and hidden encampments, I begin to make sentences about the world that lurks just behind this one. It was where people used to live, where they seem still to be living. The ancient wilderness stretches out just beyond the screen door.

5

Back to the Country

To THE NEW WORLD OF THE POSTWAR SUBURBS THE OLD WORLD came calling. A collection of songs transferred from old 78s, eighty-four of them—discarded dance tunes and country blues, murder ballads and gospel hymns and comical numbers from an earlier era of commercial recording—was released in 1952 by Folkways Records under the title *Anthology of American Folk Music*. The assembler was Harry Smith, then twenty-nine years old, a collector, underground filmmaker, occult philosopher, fabulist, and scrounger who sometimes claimed to be the illegitimate son of the satanist Aleister Crowley and who by the time of his death in 1991 had earned the nickname "the Paracelsus of the Chelsea Hotel."

The anthology identified him only by name, but the self-designed booklet accompanying the set's six LPs signaled the presence of a deep and deeply eccentric scholarship. The booklet's idiosyncrasies ranged from headline-style summaries of old ballads—ASSASSIN OF PRESIDENT GARFIELD RECALLS EXPLOIT IN SCAFFOLD PERORATION, or ANNIE UNDER GRASSY MOUND AFTER PARENTS NIX MARRIAGE TO KING—to a wildly methodical cross-indexing: "Bible history quoted on record . . . Broken promise mentioned on record . . . Death instructions given on record . . . Echo-like relation of voices . . . Humming, records featuring . . . Mountain vantage point theme."

In passing, Smith displayed an offhand familiarity with the corpus of early recordings and with all relevant printed sources.

Many of the performers featured in the anthology—they included Mississippi John Hurt, Uncle Dave Macon, Dock Boggs, Henry Thomas, the Carter Family, Furry Lewis, Blind Lemon Jefferson, the Memphis Jug Band, Charlie Patton, Clarence Ashley, Cannon's Jug Stompers, Sleepy John Estes—would eventually become more or less celebrated, even if their music was never to be widely heard over the airwaves or in the aisles of supermarkets. In 1952, however, such music was more likely to be found, if at all, in attics or thrift shops or abandoned warehouses. It was the sound of cultural obsolescence, products no longer fit for broadcast or mass entertainment. Unlike the collections made in the field by such folk-music specialists as Alan Lomax, they were all commercial recordings made between 1927 and 1932, a period when previously marginal country music was recorded on a large scale as record companies discovered the potential of rural markets and when, as Smith noted, "American music still retained some of the regional qualities evident in the days before the phonograph, radio and talking picture had tended to integrate local types." By the simple act of bringing these selections together, Smith essayed something like a one-man cultural revolution. Its effects were felt gradually, as the collection worked its way in subterranean fashion from one newly formed folk music devotee to another. Years later Peter Stampfel (of the Holy Modal Rounders) said simply, "If God were a DJ he'd be Harry Smith."

That was one way to think of the collection, as a supernatural jukebox blasting out favorites for the dead, the old dead, from the time before there were jukeboxes, especially since so many of the songs have to do with death in every form, by drowning, by train wreck, by outlaw's or assassin's bullet, by self-inflicted stab wound. Dock Boggs, coal miner and moonshiner, set the pace in his knife-edge drone:

> *Go dig a hole in the meadow, good people*
> *Go dig a hole in the ground*
> *Come around all you good people*
> *And see this poor rounder go down.*

That was the kind of party it was, and in 1952 or 1962 or whenever you came upon it the jolt was perceptible. It would remain so, since the accumulated bloodlettings of neo-noir, neo-Gothic, post-punk, and hip-hop would make it no easier to accept the direct encounter with last things that such songs propose. In that light even the merriest music—the dance rhythms of Prince Albert Hunt's Texas Ramblers or Hoyt Ming and His Pep-Steppers, the children's song "King Kong Kitchie Kitchie Ki-Me-O," the protracted comical adventures of drunkards and lechers—acquired an abrasive edge. The soothing and hypnotic aural environment to which so much latter-day pop music accustomed us would make this music permanently exotic: it felt like a music in which the world could not be escaped.

To speak of an abrasive edge is another way of saying that this was music about being wide awake. It was always at peak; it refused to become subconversational pulse or trickling background rivulet. Insistence, emphasis, exhortation: these were the qualities that united an otherwise utterly disparate collection of performances. Geographically, the performers came predominantly from the American South—from Lake Providence, Louisiana, to Burton's Fork, Kentucky—but also from as far afield as Los Angeles, St. Paul, and Cincinnati. They worked, among other things, as coal miners, ministers, carpenters, mill hands, tenant farmers, and, yes, cowboys. Many were professional or semi-professional musicians, traveling with medicine shows or performing on the street. What these recordings captured was not the folklore of private pastime or family lore but the repertoire of public performance.

The anthology's temporal reach extended both forward and backward. It consisted of songs that were recorded in the 1920s and '30s, were collected in the 1940s, and attained wide if covert influence in the 1950s and '60s. But for many of the musicians represented, 1928 was already the aftermath, the last time it was possible to retrieve an echo of a world whose rapid disappearance was signaled by the very fact that these songs were being recorded. That world stretched from the late nineteenth century, when the style of performers like Henry Thomas and Uncle Dave Macon was already taking shape at barn dances and tent shows and political rallies, to the eve of World War I;

an era when the hot news was of the depredations of Cole Younger in the 1870s, the assassinations of Garfield and McKinley in 1881 and 1901, the death of Casey Jones on the Illinois Central Line in April 1900, the sinking of the Titanic in 1912. Even those bulletins were late accretions to a body of knowledge extending back toward Indian war whoops, medieval enchantments, John the Revelator and his "book of the seven seals." We were in a place where history survived only by being transmuted into rhymes, charms, complaints, exorcisms, prophecies.

Purely as an arrangement—a profoundly satisfying juxtaposition attentive to echoes, responses, thematic parallels, and who knows what hermetic alchemical principles smuggled in by Smith—*Anthology of American Folk Music* itself functioned as a work of art. Designed to be heard precisely in the order laid down, it anticipated the sort of musical collage that would become perhaps the most widely practiced American art form: the personal mix tape of favorite songs that serves as self-portrait, gesture of friendship, prescription for an ideal party, or simply as an environment consisting solely of what is most ardently loved.

Smith's concept was vaster but equally personal. The songs did not so much refer back to an earlier America as reconstitute it. A single person was here mapping a lost or at least forgotten domain not in the name of tradition or collective will or social or musicological theory, but merely out of his inexplicable sense of how everything falls into place. The elements were together because they belonged together; he knew. The anthology resonated with the demiurgic thrill of holding those elements in hand; it registered a search for hidden correspondences and occulted communications, and Smith moved as easily among its implications as a shaman rapidly switching voices during a dialogue with spirits.

That was pretty much what it seemed like to its listeners, even a decade after its first appearance: the soundtrack of a resurrection, an unbottling of hidden identities. After ten years, however, a whole culture had taken shape along the lines indicated by the anthology. The dead, it turned out, weren't all dead. Lost singers (Clarence Ashley, John Hurt, Dock Boggs, Furry Lewis) were found, lost careers revived in the form of albums and appearances at nightclubs and folk festivals. Ancient became contemporary in albums like *Mountain Music Bluegrass Style* (1959) or *Old Time Music at Clarence Ashley's* (1961–63); the emergence of young stars like Bob Dylan and Joan Baez helped prompt an explosion of youthful guitar and banjo and harmonica players; and at the triumphant Newport Folk Festival of 1963, the joining of old (Ashley, Boggs, Hurt, Bill Monroe, Mother Maybelle Carter) and new (Dylan, Baez, Judy Collins, Peter, Paul, and Mary, Ian and Sylvia) seemed to augur the formation of a new culture. It came to your doorstep, into your living room: the talk was suddenly all of picks and frets and capos, and there was, it seemed, a harmonica on every sideboard. With newly acquired technical skills came a newly acquired repertoire of attitudes and allegiances and made-up histories that came to feel like memories. The implications of that rebirth would remain for many unresolved, inseparable from all that came next. The 1997 re-release of the *Anthology of American Folk Music* in compact disc format inevitably raised as many questions about the late '50s and early '60s as it did about the late '20s and early '30s, evoking nostalgia for what was already a displaced nostalgia, as if the music were a treasured memento of an alternate life.

The CD box set of the anthology was an advanced specimen of the form, featuring a video and photographic appendix on CD-ROM, a book-length collection of essays and interviews, and detailed notes to each track (supplementing, updating, and sometimes correcting Smith's own notes, reproduced in facsimile) that together constituted a study guide to the field. The entry for Charlie Patton's "Mississippi Boweavil Blues," for instance, identified fifteen other sources for Patton recordings and thirty-five other recordings of this and other boll weevil–related ballads, by artists ranging from Blind Willie McTell to Brook Benton. Each song became an entryway into a potentially unfinishable research project.

It provided further confirmation that the CD box set had become, in terms of reverent attention to detail, our moment's equivalent of the medieval illuminated manuscript. It was not enough to have learned how to capture sound; there must be an appropriate monument to enclose it and keep it from ever escaping again, to stabilize what would otherwise remain a drifting accumulation of sound effects. Hearing is the most slippery and intangible and therefore most haunting of experiences; and we have heard so much, more than we can remember or even process.

If the technology of recording and broadcasting has probably not made the world any noisier than it was—in some ways, as brass bands in the piazza give way to brass bands in someone's headphones, it has made it quieter—the noise has at any rate become denser, and harder to interpret. Sound as a measure of location—a fairly direct clue, in simpler days, to what was coming this way and how soon it would get here—has been compromised ever more drastically by telephone, phonograph, radio, and their generations of offspring. Some point of no return was reached when you couldn't tell the phone beeping in the movie playing on your computer from the phone beeping in your pocket. Edgar Allan Poe was by his own account driven half-mad by the infernal din of horses' hooves on cobblestones in 1840s New York, but at least he knew where the noise was coming from. In the urban infernos delineated by Balzac and Dickens, however convulsive and hallucinatory they may have been, sound was still 100 percent live and therefore a reliable tool for navigation; at the very least, a shriek might guide you to (or away from) the scene of a crime, or the roar of a mob alert you to an approaching riot.

Modern sound technology offered new improved forms of disorientation, impossibly distant sounds, pre-recorded whispers, street barkers piped into private dwellings, speeches from a podium whose center was everywhere, beeps and sirens that cut across space so sharply that their point of origin became indeterminable, canned laughter echoing down airshafts, canned music doing battle with other canned music in the discontinuous spaces of our own city, the multichannel not-quite-all-here city of Burroughs or Pynchon or Perec, where we spend much of our lives listening to what is not here, is no longer here, never was here to begin with.

Long usage blunts the anomaly of this, so that by contrast those moments when one may have grasped the oddness of the recording era's wraparound wall of sound can seem in retrospect like flashes of mystical insight. A minor instance: on his 1957 album *Bonjour Paris,* Michel Legrand began his arrangement of "J'ai Deux Amours" with an ingenious reconstruction of the sound of an early (circa 1920) acoustical recording, complete with meticulously simulated surface noise, before gliding into a stunning demonstration of late-'50s hi-fi in its thennovel richness of tone and breadth of spectrum. At the time, the idea may have been to contrast the almost comical poverty of the old with the splendor—growing rapidly more splendid in those heady days of Dynagroove and Full Dimensional Sound—of the new. But the device also served, intentionally or not, as an alienation effect. It made the listener abruptly aware that this was a recording, and that if recording had a future it also had a past. Oddly, the shrill and spectral past— even in this ersatz, mimicked form—seemed more real than the dynamic, naturally balanced, full-dimensional present of 1957.

That contrarian impulse to travel against time's current—to gravitate toward the noise and detritus filtered out by the culture of Dynagroove—was crucial to what became, after a lot of listening to a lot of old records, the early '60s folk revival. The road to the future lay in the past, among forebears so forgotten that they had become alien, so alien that they could almost be invented. Early listeners agreed that the Smith anthology's initial effect was of uncanny strangeness. It seemed a repository of "lost, archaic, savage sounds" or, in the words of filmmaker Bruce Conner, "a confrontation with another culture . . . like field recordings, from the Amazon, or Africa, but it's here in the United States!" "Who is singing?" Greil Marcus asked. "Who are these people?" That was Harry Smith's idea: "It sounded strange," he said of the blues record that provoked his collecting career, "so I looked for others."

Folk music was not supposed to be strange. The folk music that Smith's younger listeners were likely to have heard in the 1950s—perhaps in elementary school, perhaps in summer camp—was purveyed by such intermediaries as Pete Seeger (both alone and with the folk quartet The Weavers), and Burl Ives, and Carl Sandburg. It might be droll, rambunctious, plaintive, bawdy, morally indignant, or nostalgic—it might, if you were an urban type with what you considered more advanced tastes, be faintly embarrassing—but it was music designed to restore a sense of intuitive collective warmth, as if everyone listening could be brought back into some lost circle of fellowship. The fifth-graders who sat listening to scratched LPs of Burl Ives singing "The Blue-Tail Fly" or "The Streets of Laredo," or the Weavers segueing from "Goodnight Irene" into "Tzena Tzena," or Woody Guthrie singing "This Land Is Your Land" surmised that folk songs emanated directly from the collective anonymity of The People, floated freely in a timeless inaccessible realm where folk life replicated itself from generation to generation, until some dedicated collector bothered to write them down. Emissaries carried them from those regions into ours, so that we might come to know our distant kin.

It all had to do with "the country"—but what country, whose country? For so many of those drawn into the folk revival, the very idea of the rural was something constructed out of artifacts and catchphrases. It wasn't just a matter of accents and peculiar sayings but of different worldviews, different systems of thought. There was not so much a dividing line as an abyss between the two cultures. For a postwar generation of urban and suburban children, the mountains and creeks and hollows of the songs might as well have existed on another planet.

I remember an elementary school textbook in which Jimmy and Judy from the big city went to visit their cousins in the country to find out the source of their milk and eggs, a visit that provided the occasion for a dialogue on the many differences between city and country. For a suburban third-grader, both city (skyscrapers, elevated trains, smoky harbors, suspension bridges) and country (barns, tractors, silos, haystacks) were exotic. In fact it was in trying to puzzle out a middle ground between these starkly opposed terms that the meaning of "suburb" began to dawn. Jimmy and Judy told their cousins about the technological marvels of the metropolis, but the country ultimately got the better of the comparison. The city kids were dazzled by a succession of miracles—"Oh, look at the pretty chickens!"— while the country folk exhibited an air of laconic and undemonstrative wisdom, secure in the knowledge that the old homestead was the ultimate source to which the city had finally to pay homage. Back to the land! "Lordy, where on earth did you think bacon came from?"

Mythologies of that sort had piled up like so many layers of insulation. The material collected by Harry Smith was new information, incomparably harsher and more tumultuous, as if intended to convey, "Everything you know is wrong." What folk were these? The mood was not necessarily either collective or warm; more often it conveyed isolation, fear, even madness. As for intuition—the sort of instinctive and essentially impersonal expressiveness that was supposed to be the very definition of folk music—it was hard, given the almost freakish individuality of many of the performances, to avoid the sense of a craggy and fully conscious artistry.

In the '30s and '40s, under the influence of performers such as Pete Seeger and scholars such as Alan Lomax, folk music had been purveyed in more or less Marxist terms, as an expression of sweeping social forces, the soundtrack of a narrative marked by clear moral roles. (The breadth of vision of a Lomax or Seeger was in turn, inevitably, reduced to more simplistic terms by those whose agenda outweighed their knowledge.) Smith broke down that sense of large-scale evolution into molecular units, suggesting that the process was immeasurably more complex than the available schemata could account for. He ignored ethnic or geographic or chronological pigeonholing in favor of a tripartite division of his own invention, into Ballads, Social Music, and Songs. Ballads told stories, whether of murderous gypsies or hapless sharecroppers; social music ranged from square-dancing to apocalyptic preaching; as for songs, the most wide-open of the categories, ranging from "I Wish I Was a Mole in the Ground" to "See That My Grave Is Kept Clean," they turned out to contain an unsuspected freedom of poetic association. Everything about Smith's presentation implied that to hear these at all, you had to forget categories and listen to each cut as the record of a distinct and mysterious event.

Smith's most utopian gesture was to posit an American Folk Music without racial divisions. Careful to note every other detail about the records' original release, he ignored the separation of country recordings into "race" and "hillbilly" categories, which record companies had enforced from the outset, even if the recordings were sometimes hard or impossible to separate by ear. Race records would evolve into modern blues and rhythm and blues, their hillbilly counterparts into commercial country and western; half a life could be spent tracing the development of one strain or another. Much research effort has gone and continues to go into separating out the strands of American music, to intercepting the West African praise song or Irish fiddle lament before they collide, or surprising a square-dance tune in the act of acquiring (or discarding) a blues inflection. Smith's arrangement suggested that—since every imaginable kind of crossover had already happened, had never stopped happening—there was more to be gained by listening to the records as singularities, categories of one, rather than as specimens of one type or another.

In terms of the mainstream culture of 1952—or 1958 (the year the Kingston Trio, with their monster hit "Tom Dooley," became the living embodiment of folk music) or 1962 (the year Bob Dylan released his first album)—all these performers, whether black or white, were united in common strangeness. To gauge the surprise, it would be necessary to reinhabit the sonic universe of late '40s/early '50s pop music, whose perfected mellowness—a Modernaires or Mel-Tones kind of mellowness—was achieved at the price of a narrowed spectrum that excluded broad areas defined as noise. Even silence could qualify as noise, dead air, a disturbing spareness or starkness of tone. In those days when cowboys rode the range they brought their orchestra and echo chamber along.

It was as if the past was meant to survive only as a point of reference—at most as old songs done in new ways—not as something actually to be listened to. "Tennessee Saturday Night," a 1947 country-and-western hit about the rough and rowdy ways of backwoods folks ("When they get together there's a lot of fun / They all know the other fella packs a gun"), was sung in suavely self-kidding fashion by Red Foley, the already old-fashioned fiddle solo emanating from some harmless country of recollection. Most of the Smith anthology qualified by hit-parade standards as noise: grating, rasping, screeching, out of tune, out of time. The crushed-rock voice of Blind Willie Johnson, the wailing tambourine-accented calls and responses of William and Versey Smith as they memorialized the sinking of the Titanic, Dock Boggs with his voice made for what Greil Marcus describes as "primitive-modernist music about death": these came from somewhere off the map.

In short order an underground army of mapmakers emerged, finding trails within the rapidly expanding recorded archive of old-time music—who could have imagined so many recordings had been made?—foraging for information that no one else had deemed worthy of organizing. A sort of do-it-yourself free-floating academy devoted itself to the tracking of variants and antecedents, chord changes and tunings, false labels and reversed identities: to determining the contexts in which the protagonist of "The Girl I Left Behind Me" either "read on a few lines further" or "rode on a few miles further" to find out the truth about his abandoned girlfriend, to pondering whether John Hardy (or was it Johnny Hard) carried "two guns" or "a gun and a razor" every day, to meditating on the non sequitur in "Little Sadie" when Sadie's murderer is accosted by a sheriff—"He said, Young man, is your name Brown?"—and replies, "Yes sir, yes sir, my name is Lee." Through this door you could enter history as it was in the act of changing and come to inhabit the old language before the smoothing-out of dialects. In that area of mutating information—conceived as an outlying borderland just beyond our settlement—fifty miles might make all the difference in how a particular story turned out.

All the scholarship in the world could not keep nonspecialist listeners from finding in the songs the ingredients for a narrative as thoroughly imaginary as *Ivanhoe* or *Ernani*. For a generation that lacked much sense of common national tradition it became the equivalent of Percy's *Reliques of Ancient English Poetry* or Grimm's fairy tales. Smith's collection, and the other sources to which it pointed the way, opened up a secret literature, the poetry of an America that had been successfully excluded from the written record. Here was a down-home lexicon of fundamental terms: the river, the mill, the tavern, the mountain, the old dusty road, murders, bird calls, corn whiskey, graveyards, the train that carried my girl from town, journeys by sea to London Town or overland to the other side of the Blue Ridge Mountains. It was like an induction into a space constructed by ritual gestures, droning modal chants of indeterminate function—

Same old man
Living at the mill
The mill goes around of its own free will

—which revealed what the listeners had least expected, a form of abstract art.

This body of songs proposed an aesthetic that promised to be actually usable. In some sense they were songs without authors, or songs that questioned the notion of single authorship and made it seem a rather bland and decadent subspecialization; songs that interpenetrated one another, words that went drifting and changing, disparate stories that were grafted together to generate further songs in a process that could have no end. Verses torn from their context—but then many of these verses had been adrift for a long time—seemed at once archaic and freshly concocted:

Like a mole in the ground
I'd root this mountain down

or

Single girl, single girl
She's going where she please
Married girl, married girl
Baby on her knees

or

I've been to the east and I've been to the west
I've been this whole world round
I've been to the river and I've been baptized
And now I'm on my hanging ground

or

A railroad man

He'll kill you when he can
And drink up your blood like wine.

Out of the swirl, chunks of phrasing bobbed up—"old plank road" or "new river train"—with the inscrutable force of half-understood ideograms.

The element of unknowability, of unlimited suggestiveness, was essential to the allure. A web of allusions stretched beyond any living person's ability to make the connections. Even when the songs dealt with recognizably real events the effect was dreamlike. The horror of the Titanic disaster lived on as inconsolable moaning chant in "When That Great Ship Went Down," as if the ship would never stop sinking. When the wife of the assassinated McKinley confronts his killer in "White House Blues"—

Look here, you rascal,
See what you've done
You shot my husband
And I've got your gun

—we seem to be in the middle of some extraordinarily strange puppet play or verse chronicle. By contrast, Edwin S. Porter's 1903 film version of Czolgosz's execution, a harbinger of the modern with its laboriously faked verisimilitude, has a far more cut and dried and therefore unintentionally comical effect. The old songs were never comical except when they wanted to be.

The process by which folk music (however defined) came to enjoy its brief moment of ascendancy in the late '50s and early '60s was more circuitous and complex than most knew or cared to know. To learn all of it would have been to plunge into the specifics of a past that was more fun when it was left beautifully vague, when it was allowed to consist, in Robert Cantwell's words (in his passionate and absorbing study of the folk revival, *When We Were Good*), of "a tissue of illusion, of mountain cabins and southern canebrakes, desperados, tramps, maidens, farmers, banjo pickers, and wandering blues guitarists." A generation tentatively sketched out, on beach or in woods or down in the basement, a future of kazoo music and choral chant by the fire. An alternative autobiography was put together out of crimes and executions and haunted loves, a romance of bitterness and devastation and exile. The song was there to be entered again and again, an impersonal one-size-fits-all space where one could paradoxically feel most at home: "I am going down this road feeling bad." "Gonna build me a log cabin / On a mountain so high." No questions asked, no details needed. Wasn't that what folk music was for anyway, to be taken and changed into whatever one needed it to be?

Later, after the triumph of Pop around 1965, there would be relief for the young fans in realizing that they did not finally have to become coal miners or tenant farmers. A pinch of reality is just what fantasy needs to give it an aura of substance, and what a fantasy it was, with its dizzying cascades of stereotypical figurines and toy sets, gambler and floozy and moonshiner and deranged preacher, roadhouse and scaffold, mountain cabin and pitch-dark piney woods. In a 1960 article in *Mademoiselle,* Susan Montgomery registered a disenchantment with the scene, which would later read like an advance judgment on the decade to come: "This generation of college students . . . is composed of young people who are desperately hungry for a small, safe taste of an unslick, underground world. Folk music, like a beard or sandals, has come to represent a slight loosening of the inhibitions, a tentative step in the direction of the open road, the knapsack, the hostel."

It was a virtual South, then, existing in a virtual past; but then they always were. Delve the fantasy to its roots and you find another fantasy; look for untrammeled folk expression and you find one form or another of show business. Robert Cantwell, tracing back the folk lineage, found himself back among the artifacts of nineteenth-century blackface minstrelsy: "The cabins, cottonbales, wagons, steamboats, and rail-fences . . . the piquant genre images of corn and cottonfields, the welcoming old plantation home, the harvest moons, the barefooted children, the magnolia, honeysuckle, and wisteria vine, all the wistful longing songs addressed to them, and the very 'South' itself, magically invoked by mere names, Kentucky or Carolina or Alabama—are the visual and linguistic coinage of the minstrelsy that has been circulating in America for a century and a half in thousands of forms beyond the stage itself." Copies, parodies, reversals, deliberate distortions, whatever was required to tone down, jazz up, smooth out, mess around, or make over: this had been the process of American music, of American entertainment, for so long before anyone took note that the recorded history could never be about anything but mixes, hybrids, crossovers. Pure strains could be imagined but not really experienced, since the moment they hit the air they became part of the fusion.

In America the primary imaginary purity was traditionally racial, although there were plenty of other purities—of region, of religion, of occupation, of technique, of sheer feeling—to extend the metaphor. Theodore Roosevelt, for instance, wrote an admiring preface for *Cowboy Ballads* (1912, by John Lomax, Alan's father), drawing attention to their echo of Anglo-Saxon outlaw ballads (a possible nod to the support Roosevelt had gotten in Missouri from Jesse James's brother Frank). The revival of traditional mountain music that flourished briefly in the 1920s received enthusiastic support from Henry Ford and the Ku Klux Klan, while the founder of the Archive of Folk Song spoke ominously of the threat of "Hebrew Broadway jazz" and the composer Lamar Stringfield wrote (in 1931) that "since the emotions of the Negro race are foreign to the white man, an essentially Anglo-Saxon nation derives its nationalism in music only from its own people . . . Naturally, the least affected of the folk-music that now exists in America is preserved by people in the mountainous country, or on the plains." You had only to listen, for instance, to the African-American stringband music of Nathan Frazier and Frank Patterson recorded, almost at the last possible moment, in Tennessee in the early '40s—versions of "Dan Tucker" and "Bile Them Cabbage Down" and "Corrinne" that suggested the hidden origins of supposedly "pure" hillbilly music—to give the lie to the Anglo-Saxonists. But to do so you would have had to be digging pretty deep into the archives of the Library of Congress, on a mission with few sponsors.

In the '30s and '40s, folk music would be reclaimed for the left, a story full of unexpected oddities and digressions. The musicologist Charles Seeger and his son Pete got their first taste of folk music at the

New School for Social Research in 1931, listening to Thomas Hart Benton sing "John Henry"; and Leadbelly really was prevailed on to dress in convict stripes for some of his public performances after Alan Lomax had managed to get him sprung from Angola Prison. Whether or not the left-wing folk song movement was the best idea the American Communist Party ever supported, it was certainly the most successful. At high tide the movement made inroads into radio (the Almanac Singers on the Navy Department's *Treasury Hour,* Woody Guthrie on *DuPont's Cavalcade of Stars*) and Broadway (the Burl Ives musical *Sing Out Sweet Land!*). Eventually, the Weavers, who had taken their name from Gerhart Hauptmann's 1892 protest play about the class struggle in Silesia, found their hits covered by the likes of Mitch Miller and Vic Damone; if the people's music was not to be enlisted in the service of ideological crusades, then it was to be looted for whatever saleable tunes it might have to offer.

But then every stage of the process reflects singular inflections and deformations. It was in the form of rousing singing groups, redolent of collegiate glee clubs—the Kingston Trio, the Limelighters, the Brothers Four—that folk music muscled its way into the charts in the next decade. Softened up by "Tom Dooley" and "Greenfields," pop fans were ready for Baez and Dylan and the Newport Folk Festival ensemble, by which time folk music was inextricably entwined, again, with political action. Some would forever recall the resistance in Washington Square to Park Commissioner Newbold Morris's order to ban folksinging in 1961—the protestors beaten while singing "We Shall Not Be Moved"—as their first taste of what the '60s were going to be like.

Eventually even the folk revival would become ancient history. They all have their box sets now—Leadbelly, the Weavers, Alan Lomax, Pete Seeger, Woody Guthrie, Bob Dylan—row upon row of freeze-dried echo chambers. The metallic wheels have that gleaming, hygienic impersonality by which we recognize the new technologies: the home entertainment library is now ready to be loaded on the rocketship. We have entered an Alexandrian phase—or is it a Noah's Ark phase?—of storing and classifying and anthologizing the works of the past, and discover that an Alexandrian life has its distinct charms. The generations become coeval; whether you reach for the '20s or the '50s or the '70s may indicate no more than your taste in hats or song titles or cover designs. Last week you were in Zaire 1980, the week before in Paris 1952. Now, on a whim, it's Kentucky's turn; it is only a matter of determining where to set the dial of the time machine.

Differences were formerly mediated by physical space. If you wanted to hear mountain music you went to the mountains. Researchers of the heroic age—the Lomaxes and Seegers and Rinzlers—invested their physical being in the music. Free now to drop in anywhere unannounced, we listen in their secret fastnesses to Tibetan lamas or Moroccan jajouka musicians or the throat singers of Tuva. Like Johnny Mercer's old cowhand, we know all the songs that the cowboys (and the yak herders) know because we learned them all on the radio. Long familiarity with the industrial cycles of pop permits us to observe the rough being made smooth while calmly anticipating the moment when there will be novelty value in making the smooth rough again. Blues goes lounge, lounge goes industrial noise, industrial noise prepares to merge, perhaps, with Gregorian chant. Our new tradition, however designated—fusion, crossover, sampling, mix—amounts to hardly more than a drastically speeded-up version of the way things have always happened. If a band in Madagascar plays the Bobby Fuller Four's "I Fought the Law" on traditional instruments or a London-based bhangra group fuses Punjabi folk music and James Brown grooves or an even newer group mixes all of the above in brief unrecognizable fragments, the process hardly differs from, say, an obscure Alabaman band of the 1920s lending Hawaiian inflections to a revamped English ballad whose original subject, somewhere back in the Middle Ages, was the blood libel of Jewish ritual murder.

As told by Richard A. Peterson in his book *Creating Country Music,* the formative stages of commercial country music—from Fiddlin' John Carson's pioneering recordings in Atlanta in 1923 to the posthumous mythologizing of Hank Williams after his death in 1953—consisted of a series of transactions, marketing decisions, calculated changes of costume and instrumentation and repertoire in response to outside pressures.

In the mid-1920s the rapidly expanding record business was hungry for material and newly aware of the potential of specialized audiences. The companies recorded almost anything they could think of, on an extraordinary scale; over 10,000 new recordings were released in 1929 alone. One can almost hear the executives at Columbia or Vocalion planning their strategy: "Let's round up as many of these hill people as we can and see what they've got." The company scouts went out and found music that could be scooped up with a minimum of effort. Reading of the historic 1927 sessions in Bristol, Tennessee, at which Ralph Peer of Victor discovered Jimmie Rodgers and the Carter Family, or other similar corporate forays, it is hard not to think of those scenes in old Westerns where the trappers come to the company depot to have their furs assessed and to be duly short-changed. The scouts who snapped up the music were mostly indifferent to it, as Polk Brockman, responsible for getting Fiddlin' John Carson recorded in the first place, freely acknowledged: "My interest in hillbilly music and black music is strictly financial."

The idea was not to launch musical careers but to take what the musicians already had and see what could be made from it. As Frank Walker of Columbia Records commented: "Their repertoire would consist of eight or ten things that they did well and that is all they knew. So, when you picked out the three or four that were best in a man's so called repertoire you were through with that man as an artist . . . You might come out with two selections or you might come out with six or eight, but you did it all at that time." The Clarence Ashleys and Mississippi John Hurts sank back into obscurity for the next three decades.

It was a novelty to put old hearthside favorites on record, but the novelty was soon exhausted; most people did not want multiple versions of old murder ballads and square-dance tunes. The charm of Uncle Jimmy Thompson's old-time fiddle music wore off quickly when he appeared on the Grand Ole Opry's first program in 1925. In Peterson's account, "Uncle Jimmy started right in playing a string of jigs, breakdowns, and hornpipes. When after two hours George Hay, the announcer, tried to get him to conclude his performance, Uncle Jimmy said he knew 2,000 tunes and was just getting limbered up." The Grand Ole Opry continued to pay lip service to its folk origins while moving as rapidly as possible toward smoother, more radio-friendly sounds. From the early '30s on, the music that got heard was mostly music tailored for the new marketing channels; songwriting became the basis for the industry, making old-time music a style—a "renewable resource" (in Richard Peterson's phrase)—rather than a fixed repertoire of inherited songs from which no copyright advantage was to be derived.

What we heard on the Smith anthology was how people sounded before they knew how they sounded, in the same way that the first movies briefly caught the demeanor of people who had never seen anyone on film. The vocal styles had not been corrected by reference to recorded music or adapted to the microphone. All that was about to change irrevocably, as singers learned how the voice could be something separate from its body. In his autobiography *Truth Is Stranger Than Publicity,* Alton Delmore of the classic country duo the Delmore Brothers tells how at their first recording session in 1931 they heard their recorded voices for the first time, and how in that instant everything changed for them. They didn't know their own voices: "There was something divine in that little can [the recording equipment] . . . that helped us immensely and changed us from two country farm boy singers to something 'up town' and acceptable to listeners who bought records and listened to radio programs. That was the whole secret of our good luck. Our voices took well to the microphone."

It is a moment in the history of disembodiment, the history of recording: the birth of the voice as unhinged object, linked to no particular point in space or time. By a series of incremental steps we end up in the never-never world of overdub and multitrack—from Bill Evans playing duets and trios with himself, Hank Williams Jr. and Natalie Cole singing duets with their dead fathers, Frank Sinatra singing duets with people he may never have met, down to the completely concocted ambient landscapes of technopop, electronic collages deliberately inhabiting the land of Nowhere, records that are not records of anything but their own existence.

Go back to the genesis of recorded sound. On a July night in New Jersey, in 1887—make it a Gothic night, afflicted with lightning and bursts of thunder, a night when Victor Frankenstein might have been at work in his lab—Thomas Edison shouts into a telephone speaker attached to a diaphragm, to which in turn an indenting stylus has been affixed. A strip of paraffin-coated paper is positioned under the stylus: as he shouts, the paper is pulled along so that the stylus leaves a trail of agitated markings. A moment later, when the stylus is dragged back through the gouges, the assembled lab workers hear an echo, ever so faint and misshapen, of that shout. Edison's assistant remarks, "Golly, it's there." A tiny cosmic fracture has occurred. "It's there": not only the shout but the time in which the shout was made. On a small scale the order of things—the flow that hitherto only went one way—has been reversed.

It must have been a very long time ago that Moe Asch, the founder of Folkways Records, could have said: "I always believed in the 'one mike' theory—I hate the stereo recordings, and mixing can never give you the accurate sense of the original sound. A hundred years from now it is as natural as the day I recorded it." Once there was an emotional—not to mention a political—stake in having a sense of the reality on the other side of the mike, in visualizing the musicians actually playing and singing, in imagining their likely surroundings—even if many of the songs on *Old Time Music at Clarence Ashley's* were really recorded not in the archetypal wood-frame house on the cover but in a Los Angeles recording studio; even if the *Beach Boys' Party,* with its aura of background chatter and fizzing soda pop, was no more actual than sitcom laughter. It was around the time of that party—1966 or so—that the Moe Asch idea of "natural" sound began to slip into an unattainable archaic realm. There were too many options on the gizmos for anything ever to be natural in Asch's sense anymore, and it was too much fun exploring the unnatural. Recording as constructed artifact began to replace the ideal of recording as preservation of a moment in time.

Yet we go back looking for what was preserved, a life sustained beyond its limits and with which we can achieve the most intimate of fusions through the relation of sound and ear. It becomes a matter of awe that the voice of the other, the fingers of the other moving on the strings, actually vibrate in the body of the hearer, in the absence of the world in which the sound originated. All gone, those mills and wagon-yards and cheap hotels, gone even the music halls and recording studios, along with the life that sustained them, save for what a machine has captured: Uncle Dave Macon shouting "Kill yourself!" in enthusiastic exhortation, or Henry Thomas blowing a reed-pipe solo as if nothing else existed. The mystery of it deepens as we drift further from the original moments thus kept uncannily present.

The notion of lineal descent in art derived from a culture of apprenticeship becomes unwieldy when any given listener gets signals simultaneously from every direction. In the strange museum that technology opened for us, we relive earlier stages of the mixing process, wind the tape back in godlike fashion to one segment or another of the flux, tracing tones and patterns as they bounce from Swiss yodelers to Jimmie Rodgers and from Jimmie Rodgers to Doc Watson, from Blind Lemon Jefferson to Bob Dylan to the Four Tops, from gamelan music to Debussy to the Ivory Snow commercial, from Luisa Tetrazzini to Louis Armstrong to Billie Holiday, from Arnold Schönberg to Ennio Morricone to Lee Perry and the Upsetters. We are drawn to the beginning of our world—understood as somehow synonymous with the core of feeling—only to find a past that changed forever in being captured. The technology that lets us hear the songs also rapidly undermines the conditions in which they were created in the first place. Go back as far as possible and you find already only an echo of some unknowable music, wilder and richer.

DEVELOPMENT

6

Top Forty

IT IS JUST ANOTHER MORNING IN JUNE 1961. FIVE MARITIME workers' unions have struck all three U.S. coasts despite a plea from President Kennedy. Veteran observers remain confident that Soviet premier Khrushchev will soften his demand that the West leave Berlin. U.S. ambassador Adlai Stevenson is under heavy guard in La Paz, Bolivia, following anti-government riots, and will travel tomorrow to Peru where Communist students have threatened to make trouble. Twenty suspects described as youths, most of them teenagers, have been arrested by narcotics squad detectives in a $15,000-a-week heroin operation in Bay Ridge. In Manhattan, meanwhile, my father is doing what decades of radio experience have enabled him to do: read the weather report as if it were a form of poetry, a free-verse improvisation bouncing off a prerecorded jazz vocalist (was that Ella going by so quickly?) as she lets fly with "It's a Lovely Day"—

> *It's a beautiful day,*
> *sunny, pleasant, afternoon temperatures*
> *high in the seventies—*
> *clear and cool again tonight,*
> *good sleepin' weather,*
> *tomorrow about 80 degrees,*

a nice sunny blue-skies Saturday,
looks like a good weekend—
winds from the northeast at 9 right now,
humidity 53 percent,
WMCA temperature is 58 degrees—

He functions as a stand-in for the weather itself. His program's cluster of patter and news flash and stockpiled rhythmic interpolations—"Top of the morning to you no matter where you are, at work, at home, or in your car"—tosses about as naturally as branches in this June breeze. Radio is an air shaft open on the world. You're allowed to listen in on whatever is happening out there, or more exactly, in there. "Being Joe O'Brien," according to the station's publicists, "is like being a traffic cop in the grandest sense of the word. In the largest city in the world. It means telling a lot of people all about the day they're about to live."

What you hear is the day you ought to have lived, that you would have lived had you not been too busy driving to work, or dropping the laundry off, or trying to finish the science homework, or getting caught in traffic on the crosstown bus. Since you can't quite be there to experience the hours as they pass, you're given moment-by-moment reports on how things are going down. And if nothing is happening, the man behind the mike will dream up something just for you, an alternative day punctuated with happy-go-lucky outbursts and obscure surprises.

The radio show is a collage always in the making, an art work that manages the flow of information and music. It never quite turns into an object. No time! When you start to think about it, it's already in the past. It consists of the process of making itself happen and then making itself disappear so the next one can start: no regrets, only anticipation. This is no representation of a world; it *is* the world, unfolding in real time.

It is a miniature city. On closer examination this city is made up of random units, odd coils and bolts of spots, songs, jokes, jingles, fast-breaking news bulletins, public service announcements, station breaks. The art is to drop them in seamlessly, with bracing ease and exuberance, allowing no distinction between what is live and what prerecorded, slot each in the right place and give all of it the semblance of rolling along of its own momentum. It should give the impression that the components hop around as freely and goofily as the teapots and knives and spoons in a Disney cartoon. The deejay's talk ties it together, persuades you these pieces belong to a continuum in which connections flow back and forth. Take away that will to flow and nothing would remain but an inert heap of loose parts.

Music is a major part of the radio fabric but not yet the sole point; there are revolutions yet to come. Music is simply the biggest of the elements intended to establish that here, on the other side of the mike, is the natural home of optimistic energy, of the spirit that makes it possible no matter what the circumstances to get through the next hour. Slackness is not allowed. The thing coming right up will always surpass what went before, and the best of what went before is in any event always about to be brought back as if it had never left. The world is not permitted to disappoint. It is not even permitted to catch its breath. There are no tired deejays. Sentinels of temporality, they are always wide awake and wired, ready to go a bit faster than the ear can follow. By the time the listener gets to the end of what was being said, something else has already begun. No use thinking about lost moments, this new moment is all there is. Here the present does not emerge from the past, it only emerges into the future. The past doesn't exist, baby! Don't tell me about last night, tell me about the one that's coming up!

It can only be good, whatever it is. The deejay's task is to persuade the listener that all instants are created equal, that even the commercials—don't turn the dial!—have a natural right to exist and flourish. The music on the records receives scarcely more airplay than the music in commercials, music often better produced and more complexly arranged. The deftest technicians have given themselves over (or rather for the right price have allowed themselves to be given over) to sodas and automobiles, deodorants and cigarettes and discount furniture outlets. In 1961 this secret mandarin class of composers and arrangers considers the most popular records far too juvenile, too primitive, for selling quality products. They still don't think they're selling to kids.

So we segue from "The Mashed Potatoes" or "Short Shorts" to a Salem commercial in which a "hot" Gene Krupa–style big band drum break dissolves refreshingly into a segment of "cool" guitar and vibes-drenched West Coast '50s jazz to demonstrate through a fusion of word play and musical joke the cooling effect of Salem's menthol filter on your cigarette break: a pretty hip concept for AM radio—almost "too hip for the room"—but if you didn't get it, it's over in a flash anyway, even if while it lasted it was a music drama with its own native dynamics and emotional climate. The commercials are home to a heavily arranged, perfectly balanced studio sound that is in the process of being dislodged from the charts by what might be untrained teenagers singing in a subway corridor. "That sounds like it was recorded in a bathroom," a professionally trained musician remarks in disgust, and it might well have been. Reverberance is where you find it.

The new music isn't art; it isn't even "pop," a concept yet to be refined. It's entertainment, vulgar fun, stuff that will make large amounts of money for invisible entrepreneurs clustered as likely as not somewhere near the gangster end of the capitalist spectrum. (What is "The Peppermint Twist" if not a musical advertisement for a mob joint?) "Alan Freed took the rap for the rest of the crooks," my father confides, "because he was too stupid to avoid getting caught. Small potatoes. There were plenty of them. You want dumb? One guy took his payoffs in checks. The big thieves are still raking it in, only they're smart enough not to put it in writing." Where there's music, there's gangsters—that is to say, everywhere. Frank Tashlin's mid-'50s rock musical *The Girl Can't Help It* even made a joke out of it, with jukebox racketeer Edmond O'Brien finding his true calling as a rock and roll novelty act.

The kids don't know or care. Strictly speaking, this is music for teenagers and no one else. If you considered yourself a serious person, there are after all plenty of other things you could be listening to—Stan Getz, *Candide,* Ella singing the George Gershwin songbook, Van Cliburn, the soundtrack to *Black Orpheus*—anything but the "neanderthal banging" of "adenoidal amateurs singing music for morons." Jungle music! But even if the jungle was invoked—so tastefully, with such good humor—in the Tokens' "The Lion Sleeps Tonight" and the

Vibrations' "The Watusi," compounded by the Orlons' "The Wah-Watusi," hardly anyone notices that the "mindless noise" and "primitive beat" to which editorialists have been objecting for nearly a decade is now rich in invention and ornament, densely textured, decked in chimes and trills even as it moves—in the work of Barbara Lewis or Ben E. King or Curtis Mayfield—into emotional spaces far removed from anything that had ever been called rock and roll.

Most of the people listening—on the beach, in the parking lot, on the roof, behind the stadium—are oblivious to where the music ultimately is coming from. The records speak for themselves. How many aside from local fans know that the Rocky Fellers are Filipino, that Freddy Cannon is an Italian from Boston or that Chris Montez is a Mexican from Hawthorne, California, attending the same high school as the Beach Boys, that the Angels are white and the Cookies black? They're all on the radio. The listeners seek and find an intimacy without knowledge, without identity, without any details except those of which the song consists. They know even less of the people behind the scenes, the producers and writers and arrangers and instrumentalists: Phil Spector, Burt Bacharach, Quincy Jones, Carole King, Barry Mann, Cynthia Weill, Luther Dixon, Ellie Greenwich, Carl Davis, Johnny Pate, Hugo and Luigi, Jack Nitzsche, Earl Palmer, Hal Blaine, Carol Kaye, not to mention the emerging industrial-strength music machines of Tamla-Motown and Stax-Volt. It is just before the moment when self-conscious, publicly proclaimed artistic ambition enters the formula.

The competitive energies of the Top 40 era are brought to focus by the brevity of 45s. Two minutes and 30 seconds of concentrated power and with luck you might get a career out of it. The deejays in their off hours sit with a stack of demos, taking records off after a few bars. A song has to be "on" from the first note even to qualify. Sometimes it's removed so quickly it's hard to believe they could have heard anything at all. A single note, or the absence of a single note, can do it. A beat held back a fraction of a second too long, a melody line digressing from its appointed mission: such are the infractions that can send a potential "sure shot" into the reject pile. "It waited too long before beginning. In radio there isn't time for that."

Before and after the songs (and on top of the songs, the deejay continuing to talk as the first notes play and picking up the talk again before the fade-out, indulging in some good-natured needling at the expense of a tearful love ballad—"just kidding, Little Anthony"—and tossing in a few enthusiastic cries of assent—"yeah, man!"—in the middle of the drum break) there is that other, sometimes recalcitrant material to be inserted. The deejay's real labor is to blend, with art and at high speed, all the mandatory ingredients into a consistency neither too monotonous nor too startling: weather reports, traffic alerts, quiz questions with a sweatshirt going to the first lucky listener to call in, announcements of upcoming record hops where the whole station line-up will be there to keep things jumping. He must read with some degree of conviction—Tennessee Williams was never like this!—relentless advertising copy, spots for restaurants ("Open until twelve every weekend for your dining and dancing pleasure"), spots for cigarettes ("The best tobacco makes the best smoke"), spots for discount men's clothing outlets ("Come to John's Bargain Store!"), spots for furniture with easy payment plans available, spots for easy loans with no credit problems "even if you've been refused credit before." This is a message to everybody out there in radioland, if you can hear the sound of my voice there's an outlet near you, just look in your yellow pages or call this number, we've got more music coming right up, first on your dial at the home of the hits where the tunes just keep on coming, here's one by a little lady who came out of nowhere and took her home state and then the whole nation by storm, in a new and very swinging rendition of the Mills Brothers classic "Lazy River"!

My father has mastered a repertoire of catchphrases that he summons up as needed, like the formulaic verse phrases with which Balkan poets once filled out their epics, or the come-ons and canny improvisations of the accomplished carnival spieler. They enable him to fill any uncomfortable pause—and in radio virtually any pause is uncomfortable, any silence longer than a microsecond verges on becoming the dreaded Dead Air—with wit, or with a cadence or tone approximating wit: "It doesn't have to be funny as long as it sounds funny. Timing is everything." Strung together, they become a kind of folk repertoire, fragments of the Ultimate Spiel: "When you're hot you're hot"—"Ah, those were the days—and the nights weren't so bad either"—"He can't get arrested"—"Now I'd like to do a medley of my hit"—"Don't fail to miss it if you can"—"Last of the big-time spenders"—"A man who became a legend in his own mind"—"This guy can't get enough of himself"—"Beaucoup de glick and molto mazel"—"I'm Joe O'Brien, I guess you know who you are"—"And if you were listening in the car, thanks for the ride."

These last few years the pace has been steadily speeding up. How did the world put up so long with such slow tempos? Suddenly everybody wants to jump in in the middle, or just jump. It's all over with that "Tennessee Waltz" schtick. When Joe makes live appearances— and there are more of them all the time—at high schools, record stores, street festivals, emceeing record hops where the headliners might be the Shirelles or the Jive Five or the Exciters or the Isley Brothers, he comes back with adrenaline pumping from contact with the fans. They have such commitment, they're so into the music. There's a party going on, and the jubilance is catching: he's visibly rejuvenated as much by the audience—"the kids"—as by the music, elated even from the sidelines by the dancing. What he came to sell he ends up sold on, and carries the energy of it back with him.

The new music feels even livelier for being mixed with so much else, old music, odd music, accidental music. In a given week, the teen sounds of the Regents ("Barbara-Ann"), Gary "U.S." Bonds ("Quarter to Three," one of the most crudely recorded disks ever to make the top of the charts), Bobby Lewis ("Tossin' and Turnin'"), Dee Clark ("Raindrops"), and the Shirelles ("Mama Said"), and the teen-by-adoption R&B sounds of Ernie K-Doe ("Mother-in-Law") and Ben E. King ("Stand By Me") jostle against records by Steve Lawrence, Pat Boone, Andy Williams, Lawrence Welk, the McGuire Sisters, and the Clebanoff Strings (doing the theme from *I Love Lucy*). There is also room in the Top 70 for blues (Etta James, Slim Harpo), jazz (Eddie Harris), and country (Patsy Cline and Faron Young).

Sometimes the mix gets downright weird. A rough-and-ready kind of fusion crops up in gimmicky crossovers like "The Boll Weevil Song" (folk goes R&B), "The Bilbao Song" (Kurt Weill goes Las Vegas),

"Summertime" (Gershwin goes doo-wop), "Temptation" (the '20s go country), "Nature Boy" (Bobby Darin sings Nat King Cole), and "San Antonio Rose" (Floyd Cramer brings back western swing). The top-selling album is Frank Sinatra's *Ring a Ding Ding:* this hour is, among other things, the apogee of the Rat Pack. It is still a time when all the rock and rhythm and blues and doo-wop on the radio can be drowned out by Jane Morgan's massively exuberant "Love Makes the World Go Round."

The songs are what people's lives are dressed in. Each picks what he can use out of the line-up of hits. By the songs' advent and displacement and revival you can trace movements of peoples, the aging and disappearance of generations. The older ones go away into marriage and jobs, become clerks, uncles, customers for life insurance, their discarded youths a residue haunting jukeboxes in the form of Bunny Berigan's "I Can't Get Started" or Glenn Miller's "Elmer's Tune" or Frank Sinatra's "My Blue Heaven." Those are the songs that show up when the bar is half emptied out and there is enough silence for the past briefly to become audible: "Can we hear some real music now?" They stick around for decades that way. Their deep sonic undercoat—vibrant with trombone and cello even on the most worn-out pressings—still shows through the faster, flashier overpainting of the music made for those who just arrived on the scene: the transistor radio music of the Cookies and the Crystals and Jan and Dean and Gene Chandler.

Now the juice is coming from the young ones. The industry is getting high on that surge. At some point pop music became teenage music, and the change is turning out to be permanent. To have a nineteen-year-old like Paul Anka headlining at the Copa is only one symptom. Before, there was just music. The deejays counted heads and didn't worry about age; the only thing that mattered was how many people were listening. It would have been absurd to think that younger ears were somehow more desirable, as long as the ears were there to hear the pitch, whether for Wheaties or Crisco Oil or Lucky Strikes.

But the children had been listening all along. They were perhaps the unintended audience on the receiving end of radio, foraging among that mess of sounds the same way they would crawl around in the garage or the basement looking for discarded junk that they could use for their own purposes. Doubtless they heard some things differently than intended, but it was all part of the process by which they would make the radio business and the record business their own domain, a world where they felt so comfortable it might have been designed for them.

At the start they fed on the ridiculous. In the period that would later be perceived as rock and roll's heroic interlude, from about 1955 to 1957, they were glutting themselves on the funny stuff the songs were packed with. For the youngest listeners, the impact of the new sounds had a lot to do with the way they deformed language. Phrases like "see you later alligator" or "you ain't never caught a rabbit" and "I saw Uncle John with Long Tall Sally" and "be-bop-a-lula" and "bony moronie" and "don't step on my blue suede shoes"—and with them, hardly differentiated, other phrases like "killed him a bar when he was only three" or "papa loves mambo" or "hot diggity dog ziggity boom"—were new and welcome additions to a world created especially for children to get lost in, the world of nursery rhymes and animated shorts and funny animal comic books. "Shake rattle and roll": it added up to a noisy hilarious sound, something that made speech crack open.

A cartoon world of warped language and hilarious masquerade bubbled up in a stream of novelty records whose early specimens included "Stranded in the Jungle" (The Cadets, 1956), "The Flying Saucer" (Buchanan and Goodman, 1956), and "Transfusion" (Nervous Norvus, 1956), making savagely tasteless comedy out of an auto smash-up. The trend peaked in 1958 with "Short Shorts" (The Royal Teens); "Dinner with Drac" (John Zacherle, known for his ghoulish comedy routines introducing TV showings of old horror movies); "Witch Doctor" (David Seville); "The Purple People Eater" (Sheb Wooley); "Splish Splash" (Bobby Darin), a novelty record only by virtue of its comical bathtub setting; "Chantilly Lace" (The Big Bopper), a novelty chiefly because of the artist's name; "Beep Beep" (The Playmates); and "The Chipmunk Song" (The Chipmunks).

With Leiber and Stoller songs like "Yakety Yak," "Charlie Brown," "Along Came Jones," "Idol with the Golden Head," and "Poison Ivy," the Coasters gave the novelty genre something like the stature of satirical art, within the limited expectations of early '60s pop. The trend trickled away to the sound of nuisance records like "Kookie, Kookie (Lend Me Your Comb)" (Edward Byrnes and Connie Francis, 1959), "Seven Little Girls Sitting in the Back Seat" (Paul Evans and the Curls, 1959), "Itsy Bitsy Teenie Weenie Yellow Polka Dot Bikini" (Brian Hyland, 1960), "Mr. Custer" (Larry Verne, 1960), and "Yogi" (The Ivy Three, 1960).

The invocational power of nonsense phrases like "papa oo mow mow" and "rama lama ding dong" and "shimmy shimmy koko bop"—not to mention "Sh-Boom"'s fantastically extended "a lenga-luh lenga-luh lenga-luh lenga-luh, wo wo dip, shuh-bay boo-doh boo-dip"—was joined to the thousand and one mind-suspending mantras of doo-wop. Kids could always use catchphrases. What better way to fill dead air at parties than a basso interjection of "Te-quii-laaah" in the manner of the Champs, or "Why is everybody always pickin' on me" from the Coasters' "Charlie Brown"?

Funny words, funny voices, funny noises: there were few places where some kind of silliness could not be harvested. The novelty-record narratives about jungle witch doctors and flying saucers from outer space (the punch line of the moment was "Take me to your leader") and comic-strip cavemen (the Hollywood Argyles' sublime 1960 release "Alley-Oop"), Stan Freberg's comedy records parodying the echo effects in "Heartbreak Hotel" and the "bubble machine" of Lawrence Welk and his Champagne Ladies, the fairy tales told in "hip talk" in the manner of Steve Allen or Al "Jazzbo" Collins, linked up with comic book fantasies from *Uncle Scrooge* to *Little Lulu,* the silliness of old stars dressing up in ridiculous costumes for guest appearances on *Masquerade Party,* the commercials with their population of talking breakfast cereals and humorous cigarettes.

For a child the irresistible reason to watch or listen to anything was because it was funny, not because it was pretty or inspiring or deeply moving. If you did find yourself, to your own surprise, deeply moved by some song about church bells or last good-byes, you'd be inclined to keep it to yourself. Kids got together to laugh, not cry. So did everybody else. A mocking comic sense floated freely from *Mad* to

Steve Allen's Sunday night variety show on NBC to the movies of Jerry Lewis and Dean Martin.

America fostered oversized hilariousness, huge grotesqueness. It was all a laugh. The commercials on television and radio were funny; big-breasted blondes were funny; cops and private eyes were funny; Indians in war bonnets were funny; husbands were funny, mothers-in-law funnier; and teenagers, with their hairstyles and lingo and hysterical tears were funny up until the moment when puberty revealed that the moans and lonely teardrops were a manifestation of genuine suffering rather than episodes in a stylized cartoon. "It looks like raindrops falling from my eyes": until one day you wake to find that Dee Clark is not joking.

The teenager is the one who loses his sense of humor. Listening with desperate concentration to the same song over and over—radio won't do anymore; he has to have his own record player so he can hear what he needs when he needs it—he initiates a practice that will be extended into the rest of life. The haunting melody takes up residence inside him. What he hears in it doesn't change. The past is here made prisoner, except it isn't even the past anymore. There is just this blind wall of song, the permanent night into which he wants to stare. The teenager, technologist of obsession, learns how to manipulate his own feelings with the proper ordering of playlists. He builds his nostalgia around himself, having no idea of how much time he is going to spend there.

In Stanley Kubrick's *Lolita* (1961), when James Mason's Humbert bonds with his image of Sue Lyon's Lolita, sprawled in her bikini in the backyard, she is listening to her favorite idiotic music on her transistor. He hears the music—Nelson Riddle's "Lolita Ya Ya" theme, with its high-pitched chorus of mechanically speeded-up wordless vocalizers, Chipmunk music for the spiritually adrift—"*Yaaa yaaa, ya-ya-ya-ya yaaa yaaa*"—even before he sees her. Later, as he soaks in the tub enjoying his new freedom after her mother's death, the music recurs. The melody, so like a jingle for a candy bar or a pack of menthols, is the nearest thing to possession: of a person, a feeling, a moment. Later it will become a mockery he must convert into a solace, throwing himself on the mercy of a heartless pop product, a cheap and common toy of a plastic disk embodying the brutal dominance of mindless cadence and nonsense syllables. Picture him sneaking into her empty room to play the record on her abandoned music box, an act at once of mourning and of symbolic reunion.

But then a teenage boy might well find that nothing can be more intimate than rummaging through a girl's record collection. In these grooved surfaces are embedded the emotions they elicit from her, in her imagined privacy. By playing her records, absorbing the same sounds that she has absorbed, he becomes her, keeps her inside himself. Sound is the conduit between worlds, or at least between nervous systems. To these same trills her bones have thrilled. In the same half-swallowed sob both of them, separately, have nearly wept. Alone together! In different places, the same sounds find the same pressure points. They become one by inhabiting the same virtual listening booth. Music is a body.

The boy is alone (of course). He wants to participate invisibly in the *Pajama Party* pictured on the cover of a Roulette album of the same name, a doo-wop compilation featuring Frankie Lymon and the Teenagers, the Cleftones, the Heartbeats: "Little White Lies," "Woo Woo Train," "Don't Say Goodnight." This must be the place: "An evening of cokes, conversation and just plain lolling around listening to the record player . . . The Pajama Party is a teen-ager's frolic and it's easy to get into the spirit of it . . . The right record sets the mood, makes everybody happy and keeps the party rolling at a wonderfully snappy pace."

The walls are decked with pennants, pom-poms, and souvenir figurines. A portable record player on the white dresser plays a 45. The girl in the blue floral pajamas is showing her companions a pink prom dress (to go with the pink high heels she's modeling). Another girl holds up a hand mirror so she can take in the full effect, while the girl sitting on the floor in the yellow baby doll outfit (the one who's carefully positioned in front of the others) gazes up at her friend with mysterious wistfulness. A plate of improbably shiny red apples sits on the white chenille rug adjacent to the bare right foot of the girl in the baby doll, as in some Renaissance catalogue of allegorical emblems.

It is easy enough to imagine what their record collection might consist of by 1963, even if this Roulette album, with its line-up of tired oldies, lags well behind the curve. The soundtrack of their lives might be released as *Havin' a Masterpiece Party,* the rug in the cover photo scattered with Imperial and Atco and Chess and Brunswick and Tamla and Minit and Philles and Scepter and Dimension and Cameo and Volt releases. Forget about the Cleftones, or the endearingly named Monotones: this is no longer the age of doo-wop or novelty or mindlessly repeated nonsense choruses. The repertoire of Top 40 has evolved—in studios from New York to Los Angeles to Memphis to Chicago—into orchestral dances that carry a carefully restrained sadness in their horn figures, muted dirges for lost love that can turn on a dime into savagely exact delineations of vengeful triumph, ballads turned inside out to become sequences of florid variations, doom-laden soundscapes lit by sudden moonglow, rooftop serenades, ecstatic gospel hymns, and finally, from within echoing dance halls, the very cadence of the galaxies continuing to roll out all night long. It will be a long night, because they have a lot of listening to do.

The choral hooks reach out through a static of traffic signals and weather alerts: the Drifters' "Na-na-na-na-na-na late at night" (at the beginning of "I Count the Tears") or Claudine Clark's "I see the lights, I see the party lights" or the Orlons' insistent "Don't Hang Up." If you don't find them right away they come looking for you. The refrains are intercepted cries. You may not even know you intercepted them until, years later, you hear the phrase and the implanted emotional complex surges up. They are a summons: if not quite to the voodoo assembly to which jungle drums lured the cast of movies like *I Walked with a Zombie*, then at least to the irresistibly desirable space lit by Claudine Clark's party lights, "red and green and blue," or to the campfire where the Impressions' "Gypsy Woman" dances until dawn, "all through the caravan."

What a night one might make of it, shuffling through that pile of 45s to pick out, first, a few numbers to get the engine going. Start with a taste of the surf guitar emanating from southern California, Dick Dale's electronic Middle Eastern fantasy "Miserlou" or the Chantays' "Pipeline," a shot of reliably streamlined and impersonal wave-pulsations, before coming back to land—to earth—with Booker T. and the M.G.s' "Green Onions" and James Brown's "Night Train." By now they are dancing, hesitantly at first, to the already nostalgic rhythms of the Vibrations' "Watusi" and Sam Cooke's "Chain Gang," with its chilling clank of metal on metal (a lead pipe banged on the base of a microphone), Benny Spellman's "Fortune Teller" with its otherworldly backup singers dragging in a lost world of New Orleans prophesying. The dancing picks up speed with Little Eva's "The Loco-Motion," Ray Barretto's "El Watusi," the Isley Brothers sustaining the Latin groove with "Twist and Shout," King Curtis's saxophone on "Soul Twist" beginning to elicit actual yelps of excitement, and then Junior Walker blasting even King Curtis out of the way with his unrestrained blowing on "Brainwasher," as if he has set his sights on the other side of the sky and has to play very fast and very hard to get there in time. They have to pause for a moment after that, modulating into the slower and more enveloping impulses of Bob and Earl's "Harlem Shuffle."

Now their resistance has melted sufficiently to respond to a sequence of ballads: Dell Shannon's "Runaway," if only for its shrieking organ and the yodeling upper reaches of Shannon's singing; the plaintive hermeticism of the Beach Boys' "In My Room" spiraling toward an even higher pitch that translates the very idea of weeping into eerie abstraction; Gene Pitney's "Town Without Pity"; Chuck Jackson's "Any Day Now"; "Strange Feeling" by the physically corpulent, vocally ethereal Billy Stewart, with its hovering chorus of women and the singer's transmutation of "feeling" into "fee-fa-fee-fa-fee-ee-ling"; the Drifters' "Up on the Roof" to help them feel the weather around them, the air of cities blowing through even suburban windows; Ben E. King's "Stand By Me," a song sung at the brink of the end of things, when "the land is dark and the moon is the only light we'll see," a song to hold a few things together in the midst of some ultimate foundering; followed (logically enough) by Skeeter Davis's "The End of the World," if only because the evening is not complete without that angrily self-centered vision of the whole universe tumbling into oblivion because her love affair fell through.

Maybe around this time the girls at the pajama party turn to the records that sound more or less like themselves, or as they would sound if they had Luther Dixon or Carole King or Berry Gordy providing material for them and taking a hand in the production. The boy singers wept; the girls growl when they do not scream. Here are the Cookies' relentless "Chains" (they sound tough even when they're in chains) and "Don't Say Nothing Bad About My Baby," the latter with its unmissable warning: "He's true, he's true to me, so girl you better shut your mouth." Here too the Exciters' "Tell Him" ("I know something about love"), the Marvelettes' "Strange I Know," and the rest, the Chiffons, the Angels, girls with large hair and possible concealed switchblades, girls on the march, backed by strings and kettle drums, the Crystals and Ronettes and Darlene Love singing as if to force their way through the muffling layers of Phil Spector–induced overload.

At the pajama party they come around finally to the Shirelles because it takes a lead singer like Shirley Owens to make nonsense of the idea of a "girl group." This is no girl, even if the backup on "A Thing of the Past"—the three-note setting of "Our love's becoming a thing of the past"—sounds at first like some elementary school sing-along. The scars of experience become audible soon enough with the emergence of Shirley Owens's unmistakable husky voice, nearly cracking with painfully acquired wisdom, describing how "your kisses taste like it's goodbye." A chorus later, she's rising into a falsetto whisper, urgently confiding that "this is the moment to decide," and finally rising into a tearful shout—"darling, tell me that I'm dreaming 'bout it"—that forces the song into further depths of feeling even as it abruptly cuts short. With an ending like that, the only recourse is to find the final phrase and play it again, as if this time the passage might be miraculously extended, the needle permitted to extract some additional hidden layers of wrenching improvisation beyond that handful of notes. The question of why the songs have to end at all sometimes haunts them even in the middle of listening.

If anything can follow the Shirelles, it can only be the Jaynetts' "Sally Go Round the Roses," a dream ballad that sounds like a whispered death threat, sung by friends whose helpful advice rises into desperate cries of warning: "Sally don't you go, don't you go down-town. . . . Because the saddest thing in this whole wide world is to see your baby with another girl." Sally must be in deep trouble. The final hypnotic repetition of the title phrase begins to resemble the melody that haunts a trauma victim, or that whispers unspeakable remedies to someone near inner collapse. Where did this song come from?

They could go on for hours, in so many different directions. Maybe they feel like veering into the raucous comedy of the Rivingtons' "Papa Oom Mow Mow" or the Trashmen's even more grotesquely exaggerated variant on it, "Surfin' Bird." They might put themselves in a kind of trance state with five or six repeated playings of the Kingsmen's "Louie, Louie," the noisiest and most amateurish record they have ever heard ("I bet you could play drums like that, Laureen!"), a record with the mysterious capacity to sound refreshing no matter how often they play it. After another quick snort of surf harmonics with Jan and Dean's "Surf City" and the Beach Boys' "Surfin' U.S.A." it's time to dance again, but with a difference: the "place right across town" into which Major Lance's "The Monkey Time," with its triumphant horn figures, brings them turns out (when you listen in the middle of the night, with the lights a little low) to be a cavernous space, with a dance floor of epic proportions. The dance floor is crowded with human hearts—everybody! they've all been admitted!—joined in the dark:

> All I know is when the beat brings a feel
> It's hard to get parted.

Then Major Lance moves into even more mysterious territory, bringing the dance orchestra out into the open air in "Um, Um, Um, Um, Um, Um," into the park where a man—a lost soul, a failure at life—sits moaning on a bench at dusk. There has never been a more mournful shuffle, as the maracas delineate a slow disconsolate dance.

The air of suffering brings them up short. They are glad now that they saved the best ones for the very end. Now they are ready to feel what no songs ever gave them before, not until the arrival of Betty Everett's "You're No Good" and Otis Redding's "That's What My

Heart Needs" and Maxine Brown's "Funny" (with its bitter laugh coming close to a dangerous breaking point). In Barbara Lewis's "Hello Stranger" they hear a forecast of future adult sorrows they can only imagine, as the lovers meet up after what "seems like a mighty long time"—a matter of years, decades perhaps, surely not the weeks or months by which these girls measure their tentative involvements—and the singer can only bridge the gap in time by singing "I'm so happy" in a tone that suggests she has just plunged a poiniard into her heart up to the hilt. For balm to that anguish, put on Mary Wells's stylish and poignant but lighter, blessedly lighter (it could be the Girl from Ipanema singing), "You Beat Me to the Punch." (It does sometimes happen that the girls get the last laugh.) Inevitably they're drawn back to the Motown stack. Nothing else can close things out like Marvin Gaye's "Can I Get a Witness" or the Miracles' "I Like It Like That" or—but here they run out of superlatives, they just keep playing it over and over—Martha and the Vandellas' "Heat Wave." They are jumping; they are burning; the music doesn't stop until the break of day.

Outside the window, clinging to the fire escape or crouched in the flowerbed outside the ground floor bedroom, he gazes in wonderment up to the moment when the dream dissolves in dawn.

7

Seven Fat Years

ON A SUMMER AFTERNOON IN 1964 I WENT TO A NEIGHBORHOOD movie theater to see the Beatles in *A Hard Day's Night*. It was less than a year since John F. Kennedy had been assassinated. Kennedy's death, and its aftermath of ceremonial grief and unscheduled violence, had if nothing else given younger observers an inkling of what it meant to be part of an immense audience. We had been brought together in horrified spectatorship, and the sense of shared spectatorship outlasted the horror. The period of private shock and public mourning seemed to go on forever, yet it was only in a matter of weeks that the phenomenally swift rise of a pop group from Liverpool became so pervasive a concern that Kennedy seemed already relegated to an archaic period in which the Beatles had not existed. The New York deejays—my father among them—who promised their listeners "all Beatles all the time" were not so much shaping as reflecting an emergence that seemed almost an eruption of collective will. The Beatles had come, as if on occult summons, to drive away darkness and embody public desire on a scale not previously imagined.

Before the Christmas recess—just as "I Want to Hold Your Hand" was finally breaking through to a U.S. market that had resisted earlier releases by the Beatles—girls in my tenth-grade class began coming to school with Beatles albums and pictures of individual Beatles, discussing in tones appropriate to a secret religion the relative attractions of John or Paul or Ringo or even the underappreciated George. A month or so later the Beatles arrived in New York to appear on the Ed Sullivan show and were duly ratified as the show business wonder of the age. Everybody liked them, from the Queen of England and the *New York Times* on down. My parents and their friends, who ordinarily might have sat around listening to Edith Piaf or Charles Aznavour or Barbara Cook, were now pausing in their conversation to register enthusiasm for "And I Love Her."

Even bystanders with no emotional or generational stake in the Beatles could appreciate the adrenaline rush of computing how much this particular success story surpassed all previous ones in terms of money and media and market penetration. It was moving too fast even for the so-called professionals. The Beatles were such a fresh product that those looking for ways to exploit it—from Ed Sullivan to the aging news photographers and press agents who seemed holdovers from the Walter Winchell era—stood revealed as anachronisms as they flanked a group who moved and thought too fast for them. (Or so it seemed at the time. The anachronisms worried about it all the way to the bank, while the Beatles ultimately did their own computing to figure out just how badly they had been shortchanged by the industry pros.)

And what was the product? Four young men who seemed more alive than their handlers and more knowing than their fans; aware of their own capacity to please more or less everybody, yet apparently savoring among themselves a joke too rich for the general public; professional in so unobtrusive a fashion that it looked like inspired amateurism. The songs had no preambles or buildups: the opening phrase—"Well, she was just seventeen" or "Close your eyes and I'll kiss you"—was a plunge into movement, a celebration of its own anthemic impetus. Sheer enthusiasm, yet tempered by a suggestion of knowledge held in reserve, a distancing that was cool without malice. When you looked at them they looked back; when they were interviewed, it was the interviewers who ended up on the spot.

That the Beatles excited young girls—mobs of them—made them an unavoidable subject of interest even for young boys, even if the boys might have preferred more familiar native product like Dion and the Belmonts or Freddy Cannon to a group that was foreign and long-haired and too cute not be a little androgynous. The near-riots that accompanied the Beatles' arrival in New York, bringing about something like martial law in the vicinity of the Warwick Hotel, were an epic demonstration of nascent female desire. The spectacle was not tender but warlike. The oscillation between glassy-eyed entrancement and emotional explosion, the screams that were like chants and the bouts of weeping that were like acts of aggression, the aura of impending upheaval that promised the breaking down of doors and the shattering of glass: this was love that could tear apart its object.

Idols who needed to be protected under armed guard from their own worshippers acquired even greater fascination, especially when they carried themselves with such cool comic grace. To become involved with the Beatles, even as a fan among millions of others, carried with it the possibility of meddling with ferocious energies. Spectatorship here became participation. There were no longer to be any bystanders, only sharers. All of us were going to give in to the temptation not to gawk at the girl in Ed Sullivan's audience—the one who repeatedly bounced straight up out of her seat during "All My Loving" as if pulled by a radar-controlled anti-gravity device—but to become her.

I emerged from *A Hard Day's Night* as from a conversion experience. Having walked into the theater as a solitary observer with more or less random musical tastes—*West Side Story, The Rite of Spring, The Fred Astaire Story, Talking Dustbowl, Old Time Music at Clarence Ashley's,* the soundtracks of *Black Orpheus* and *El Cid*—I came out as a member of a generation, sharing a common repertoire with a sea of contemporaries, strangers who seemed suddenly like family. The four albums already released by the Beatles would soon be known down to every hesitation, every intake of breath; even the moments of flawed pitch and vocal exhaustion could be savored as part of what amounted to an emotional continuum, an almost embarrassingly comforting sonic environment summed up, naturally, in a Beatles lyric:

There's a place
Where I can go
When I feel low . . .
And it's my mind,
And there's no time.

Listening to Beatles records turned out to be an excellent cure for too much thinking. It was even better that the sense of refreshment was shared by so many others; the world became, with very little effort, a more companionable place. Effortlessness—the effortlessness of, say, the Beatles leaping around a meadow with goofy freedom in *A Hard Day's Night*—began to seem a fundamental value. That's what they were there for: to have fun, and allow us to watch them having it. That this was a myth—that even *A Hard Day's Night,* by portraying the impossible pressure and isolation of the Beatles' actual situation, acknowledged it as a myth—mattered, curiously, not at all. The converted choose the leap into faith over rational argument. It was enough to believe that they were taking over the world on our behalf.

A few weeks later, at dusk in a suburban park, I sat with old friends as one of our number, a girl who had learned guitar in emulation of Joan Baez, led us in song. She had never found much of an audience for her folksinging, but she won our enthusiastic admiration for having mastered the chord changes of all the songs in *A Hard Day's Night*. We sang for hours. If we had sung together in the past the songs had probably been those of Woody Guthrie or the New Lost City Ramblers, mementoes of a legendary folk past. This time there was the altogether different sensation of participating in a new venture, a world-changing enterprise that indiscriminately mingled aesthetic, social, and sexual possibilities.

An illusion of intimacy, of companionship, made the Beatles characters in everyone's private drama. We thought we knew them, or more precisely, and eerily, thought that they knew us. We imagined a give-and-take of communication between the singers in their sealed-off dome and the rest of us listening in on their every thought and musical reverie. It is hard to remember now how familiarly people came to speak of the Beatles toward the end of the '60s, as if they were close associates whose reactions and shifts of thought could be gauged intuitively. They were the invisible guests at the party, or the relatives whose temporary absence provided an occasion to dissect their temperament and proclivities.

That presumption of intimacy owed everything to a close knowledge of every record they had made, every facial variation gleaned from movies and countless photographs. The knowledge was not necessarily sought; it was merely unavoidable. The knowledge became complex when the Beatles' rapid public evolution (they were after all releasing an album every six months or so, laying down tracks in a couple of weeks in between the tours and the interviews and the press conferences) turned their cozily monolithic identity into a maze of alternate personas. Which John were we talking about, which Paul? Each song had its own personality, further elaborated or distorted by each of its listeners. Many came to feel that the Beatles enjoyed some kind of privileged wisdom—the evidence was their capacity to extend their impossible string of successes while continuing to find new styles, new techniques, new personalities—but what exactly might it consist of? The songs were bulletins, necessarily cryptic, always surprising, from within that hermetic dome at the center of the world, the seat of cultural power.

Outside the dome, millions of internalized Johns and Pauls and Georges and Ringos stalked the globe. What had at first seemed a harmonious surface dissolved gradually into its components, to reveal a chaos of conflicting impulses. Then, too often, came the recriminations, the absurd discussions of what the Beatles ought to do with their money or how they had failed to make proper use of their potential political influence, as if they owed a debt for having been placed in a position of odd and untenable centrality. All that energy, all that authority: toward what end might it not have been harnessed?

Seven years later, when it was all over, the fragments of those songs and images would continue to intersect with the scenes of one's own life, so that the miseries of high school love were permanently imbued with the strains of "No Reply" and "I'm a Loser," and a hundred varieties of psychic fracturing acquired a common soundtrack stitched together from "She Said She Said" ("I know what it's like to be dead") or the tornado-like crescendo at the end of "A Day in the Life." Only that unnaturally close identification can account for the way in which the breakup of the Beatles functioned as a token for every frustrated wish or curdled aspiration of the era. Their seven fat years went from a point where everything was possible—haircuts, love affairs, initiatives toward world peace—to a point where only silence remained open for exploration.

All of this would eventually settle into material for biographies and made-for-TV biopics. Generations yet unborn would be rehearsing the story. In the final years of the twentieth century, the number of books on the Beatles began to approach the plateau where Jesus, Shakespeare, Lincoln, and Napoleon enjoy their bibliographic afterlife. The surviving Beatles themselves seized hold of the opportunity to control their own story with an elaborate project consisting of *The Beatles Anthology,* a six-CD compilation of outtakes, alternates, and rarities released in 1995, an accompanying video series, and finally the book version of *Anthology,* published in 2000. If *Anthology* had any claim, it was as *The Beatles' Own Story,* an oral history patched together from past and present interviews, with the ghost of John Lennon sitting in, along with an already ailing George Harrison, for an impossible reunion at which the old anecdotes were to be told one more time, and occasion provided for a last word in edgewise about everything from LSD and the Maharishi to Allen Klein and the corporate misfortunes of Apple.

Reading something like a *Rolling Stone* interview that unaccountably went on for hundreds of pages, the book could hardly compare with the authority of the previously hidden recordings included in *The Beatles Anthology.* Those recordings—from a crude tape of McCartney, Lennon, and Harrison performing Buddy Holly's "That'll Be the Day" in Liverpool in 1958 to John Lennon's original 1968 recording of "Across the Universe" without Phil Spector's subsequently added orchestral excrescences—were revealing and often moving, and left no question that the Beatles were no mirage. Indeed, even the most minor differences in some of the alternate versions served the valuable function of making audible again songs whose impact had worn away through overexposure. In the print-version *Anthology,* the Beatles were limited to words, words whose frequent banality and inadequacy only increased one's admiration for the expressiveness of their art. People who can make things like *With the Beatles* or *Rubber Soul* or *The White Album* should not really be required also to comment on what they have done.

As they rehashed their career, it turned out that most of what they had to say that was interesting came early. Before *Love Me Do* and Beatlemania and the first American tour, the Beatles actually lived in the same world as the rest of us, and it was their memories of that world—from Liverpool to Hamburg to the dance clubs of northern England—that were most suggestive. The earliest memories were most often of a generalized boredom and sense of deprivation. A postwar Liverpool barely out of the rationing card era, with bombsites for parks (Paul recalled going "down the bombie" to play) and not much in the way of excitement, figured chiefly as the blank backdrop against which movies and music (almost exclusively American) could make themselves felt all the more powerfully. "We were just desperate to get anything," George remarked. "Whatever film came out, we'd try to see it. Whatever record was being played, we'd try to listen to, because there was very little of anything . . . You couldn't even get a cup of sugar, let alone a rock 'n' roll record."

Fitfully, a secret history of childhood music took form: Paul listening to his pianist father play "Lullaby of the Leaves" and "Stairway to Paradise," George discovering Hoagy Carmichael songs and Josh White's "One Meatball," and Ringo (the most unassuming and therefore often the most eloquent speaker) recalling his moment of illumination: "My first musical memory was when I was about eight. Gene Autry singing 'South of the Border.' That was the first time I really got shivers down my backbone, as they say. He had his three compadres singing 'Ai, ai, ai, ai,' and it was just a thrill to me. Gene Autry has been my hero ever since."

Only John—massively indifferent to folk ("college students with big scarfs and a pint of beer in their hands singing in la-di-da voices") and jazz ("it's always the same, and all they do is drink pints of beer")—seemed to have reserved his enthusiasm until the advent of

Elvis and Jerry Lee Lewis and Little Richard: "It was Elvis who really got me out of Liverpool. Once I heard it and got into it, that was life, there was no other thing." If one could imagine an alternate future in which Paul played piano for local weddings and dances, George drove a bus like his old man, and Ringo perhaps fell into the life of crime his teenage gang exploits seemed to portend, it was inconceivable that John could have settled into any of the choices he was being offered in his youth.

None of them ever did much except prepare themselves to be the Beatles. Their youths were devoid of incident (at least of incident that anyone cared to write into the record) and largely of education. John, the eldest, had a bit of art school training, but for all of them real education consisted more of repeated exposure to Carl Perkins, Chuck Berry, and Frank Tashlin's Cinemascope rock 'n' roll extravaganza *The Girl Can't Help It*. On the British side, they steeped themselves in the surreal BBC radio comedy *The Goon Show*—echoes of the non sequiturs and funny voices of Spike Milligan and Peter Sellers would be an abiding presence in their work—and in the skiffle craze of the late '50s they found a point of entry into the world of actual bands and actual gigs.

"I would often sag off school for the afternoon," wrote Paul, "and John would get off art college, and we would sit down with our two guitars and plonk away." Along with the younger George, they formed a skiffle band and played local dances, and after some changes in personnel officially became, around 1960, the Beatles, in allusion to the "beat music" that was England's term for what was left of a rock 'n' roll at that point almost moribund. Hard up for jobs, they found themselves in Hamburg, in a series of Reeperbahn beer joints, and by their own account were pretty much forced to become adequate musicians by the discipline of eight-hour sets and demanding, unruly audiences. Amid the amiable chaos of whores, gangsters, and prolonged amphetamine-fueled jamming—"it was pretty vicious," remarked Ringo, who joined the group during this period, "but on the other hand the hookers loved us"—they transformed themselves into an anarchic rock band, "wild men in leather suits." Back in the U.K. they blew away the local competition: "There were all these acts going 'dum de dum' and suddenly we'd come on, jumping and stomping," in George's account. "In those days, when we were rocking on, becoming popular in the little clubs where there was no big deal about the Beatles, it was fun."

Once the group got back to England, the days of "sagging off" and "plonking away" were numbered. As their ascent swiftly took shape—within a year of a Decca executive dismissing them with the comment that "guitar groups are on the way out" they were already awash in Beatlemania—the life recalled in their reminiscences had less and less to do with anything other than the day-to-day business of recording and performing. Once within the universe of EMI, life became something of a controlled experiment, with the Beatles subjected to unfamiliar sorts of corporate oversight. Paul recalled: "We weren't even allowed into the control room, then. It was Us and Them. They had white shirts and ties in the control room, they were grown-ups. In the corridors and back rooms there were guys in fulllength lab coats, maintenance men and engineers, and then there was us, the tradesmen . . . We gradually became the workmen who took over the factory." If they took over, though, it was at the cost of working at a killing pace, churning out songs, touring and making public appearances as instructed, keeping the merchandise coming. It could of course be wondered whether this forced production didn't have a positive effect on their work, simply because the work they were then turning out—everything from "Love Me Do" and "Please Please Me" to *Rubber Soul* was produced virtually without a break from performing or recording—could hardly be improved.

It is the paradox of such a life that it precludes the sort of experience on which art usually nurtures itself. The Beatles' latter-day reminiscences evoked the crew members on a prolonged interstellar flight, thrown back on each other and on their increasingly abstract memories of Earth, and livening the journey with whatever drugs or therapies promise something like the terrestrial environment they have left behind. In this context, marijuana and LSD were not passing episodes but central events, the true subject matter of the later Beatles records. In the inner storms of the bubble world, dreams and private portents took the place of the comings and goings of a street life that had become remote.

The isolation became glaring in, say, Paul's recollections of 1967: "I've got memories of bombing around London to all the clubs and the shops . . . It always seemed to be sunny and we wore the far-out clothes and the far-out little sunglasses. The rest of it was just music." One could be sure that the "bombing around" took place within a well-protected perimeter. It was around this time that the Beatles pondered the possibility of buying a Greek island in order to build four separate residences linked by tunnels to a central dome, like something out of *Dr. No* or *Modesty Blaise,* with John commenting blithely: "I'm not worried about the political situation in Greece, as long as it doesn't affect us. I don't care if the government is all fascist, or communist . . . They're all as bad here."

Finally the Beatles were in no better position than anyone else to get a clear view of their own career. "The moral of the story," said George, "is that if you accept the high points you're going to have to go through the lows . . . So, basically, it's all good." They knew what it was to have been a Beatle, but not really—or only by inference—what it looked like to everybody else. This led to odd distortions in tone, as if after all they had not really grasped the singularity of their fate. From inside the rocket was not necessarily the best vantage point for charting its trajectory.

Paul's comments on how certain famous songs actually got to be written were amiably vague: "'Oh, you can drive my car.' What is it? What's he doing? Is he offering a job as a chauffeur, or what? And then it became much more ambiguous, which we liked." As much in the dark as the rest of us as to the ultimate significance of what they were doing, the Beatles were all the more free to follow their usually impeccable instincts. So if John Lennon chose to describe "Rain" as "a song I wrote about people moaning about the weather all the time," and Paul saw "A Day in the Life" as "a little poetic jumble that sounded nice," it confirmed that any enlightenment about deeper significance was best sought by listening to the records. (John, again: "What does it really mean, 'I am the eggman'? It could have been the pudding basin, for all I care.") The band doesn't know; they just write them.

In the end it was not the music that wore out but the drama, the personalities, the weight of expectation and identity. By the time the Beatles felt obliged to make universally acceptable exhortations like "all you need is love" and "you know it's gonna be all right," it was already time to bail out. How nice it would be to clear away the mass of history and personal association and simply hear the records for the notes and words. Sometimes it's necessary to wait twenty years to be able to hear it again, the formal beauty that begins as far back as "Ask Me Why" and "There's a Place" and is sustained for years without ever settling into formula. Nothing really explains how or why musicians who spent years jamming on "Be Bop a Lula" and "Long Tall Sally" turned to writing songs like "Not a Second Time" and "If I Fell" and "Things We Said Today," so altogether different in structure and harmony. Before the addition of the sitars and tape loops and symphony orchestras, before the lyrical turn toward eggmen and floating downstream, Lennon and McCartney (and, on occasion, Harrison) were already making musical objects of such elegant simplicity, such unhectoring emotional force, that if they had quit after *Help!* (their last "conventional" album) the work would still endure.

Paul McCartney recollected that when the Beatles heard the first playbacks at EMI it was the first time they'd really heard what they sounded like: "Oh, that sounds just like a record! Let's do this again and again and again!" The workmen taking over the factory were also the children taking over the playroom, determined to find effects that no one had thought of pulling out of the drawer before. They went from being performers to being songwriters but didn't make the final leap until they became makers of records. Beyond all echoes of yesterday's mythologized excitement, the records—whether "The Night Before" or "Drive My Car" or "I'm Only Sleeping" or any of the dozens of others—lose nothing of a beauty so singular it might almost be called underrated.

8

Along the Great Divide

NO MATTER WHERE THE CONNECTION STARTED — WITH ELVIS or Bo Diddley or the Beatles, the Byrds or the Monkees or the Archies—the history of rock and roll inscribed itself in the nervous system of whoever passed through it, to persist years later as a network of potential responses and unbidden flashbacks. Sometimes the resurgent impressions might be connected with public events: the memory of watching a crowd of teenage girls storming New York's Paramount Theater for a glimpse of Eric Burdon and the Animals (it wasn't so much Burdon as the group's more obviously pretty bass player Chas Chandler that they were looking for), or of bursting into startled laughter as Bob Dylan launched in a Forest Hills auditorium into the as yet unrecorded "Your Brand-New Leopard-Skin Pillbox Hat," or of sprawling on the floor of the Avalon Ballroom amid a sea of strangers, like a vast stoned kindergarten class, as Janis Joplin tore "Down on Me" to pieces. More often the crucial moments were less planned and less collective, and more often they had to do not with live performances but with recorded music forcing its way into your ear. It was a matter of tiny accidental collisions, like a saxophone solo on the radio (Junior Walker's on "Come See About Me") blowing away the intricacies of your latest personal crisis, or (years earlier, before you had much idea what a personal crisis was) a refrain from the open window of a bus—the Orlons chanting "South Street, South Street"—beckoning hauntingly toward the unknown.

Songs glossed whatever place you happened to be in. The way the mere fact of living in a large city was transmuted by the Rolling Stones' "Get Off of My Cloud" into a stylish futuristic bleakness became in the same instant like a new way of perceiving space—

> *I sit at home looking out the window*
> *Imagining the world has stopped*

—while the torpor of summer was (as if you'd never really felt the warmth of the air before) given structure and a sense of mission by Archie Bell and the Drells' "Tighten Up." It wasn't a question so much of what you looked for as of what found you. Sounds went after you: intrusions, alarm bells, outbursts, the hoots and shrieks of party-goers, seductive hisses, warped laments, furtive tweaks, a phrase ripped from its context or the thud of a bass line sturdy enough to order the world. It was a music of impatience, of insistence, and for a time it seemed to be a one-size-fits-all soundtrack for the world.

In the retrospect of anyone's life, the elements of the music track accumulate as promiscuously as the heap of records on the rug after a party. What those who attended this particular party couldn't have guessed was that the playlist would repeat for the next thirty years, tempering nostalgia with an echo of the old line: "How can I miss you if you won't go away?" From oldies stations to television commercials to movie soundtracks, the '50s and '60s and '70s never stop playing. Video histories of rock have proliferated so much that at almost any hour the career of some band or the destiny of some stylistic trend is unspooling on one cable channel or another. Disco rises; Glitter falls; stars are born, stars are murdered or in various ways murder themselves, stars return from living death with a new manager and a new album; nothing will ever be as it was but the music goes on forever. The giddiness of show business, with its steep ascents and equally precipitous falls, its full-blown ecstasies and harrowing abysses, provides material for a thousand chronicles as entrancing as the ancient roller-coaster rides of *Tamburlaine* or *Richard III*, with the added democratic attraction that absolutely anyone can grow up to be a rock star. The history of rock and roll is the great melodrama and the great celebration; nostalgia for an irrecoverable past dissolves in the promise of perpetual rebirth as new styles and new superstars emerge on cue.

It is a story with no real beginning or end, that starts when you happen to tune in—or in this case when a generation of teenagers happened to tune in—and ends, presumably, when you've lost the desire to keep listening. The possibility of such a loss of desire would later become unavoidable for those who tasted fully the string of conversion experiences that once made rock and roll so exciting. For them the spine of the tale would remain the heroic arc of rock's rapid early evolution as perceived by the generation that grew up with it, a generation persuaded more than once that the onset of a new heaven and new earth could be detected in the cadences and textures and sheer volume of "Tutti Frutti" or "Twist and Shout" or "2000 Light Years from Home." Here was music to dispel the haunted past and smash the world open, mass-market party music transmuted into ritual you were permitted to make up as you went along.

Finally it was a revolution televised once too often. The way stations of rock history have acquired a weary inevitability. Elvis will appear on the Ed Sullivan show, again; disc jockey Alan Freed will convert young white listeners to rhythm and blues before being destroyed by the payola scandal, again; the Beatles will invade America, Bob Dylan will go electric to the chagrin of Newport folkies, the Altamont festival will collapse in apocalyptic violence. These moments have long since assumed the portentous historical weight of, say, the Battle of Midway; merely to allude to them is to evoke a whole tradition of grandiose recapitulation.

What is striking is how vividly each such episode imprinted itself from the start. In the public culture of the '60s, a collective symbolic theater in love with its own devices, a domain in which everyone was raptly studying everyone else's moves, even peripheral accidents and misfortunes could be given meaning and incorporated into the unfolding drama. Subsequent retellings of the rock and roll story have refined it into the chronicle of a sequestered analogue world, with its own allotment of violent tragedy and its own brand of moral uplift, its own parades and nagging philosophical doubts. It also has its innumerable splinter sects—as I write this sentence a hundred more are being formulated—through whom the earlier history is not merely redefined but restaged.

In this tradition it is mandatory always to begin at the beginning, as if every take were the first ever. Each new subgenre aspires to duplicate the shock value achieved in a now legendary time by the invention of rock and roll, back when the music really had adversaries. The primal smash-up stays in place as a symbolic moment of cultural violence to be reenacted over and over. What contemporary rocker would not cherish, more than any endorsement, the overwrought dismissals once elicited from Frank Sinatra ("It fosters almost totally negative and destructive reactions in young people . . . It is sung, played and written for the most part by cretinous goons") or Sir Malcolm Sargent ("Nothing more than an exhibition of primitive tom-tom thumping . . . Rock and roll has been played in the jungle for centuries") or Miklos Rozsa ("The most God-awful noise mankind has invented since leaving the jungle")?

Instead—no matter how recklessly they push the limits—they are likely to find themselves part of a blandly acceptable subdivision of the industry that embraces television, advertising, and fashion, an industry content to purvey whatever brands of accessorized rebellion move the most units off the shelves. As the pioneering Top 40 radio programmer Todd Storz remarked a long time ago, "I do not believe there is any such thing as better or inferior music . . . If the public suddenly showed a preference for Chinese music, we'd play it."

Even after a lifetime steeped in rock and roll it is possible to remain uneasy with the very notion of such a category, especially since its long dominance has served so often to keep potential listeners roped off from other kinds of music. No term is more elusive; a 1995 rock critics' poll by *Mojo* magazine to determine the "100 Greatest Albums Ever Made" gave the first three spots to the Beach Boys' *Pet Sounds* (1966), Van Morrison's *Astral Weeks* (1968), and the Beatles' *Revolver* (1966), eclectic and experimental works far removed from the rhythm revolution ushered in by Little Richard and Jerry Lee Lewis. Of the one hundred albums on the list, only eleven, it might be noted, were released after 1980.

The question remains whether one can even speak of a genre. Rock begins as a slapped-together mix of blues and boogie, country and pop, gospel and rumba, and ends up as pretty much anything that can be marketed under that name. Attitude in the end is all. If attempts to define rock begin with the concrete—with discussions of specific audiences, production companies, radio stations—they tend to drift toward a separate and ineffable reality, along the lines of H. G. Koenigsberger's notion of "the rise of music to a quasi-religious status and cult, as a psychological compensation for the decline of all forms of traditional religion." Any attempt to nail the music down is too restrictive for a culture whose whole point is to find out what happens when every form of restriction is removed. What if there were no rules, no limits, no qualifications for either listening or performing? The critic Robert Christgau invokes rock's "irresistible energy and mysteriously renewable spirit," and the late Robert Palmer declared, "Rock and roll was our very lives, our reason for being. Rock was our religion." Rock finally is a music definable not by the kinds of sounds it makes but by how those sounds have been used by their listeners, whose desire constitutes the music's real history.

There is a certain arbitrariness about where that history might begin. If you really wanted to you could go back to Cab Calloway in the '30s or Emmett Miller in the '20s or "Eli Green's Cake-Walk" in 1898; you could go back to Mali or ancient Sicily or the ports of call dotting the Indian Ocean. James Miller in his rock history *Flowers in the Dustbin* starts in December 1947, with Wynonie Harris, a thirty-two-year-old singer who adopted the nickname "Mister Blues," recording "Good Rockin' Tonight" for Syd Nathan's King label in Cincinnati, Ohio. "Good Rockin' Tonight" is one of a thousand up-tempo blues numbers that had been rolling off bandstands and out of jukeboxes for decades, a song that could have been sung by Joe Turner back in the heyday of Kansas City jazz, an excellent record— relaxed and comfortably swinging, moving so securely in its groove it has no need for strenuous emphasis—in a genre in which, at that time, such excellence was almost routine. It was certainly not an isolated sign of life; the late '40s were an era of unparalleled variety and invention in American music, whether the inflection was gospel (Sister Rosetta Tharpe's "Up Above My Head," 1948), bebop (James Moody's "The Fuller Bop Man," 1949), western swing (Tex Williams's "Cowboy Opus No. 1," 1949), Afro-Cuban (Machito's "Gone City," 1948), or Hollywood noir (David Raksin's theme for *Force of Evil,* 1948).

Could I have tuned in every sound that was entering the world at the same moment that I was entering it, I would have heard all at once what it has taken the better part of a lifetime to begin to catch up with. Then again, all those sounds played back to back might well take a lifetime to listen to. Part of the oddness of the present archival era is the way it makes it possible to reconstruct, for instance, a virtual 1948 encompassing everything one might conceivably have heard but would have been unlikely to perceive as part of a single entity. These little time machines are so hard to resist. By slowing down history long enough to wallow in a particular moment we impede the flash-flood pace of time's progress.

The A List of radio hits had a curiously backward-looking tone in 1948, perhaps attributable to postwar malaise. Perry Como successfully resurrected a 1902 operetta tune, "Because," while a deliberately "retro" reading of the 1927 "I'm Looking Over a Four-Leaf Clover" by Art Mooney rode the charts for eighteen weeks. Bing Crosby got further mileage out of "Now Is the Hour," an adaptation of a Maori melody that had already been a hit in 1913, and Frankie Laine brought back "Shine," written in 1925 as a blackface number for Ford Dabney and reprised successfully by Bing Crosby and the Mills Brothers in 1932; Laine's version—in an almost subliminal acknowledgment of racial sensitivity—is deftly trimmed of lines like "just because my skin is shady" (a line that Dooley Wilson had sung only five years earlier on the soundtrack of *Casablanca*).

Yet if some care was taken not to offend too blatantly, the fact remained that relatively few black artists were likely to be heard on most radio stations in the country. A major exception was Nat "King"

Cole, whose 1948 hit "Nature Boy" feels in this particular hit parade like an anomalous tremor from outside the system. Written by the Hollywood mystic Eden Ahbez (or more properly "eden ahbez"), supposedly left by the songwriter on Cole's doorstep without further commentary, the song imparted a jolt of esoteric revelation (secrets of divine love made audible!) into a world otherwise dominated by "The Woody Woodpecker Song" and "Buttons and Bows." There were a few other more lasting gestures as well, a handful of songs new that year that would keep on playing for the next half century: "It's Magic," "But Beautiful," "Tennessee Waltz." (Compare the hit lists from 1928 or 1935 to see how drastically the production of future standards had slowed.)

In another sphere, specialists continued to craft the wraparound sound that Hollywood had by now learned to integrate more insidiously than ever into each shifting emotion of its movies: Franz Waxman *(The Paradine Case, Sorry Wrong Number, No Minor Vices)*, Dimitri Tiomkin *(Red River, Portrait of Jennie)*, Max Steiner *(Treasure of the Sierra Madre, Key Largo, Johnny Belinda)*, Victor Young *(The Big Clock, The Emperor Waltz, Miss Tatlock's Millions)*, Hugo Friedhofer *(Joan of Arc)*, and the astonishingly busy Miklos Rozsa *(A Double Life, Secret Beyond the Door, The Naked City, Command Decision, Kiss the Blood Off My Hands)* and Alfred Newman *(Call Northside 777, The Snake Pit, Yellow Sky, The Iron Curtain, Cry of the City, Sitting Pretty)*. Fred Astaire was singing "Easter Parade" in *Easter Parade*, and Marlene Dietrich was singing "The Ruins of Berlin" in what looked very much like the ruins of Berlin in Billy Wilder's *A Foreign Affair*. On Broadway, *South Pacific* would open a year later and become the first original cast album on LP; Kurt Weill was gearing up for *Lost in the Stars*, his musical adaptation of Alan Paton's anti-apartheid novel *Cry, the Beloved Country*, a show into which he would deliberately avoid incorporating anything resembling actual South African music. Les Baxter was scoring Harry Revel's compositions to produce the calculatingly layered mood music featured on *Perfume Set to Music*, a historic attempt to establish audible equivalents for the fragrances of Corday, finding for example in Toujours Moi "a mood that is deep and mysterious . . . enhanced by overtones of Theremin, Novachord, French horn and harp." Around and under everything else were the barbershop harmonies of radio commercial jingles like those Orson Welles satirized in *The Lady from Shanghai*:

> *Glosso-Lusto in your hair*
> *Keeps it Glosso-Lusto bright,*
> *G-L-O-double S-O-L-U-S-T-O*
> *Is right—*
> *Glosso-Lusto!*

Meanwhile, in a world outside the self-enclosed domains of M-G-M and network radio, there was the revolution represented by Charlie Parker ("Barbados," "Ah-Leu-Cha," "Parker's Mood"), Tadd Dameron and Fats Navarro ("Symphonette"), Fats Navarro and Howard McGee ("The Skunk"), Fats Navarro with Earl Coleman ("Yardbird Suite," "A Stranger in Town"), James Moody's Modernists ("The Fuller Bop Man," "Moodamorphosis," "Moody's All Frantic," "Tin Tin Deo"); Machito and Tito Puente and Chico O'Farrill were weaving Cuban music into the texture of New York modernity in collaborations with Dizzy Gillespie and Charlie Parker ("Mango Mangue"); and in the world of country music, held equally as much at bay by mainstream radio, there were Bob Wills, Red Foley ("Tennessee Saturday Night"), Hank Williams ("Honky Tonkin'"), Tex Williams and His Western Caravan ("Artistry in Western Swing").

The sound that wasn't on the radio in the dining room was the rock and roll that was already going strong but hadn't yet undergone a marketing revolution. If I could have floated into one of the bars on the other side of Northern Boulevard I would have heard it: Amos Milburn ("Chicken Shack Boogie"); Louis Jordan ("Barnyard Boogie," "Reet, Petite and Gone," "Run Joe"); Memphis Slim, Ivory Joe Hunter, Nellie Lutcher, Roy Milton, Bullmoose Jackson, the Orioles ("It's Too Soon to Know") and, of course, Wynonie Harris's "Good Rockin' Tonight." And for good measure could have heard the blues records of Muddy Waters and Sonny Boy Williamson and T-Bone Walker, and the gospel of Sister Rosetta Tharpe:

Up above my head
I hear music in the air . . .
And I really do believe
I really do believe
There's a heaven somewhere.

All this in a year when, in compliance with a union-decreed ban on recording, dues-paying musicians weren't supposed to be making records at all; most of the hits had been rushed through in late '47 to get around the impending labor action. It was also the year that the first LPs came on the market, followed a month or so later by the first 45s. The Folkways and Vanguard labels were starting up; network television programming kicked in that fall. Somewhere in the wreckage of Nazi Germany, Richard Strauss was writing his *Four Last Songs*.

Like everything else you are given it in pieces, knowing nothing of origins or pedigrees. Every song was old, every song was current. The world had been going on forever and everything was constantly being born, a little brighter and a little louder each time out, and possibly a little more desperate.

Whether it was the end of the war or the atom bomb or the advent of the United Nations or network television or long-playing records, musicians in every genre seem to have felt the imperative to be as modern as the cover art on those early LPs. Their stylized poster style made abstract fetishes out of el trains and cigarettes and martini glasses, blues singers and gypsy dancers, keyboards and conga drums, the faces of Billie Holiday and Xaviar Cugat and Gene Krupa, the fingers of Art Tatum and Meade Lux Lewis. It is tempting to pause on the threshold, steep yourself in the sum total of the music of that moment, and think idly of the potential musics that could have been: why not, side by side with rock and roll, cowboy bop or Caribbean big band or electrified Parisian cabaret or twelve-tone tango or shakuhachi blues as Top 40 material? Why not a yet wider range of forms, more varied instruments, weirder textures, rarer harmonies?

A record like "Good Rockin' Tonight" was part of the landscape, a restricted part. The reality underlying the classic recordings that now fill box sets in every chain store nationwide can be summed up in a single sentence by James Miller: "Distributed primarily on jukeboxes located in Negro clubs and bars, none of these pioneering 'rock' records reached the larger white audience." The real story of rock and roll is how, in the seven years between Harris's record and Elvis Presley's cover version of it in 1954, the landscape changed. Up until 1948, for instance, the industry magazine *Billboard* featured a single jukebox chart topped typically by Bing Crosby or the Andrews Sisters, icons of the genial mainstream; only in that year did the magazine acknowledge other markets by adding charts tracking "race" and "folk" records (categories soon amended to "rhythm and blues" and "country and western").

What the chart numbers registered was that the records were reaching unintended audiences. While the majors continued to focus on material like the Ames Brothers' "Sentimental Me" or Vera Lynn's "Auf Wiederseh'n Sweetheart"—the dross of a songwriting era notably lacking in Gershwins and Porters—the ears of younger white listeners escaped into the black music released on smaller labels and played on local radio stations whose signals often reached far beyond Memphis or Nashville or Cleveland. A radio empire of the night effected a crossing of racial lines despite the efforts of the mainstream music industry to keep its audiences separated. Little Richard and Chuck Berry broke into the pop charts, just as white country musicians like Elvis Presley and Carl Perkins were adapting rhythm and blues into the breakthrough rockabilly hits of the mid-1950s. The major companies would take years even to grasp what had occurred, letting small labels reap the early profits of rock and roll.

The penetration of white radio by black music was the single great fact, ultimately enabling artists on the order of Smokey Robinson, Aretha Franklin, James Brown, Marvin Gaye, Otis Redding, and Curtis Mayfield to reach a huge and all-inclusive audience. (Ray Charles had already found another way in, without benefit of the rock and roll revolution.) In 1956, Elvis Presley—still known by some as "the King of Western Bop," headlined by *Life* as a "Howling Hillbilly Success"—defined what he was about with remarkable bluntness: "The colored folks been singing it and playing it just like I'm doin' now, man, for more years than I know. They played it like that in the shanties and in their juke joints, and nobody paid it no mind 'til I goosed it up. I got it from them." Ironically enough, "rock" would eventually become a marketing term implying music made by and for white people, differentiated from the myriad forms (disco, funk, rap) that black musicians would continue to evolve. There was nothing new in such a racial crossover: it was the permanent condition of American music, which had always been a laboratory for revealing what happened when African and European musics mixed with a freedom often ferociously resisted in other spheres of life. The major difference this time was that there were more potential listeners, young ones, with a lot more money to spend. "I've got some money in my jeans," sang Eddie Cochran, "and I'm really gonna spend it right."

Myths need points of origin, however, and in rock history the primal place tends to be Sam Phillips's Sun recording studio in Memphis, for which Elvis made his first recordings. Operating in a tiny space and with the most rudimentary equipment, Phillips launched the careers of Elvis Presley, Jerry Lee Lewis, and Johnny Cash, having already cut pioneering sides by blues singers B. B. King, Howlin' Wolf, Junior Parker, and James Cotton, among others. A record Phillips made in 1951, Jackie Brenston's "Rocket 88," featuring Ike Turner on piano, is a frequently cited prototype of rock and roll; five years later Carl Perkins became the first country singer to make the national rhythm and blues charts with "Blue Suede Shoes," a record that sold more than a million copies.

The legend of Sun has everything to do with the atmosphere of laid-back improvisation evoked by Scotty Moore, Elvis's original guitarist: "We had absolutely no material going in. We'd just go in and start kicking things around . . . Every session we did on Sun was done the same way—just through trial and error until something would just finally click." A recording studio where schedules didn't matter, where there was all the time in the world to "kick things around"—rip songs apart and reassemble them, bang out stray sounds until they coalesced—suggests a pastoral paradise or paleolithic cave of music-making. Those early days at Sun, culminating in Elvis's first recordings, have subsequently been studied as assiduously as the origins of World War I. Every bar of "That's All Right" and "Baby Let's Play House," each slur and shout and half-swallowed howl has been parsed as if to tease out the alchemical transmutation taking place. In many such accounts, the birth of a singing style is taken to register the moment when an atrophied culture is swept contemptuously aside, as all the American voices separated or suppressed or held in contempt converge to celebrate a new day in a new all-purpose language.

But what if, instead of taking the Sun sessions as the triumphant dawning of an era, we saw them as something of a last gasp, a final burst of raw improvised sound before the time of the Great Homogenizing? They were still part of that undercurrent of American music documented by the mountains of 78s from which Harry Smith had compiled his Folkways anthology of folk music, the blues and jug and string band music that (as the recording industry retrenched during the Depression and as a streamlined pop industry rolled over the airwaves) had retreated into local crannies. When Sam Phillips opened his studio to every residual sound that came through his door, he merely extended an ongoing fusion. The sonic landscape of the years between Wynonie Harris's "Good Rockin' Tonight" and Elvis Presley's "Good Rockin' Tonight"—that part of the landscape unlikely to show up on *Lucky Strike Hit Parade* or *Chesterfield Supper Club*— encompassed, to cite a few random examples, Jimmy Witherspoon's "Ain't Nobody's Business" (1947), Pee Wee Crayton's "Blues After Hours" (1948), the Delmore Brothers' "Pan American Boogie" (1949), John Lee Hooker's "Hoogie Boogie" (1949), Hank Williams's "Mind Your Own Business" (1949), Wild Bill Moore's "Neck Bones and Collard Greens" (1950), Duke Ellington's "C Jam Blues" as performed by Ole Rasmussen and His Nebraska Cornhuskers (1952), the Korean War blues anthem "Drive Soldiers Drive" by "Little Maxie" Bailey (1953), Del Thorne's admonitory juke joint travelogue "Down South in Birmingham" (1953), Johnny "Guitar" Watson's "Space Guitar" (1954) and its country cousin "Stratosphere Boogie" (1954) by Speedy West and Jimmy Bryant.

There were not dozens but thousands of such records, jukebox music, honky-tonk music, barn dance music, music designed to go well with dancing and drinking and carrying on, churned out by countless small labels: King in Cincinnati, Excello in Nashville, Duke and Peacock in Houston, Modern and Aladdin and Specialty in Los Angeles. No one person was likely to be listening to all of that music, localized and hidden as it often was; no one was writing books or publishing glossy magazines about the people who made it. Except for those directly involved, no one was apt to think about the music at all except as scattered pockets of indigenous noise. Not many foresaw the imminence of the moment when a bit of genuinely strange back-country swamp-trance invocation like Bo Diddley's "Who Do You Love"—

Tombstone hand and a graveyard mind
Just 22 and I don't mind dyin'—

would be transformed from the Other into the Main Thing.

What happened next was a business revolution, forced by a realization of the size of the potential audience. Within a year Elvis went from being a small-time country music phenomenon to becoming the unavoidable defining figure of a dominant teenage culture sweeping all before it. It was his singular ascendancy that identified rock and roll forever with a new kind of idolatry, a cult of unprecedented stardom fed by unimaginably wide diffusion, as the music spilled far beyond the "rural rhythm field" where it had been nurtured. It became clear that honky-tonk could be sold as the New Teen Sound, and that the Elvis of Sun's "Mystery Train" and "Good Rockin' Tonight" could, with a few adjustments, become RCA's Elvis, a smoother product cutting across regional and class lines. It wasn't only the music but the whole culture that had changed its name: rock and roll wasn't a niche, it was going to be the whole picture. The performers converged on a national public square that in a few more years, with the advent of the Beatles and the Rolling Stones, would become a global public square. For a time it would seem that there was one universal audience watching a single show: the Great Play of the World, waking dream, unique puppet show, mirror of attitude, school of gesture, showcase of fabrics and accessories, discount warehouse of fantasy roles.

Anyone who was alive around 1955 can remember the nearly simultaneous emergence of "Crazy Man Crazy" and "Long Tall Sally" and "Be Bop a Lula," the sense of noise unleashed and nonsense set free, the invitation to go wild extended in Jerry Lee Lewis's "High School Confidential":

> *Go get your bopping shoes*
> *Before the jukebox blows a fuse.*

It didn't matter what you thought of it: it wasn't asking your opinion, merely saying that this was what the world was now. Rock's exhilarating ascent created an impression of being inducted into a central space where you could lose anything you wanted to lose, from inhibitions to name and prior history. Dissolution as uplift was the dream that for a while forced its way into the real world. The '60s proposed a possibility of endless anonymous collective merging that rock alone among cultural forms has tried to sustain without dilution, each generation of youth inheriting the attempt as the privilege of its order.

The music was of course not simply nameless swirl and head-knocking backbeat; it had acquired complexities and elongations, political missions, liturgies and robes and masks. Lyrics had evolved from the equivalent of "Meet me on the corner and don't be late" into increasingly baroque variants of Jimi Hendrix's "Is this tomorrow or just the end of time?" Music was scarcely the point by now: this was literature, theater, religion, noise opera, political action, erotic paradise. It contained the promise of perpetual new inventions, new social relations, even as it drew into itself whatever of the past could be salvaged, from cowboy campfire songs to Vedic chants. To the giddily contagious grandiosity of that moment—the certainty that music was reshaping the world as irrevocably as it reshaped the consciousness of the stoned dancers caught in its flow—the only dramaturgically appropriate follow-up was steep descent and radical dispersal, the fall commemorated by so many histories and memoirs. There is no substitute for cosmic fusion, and whatever comes after tends to seem like a footnote to a sacred text.

A more lucrative footnote would be hard to imagine, of course, as the major labels freed themselves of hidebound anti-rock holdovers and finally succeeded, in the early '70s, in getting a handle on the product they were selling, achieving—with the help of terminally hip, cocaine-addled sales reps and producers—full mutual interpenetration of rock underground and global industry. The revelries were reorganized under the auspices of Dionysus Incorporated, and excess itself reconfigured as an ostensibly rational, assembly-line procedure. Stare at the music industry long enough and the music itself seems an accidental by-product of an impossibly turbulent and treacherous skein of mad transactions and delusional ambitions, an out-of-control mix of farce and bloody melodrama whose participants are blown about as helplessly as Dante's Lustful.

The scale changed. A moment ago you were getting down with your friends and neighbors on the corner, or in church, or at a barn dance, or at a high school hop, or in your living room; now you're in the midst of an army of strangers at stadiums and streamlined clubs and revival-style raves, getting high on sheer acceleration and the press of crowds. The music reaches into more and more places but at the same time comes to the listener from farther and farther away. If archaic music consisted of songs sung at harvests, we have progressed to harvest songs adopted for performance in dance halls and from there to songs about dance halls performed nowhere in particular, perhaps not performed at all but merely pieced together from a menu of morphable blips. You stick them in your ear and stroll into the field, or into where the field used to be before they built the Wal-Mart.

The term "rock and roll" long ago lost its utility as anything but a commercial subdivision of a field Balkanized into sliver-audiences. By the end of the '70s, rock was already a dubious label for defining a scene that encompassed (along with much else) disco, the Philly sound, reggae, a resurgence of cabaret, a range of jazz fusions and electronic experiments, and the earliest hip-hop. Since then, the subspecies of music have only gotten more fantastically variegated, or at least their names have. For one example, a recent study of techno and rave music lists over forty allegedly distinctive genres, ranging from New York Garage and Ambient Techno to Darkcore, Terrorcore, and Horrorcore. Ineluctably the rock and roll moment—the great convergence of mid-century pop—begins to take its place as another episode in a serial with no end. In New York, the new oldies station in town features late '60s and early '70s soul, funk, and disco, while excising the treasured masterpieces of rockabilly and doo-wop under the sardonic slogan "Elvis Has Left the Building."

It is possible to imagine a history of rock and roll that would not be about superstars or record labels or *Billboard* charts at all—not even about the armies of aspirants and small-time contenders and might-have-beens who in many ways are even more important—but about the use that listeners made of music. Such a project, however, would resemble a history of lighting effects, or sex acts, or breathing. It would be a history, finally, of the desire to bury history, to be free once and for all of an imposed narrative. To remain rock and roll, whatever is being said must be true to the code summarized with comic aplomb by Ian Dury in 1977:

> *Sex and drugs and rock and roll*
> *Is all my brain and body need*
> *Sex and drugs and rock and roll*
> *Is very good indeed.*

More than any musical trait that invitation to unhindered interpersonal meltdown—culminating in the fenced-in desert frat party of Woodstock '99, looking in the video clips like a fiesta in an internment camp—keeps the idea of rock and roll alive. It is the promised paradise where everybody gets a chance to "crash out" like an escaped con in a '30s gangster movie: the one paradise that is not merely promised but—such as it is—delivered.

The ultimate rock history would be a history of the listener's body as transformed by music, or of the imaginary body that the music makes possible, and that the listener can select from an expanding menu of options, in an era when music is often experienced as a literal appendage, attached via Walkman or Discman. What kind of body do you want? Pick your desired model of nervous response from the rack. The ideal record can be relied on to deliver a jolt of gratuitous excitement unencumbered by relationship or history. You play it to enhance an excitement you already feel, or to revive an excitement you have unaccountably lost. This is revelry you can swallow like a pill, like the Who record called "Instant Party." At the push of a button you are lost in a nerve dance, fused effortlessly with bass line or falsetto refrain or repeated intrusive jangle.

You don't listen to this music; you assume its identity. You virtually inhabit it. The digitalized home of the future is set to function as resonating chamber for the sounds piped in by request from Disembodied Music Central, far from any hint of taverna or roadhouse or rocked-out stadium. But then the places have always finally been imaginary, reconstructed in memory, or never experienced except through songs: At the Hop, On Broadway, Under the Boardwalk, In the Basement, Out in the Street, In My Room. The festivals and orgies (rock history's cinematic high points) provide an ornamental backdrop even as the music filters into the drabber confines of office life, apartment life, subway and airport life, as roots music gives way to rootlessness music. A whole population, adrift with headphones, continues to tune in to the permanent all-night party in the Grand Virtual Ballroom of the Twentieth Century, a party that goes on without regard for the collapse and disappearance of some of the guests and their replacement by new recruits. Those who have stayed longest may find the drastic changes in tempo and texture disorienting, perhaps around the time "Let's Have a Party" (Wanda Jackson, 1958) is replaced on the turntable by "I Wanna Destroy You" (The Soft Boys, 1980).

For each listener what sticks is the imprinting, the earlier the better. You don't forget songs, you merely lose contact with them. The connection can be renewed at any point in life as if nothing had changed, and no more exact retrieval of experience is possible. Everything comes back, and then the comebacks come back: the '50s theme from I Love Lucy mutates into a '70s disco record that surfaces again in the '90s as a classic oldie, and late at night in the summer of the first year of the new millennium an easy-listening arrangement of Van Morrison's "Wild Night" fills every corner of the underground concourse of the World Trade Center.

An extended web of chance encounters makes the music's real history. What you remember in the end is not the power of a single song but the environment created by many songs reacting to one another: a transitory world, but haunting in the memory of its richness and extensiveness. It was only after buying a good many records, apparently at random, that I became aware that I had, almost somnambulistically, reassembled the playlist from a certain memorable party in the fall of 1965, in a labyrinthine apartment off Central Park West. The efforts I had taken for research had been driven by the unconscious desire to hear once again, in an order of play determined by purely personal considerations, Wilson Pickett's "In the Midnight Hour" and the Premiers' "Farmer John" and the Righteous Brothers' "Little Latin Lupe Lu," Ray Barretto's "El Watusi" and the Contours' "Do You Love Me" and Sir Mack Rice's "Mustang Sally." That was the night we lost ourselves definitively in shadows and noise, the night the cops finally showed up to quiet things down, the night when the music seemed—as it would never quite so perfectly seem again—the solution and dissolution of every perplexity.

9

Central Park West (Side A)

*[*CUE: JOHN COLTRANE, "CENTRAL PARK WEST," RECORDED October 1960.]*

The needle hits the groove and it begins. It's the same every time. John Coltrane plays "Central Park West" and by an accident of title— as if his Central Park West were mine—opens up lost space. The wordless ballad sings about what flourished and was buried there. Right here, transmuted into pure tone, are the words that drifted away. Here are the secret rites and conferences and exchanges of the apartment-dwellers. Here is the life that took a structure of stone and plaster for a figure of its own durability.

Now only the notes remain—Coltrane's notes—and the notes have nothing to do with any of it. They have their own fate, unconnected except for an arbitrary link that I invent and then reaffirm by playing the record every time that mood hits. I appropriate the music because I have a use for it. "Central Park West" could have been the theme playing over the credits in the movie version of our lives on Central Park West, the movie that young people expect their lives to become. Coltrane's ballad is what that world might have been if the hesitations and accidents had been edited out, the miscues translated into calm assured clarity, the passing joy or compassionate connection grabbed hold of and held tight instead of being allowed to dissipate into smoke and small talk. It is night on Central Park West, forever. We can live in it permanently now.

John Coltrane plays "Central Park West." The pitch is exact, the timbre undecayed. In that clear presence, nothing changes. But the people who listened to it back then? Either disappeared altogether or changed into these latter-day beings who can scarcely recall what they might have said or felt on one or another of those evenings. They become repositories of echoes and outtakes from which, if there were time and strength enough, it is tempting to think that a lost original might yet be reconstructed.

[Cue: Max Steiner, main title music, The Hunchback of Notre Dame, 1939.]

This is fiction. In a new space (a space I invent, and call that invention memory) the family arrives with cartons of books and costumes, piano and sofas and box sets of Richard Strauss and Benny Goodman. The family has gotten smaller since moving from the island and shifting its ground with disconcerting frequency from one temporary dwelling to another before alighting here on the Upper West Side. In the course of a few years of restless migration within Manhattan, Ruth has left the household where she worked for so many years to get married and move away, Bob too has married and set about making a place for himself in the world of music publishing and arranging with which he has already acquired such professional familiarity. Joel has a room set aside for him but will occupy it only from time to time. He'll return from somewhere to go somewhere else, disappear into California for six months, show up unannounced one midnight with a trunkful of innovative records that nobody has heard of yet. Eventually, after a year or so, he'll settle in his own place downtown, a cramped walkup whose walls and surfaces will fill soon enough with records, magazines, paperbacks, and so much else, flutes, figurines, tasseled hats, curious carved sticks, found objects to be given new life by incorporation into his space.

The new home off Central Park West has space enough to dwarf any furnishings. Seen for the first time late at night, its vaulted rooms seem lifted from a chateau. The morning after the voluptuous dark-

ness of the night arrival reveals it as a stone eyrie that still looks pala-
tial as light invades it through the high windows. From its parapets
neighboring castles are visible: this is the stone city, built to last if
only as a ruin. The scale seems to demand a corresponding scale of
emotional life. What kind of actions and gestures will it take to live
up to these rooms?

The bank of windows looks down over the Museum of Natural History. In the museum's faded splendors—the dioramas of stuffed okapi
and bongo in simulated African foliage, the life-size figures of Pacific
Coast Indians in canoes, a bronze Theodore Roosevelt on horseback
and flanked by native subjects at the head of the imperious front
steps—we will come to find remnants of a world-system so out of date
as to be almost comforting. This is that past we heard about—with its
wars and professorships and ethnographic expeditions, preserved as
if the engines still hummed—the past where we had always secretly
wanted to live. Among the richly draped remnants of a gilded civilization the young are free to imagine new regimes, borrowing whatever tints and patterns they like from the old.

The building into which we have moved as if into an inheritance is
itself a museum of sorts. A monument of the Gothic Revival, its shadowy medieval lobby would be suitable for monastic vigils and extended duel sequences. It might have been the set for a black-and-
white movie based on Victor Hugo or Alexandre Dumas. Was that a
Gregorian chant echoing from the crypt under the elevator shaft, or
merely a lush Max Steiner imitation of a Gregorian chant? Wasn't it
Archbishop Frollo who emerged from the hidden alcove to the right of
the gilded doorway, his mind intent on the slaughter of heretics? It's
a space for conspirators, prelates, hired assassins, rogue poets, or for
the Bohemians of the Gilded Age who would dress up as such in midnight masquerades.

The neighbor with whom we are to share a floor is a long-term
tenant, a high-living 1920s illustrator secluded now in draped and
mirrored retirement. When he shows up on television one night in
an old movie musical, trading quips with Jack Benny and the Yacht
Club Boys, it is like a confirmation that we have moved into the past,
become part of history. We have left the suburbs, where history did

not exist, for the city, where it is made, or rather of which it is made.

[*Cue:* West Side Story, *"The Dance at the Gym," recorded 1959.*]

Just outside, down the block, down most blocks, are the fringes of the Dark City of B-movie and cop-show legend, where tourists who ignore the warnings find out why they would never want to live there. This *City Destroying Itself* (as a best-selling social tract has it) is beset by rumors of rapists, armed bandits, college girls slaughtered in their apartments. People talk constantly of the city's dangers and annoyances. There is a sliding scale that extends from atrocious murders and assaults to lines at supermarkets, stalled subways, and every variety of insolence and madness in public places. Prowl cars circle the park. Doctors dress down and carry their medical supplies in grocery bags to deter marauding addicts. Cab drivers rage against the mayor: "It's that Lindsay. This used to be a nice place to live." There is a siege mentality marked by a general obsession with locks, bolts, window guards. Easy enough, from within the circle of light, to sketch out a world of playgrounds commandeered for gang wars by teenage wolf packs, street-corner drug dealers, diners with bullet holes in the walls, frighteningly defective subways and menacingly unlit parking garages, discarded syringes, deranged beggars. It's already a movie, a whole string of movies, *Crime in the Streets, The Young Savages,* not to mention *West Side Story,* filmed only a few blocks away just before they tore down those mean streets to build Lincoln Center.

Yet all that is kept at bay—by what? A contrary fantasy that might be compounded of Theodore Roosevelt, Chinese screens, piano music drifting from hotel lounges, the mournful tenderness of *Mood Indigo* and *Autumn in New York* seeming to provide an accompaniment for the early summer evenings when the lights first go on, and Central Park itself (by day at least, before the predators come out) with its often nearly deserted paradise of arches and lakes, its ancient colonnades and cascading meadows. The pleasure of life here frequently consists of imagining the pleasure of other people's lives: Audrey

Hepburn accompanied by the music of Henry Mancini, turning the city into her gleaming playground.

The dark city has only one unavoidable risk: that one might come to fear it. From that moment, if it arrives, farewell to tranquility of mind. Once the sense of dread has been permitted to insinuate itself, no stairwell or deserted stretch of pavement is without its peculiar terrors. Note, in the faces of frail elders and embittered shopkeepers, the look of infinite mistrust. They have become prisoners of their own dread. Absence itself—of people, of lights, of noise—is terrifying. The invisible assailants are hiding; they're around the corner; the street itself is a trap. Take a train, but which train, and from which end of the platform? Walk slowly or quickly on the winding metal stairs that connect distant lines?

How much better to live in a breezy continuum of unhesitating rashness, letting the possibility of random evil figure as no more than invigorating mental punctuation. Intrusions do occur: think of them as percussive accents. Random gunshots are fired at odd early morning hours from a source never identified, somewhere in another building, some space on the other side of our thick-walled compound. Professional thieves—picture them wearing dark tailored suits, thin ties, Italian shoes, and the inevitable sunglasses—slip in during a doormen's strike while the family is on vacation to strip the apartment systematically of every half-way valuable heirloom (there aren't many), every rare coin stashed in childhood collections, and every piece of genuine jewelry, carefully distinguishing and rejecting the costume gems accumulated in the course of my mother's theatrical life.

We exist in a semblance of serenity and comfort, all the same. Where we live could be the country; with the park, and the trees around the museum, it practically *is* the country. We aren't even aware of the serial killer living in the residential hotel next door. He's on staff there, a handyman dedicated to the silent removal of lonely elderly women from the world. He works so discreetly that some years go by before the deaths are identified as murders. Only in retrospect will we wonder if the residential hotel's desolate air—we took it for granted, an almost emblematic grimness consonant with the rumor that Theodore Dreiser had lived there once—was already whispering news of murder to the neighborhood.

[Cue: Tito Puente, "Night Beat," recorded 1957.]

The wide windows make a convenient observation post. We see and are not seen. After midnight, crowds of dancers—a calligraphy of scarves and red leather shoes and enormous floral hats—pile out of taxis into the basement-level mambo club next door. Gigantic floats gather on the side street the night before the Macy's Thanksgiving Day parade. Disney characters bob, grinning in the wind against the ropes that tether them, a sight to terrify any stoned or unwary traveler turning the corner at four in the morning to find his path blocked by a gigantic duck.

Yet fully half the world seems asleep all the time. How can any city, least of all the city that accounts itself the busiest in the world, be so quiet? When you have lived here long enough, even the honks and the pneumatic drills acquire a strangely lulling effect. With hats and briefcases the men go about their business as if napping. The women disappear into discreetly decorated shops, or step into taxis on their way to undisclosed destinations. The half that isn't asleep often likes to conceal its enjoyments. Stray chords escape from camouflaged doors. You detect gleams of color through windows left open a crack. At strategic points in the most outwardly placid neighborhoods, a few inches below the surface, there is a muffled throb of enclaves.

Across the street, one October night, adventurous thieves—is this a *Spider-Man* comic, or a game of Clue?—steal the Star of India from the museum, climbing down the wall. They would have been in plain view, had I not been too busy watching *The Best of Broadway* on Channel 7. The caper itself seems a worthy subject for one of those movies that night after night provide the most royal of entertainments, decades of images and story lines served up for the indolent young to revel in. Only later will the master thief be identified as Murph the Surf—even better!—a name suitably raffish for the modish allure of movie jewel thieves, sophisticated rascals who give ordinary life an indelible comic twist, put-on artists with class. (In real life the case would degenerate soon enough into an uglier strain of paranoia and violence, but that was in another state and—things moved so quickly—already another era.)

These corridors and alcoves and window seats and living rooms divided by French doors will always, no matter how long inhabited, seem like a slightly grandiose stage set fit for melodramatic gestures and romantic escapades. It is here that the impending changes will come upon us. Was it we who were napping? So swiftly and stealthily does the decade work its transformations that it is already nearly over before any of us realizes the scale of what we have been living through: it wasn't just us, it was happening everywhere. The late '60s brought an imperative to rearrange one's identity as the moment demanded, and the uncomfortable sense of being always a bit behind, so that it was always already time to rearrange it again. At almost every minute even the definitions of words were changing.

We measure that speed by comparing it to the enduring and unmoving past the apartment evokes in so many of its furnishings. How many times the eye surveys, as if from the comfort of a mountain gazebo, the timeless Empire of the Parents. A slow turn of the head takes in the Chinese screen with its horsemen and palanquins and mist-hidden temples, the bronze statuette of Shakespeare rescued from a New England antique shop, the Renaissance maps of Europe and the New World with their quaint inset portraits of Jews and Turks and cannibals, the rows of play scripts by Shaw and Rattigan and Coward, the floral prints and Dutch interiors. The view from the grand piano is a sweep of carpeting and vases and brass candlesticks. The memory of an Edwardian era never actually experienced hovers over what might from some angles serve as a set for *Candida* or *The Winslow Boy*. It is designed for perfect comfort, an ashtray conveniently placed to prevent a single ash from falling on the varnished coffee table, the lamps adjusted so that one can read comfortably on the sofa, even if the book turns out to be as disconcerting as Ginsberg's *Reality Sandwiches* or Burroughs's *Nova Express* or Selby's *Last Exit to Brooklyn* or Genet's *The Thief's Journal*.

The plenitude of the past was not intended for us, but (lucky accidental inheritors) we can appropriate pieces of it. What hours are spent imagining new uses for these neglected legacies: the antique ivory letter opener, the incomparably delicate paper of the book of woodblock prints printed in Japan in the 1920s, the silk scarf that might have belonged to Flora Tosca or Isadora Duncan, the stereopticon views of St. Petersburg and Shanghai, a world of steamer trunks and seaside hotels to be reentered only in waking dreams. The dreams borrow freely from Alain Resnais's *Last Year at Marienbad,* the dance of Salome whether in the colors of Gustav Klimt or the morbidly lovely prose of Oscar Wilde, the sparkling eyes of Parisian chorus girls as conjured in the music of Offenbach. That masquerade—in which sex is inextricably interwoven with champagne and opera and the occasional fatal duel—has the density of a world we hope one day to inhabit. We might have to build it first, of course: make our own ballrooms, our own galleries full of voluptuous mythological images, our own mesmerizing flute music. In the meantime the Chinese screen will do fine. The pillows couldn't be more comfortable.

[Cue: Johann Sebastian Bach, "Sonata no. 1 in B minor for violin and harpsichord."]

The layout, the carefully considered functioning of each room, has taken shape under my mother's close scrutiny. There is no effect of lighting or composition that she has not weighed before making an absolute (even if never fully verbalized) aesthetic decision about what works: comfortable but not cumbersome, shapely but not smothered in detail, and above all with enough open space. Now that she is apparently on the verge of giving up her life as an actress—there will be one last season of summer stock, and that's it—she can devote herself to the ordering of the household almost as a full-time occupation. At first it seemed incredible that she would deny herself those alternate lives, with their tragic crises and comic flourishes. Isn't it the latent presence of that counter-world of theatricality that has imparted a measure of enchantment even to the most ordinary household scenes?

That she went out into the world to assume roles suggested a privacy that was understood to be necessary to any artist. It was not enough to be your outward self, you had to guard some other part for the higher purpose: to leave the world behind in order to make it over. To rehearse, learn lines and cues, acquire accents and postures, smoke a cigarette while waiting for the curtain go up: this was to be already in transition to that other higher plane of performance. Once there, she was no longer the same person. It seemed an unthinkable resignation to renounce that metamorphosis. Wasn't it the crucial act in life to go through the door, to become that other person, whether through playing a part or playing music or becoming lost in the act of writing? There was an inviolable privacy at the heart of being an artist, something beyond explanation no matter how much we loved explaining things.

Or maybe her renunciation of the stage is not so much a denial as a further evolution into another and more austere conception of art. Henceforth she will devote herself to remaking the space around her. Piece by piece she constructs a world of tactful beauty, a world existing under the sign of solace rather than glitter. The surface comforts are braced by a certain Early American rigor not to be deceived by the frauds and delusory vainglories of the fleeting world. The decor amounts to a meditation, a spiritual discipline even. But how many years will it take for me to get any sense of that? I'm too busy trying to be at ease with chaos, acquiring a flair for as much messiness as I think I need, the swagger of flicked ashes. It's not the moment for me to appreciate that from her point of view, there is a design that needs to be renewed every day and that part of the design has to do with eliminating superfluous details.

Every object displaced or put awry mysteriously finds its intended home again. I see this tidying up as compulsive, never more so than when I discover how exactly I've learned to imitate it. It's a world she's maintaining, as if from moment to moment, but is it my world? As much as I feel hemmed in, I also have to admire the harmonious resolution she works out among those objects. I'm imagining chords. Bach hovers in the air around her. Her manipulation of space is, in fact, her own form of music, enacted in silence. It's the architecture that all of us in the family inhabit. The silence is necessary to counteract the constant noise of the men in the apartment, noise that must always be kept somewhat under control: "Can't you turn that down a little, dear?" "*Sotto voce,* please." "I'm afraid I suffer from acute hearing."

No way to reach any of this but through music, incantatory music. Like music, what is lived exists forever and only in the present, only for as long as I can sound it.

[Cue: Conversation and ambient noise, home recording, c. 1965.]

The most intimate sound (could it be recovered) is the play of voices talking not so much with as past one another. The high ceilings do wonders for vocal projection. Each of us has a distinct style of speech, as if each were a character in a different play. This small and close-knit household contains a remarkable range of fully evolved jargons. It's as if we had each cultivated our own argot, with its special vocabulary and unique tonal system. My father, for example, can't help retaining a good deal of the language and cadence of his radio show. Those jokes and interjections—the bad puns deployed according to opportunity (like saying "you're welcome" whenever somebody happens to use the word "tanks," something that happens with uncanny frequency), the historic ripostes and punch lines of everyone from George Bernard Shaw to Fred Allen, and if all else fails, the all-purpose nonsense words like "franacapan" and "ring-a-ding" and "beanbag" that can give any sentence a slightly disorienting accent—have, after years of ad-libbing, become almost part of him. He brings home with him as well—if we're talking business, and don't forget that *gesheft is gesheft*—just a trace of the jabbing rhythms of the marketplace, the hardboiled comebacks that are the mere common courtesies of the music industry; but he can also drop them at will, demonstrating that it is merely another role, an assumed persona.

At the dinner table he can be a monologuist of perfectly timed transitions and exactly placed anecdotes that lead from the nightlife of the big band era or the culinary delights of Portugal into larger questions of political corruption and religious hypocrisy. "Organized religion is the oldest racket in the world." Consider—if you must—the parade of the pompous and unctuous who remain the same in every historical period—Lord Acton said it all, absolute power corrupts absolutely— and the churches do nothing but feather their own nests. But we don't have to worry about them; we can enjoy our own freedom of thought right here. "And now that we've solved all the problems of the world, let's have some more wine."

The flow of it is what he loves, the constant affirmation that any present occasion ought to be celebratory and, if possible, more than a little comical. More than decoration, it's a technique for survival. "If it works, don't knock it." "Don't overdo it, leave them a little hungry." "Sometimes people have to be chivvied along a bit." Sorrow doesn't sit well with him. Life is what moves forward, with the momentum and economy of a practiced performance, anything it takes to avoid the circular doldrums of, say, the characters in a Eugene O'Neill play. Given a choice, he'd prefer the speed and polish of Noel Coward: whatever delights and pays off at the end of the second act, whatever conquers the beast of boredom waiting to devour life and turn it into something like a slow afternoon in the Yonkers of his childhood, the storefronts and playgrounds where people turned petty or plaintive simply because they had nothing interesting to think about. The art of living consists of tricking life into honoring its evasive promises.

Joel counters with a stylized hipsterism whose tempos work at cross-purposes to Noel Coward. It's a feinting maneuver, reminiscent of the boxers he admires, the ones who stay in the game by staying light on their feet. He has long since assimilated his own influences— the list might at different ages have included Lester Young, Lord Buckley, Babs Gonzales, Lenny Bruce, Jack Kerouac, Jack Teagarden, Chet Baker, Samuel Beckett, Henry Miller—and the residue is a seamless blend, an idiosyncratic and pervasive texture, as much a play of accents as his own drumming. It is music that incorporates, for its lyrics, the self-invented field of knowledge in which he has made himself expert: a knowledge that there is no school for, encompassing music, movies, comic books, modern history of a type not found in textbooks, a history of crimes and anomalies and confidence tricks and lost or discarded tribes.

He is an expert whose expertise often has no obvious practical application. It exists for the sake of long free-form improvisations that leap from Bud Powell to Dr. Strange to the origins of bluegrass, from middleweight champions of the late nineteenth century to minor character actors of the early sound period, the writings of Anaïs Nin and D. H. Lawrence and Mickey Spillane. Such a solo can begin and end anywhere, and as it spirals it weaves into itself antique one-liners ("That gag has whiskers!"), and songs retrieved from yellowed sheet music, and movie dialogue—the speech before the showdown in a B western or a gangster's desperate dying question—remembered word for word.

It teems, too, with news of the world that is springing up around town. There are new musicians, new phraseology and new ways of shaking hands, new political issues and styles of clothing, new kinds of jokes (sometimes disguised as witlessness to exclude the uninitiated). The bulletins tumble out urgently. He is the one who knows that changes are occurring under the surface of the way things used to be done, and he has come to let us know that everything is going to be different. This can lead to arguments. When father and son face each other at the table, sometimes it ends in shouts and recriminations. The fiercest disagreements—because the new world can be a rude and disrespectful place—turn out to be about language: "Don't talk that way in front of your mother!" It is a battle of mutually incompatible styles that nonetheless have the closest of relations being joined at the root.

To my ears, Joel's speech amounts almost to a separate dialect. When I catch myself trying to imitate it, the result of that attempt seems a variant of a variant, a literary version that fails to catch the lilt of its model. Listening to myself talk—at sixteen it is impossible to do otherwise—I hear an artificially constructed mode of speech, acquired more from books than by ear, larded with parenthetical filler—"as it were," "so to speak," or "relatively speaking"—that make it sound as if I had been reading too much Aldous Huxley or had taken as a role model the bookish, Freud-spouting adolescent in the movie of *The Thin Man*. To chip away at that takes self-imposed speech therapy. Self-consciously I interpolate what I take to be the language of the streets and coffee shops and bus terminals, piling one kind of artifice on another to end up with something approximating the natural. It's work, and when the effort fails—in the presence of spontaneous feeling, sudden upset—the result is embarrassed silence or a stammering flurry of more or less abstract approximations of what I haven't found a way to say.

The three males manage somehow, most of the time, to summon up an exuberance that can be almost like vehemence. At its best the talk takes on a life of its own. We're collaborators, we cap each other's thoughts when we aren't stepping on each other's lines or topping each other's jokes. We're caught up in a conversation that evolves from a description of the world to what feels more like the creation of a world, our private world. It's chamber music, arranged for distinct voices—spontaneously arranged, after long practice—in the relaxed but close harmony associated with family acts.

Mom's style is not to shout like the rest of us, maneuvering for a point of entry, and so her role can seem more like auditor. Or is it precisely her attention we're competing for? She alone appears, if casually observed, to speak in a direct if old-fashioned style. Her speech is still larded with quaint country sayings, "Lord love a duck" or "I declare," and free from the obscenities that the men find necessary for emphasis. "Shoot" or "sugar" are her expletives of choice, and any line of talk that gets too crudely explicit is cut off with "Save it for the boudoir!" Yet she as well has practiced for years the art of acting. Into her phrases creep echoes of the parts she has played—is it Blanche Du Bois? Miss Gooch from *Auntie Mame*? Mrs. Wendyce from *Dial M for Murder?*—so that even at the highest pitch of emotion some artifice enters in.

Having at various points accommodated itself to the dramatic language of Shakespeare, Tennessee Williams, George S. Kaufman, Agatha Christie, her speech ever afterward bears the traces of that discipline even when she's talking about the most minor details of daily life. What she has to say is never an outburst. It is more like a set speech, the line readings so calibrated that there is an implicit irony, as if she herself knows very well that she has said this before and will say it again—whether it is "Alcohol *dulls* the senses" or "Nothing is harder than having just enough money" or, simply and often, "Never assume"—but it is what the part demands.

She knows there are places where wit and argument can't take you, but there's hardly a pause long enough to let her even begin to talk about what that might be. It might come out as a spontaneous musing about inmost religious beliefs that she prefers not to define too closely. It's enough to indicate that they exist and that they concern the fundamental mysteriousness of what is. For a moment she has gone beyond table talk, and everybody else goes silent or looks for a way back into bantering humor.

Consequently discussion is never a simple thing. It would require a cultural translation from one dialect to another. Sometimes I feel inclined to serve as such a translator, at those moments when I sit at the edge of the room watching one assertion fly entirely past its intended recipient, who in turn sends a counterlob designed to elude the other's system of defenses, his repertoire of signs; but not being exempt from the linguistic limitations around me, I can hardly put myself totally outside the closed circle. Everything becomes an argument over basic terms, and the conversation sometimes cannot even begin because the vocabularies are mutually exclusive. We are living, after all, in the era of the Theater of the Absurd; the circularity and ineffectiveness of conversation is a commonplace regularly discussed in the arts pages of the *New York Times*. Anyway, we are all theatrical enough to hear the potential dialogue—whether by Beckett or Ionesco or Jack Gelber—in our own conversation. If the talk takes a particularly unlikely turn—what were we supposed to be talking about?—Mom will unfailingly remark, "Put it on a stage and no one would believe it!"

So the talk proceeds on its careening course, punctuated with shouts, and hinging, more often than not, on music. The music business, and the way it treats musicians, always provides something to argue about. "Listen to this! Tell me this isn't genius!" "If enough people feel that way maybe it'll pay for the studio overtime." "You're talking about gangsters! I'm talking about art!" "Talk about art as much as you like, but it's a business too. A lot of it is about showing up on schedule." "You're not seriously comparing Lesley Gore with James Brown . . . " "Look, the James Brown band may be the greatest, but they couldn't read Lesley Gore's charts . . . The first show was a disaster." "Lesley Gore should feel honored to work with James Brown. They should have fired her and let the band play their own stuff!" "I'm sorry that the world isn't arranged totally to your satisfaction." "Dig what D. H. Lawrence wrote: 'You cannot dance gaily to the double flute and at the same time conquer nations or rake in large sums of money.' Just dig what that's saying."

[Cue: Experimental recordings incorporating verbal messages from deceased subjects, recorded in Romania, circa 1963.]

If the talk reverts constantly to records it's because the records keep flowing in. There's always a pile of new ones next to the cabinet or stacked up by the piano. They are the noise the world is making right now. It's like an advance warning system. At times the record player serves as a kiosk where residents and visitors gather to share impressions of how things sound like they're going. But at other hours—later and more isolated—it's more like the pool where the stroller in this theme park, finding himself alone for a few minutes, pauses to catch a glimpse of his own reflection. There's a moment of strange calm as the needle makes contact with the vinyl. Different people listen to the same records for different reasons and at different times of day. A given record might be assessed for its radio suitability; contemplated as a possible addition to the repertoire; considered as material to be adapted to another style or instrumentation; studied as an indicator of what the public is going for; played for pastime, or for party music, or (with whatever degree of wishful thinking) for seduction music; or, after midnight, plunged into in an act of solitary communion. As each listener weighs the music, he is also weighed by it. Which is heavier, the listener or what he listens to? Which cuts faster and deeper? Is the music too slow, or is he too fast?

We're surrounded by one another enough of the time that it's striking when someone withdraws, plays music for himself alone. Dad sits back with eyes closed listening to one of the Mozart divertimenti that he has taken to putting on late at night. Mom practices her castanets to the flamenco that she has begun to study with undemonstrative seriousness. I have the impression of being shown a representation of their feelings. It's his divertimento, her flamenco: I'm hearing the music through the medium of their sensibilities, as if eavesdropping on what they hear. Different musical selections are like foreign phrases in a guidebook, ways to get across what cannot otherwise be said. "If you really want to know how I feel, listen to what I'm not saying, what I'm letting Piaf or Teddy Wilson say." In this way—this way of pointing a bit to the side, leaving a great deal to mute inference—we converse from year to year.

The point where the music starts is like the brink of a well. What is to be scooped from down there in the underground river of sound? Where's the pulse? To watch the record as it spins is to reinforce the idea that a form of divination is in process. Stare into the circle and wait for the message to emerge. A psychic researcher claims to have recorded the voices of the dead and releases sample excerpts on a 45: authentic Romanian revenants emitting barely audible hisses, like field mice trapped in a wind tunnel. It sounds like the voice is saying, "Kafka . . . Kafka . . . Kafka."

But then sooner or later all the records will contain the voices of the dead, will speak as it were from the beyond. Life-energy is pressed into the records' surfaces. Actions of living people—cries, moans, gasps—have been artificially preserved so that they can be repeated on command, as in a mad scientist's dream. Science proved that ghosts don't exist and then, as if to compensate, turned around and invented real ghosts. The coiled-up carnivals are set in motion with a button, fulfilling the prophecies of futuristic living that used to fill glossy magazines: "A symphonic orchestra will play for you in your own living room, as soon as you open the door." On Central Park West, in this movie set of an old castle, we are already living, behind the thick yellow curtains, an anticipation of the automated planet.

Real time happened one day at a time. Played back as music, everything is accessible at once. There is a box of records, some cracked, some overlaid with surface noise. They outlast talk, outlast breath. The altar survives its worshippers. Cracked and mossy, the nymph's fountain endures.

[Cue: Station identification jingle, WMCA, New York, 1965.]

Each member of the household operates in a separate sphere, working at a distinct task. For Dad the sphere is always partly public, even when he's home. Lately there's too much going on for him to keep his attention averted for long; after thirty years in radio he's watching the music business become something like the center of the world. To be a disc jockey at this moment is to find himself at the hub of a trans-formation that keeps expanding. Can we still be talking about music? "It's unbelievable how big this thing has gotten." The word "popu-lar" isn't enough anymore. "Popular" is an appropriate word for Doris Day comedies, *Mission: Impossible,* Colt 45. This music business thing, on the other hand, is more like global takeover.

Were Margaret Whiting or Kay Kyser ever the defining emblems of their era? Did anybody outside of a few hard-core fans think that Perry Como was the center of the world? We have reached an increas-ingly strange place where rock and roll bands and folksingers become the acknowledged legislators of new codes of speech, new orders of decorum. Background has become foreground. The hit parade *is* the news, and the numbers are getting to be beyond belief. "Do you have any idea how many records Motown sold last year?" The Morning Man watches in fascination the turning wheel on which he himself is carried along.

The rounds of his daily life interact with the larger rhythms of the music business. Part of the fascination is in knowing it's an utterly un-caring force, the big casino whose chips are stacks of demos, the Sure Shots and Plug Sides and Hot Picks churned out week after week. Is it a hit or a miss? This close to the center, the mechanism can be in-toxicating. It is 1965, or 1966. Billboards with his face are plastered at train stations like election posters: WAKE-UP ARTIST. There is a rich flow of high-cost freebies, pocket money in this industry: the filet mignon packed in dry ice (a personal token of appreciation from Berry Gordy Jr. to the disc jockeys of America), the case of Haut-Brion by way of Christmas greeting, the comped evenings at the Rain-bow Room among the expense-account suits gathered to hear Mel Tormé or the Dells. Framed platinum records honor his role in pro-moting the careers of Vikki Carr and the Singing Nun and Jimmy Rosselli. Personal appearances proliferate; the fan mail triples. Under everything is the perpetual grinding of the charts, the spinning of Fortune's platter.

When you think about it for too long the radio business dissolves into an abstraction, an invisible network. Yet its material tokens are scattered around the apartment, small indications of how far and wide the empire extends. Every demo and lead sheet, every record hop poster and promotional glossy and weekly chart—STATION USE ONLY—is an artifact of that circuitry of power. From inside the center—and simply to be living in the apartment feels like being inside it, most days—it's possible to imagine the multiplying interconnections, from the corporate level, at which Paramount buys Stax and Gulf, and Western in turn buys Paramount, to the B-movie stratum of the scattered operators scrounging in the shadow of the conglomerates: the independent producers, the middlemen, the semi-legal extortionists and flimflam specialists, the packagers and repackagers, the discounters and salvagers finding money in music like those people who walk with metal detectors on the beach to find coins in the sand. There have never been so many coins in the sand.

People are beating their brains out figuring how to make a bundle selling hits from ten years ago on late-night television, make a bundle writing the diet soda theme or placing the instrumental version as a movie theme, make a bundle licensing somebody else's song to a third party, make a bundle getting an exclusive U.S. distribution deal on the Italian novelty record that's turning into a freak international phenomenon. Nothing succeeds like success! Everybody loves a winner! Write a tune and if it's catchy it will penetrate everywhere—as long as you can get it recorded, and get it played, and get it distributed, and as long as somebody doesn't prevail on you somewhere in that process to sign away your rights, and as long as you can get your money out of the distributor. "You've got to get a piece of the action. Otherwise it's nickels and dimes." "You sign with that label, you might as well hand them your watch and your wallet while you're at it."

The intersection of music and money: an eight-thousand-page epic without a hero, but with room for a constantly shifting cast of players major and minor, and more than its share of violence, betrayal, madness, wildly lucky shots. Chapters of it pop up in conversation over five o'clock cocktails or the after-dinner shot of Grand Marnier. "What ever happened to him?" "It's a sad story . . . He ended up believing his own publicity." Or "He sold out his publishing rights for

peanuts when the wise guys already knew that EMI was going to option the songs." Or "She changed labels, but she didn't realize she
couldn't take her arranger with her. Never charted again. She never
did quite figure out what happened to her."

There are so many cautionary tales about the professional ruts and
isolated lounges and bottom-of-the-bill dead ends that even the most
talented can tumble into. There are strata—and strata under the
strata—of chicanery and red tape where you can beat on the door
without ever getting a look-in, your talents wasted on soundtracks
for industrial films or jingles for local retailers or uncredited behind-
the-scenes doctoring of arrangements credited to famous alcoholic
composers. Jazz musicians who studied harmony with Milhaud end
up playing the theme from *Exodus* at bar mitzvahs in Westchester—
if they're lucky. If they're luckier they get tapped for the house band
on late night talk shows, or get on the A list for commercial calls, so
they might just have time to make it to the Vanguard after wrapping
up the shaving cream spot—and for musicians that is what is called
success.

[*Cue: Bill Evans Trio, "My Foolish Heart," recorded at the Village Vanguard, 1961.*]
Musicians! The conversation can never get too far away from them,
and the troubles they drag around with them like a birthright. They
get nothing but the tough breaks. If management doesn't screw
them, Local 102 will. "What else is new? So life is not fair." They
have to make a world of their own to compensate for the injustices of
the one they work in. In the privacy of living rooms and lofts they
reinvent the out-of-the-way joint where the musicians go after hours
and jam until dawn, the smoky utopia where James Mason sought
out Judy Garland in *A Star Is Born,* where Kirk Douglas started to
unravel in *Young Man with a Horn,* where the doped-up Elisha Cook,
Jr., "real, real gone" into his drum solo, ripped apart at the seams in
Phantom Lady.

The musicians sit around in their private world making jokes, no
matter how ancient. It's a caste privilege. "He thinks time is a maga-

zine." "(In a tone appropriate for *King Kong* or *Jungle Moon Men*) I don't like the sound of those drums. —That's okay, he's not our regular drummer." "You hear the one about the new group? Their album wasn't released, it escaped." "The record company pulled a switch, they kept the album and released the group." Or else it's shop talk. "Doesn't anybody here know the changes to the bridge on 'Skylark'?" The musicians have to talk among themselves, there are too many things that only they will ever notice: the way he handled the third bar of the intro for instance, slightly off-key, but you could tell it was deliberate. Was that really Brad on that Burt side? Art got hit in the head that afternoon so Kenny subbed for him at the session but he played just like Art, they played it for Art after the bandages came off and convinced him he'd actually made the date, forgot it because of short-term memory loss from the concussion. It ended up in his discography!

They know they are the permanent outsiders. Producers and promoters need their skills but don't want them getting the whip hand. Margin wanderers from beyond the loop, they are most at home moving from town to town. The musician is the subversive onlooker, the derisively comic wise guy, like the hotel piano player playing "Somebody Stole My Purse" after Ray Milland desperately turns thief trying to buy himself a drink in *The Lost Weekend,* or Hoagy Carmichael's Cricket sliding into a funereal vamp after the crooked American tourist gets caught in the crossfire in *To Have and Have Not,* until Bogart has to pull rank: "Cut it out, Cricket."

The musicians will go too far if somebody more responsible doesn't rein them in. Somebody—the mobbed-up club owner, the hotel manager, the booking agent, the record company executive, the hidebound bandleader—is always trying to stop them from playing what they need to play: "You've been in show business ten minutes and you're going to tell me about audiences?" "I don't care about audiences! I just want to play what I feel!" "Look, kid, you see those people out there? They've got troubles of their own. They came here to have a good time. Maybe they don't want to know a thing about your feelings. Anyway, it's a take it or leave it proposition." It happened to them all, in movie after movie: Elvis Presley, Gene Krupa, even Benny Goodman.

[Cue: Booker T. and the MGs, "Home Grown," recorded 1963.]

Yet the musicians are going to change the world. Their moment has arrived. The apartment teems with musicians, Joel's friends and collaborators. They come and go at improbable hours, unpacking their violins and guitars and saxophones, their frets and mouthpieces and sheet music, their drugs and their Budweisers, their Fats Navarro and their Blue Sky Boys and their Lightnin' Hopkins. Raised on old-time music and jazz and with no help from anyone else (no schools, no institutions had the slightest interest in anything like that, and if they did they'd get it wrong anyway, they always do), the musicians have turned themselves into independent scholars of rare mandolin solos and Russ Freeman B-sides. They share whatever they know with one another: chord changes, picking techniques, inside stories about the renowned and obscure, what Monk said between sets last Friday, the greatest dobro player never recorded. And songs: whole songbooks. They are fast and omnivorous. There is too much to know and they want the whole repertoire.

Now, since the Beatles thing started, if they want bookings they have to study the new English models of pop music. Putting aside *Down Beat* and *Metronome,* they pore over *New Music Express* to see what the London critics—arbiters of the pop revolution—are going for. They learn to compete with teenagers who can't play more than two chords and have never heard of Roscoe Holcomb or Bukka White or Lenny Tristano. They look in amazement at what is climbing up the charts in *Billboard* and *Cash Box*. With music this simple shouldn't the real musicians be able to take over? "Hell, I've forgotten more chords than they'll ever know." But nobody's handing out the key to the recording studio.

There are gigs, to be sure. There are second-tier Catskills resort hotels, and go-go bars in midtown, and teenage hops in the outer boroughs, and sound-track sessions producing the requisite cocktail jazz for movies like *Touch of Her Flesh* and *The Degenerates*. There will be more, and better, once you get your name around. Everybody needs to dance, now that they've made the steps ("what steps?") so easy that anyone can do it. Arthur opens—it is May of 1965—down on 54th Street, where El Morocco used to be; and soon enough Joel and his newly formed band, the Kingbees, will be there, playing their blues-and-jazz-infused version of The Big Beat. This springtime the new glamor is rising out of the ashes of the old: Sybil Burton, newly separated from Richard, has teamed up with Roddy McDowell (another survivor of the gaudy debacle of *Cleopatra*) to create a space where Rudolf Nureyev can reveal himself (according to the *New York Times*) as "the liveliest Frugger of all," where the stepdaughter of the Duke of Bedford can dance in her "well-above-the-knee knitted dress," where Senator Jacob Javits and Tennessee Williams and Baby Jane Holzer find themselves sloshing around together in a sea of Courrèges boots and Pucci print jerseys. There goes Leonard Bernstein; they say Mike Nichols has a piece of the place.

This is the moment when everybody is about to be famous. The band has everything required to turn the night at Arthur into pure exhilaration. They encore with the Chuck Berry tune and everybody's dancing, nobody's ever heard anything better. The older patrons, the ones with money, are shuffling off their silly private rules, their trivial codes of etiquette, the social distinctions that gradually cut them off from the rest of the population. The young have what the old ones need and can't supply for themselves. They are master technicians commissioned to provide dance music for the rulers of the world. Keep it tight and funky and joyful, and go on all night like that, until every night's a wedding party. All it requires is to be initiated into the codes, to have the key to the secret Memphis drum patterns, the Detroit bass figures, the New Orleans chordal spirals.

The musicians have knowledge, skill, experience. So how come their single didn't make the charts? Deliberate art can only penetrate so far into an area ruled by mysterious capriciousness. How anything gets up there remains unknowable, pitched somewhere between a roll of the dice and divine predestination. They stare at the slots as if at a billboard flashing: Your Name Here. Why not? The new art is simplicity itself. It's beyond words: you've got to develop a sixth sense for what makes things click. It's Zen! Get that baroque junk out of the way, that grammar and filigree of bebop fussiness. Too much detail, nobody cares. That's what killed the big bands, too many notes, too many horns. Make it simpler than you know how, and it's still not simple enough. Listen to "Farmer John" again. They *like* it crude like that. A single hook makes the world yours. Can you believe what "yeah, yeah, yeah" did for the Beatles? Pete Townsend stuttering on "My Generation": that's all it took.

Mistakes make the world yours! The singer comes in at the wrong bar of the Kingsmen's "Louie, Louie" and it sounds like deliberate artistry. Well, they say Shakespeare never blotted out a line. The bronze statuette of the Bard, perched on the bookshelf, remains imperturbable as Gary Abbot launches, again, into his spastic, incomparably primitive drum outburst. For this you studied Max Roach, Kenny Clarke, Art Blakey? So you could unlearn every nuance of timing, every delicacy of pressure, in some college of musical stupidity, for the amusement of drunken high school students celebrating Prom Night with an orgy of vandalism?

Soon enough the musicians are bound to come to know firsthand the melodrama of commercialism they always heard about, the one they thought they could evade. They will live through episodes of glad-handing tactics that abruptly turn cutthroat, arm-twisting at clandestine meetings: "We'll sign you if you get rid of the bass player, I know he's your friend, kid, hey listen it's a tough racket." Purloined visions: a tape-recorded dream journey (it was the bass player's masterpiece) will be sold to offshore pirates, released under another name. The songwriter will end up signing away the publishing rights to a so-called independent production company: "That's another term for criminal conspiracy to defraud." Musicians give in to delusions that will quickly become disappointments: "They promised us the Northeast! The tour, the album, the whole thing!" "They gave the song to the other group!" "They claim they own the tapes!" "They cancelled next Friday!"

You could break your head against the wall. Or else learn how to play the game, make a few bucks even if you have to submit to constant humiliations, agree to wear costumes, undergo foolish haircuts, pose for promo shots designed to make the group look like the new contenders challenging the Lovin' Spoonful or Paul Revere and the Raiders. "That kind of thing is selling, what more do you need to know? You don't like the suits? You prefer those suits the guys wear that do the mopping up? Look at the numbers. Look how many units of that record that you hate so much are moving off the shelf. What do you guys think, this isn't a business? What are we doing, are we here to lose money? You tell me, I want to know what you think. Are we here to lose money? Give me a break please, I bust my chops for you and you talk about free expression? What free expression? The studio time doesn't cost me? The promo doesn't cost me? Tell it to the rack-jobbers."

10

Central Park West (Side B)

[C UE: THE BEACH BOYS, "SURFER GIRL," RECORDED JUNE 1963.]
Records are perfect and self-contained. The events they memorialize are messy, unfinished, often not events at all but slivers of possibility salvaged from everyday chaos. Somehow out of that process a song was made to stand for someone, and years later the song—all that tangibly survives—has more the effect of blotting out than of reviving what was once a presence. The sixteen-year-old boy that I was has become distant enough that I know him chiefly by what he collected: tastes, mental associations, recollections of thwarted impulses, fragments of conversation committed to memory. I study the record collection left to me by that individual, looking for bits of the lost live moments that may still adhere to it, and find just as frequently the fantasy literature into which he tended to translate those moments even as they were happening. It was the songs above all that facilitated that translation.

This is the description of a movie, a tenth-grade epic: Susie, the classmate I have admired in silence, smiles in the stairwell. She's started talking to me in the middle of the noise of students shuffling between Geometry and European History. The conversation is rushed because we're heading toward different floors, and I have to ask her to repeat everything she just said anyway. I've scarcely heard a word. The smile drowned out everything else.

Time freezes. The few instants that constitute this "event" are carefully spliced out of the reality that framed them and carried home to be projected repeatedly, like the traveler's eight-millimeter footage of his trip to Niagara Falls. The soundtrack—the result of spontaneous association—is the Beach Boys' "Surfer Girl." Why not? The great American smile that Susie beams at me if only for a second radiates as much as I can imagine of easy good nature, free enthusiasm, liveliness and generosity and roguish invitation. Perfected in memory it becomes an ocean, the only ocean. Everything I ever wanted is standing in front of me; and somewhere a jukebox button in my brain is being pushed:

> Girl, surfer girl,
> My little surfer girl.

Is it the blonde hair, the frank eyes, the hint of teasing laughter? The universe's hidden door has opened. There are no limits on what is being offered.

I do not know who she is. I will never know who she is. I will study a thousand marks and signs and traces.

Until now I had not properly grasped what songs are used for: to stop moments from passing. The song is the place where perfection stays. Outside the song is where it evaporates. Because the moment is already going; it's gone. I can't really remember what it was like, only that it was a shared space one degree removed from this world, and that we both knew it. I want to continue to be there. A song can help because, when used as intended, songs suspend time. If necessary they rewire time to make what didn't happen happen. It's a game devised by one of those mad scientists who are always on the lookout for another way to resurrect a lost loved one.

Why music? Because like that moment on the stairs it's one degree removed from everything else.

[Cue: Gene Pitney, "It Hurts To Be In Love," released September 1964.]
"Everything else" encompasses uncompleted science projects, pop quizzes on the consequences of the Congress of Vienna, a medicine

cabinet supplied with skin creams and foot powder, the sexual terminology buried in manuals in which "marital fulfillment" is mapped with the ponderous exactitude of a textbook on hydraulics, and the sexual exploits, real or imagined, whose details are exchanged among classmates like combat stories from the front in a war defined largely by long periods of reconnaissance and uneasy truce. Where have you been? Where will you get to? Who knows who to believe, or what side anybody is on?

The outside world is apparently obsessed with young romance; from songs and movies you could figure that no one had anything better to contemplate than the first kisses or last good-byes of teenage lovers. At the same time it is determined to make it as difficult as possible for them to realize their calling. No actual place or time has been set aside for lovemaking that can only take place against the most demeaning odds. Kids spend their waking hours scheming, however fantastically, to bring the right person to the right place, at the hour when the apartment will be unguarded, the parents out shopping, the other parents still unaware that Music Club was cancelled; or else they simply fantasize about situations that are sadly far from being realized. At best they make do with humiliating constraints and ungrateful time frames, and even in a moment of triumph may find that the most humiliating constraints are the ones hard-wired into their own or their date's nervous system, the inner limits they find out about only when they try to go beyond them.

All of this is what Gene Pitney has attempted to express in his record "It Hurts To Be In Love": and when sung words have gone as far as they can go, a flute solo comes in to embody what is truly unsayable. The flute is there to annihilate the whole thicket of uncomfortable details: its sustained insistent tone is the voice of passion, declaring that it wants to erase whatever gets in its way.

[Cue: The Zombies, "She's Not There," U.S. release November 1964.]
Hearing the Zombies singing "She's Not There" for the first time—

> *Well, no one told me about her,*
> *The way she lies,*

Well, no one told me about her,
The way she cries—

it seems unprecedented that a song should dare to suggest a complicated cruelty that is somehow coldly beautiful and to turn that complex of jangled response into something like an intellectual statement. Intellectual? Well, angular, let's say. Deliberately asymmetrical. To be discussed: Can the singer be said to love her at all in any commonly understood sense? If what the song states cannot adequately be paraphrased, does that mean it isn't stating as much as I think it is? There is nothing to be done except play the record again and join in the nods of approval at how exactly judged each of its moves is. It's either think about the Zombies or think, fruitlessly, about her again. She just left the room.

"Just left the room": a single fragmentary element of that high school geography built up out of "poked her head into the room and went out again without saying anything," "turned the corner at the end of the hall and must have deliberately gone the other way," "didn't show up for school and nobody could say exactly what was going on." Or knew and wouldn't say. Or hadn't told how they actually felt because it might be taken the wrong way. Life resembles "Surfer Girl" less and less these days. Where are the promised twilight kisses and long walks by the ocean, the color-saturated happiness that translated movie romances into the Beach Boys' falsetto harmonies?

To know her at all is to engage with the stories about the suicide attempts, the stories about the madly controlling parents. There's the night of barging through a door at a party to find the loved one in a stranger's bed, the humiliated retreat with its toxic mix of jealousy and shame—nothing like social bungling to tear at the soul—and then another night when, as we lie together for the first and only time, the telephone is ringing and someone is knocking drunkenly on the door of the bedroom where we've taken refuge—her mother is hysterical and threatening to call the police, everything has all at once gotten mysteriously crisis-ridden—and then everything, just as mysteriously, is torn apart forever.

"She's Not There" exists both to certify that such things are real and to translate them into a tolerable, ordered, limited form: canned suffering.

[Cue: Reprise, The Zombies, "She's Not There."]
Some records have to be played more than once.

"She's Not There" marks a new era. New eras begin frequently these days, sometimes two or three times a week. Ever since the summer of the Beatles' *A Hard Day's Night* and the Beach Boys' "I Get Around" there hasn't been time to look back. There are laboratories scattered around the world where experiments in sound are being conducted, and we are constantly testing the results. No sooner do you get accustomed to the Supremes' "Where Did Our Love Go" then you're given Dusty Springfield's "Wishin' and Hopin'," the Animals' "House of the Rising Sun" (a folk song about a whorehouse becomes a four-minute plus Top 40 single as if to exemplify the sheer unlikeliness of the ways in which pop music is changing), Manfred Mann's "Do Wah Diddy Diddy," the Drifters' "Under the Boardwalk," Martha and the Vandellas' "Dancing in the Street," and Ronny and the Daytonas' "G.T.O."—and only a month or so has passed. Everybody is having a great time.

Little operas, little engines. *Tristan and Isolde* in the palm of your hand; the California coastline in 2:03 flat. The Kinks, the Rolling Stones, and the Zombies all hit the charts in the same month, mixed in with the Larks ("The Jerk"), the Righteous Brothers ("You've Lost That Lovin' Feeling"), Marvin Gaye ("How Sweet It Is"), the Temptations ("My Girl"), the Impressions ("People Get Ready"), and Junior Walker ("Shotgun"). Every note of every one of them requires close personal attention. Each of our days engages with the ongoing impact, talking it over, laying it on those who haven't heard it yet (*"What?"*), test-driving it at different hours and with each shift in emotional climate. Does it work? How does it work? What is it doing? How can I properly express what it's doing? It's blowing me away. It's knocking me out. It's destroying me. It's tearing me up.

Then Bob Dylan—that folkie with the uningratiating voice—surfaces transformed from the folk revival world that had never really gone away. Steve Cropper, the guitarist of Booker T. and the MGs, says in an interview that he drove off the road the first time he heard "Like a Rolling Stone" on the radio. It sounded that different. Dylan certainly gives everybody enough to talk about: hours and hours on the implications of every phrase. He's proposing a new listening experience, in which the words nail the listener's thoughts even as they form, derail them by punning on the listener's own hidden intentions, the ones he hasn't expressed even to himself. If you're not in the mood it can be like being sucker punched by a peculiarly unreliable kind of wise guy.

The sense is that everything is coming out in the open. An inevitable process has started. Whatever was hidden one day will be exposed the next, including ourselves. Once we tested records; from now on they'll test us.

[Cue: The Impressions, "Gypsy Woman," released 1963.]

Late at night—after (as Chuck Jackson sang) "the blue shadows fall all over town"—a different playlist kicks in. The songs suitable for midnight seem mostly to be written by Curtis Mayfield ("Gypsy Woman," "I'm the One Who Loves You," "Nothing Can Stop Me," "Um Um Um Um Um Um," "Minstrel and Queen") or Smokey Robinson ("My Girl Has Gone," "Don't Look Back," "A Fork in the Road," "I've Got to Dance to Keep from Crying," by way of leading up to the ultimate lament, "Ooo Baby Baby"). These are sounds made to order for lacerated would-be lovers who derive strange satisfaction from savoring the loss of what was scarcely possessed. It doesn't help that the songs are so beautiful, holding out the promise that to surrender blindly to them is to experience the equivalent (in some peculiar analogue world) of surrender to the beloved. Instead they go nowhere, again and again. It's like the scene in *The Girl Can't Help It* where Tom Ewell self-pityingly plays Julie London's "Cry Me a River" only to find Julie herself—in costumes and postures borrowed from her album covers—materializing in every corner of his apartment. You plunge off a bridge into water that turns out not to be there: it's just a rug. In the privacy of your own home you begin to approximate one of those guys you've seen in the bars, the ones who return night after night, decade after decade, to that jukebox on the Street of the Lost where Ray Charles sings, in perpetuity, "Drown in My Own Tears." He's digging into his pocket for another quarter. "Say, mister, I guess you must really like that song."

For Susie, when she comes over to the apartment, I can't play either "Surfer Girl" or "Gypsy Woman": or rather, I do play them and it doesn't mean a thing to her. She likes them well enough but for her they're superfluous. She wants something harsher, more sarcastic, a real challenge to the status quo. She doesn't need some singer's mimicry of pain; she's actually hurting. The fact of her discomfort with existing—it's what there finally is to talk about with her—becomes a way of judging how real other things are. Is a given song worthy of her pain, is it devoid of even a gleam of hope? She requires a music of scars and overcast skies, a music serious enough to match a gaze that discerns every form of joy and beauty except the ones that might belong to her share.

Having fallen in love with the person she momentarily seemed to be, I continue to look in her direction in the hope of coaxing the illusion back to life. It isn't difficult to do, sometimes for hours at a time. She has mastered the art of mirroring other people's desires. Or can that be called art which is more an intuitively chosen doom? Her perfect glance is an assurance of mutual communication and effortless good will. Not only are we on the same wavelength, but there is no other wavelength. The twinkling grin signals complicity in a conspiracy of hipsters and rule-breakers. It is her peculiar happenstance to embody for every guy who comes near her the girl of his dreams. Her presence makes the party a delight.

Youth as image of renewal: that's how they see her (especially the older ones), and before they've even crossed the room they've got their hopes up about how life is going to be changed by talking to her, sharing a cigarette, moving out on the fire escape to have a chance for a more private conversation. They've never met anybody so sensitive. They've never met anybody who made the idea of hanging out seem quite so promising, as if they'd been waiting a lifetime to unburden themselves to her. She'll understand, and they'll understand her in return. I continue to believe it too. I would like to explain to her how thoroughly, when Marvin Gaye sings about how "each hurt just makes my love stronger than before," he seems to be describing my feelings about her. Instead I announce, probably not for the first time, what an utterly amazing record "Ain't That Peculiar" is; how complex; how modern; embodying how unobtrusively what formal perfection.

[Cue: "Baila Bailando," from the soundtrack of Dark Passage, *1947.]*

What wasn't meant to happen will warp instead into a tortuous attachment, mixing intellectual friendship and nagging obsessiveness. A dissatisfaction that seems both inevitable and of no imaginable use mutates into something that resembles treasured companionship. What we do is smoke cigarettes together. It's a philosophical act, a way of coming to grips with the real. We stare each other down and smoke. No small talk: the subject is dreams or death or the myth of the double, the problem of language, the nature of reality. That last one is our favorite; when we get to the part about being and nonbeing we're practically vibrating. Our vocabulary thrills us. I dig up sentences she'll like—in Baudelaire, De Quincey, Rimbaud, Burroughs—as if swapping aphorisms about nothingness were a muted but undeniable sexual kick.

My secret hope is to amuse her for a while, to ease her into an admission that, at least in principle, happy endings do sometimes occur. The lovers go to Brazil to savor a rum-flavored sunset; from the window of their downtown hotel the streets become a carnival of wit and splash; the world is as green as the line of whimsical trees bordering a toy city in a Paul Klee painting. We could begin all over again. And then the music starts: like in *Dark Passage* when Lauren Bacall walks into the South American dive after how many years of anxious separation to find Bogart waiting for her, just as the house band strikes up the rumba that signifies life itself.

Shortcuts don't work. Isn't such easy musical bliss only for those who have already reached their port? Bogart and Bacall paid for that reunion with sacrifice. People have to make music theirs through harder labor than savoring the fadeout of a 1947 Warner Brothers picture. "You've got to earn it," sing the Temptations.

[Cue: The Zombies, "Tell Her No," released February 1965.]
The world hasn't even started yet—the world that in the chrysalis stage of humans is an inseparable mingling of personal desire and public destiny. The dance is not until next week but everything has changed simply by the knowledge that that night will arrive. Anticipation and dread: anticipation of bliss, dread that bliss will somehow be forestalled, stolen. Everybody loves everybody, everybody suspects everybody. All the boys are jealous of each other. Even their friendliest dealings are marked with the suspicion that the other would never hesitate to seduce the girl of his friend's dreams. When the Zombies sing "tell her no"—tell her you won't go into the bedroom with her, because your best friend really likes her—it sounds like the most forlorn of hopes. That would be expecting far too much. Courtesy is for the old, the established, those who have already gotten what they need. The young have no choice but to be ruthless.

Now is when the apartment off the park reveals itself as the friend of lovers, the place where they can gather in the evenings. By a happy chance, the plan divides into two wings. The walls are thick, the soundproofing nearly absolute; and after the parents retire to their side—early because my father, as morning man, must be up at dawn every day—the space on the other side of the barrier is inherited by the young. Its alcoves and antechambers, its tiny nineteenth-century maid's room off the kitchen, provide multiple opportunities for evasions and experiments, while the others hang around near the record player in the grand ballroom that is the living room.

Some must always watch while others slip away. Which couple will be the first to abscond? Every occasion is a different lottery. Under the surfaces of friendship lurk the calculation and urgency of the obsessed gambler prepared to throw his life away for a single chance. The hurdles are both large and small; nothing is trivial, or rather it is exactly the trivial things that trip you up. The fear of being understood too well makes even the most intimate get-togethers uneasy. It would not do to have your naïvety exposed, for example by making it obvious that you haven't quite grasped the double meaning of that Stones lyric. A free-floating contentiousness probes neighboring defenses. They look for anything that resembles an advantage in the sexual war of all against all. It is called a party.

Find a partner and the laboratory of love can still be cruel. In this school the instructor often knows nearly as little as the student. They fumble with each other's bodies, bruise and chafe each other in their excitement. They must learn to bite either not so hard, or harder. Layers of shyness and hesitation must be stripped away like coats of paint that yield only to repeated scraping. The hooks of clothes and the complexities of condoms and diaphragms are nothing to the inner wiring of diffidence, the dull persistence of dread. Between the anticipation of pleasure and its realizing, the path is rarely as clear as they want it be. What's the encumbrance? Nerves? Habits of thought, the habit of being closed, the habit of looking away? Each runs into the inconvenient business of being a person. They try not to get in the way of their own pleasure. How blissfully easy everything would be without these words in the head, these gestures that seem almost rehearsed, these indelible distortions of memory.

[Cue: Smokey Robinson and the Miracles, "I Like It Like That," released June 1964.]

It's as if they needed different bodies, different responses, and instead must mess around with the ones they have, gigantic and labyrinthine as they are, looking for lines and passages they never knew existed. With relief they stumble upon clearings. More tentatively they negotiate zones of numbness, or find in themselves brutalities they didn't expect. Who *is* this person? Music helps, and not only because it drowns out incidental gasps and thuds. In this matter of love, music is not mere background or mood-setter, it is guide, tutor, the only true manual. It opens doors otherwise imperceptible, especially with the help of some wine and marijuana. But which music, and how applied? In dance records, if fast enough, we can lose track of our baggage of premonitions. Slowing it down by imperceptible gradations can provide an incomparably slow unwinding—slow like the tempo of evolutionary change, like the erosion of rocks by sea-wind—to the speed of love.

High school students. We gather in our bodies in the darkened living room, armed with beers and Kools, trying to discern ritual pattern in what the music attempts to create for us. It begins, signaled by the simple, almost somber unaccompanied guitar figure that opens "I Like It Like That," just before Smokey comes in singing in a tone so attenuated it's like it's being pulled out of him:

> Clap hands now, everybody
> We're gonna have some fun tonight
> We're gonna sing, shout, and knock ourselves out
> Everything's gonna be all right

"Everything's gonna be all right": the tone acknowledges that "everything" is in fact threatened, steeped in potential grief. You could lose so much. Never mind. "Everything"—it won't take long, it's already happening—is finally going to come out of its shadows, out of its closet, ushered in with murmurs and handclaps and interjections of "Smokey!" This record is precious to us because it lays down an order:

> Every man find himself a woman
> She doesn't have to be a beauty queen
> If when she holds you tight she makes you feel all right
> Every man that I've ever seen
> Has got to say I like it like that

Somebody had to say it. It is the signal, the gong-note for the dimming of lights. The lovers find their way out of the central circle into whatever scattered spaces they can find among chairs and alcoves. They leave the imagined fire around which the crowd gathers—the "campfire light" of the Impressions' "Gypsy Woman," light by which the singer caught sight of

> a lovely woman in motion
> with hair as dark as night

—to venture into darkness that promises an intimacy beyond further telling. The story is to be read between the notes, in the spaces made by gasps, sighs, a sob barely held back.

[Cue: Smokey Robinson and the Miracles, "I'll Try Something New," *recorded 1962; reissued 1964 on* The Miracles' Greatest Hits from the Beginning.*]*

The voice permits us to imagine a sea into which you might fall to die and be reawakened, a sky that is home. In the new sky you say goodbye to everything, beginning with your name. The world is cleared of hangers, lists, buttons, vents, hooks; no more wires; the memoranda are erased by water; the voice goes and lets go. Permission is given to breathe deep.

The most mysterious of these voices carve cities. With eyes closed we're moving through skylines, canals, tremulous walkways. Curtis Mayfield, Marvin Gaye, Barbara Lewis, Martha Reeves, Smokey Robinson. These are planets. A shape-shifting is made audible. Stippled ceilings, carved bridges where they come to rest: those are momentary resting points before the next somersault. The sinuosity of the vocal line is establishing a model for the whole body, for the spirit: learn to unfurl and extend, it's saying. Achieve the form of cloth in wind; of reed swaying in current; of flame. The voice is on fire. Hear what it sounds like for shimmying flame tongues to lap at the edges of night. With what delicacy matter is consumed. As if being could escape into the note, soar beyond itself, yet remain a body. Listen again to Smokey as he vaults inside his own sound, or (another way) moves in the crystal vault his sound makes. The shuddering flute-sounds *are* him, are spun from him. He sighs in tones. The gasps have pitch. This is a music of transformations.

If Smokey reveals in an interview that he writes happy songs when he feels sad and sad songs when he feels happy, it confirms what the songs have already said: "I've got to dance to keep from crying." By the same token the tears embodied in the upper falsetto reaches of "Ooo Baby, Baby" would be in some sense a deep laughter, a surfacing of joy too intense to be expressed as anything but sorrow.

Their ears still ringing with the noise of tambourines, lulled by bass and chorus, the masquers disperse. They are intent on losing some further layer of virginity somewhere in the realms (now broadened by darkness) that lie between the refrigerator and the television set and the coffee table, realms to be made over as much as possible into that "Venus or Mars" of which Smokey sings in "I'll Try Something New," where "every day we can play / on the Milky Way," into whose midst he emerges from the heart of the subaqueous:

> *I will bring you a flower from the floor of the sea*
> *To wear in your hair.*

We do our best to swim along. Become fluid as sound. Find the cadence that permits spontaneous chant.

"Waiting for the rising sun," the Impressions are singing (it's "Gypsy Woman" yet again) as the ashtrays are cleared, the pillows put back in place, the last beer can disposed of before dawn breaks through and the adults begin their rounds. It's clean-up time. The generations barely avoid brushing against each other in the brief interval between shifts. Soon the music will start up again, the morning radio bringing early word of four-car pile-ups and failed missile pacts. Dad is already on the air, well into his day before the rest of them even open their eyes. By midday he'll be lunching on escargots and martinis, or sitting through the Monday ratings run-down, maybe hearing about someone else losing time slot or salary or billing through the whimsical judgments of corporate decision-making informed by implacable marketing science.

By then the musicians from my brother's band, the Kingbees, may have drifted up from downtown or down from uptown to hang out and listen to playbacks of their gig the night before, testing the effectiveness of their arrangement of Ernie K-Doe's "A Certain Girl" or John Lee Hooker's "Bottle Up and Go" before riffling through stacks of promo records to find the gold: the new Van Dykes release, the new Etta James, the new Otis, the new Burt Bacharach song sung by Jackie De Shannon. They're preparing for one night while recovering from another. The blinds are drawn to keep the sun out. Is it too soon for night?

[Cue: The Kingbees, "Four in the Morning," unreleased demo, 1965.]

It's summer. Another year passed while they were listening to records. The younger kids—high school's over with by now, though autumn still seems far off—will gather around the musicians to study their moves and provide an audience. Joel manages a constant play of metamorphoses—starting with name: he is now Bishop, because somebody thought a cloak he wore once made him look like a bishop—and his role changes hang on the adjustment of an ascot or medallion, an unexpected guava-colored splash, a modulation of accent or facial hair that changes a Prussian officer into a Dodge City gambler. The effects are completed as often as not with wardrobe salvaged from the back of the closet, the castoffs of four decades, the Shriner's tie, the golf hat with the scarlet tassel, the leather driving gloves. The characters he mimes—not so much impersonated as freshly invented—reel in and out of existence so fast it would seem rehearsed except for that air of rough exuberance that proves it's all improvised.

Somewhere nearby where he can reach it is a cascading pile of 45s, scooped up from among a dozen such piles: René Hernández, the Manhattans, Gene Ammons, Albert Collins, Lord Invader, Eddie Jefferson, Buck Owens, Sugar Pie De Santo, chosen almost randomly from hundreds of instances. He's just remembered the name of an accordion player who died in Missouri last month with all his recordings out of print. This morning, while seeming to watch a *Jungle Jim* rerun, while doing the things that musicians do (wait around until three, listen to the tapes, wait for Mike to call, remember to pick up some soda on the way out), he was thinking about how chord changes affect the space in a room. Now, in the guise of a melodica version of "Ruby My Dear," he is sketching a tonal portrait of our grandmother's childhood in Hungary.

These improvisations mingle with pieces of his life in these last few complicated years that seem to have moved too fast to track: the time he played drums behind the Cadillacs (of "Speedo" fame) at a high school dance, the summer he was supposed to graduate from high school but ended up in Los Angeles listening to Teddy Edwards and Billy Higgins at the Venice West, or catching Dexter Gordon in the West Coast production of *The Connection,* and then back home where he played a gig doubling on drums and vibes on a floating bar while attending summer school by day. Sitting up listening to Alan Freed and Jocko; hanging out at Indian Joe's record store in the West 40s; picking up mandolin and a little banjo and learning folk songs from an old Communist; learning about African jazz from Hugh Masekela and Cuban jazz from Eddie Palmieri, not through formal study but just by hanging out; managing a movie theater on Avenue C and getting badly beaten by some locals who didn't like the company he was keeping; in the hospital and then on an island off the Baja coast, getting crazy; getting high; shooting a pistol off in an empty house; driving through Mississippi singing Hank Williams songs in road houses; watching a movie in the snow at a drive-in in deep winter. The scenes come out in a different order every time.

He demonstrates the total malleability of surfaces. Disruption is life. His musical transformations are of the same order. He segues from suggestions of Jack Teagarden to Uncle Dave Macon, from tourist lounge calypso singer to a scatting vocal setting of Sonny Rollins's solo on "Strode Rode" to a fragment of an Alban Berg-like wail of atonal Central European anguish in mock German, with spoken interludes ranging from punch-drunk prizefighter to George Sanders welcoming you to Saturday night at Club Macumba. Everything truly alive is in some sense made up on the spot, out of whatever happens to be around. The band is rehearsing, making themselves acceptable for the club audience, hoping to stimulate some airplay for their second single, but that audience will never see the chaos that gets edited out. This is perhaps the real artwork, but it dissolves in air.

[Cue: Ambient recording, chanting, finger cymbals, bongos, and other; Central Park, April 1967.]

The apartment is littered with accumulations of what was recently new. Falling into place year by year, they form momentarily startling combinations. For some time now the culture has been about juxtaposition. Pieces are thrown out like cards in a fast-moving game whose rules are reconfigured at each hand: the new Godard, the new Lichtenstein, the new *Realist,* the new Beatles single, the new Tom Wolfe article, the new Ginsberg poem, the new Sam Fuller movie, the topless bathing suit, the solarized publicity photo, the Green Beret who said "I QUIT!" on the cover of *Ramparts,* the newest and even more absurd-looking long-haired band to hit the Village club circuit—is it the Barbarians, the Mojo Men?

It's not so much what things are as what they border on. Boundaries melt: clubs, scenes, happenings, the Bob Dylan album incongruously displayed at Womrath's, John Lennon on acid, revolutionaries marching on the Selective Service offices, drag queens on guitar and bass, all are to be mixed together. What comes out of that will be the new synthesis, the spine reconfigured, perception alchemically remodeled to conform to the swivelings and drippings of the natural world. Who would have foreseen that inanimate objects—like that smooth rock you turned over and over in your hand for two hours the other night—would turn out to be *reading matter* as extensive as the Encyclopaedia Britannica? Take a feather—the one you found in a drawer, souvenir of a trip to Florida—think about everything that's going on there. You could spend years on it. And music? Every tone's a divine aperture. Every time the hand moves over the guitar strings you see arcs, flowerings, widening rings, flamboyant geysers.

One morning, home from college on a visit, I slip through the Gothic movie set of the lobby to meet some friends in the park. It's just after Easter. The Sheep Meadow hums with tambourines and flutes and bongos. Clusters of newfangled gypsies and saddhus and ecstatics newly arrived from the coasts of Nebraska or Ohio mingle with the dross of dorms and crash pads, the children of Upper West Side intellectuals and suburban CPAs, veterans of music festivals and socialist work camps, drug dealers, photojournalists, old poets. The new air on the rim where the meadow dips: we'd like to carry it away with us to wherever we're spending the night.

On those nights when we find ourselves hanging out at the apartment again, a group of us like the "old times" of fourteen months ago, we settle back into that space like a palace of slightly shopworn ex-

pectations. Depending on the mix of chemicals, the scenes have disconcerting ways of dissolving—or not dissolving—into each other.
One drug meets another in the hall and it's like two worlds staring at
each other in mutual incomprehension: the opiated and the psy-
chotropic, looking for a few common definitions to negotiate the distance. Go to the kitchen for some orange juice and you come back to
a different world already. The gods and goddesses of the night sky sit
around in the living room, lost in smoke and bowls of crackers, awash
in wine and alto saxophone. They discuss ancient history: what was
happening forty minutes ago. There's thunder. It's daytime, after all:
they'd forgotten. It got dark at midday. "The six-day war began and
Donald was freaking out on acid and thought it was World War III. It
took a long time to calm him down." "And then her friend couldn't remember how to talk, and when other people talked to show him how
it's done it only made things worse. He stood in the middle of the
kitchen with his mouth open, unable to form words, terrified." "He
put on *Sergeant Pepper* because he thought it would be like hanging
out with friends. Later he said he never heard anything so full of hate
as the voices of the Beatles."

Play something soothing at times like this, it's too early in the
morning for the Mingus or the Ornette Coleman. We surely don't
need the Stones, or any of those Dylan records: they've been playing
around for so long that you never know what unpleasant personal association they're going to remind someone of. "Ruby Tuesday" might
turn out to be a trigger for just that experience you were hoping
you'd never have to relive. Try some flute music; a sweet singer; something Brazilian, so the words won't get in the way. The idea is to calm
down enough to face going out on the street. "What? Outside? I don't
think so, I want to stay here." "*But this isn't our space.*"

So we slip into the blinding sun of that other New York inhabited
by people who have a different sense of what time it is, people who go
about their business apparently without feeling like they're wading
through chaos at every step. It's so ordinary on the street—smell
those Sabrett hot dogs—that it's almost festive. It isn't bad out here!
Or is that because the cab driver is playing the Joe Bataan cover of
"Gypsy Woman," the Latin version that makes it sound happy instead

of mournful? And follows it up with Johnny Colon's "Boogaloo Blues," with its lighthearted story about a hippie chick offering some free love while under the influence ("LSD has a hold on me . . . LSD has a hold on me"), to insinuate that all you needed finally was to relax a bit for the whole set-up to show a mellower face?

[Cue: Tim Hardin, "It'll Never Happen Again," released July 1966.]

For the young, each intimately known individual is a general term. When they talk among themselves they parse the qualities of Steveness, Janet-ness, Meg-ness. Every friend and rival embodies some irreplaceable value. When a person changes radically it's like the death of a word or an idea. Now Susie begins to change, or is it only that we begin to see her differently? She had gone missing—sequestered by parents, sometimes incommunicado under doctor's orders, submitting more or less voluntarily to treatment—but she emerges back into our midst now, and when we have occasion to go around town together she still seems central to what we take for our world—the perfect ornament of the time, an emblematic figure like those long-haired love goddesses and runaway flower children with whom movies and magazines are full. She's still capable of a stoned giggle that makes it seem as if the world could be reinvented right where we sit, and a glance of penetrating sincerity that suggests it would be worth the upheaval.

She's part of people's histories, and the history goes on. They continue to fall in love with her, or talk about the time when they did. But a new note of impatience comes out when people talk about her, a reluctance to get too close. What is it with her, anyway? Everybody has a theory or an example. Some of them they even discuss with her: "But you end up going around in circles." Nothing, beginning with herself, will ever quite satisfy her. At a certain point—as if she was obeying a hypnotic suggestion, the implanted orders of a malevolent doctor—she turns on herself. Fun isn't enough fun, the revolution is not revolutionary enough, and the fact that boys have a predictable habit of falling for her isn't, finally, helpful.

There are those moments late in the evening when her face changes suddenly, like a mask dropping. The look that surfaces shuts out every other look: the look turned inward to devour itself, the smile turned bitter and self-mocking. The exchanges go around and around and they end in silence. The story has already been written and has an unsatisfactory ending. Everybody's her therapist. "Why can't you resign yourself," they might be saying, "for your own good, to be the person I once imagined you to be? Submit to being saved: be the lost child rescued, the invalid restored to perfect health and capable finally of enjoying springtime at the sanitarium, the victim of Mesmerism from whom the hypnotic spell has been lifted, the woman brought literally back to life like at the end of the Carl Dreyer film. Some day you'll smile again. Look in the mirror: can you see it, that preliminary glow of returning vitality?" Everybody wants to help.

I'm still hearing descriptions of her in songs, but they're different songs. She's the one who "knows what it's like to be dead" in the Beatles song. She is Dylan's sad eyed lady. She's encoded in the way Tim Hardin sings "all the pain, always rain" when recalling "our first affair," in his characteristic tone of heroin-flavored tenderness steeped in angry suspicion. She'll always be there, in every subsequent replay. Why do the songs attach themselves to her? Does she require that extension, that filling out, to make up for a certain sense of hollowness, as if everything about her that you could apprehend were an elaborate disguise of what perhaps you didn't want to apprehend because it would shatter a cherished image?

[Cue: The Flying Machine, "Baltimore Oriole," rehearsal tape, New York City, July 1966.]

My brother is by now involved with a new band that formed out of the wreckage of the Kingbees, who broke up after their single didn't chart. This time the material is mostly original, written by a young songwriter who's just come to town, a childhood friend of the guitarist. He already has a whole catalogue of finished songs, and no one doubts that these are "real" songs, the kind that can go anywhere in the world without having to be explained or hyped. A small circle forms around the band; we go to the Night Owl night after night to hear the same songs, anticipating, in the strange way that fans have, that our own lives will be uplifted if this group—our team—can succeed.

Susie goes to hear them and is immediately fascinated by the song-writer. James is eighteen; his air of bashful self-containment masks a quick intelligence; he writes sweet and melancholy ballads that suggest a condition of mourning for a life barely lived yet. When he sings Hoagy Carmichael's "Baltimore Oriole," he could be serenading her in the only way that seems appropriate. It's a song for somebody who's absent, who left the nest: "Bring her back home, 'cause home ain't home without her warbling." Always the perfect listener, she's found something she wants to listen to.

He's written a song about the mental hospital where he spent some time not too long ago, and with its mix of comic mockery and self-pity it might have been written for her. They sit quietly together and discuss modes of sadness, retreat, loss, as if together they were going to attain a perfect philosophical understanding. He wants to study biochemistry, get to the bottom of the chains of transmissions that we're caught in. She loves his seriousness. "What's with the two of them?" "They seem to recognize each other." Or is it that she sees in him a sorrow improved upon, made livable, even (if such a thing can be) capable of soothing? There's a relief in seeing them together, even if it's tinged with an ember of jealousy that refuses to quit; someone else is taking over the responsibility of keeping her interested in being alive.

So for a time—just a few months really, but time seems to expand for that little while—a feeling of what could almost be optimism takes hold. Success is at hand. Music really will save the world, in the first place by saving the musicians who create it. New songs will be written, sorrow will inspire the art by which it will in turn be healed. Isn't this what each of us has been trying to do however tentatively, to transmute anger and self-loathing and uncertainty, splinters and exposed nails, into the magic feature-length eight-millimeter dream adventure, the magic twelve-page poem assembled from fragments of William Blake and William Burroughs, the magic collage of odd pictures and headlines ripped out of magazines, take-out menus, match packs? Only find the form and you can go across the threshold. The world will be saved by technique, by the deftly placed note that makes the whole tune inevitable.

[Cue: The Rolling Stones, "2000 Light Years from Home," released December 1967.]

Six months later the comings and goings are more hurried, the music caught more on the wing: pieces of songs there isn't time to live with. The apartment's space fills with rumors of disrupted plans. The telephone keeps ringing with more complicated news for someone who isn't here right now. The small appointments and decisions are part of a larger scheme in which destinies are hoisted into place as if with giant winches and pulleys. The characters can't seem to break out of what has been scripted for them, and on top of that they've forgotten their lines. Their lives resemble music less and less, not even the music they are playing. People are condemned to their own behavior; they work at making problems for themselves, and they don't know how to stop. The sybaritic psychiatrist falls in love with his schizophrenic patient and loses his license. The seeker after Eastern wisdom allows herself to be seduced by her eighty-year-old guru only to find that he has served all her friends the same way. The grad students are enlisted by a free-associating harmonica player into his campaign to become world savior. The Jew becomes a Buddhist. The Buddhist becomes a road manager. The cameraman loses his job because of personality problems. The musician loses the only copy of the session tape in a taxi. The valedictorian from Illinois becomes a gunshot casualty of the methedrine trade. The prom queen becomes an earth mother in the hills of California. The artist's model who thought that song on *Blonde on Blonde* could have been about her becomes a call girl in another city. The movie star's illegitimate daughter takes the wrong drug by mistake and gets sick in her Columbus Avenue walkup. Snow begins to fall. Everybody has a cold that lasts forever, or is that really a cold, those shakes, those sniffles? Everybody had trouble sleeping last night and so they didn't.

The musicians all seem to have become confirmed junkies. They gorge on candy bars and wear long-sleeved shirts in July to hide the track marks. Then they decide that the negative effects of heroin can be reversed by a rigorously applied macrobiotic diet. People drive upstate to sell acid to college students and end up getting stopped by a rural highway patrol and busted on a trumped-up vagrancy charge.

Parents hire lawyers so their kids can beat drug possession raps or simply consign them to granite fortresses of psychiatry on Long Island. It's Christmas time. In midtown lounges the execs and the operators are listening to a jazzy interpretation of "Something's Gotta Give" or "Put On a Happy Face." It gets harder to separate out the overlapping conversations. "He said he'd stop." "He said he wants to come back." "She's going to be committed again." "Don't do that or I'll have to stop seeing you." "The record company said no." "If I'd known about this drug business I wouldn't have had children in the first place." "If she asks for me tell her you didn't see me, okay?"

When was the last time the pieces fit together? Was it that moment before Otis Redding's plane fell into Lake Michigan, the unanticipated disaster presaging the all too accurately anticipated ones?

[Cue: Jimmie Rodgers, "In the Hills of Tennessee," recorded December 1932.]

The gloss of the long moment when show business seemed fun—the moment I glimpse in publicity photos of my father posing with the Beatles, the Rolling Stones, Jimmy Durante, Engelbert Humperdinck, Wayne Newton—the sheer silliness of it: it gets old with surprising suddenness. Anyway, where is Jimmy Durante when you need him? How much can he help? Show biz: it was an exciting illusion sustained by the enthusiasm of the guys behind the mike. Now it gives way to what it always was, the business of money, the mechanization of playlists, the erosion of spontaneity by work rules and management-sponsored psychological profiles of the listening audience.

It must have been a very long time ago that people cobbled their own scripts together, begged or borrowed or even wrote their own jokes, ad-libbed until dawn if necessary. One afternoon my father remarks that he's tired of wearing a watch, and at that moment looks as if he's had enough of agents and promo guys and programming execs. Enough of everything perhaps except telling jokes, because there are never enough of them. Now he's begun talking about the pollution of pond water, the loss of wetlands, acid rain, the problem of nuclear waste, the diminishing quantities of kelp: "If the ocean goes, it all goes."

Once it appeared as if everyone—everyone in the family, and their chosen friends, a whole subculture of mutually agreeable people—could be lifted together to another plane. In that zone of earthly enjoyment, everything truly fun and rewarding could come into deeper focus. The possibility of fame had something to do with it, and what it could bring: banquets, awards, conversations with remarkable people, trips to hotels equipped with fountains and gardens, the best parties in the world. Our own parties—like the one when the police came at midnight after the ecstatic sequence of Sir Mack Rice and James Brown and Lee Dorsey and Booker T. and the MGs at full blast proved too much for the other inhabitants of West 77th Street—were rehearsals for some larger festival that would go on for days, weeks, years. But any worldly success would only be a natural by-product of our enthusiasm and mutual affection. We lived as if we anticipated a world of exhilarated tenderness punctuated by brilliant invention.

For every family, every group, there is a myth of continued collective ascent that at some point stops being plausible. A shared destiny splits into separate roads. The notion of a central meeting place is replaced by parallel corridors that may never reconnect. One or another straggler wakes as if from a long sweaty nap in a room he doesn't know and retraces his steps through a museum of debris that harbors forged prescriptions, pornographic novels, scars, chewed-up fingernails, confessional poems, postcards that tell too little, hotel receipts that tell too much, discarded drafts of suicide notes. Private spaces fill with clutter. People wave to each other at the airport or leave notes next to the phone. He's looking for somebody and remembers that he forgot to say where he would be. Maybe they neglected to write down the number.

The band is dissolving: the sessions went badly, the single flopped, the label withdrew its support but kept the tapes for possible future exploitation. It's a coming apart that happens in slow motion. The weather is nice but everybody feels sick. Their skin acquires a prison pallor from long afternoons of fitful nodding and sporadic talk of action, regrouping, ideas for movies, ideas for moving to a different city. Go to California. Use the existing material for a soundtrack. Get a different producer interested. With the lights dimmed, they sit around playing an old Jimmie Rodgers tune on acoustic guitars. It's a beautiful song, and it's hard to believe that anything could be wrong:

> *I know I'm going to find my paradise lost*
> *In the hills of Tennessee.*
> *I know I'm going to find my seventh heaven,*
> *It's just a cabin, my seventh heaven.*

Susie strolls over from the other side of the room and joins in tentatively on the chorus: a scene of pastoral calm.

[Cue: Country Joe and the Fish, "Not So Sweet Martha Lorraine," released 1967.]

She doesn't come around so much these days. Her face is altered, puffy from medication. Her musings on the soul and world peace sound as if she herself puts little credence in them. There's a song by Country Joe and the Fish—"Not So Sweet Martha Lorraine"—that people admit (almost guiltily) reminds them of her, almost every word of it:

> *Knowing that it's hard to find*
> *Stuff way back in her mind,*
> *Winds up spending all of her time*
> *Trying to memorize every line,*
> *Sweet Lorraine . . .*
> *Sweet lady of death wants me to die*
> *So she can come sit by my bedside and cry . . .*
> *Then softly she will explain*
> *Just exactly who was to blame*
> *For causing me to go insane*
> *And finally blow out my brain,*
> *Sweet Lorraine . . .*

She had already acquired the air of foreboding appropriate to a Gothic story, a story about a curse from which everyone wanted to save her. Now, more cruelly, she becomes the object of a blame never quite stated, as if her pliable charm, her irresistible sensitivity and sincerity were nothing more than the obverse of a face never seen but terrible to imagine, a face consumed with the need to destroy. People lose patience: too many "strange head trips." Inwardly perhaps they blame themselves. One asks himself if things would be different if he hadn't broken up with her so abruptly, another if he hadn't sold her those tabs that were possibly tainted and certainly couldn't have done her any good, another if he hadn't allowed himself to get bored with problems that he no longer felt he could do anything about, and anyway he'd found another girlfriend.

She traces wriggling floral complications down the side of a sheet of paper and fills the space between the patterns with scattered pieces of a poem that will never be properly assembled. It seems like so much effort now to get a conversation going, because every conversation had always implied that right this moment we were going to start everything again with a clean slate, that the beginning of the world was located just on the other side of an invisible line if only we could cross it. I'm wondering what she is going to be when she grows up. All she had ever succeeded in doing was embodying boundless promise. The energy needed to sustain that feels like it's fading, and in the soulful exchange of glances it's no longer clear what is being exchanged. The conversations get hard because it's difficult to end them, to find a way out.

All it takes, finally, is one moment when you really don't want to live anymore. This thing-ness involved in being a person gets to be too thick and sticky a medium. She's getting ready to step up to the turnstile where history is finally abolished. With a single gesture the whole miserable century and its train of massacres and mind-control factories can be erased. Who needs it anyway, that enormous ball of pain embodied in Bellevue and Treblinka and the United Nations? Turn off the faucet. Curtail the flow of words at their source. (They never did anything except fill up time, they never did change a thing. So much for Baudelaire and Rimbaud . . .) Nobody ever has to worry again.

She will be removed by progressive stages from the action, remanded to parental control again, taken to hospitals again, and will continue to cover sheets of paper with poems about death and flowers. Let out again to get lost again, she will eventually, on a morning like the others, take herself out of things by stepping off the platform as the train comes into the station, a few days after the Soviet invasion of Czechoslovakia.

On another day, only a year or so later, I turn on the radio and hear the song that did finally, inevitably, get written about her. It had always seemed as if she was the sort of person that people write songs about, if only because they can't think of what else to do on her behalf. James, whose songs, properly recorded at last, are now reaching an immense audience, has encapsulated her death and the band's undoing into a ballad that will be heard on every jukebox in America: "I've seen fire and I've seen rain . . . "

Right away I have a premonition that this song isn't going to go away. I'm going to be hearing it for the rest of my life, over breakfast, while waiting to take money out of the bank, while preparing for takeoff, emanating from the speakers in an otherwise almost deserted shopping plaza. Musicians who weren't born yet the day she died will open their sets with it. Rock critics will resent its success, blaming it for the sidelining of harsher, more rebellious kinds of music. Elaborate and utterly fanciful theories explaining what it's really about will be posted on the Internet. In different contexts it will find new applications, finally even coming to seem like an appropriate record to play in commemoration of the attack on my city in September 2001. It will become common property, and thus a curiously alien object, no matter how much I admired it on first hearing. It's an artifact connected to my own life. Yet for that very reason it can never possess the mystery of the other songs, the ones whose meanings I purloin and invent and remake. Every other song can be a paradise of the imagination, but not this one.

[Cue: Every Mother's Son, "Come On Down To My Boat, Baby," released June 1967.]

But all that is yet to come. We're all still fine. I walk home early through winter drizzle one morning, after a night of fine talk that enthusiastically hurtled nowhere with the help of a snowy pile of methedrine, and as I enter the dark warmth—everybody else has gone to bed—wonder at how the apartment continues to sustain itself. The space made safe for Duke Ellington, *A Midsummer Night's Dream,* and Chinese art, with its lamps and fringes, glazed blue dragon and hand-carved ibis, Roman fountain painted on an ashtray, cut-glass decanter waiting for the Spanish brandy that might fill it, continues to speak of a world of quiet enjoyment. Impossible to believe that such a world could be swept away and never seen again.

Soon enough—in a few months, as it turns out—the apartment will be vacated. Circumstances shift, the space is more than anybody needs, there's a cheaper if blandly utilitarian place on the other side of the park. The furniture will be crated, the books and dragons and souvenir ashtrays boxed, the grand hall saluted in parting. Everything is still looking pretty good. My father's radio job will be replaced by another radio job that pays better, for a while. Joel will go to California to live the life of a successful rock musician, for a while. The space is just a space. So, it's shrugged off after a thousand days or so, leaving barely a remnant—we didn't even bother to photograph things in those days, there was too much going on—except for those records that in later years will be played again and again. I will play them in the useless hope that music might body forth such a space again, complete with its smoke and talk and promises of kisses and dances and embraces. And, best of all, its future: a future like nothing that would ever exist.

The records are still around. Recorded music, unlike time, doesn't have to end. It can begin again and begin anywhere it likes. Start—or end—with a single moment isolated from everything else. My mother in the kitchen, having gotten up in the middle of the night to make my father's breakfast, listening to his show as she does each morning. It's one more of those mornings, and she's listening to a song she admits she really likes:

> *Come on down to my boat, baby,*
> *Come on down, let's sail away*

It's the summer of 1967 and the group is Every Mother's Son, sounding very much as if it were still 1964 and it were still appropriate to be producing second-tier knockoffs of early Beach Boys album cuts. The song might be the soundtrack theme for a particularly vapid beach movie in which Troy Donahue and his pals invite Suzanne Pleshette and her pals for a cruise of the Florida Keys. The fisherman's beautiful daughter stands on the dock; the boy wants to go away with her, but she's out of reach until the very end of the last reel. Mom simply likes it, no reason given or asked. Maybe she senses that this is one song that no one else will claim, a song for which indeed no claims can be made. It's a free gift—of no perceived value—beautiful in its lack of any major significance.

There they remain, those people who were us. A person lets the songs enter him and mark him. How can he foresee a moment when he will try to forget some of those songs? When some of the songs with which he is forming such close relations will become as unpleasantly familiar as a roommate to whom he told his secrets one unguarded night in his first year of college, and then decided he didn't like after all. Or as painfully familiar as a party he would prefer to forget, the one where things didn't go well, after such a fabulously promising start. Shouldn't real freedom include freedom from memory? One day it may seem more desirable to find music devoid of personal associations: songs without lyrics, songs with lyrics in languages one doesn't understand, songs that undermine the possibility of emotional bonding, songs of affectless irony, fast, cool, voluntarily vacant, songs that will remind you (you assure yourself) only of what you deliberately and judiciously put there in the first place, after you grew up and achieved a significantly heightened degree of control over your surroundings.

In any case, music brings back nothing.

RECAPITULATION

11

The Lonely Sea

DEAR RHONDA,

I write this letter from a need to describe how certain records sounded once. Apparently I can find my way back into that response only by passing through some of our common memories. Of course I could pick up the phone instead, but that probably wouldn't be a satisfactory solution. We would find ourselves stranded in the present, negotiating our distance from each other and from old music and almost forgotten events, with no easy access to moments—fairly ineffable moments to begin with—that occurred decades ago. Simply to agree on a vocabulary, a common chronology, would no doubt be a stumbling block. "I don't remember it that way." "I never experienced it that way in the first place." "That isn't when it happened." "It didn't happen." Some conversations are best conducted at one remove.

What I need to talk about is the Beach Boys. You of all people will understand the inexorability of that need. Not the Beach Boys as they are (well, these days they mostly aren't) or were, but as we imagined them, remade them from within ourselves. I need to recover parts of a world that may still exist, disguised as parts of Beach Boys songs. Inside those songs, I know, can be found whatever is left of whole days and weekends and seasons otherwise beyond retrieval. The trick is to locate the seams in the music that will permit an unraveling of what was woven into it. We hide so much in that way, as if to protect something precious (and maybe slightly threatening) from outside forces that would root it out and destroy it.

Our record collections are libraries not only of lost sensations but of lost ideas, lost theories about the nature of things. A fragile metaphysic—the gossamer speculations of a stretched-out and mostly pleasurable afternoon—was sustained, perhaps provoked, by certain chord changes. Now all we have are the chord changes. We value them inordinately because they are connected to something even more valuable that we can't quite have but can only approximate through this token, like the uniquely suggestive bit of driftwood carried home from Montauk so as to import the seaside to Second Avenue. The effect is all the more frustrating because most of these ideas and understandings were never spelled out in the first place. They hovered in the air around the record player. There was perhaps a smile of mute assent, mute because it did not seem necessary at the time to speak. Instead we communicated through our selection of tracks, like in the Godard movie where the quarreling lovers carry on a conversation by pointing to the titles of books.

"You of all people will understand." What a presumptuous and no doubt misguided statement. Probably you have only a faint idea of what the Beach Boys meant to me even back then (aside, that is, from what I claimed, vociferously, that they meant to me); just as I must rely on imagination to tease out hints of what, really, they meant to you. Two people focus simultaneously on the same object—let it be "Don't Worry Baby"—and are sure they have attained a shared knowledge. Facile assumption, extrapolation, inspired guesswork: that's all such knowledge counts for. The intuitive certainties of romance are extended to adjacent phenomena, initiating the possibility of an eroticized world characterized by the glistening transparency we detected in "Catch a Wave" or "Don't Back Down." To play those records—set those particular sound waves in motion—was perhaps our way of letting the air itself participate in our lovemaking.

To love is to share: that's what we've wanted to believe, and so the emblematic gesture of our lives—all of our lives—has been to play records for one another. What was enjoyed in solitude was never enough. Listening became authentic only when two or more people participated in it. Our eyes confirmed, with locked glances, what our ears absorbed in common: a disembodied mandala, displayed momentarily in the Museum of the Air Between Us.

So lovers need music more than anyone. Any other form would be too gross to suggest the implications they breathe in and out almost casually. Do you remember lying on the floor lost in each other's eyes as we heard, for the thousandth time but as if the first time, the Beatles singing "Things We Said Today"? The intensity with which we pretended that our own immediate reality was embodied in "we" and "today"—they were singing about us! right at this indelible moment!—was compounded by the simultaneous realization that while this moment was fleeting, was already evaporating in the instant we became aware of it, the record would always be there. Years later it would be the reliquary of a union otherwise dissolved. A song becomes sacred to the memory of a kiss, or at least that is the way a fourteen-year-old girl might record it in her diary. The first premonitions, by the young, of the horror of time's passage are as beautiful as carnival masqueraders. Flashbacks—the kind accompanied in movies by soft focus and a dense cluster of violins—are anticipated like parties. Won't it be fun to have a past? To be haunted by the smoke curling from long-extinguished cigarettes? To be launched into inexhaustible meditation by the opening bars of a once familiar song?

The Beatles, of course, belonged to everyone; that was their peculiarity. The Beach Boys by contrast suggested a more rarefied indulgence. To enter their domain fully involved an initiation. Not that they were hidden: they were rather, at the outset, the very emblem of obviousness. Our journey consisted of finding, in the heart of that obviousness, what was most secret. For example, even when they sang in "Our Car Club" about some unspecified but no doubt grueling hazing ritual—

We'll have the roughest and toughest initiation we can find
And if you want to try to get in we'll really put you through the grind

—there too was beauty of the most delicate kind, disguised as a celebration of brutality.

In the beginning—pouring suddenly like Hokusai's Great Wave out of the radio, changing the quality of the bus ride home through Manhattan congestion as they emanated from someone's transistor—the Beach Boys were simply California, the Golden West of beaches and movies, not the literary bohemian West Coast of Gary Snyder or City Lights Books, but a country of orange groves and parking lots, vast high schools like the one James Dean attended in *Rebel Without a Cause,* highways winding alongside the ocean. *Rebel* was very much the movie from which the Beach Boys had emerged, the movie to which their music in the beginning seemed an augmented soundtrack. The connection was confirmed by "A Young Man Is Gone," a retelling of James Dean's life to the melody of "Their Hearts Were Full of Spring." But this was James Dean as reimagined for some Golden Book—*A Child's Introduction to Violent Death*—some elementary school transformation of youthful self-immolation into a form of choral calisthenics, as free of trouble as a round of hopscotch or marbles.

Rebel Without a Cause had combined, in hallucinatory fashion, two quite different things. On the one hand there was the cult of the dead teenager, the religion of vulnerability and wounded anger, the hideous puppet show of the middle-class parents reduced to impotence, the need to invent a new family in which young people could nurture each other without interference from the world of teachers and psychologists and security guards. It offered a universe on the scale of our hitherto unexpressed self-pity, with ourselves in the starring roles and everyone else on the periphery of a space cleared for the enactment of our tragedy. (Natalie Wood waving her arms to start the cars on their fatal "chicken run" looked like an ancient statue of Hecuba or Cassandra, the marble dyed with lipstick and nail polish.) On the other hand—and this was more important, finally—there was Cinemascope, the color red, the planetarium with its light show of cosmic destruction, the choreography of the sleek cars driving in darkness toward the abyss, the scoops of light and space that the camera gathered up in its swivels and spiralings. A landscape reinvented by Frank Lloyd Wright, mixing indoors and outdoors in a great airy construction, with enough open territory to soak up any amount of adolescent sorrow. It was the modern world, and it was going to be ours. The empty house—the parents away for the weekend—beckoned like an apparently undefended beachhead.

That great surface stretching across the wide screen was as attractive as a drug. One day I encountered a similar surface in another medium, hearing Jan and Dean's "The Little Old Lady from Pasadena" for the first time. It was only by accident that the record that turned me on to the Beach Boys' sound was not by the Beach Boys. It hardly mattered, since one could already have spoken of a School of Brian Wilson, diffused through the likes of the Hondells ("Little Honda") and Ronny and the Daytonas (the magnificent "G.T.O."). "The Little Old Lady from Pasadena" sounded, that first afternoon, like a new kind of Handel, a Bach chorale for freeways. A wide sound—liquid organ chords and savage falsetto—compacted. The light streaming into the living room as I played the 45 merged with another light, the imagined wide-open sunshine reflected off a Pacific coast I had not yet seen but could now, with the help of Jan and Dean, begin already to inhabit.

It was an opening up of the world. Who could have expected it to happen quite like that, with such unlikely accoutrements, those nasal vowel tones that would some day seem lovely, those evocations of an unknown geography ("she's the terror of Colorado Boulevard"), that veneer of Saran-Wrapped hygiene? This was supermarket beauty. It was a product imported from the world of the beach movies—the dismal teen comedies that always showed on the same bill with the movies that had drawn us in, the ones about vampires and zombies—transformed when I must have been looking away for a minute into something I actually enjoyed. "Enjoyed" is too weak: I was fascinated. What was it about that sunshine that made it as mysterious as one of the Edgar Allan Poe stories on which the horror movies on the bill with *Bikini Beach* and *Palm Springs Weekend* had been based?

The American mythology of the body, once fearsome, cluttered as it was with the machinery of sex manuals and deodorant applicators, could now be made ours. We were all, inwardly, Annette Funicello. Or had blonde hair, worked as lifeguards, lived on vast campuses near the Pacific, carried boards or other complexly simple equipment. Sex here was not the end of innocence but the embodiment of innocence, not the end of childhood but its expansion into further fields of action. Childhood did not end, it merely widened and merged into marijuana and the ocean and all-night parties: a noisy Pop Art comedy with moments of unexpected tenderness. You hadn't known you cared about the puppets until that scene by the car door, near the cliff's edge, when Suzanne Pleshette managed to say something that might almost be serious: "Look, you don't have to play games with me, it's about more than beach parties, just be yourself." Those things I had felt distant from—cars, sports, team spirit—had become the material for these permanently wonderful objects. It became possible to stroll through an outdoor church decked not in saints' lives or apocalypses but images of root beer and drive-ins and car-crazy cuties with candy-apple lips. Had people been inventing a new kind of body out there that could feed on artifice and thrive?

Years later, hitchhiking up the legendary coast, you and I saw the real surfers and surfer girls at Isla Vista, and they looked exactly the way they were supposed to. We didn't have bodies like that, of course. We were thin and pale and dark-haired in contrast to those tanned, full-bodied, sandy-blond creatures, and thus presumed ourselves to have problems they couldn't dream of. The song title "The Lonely Surfer" had seemed humorous because it was hard to imagine people who looked like that ever being lonely. (Actually, he was lonely simply because he found himself in New York City.) They were born for group frolics, line dances, swimming pool shenanigans. Didn't their physical self-confidence constitute a natural antidote against unwanted solitude? And didn't that imply a different kind of consciousness, something like a satisfied hive mentality that could glut on sensual joy without any finicky or self-doubting reservations? Half of what we heard in the Beach Boys was that kind of cartoon: the other half was its mysterious flip side, full of concealed sorrows and eccentric reveries.

I didn't fully register the Beach Boys the first time around, any more than one fully registers one's youth the first time around. It's in the playbacks that the patterns come out. Back then the Beach Boys, as far as I can recollect, were a brand name denoting a certain kind of reliably attractive object, a sound-sculpture that sounded good in the most unexpected contexts, and that could take people by surprise. Listening to their music was a form of fun. It went with six-packs. Part of the fun was conceptualizing them as teenage geniuses, high school kids who invented their own peculiar variety of classical music. "I Get Around," "Little Deuce Coupe," "Wendy," "Fun, Fun, Fun": these were high school operas by kids who obviously went to a different kind of high school, its Cinemascope-and-Technicolor parking lot crowded with Eldorados and Mustangs. Their singing was in the first place a feat, something to earn a trophy for the mantelpiece, like coming in first in the statewide swim meet. Admire the workings of a nifty machine. Notice gradually that the parts fit into place even when they seem deliberately random, and how the instruments are in there too, and that emotions creep in that can't be mistaken for formulaic paste-ons: they're more elusive, more troubling, and in some way they're built into the structure. In the after hours, listening again, become aware of secret jokes planted in the fade-outs, tiny sublayerings designed to test if you were paying attention.

At that time, the individuality of Brian Wilson was clear to people in the music business but not so much to everyday listeners, or at least it hadn't yet taken on a cult-like aspect. We had heard that he didn't tour with the band anymore and may have heard rumors of his 1964 breakdown—the time he got off the plane at the last moment before takeoff, overcome by sudden overwhelming terror—but we had not yet formulated that mixture of whimsy and reclusion, technical acumen and soulful melancholy that would make up the iconic Brian. It was impossible not to be aware of a controlling intelligence, musical intelligence that is, although at the time I was mostly conscious of gimmicky things like the startling modulation toward the end of "Dance, Dance, Dance." The more mysterious beauties crept up on you, and the beauty was mingled with an equal measure of oddity: the droning modalities of "Don't Hurt My Little Sister," echoing some Arabian Nights soundtrack, were set off by the poetic shock value of repeating the title phrase over and over in undulating chorus. Did they realize how weird it sounded, or were they drifting ever deeper into a trance that might pass for normal in that golden light?

Beyond the sweetness (but you had to listen closely to catch it) there were those other more perplexing elements, the harmonies distorting into burlesque falsettos, the peculiar textures stitched out of pops and plucks, giggles and slurps, the mood-wrecking bursts of caricature. Beneath lyrics that were calmly inane—

> *She's my girl and I'm good to my baby*
> *And I know she's happy with me*

—the instrumental tracks painted an aquarium of elusive and contradictory emotions swirling in and out of one another. "It's all in the back of my mind," Dennis was singing, and at the same moment the strings in the background were slurring toward some other melody (the one hidden still further in the back of his mind): the effect was like a smash-up that managed to sound exquisite, delicate, lighter than air.

In May, as we were graduating from high school, they released something called *Pet Sounds,* which on a first, rather inattentive hearing sounded a lot artier than the early stuff; listening with only half an ear it seemed as if the band might be losing touch with the pulsing energy that we prized so much, but there wasn't time to focus on it then. There was so much else going on.

My next, and decisive, encounter with the Beach Boys came under different circumstances about a year and a half later. Timing is everything; although, when the subject is the release of the album *Smiley Smile,* "timing" is perhaps too cruel a concept to bring into play. It was to have been released at a different time; it was to have been an altogether different album, the mythic *Smile;* when it did come out it crept into the world in so muffled a fashion that it might as well not have come out at all. That original failure of timing would be compounded over the years as rumors periodically circulated that "they" were finally going to release *Smile,* while pieces of that lost splendor turned up in one form or another on subsequent Beach Boys albums, haunting suggestions of a not quite conceivable masterpiece. (Only when more or less complete bootlegs became available could one grasp that *Smile* was unfinishable and therefore unreleasable in anything but a modified, reduced, translated form, that the "complete" album was the ultimate ineffable artifact.)

For me the timing couldn't have been better. Far from any surf, living alone in an autumnal dorm room with a window looking out on modernistic sweeps of concrete, my own personal meltdown well under way, I was sufficiently defenseless—cracked open so to speak—to make a good listener for that most unexpected of albums. The day I bought it I remember being struck primarily by the Henri Rousseau knock-off on the cover, with its infantile jungle populated by grinning elephants and giraffes. On the back, some words attributed to Indian Wisdom: "The Smile That You Send Out Returns to You." I had no fundamental objection to the sentiment and wanted to bring that tropical vegetation back to my cell, to console myself with its comforting associations of children's zoo or fifth-grade art class, not to mention the curl of smoke issuing from the cozy cottage way in the back of the jungle. Flowers, birds, smiles, the promise of warmth: if this was how the Beach Boys had reinvented themselves—since at that moment no one had any choice but to reinvent himself—it would be interesting to know how they had done it.

I don't know what kind of music I expected, but within minutes expectations became irrelevant. What was going on here? The implicit strangeness had become explicit. Brian had produced an entirely idiosyncratic version of psychedelic music, relying not on reverb or tablas but on his own quirky ingredients, ukuleles, melodicas, soda bottles, chomps, bangs, animal noises, fragments of barbershop harmonizing. What sounded like helium-induced chipmunk voices laughed themselves silly over a stream of cartoon music that might have been created by sixth-graders sniffing glue behind the tool shed. The album's logic was along the lines of a children's puzzle that asks "What's wrong with this picture?" ("Kangaroo is wearing a hat. Postman delivers letters with his foot. Church steeple is upside down.") It was a public disintegration, summed up in the mad refrain of "She's Going Bald":

You're too late, mama,
Ain't nothin' upside your head.

Sounds. It was about sounds in the head. Whistling noises, nearly inaudible laughter, pieces that might have been part of songs set adrift in some studio tank made up to look like the ocean, words divorced from their meanings so you got to hear what they really sounded like. ("When she saw her shiny forehead didn't stop. . . .") The Beach Boys? If these were the Beach Boys, who had those other guys been? It might have been called *Music To Forget Your Name By.* Those other acid-head musicians suddenly looked tame, the ones who with one eye on the exploding inner cosmos had managed, pragmatically, to keep the other on the marketplace. Brian and the boys—or was it after all just Brian?—had let themselves become unmoored in a way that felt final, beyond rescue. What did you come back to after you let yourself go out that far?

Smiley Smile was the token that made it imperative (by affirming that yes, the oddness was real, you hadn't merely imagined it) to go back and listen to the rest of the Beach Boys catalogue as if for the first time, starting with *Pet Sounds* and moving all the way back to "The Lonely Sea," that piece of primitive profundity in which the very young Mike Love assumed an absurd juvenile basso, like a junior high kid doing *King Lear,* thereby disguising as prank a true summons from the deeps. There had always been more than there seemed to be. Listen to *Pet Sounds* again—is this the twelfth time, or the twentieth, this week?—and then, with your head full of those solemn melting harmonies, go back to "This Car of Mine" and "Custom Machine" and "No Go Showboat" to hear what you hadn't noticed before. Songs about cars? Can it be? More like songs as cars: vehicles out of the *Mahabharata* or *Odyssey,* in which a god would traverse continents or inspect polar zones. The ethereal musical settings lavished on words like those of "Custom Machine"—

> *Well, she's got Naugahyde bucket seats in front and back*
> *Everything is chrome, man, even my jack—*

brought chromium and metal flake paint into the realm of the numinous, offering not heavy but soft metal, metal manufactured in Oz or Shangri-La. These streamlined machines were impeccable and detached: "I'll let you look, but don't touch my custom machine." How could one have touched what existed only as sound patterns? The "No-Go Showboat," a beautiful but nonfunctional hot rod, was a perfect metaphor for Brian's crystalline, otherworldly musical structures:

> *Whitewall slicks with racing mags,*
> *She's just for looks, man, not for drags . . .*
> *When it comes to speed, man, I'm just out of luck,*
> *I'm even shut down by the ice cream truck.*

This archaeology of Brian Wilson provided the strange sensation that at the very time that everyone was moving forward, into new identities, new decibel ranges, new scales of Dionysiac self-abandonment, a hidden truth was to be found in what had already been tossed aside, the pop hits of five years ago. Perhaps the secret instructions were: Don't follow the noise, follow the trail of hidden silences.

What brought us together in the first place was sudden death. The friend we both loved had hurled herself out of the world. That was the premise of everything that followed, for a while at least. It was as if we had met at the edge of an abyss and continued to hang around in that neighborhood for a term, feeling vaguely that it might be a good idea to move on but having no precise destination in mind. Periodically one or the other of us might glance back toward the fissure, or take an exploratory stroll near the rim to test our reactions. The event infused everything, including the way Beach Boys records sounded. Or was it that Beach Boys records already sounded like that, and so naturally became indispensable to us?

It was an incomparable joy to find that you were already there. You already understood thoroughly the secret pathways embedded in such tracks as "Pom Pom Playgirl" and "Let Him Run Wild," and (with a philosophical sophistication informed by Heidegger and Wittgenstein) could negotiate effortlessly the paradoxes of brilliant stupidity, coarse subtlety, tender power, meditative hilarity. To listen together was a rite of confirmation, in the course of which we laughed a lot, like the anonymous participants in that *Beach Boys' Party* that we so frequently attended. Our delight had partly to do with the idea of finding beauty where it was least expected, the idea that beauty was hidden in plain sight in the unlikeliest places, and that it might be closely connected with the banal and even the ridiculous. We were determined to have fun. It was almost a religious aspiration.

The fact that your name figured in the title of a Beach Boys song was the final touch of poetic perfection. Even better that it happened to be the song in which the man (or, rather, Boy?)—who has been "out doing in my head" in a prolonged fit of self-pity after a break-up—turns to another woman for help, as if she were a nurse or therapist on call. It was another one of the songs we loved for their dumb honesty, their guileless delineation of male assumptions. There were other, better ones, above all "She Knows Me Too Well," in which the singer berated himself for attitudes that he was clearly not about to even contemplate changing:

> When I look at other girls it must kill her inside,
> But it'd be another story if she looked at the guys.

She knows me too well: she is so intimately aware of my moral failings (my relentless self-absorption, the double standard I preserve like a cherished tradition, my unspoken underlying vulnerability for which I punish her, the sense of dread that not even lust fulfilled can entirely soothe away) that she can read these as expressions of love. It was of course among the most beautiful—divinely beautiful, it often seemed—of Brian's songs. The falsetto at the fade-out aspired to compensate for all frailties, all shortcomings, to simply erase every uncertainty with a wave of feeling.

We were convinced that the key to final aesthetic understanding (assuming, as we did, that such a key existed) was to be found here, if only one knew where to look. An alchemy, a mating of opposites, a paradoxical marriage: under a patina of easy prettiness lay a hard beauty. Rigor! Classical toughness! The twisty midpoint where form is created! Looking at it that way you could find beauty equally in the creamy doo-wop lyricism of "Hushabye" or in the minimalist grotesquerie of "I'm Bugged at My Old Man." The rasp was the necessary counterpoint to the ethereal swell. It was needful that streams of unimpeded sweetness should coexist with sneezes, burps, kazoos, hammers, soda bottles. It no longer seemed extreme to posit *Beach Boys' Party* as the precise aesthetic counterweight to *Pet Sounds,* the anti-*Pet Sounds* that for control of surface substituted a willed chaos of bad jokes, interrupted or distorted lyrics, random party shuffling and chattering. By such a circuitous route it reached the same sublime as the other, but this time without tears.

Wild Honey had just come out, and soon *Friends* followed. The once numerous legions of Beach Boys fans were getting thin on the ground. With remarkable speed the band had managed to achieve a cult status that verged on the esoteric. We spent a rapt afternoon smoking marijuana and listening to *Friends*—an LP whose remarkable brevity was encapsulated in a fully formed opening song precisely thirty-eight seconds long—over and over. (Brevity was added to the list of virtues driven underground in the age of the twenty-minute guitar solo.) It was still possible to believe that the Beach Boys were in the early stages of a process that would yield, say, a dozen more albums equally surprising and equally sublime. Already it was a secret world, now that the Beach Boys had fallen into a side pocket far removed from that noise, out on the highway, of Cream and Hendrix and the Jeff Beck Group. How many were there of us, four, five? A whole summer was spent on *Friends* and *Pet Sounds* and *Smiley Smile* and *Wild Honey,* the spaces between them filled in with the early albums in which we continued to savor newly appreciated harmonies or fade-outs or unfathomably peculiar lyrics or funny voices or eccentric instrumentation.

We even made a few converts, lured a few people away from Moby Grape and King Crimson long enough for them to submit, then surrender, to *Pet Sounds.* The seriousness with which we molded ourselves to the contours of that canon, alternating flurries of exegesis with silent prayerful listening, might well have been mistaken for the proceedings of a Bible Study group very far out on some sectarian limb. We lived near water that summer—in a rented apartment above a Dodge showroom next to where the ferry docked, adjacent to a strip of beach punctuated by fuel storage tanks—so that it felt appropriate for the soundtrack of our lives to be "All Summer Long" and "Girls on the Beach."

We loved the sound. We loved the materiality of the voices and instruments and other sound-sources brought into the record. We loved, almost embarrassingly, the very breath of the singers, mere inhaling and exhaling, as if simply being thus barely audibly alive were the final music. But it wasn't "simply" breathing, it was the deliberate decision to record breath, the specific texture achieved in the mix. Not the idea of the thing but the thing itself: *musique concrète,* an object, a texture, a pressure: or, even better, the removal of pressure that allowed sounds to issue unimpeded. When we came upon those lines of Hugh MacDiarmid—

> *The inward gates of a bird are always open.*
> *It does not know how to shut them.*
> *That is the secret of its song*

—we thought we had found a new way of conceptualizing what made the singing on "The Warmth of the Sun" and "Why Do Fools Fall in Love" and "God Only Knows" unmistakable.

In that soundscape we lived. It had dimensions we could move around in. The atmosphere was different there; it made the body feel different. The pleasure of the ear was not to be subsumed under some big idea: the pleasure was itself the big idea. (That Brian Wilson was deaf in one ear took on a symbolic import, as if to underscore that he had made better use of one ear than most others of two.) We wanted to find a way to dissolve whatever barrier still separated hedonism from spirituality. Listening to this music was like being in church and being at the beach in the same instant. There was a spinal bliss that came out one way as Meister Eckhart, another way as surf songs. We secretly hoped that the ocean music of "Don't Back Down" and "Hawaii" would keep us healthy, fill our lungs with the sea air we thought we needed to be fully alive. It was a sound we could happily drown in: an annihilating liquefied sweetness, canned music for some Polynesian castaway life, yet yielding a final aftertaste superbly dry and exact. The instrumental "Let's Go Away for Awhile"—aside from making us wish that Brian Wilson had spent more time writing music without voices—seemed to announce that it wasn't enough to gesture in the direction of paradise, or (worse) to deny its existence: you had to take possession of it, even if it meant constructing it for yourself.

The ripples of that tropical surf might be the last dawdling vibrations of some Gnostic emanation. A molecular poetry, modular and self-sustaining, had been allowed to escape, like the light of an ancient star, from that Void whose centrality we found curiously reassuring. Was there a difference between lushness and nothingness? Didn't the most austere mystical vision of the heart of creation merge, at the very crux where "is" met "is-not," with a hand-tinted postcard from Maui printed in 1905? We wanted the view at land's end—the Pacific sunset, the physical beauty of the surfers and surfer girls, the wide screen filled with nothing but salt and emptiness—to be a pictogram of the mind's end, the place where thoughts came to find fulfillment in realized form. Did it matter if the form resembled, playfully, a Ferris wheel or a drive-in, a fast-food restaurant or an elementary school playground?

Amid such imaginary haunted piers and seaside arcades we walked the night. The blending of the voices of the Beach Boys floated through those spaces like the emanation of a dematerialized pipe organ. The space between the voices, the space between the notes: there was a bottomless theme for meditation. We imagined Brian Wilson as the orchestrator of ether, the architect of intervals. He could move and work in an environment that to most outsiders seemed nothing but empty air.

The beautiful object replaces something that no longer exists. Therefore the anthem of this subculture had to be "Caroline No": the song as act of mourning, a grief never to be resolved. A wound was made to sound permanently beautiful. Was it all the time, still, our dead friend we were mourning, to the tune of that barking dog and lonesome train whistle disappearing into the void, again and again at the end of the album's last cut? By repeated listening were we attempting to get used to the idea of a death to which we still chose to remain unreconciled? Or did we mourn merely the banal fact of time passing, of the young girl cutting her hair short, of the dematerializing of a never quite real geography of swings, water fountains, hot dog stands? Volley ball games at dusk? Driftwood fires under the boardwalk? Bicycle moving out of visual range on the other side of the hill? The unforeseen evaporation of childhood, and nothing more?

We had all lost one thing or another. Why then did we feel such unnatural pity for Brian? Why did he seem to have lost more than the rest of us, or to be less able to bear any loss at all? Our own sensitivities were deflected onto his, understood to be so immense that when a girl cuts her hair short it's the end of life. There was the question of how much his evident unhappiness had to do with the music. Would a happy Brian have been capable of the symphonies and oratorios we dreamed of? Could he have stretched those seconds of musical joy into hours of compositional development?

The cult of Brian, as it took shape, devoted equal attention to personal suffering and formal genius, a genius in itself not maudlin but rather dry, humorous, and endlessly inventive. It was important for us to find peripheral evidence of his artistic single-mindedness, as if to assure us that we weren't dreaming. We read in awe of how he constructed the arrangements of *Pet Sounds* part by part, teaching each musician separately in order to realize a unity already constructed in his head. We were fascinated to learn of his habit of thinking through a compositional problem by pounding away at the piano, playing an entirely unrelated boogie woogie pattern. At the same time we took note of everything that signaled his capacity to become lost. There was a terrifying anecdote about his being given a globe; he turned it around, trying to determine, he said, whether there was any point on earth that sunlight never reached. He was either a talisman against suffering, or else a talisman designed to induce a suffering that, it was hoped, would lead to the same kind of aesthetic satori. When we named a stray cat Brian Wilson, was it to invoke his presence, or to placate the stubborn trace of sorrow we had come to associate with his name?

We played—but already more uncomfortably—with a notion that absolute artistic judgment and a kind of scary holiness were so closely linked as to be nearly (but never quite) identical. The injection of Charles Manson into the Beach Boys saga raised the issue in almost too archetypal a fashion. After Manson's arrest for the 1969 Tate-LaBianca murders, the inimitably sordid account of Dennis Wilson's long-term seduction by the Family began to emerge despite every effort by the Beach Boys and their industry allies to keep a lid on it. It was disturbing to learn long after the fact that as we listened to "Cease To Resist" on *20/20* we had been subjecting ourselves to Manson's uncredited, only slightly modified serenade (his more characteristic refrain was "cease to exist"). We imagined the silent duel between Brian and Manson: Manson, having already seduced Dennis, tries to lure Brian into the web of fascination, under the guise of one artistic genius speaking to another in terms he would understand. Our cartoon version of it became a Tibetan showdown between black magic and white magic, diabolical music and angelic music. It seemed important to make such distinctions, even if we had to concoct the evidence. Whatever we had been looking for in the Beach Boys, it wasn't the face of evil.

It was getting harder to keep the faith, in an era when, as a friend remarked, "each new Beach Boys album makes the last one sound so much better by comparison." The Maharishi stuff had already made it hard. (Years later Brian would acknowledge, "Meditation didn't do shit for me," but at the time we had no way of knowing.) If being a Beach Boys fan had had something of the qualities of a cult, with the encroachments of what seemed like corporate mysticism it now came dangerously close to being a subset of a larger cult, a real one this time, with actual recruitment programs and special schools and didactic hooks interpolated in song lyrics. Was it an omen that the song called "Transcendental Meditation" was the worst thing on *Friends,* a numbing jingle totally at odds with the delicate spaciness of the rest? If cars had prompted ethereal grace, mystical experience (or the longing for such) precipitated anthems of startling unpersuasiveness. The terrible lyrics about feet and food and student demonstrations made it harder. We went to the Fillmore East concert to cheer them on, amid a more or less unfriendly crowd of East Village hipsters, and came back only half persuaded ourselves.

Sunflower, inaugurating what was to have been the glorious era of Brother Records, an independent company intended to free the Beach Boys from corporate dominance, was a beautiful record, mostly, sort of, with reservations. We detected something different about the sound: it was colder, more deliberate, less open to inspired impulses. It was trying to sell itself in a way that felt uncomfortably calculated. Was this what decadence sounded like? Or was the discomfort related to an awareness that our own relationship had likewise taken on a more self-conscious tone? Now that we were out of school, living together in the city and dragging ourselves out of bed to get to miserable jobs selling encyclopedias or typing up surveillance reports, we had to make more effort to find the flow that had once come naturally. In the same way we had to look harder, in each Beach Boys album, to find those one or two things so fine that they made up for the rest of the record. Tiny songs like "Meant for You" and "I Went to Sleep" and "All I Wanna Do" suggested a movement inward rather than outward, exactly the reverse of the School of Adrenaline that dominated at that moment. We were being taken inside something, being shown spiral patterns, potentially never-ending ripple effects from deliberately microscopic arrangements of sound. Weren't five or six minutes like that, unobtainable anywhere else, worth the price of a record? Did it matter if the sound of wisdom came from someone who might be utterly adrift?

On the one hand there is the wonderful condition in which you have the irrational but exhilarating conviction that you have chosen—or lucked into—the right partner, the right philosophy, the right location, the right band. Life moves forward on all fronts. Every day brings new insights. Appetite is robust; nuances are appreciated. On the other hand there is the slow seep of poisonous uncertainty. One day more or less everything went well; the next, there is virtually nothing that is not contested, threatened, soured. In a bad moment a new cult forms, the cult of how you felt last month. There is no restoring the lost feeling. You bang on a door now permanently closed, as disappointment curdles into barely controlled rage.

When *Sunflower* came out we were living across the street from a mental hospital, and there is no question that the nightly cries and howls from its wards added another layer to the music. Once we had felt we entered music; now there was a gathering impression that we used music to drown out other sounds, other thoughts. There was an LP of ocean sounds that we played to create the illusion that we were still living at the beach. When things go wrong people ask too much of music, as of sex, or drugs, or the wine we consumed so generously but to so little purpose. Drugs always fail; it's a commonplace that the first ecstatic experience can never be recaptured, and that the attempt to do so only leads to higher and more frequent doses. But for music to fail is as intolerable as for love to fail.

The beloved song can turn into the mocking sound of childhood's music box, knocked from a shelf and starting to play unbidden, in some Italian psycho-thriller where it becomes a signal of the inner splintering that will lead to murder. Then it soothed; now it jabs. Hearing Brian sing "'Til I Die" on the *Surf's Up* album we felt a sense of dread:

> *I'm a cork on the ocean*
> *Floating over the raging sea . . .*

Who was that singing, Hölderlin on the edge of his madness? Here was a lullaby for an abandoned baby, heading toward the falls in his tiny boat. The beauty we had imagined was here laid bare, and it was a description of some kind of death. The siren song led toward the rocks: "It kills my soul, hey hey hey." A last harmonic overtone, gone the way the train went in "Caroline No."

The music had passed out of range like a lost radio signal. In time even the thought of it was lost: it was an ellipsis signifying "no point in going there again." Some time in there—was it before or after the release of *Carl and the Passions,* that most disappointing of Beach Boys disappointments?—we began living in separate apartments, and consequently whatever music we had shared underwent a sea-change. What had denoted the future denoted the past; the symbol of opening became an emblematic padlock. Whatever rumors circulated about Brian—his collapse, his vanishing into his bedroom for years at a time—served as a terrifying reminder of how badly the most splendid hopes could fail. We were losing him; we had lost him. A few fragments escaped: the music to a solipsistic fairy tale about a transistor radio was a last faint message, almost lost in transmission, the echo of an echo of childhood.

What had Brian been for us if not the sacred child, enduring loneliness for the sake of everyone else, commissioned to transmute isolation into beauty? It came down to the timbre of that sustained falsetto note, lingering on an unbearable (unbearably sad, unbearably pleasurable) awareness of unfulfillable longing. Stop time; bring back the lost world. Nothing else will assuage a nostalgia as big as the ocean. But childhood, thus imagined, offered nothing at all. One might as well seek to become Pinocchio again, waiting for the redemptive voice of Jiminy Cricket to penetrate the whale that had swallowed one whole.

You could find yourself listening to a record looking desperately for reassurance, in the spirit of some cultists I knew once who chanted to each other over the phone in the middle of the night to help each other get through patches of anxiety. The sustained tones shut out the disagreeable thoughts that reminded them of their names and addresses, even if it drove one of their roommates almost over the edge: "It's like listening to cats in heat! Except cats don't have to take special courses to learn how to sound like that!" Even the sweetest sounds in the world (think of New Age music) could become ugly if you got too dependent on them. Mandalas designed to instill meditative calm could turn hideous; flowers became overscented intrusions; even sunlight could start to feel like it was in the way, too hot, too bright. The beautiful object was still there but it didn't look beautiful anymore. Outright loss would have been preferable.

Somewhere in his lonely room Brian was playing "Be My Baby" every day, in the same way that we once played "Caroline No" every day. What could it possibly sound like after so many repetitions? The durability of recorded sound was meant to be a hedge against disappearance. Feelings would be preserved in their first freshness: a whisper cast in bronze. Eventually our turn would come to discover that the agelessness of recorded music, whatever solace it offered, could also taunt. The old songs enjoyed an eternal youth denied both to their creators and to the listeners whose advance toward decrepitude would be cushioned none too subtly by the time-denying playlists of oldies stations. It was as if a cheery soundtrack continued to play while the romantic comedy for which it had been designed turned unaccountably into a drama of decay and failed aspirations. All the more reason, then, to listen to some new music for a change.

Little by little it became possible to forget Brian and his brothers. There were a good many other thrills, more complex, more adult, more convincingly erotic, more authentically political, more profoundly exotic, more radically savage. We didn't need him anymore. If he appeared in dreams now, it was almost in the guise of an old school friend who had been slighted, his phone calls unreturned, his letters unanswered, the traditional reunion ignored. Still, the dreams did come, in which new albums were played for the nocturnal visitor, uncanny new combinations of textures, wordless mantras, symphonies for water drum and resonator. In one of the dreams the music emanated from a piano, surrounded by a crowd. It took some time to wade through that mass of onlookers to get a look at the face of the piano player, Brian: disheveled and utterly gone, beyond the beyond.

One day, many years later when we had almost forgotten how passionately we would once have cared, his "autobiography" came out. It was a ghost-written book whose novelistic slickness gave little hint of having emerged from Brian's consciousness, a collage of cullings from old press clips that forced the question of how much of the material reflected what Brian actually remembered. The book eventually was taken off the market because of legal problems. The Beach Boys were all suing each other for complicated reasons, including Brian's long involvement with the Mabuse-like Dr. Eugene Landy, whose figure loomed on every other page of the book and whose inordinate influence on Brian as both therapist and business partner had triggered a bid by one of Brian's cousins for conservatorship of his affairs.

The essence of those pages could be distilled in a few phrases that confirmed what we already knew. They were all about music. He did not seem especially comfortable on any other subject. Neighborhoods, schooling, the Southern Californian milieu, lovers, fans, the record business, his brutal treatment at the hands of a father vicariously realizing his ambitions through his more talented sons—everything might as well have been happening on another planet. Whether it was hard-core solipsism or evidence of his direct line to the music of the spheres, Brian only sounded like himself when he was talking about the sounds in his head: "As far as I can remember, I've always heard music, faint strains of melody floating in the background, the volume vacillating according to my mood. Early on, I learned that when I tuned the world out, I was able to tune in a mysterious, God-given music. It was my gift, and it allowed me to interpret and understand emotions I couldn't even articulate." Elsewhere he referred to "a twenty-four-hour radio station that played even in my sleep."

The most intimate revelations he could possibly make had to do with his most profound influences, which turned out to be *Rhapsody in Blue* ("I still hear every emotion I've ever experienced in that piece") and the 1956 album *The Four Freshmen and Five Trombones*: "Some people have religious experiences. . . . For me, that record was life-changing." That a lifetime's art had been nourished on such scanty fare—half an hour of Gershwin, some harmonizations of Kurt Weill ("Speak Low") or Jerome Kern ("The Last Time I Saw Paris"), and of course Phil Spector's "Be My Baby"—seemed a perverse confirmation of what we had always known about Brian's capacity to reconstruct the universe out of its tiniest elements.

Despite the twelve-steps optimism of its latter pages, the book couldn't help but exude a bitter aftertaste. Listening to that music years ago, we thought we heard the beginning of the sound of the future; this was what the future had turned out to be. The book wasn't so much an adjunct to the music as the description of a depleted mutilated world from which music had been excised. Its subject, intentionally or not, was life without melody, harmony, or a sustaining rhythm. At its dark center Brian became a Beckett character, mired in filth and at times nearly catatonic. What survived was the compulsion to ingest anything that came to hand: booze, dope, Big Macs, cigarettes, coffee in forty-cup urns. In symbolic defense against the world's efforts to devour him, he ballooned to 340 pounds.

Madness is the least interesting of conditions. We already knew that. Grinding boredom is its essence. The tuner on the all-night station breaks down, and the orphic head-music is buried under layers of static, screams, cackles, the chattering of goblins and demons. Toward the end—shortly before the "happy ending" where he was whisked off to Hawaii (of course) for the intensive therapy that he claimed had saved him—Brian described escaping from his guardians and walking out alone into America, bumming drinks in bars, listening to the same song over and over on the jukebox, finally "plodding barefoot through dark, empty, cold streets, in an unfamiliar city, babbling strange, nonsensical thoughts out loud." It could be a warped episode from *Meet John Doe* or *Sullivan's Travels*.

This was not a life destined to become an Oliver Stone movie. It forced prolonged contemplation of the least photogenic side of '60s excess, not the side that went noisily public, that screamed and flaunted itself and expired in a colorful burst of exhibitionism, but the side that curled up within itself and forgot to come out again, that smoked pot every ten minutes for the next few decades, that kept replaying a small pile of sacred 45s as if to keep time at a standstill. Wrapped in his long silence, Brian Wilson remained huddled in his burrow like a Japanese soldier gone to ground, still unaware that the war was over.

But that, of course, was not the ending either. It was a bit like that John Ford movie in which, just when you thought John Wayne's cavalry career was washed up for good this time, the government courier came riding in with fresh orders. Brian's reemergence hadn't even really begun. A new generation had discovered the '60s hits and turned the Beach Boys (mostly without Brian) into the most successful of oldies acts. Unreleased material began to surface—big chunks of *Smile,* a fascinating fragmentary version of Bacharach's "Walk on By," songs from an unreleased solo album called *Adult Child*. These solo tracks were sung in a voice nearly unrecognizable, destroyed by chain-smoking and misery into a hoarse parody of that earlier cherub tone. It was a voice more or less appropriate to a song like "It's Over Now," which placed its still powerful lyric line ("shades of blue and purple haunt me") at the service of terminal depression: "Heaven is far away." Biographies would be written, movies made, including a dramatized made-for-TV version of the whole Beach Boys saga. The Beach Boys, as entity, gradually dissolved; Dennis drowned in a drunken accident,

Carl died of lung cancer; Mike Love and Al Jardine toured with competing versions of the group (Al's was called Beach Boys Family and Friends). Brian turned out to be the most durable of survivors. A decade later there were a pile of solo albums, released and unreleased, a documentary film *(I Guess I Just Wasn't Made For These Times)*, a collaboration on songs written by Van Dyke Parks *(Orange Crate Art)* that turned out to be the most cunningly crafted homage to Brian's own songwriting. The ruined voice was even beginning to reclaim a little—but even a little was precious—of its lost expressiveness.

At the end of the century, there was Brian—stiff in his body language, tentative in some of his vocals, assisted by backup singers when it came to the high notes he couldn't hit anymore, but very much there—at Jones Beach presenting a live performance of *Pet Sounds*. Brian at Jones Beach: nothing could have been more appropriate than that same Jones Beach where we might once have indulged our feeble simulacrum of surf culture, sprawling in sunglasses reading movie magazines and drinking beer out of paper cups through long August afternoons. By the following spring Brian would be playing Radio City Music Hall with a cast of supporting stars come to pay homage: Carly Simon and Ricky Martin, Aimee Mann and Sir George Martin, Dennis Hopper and the Go-Go's and Billy Joel. Everything else had been an interlude, an unusually protracted intermission now consigned to oblivion. We were back in the eternally glorious present of Hitsville, where no sorrow goes unconsoled for long, and fame makes all pain bearable. Another story, another happy ending, another opportunity for television specials and shrink-wrapped reissues.

I remember once playing you a lovely Brian Wilson instrumental— a true rarity!—called "After the Game." After a moment of silence you remarked, "I guess they lost." To children the thought of losing can be unbearable. Beauty—the achieved materialized beauty of a one-minute-and-fifty-eight-second B side—is a form of insurance against such loss. Perfect sounds are assembled into a defensive perimeter against raiders from the chaotic wastelands.

Saved by music. But what exactly can be saved?

The noise of the ocean. That exact roar: like sandpaper. And then the long tidal sigh.

12

The Rabbi's Playlist

H ERE I WILL CALL HIM THE RABBI. THIS WAS THE SECRET name I had given my friend. It remained secret because I would never confess to him that there were times when, as I watched him formulating an assessment—as he sifted through his opinion of a poem, a bass solo, or the temperament of a mutual acquaintance—he seemed as learned and discriminating, and (weirdly, given his relative youth and inexperience) nearly as ancient, as one of those legendary Talmudic exegetes of Andalusia or medieval France. In prolonged hermetic studies whose object might be anything from Su T'ung-po to Dean Martin, he had acquired a method, a science of balance. His delight in exact detail did not preclude an appreciation of overall effect. The considered serenity of his judgment was the more remarkable for encompassing even his own long-nourished and inconsolable unhappiness. With what appeared to be humorous detachment he contemplated his own insomnia, hypochondria, sexual dissatisfaction, and professional failure; his crippling inability to put himself forward in the crucial transactions of love and commerce; his progressive burrowing into a solitude ever more rigorous; his sense of having been allotted futility as the only mode in which he could expect to realize himself.

He was not a likely candidate for dispensing counsel, but wisdom is to be received when and where it is found. "What is the remedy for those whose souls are sick?" wrote the philosopher Maimonides. "Let them go to the wise men—who are physicians of the soul—and they will cure their disease by means of the character traits that they shall teach them, until they make them return to the middle way." In college I had known him as a poet haunted by the uncanniness of bare trees and tar roofs and broken plaster. He spent days taking words out of his poems, stripping language away until he succeeded in describing scenes in which nothing quite ever happened: cities whose inhabitants appeared to have unaccountably abandoned them, the slightly frayed lobbies of residential hotels whose quiescence suggested a catastrophe either already past or not quite arrived. He was a musician as well— only in the most private sense, playing acoustic guitar with and for a few friends—who in an era of strident display (it was the apogee of bands who identified themselves with lead and iron, and of virtuosos who understood everything about their instruments excepts the virtues of concision and understatement) preferred a style undemonstrative, restrained, never any louder than it needed to be.

Now we were to be neighbors. A few city blocks separated our respective low-rent walk-ups, crammed with books and LPs, and I fell into the habit of visiting him once or twice a week. When I got tired of listening to records by myself I would stroll up the avenue to listen to records with him. I came to recognize him as a master of the art of solitary listening. For some people, music has to do with parties or loving embraces, and when they listen alone they listen chiefly for the memories or anticipations that music extends and deepens. Music is a social fact for such listeners, even when there's nobody around. The Rabbi by contrast reserved his meditations for the way a song sounds when it is all that stands between you and the end of life. This level of listening was exactly what I needed.

I was living by myself after what felt like the unanticipated collapse of previous plans and arrangements, romantic or educational or artistic. It was an occasion to think all over again about the music that emerges from the background, when everything else is taken away, and assumes command. What is to be gotten from music at such a juncture, and how do you get it? Or can you be said to get anything at all if there is no partner, no company to share the experience? When Count Basie was recovering from a heart attack and spent long periods by himself, he never touched the piano because, he said, he could not imagine music as anything but interplay between musicians.

Listening alone did seem to encourage the thought of final confrontations. Was that going to be the last thing we did before we died, listen one more time to our favorite cuts from the greatest hits collections? "Green Onions," once more? "He's a Rebel," once more? "Surf's Up," once more, *in extremis*? It was a peculiar substitute for litany, in a culture where homemade forms of worship proliferated. In the absence of communal religion, private shrines proliferated: to Bud Powell, to Carmen Miranda, to Buddha, to Shango, to Fred and Ginger, Jimi and Janis, to James Dean and Robert Johnson and the Road Runner. Music tied the trappings together.

What terror, all the same, lay in those darker moments when the act of shuffling across the room to turn the record over felt suddenly like the inured behavior of a sedentary retiree. Imagine becoming the aging Irish bachelor who beguiled the hours in his rented room in a Limerick hotel listening to his collection of Broadway shows, *Show Boat, South Pacific, Kiss Me Kate,* the records he had carried in his suitcase for half a century, played on a portable turntable suitable for teenage parties in the Eisenhower era; or the decrepit couple (caretakers of the funeral parlor next door to my East 7th Street apartment) whose afternoon drinking sessions were audible across the airshaft, buried in their accumulation of remote recollections, as they listened to scratchy 78s of the Casa Loma Orchestra. What travesty of Extreme Unction would it be to die, alone, amid the echoes of "The House Is Haunted By the Echo of Your Last Goodbye"?

Yet here we washed up—at the end of a summer or a relationship or a life—with little to rely on except our record collections, our tape compilations. Unexpectedly we found ourselves inhabiting private soundtracks in which emblematic songs were pressed each against each in sweetly heterogeneous juxtaposition. Music was at once shelter and what was sheltered. A record collection was the most intimate possible disclosure of bents and preoccupations, a map of what pleased you: better than that, it was the substance of what pleased you. Even the most obsessive and isolated found some sort of companionship in music. Songs were more loyal than dogs. "He loved his music," people would always say of the suicidally withdrawn high school boy, up in his room grinding his teeth and playing air guitar for hour after hour right until the day he blew his own or someone else's brains out.

To come home to your favorite records was the opposite of sitting in an office sorting out inventories of plumbing parts or typing up transcripts of polygraph tests or coding the new batch of market research questionnaires in the presence of a radio that was never turned off. In the early '70s this was often a matter of being forced to listen repeatedly to songs like "Baby I'm A Want You" (infantilism recast as ultimate sincerity), "I'd Like to Teach the World to Sing" (a Coca-Cola jingle transformed into the kind of song that a chorus of Chinese orphans might have sung in a late '50s movie about missionaries martyred by Communists), or "Last Song" (a stalker's anthem in which it was not clear whether the assertion that "this is the last song I'll ever write for you" was a threat or a promise).

Revulsion was only the first stage, however; then came the guilty secrets. If it wasn't Peter Frampton or Electric Light Orchestra or Abba, it was America or Helen Reddy or Bachman-Turner Overdrive. In secret I tested what it was like to listen to "You Ain't Seen Nothin' Yet" or "Evil Woman" twelve times in a row. I had to admit the stuff was getting to me. Not only the loud fast stuff—that was easy to live with—but the maudlin stuff, the self-pitying stuff, the ostentatiously sensitive stuff. I was a guinea pig in an uncontrolled experiment, and it was time to fight back as best I could.

The options were limited. Since the radio at work could not be turned off, I could either tune in or tune out: surrender or resist. The test of character was whether I could avoid paying attention to every note— every glide and inflection and expressive rasp and melismatic slur, every self-conscious variation of pitch or idiosyncratic deformation of vowel sound—of Dave Loggins or Melanie or Maria Muldaur or the lead singer of Looking Glass. Sometimes I felt licked before I started. "Brandy" came on at first light with the clock radio, and the day was shot.

What was I resisting, anyway? Was there really a difference between the songs I could sort of accept and the songs that seemed to eat away at any sense of autonomous self? Between Chicago's "If You Leave Me" and Climax's "Precious and Few" (as long as the idea of a band called Climax were not already portentously absurd enough)? Between the Eagles' "One of These Nights" and England Dan and John Ford Coley's "I'd Really Love to See You Tonight"? Between Fleetwood Mac's "Go Your Own Way" and Barry Manilow's "Mandy"? If the music kept nudging long enough, the will to remain separate would collapse altogether. Like one of the citizens taken over by the unearthly group-mind in the 1956 movie *Invasion of the Body Snatchers,* I would come to find solace in "Muskrat Love": "Relax, it will make you feel better." Except it wouldn't, and I would wake up in the middle of Friday night raked over by the depressive refrains of "It Never Rains in Southern California" or "Rainy Days and Mondays Always Get Me Down." The voice of Karen Carpenter seemed peculiarly the sound of a gentle slide into final despondency, the interior monody of a woman who stares into the downpour through the kitchen window, nursing her second cup of coffee to avoid acknowledging that she simply isn't able to get up and do anything.

That monstrous bog of emotion that the songs chose to wallow in: "Feelings"! "Hooked on a Feeling"! "More Than a Feeling"! "Alone Again"! "All By Myself"! Where did they think that sort of feeling would get them, if not deeper into the downward loop? "Please come to Boston," the singer ventured in a desperate quaver. Fat chance. Give it up, stop whining. If feeling is mandatory, go for the "emotional content" that Bruce Lee demanded of his kung fu students in *Enter the Dragon.* The heart beaten down by outpourings of heavily orchestrated weepiness regained strength from Carl Douglas's disco hit "Everybody Was Kung Fu Fightin'": here was encouragement for the flagging resistance fighters, an occasion to lose any sense of personal anguish in the collective stratagems of a corps of dancing ninjas.

All this had to be talked out, and the Rabbi and I spent many an evening recapitulating our relations with the music of the hour, whether painful or unexpectedly agreeable. The simultaneous emergence of more than acceptable records like War's "The Cisco Kid" and Stealer's Wheel's "Stuck in the Middle with You" almost succeeded in drowning out the ineluctable stridency of "Tie a Yellow Ribbon Round the Old Oak Tree"—a song that only a few years later would recur nightmarishly as the theme song of American public response to the Iran hostage crisis. That's what fans were supposed to do, give grades to songs, like on an old television show. "For its unusual arrangement, its superior complement of studio musicians, its interestingly muted suggestion of a warped viewpoint, and its tactful brevity, I give it an eight."

Mostly we complained. The era had become overbearing, that much was clear, but at what point exactly? When massive amounts of money were funneled into the pop music industry at the precise moment when the aesthetic elan of the mid-'60s had about run its course? Or was it when large numbers of people grasped that Woodstock was not the beginning but the end of something, and found themselves searching restlessly for some more permanent identity? Or when the notion that Rock (as it now, with minimalist tastefulness, had to be called) was Art became the credo of every record company apparatchik and marketing wise guy? If it wasn't supergroups and giant guitar solos, it was Deodato with the disco version of Richard Strauss or the gang of sensitives pouring out their dissatisfactions in well-crafted, savvily produced ballads featuring an inevitably "tasty" guitar solo.

If any thread existed it was still to be found in black music, more than ever in fact. The '60s rockers had made much of their incorporation of Howlin' Wolf and Sam Cooke and Otis Redding. The black artists who followed went them one better by taking Art Rock to its culmination in Marvin Gaye's *What's Going On* or Stevie Wonder's *Talking Book*. At the same time they managed to maintain the level of exact sustained excitement that had once been the justification for the whole rock and roll extravaganza and that had subsequently drowned in overproduction and histrionic exaggeration. Within a single year (1972) there were singles like Betty Wright's "Clean Up Woman" and the O'Jays' "Back Stabbers" and James Brown's "Talking Loud and Saying Nothing" and Curtis Mayfield's "Superfly" and Marvin Gaye's "Trouble Man"—or, in a sweeter vein, the Chi-Lites' "Oh Girl" or the Spinners' "I'll Be Around" or Billy Paul's "Me and Mrs. Jones" or the Stylistics' long-form masterpiece "People Make the World Go Round"—records without which life (or radio life) would have been in some fundamental way unlivable. These were received by us with prayerful gratitude: as long as such music existed, we were not altogether adrift, a sense of shape and cadence and beauty of tone would continue to inform our days.

But why should we even be worrying about the health of the pop music industry? The idea that our fates were bound up with the culture that happened to be popular at any given moment seemed an imposition, a marketer's dream disguised as a political insight. What we really liked was to listen to things that were off the charts entirely, that had never been on the charts in the first place. It wasn't so much about music as about singling out peculiarities of presentation and response.

By now I had a good idea of what would appeal especially to him, could guess it so well that, if I chose, I could listen as if through his ears. Any kind of incongruity appealed to him enormously. He spoke with fascination of having seen Pete Townsend perform a reverentially acoustic version of "Begin the Beguine," in homage to Townsend's guru Meher Baba by whom the song had been interpreted as a cosmic allegory. He was drawn irresistibly to curdled whimsy, self-parodying nightclub hamminess, the performer reveling in his own fakery. Even more than that he appreciated the performer not even aware of his fakery, sweetly awash in his own poetic pretensions, oblivious to the opportunism of his political stances. The splendid idiots, the Rock Poets, gave us as good a laugh as we got in those days.

Unintended ramifications and unscheduled intrusions—bits of the world accidentally getting onto the tape—fascinated him. He would savor, on their live recording of "Without a Song," not simply the artistry of Tony Bennett and Count Basie, but the almost menacing echo of the crowd, the whistling and hooting that the liner notes described as "restless excitement and enthusiasm." That sound you heard was the aftermath of "one of the big football weekends in Philadelphia." The dissonance between what Tony Bennett was singing about—corn and grass and rain and plowing—and what was going on in the world of the early '60s frat boys we presumed to be milling about in the Latin Casino registered as the contrast between Bennett's exalted tenor and the disturbing texture of the audience noise that the music barely held in check.

In the same way that children gravitate to novelty songs and nonsense refrains, he was grateful for anything that resembled humor, deliberate or otherwise: the Lumberjack song from Monty Python; Mel Brooks doing the lounge singer bit in *High Anxiety*; the Bob Dylan late-night record offer parody from the National Lampoon album *Radio Dinner* ("Hi, remember me? I'm Bob Dylan . . . "), or for that matter Dylan's own bizarre reading of Simon and Garfunkel's "The Boxer," himself both Simon and Garfunkel, like a kid playing with his new multitrack recorder, or the tone of oblivious Southern California philistinism that the Beach Boys brought to their cover version of "The Times They Are A-Changing." He treasured the deployment of nonsense phrases made to sound meaningful, like the "for cram and for dorsn" fade-out at the end of "Desiri" on Frank Zappa's *Cruising with Ruben and the Jets.*

He scanned the spectrum for idiosyncrasies; travesties; the misbegotten products of weird turns in marketing strategy or contractual obligation. What caught his attention might be the merely odd: Nat King Cole singing in Spanish (*"cuando calienta el sol aqui en la playa"*) with clipped vowels that made him sound—or so my friend insisted—weirdly like some '30s-movie Englishman, C. Aubrey Smith, or Lionel Atwill. (This thought would invariably remind him of the Lenny Bruce bit in which he wondered why all rabbis read Hebrew with a British accent.) He could play a record again and again for the sake of one unexpected detail of phrasing, where the difference between the beautifully absurd and the absurdly beautiful became both indeterminable and crucial. He could go on at length about the peculiar inward stutter induced by the phrase "that the" in Ray Charles's recording of the theme song from *The Cincinnati Kid*: "I'm talkin' 'bout that the Cincinnati Kid."

It hardly mattered whether such moments were the product of art or accident. The instance of the lead singer coming in too early in "Louie, Louie" and dropping out again after realizing his mistake was only the most celebrated of the minor felicities of sheer unpreparedness that could be gleaned from careful listening. He loved the way inadequate judgment could unknowingly lay itself bare in the form of language just slightly abused, hyperbole collapsing under its own weight in titles like "More Than a Woman" or, even better, "More Than a Feeling": miscues, embarrassments, overreachings, each one a little rip in the universe.

He could give himself a fit of the giggles imagining Robert Merrill doing an operatic version of "Shame, Shame, Shame" on TV, in the overblown style usually lavished on "Eleanor Rigby" or "Yesterday" by opera stars filling out the guest lists of late-night talk shows: "You know, Merv, some people criticize today's music and say it doesn't compare to the masterpieces of the past. But I believe that some of today's song creations will live on, and so I'd like to conclude with a very beautiful contemporary melody by Shirley and Company . . . "

He'd wake up laughing in the middle of the night at the thought of mutating an annoying song lyric into "I've been through the desert on a horse with no legs." You had to destroy the songs by remaking them, as a form of psychic self-defense. The unavoidable Ray Stevens hit had to become "Everything is beautiful . . . In its own fucked-up way": all that surprised was the assured bitterness with which he sang the line. It raised the question of how deeply it was possible to hate a song. So deeply that your nerves would tighten into a knot and your insides develop scar tissue?

Discussions of music tended to become formulations of a taxonomy of different levels and degrees of craziness. Do you mean crazy like Syd Barrett or crazy like Wild Man Fischer? The derangement deliberately cultivated to generate surrealistic song titles or the patches of emotional flatness showing through a deceptive gloss of team spirit? The broken-plaster wilderness of electroshock or the wilier dexterity with which a splintering solipsism could disguise its own approaching submersion as civilized playfulness?

He appreciated the strangeness of Dan Hicks and His Hot Licks, a group whose good-timey jazz-folk harmonies masked intimations of fracture that he could spend hours obsessively mapping. Give way to the easygoing patter of "Canned Music" and "Walking One and Only" and "I Scare Myself" and you might find yourself in the heart of an isolation ward from which there was no return ticket. "The Laughing Song," indeed: here grin was rictus. "My radio's on and the music's insane, the music's insane": the author of that line was privileged even among all the others—from Van Morrison ("Caravan") to Donna Summer ("On the Radio"), not to mention the San Francisco poet Jack Spicer—for whom radio stood guard like some Egyptian god, rasping out orders and indecipherable codes, at the crossroads of being and annihilation.

Even between close friends, a darkness surrounded the act of listening. To sift through someone's record collection was to imagine his unconfided dreams. What did the other *really* hear? "Wait—listen to what happens right after the bass figure repeats for the third time—a scraping whisper under everything, for a split second? Now!" Even if you knew what the sound was, you couldn't tell how it sounded in someone else's ears.

So we would talk—as if zeroing in on the heart of an otherwise unspeakable mystery—about the slow fade-out of the record as a model of paradise. The slow fade-out: where everyone got a chance to go wild, bang the piano into another dimension of dissonant abandon, drive the vocal variations to the other side of language, break the words down, take apart the feelings themselves. This was something that only happened on records. It was as if the musicians disappeared into their own sound, continuing the song forever in some mythological underworld. We were sharing the kind of thing you would come upon only by listening alone, without the distractions of company and conversation. It was rescued from solitude, this entry point where the sound withdraws into the beckoning inaudible Island of the Blessed.

Of course there was more to life than that. He filled his head with Paul Celan and Spinoza and Piero della Francesca; Coltrane and Dolphy and Bill Monroe; bird song, floral displays, mountain ranges; Romanesque arches and Baroque fountains; philosophical serenity and the archaic science of beauty; the verbal interplay of the Marx Brothers and the austere discipline of post-metrical verse; right proportion, perfect brushstrokes, Zen spareness. But that wasn't enough, even perfection wasn't enough.

There needed to be things that no system of thought could ever have allowed for: the voice in the background, while Kool and the Gang kept the universe in balance by repetitions of

> *I can't get enough*
> *Of that funky stuff*

calling out in response

> *I tried, I tried,*

or the unaccountable fragile sublimity of the Channel Lumber jingle in which ethereal voices chanted, to ghostly surflike accompaniment:

Channel, Channel,
Channel, Channel,
A whole lot more more
Than a lumber store.

Back in my own apartment, the door locked and the record player on, I thought a lot about the invention of the locked-in auditor and what a technical triumph it represented. The whole civilized apparatus existed to make it possible for people to be free-standing units. The solitary listener had never existed until now, unless you counted the lone musician playing to himself: "While passing the long hot days in the shade, musicians often play for their own enjoyment in the style heard here. This music, like the sounds of birds and insects, has no formal beginning or end." Elsewhere the same notes (to the Nonesuch compilation *Africa: Drum, Chant and Instrumental Music*) reinforced the impression with this sentence: "The eight-year-old Djerma boy who performs this solo spends virtually all of his time improvising on his instrument."

It was one thing to imagine a life lived entirely in music—to think of Eric Dolphy practicing almost continuously when he wasn't performing, so that the recordings amounted to brief excerpts from an extended piece of music that was his life; or of Stevie Wonder building up soundscapes track by track, effect by effect, working alone in darkness, the harbinger of generations of technical wizards who would gradually do away with the need for performers or even instruments.

If even the creators of music were learning to do without scoring, without writing, without playing, perhaps the listeners could go one better and establish themselves as the ultimate creative force. To select the sounds, out of a forever expanding library: wasn't it godlike, this cosmic passivity? If not, why had this equipment been invented, this array of personalized space capsules? If we could not conveniently steal away into the emptier reaches of Upper Volta, we could at least rig up an electronic savannah with near-perfect acoustic fidelity.

Being alone did tend to distance you from where the music was coming from. At times, in an effort to get a bit closer to the source of what you were hearing, you might find yourself reading the liner notes with obsessive attentiveness—as if liner notes could save you! At least they kept you company. Reading them over and over, you developed an intimacy with their random bits of reportage, chit-chat, bad poetry, murky political slogans or notes toward a new world religion, in-jokes about the recording session, salutations ("Hi Deb!"), Islamic prayers, technical remarks, effusive flights of praise, grand theoretical pronouncements about the origins of Dixieland or the necessity of serialism, music critics settling old scores about who played piano on some crucial early bebop session, or (best of all) utterly mindless copy written or dictated or ghost-written in the name of some deejay or associate producer: "In my many years in the music business it has been my privilege to meet relatively few artists to whom the word 'overnight sensation' could be applied . . ." The words (the more random the better), the packaging, even the familiar nicks and skips of records played a thousand times: these were last links to a world getting more hypothetical by the day, the world where real people got together in real places and made sounds.

But in many ways it was more appealing to build a new world out of the fragments. Put them together according to your needs: string together the fetish-songs denoting a particular person, a particular desire, a love affair consummated or otherwise. The song was present, the singer was absent, the person the singer sang about was even more absent. "She's Not There," "The Things We Said Today": everything had already vanished. "The Way You Look Tonight": gone. "They Can't Take That Away From Me": they already took it. The song, ultimate analog, made what wasn't there somehow stay put. After her brother died a girl I knew played the song that coincidentally bore his name many times, for many years.

Item by item you built up a box of magic songs. The titles and artists printed on the labels were strictly for the regular customers. Once they became part of your private domain they acquired magic names: the coincidence song, the talisman song, the voodoo curse song, the violent revolution song, the sexy daydream song, the song with the key to the encrypted name. The original recording evolved into a dream song tailored to your own peculiar requirements and providing entry into imaginary lives. Incorporeal ethnographic fictions configured themselves into narratives of empire and voyage, orgy and divine revelation, catastrophic battle and the reunion of scattered communities. Side A, Band One: The Flight Across the Mountain. Band Two: The

Fire at Midnight. Band Three: The Closing of the Shutters. Band Four: The Awakening of the Birds. Band Five: The Death of the Messenger. Bonus Track: The Wagon on the Hidden Road.

I made the pilgrimage to his apartment every few days, and then every few weeks, every few months. My own life was changing, in tiny increments, but in that place there was a sense of gathering immobility. Time stood still. We would again compare notes on what records we were listening to, a discussion that reverted helplessly to the same beloved anomalies. At what point did his apartment come to seem a place under siege, to evoke those horror movies in which palazzos accumulate thickly matted layers of dust and every door squeaks as if being opened for the first time in centuries? An accclerated aging process appeared to be going on, as if not years but decades had passed since we initiated this dialogue. We would emerge into daylight and disintegrate like fugitives from Shangri-La or the lost kingdom of Kôr. I thought of the aristocratic hero of Satyajit Ray's *The Music Room,* who created a world of continuous sound into which he could withdraw. He lost himself in music while his mansion imperceptibly became a sealed-off place.

Ancient courts knew music as a protective buffer. Serenades and divertimentos could blot out the noise of approaching armies or other, more local disturbances. The solitary monarch could enforcc a silence nowhere else obtainable: not a whisper was to infringe on the resonance he sponsored. Thus might one imagine Charles I savoring the dreamlike continuum of Lawes's viol interludes with their promise of an ethereal existence indefinitely sustained. In the listener's hermit kingdom he summons as to his court the bronze cymbals of the Mycenaeans or the water drums of the Han Dynasty.

In the end he turned the record off, turned himself off. Naturally it happened when I had turned aside and was no longer paying much attention. For a long time things had been getting on his nerves more than before. He complained about the power of advertising: "I know it sounds like an exaggeration, but it's really as bad as Nazism. It's as if they're trying to tell you that you don't exist; they want to appropriate even that last part of your mind that doesn't care about what they're saying." Of course everyone complained about advertising, but not everyone suggested that advertising was making life genuinely unbearable, or at any rate they didn't say it in a tone that indicated they really meant it. His routine was governed by indecipherable compulsions. When he turned down a final dinner invitation it was for the most deadly serious reason: "I have to stay home and watch *Dallas Cowboys Cheerleaders II.*"

There was an anecdote he had often told about the time he visited the blind guitarist Doc Watson in his hotel room. Doc had told him to come in, the door was open, and he was momentarily startled to find himself in a pitch-dark room. There was no obvious point to the anecdote beyond the fact that blind people don't need lights, but with each retelling the shock of that abrupt darkness seemed more acute and inexplicable.

Years after he hanged himself I imagined writing him a letter, a late bulletin of news from Earth:

A lot happened since you cut out, unimaginable things that rapidly became imaginable. There is no Yugoslavia anymore! Zaire became the Congo again! The premier of Israel was assassinated by a Jew! The more time passed, the more uncannily strange it got. And so many people left the planet. Frank Zappa died. Klaus Kinski died. Carl Wilson died. You would have loved *This Is Spinal Tap.* How could you have known that in your distinctly private way you were exploring a sensibility of ironic collage that would take over the culture, that you were (as if you cared) so triumphantly ahead of the curve? That lounge music and the other stuff we reserved for private amusement, the unthinkable delights of Las Vegas and Hollywood and Broadway, would come back with a veneer of aesthetic seriousness?

At any rate, before I close—and it would have been so interesting to discuss this—you should know that I finally decided it's impossible to listen to music alone, least of all when you are alone. You listen always as if with a companion whom the music almost evokes, almost is—because, after all, as Tony Bennett put it,

> *When things go wrong*
> *A man ain't got a friend*
> *Without a song.*

13

The Year of Overthrowal

[Cue: Explainer, "Table Is Turning," released 1980.]
Prophecy comes out of a radio:

> *There was a wheel the Bible say*
> *That keep spinning every day*
> *Today you rule a kingdom*
> *Tomorrow you the opposite position*

The jukebox (sum total of the music playing in the world right now) is a single text and it's alive. Alive: what a terrifying concept. When the music shifts there is no telling what it will shift into. What if the songs added up to a single immense poem, stitched together like the ancient epics stanza by stanza? And if we were living inside it, not knowing how the story will turn out, or even which story it is?

The ancient epics offer no escape from the reality they propose. The geography of such poems is coextensive with the world in which they exist. Helen and Achilles and Cassandra—the founders of the empires of Mali and Persia—the conquerors of the Etruscans and the Gaets—sacred criminals, blasphemers and adulterers, fatally wounded heroes, oracular virgins, inventors of stratagems, secret traitors: their force is still spread among us, they gave birth to us, we cannot escape from the consequences of their actions. But what if it continued like that, what if the mythical past had never ended? A system of omens and dooms continues to operate under the surface of an apparently deforested and freshly paved world. How would we know, how would we find out?

We would have to listen for the rhythm. Cadence is destiny. At the appointed moment the Pope dies; at the appointed moment the flute part comes in. It's about timing, backbeat, vatic ictus. From grooves come events. Vamp until ready for the realities not yet released, of which we can glimpse only the trailer. SOON TO BE A MAJOR MOTION PICTURE: the breaking of the vessels, collapse of walls, smoke in the streets, fields where mad kings eat grass. "Today you rule a kingdom, tomorrow you the opposite position," sang the Explainer (Winston Henry) in Trinidad in 1979, because '79 was The Year of Overthrowal and, the way the song's title tells it, "The Table Is Turning." (Two years earlier, '77 was to have been, according to the Jamaican group Culture, the year when "two sevens clash" and the signs of apocalypse proliferate.) For the Explainer, a hidden rhyme scheme (controlled either by the wheel of fate or the logic of historical inevitability) connects the more or less simultaneous downfalls of Idi Amin, Emperor Bokassa, the Shah of Iran, Anastasio Somoza, and Eric Gairy of Grenada:

> *The way the world is going on*
> *All who up start to fall back down*
> *This might sound like fallacy*
> *But '79 proved this to me.*

The Mighty Sparrow, on his competing record "Wanted Dead or Alive," chimes in with his own rundown—"The rule of the tyrants decline, / The year 1979. / From Uganda to Nicaragua / It's bombs and bullets all the time"—adding for good measure South Africa's Voerster, Rhodesia's Ian Smith, Dominica's Patrick John, Pakistan's Ali Bhutto, Ghana's Achimpeong, and South Korea's Park Chung Hee:

So they corrupt, so they vile
So it's coup after coup all the while.

Songs mark a secret calendar. Their structures already save a place for what happens before it happens.

[Cue: The Wailers, "Mister Brown," recorded 1970.]
    Hearing the Wailers for the first time exposed an underlying metric. The inexorable bass line pulsed from under layers of jumble. This is what it would sound like if everything else were turned off and you could hear what was trying to get said. But what exactly was it saying? A sequence of doom-laden organ chords with a wind machine howling in back of them opens a space for the question: "Who is Mister Brown? . . . Mister Brown is a clown / Who rides through town in a coffin." Listen to the same song twelve times in a row trying to understand the lyrics, moved especially by the ones you can't catch: brainwashed by "Brainwashing." When Bob Marley sang about "jamming" I thought for a second he meant the kind of jamming the Russians and Americans did to each other's radio broadcasts in the Cold War. The idea was to interrupt the regular programming.
    The poems that we know consist of everything that has already happened and that has been tabulated in books. The poem we might possibly inhabit consists of everything that has not yet happened, or has just started to happen, the names that cannot be looked up in a book, the wall writing that went up last night. Nothing more unsettling than that the world should be such a poem, that it should move forward, that irrevocable chasms should open inside it, armies clash, temples burn, families divide, walls of separation rise stone by stone. You'd probably be more comfortable with the same old song, love's old sweet song, the old oaken bucket, the songs that mother sang, the songs that echoed once through Tara's halls, "Silent Night," "Easter Parade," "Yesterday": the unchanging past that you can move around in for the fun of it, rearranging, jazzing up, shifting beats, adding parts, updating lyrics, without ever disturbing the foundations.
    The musicians are listening for symptoms of disturbance. Their ears are trained to detect cracks, frayings, the trembling of fault lines, the

faint hum that signals metal fatigue. All the musicians, potentially, are prophets. The crucial communication—the recognition of an unseen pattern, the breaching of an unperceived layer—might come to any of them, from the half-mad street corner organ grinder to magisterial inventors like Billy Strayhorn or Bernard Herrmann. It might come to Albert Ayler or Pharoah Sanders or John Gilmore, blowing as if to level the walls of a besieged city, or as if to exemplify those "winds of change" that Prime Minister Harold Macmillan had talked about in what seemed like another life (Africa '58). Here indeed are those winds—"instruments" indeed, but of what unknown forces?—making as if to mold new worlds in the manner of cosmic glassblowers.

No telling what form the message will take. It might come as a movie theme song. It might be a soap commercial, it might be a melodica solo invented by an illiterate shepherd. The singing beggar in the Indian movie is really an avatar, recognizable as such by the mysterious song he repeats at unexpected intervals. While the other characters are getting betrothed and jilted, enriched and swindled, disinherited and exiled and tragically estranged—suffering amnesia in train wrecks and forgetting their identity for reels at a stretch—he's meanwhile everywhere, far beneath the narrative. He's the vegetable man, the raggedy taxi driver, always with the same wink and the trademark warble: "Don't worry, baby, it's only a dream; I'll be singing my song until the end of time; people come and people go, the song goes on forever."

He sees everything, even the future: "Twenty, thirty years later you'll come to the same corner and nothing will have changed, except that by then you'll understand what the lyrics mean." That's how the gods talk to people. They work their way into the minds of singers who do the talking for them under the guise of letting themselves go on, pouring it out like Jessie Hill for Minit Records in 1962:

> I won't stop trying
> Till I create a disturbance in your mind.

Broadly speaking, songs are either love songs or not. The love songs are timeless, so it's easier to deal with the choices they present: the only question is of happiness or sadness, the toss of a coin. I saw her walking. I looked for her and she wasn't there. Yesterday was happy, but today is sad; today started out sad but tomorrow will be happier. A thousand years come and go and the lovers are still meeting for the first time or just starting to complain or allowing themselves to remember what it was like before the split.

The other songs, by contrast, have the dangerous quality of existing in time. They even have a jump on which way time is turning: they have a connection, occult or otherwise, to events that unfold, so that with them it's a matter of truth or untruth. The chill down the spine comes from wondering what would happen—what kind of world would I come to inhabit—if I believed the lyrics. The prophet speaks, but does he speak true? Is London really burning? Is Afrika burning? Is there a train that's coming? Are we spirits in a material world? Is America waiting for a message of some kind or another? Is the table turning? What's going on? How long has this been going on? Does anybody really know what time it is? Is there really a wheel that keeps spinning every day?

Each song is a proposition. I want to make a string of those propositions, so that when scanned in the correct order it offers a theory of everything that happens. But like the necklaces that children make from interlocking plastic beads, the string comes apart at the slightest pressure. Disconnected facts and rumors and prophesying insights—geometric patterns carved into the Andes, unnatural proliferations of rabbits and mice, high rises whose windows keep falling out, Caribbean death squads, Fleetwood Mac singing about the Bermuda Triangle, the plots of Italian Westerns, the fall of Allende, the Honeydrippers singing "Impeach the President"—are heaped on the rug like a pile of popped beads. The residue of Bible study, Marxism-Leninism-Mao Thought, numerology, the graphs scrawled in chalk on city sidewalks by a night-wandering psychotic, dirty jokes, inspirational mottoes, and what somebody on drugs might glean from rapidly scanning newspaper headlines mixes into a sauce in which the future will be cooked up. One thing is certain: if something unbearable is happening somewhere, it will find its way into a song, even if by the time the song reaches your ears it will sound like a baby's lullaby or an invitation to a dance party.

[Cue: Andrea True Connection, "More, More, More," released February 1976.]

Once there was a music that seemed to promise that the future would be without language and therefore without pain. They called it disco. It was not the murder of language, only its seduction into a state of permanent erotic mindlessness. No need to talk, unless it makes you happy—"yeah, baby, please, that's right, uh huh"—no need even to have a name. Just call yourselves The Party Freaks. Here comes the express. Once you get started you won't remember what the big deal was supposed to be about the differences between states of being, intentions, destinations. In the new world you've already arrived. If the hook is what connects you to the song, makes you want to listen to it in the first place, why not repeat the hook over and over, all night if necessary? If structure limits or interferes with pleasure, invent a structure with no end or beginning, complete at every instant, part of a long chain of moments of pleasure.

Perform an experiment on yourself. Experience the radicalism of total surrender. Dismantle whatever gear it was that you thought held you together. Of what do you consist, after the ledges have been cleared, the connecting doors removed and the hinges unscrewed, the small accumulations of pocket litter and personal documentation discarded? "Baby, you know my love for you is real," sings the porn star Andrea True in her new incarnation as disco diva. It's real even if it's only a movie—"get the cameras rolling, get the action going"—which makes everything in life much simpler. A new aristocracy fueled by cocaine and margaritas plays with the opulence of a tacked-together palazzo, headquarters of a piratic successor state picking up the pieces in the wake of the Indochinese disaster. "We reinvented the world last night, it was wild." Stockbrokers and gangsters grin at each other in an after-hours club on Varick Street to the tune of "Cherchez la Femme":

> *Blowing his mind on cheap grass and wine,*
> *Oh ain't it crazy baby . . .*

They're all the same,
All the sluts and the saints.

In the paradise of equivalence everything always adds up right. There are no odd or even numbers and therefore no possibility of error.

The epic sound system announces its capacity to exist forever. There shall be no dawn. In the recesses of night, successive layers of personality can be taken off like wigs and garter belts. Language? Did somebody say "language"? Words are other wigs, other garter belts. "If I ever lose this heaven I'll never be the same." In here we translate every term into every other term. If you forget one you can pick it up on the way out, if you can still reconstruct how it used to be before you came in here. Otherwise you can start over again. Everybody's joining in, even the jazz musicians. This is the era when it seems as if almost every album could be called *Cosmic Funk*, although only one actually is. All over town the tunes are melting.

[Cue: Shadow, "Don't Mess wid Me Head," recorded ca. 1980.]
As the all-night dancers push themselves beyond the possibility of closing time—"We're lost in music"—there comes news from Iran, by way of the Mighty Sparrow:

The Shah have a short time to live
Because the Ayatollah don't forgive
When you see church ruling state
With pure vengeance and hate
Situation must be explosive.

Not long after the revolutionary regime of the mullahs takes power, the Ayatollah Khomeini declares a ban on music, especially the imported kind: "All the corrupting Western songs must go." (Does he mean the Beach Boys? Nancy Sinatra? Sister Sledge? Al Martino? Loretta Lynn? Funkadelic? *All*, did he say all? Could he possibly mean Stevie Wonder or Marvin Gaye or James Brown? For that matter does he mean the Mighty Sparrow or the Explainer? Or is it the amalgam into which all of them coalesce for an ear that never cared in the first place?) Starting as he means to continue, the Ayatollah establishes an order of silence, permitting not so much as the muffled bass groove leaking through the sealed doors of a private club. Last Tango in Teheran: the marching song of this revolution is the absence of song, the shattering of the pleasure dome within which "Disco Inferno" had a moment before been churning out in a continuous loop, to yield a morning after of bracing air and broken glass. It's history happening. It can make things get quiet in a hurry.

"Well, it's been building up inside of me for I don't know how long," as the Beach Boys sang in "Don't Worry, Baby." Only this time it's building up *outside* of you and the message is more like "Worry, Baby." "Nothing will be as it was," sings Milton Nascimento in Brazil.

> *What is wrong with the world,*
> *Like everything gone out of control,*

sings the Trinidadian soca star Shadow, and he has only one suggestion: "Don't Mess wid Me Head." But everybody does, anyway. The signs are everywhere. KEIN ZUKUNFT. NO FUTURE. NO MORE LOVE SONGS. It has been a long intermission and now it's drawing to a close.

A Japanese comic book about the impending world economic crisis tells of the Italian banker with close ties to the Vatican who hanged himself under London Bridge. It has something to do with the mysterious death of John Paul I in the autumn of 1978. It has to do with numerology (everything has to do with numerology). It has to do with the Freemasons (everything has to do with the Freemasons). It has to do, naturally, with the Book of Revelation. (Isn't that what they were talking about on the fade-out of that Stevie Wonder record, or was it the fade-in of that Curtis Mayfield record?) If you understood, you would have no trouble understanding.

Nine hundred cultists die in the jungle, drinking their poison Kool-Aid after killing the U.S. congressman who had come to investigate them. The news of it emerges like a new song, like a new kind of song. We thought we were living in our familiar world—whichever that might be—and really we were living in Jonestown. Some people always knew that. It shouldn't have been so hard to figure out, what with the paranoid theorists running in and out of the copy shop with their urgent letters about secret lists and flying saucers and electrodes implanted by the CIA, or the emissaries from the Children of God making multiple copies of joky newsletters about the need for members to turn their children into holy prostitutes. Or the guys in the ski masks, or the hunger strikers in the German prison, or the Italian Fascists who blew up the train station in Bologna. Or the Munich Olympics, or the Greensboro massacre. These people who aren't kidding, and who aren't singing either.

All over the planet in 1979 the Bee Gees are harmonizing on "How Deep Is Your Love?" You hear them in the taxis of New York and the coffee shops of Rome, in hair salons and the waiting rooms of consulates, in underground shopping centers and open-all-night fast-food outlets, on a plane flying low over the glistening Canadian tundra, on a vessel making its way westward in calm seas toward the port of Nakhodka. If the world manages to hang together it's on a thread of disco so homogenized it belongs everywhere and nowhere. It has a smooth feeling. It disrupts nothing. It's at home in Lapland and the Comoros. It's as generic as a dip in the pool or a continental breakfast at any one of over five hundred locations worldwide.

In Osaka "How Deep Is Your Love?" fills the lobby of the theater where several hundred people are lined up to get a look at *Saturday Night Fever,* while around the corner the *jôruri* who provides narration and sound effects for traditional puppet plays chants to an almost deserted house, mostly a bunch of formally attired old women who fan themselves and have never heard of disco. The Japanese game parlors pulse with electronic blips as the compulsive players of Space Invaders sit hunched in front of the screens. Pink Lady, two young women in short skirts who chirp upbeat songs with the enthusiasm of cartoon characters and look like a schoolgirl's fantasy of Las Vegas lounge entertainers, smile and pose on every available television screen and magazine cover. What bubble world is this? The electronic pop music of Ryuichi Sakamoto and Yellow Magic Orchestra invites you aboard a toy train of rhythm, a bright abstract monorail heading toward a future whose ragged elements are airbrushed out to reveal a luxury suite of pure design.

In Russia the night swarms with black marketers looking for Japanese felt-tip pens, or anything Japanese. In Russia all the elements appear to be ragged. The shelves in the Moscow grocery store are bare except for a huge consignment of beets imported from Bulgaria, and the TV in the hotel lobby shows a three-hour tribute to Soviet war films of the past half-century. The triumphant movie themes blare at top volume. Nobody is watching, nobody is listening. In Irkutsk the authorities have set up a wooden platform in the square for a public dance. The featured rock band consists of soldiers in uniform playing a pretty good imitation of Manfred Mann's sound from 1964. From the way the local youth get into it I can almost believe the '60s are just arriving, that the era of my youth has started over again in this place where time stopped some time ago.

Eras overlap messily. In a neighborhood of south London, people are still living in prefab housing left over from the war years, and in the smoke-filled local a piano player gets the patrons going (some of them look like the original cast of a 1952 Ealing comedy) with a late-night sing-along of "Knees Up, Mother Brown." The next morning I read that in the tube station around the corner from the pub a Pakistani on his way home from work was stomped to death by four young men in boots, probably while I was knocking back a pint with the nostalgic comfort of living inside someone else's imagined past. A year later the Clash releases "Clampdown," their warning cry about the Fascists who walk the streets of London. Nothing suggests exaggeration.

The writing is on the walls all over the Lower East Side: THE PARTY'S OVER, accompanied by the symbolic logo of an inverted cocktail glass, and a date: 1933. The Nazis! For years there have been rumors that the Nazis would somehow come back. Has the moment come? It's an ad for a punk band called Missing Foundation. Are the punks Nazis? Isn't this what they always said would happen? It had to happen. Once the Flower Power of the '60s had mutated into the design elements of a commercial for "organic" shampoo—a New Age recipe for resilience, luxuriance, and that shiny healthy look—some felt it was time to move on to the adoption of slasher movies as aphrodisiacs. Those people in the audience can change their natures as quickly as they change their politics, and do it as quickly as they change their songs: and they do that all the time now. The records go on sale and two weeks later they've disappeared. Everything is a limited edition. The records themselves are exercises in hard-core brevity. Get them while you can.

The excitement of a temporary world is contagious. When Talking Heads releases "Life During Wartime"—

Ain't got no speakers, ain't got no headphones,
Ain't got no records to play

—it's a joke, because you couldn't be hearing the record without speakers, or if the record didn't exist. At the same time it's partly a joke about not really being a joke, or at least providing the momentary cheap thrill of imagining that it isn't a joke. Or whatever. Anyway, it's pretty funny.

In Toulouse the walls of the cathedral have been damaged by anti-clerical activists. In the local bookstore they sell comics in which the heroic Languedocians go down to defeat and massacre at the hands of the Catholic Northerners from Paris. It happened eight hundred years ago. Someone scrawled LANGUEDOC LIBRE on the wall. All the walls in town are covered with writing: there is a war of slogans. The neo-Fascists use white paint for their Celtic crosses. The Maoists and the radical feminists use red paint: C'EST LA GUERRE DES LILITH. Specters are haunting Languedoc: Lilith and the slaughtered Albigensian heretics. In the main square outside the cathedral a book dealer with an odd pointed beard—he might be the secret leader of a chiliastic coven that meets in the crypt under the cathedral—is offering for sale, among many other items, a volume of French pro-Nazi literature from the mid-1930s. "C'est un bon bouquin, ça," he tells me, it's a good little book. What does he mean, exactly? Perhaps the effect would be different if it weren't for the pointed beard and what it does to his carefully controlled excuse for a smile.

A preternatural calm warmth settles over the southern coast, an undeveloped beachfront near Gruissan. A beautiful young woman, long-haired, entirely nude, walks along the Mediterranean with a gigantic black mastiff on a leash: the young Aphrodite with the Hound of the Baskervilles. In the background, at the makeshift drinks stand, Bob Marley records play in rotation. At the movie theater, which resembles a concrete bunker, *Carrie* is showing, with its ballet of the girls' shower room disturbed by menstrual blood. "Exodus, movement of Jah people." Nothing moves in the heat. In the shack that passes for a restaurant, a German tourist complains about the quality of the sausages, complains so relentlessly that finally the French cook, a weathered hulk, emerges from the kitchen and listens in silence while the tourist goes on: "In my country we give food like this to *animals!*" The cook maintains silence, looking at him as if measuring his throat for the knife, or as if remembering the throats of the tourist's compatriots that in former years he might have already slit. He takes the sausages back into the kitchen.

In Ayacucho, the young Indian men ride motorbikes and act out scenes from kung fu movies: *Seven Blows of the Dragon, Legendary Weapons of China, The Flying Guillotine.* They go underground and surface as foot soldiers of Sendero Luminoso: a Maoist army spreading through the Andes. In Manhattan, wall posters appear all over the East Village, posters that might almost, with the lovely phrase SHINING PATH and the lovely image of the sun rising over mountains, be mistaken for the advance publicity of yet another meditation school, some even more advanced Institute for Inner Harmonics.

A graduate of Bible study classes in which John Lennon was vilified as a tool of Satan turns up at the Dakota with a gun. The chief songwriter for Joy Division (an English rock band named for prostitution units in Nazi concentration camps) hangs himself after writing "Love Will Tear Us Apart." They mean it, they aren't kidding. None of them are kidding.

In midtown Manhattan nothing moves. The streets are jammed up with people assembled to call for a nuclear freeze, except that most of them never get to assemble. Efficient crowd control keeps the majority sidelined in side streets, calmly passing the day waiting for a turn that never comes: a kind of anti-demonstration, silent and well behaved. Downtown at a block party in a vacant lot a DJ is playing Twilight 22's record "Siberian Nights," proto-rap that keeps insisting: "And nuclear winter gonna freeze your brain!" The Jamaican dub masters Clint Eastwood and General Saint chant as if in response: "They even planning a neutron bomb . . . But we can't take another world war." On Avenue C the drug carnival goes on all through the night, people passing money through the slots where the bricks have been removed, getting crack in return.

[Cue: Tangerine Dream, main title theme, Sorcerer, *released 1977.]*

A movie like William Friedkin's *Sorcerer* is the perfect drug for a moment that cannot decide whether it is after the end or before the beginning, and whose motto might be: In the Meantime. A remake of the old French movie *The Wages of Fear, Sorcerer* manages to turn what was social protest into a rock and roll experience of slow death punctuated by explosions. It is a movie in which only unpleasant and destructive things happen and whose only real theme is sensual gratification. Four men go into the jungle and only one comes out alive, so he can be casually assassinated (it's irony, man) just when he thought he'd made it. You can't win, but you can experience pleasure while losing, especially when the music is wall-to-wall electronica by Tangerine Dream. It's music to drown in at two in the morning after everybody else went home; music that promises never to remind you of anything.

Learn how to relax and enjoy catastrophe, and the rest is easy. Soon you can even stop worrying about the neutron bomb and spend more time thinking about cocaine, Lycra spandex, and Godard movies as ancient artifacts. Who said fun was dead? Not the new dandies, the priests of retro aestheticism, the wearers of thin ties and black jackets modeled on what Eddie Constantine wore in that early Jess Franco spy thriller, the young cultural archeologists in horn-rims who study the mutations of mood music and find out the secret meanings in the film scores of Henry Mancini.

In between the changes of scene and the collapse of states, I had forgotten to keep track of the passage of time. It happens. I'm startled back from a reverie of continual forward movement by the emergence of the new young, who grew up while I wasn't looking in that direction, and who have come to signal an irrevocable transition. They have evolved into their versions of the movies my friends and I watched back in high school. To seal a process of defamiliarizing that is already well underway, they will reinvent our past. They appropriate the songs from our private jukebox and remix them to bring out different sound values, different emotions. What we once did to the '40s they're doing to the '60s. They make Burt Bacharach strange the way we made Glenn Miller strange. They will tell us what it meant, as if our having been there must necessarily cloud our perception. To realize that in some sense they're right begins to instill a new detachment. The years are gone and they don't belong to us anymore, not any of them.

14

Ambient Night at Roots Lounge

T HERE IS A MOMENT DURING THE FADE-OUT OF "MR. PITIFUL" when Otis Redding sings:

And I want to tell you right now
Everything that's going through my mind.

Through yet one more rehearing the phrase still shocks, because by the time that moment comes around you are so full of everything that's going through *your* mind (everything prompted by the still miraculously gratifying interplay between what Otis is singing and what Booker T. and the M.G.s are playing, and by the buried personal associations that the record inevitably stirs into fitful life) that once again you have forgotten that it's music. You thought it was the world that you were caught up in, instead of a record. You can't believe that it's happened again, that it happens every time, and that you never learn.

At such moments you are thinking and listening at the same time; except that listening shuts out thought, and thought shuts out listening. Or, listening shuts out one thought to clear the way for another thought to emerge, only once it emerges it tends to shut out the listening that gave birth to it in the first place. Really to listen would be to stop thinking altogether. So it goes in like fashion with all the oppositions: the listener tries to melt and resists melting, looks for history and tries to erase history, summons up images while systematically distorting them or replacing them with fresh fancies nudged into being by a chord or a quaver, and then wonders how fresh they really are. Hasn't this happened before, as in one of those recurring dreams? Doesn't it perhaps happen exactly like this, every single time you submit yourself to music?

In that space between listening and not-listening a story is invented but only obliquely perceived, the visible obverse of the sounds. You don't know if the story is created by the music or partially blotted out by it. You tell yourself, "I'm doing something: I'm listening to a record." Or else: "I'm not doing anything, I'm listening to a record." So you don't know what you want, to start listening or to stop listening.

Maybe you have to stop before you can start. Because you are always listening, even (or especially) when you don't want to. The program doesn't let up. Keep your dial tuned to Inner Radio and the stuff pours through the static. You can lie awake in the dark and let someone else (a late-night voice at home with itself and with nothing else) take care of changing the records, completing the thoughts, keeping track of what time it is or isn't.

A man who exists only as a voice on the radio has no body, no history, only a recognizable drawl, an impatience with silences, a quick brutal laugh as punctuation between his anecdotes and his announcements. Even the bad jokes are good. He will walk you through the history of music as if it were the history of the world, and as if both were nothing more than the history of this particular evening, the story of how you will somehow reach dawn.

"We've got a non-stop lineup of volunteers for your ears, the Sultans of Soundtrack, the Pashas of Playback, from the fall of night to dawn's early light, from morning musk to purple dusk, this here is yours truly DJ Rerun . . . And coming right up is the rest of the lineup of stars . . . We got DJ Revamp, DJ Exit Ramp, DJ Modulator, DJ Byproduct, DJ Fossil Fuel, DJ Aftertaste . . . They'll tell you how to put more slither in your zither . . . More stalk in your walk . . .

"Ahoy there . . . DJ Rerun on the dial . . . With a sidecar full of meltdown music for that very special clambake . . . Or merely for grooving in the solitude of your hammock . . . While toreadors of the stratosphere skate on the thin ice of the outlying satellites . . . We're going to be up all night so let's get started . . . Up all year if need be . . . And it may take that long because I've got a stack of mysteriously twisted sides here that insist on being played . . . That's right, they put a gun to my head . . . It happened while you were waiting around to be rescued from the jungle of time where your plane crashed . . . Only five can go back to civilization . . . The rest of you are going to be stuck there forever with whatever tapes you brought with you . . . Good thing you chose the cuts wisely . . . You did, didn't you? Never mind, DJ Rerun is here to pick up the slack . . .

"We got all kinds of music, we got bar songs, we got praise songs, we got Greek gangsters and people from outer space, harmonica solos and funny songs about food, greatest hits of Mexican surf bands, Russian soldiers singing Chinese folk ballads, Alabama gospel records from before recording was invented, voodoo rites with strings, Mantovani without strings (that one is really wild), the lost Frank Sinatra–Ravi Shankar tapes, *Tangerine Dream Unplugged,* all kinds of novelty items . . . You never heard anything like it . . . Except maybe in the soundtrack of your own nightmares, heh heh heh . . . *(slips into Viennese psychiatrist voice)* Let's face it, my friend, you vould haff to be pretty sick to be listening to zis program in ze first place! . . . *(preacher voice)* This is the music of perdition, my friends . . . What you call 'a good beat' is nothing but the sound of Satan's footsteps as he sneaks up behind you . . . *(ayatollah voice)* All the corrupt western imperialist good-time music must go . . . If you can hum it, we burn it! . . . *(noise of automatic weapon fire)* Don't worry, the Navy SEALS dropped us some Walkmans! . . . First off we'll be listening to the '80s classic 'Voodoo Economics' by the Rent . . . "

Think of it as the musical unconscious, the sound of auditory residue, this radio station that will not permit itself to be turned off. It is landfill that constantly shifts and reassembles, built up from what sticks to the ears. It proliferates in the gap between deliberate listening and involuntary overhearing. The scrap heap heaves and grinds, and its movement is like the slow shrug of tectonic plates. Bits of songs are threshed in the shifting—you probably got the lyrics wrong—and mingle promiscuously with advertising jingles and ancient snatches of operetta and hurdy-gurdy repertoire, well-worn scat phrases and doo-wop hooks. Under it are the mindless chants that surge up from your own head, the tiny repetitive almost mad songs that you and everybody else serenade yourselves with on bus or at desk or while doing the dishes, grateful that no trickster can embarrass you by cranking up the volume on what's playing in your head.

So listening has always in a way meant unlistening. You need ears cleared of that rattling debris to receive new signals. Blow the tunes out, avoid classifying, distrust the old information, the old responses. Make as if your instructor, Bruce Lee, had whacked you on the head because you said something about "thinking." "Don't think, *feel!*" Sabotage your own expectations. Abandon the shapes and rhythms you keep expecting the music to fall into. Having destroyed your thoughts, destroy your feelings too, destroy every impulse to classify a random cluster of sounds as "cheerful," "mournful," "defiant," "wistfully bewildered," "laid-back," "seductive," "transcendent." Move into the country where feelings are as unreadable as mountains in a stretch of country unknown to you. Become hollow. Make room. Learn to despise your own internal protests at what bores or irritates you with its unfamiliarity. Be shaped by strangeness. Love what abrades. The future can come into being only by stripping away what was formerly locked in place.

You keep telling yourself you have to smash history, no matter how much you loved the old episodes. But you keep building more history, making it up out of the imagined connections between pieces of music. Nothing but stories, and all the stories are about origins. The future is back there, only a few thousand years on the other side of what you were listening to a moment ago. Behind Monteverdi's *Orfeo* you find Dufay's motets, and behind the motets a medieval dance music revealed in turn as a remnant of lost Greco-Arabic melody. The thirteenth-century English lament "Brid on a Breyre" might have been adapted from an Algerian shepherd's hillside solo, a repetitive high-pitched wail that traveled the circuitous overland routes that allowed an ancient pastoral jazz to permeate—ever so slowly—each gulf and hilltop enclave. Music is the voluptuous traveler. It goes away and leaves itself behind at the same time.

You find a different kind of history book in Henry Cowell's Folkways compilation *Folk Music of the Mediterranean,* itself a remnant of sorts, a 1953 project drawing on earlier field recordings that Cowell had strung together into a narrative about the secret sonic transactions connecting Libya and Greece and Albania and Provence and Morocco. Merely by listening you feel you are tracing the permutations of a pan-Mediterranean music branching off into subsidiary Serbian and Syrian and Egyptian and Italian variations, an embedded language signaling its presence through "yodelling glottal trills" and "long melismas" and "tiny slides of pitch." Go back far enough and you would be listening to the beginning of the world, the first tune, the first responsive beat.

These are so many invitations to lose yourself, or more properly to empty yourself of yourself. Once you succeed in clearing that personal baggage out of the way, you can wander freely through the sounds the world gives you as if wandering through the world itself, to discover at last whether you would recognize yourself once you got there. But nowhere is there any freedom from memories, stories, histories. In the very act of listening you weave a fantasy about what listening is, a fantasy whose very groundlessness is what draws you to listening in the first place. In the oscillating drone of Egyptian mizmar players whose circular breathing lets them sustain their tones to unbearable length you are suddenly caught up short by a recollection of the moment in Satyajit Ray's Bengali film *Pather Panchali* when the father's unbearable cry of grief at the death of his child is transmuted (dubbing as ultimate act of mercy) into a flute's wail.

In the same way the ancient drone of the Japanese gagaku orchestra—music for imperial sanctifications and exorcisms, the oldest orchestral music surviving in intact arrangements—takes up the otherwise unspeakable burden of loss at the end of Mizoguchi's *Sansho the Bailiff,* as the camera lifts farther and farther above the figures of son and blind mother embracing on a rocky deserted beach after years of separation, the only remaining members of a doomed family. Is that what music has been doing all this time, making the extremities of human feeling tolerable, bringing them into line? Tone and cadence mark the limits of what can be supported. By following the note to the end of its journey you could even learn to disappear and love it. The truly exotic, the music that doesn't remind you of music you've already heard, seems to make possible a glimpse of the kind of creature you have been all along. This is the sound that is made when you confront the only home anyone can finally claim, the edge where flat sea meets black rock.

And what can that sound be except an imitation of the non-human? What other library of samples has ever been available? Music is where you drop the bundle. Through this gate the human passes to encounter what is outside itself—birds, thunder, the crackling of fire, surf noise—and to learn to perceive its own innermost cry as audible echo, song amplified by cliff-hollow. Like Robinson Crusoe in the Valley of Echoes, the first musician stands astonished as he confronts his own voice as part of the landscape. It is a distant music beyond and perhaps more substantial than himself. His voice's echo is a thunder no less terrifying than the thunder that will send him soon enough back to his cave. Caught in the middle of those sounds, he's nothing more than resonator, thin and tremulous as a drumskin.

To the city-dweller haunted by it in his brick tree-house, the seamless primeval hocketing of the Ba-Benzélé chorales from the heart of the Congo rain forest—liquid as the intersection of bird-voices in a thicket—seems not so much singing as listening made audible. They sing like that because they hear what you will never hear, what you will only imagine through the art they have made of it. The more ancient and simple the music, the more intricately complex, something like how a spiderweb would sound. It is the music of what was destroyed in you a long time ago, a notation of jettisoned or bypassed neural possibility.

Perhaps you did hear something like it, around the time you first began to grow ears. Some kind of music was coming at you even before birth. The primal culture clash might be between the aesthetics of womb sonar (the dolphin music of internal pings and amplified gurgles that was the radio of the unborn) and the aesthetics of whatever car commercial or heavy metal pick-of-the-week the newly thrust-out ears were first accosted by. The infant emerged from the watery microtones of his original darkness begins to discover what he has gotten himself into only when it's too late. How long does it take him to measure in imagination the four thousand years of civilization and its abrasions that it has taken to turn spiderweb music into "The Ballad of Davy Crockett" or "Blitzkrieg Bop" or the network TV theme music from the Gulf War? In the same way, he will discover, the swirling convolutions of jungle mythology (chanted from dusk to dawn to nose-flute accompaniment) have been refined into the sound-bite plot summaries of made-for-television thrillers (pumped up at each shift of clue or twist of hip to hot-button synth grooves). It takes a long time to evolve from the delicate and indefinitely prolonged into the quick and vibrantly crude.

Once there was history. There were families. Signals were sent from one settlement to another. Marks were left on trees to indicate the point where the colony vanished. Now the stories are adrift. A small-town police chief investigates the spillage of lethal chemicals from an army truck. To avenge the death of their mother, two brothers plan to destroy their stepfather with the help of a beautiful and seductive woman. An FBI agent probing an industrialist's kidnapping falls for the victim's wife—the prime suspect in the case. A postal inspector tries to prevent a big mail robbery. A detective seeks a scroll that holds the key to treasure, and encounters murder. A man falls apart when he learns that his wife has tried to murder him. An evil woman uses a retired secret agent to seize control of a submarine. A battered wife is accused of arranging her husband's murder. An oceanographer tries to prove that a colleague was murdered. A brave man, with no help from anyone, confronts murderous intruders seeking to steal gold from a mining complex. A detective uncovers a vicious plot to steal a secret industrial formula. A stripper fighting for custody of her son is charged with murder after her ex-husband is killed. A detective assumes the identity of his underworld look-alike in order to infiltrate a gold-smuggling ring. A cop's widow becomes involved with the drug dealer responsible for her husband's death. Jewel smugglers search for a legendary 200-carat diamond. A biology student searches for a legendary five-ring cobra. An undercover cop infiltrates a stolen-credit-card ring. A lawyer races against time to save an innocent man from execution. A CIA agent targets gun smugglers in Central America. Ruthless people search for a lost mine in Arizona.

All the stories happen at the same time. Nothing else ever happened. The stories come into being only so that the background music will have a reason to exist, in a world that without it would be silent. Or is the noise of the shows designed to drown out the noise that would otherwise make itself heard from under the silence? People turn on the TV in empty houses so as not to hear the creaks and gusts that sound too much like ghosts or burglars. You never know when they are going to steal up on you. At some point in your trajectory, some unexpected past is going to walk unannounced out of the least likely portal. The voice of Mississippi John Hurt will issue from the inner precincts of a Buddhist temple on the island of Shikoku, to guide the meditations or beguile the lunch hour of an unseen priest. From the organ invisible in its loft in the cathedral at Albi, the one the Catholics built after they wiped out the rebellious heretics, awe and terror will emanate in the form of music that sounds like what it is: a state-of-the-art technological thrill demanding respect for an army of occupation. From a jukebox in Santa Monica at the tail end of the twentieth century Johnny Horton will intrude, singing in 1959 about the War of 1812. Johnny seems to be suggesting that history is what you can't escape from, even when it's disconnected from everything else, even when nobody on the pier remembers the War of 1812, even when it's centuries after the surrender and it isn't even clear what was surrendered:

> They ran through the briars and they ran through the brambles
> And they ran through the bushes where a rabbit couldn't go.

In a back street of Tokyo, in one of the cramped zones of irregularity surviving in the interstices of the rapidly modernizing grid, a vendor of fried sweet potatoes not so long ago wove archaic variations on the phrase "*Yaki imo! Yaki imo! Imo, imo, imo.*" The cry was so penetrating that you could hear it in an office many blocks away, and so satisfying in its slightly varied repetitions that you would have kept listening forever. A decade passes and it is no longer there to be heard. The very tones and textures the vendor found within himself have started to become inaccessible to citizens with ears full of the Spice Girls and the Chemical Brothers. In this way the street itself lost its voice. Perhaps a field recording, if anyone had bothered to make one, might find its way into the Museum of the Ancestors.

As the vendors begin to stop singing, one by one all over the planet, the cries enter the category of folkloric material, something for George Gershwin to draw on for "Here Come De Honey Man" in *Porgy and Bess,* and for Miles Davis and Gil Evans to transmute into their even more ethereal version lasting barely over a minute, the quintessence of afterecho. By 1958, when a trio of vendors walks down Elvis Presley's New Orleans block in *King Creole,* their calls— "'Tatoes . . . Berries . . . Gumbo"—metamorphose with alarming rapidity into a brief but heavily arranged Hollywood number, a touristic fantasia for drive-ins.

The cry hovers forever on the edge of the drama, determined but unable to help or change anything, a voice beyond narrative. It is part of a chorus that encompasses Mongo Santamaria's watermelon man, or Johnnie Taylor's tightened-up Stax-Volt version of him, or Miriam Makeba's berry man singing "strawberries, ohh, strawberries," or the Trinidadian soap peddler given calypso immortality by The Lion in "The Vendor's Song" of 1938. "The Vendor's Song" seems to have to do with everyone in Port of Spain being driven slightly crazy by the repeated cry of "Gold Band soap, penny for the cake": "When we heard the tune, well it really cause a mess." There is no escape from advertising—"it was even crooned by the man in the moon"—so that The Lion has no recourse but to abandon language altogether (since language is apparently good only for selling soap) and take flight into choruses of scatting.

These take their place as part of the secret history where we also find Orlando Gibbons's "The Cries of London," a documentary of Elizabethan street life, where hawkers and town criers intersect in an ordered cacophony, the random calls arranged and harmonized—

Have you any work for a tinker?
New mackerel, new.
Broom, broom, broom, old boots, old shoes,
Pouch rings for brooms.
Will ye buy a mat for a bed?
Have you any kitchen stuff, maids?

—just as Proust's narrator would convert the cry of the snail vendor below his Parisian window into "one of those mournful cadences in which the composer of *Pelléas* shows his kinship with Rameau," and just as Walter Scharf in his score for *King Creole* would turn the sounds of a New Orleans street into the musical equivalent of VistaVision.

The vendors, back in the lost world, came closest to making human voices seem of a piece with the rest of creation. Perhaps it was because they sang of sustenance itself, hanging from a pole or floating in a barrel. They carried life in the most literal sense from place to place. To that music of hunger could be joined the call-and-response music of desire that Renaissance composers like Clément Janequin constructed out of the cries of birds. The practice would be echoed, with more austere intent, centuries later—not too long after Wagner's Siegfried gained access to the meaning of birdsong by sipping on dragon blood—by Olivier Messiaen, with his thick *Catalogue of the Birds* converting the song of nineteen species—blue rock thrush, short-toed lark, curlew, buzzard, and the rest—into distinct compositions for solo piano, each piece incorporating its "soloist . . . in its habitat, surrounded by its landscape and by the songs of other birds (seventy-seven in all) from the region." Eric Dolphy sat in his room listening to the birds at his window, finding ways to play along with them, to recreate that orchestra lost since mythic times in which humans and nonhumans found ways to jam.

One way or another it has been going on forever, this attempt to ride human music back to its origin, like Orpheus soloing his way into the country of the dead. Did anyone ever figure out a better way to charm demons? By the time the twentieth century was coming to an end it felt for many like a good moment to hook up to the source again, renew the primordial compact. Forget literature. Pick up Orpheus's fiddle and play. As you walk from the subway you hear the reiterated phrase a block away, through giant speakers: "Music is the universal language. Music is the universal language." This is no esoteric philosopher or soapbox evangelist. It's the MC for a dance band entertaining tourists in front of the World Trade Center, preparing to see the new century in.

Civilization turned out to be only a roundabout way of getting back to basics. Dawn of the throat-singers! Ululation and internal echo as final hardware triumph! No machine but the body itself! The dream of a technology rooted in the body finds its only possible expression in music, a technology whose only product is air currents shaped into figures. Pry the veil between worlds half an inch apart through devious serpentine inflections of flute music, as if the reality machine itself could be seduced—like the guardians of hell by Orpheus—into momentary inattention to let what it conceals peep through. Sound is a wedge to knock the portals loose with shakuhachi voicings, so that flakes of sky can scatter down through wrenched silences. It's raining light.

What more could humans hope to produce than a noise loud and deep enough to blow a hole into the nexus where space and time lock into each other? Tibetan deep-voice chanting—in which the impossibly low note resonates at the precise frequency that generates a simultaneous higher note, allowing the singer to harmonize with himself to the accompaniment of jingling hand-bells and crashing cymbals—destroys the universe without leaving any visible damage. There was never, in fact, anything there to destroy, only "cyclonic winds of karma" through which the enlightened can hear the sounds on the other side of the divide: "They hear them all the time . . . Only in meditation are the methods of chanting and instrumental playing revealed." This is the music criticism of lamas: "Music has nothing to do with man at all, it is for the gods alone."

By the last year of the century, the music of the gods—or perhaps, to be on the safe side, a digital imitation of it supplemented by some pumped-up bass—is underscoring a car commercial, as a Chevy Tahoe effects its mystic journey across a panoramic stretch of American wilderness. OM: it is a computer-generated cowboy movie with no story other than blind smooth luxurious forward movement. A music not made for listening, but only for stimulating transcendent experience in those who practice it, has thus been transformed into one more metaphor for ultimate power effortlessly attained. The exhaustion of earlier modes of power music—John Philip Sousa or Max Steiner or Iron Butterfly—has left the field open to the wrathful aspect of Mahakala "throbbing like churning cloud" under the Western desert in oscillating pulses of Dharma.

That's a lot of car, driving off into a lot of dusk, as if without human assistance. Maybe the music is only there to keep the desert entertained. Maybe the gods themselves are at the wheel, with no need for the pitiful human who would be unworthy either of the music or the machine. It's a beginning. It's dawn on the desert. If we can go one hundred percent bionic, it won't be necessary to experience anything at all. We can let the machines do the suffering as well as the working and the thinking. Let the machines write the symphonies, for that matter. Construct software that incorporates the rules of baroque composition and generate instant ersatz Vivaldi. Meanwhile we humans—with the help of wireless electrode implants—can complete our evolution into virtual churning clouds.

You are alone on the prairie, vibrating to a music for ghosts, produced by ghost musicians. But will they not all be ghosts before long? They left their marks in the sound archives before disappearing. In a Cambodian village an orchestra of magicians drives off demons with oboe and zither and drums, working in a scale so ancient that the ceremonial music of the royal family seemed modern by comparison. Somebody working for UNESCO taped it. Probably every one of them was swept away when the Khmer Rouge came hunting down anyone who knew anything, even so much as the lyric to an old song.

In a recording studio in Kabul, the Radio Afghanistan Orchestra perfects its blend of classical style with the inflections of Indian movie music. An erotic praise song penetrates the darkness separating that recording session from the darkness of unending war that is about to fall on them, musicians and listeners alike. The song itself is swallowed up in the more agreeable darkness—to be prolonged indefinitely if possible—in which the lovers' secret meeting is hidden:

Her eyes are so inviting,
Her trouser cuffs jingling,
Beads encircle her neck,
On her mouth lipstick,
Her face adorned with beauty marks,
Under her blouse two pomegranates,
Hurrying toward a rendezvous . . .

Eventually all the old recordings will become ethnographic. The inheritors will be left with a museum of sounds now beyond producing: Last of the Blue Devils, last orchestra of magicians, last royal radio orchestra, last Hollywood soundtrack composer privy to the ancient arts of Rozsa or Friedhofer. Each fragment is lodged in the samples freezer for future restructuring and digital sweetening. Think of it as a plant specimen rescued by helicopter from a burnt-out rain forest so it can be broken down into its chemical components.

Is it to provide some residual psychic comfort that pockets of the past are kept alive, if only in a form like the Three Tenors, to provide a living myth of presence and plenitude, to prove that three more or less aged, more or less corpulent bodies can still overflow with the feeling and training required to put across "Nessun dorma" or "La donna e mobile" on a global satellite transmission? Who said the ancient world had been abandoned? You can still tune in to *Yanni at the Forbidden City* or *Yanni at the Taj Mahal*. But when will we have a live concert from within the beehive tombs of Mycenae, where a mild footfall becomes an earthshaking thud, and a single flute trill would induce a madness like that of Orestes? Even the purchasers of *Hooked on Panflute*—devotees of the instrument that has come to assume the whole burden of the archaic and remote, the instrument that is the very voice of the unrecoverable human past, of tropical rivers hidden behind vines, submerged ruins, homelands from which everyone has been irrevocably exiled—might change their minds if they could experience such a reverberant tomb. What is wanted is a past that is beautiful rather than ghastly, the brocades of the ancestors without their destructive passions: dynasties that will not crack your headphones.

It's the perfect end to the perfect century. If it did nothing else it created a paradise of listeners. People were set free to hear anything. The idea of neighborhood, of history, of time itself collapsed. Everything became available anywhere anytime in a format of your choice. Maybe that's why the World Music releases sound increasingly the same. It hardly seems to matter whether they originated in Andalusia or Mali or Albania, once the synths have done their work. It's grist for the Body Shop, or for the changing rooms at Banana Republic. We're all one, anyway, that was the idea, wasn't it? The grittiness of actual silk roads and mountain kingdoms has been thrown into the blender. The undigestible bits—the parts that sound like maybe something bad happened once—lose themselves in a refreshing and indistinguishable tonic. It's cocktail hour on Planet Remix.

The salvaged materials become part of the Sound Bank, a filing cabinet of elements that can be drawn on for any purpose. It's like an alternate nature, or perhaps like the chemistry set from which an alternate nature will eventually be created. Circular breathing that took years of devotion to attain is yours at the twiddle of a dial. The soul of anonymous island singers is plucked out of context and reconfigured into beguiling dance melodies: nothing that is human is alien to this electronic museum. Nor anything inhuman either: who needs open air when it comes in a can? Whales and dolphins! Ambient ocean sounds! Doves in a grove! A whole hill of cicadas! Bats lost in a frenzy of echolocation! Sound of sunrise in the Blue Ridge! Turn up the ocean record to maximum volume and the city disappears. In time the whale sounds themselves—the sounds, that is, that continue to emanate from living whales—are no longer required. They've been sampled and added to the mix. You'll hear something that sounds exactly like them whenever the need arises.

Merge the accumulated heritages, blend them to a homogeneous consistency, and this is what it might sound like, a tapioca pudding with hints of a hundred different spices. In the country of permanent massage the waves slap against the pier forever. The impulse to form thoughts subsides into a slow gentle slosh. There are no more words or names, only the long drawn-out gurgles that swirl in the mind of God. They sound, at this distance, like a row of washing machines in rinse cycle down at the local laundromat. Here's a universal language for you. There is no more need ever to recognize anything again, because the mix makes anything at all sound instantly recognizable. Whatever it is, it's your oldest favorite: the thump your heart loves, the sustained flutelike note that stands for every secret inexpressible feeling. This is what the world would be like without those hairsplitting details cluttering it up. Somebody would have done it sooner if they'd known how. You love it, admit you love it. If you don't, you will learn how in time.

In their virtual parade the ghost musicians go down the street blowing horns and banging drums. It's some kind of snakelike funerary procession. Went by a while ago, actually. Don't bother going to the window, they're not there anymore. Fortunately, before they stopped playing, someone recorded the last bit of it. Someone else learned how to repeat the fingerings and mallet strokes and recorded their own version of the way they imagined it would have sounded if it had been properly recorded in the first place; remixed it; laid some heavy bass under it; fed it through the giant speakers into the thick of the dancers: and here it is. The archaic forest kingdom never went away. It will be here forever, or as long as we have the machines to maintain it on life support. When we don't have them anymore we too will have become ancient, and the primitives of the future will pick over our useless equipment. Of our amps they will make chairs, or treasure chests, or altars.

Imagine a planet where no one remembers how to make any of the sounds in the archive, any more than they know how to build a pyramid. This will be a few decades or centuries down the line, after the factories close and the index of specifications becomes garbled due to faulty transmission. Doesn't anyone around here know how to make the parade play again? We lost the batteries. We forgot how to fix it. The depot shut. They mislaid the flow charts. In childhood, when the new recording devices were being invented and marketed, it was awe-inducing to contemplate a technology whose arrival certified that the future had begun. You knew at the same time that, in the wake of nuclear disaster, you could never reconstruct it. In the world after the catastrophe, you and your fellow survivors would stare like helpless natives at the scattered inert machines, the mute disks, not knowing how to make them go. Perhaps you would continue to trade them as sacred objects to which disjointed legends were attached, fragmentary recollections of the sounds they had emitted before they were silenced. Only then—the machines no longer operable, the instruments and lyrics and chord changes a memory of a memory—would it become necessary to invent music again.

The inheritors—we can almost envy them their tabula rasa—will imagine they hear voices coming out of the dead amps. What those voices intone will be memorialized as the music of a new tradition, the songs of kings existing only as legend.

On a hilltop in Urbino, above even the highest ramparts of the ducal palazzo, they're testing the sound system for the Communist picnic. The old Reds drink wine in the shade, under an array of Cuban flags, while the speakers rattle out a mix of revolutionary songs like "Avanti Popolo" and popular favorites like "Surfin' Safari," sung in English by what sounds like an Italian garage band.

In a bar in Colchester in 1998 the jukebox is playing a 1984 Malagasy version of the Bobby Fuller Four's 1964 hit "I Fought the Law (And the Law Won)"—which may have hit Madagascar by way of the Clash's 1979 cover version—before switching to Rita Marley covering the Lemon Pipers on "Pied Piper."

Tokyo television shuts down for the night with scenic views of Rome, always the same views, underscored by Respighi's "The Pines of Rome."

Meanwhile, in Venice, where time stands still, the piano player is singing "Volare" in the lounge and will continue singing it well into the next millennium.

Hungarian violins sweep through the palm court of the Hotel Imperial—or is it the Hotel Rex, the Hotel Metropole, the Hotel Luxor—and are they strings at all? Are they not a digitalized simulacrum overdubbed over a colorized long shot of a virtual lobby clotted with palm trees?

Music for tourists, except that now everyone is a tourist, and every home a hotel room. After so many years we are still, in imagination, the jaded sophisticates Elyot and Amanda on the balcony of a hotel in southern France in Noel Coward's *Private Lives,* divorced lovers (back when divorce was glamorous) who smoke cigarettes and comb for traces of residual passion while murmuring about the "extraordinary potency of cheap music." Pour another cocktail and savor "The Very Thought of You" as it steals over the railing. Duke Ellington himself loved hotel rooms best of all, their interchangeability and freedom, their indifference to the time of day. They were the perfect space in which to think up music, a space as abstract as music itself. The ballroom of the gods: a private universe where it doesn't matter what year it is. Abstraction is where you hang your hat.

You might be anywhere. Close your eyes and let the sounds construct a world. You might be heading four miles out of Fort Worth on the White Settlement Road to get to Crystal Springs—"dancing, swimming, and fishing"—to dance to the music of Milton Brown and His Musical Brownies, a fiddle-and-steel-guitar-fueled medley of "The Sheik of Araby," "Cielito Lindo," "Goofus," and "Darktown Strutters' Ball." You don't even need a car, just a radio: "This broadcast is coming to you live from the ballroom of the Ambassador Hotel in the heart of downtown Minneapolis."

Sixty years later the broadcast is still playing. You could be hiding out with Vincent Parry in his girlfriend's apartment in David Goodis's mystery novel *Dark Passage,* listening to her excellent record collection to keep from thinking of what will happen if the cops catch up with him. This is the ultimate refuge, the space within which "One O'Clock Jump" plays repeatedly, as if he could take up permanent residence in the space between Walter Page's bass and Jo Jones's drums. There are no cops in the music, not the slightest remnant of governmental structures.

In the bar in Sidi Bou Said they play James Brown all night and in the bar in Knossos they play Otis Redding all night. Someone is talking about his uncle who was arrested after the government changed, summarily stripped of his ministerial position. Worse things happened than that; they killed many people. As for him, he only had to flee to Rome for a number of years until the government changed again. The distance between the airport and the bar across from the

Pantheon—you know that one?—always reminds him of hearing Ray Charles singing Hank Williams on the taxi driver's radio. It became his personal theme song: "I'm So Lonesome I Could Cry." In the bar where you've been talking with him the band is playing "Mustang Sally" in a near-perfect simulation of the Mussel Shoals sound.

Often the customers want to purchase the music they hear in cocktail lounges and take it home—maybe the drummer has cassettes in the trunk of his car, maybe the calypso band has some locally pressed vinyl for sale—to prove that the intangible ecstasy of hanging out was something that really happened. There is no requirement even to enter the bar. Music can equally well be a souvenir of a visit never made, of taverns without smoke, without guns or B-girls, nothing but the music going full blast as long and as often as you desire.

At this hotel you are not guest but manager and sole owner. It's The House of Sounds, The Purple Magnet, Chez Margo, The Twilight Perch, The Bamboo Palace. The sets start whenever you want and can be prolonged on demand. Tear down a wall, put the window where the sea is. Bring on the virtual dancing girls. Paint the sun green and light a fire on the roof after it sets. Jack up the amplifier another notch.

Terrestrial paradise, modern-style, begins where the authentic ritual order is blurred beyond recognition. Here's where every distinction is deliberately smeared. We feel it happening and in a sleazy way are glad. Was there ever really an alternative? It got too hard to maintain the boundaries, and by then most of the boundary-keepers were dead. The saxophone underscoring Toshiro Mifune's nineteenth-century sword fights in *Yojimbo* was already a continuation of Telemann's eighteenth-century mimicry of exotic Polish dances and Puccini's Italian-Chinese music in *Turandot* and Bernard Herrmann's Hollywood gamelan in *Anna and the King of Siam*. Here is where everything begins to become infinitely malleable, infinitely recyclable, and it feels so good. Why settle for the real China when you can invent your own? Siouxsie and the Banshees invite you to "Hong Kong Garden."

Through changeless bubble worlds a resonance of hula music filters. "Chinatown, My Chinatown" brightens the back alleys of crowded, barely lit cities. If you can't have Japanese lanterns, you can at least have song lyrics about Japanese lanterns. Duke Ellington presents "Maori": the heroic musical corollary to the backdrop for a lost Cotton Club floor show, a mess of fans and painted palms. Wherever you are when you hear it you partake of the sun-splashes dappling naked bathers in the silent Movietone worlds of *Moana* and *Tabu*. To beguile the hashish dreams of Smyrna for an audience of portside gangsters, Greek tango musicians sing of Waikiki and Bora Bora: "If you want to learn how to love, come to Hawaii." Everywhere on earth, small bars transform themselves into landscapes out of "Ukulele Lady" and "Under the Bamboo Tree." Somewhere way out on Long Island, cop cars cluster in the parking lot of The Grass Hut. The song on the jukebox is "Hawaii" by the Beach Boys.

In the tourism of imagined spaces, everybody is somewhere else, always. They prefer it that way. A Japanese college student, not long after the end of the American occupation, perhaps around the time *Sayonara* was released, puts on a record of Ferde Grofé's *Grand Canyon Suite* and lies back with eyes closed feeling out the spaces of a Grand Canyon he invents for himself, savoring an American expansiveness that belongs to him alone. No passport or green card required. Ride any range you please, to the tune of Aaron Copland's *Billy the Kid* or Gene Autry's "South of the Border" or Duke Ellington's "Dusk on the Desert" or Don Redman's "Chant of the Weed" or Vaughn Monroe's "Ghost Riders in the Sky" or Elmer Bernstein's *The Magnificent Seven* or Jerome Moross's *The Big Country*. Dematerialized cowboys are free to inhabit a domain made especially for cowboys, full of air and wind and fallen boulders, its rivers clattering along snakelike bends and its canyons howling with voices, its mesas breaking off where the sky starts.

All that is needed is enough scope and depth that even those lacking a body—those ghost riders made of echo and electricity—can find enough room to gallop through it. But what could be easier to supply? If you need more it can be manufactured by the yard; it's a matter of intervals and instrumentation. There is probably already a computer program—CowboyMood or the like—that can generate it without human intervention. The desert needn't be Western: Lee Perry, in "The Return of Django," found it easy enough to transport the already transported Italian cowboy music of Ennio Morricone to the streets of Kingston, where Kool Mo-Dee found it to take it back to Harlem in "Wild Wild West."

It doesn't have to be American even by derivation. Russians have been happy to find their own nomadic cowboy music in Kabalevsky and Khachaturian, or go back to Borodin to join Prince Igor with his Polovtsian captors in a cheapo Khrushchev-era opera movie, the singers dubbed, the horsemen sweeping over the plain like something out of *Fort Apache,* and a contingent of Polovtsian harem girls looking almost like the chorus line from *Siren of Baghdad.* Somewhere at the fringes of the Russian imagination a primal Central Asia continues to call, backed with gongs and xylophones, to be turned into operas and ballets, symphonic odes and tone poems that can then be shipped to Yokohama and San Francisco and São Paulo and translated into bar songs, novelty numbers, movie themes, music for marching bands. "The Saber Dance" will finally penetrate every crevice of the planet, carrying some degraded remnant of folk tradition into every last high school band recital, or into the demented interstices of Bugs Bunny cartoons.

Elsewhere, to a blast of snake charmer music, the archaic strip club goes about its timeless business. The perverse floor show is about to begin, backed by saxophones imported from dynastic Egypt. The place reeks of incense. Cosmopolites mingle with amulet dealers and fences for tomb robbers, and the most famous courtesan in Luxor discusses philosophy with a young physician in search of Truth. "Some combo, eh, Plotinus?" On the jukebox is Alex North's soundtrack for *Cleopatra.* The alcove is lined with pictures of Liz Taylor in full regalia. The location turns out not to be Egypt at all but a cunningly decorated whorehouse in Hamburg. Some evil fucker slipped acid in your pilsener, and as it starts taking effect the sound system is commandeered by the music from Jess Franco's porn-trance horror movie *Vampyros Lesbos,* played at maximum volume, at the part where the voices go into their ambiguous chant of "we don't care, we don't care." Don't care what you do? Don't care what they do? Don't care what happens to you, never did care? You weren't quite ready, you should have paid attention back in 1978 to Wayne County's song about the legendary Manhattan barroom Max's Kansas City: "Don't forget to bring your ego trip and your masquerade mask."

It seems like a long time to be steering a path through the smoke just to get to the other side of a room so crowded now that you can no longer see the walls, navigating the trail from the Reception Bar to the Amazon Lounge, drifting through the beads and the fake lianas while somebody plays Kool and the Gang's "Jungle Boogie" on the jukebox for the third time tonight, and all the while your mind not here but at the Chicago World's Fair of 1893 watching the kootch dance of Little Egypt and catching echoes of other lost music, maybe the songs you read about in the account of James Cook's Tahitian voyage of 1769: "The young girls when ever they can collect 8 or 10 together dance a very indecent dance which they call Timorodee singing most indecent songs and useing most indecent actions in the practice of which they are brought up from their earlyest Childhood."

Perhaps the foliage is real and you are advancing with Mungo Park into a clearing in the country of the Serawoolli, somewhere on the near side of the Niger, in 1795: "I found a great crowd surrounding a party who were dancing by the light of some large fires, to the music of four drums, which were beat with great exactness and uniformity. The dances, however, consisted more in wanton gestures than in muscular exertion or graceful attitudes. The ladies vied with each other in displaying the most voluptuous movements imaginable." How long has the party been going on, and when did they stop using real drums? It's all synth, just like the vines are made of plastic. Meanwhile, up in the hills, among flints and cookpots and rusted sabers, to the tune of themes adapted from Italian westerns, people are singing about the end of the world in which their song was just remixed by the owner of the record company that has a financial interest in this very bar, these very strips of plastic foliage.

Django returns from the movie in which the Comancheros buried him alive and with a scruffy-looking band of recently recruited musicians to participate in an incredibly abrasive tribute to Henry Mancini whose highlight is a very "out" improvisation on the title music from *Hatari!* As a beat-up video on the VCR above the bar shows John Wayne's truck speeding across the dusty African plain, the music begins to mutate into some kind of droning rumba figuration, with multiple horns playing in different keys, different pieces of Mancini's melody knocking against each other in reversed or doubled form, banged around like you might be if you were riding in that truck, while in counterpoint a wall of five-foot-high drums works its way into the cadence of some royal central African progression, as if to wake a kingdom's sleeping ruler. It takes anachronistic noise to uncover everything that the movie couldn't show, every place that neither Red Buttons nor Elsa Martinelli with her baby elephants could even imagine entering.

Now it's time for even the last smeared images to go under. Here come the mutant headphones.

For a moment the names are on the table. Then, suddenly, like a pocket turned inside out, they are removed. Nothing refers to anything anymore. The warehouse is indistinguishable space. No songs have lyrics. Or they have lyrics like blank walls. I'm alone forever. The sun is on the lagoon. Welcome to the ice palace. The names are going. They go out like stars extinguishing one by one. We find ourselves living in igloo-like domes connected by windowless corridors. The wind howls in the giant garage. The way out is the way in. There is no way out. There is a sound like shapeless flakes. If you listen carefully you can hear the minerals the flakes were made from, melted-down chunks of disused temples, mountain zithers, murder ballads, genealogical anthems. We use history for body lotion. Turn the names to the wall to keep the chill out. Under the party lights the rust looks blue. There is a sound like gel. The iceberg loses its contour. In the drunken forest the trees wobble like cartoon characters. There is a sound like helium. Hard-to-remember words in the wind tunnel. This tune you don't hear, you climb inside it. Welcome to Surf City. It sounds better with the lights out. It sounds more like nothing, jacked up loud enough to make your bones rattle. You open and shut like a tent-flap knocked around in a cyclone. The howl modulates. The canvas flaps back and forth in the dark.

15

Silence in the Age of Noise

Recording changed everything. It beat time at its own game.

Permanent oldies; oldies on night call; the buttons pushed twenty-four-seven, as long as somebody is left alive to respond.

Maybe longer: even after the end of the world in *On the Beach* there was a record that kept spinning around for no one.

Didn't we use to laugh at the whole idea of oldies stations, until they started playing our own songs? Surrendering to their cycle is like being given another life to live. One year they permitted me to be fourteen again, then sixteen; now, according to their long-term marketing scheme, I'm just getting out of college.

I can remember when the favorite oldies station phrase "a blast from the past" was freshly minted, capable of surprising. For that matter I can remember when the term "golden oldies" still had the aura of what had recently been new. Language also has its hit parade, its novelty numbers, its one-hit wonders.

I will know that old age has arrived when even the oldies are unfamiliar songs of younger generations, and "Do Wah Diddy Diddy" and "Back Stabbers" are stashed away in the archive along with "Whispering" and "Alice Blue Gown," the music of a past that there is no one left to be reminded of.

It is a final indignity, the Memory Lane Massacre. You wake up in a world where you can't identify or even distinguish among any of the songs, where in fact they aren't "songs" anymore but strips of sound with no beginning or end.

Remember endings? We thought we liked them. Or at least they somehow seemed necessary. How else do you deal with the fact that the music has to stop sometime? The instruments get louder; or the singer starts to improvise more freely and excitedly; or the chorus comes in for a final reprise. It's your signal to say goodbye to the song and everything it has meant to you, until the next time.

Remember when there were happy songs, sad songs? We have moved into a new country, of prolonged and indeterminate duration. The music expresses whatever you want to project onto it. It is at once nowhere and everywhere.

But it is scarcely on the street. The dancers and drummers in the plaza have mostly packed up and departed, although a few find shelter in the subway. Even the boom boxes grow quiet in the age of headphones, where music can be piped hygienically and noiselessly into each individual head without disrupting the public sphere.

Most of those listening to music on records no longer know how to play it. Even on many of the records themselves people do not play except in the sense of making collages of earlier records. ("Do you know how many musicians have been put out of work by digital technology?" "No, but hum a few bars and I'll sample it.")

Perhaps it began when new records positioned themselves as commentary on earlier records. ("All of punk music," the earnest radio commentator—Gary Thrall, ex-bass player for the early '80s band The Simplistics—is suggesting, "is nothing more than an extended footnote to certain recordings by The Who which were themselves an oblique commentary on surf music, while at the same time all of them, the surfers, The Who, the punks, were listening to the same James Brown records.") Perhaps it began when the concept began to change from record as copy of live performance to record as thing-in-itself. But the wedge was already being driven in with the first recording.

Now the computers come equipped with machinery for creating masterpieces of sampling. Design your own trance. Maybe it will even drown out the hums and white-noise signals of the machinery on which you design it, or the city—itself rapidly undergoing a digital transformation—in which you play it back.

The push-button living we were promised in the '50s—the doors opening and lights going on by themselves, the tone arm dropping the needle onto *Mantovani's Immortal Classics* at a pre-selected volume—has pretty much arrived. Even if we don't yet live in the fully operational "smart house," we pass from smart city to smart city through smart airports, watching smart television and listening to smart music machines.

The Russian inventor Leon Theremin created not only the electronic instrument that bears his name but a range of prototypes for the world we live in: doors that open and close automatically, advertisements that switch on when approached by humans, security alarms sensitive to movement, surveillance devices capable of penetrating the U.S. embassy in Moscow.

Music was fed, in the ancient times that ended ten or twelve years ago, by the human scene around it. There was no way of getting around musicians, and the mess and confusion that pertained to them.

Records, true to the spirit of all modern conveniences, provide the music without the scene. At the very least there is then no need to wait for the musicians to show up, or warm up, or get in the mood, or accommodate themselves to the listeners' more or less inarticulate desires.

And now the record makers can dispense with musicians altogether, as if thereby to get at the music without having to deal with intermediaries. Eliminate the factor of human error, so to speak, those flaws of character or inherent biases that get in the way, the awkward aftereffects of habit and experience.

The culture that gives us these things wants to satisfy a longing for human contact that persists stubbornly, even among those who gradually have let themselves get hooked on a life with as little such contact as possible. It's a tough order to fill, unless the customer agrees to be contented with an illusion of contact. After that—once the replica has been accepted as a full equivalent of its original—the possibilities are endless. It's a matter of training.

Our childhood was a preparation for vicarious living. Gradually we were made accustomed to music without instruments, even without instrumentalists. In return for whatever loss that might entail, we get to keep the music forever. Playback is instant and on demand. As for the rest of it, how much did you really care? You have been liberated from all that smoke, all that waiting around.

Wherever we are we find ourselves pushing many buttons, until the prehensile thumb begins to feel as superfluous as the appendix. (We begin to glimpse the end of handling.) Gradually music becomes a mere substitute for silence, a sonic blanket designed to make a bit more tolerable an environment where the little noises of the little machines never stop. There are CD players that can be programmed for thirty-six hours of continuous play, and that is surely only a beginning.

Music drowns out sound, or drowns out self. When the bass makes your bones vibrate it's the most intimate possible invasion.

The new phone beeps are indistinguishable: is it sounding in the TV movie or in the room itself, and is there a difference? Sound negates sense of place. "I'm on the train": no, he isn't, he's on the phone.

A guy walks briskly along the avenue talking into his cell phone: "You're so indifferent." Or was it: "It's someone different"? The city itself is the switchboard where the operators are subjected to a thousand different randomly crisscrossing conversations at the same time.

It seems like a long time ago that rock and roll made it hard to have conversations in bars, and when booming speakers made it impossible to talk at parties or clubs. We got used to this slowly. Was it sometime in the '60s or '70s that it became normal not to be able to hear what anyone was saying, and not to care? ("A person can't hear himself think in here." "That's the idea, baby.")

At some point music becomes not the cure but the ailment. Music as annoyance: the hip-hop at deafening volume in the adjacent passenger's headphones; the music from the cruise ships that pass by the harbor apartment window all night long (the salsa boat, the disco boat, the Céline Dion boat); the pounding electronic themes of TV news shows, exploring the aesthetic of the emergency beeper (an ultimate vulgarization of the music of Philip Glass?); the mix tape of New Age synthesizer music without which your tofu would not be complete. But we were told of this long ago. In Fritz Lang's 1952 movie *The Blue Gardenia,* Richard Conte and his partner sit in a restaurant talking about a murder, and the partner is startled by the sudden intrusion of an invisible orchestra playing the Liebestod theme from *Tristan and Isolde*: "What's that?" "Music. Canned. They can everything nowadays."

During Operation Just Cause, American troops laid siege to the Vatican embassy in Panama City where General Manuel Noriega had taken refuge. On the third day they brought in the psych-warfare team to wear down his resistance with painfully loud, indefinitely prolonged bombardment with mix tapes designed to be as irritating as possible, everything from heavy metal to *Barry Manilow's Greatest Hits.* (The playlist also included, with a whimsy possibly lost on the General, Martha and the Vandellas' "Nowhere to Run" and Linda Ronstadt's "You're No Good.") Conversely, police played the favorite records of an armed and mentally troubled woman barricaded in her home in an effort to tranquilize her by restoring a sense of familiar reality. The playlist included *Barry Manilow's Greatest Hits.*

At suburban malls Beethoven and Brahms are played over the P/A systems to drive away teenage loiterers, who find the music oppressive.

Records can become a torture device anywhere at all. Tourists at a restaurant overlooking Lake Baikal are subjected to hideously distorted military music played at top volume on a broken-down phonograph, the employees apparently oblivious to the deafening sound while the westerners try to focus on their bumpers of vodka and heaping platters of goulash. A Japanese main street at Christmas time becomes a traffic jam of competing carols and seasonal favorites, "Frosty the Snowman" and "Silent Night" and "Jingle Bell Rock" simultaneously from different storefronts at the same bludgeoning volume.

The final punishment—the delayed punishment—comes when no music at all is playing. This is the moment—it's three o'clock by the luminous dial that never shuts off—when it begins to look as if you'll be up all night auditioning for *Pride of the Insomniacs* as you relive each bar of a hated tune that repeats and repeats, a perpetual-motion machine whose circular structure is sometimes even compounded by the lyrics themselves: "The Music Goes Round and Round," "Raindrops Keep Falling on My Head." "Big wheel keep on turning," indeed.

In Charles Williams's noir novel *All the Way* (1956), the insidiously circular 1934 hit "The Music Goes Round and Round"—a record whose effect is something like being strapped to a wooden horse on a carousel that will never stop—is used to drive someone mad. The prospective victim is haunted by the memory of how his brother committed suicide many years earlier after locking himself in his room and playing "The Music Goes Round and Round" repeatedly for days. Now an ingenious conspirator reawakens the old dread by making anonymous calls during which he plays the record over the phone. The whole book amounts to an arcane piece of music criticism. That Williams himself later committed suicide gives the joke an unexpected gravity.

Hell is an oldies station that cannot be tuned out.

Wasn't there a scary TV show like that, on *Panic Theater* or some such program? The radio had no controls, the sound got louder and louder, and when the tenant went to open the window to make contact with the outside world there were only thick metal panels bolted in place?

Like a car alarm echoing through the urban canyon, there plays within the skull what likewise cannot be shut off: the five hundredth chorus of "Nice and Easy," not actually a chorus but merely the bar-and-a-half that got stuck, a bit of well-crafted sonic shrapnel.

Composers often describe being kept awake by their own melodies, until they are forced to get out of bed and write them down. At some moments it becomes clear to the victimized listener that the songwriter has escaped from insomnia by inflicting it on someone else. "Put the tune in *their* brains!"

There are songs that should have a warning attached to them: Casual Listening May Result in Melody Burn. They appear scientifically designed to cause suffering, and are even proud of it, proclaiming their intention brazenly like the Electric Light Orchestra's "Can't Get It Out of My Head." Such songs suggest what a terrible thing eternity might be. Even in dreams the gears continue their infernal squeaking, and it scarcely surprises you when the doorkeeper of an oneiric tavern—the one to which you had just been admitted a second earlier— bursts into the same refrain to wake you.

Or is not something scarier at work, the activation of an embedded voodoo code that takes possession of any available brain matter? Babalu colonizing the hearer through the essentially passive intermediation of Desi Arnaz? A wrathful Tibetan deity singing about the end of the world whether you want to hear it or not, except that he has foregone his usual conduit of deep-chanting monks and weirdly recruited Barry Manilow for the purpose?

There was always music designed to make sure you couldn't hear, or even imagine, any other music. All together now: "The East Is Red," the "Horst Wessel Lied," the "Agincourt Song," the Latin hymn of the Teutonic knights making ready to devastate the people of Novgorod in Eisenstein's *Alexander Nevsky*. Or for that matter the marching song of the Russian peasants spontaneously rising up against the invader, dropping their farming tools, grabbing spears, and heading down the road to the recruiting center with the Prokofiev music to inspire them. Whether it's the Seventh Cavalry riding through Monument Valley to the tune of "The Girl I Left Behind," or the Japanese office workers singing the company song at their desks as a prelude to group calisthenics, there is nothing like a song to give an illusion of purposeful activity. The battle of anthems in *La Grande Illusion* and *Casablanca,* of Zulu chant against Welsh choir in *Zulu,* reduces war to a matter of competing sound systems. Nothing, finally, is as terrifying as the notion of music that cannot be deselected: the anthem of the army that is marching to destroy you, the hymn of the parishioners who are preparing to watch you burn. When you get to pick the music you can change history.

A lone flute from the woods signals a last inextinguishable spark of enemy resistance.

"It is the Death Song": the melancholy inexorable tune that General Santa Ana had his musicians play day and night outside the

Alamo until the siege was over, at least according to the screenplay of *Rio Bravo*. The bad guys re-created it with a local mariachi band to wage psychological warfare on John Wayne, Dean Martin, and Walter Brennan, cooped up in a jailhouse with a town full of vicious outlaws surrounding them. Gets to you.

But there will always be an old coot like Walter Brennan to start humming along—"Dang, I'm startin' to kinda like that tune," like Hank Worden as old Mose Harper in *The Searchers,* going into his travesty of a Comanche war dance at the most inappropriate moment, on the edge of massacre.

Useless to try to escape from it. It knocks unbidden and forces its patterns on us, forces us to live in the time it beats out, inhabits even its absence.

Music is such a grammar that even with all the notes taken out it still superimposes its structures on us.

Shut the music machine off. Turn out the last light. Silence and darkness. Now it begins, the real racket: distant slams and hoots, motor-cyclist revving up at the on-ramp, chamber symphony of foghorns, pleasure boat rounding the cove with a blast of technopop out on the water, elevator doors slamming open and shut as drunk or squabbling couples come home, small heavy object knocked over by household pet on the floor directly above, deep hum (nearly Tibetan) of refriger-ator, infomercial about hair implants being watched by the insomniac next door, crackling of electricals, noise of chairs and desks that some-how creak when they are unoccupied, buffeting of window by air cur-rents, gradual uncrumpling of the wad of paper thrown into a waste-basket hours ago, like a high-volume recorded transcription of a flower opening, rattle of air against glass, noise of head nestling against pil-low and of bed-frame adjusting to the body that stretches on it, noise of breath, noise of bones. No getting out of this symphony alive.

Under all, even if everything else were shut out, is the noise of the inner workshop of the body, echoing faintly from the deepest cham-bers, as if an army of workers clambered over pulleys and cauldrons, chanting their midnight work song. They are the slaves of time, bald gnomes out of a Grimm Brothers story or a Wagner opera, stirring with giant ladles and hauling cinder blocks while they keep the hum going. They labor all night in anticipation of the silence of that future day when they will be allowed finally to rest. Meanwhile they strike up another chorus. It's that Manilow thing again. It is the Death Song. When they are finished with their work the song will stop.

Silence is what was just interrupted. It's been like that always. That is how you know the silence was perceptible a moment earlier, a moment before the godlike howling of the noon whistle in a quiet suburb, a moment before the roar of a motorboat on a mountain lake in the days when such roars were new: "You have no idea how peaceful it was before those damn things were invented." "Somebody ought to make a law about it. It's getting so you can't hear yourself think anymore."

Because of people, silence is disappearing from the planet. We are the Noise-Bringers. (Our boom box is bigger than the boom box of linnet or cicada.)

In their Himalayan fastnesses the saddhus practicing their austerities hear the jets roar by. A man travels around the world with a tape recorder trying to find a soundtrack uninterrupted by some form of human machinery. He has trouble managing more than fifteen minutes of it, anywhere.

We tell time by noise. Silence appalls most by its suggestion that time is absent.

A length of audiotape, gathering sound to its surface as it uncoils: that is a lifetime. If not stored at excessive temperatures, and if the mylar coating resists any tendencies toward breaking or crumpling or warping, it is good for a program of extended duration at optimal dynamic levels. As long as it can be played back—as long as the encoded information does not wear away—the tape will be a history of what was heard.

Everything enters there. The noises register the persistence of life as on a seismograph. The tiniest shudder is identifiable by its characteristic acoustical marking. On this tape there is no such thing as dead air. Even the pauses make noise.

Sounds erase sounds, voices bury voices. The single lifetime is this field of interruptions, a carpet of distinct scratches and whistles. Here a deep hoot, there a high feverish chattering; here a guttural murmur of satisfaction as the hungry are fed, there a plaintive distant cry as the mother calls her children from play at sunset, her growing anxiety modulating into an audible change of register.

Sound penetrates where it wishes regardless of what anybody wants or doesn't want. Everything that exists keeps slamming the door as it goes by. The shape of a personality gets caught—like a sleeve on a bramble—in a single phrase, a single sigh, the lover's raucous gasp, the suicide's ironic murmur.

A small but crucial event is encapsulated in the almost childish giggle, barely held in control, of the pilot who has only a moment earlier recognized a technical problem as the plane was taxiing down the runway, and thereby saved himself and his passengers.

After someone dies his voice is what remains of him, an auditory signature in the inner ear, the timbre exactly sustained. A life extends only as long as that peculiar accent can be played back by the person in whom it was recorded.

All of it music, all the time: the roar of open countryside, the terror of uninhabited night, the hiss and clack of bare boughs set upon by wind. It lacks only a touch of orchestration, a little sweetening, the human touch.

We go looking for silence—the imagined silence, silence the pure. But what would silence be, if not the outward manifestation of absence, disappearance, death? It can be imagined in dreams: the discovery of the emptied house, in the wake of massacre or pestilence or economic catastrophe.

"Stilled the laughter, stilled the weeping." Years later the exile returns to the abandoned cottage, the deserted village. "No sound was there but the hissing of the wind among the bare boughs."

There is a different kind of silence, the silence of those places where no music ever plays, filled as they may be with every other kind of noise. If you are in one of them it is the only place, and for the rest of life you will cling to music as to a haven from that mute prohibition. (You will dream of the musical penthouse within whose soundproofed walls there is a permanent outpouring of rumba music, the satin suite made for love and champagne and top-flight orchestral arrangements.) It might have been a house with no radio or record player, or where the radio and record player were never turned on; without a piano, or where the piano was permanently draped in a dustcover. Here music died, or something died of which music would be too painful a reminder. The weight of that absence gave a sense of how devastating a single chord would be, if a child should stray in and start pounding randomly on the piano. With what panic would nursemaid or maiden aunt come rushing out to hiss, "Don't do that, dear! You'll wake them!"

Or, perhaps: "Turn that goddamn noise off!"

Noise of slaps, clatter of garbage pail lids. In some yard cluttered with broken glass, where a tenant coughs behind the curtain, uncounted years of noons and midnights collapse into a single moment, in a place where even music wouldn't help.

So turn it up as loud as possible. Open the windows while you're at it, put the speaker on the fire escape. When you hear music you know you're still alive, and the others might as well know too. Otherwise it's hard to be sure.

> The silver swan who, living, had no note
> When death approached unlocked her silent throat . . .

As death approaches, even the *mention* of Bach or Mozart can be a profound palliative, however brief the effect. To evoke even the idea of their music is to bring timelessness and freedom into a room defined by time and necessity.

In the wilderness, in a trance in the hospital, in the dead calm of mid-ocean, an encroaching silence lurks around you. Or would, but for the human ingenuity that puts a pair of headphones near every IV tank and on every airplane. It's okay, it's going to be fine: there's an orchestral tribute to Andrew Lloyd Webber on Channel 23, a brave thin piping sound. Outside the music's limits a mechanical groan thickens, the roar of ambient chaos.

Coda

THIS BOOK HAS TWO ENDINGS. ONE IS ABOUT A LAKE, THE other about a mountain. Really they are the same ending. They are even part of the story of the same day.

The first begins in a house where the silence is almost complete.

For the woman in her bedroom there is only one sound that matters, the rising and falling rasp of her difficult breaths. She has been dying for a long time, little by little: days, months, years. Now it may be down to hours, or minutes.

Through the curtains there is sun glare, the middle of an August day. Around two o'clock a shower of hailstones clatters on the driveway, as a freak storm turns summer into mid-winter. After a few minutes it melts back into bright silence. The silence is made more audible by the murmur of people coming and going in the adjacent rooms.

She looks up suddenly and asks why nobody is playing any music. "Why doesn't somebody put a record on or something?"

Why not? We have been playing music almost nonstop for half a century and more, in this house, and another house, and another house, and in the apartment with the great view of the museum, the apartment across the street from the consulate, the apartment near the movie theater, and the other spaces now rapidly receding beyond recall. It was as if those spaces existed so that sound could bounce back and forth inside them. Why stop now, at a juncture where music might count for more than ever before? When a brief sequence of notes—the merest phrase, a tiny upbeat trill—might have as much weight as a whole lifetime of listening? It doesn't really matter what the music is.

Silence, at this moment, could convey nothing but the unbearable weight of time, neither speeded up nor slowed down. Time asserting its dominion.

So, after a few moments of consideration, the silence makes room for the Dutch Jazz Orchestra playing the music of Billy Strayhorn. A collection of unknown pieces: lost music, music never played before, recovered from marks on paper, to be heard for the first time. Life, for a little while, is in session.

Having emerged from the house where my mother is dying, my wife and I drive away to the summer camp where our daughter has been staying for the previous month. In the morning we'll drive her back so that she can see her grandmother for the last time. So, a few hours later and a few hundred miles away, I find myself by a lake, and stare at it for a long time. Its surface rippled by a steady breeze, the imagined coldness of the water, the interplay between its blue and the blue of the sky, the pattern of reflections as the eye moves from shore to shore: that is what is there, and nothing more. The lake has a certain gravity, a certain inevitability. It has its limits. Its depths are fatal.

It makes a sound, a lapping or faint sloshing against the shore, the rocks, the pilings. The sound is saying nothing at all. The lake is not conveying the slightest thing except that it exists. It exists because it has to and will continue to exist as long as it has to, and not a moment longer. No effort is involved in any part of that process. It responds to forces.

I turn away having learned nothing, but with the impression that I am not likely to get any closer to what silence conveys.

✦ ✦

The second ending presents a scene of old friends seated around a table, in a house on top of a mountain. We've talked of dying, and of the difficulties that people have in doing it and in watching others do it. Decidedly, we don't know how anymore. Think of ancient funerary music, gongs and hollow logs, towers of incense. On what a gigantic scale they acknowledged the devouring presence, while we are barely able to lift our voices above a whisper.

We eat and drink and talk. Then, at an unscheduled moment, we start to sing. Who knows how it begins? The name of an old song comes up in conversation. Does anyone remember the words? And we're off. It goes on for a long time. "I Can't Give You Anything But Love," "Mean to Me," "Am I Blue," "April in Paris," "How Are Things in Glocca Morra," "That Old Feeling," "It's Only a Paper Moon," "The Way You Look Tonight," "Dancing in the Dark."

"These are the songs of my people." Our culture, it turns out, consists at its deepest stratum of whatever songs or parts of songs we can remember. It's a lifeline. As we go around the table, each of us adding another tune to the mix, I think of what people add to music, to show that passive listening is never enough. They sing or hum along, jump up in their seat for a live musician, or even a recorded musician, as if that helped to coax the music along. They play air guitar, air sax, air bass, air drums. All the desperate hand-clapping and toe-tapping: they want to offer something back to the sound and don't know how.

They sing in the shower, in front of the mirror. The bachelor does his private dance as he makes himself ready to go out into the world, imitating Fred Astaire alone in his hotel room singing "No Strings": the hope is that the song will cling to him, make him as slick and dapper and smoothly coordinated as its rhythms and rhyme schemes. The solitary among us burst into song in emulation of those movie characters who are never closer to us than when they are lost in music. The construction worker at the beginning of *On the Town* works magic on the Brooklyn Navy Yard when he sings: "I feel like I'm not out of bed yet . . ." People did that once. In old novels it happens all the time. Kids still do it until they learn how to worry about how they sound. In Liverpool the soccer fans sodden from equal quantities of ale and rain sing "You'll Never Walk Alone" in a discordant chorale. On Karaoke Night the regulars take their numbers and line up to sing along with the instrumental track of "Me and Bobby McGee" or "Wichita Lineman." But these are mostly exceptions. Most of the time people walk around as if it would kill them to make the rafters ring: a strange disappearance, as if they were studying how to be dead before the fact.

People whistle in the dark, walking past the graveyard. Lost in the woods we sing as if it would find our direction for us: "I love to go a-wandering / Upon the mountain track . . ." There is no other compass, finally. If it doesn't tell you where to go it at least tells you where you are, what you are. People sing when they no longer know who they are. They sing not to remember what was but to be in its presence.

When we do sing—unless we are children—we tend to sing the songs that have been written for us, not the ones we might make up on the spot. We grab hold of them wherever we can find them. How many are stashed away in memory, if we really tried to hunt them down?

My brother Joel, after decades of searching, has internalized a library's worth of old songs, movie ballads, '30s dance floor favorites, and will continue to keep adding to the repertoire salvaged from oblivion. We need as many as possible, having no innate equivalent of birdsong or cricket-click. Or did we lose it somewhere along the line? In exchange for language, perhaps, did we sacrifice inborn song, and must now make up the loss by trying to reinvent what was once part of us? Think of whole buildings full of songwriters, desperate for a hit, piecing tunes together out of stray changes, a bit of lyric here, a fragment of a bass line there, as if a college of linnets studied how to chirp.

I remember, in a hidden pocket of the Hudson Valley, as I strolled around the bend of a winding road by a creek, seeing a man (a Jamaican, probably, come up to harvest the apple crop) walking very slowly down the center of the deserted road. He played a guitar, a plaintive wordless ballad, for no one but himself. It was as much as music—as much as the world—could be.

I remember, in the 1936 movie *Follow the Fleet,* Fred Astaire losing his money at gambling and preparing to commit suicide by leaping from the roof of the casino, at the very moment that Ginger Rogers is preparing to do likewise. Instead they take one look at each other and launch into "Let's Face the Music and Dance." Saved by music, again.

As we are tonight—provisionally, as always—around the wooden table, surrounded by the silence of the mountain.

A JUKEBOX OF THE MIND,
1929–1982

1. In the Hills of Tennessee — Jimmie Rodgers — 1929
2. I'm a Ding Dong Daddy — Louis Armstrong — 1930
3. Mood Indigo — Duke Ellington — 1930
4. The Peanut Vendor — Don Azpiazu — 1930
5. Chant of the Weed — Don Redman — 1931
6. Out of Nowhere — Bing Crosby — 1931
7. When I Take My Sugar to Tea — The Boswell Sisters — 1931
8. Beale Street Blues — Joe Venuti & Eddie Lang Orchestra — 1931
9. El Dia Que Me Quieras — Carlos Gardel — 1935
10. Congo Bara — Keskidee Trio — 1935
11. Lulu's Back in Town — Fats Waller — 1935
12. (I've Got) Beginner's Luck — Fred Astaire — 1936
13. Four Mills Brothers — The Lion — 1936
14. The Sheik of Araby — Milton Brown and His Musical Brownies — 1936
15. Nine Pound Hammer — The Monroe Brothers — 1936
16. Fine and Dandy — Teddy Wilson — 1937
17. Opus ½ — The Benny Goodman Quartet — 1938
18. Way Down Yonder in New Orleans — The Kansas City 6 — 1938
19. Hong Kong Blues — Hoagy Carmichael — 1938
20. The Vendor's Song — The Lion — 1938
21. Jive at Five — Count Basie — 1939
22. New San Antonio Rose — Bob Wills & His Texas Playboys — 1940
23. Perfidia — Glenn Miller — 1941
24. Stalin Wasn't Stallin' — The Golden Gate Jubilee Quartet — 1942
25. The Peat-Bog Soldiers — Paul Robeson — 1942
26. I Cover the Waterfront — Billie Holiday — 1944
27. 900 Miles — Woody Guthrie — 1944

28. The Honeydripper, Part One	Joe Liggins	1944
29. That's My Desire	Hadda Brooks	1947
30. Ain't Nobody's Business	Jimmy Witherspoon	1947
31. Blues After Hours	Pee Wee Crayton	1948
32. Boogie Chillen	John Lee Hooker	1948
33. Pan American Boogie	The Delmore Brothers	1949
34. Cowboy Opus #1	Tex Williams	1949
35. Louisiana Blues	Muddy Waters	1950
36. Strollin' with Bone	T-Bone Walker	1950
37. I'll Drown in My Tears	Sonny Thompson with Lula Reed	1951
38. Flamingo	Earl Bostic	1951
39. C Jam Blues	Ole Rasmussen and His Nebraska Cornhuskers	1952
40. Stratosphere Boogie	Speedy West and Jimmy Bryant	1954
41. Lullaby of Birdland	Sarah Vaughan	1954
42. I Got a Woman	Ray Charles	1955
43. It's Only a Paper Moon	Nat King Cole	1956
44. Who Do You Love?	Bo Diddley	1956
45. Key to the Highway	Little Walter	1958
46. Voodoo Boogie	J. B. Lenoir	1958
47. Sweet Little Sixteen	Chuck Berry	1958
48. Tequila	The Champs	1958
49. Let's Have a Party	Wanda Jackson	1958
50. High School Confidential	Jerry Lee Lewis	1958
51. Bird Dog	The Everly Brothers	1958
52. Spring Can Really Hang You Up the Most	June Christy	1958
53. I'll Go Crazy	James Brown	1959
54. Just Before Dawn	Clarence "Gatemouth" Brown	1959
55. Hushabye	The Mystics	1959
56. I Count the Tears	The Drifters	1960
57. Chain Gang	Sam Cooke	1960
58. Gypsy Woman	The Impressions	1961
59. A Thing of the Past	The Shirelles	1961
60. Two Lovers	Mary Wells	1962
61. Any Day Now	Chuck Jackson	1962
62. A Certain Girl	Ernie K-Doe	1962
63. Party Lights	Claudine Clark	1962
64. The Locomotion	Little Eva	1962
65. Brainwasher	Junior Walker & the All Stars	1962
66. Sally Go Round the Roses	The Jaynetts	1963
67. Don't Say Nothin' Bad About My Baby	The Cookies	1963
68. Little Latin Lupe Lu	The Righteous Brothers	1963
69. Can I Get a Witness	Marvin Gaye	1963
70. Live Wire	Martha and the Vandellas	1963

71. It's All Right	The Impressions	1963
72. Hello Stranger	Barbara Lewis	1963
73. Um, Um, Um, Um, Um, Um	Major Lance	1963
74. El Watusi	Ray Barretto	1963
75. No-Go Showboat	The Beach Boys	1963
76. Chinese Checkers	Booker T. and the M.G.s	1963
77. I Like It Like That	Smokey Robinson & the Miracles	1964
78. Soul Serenade	King Curtis	1964
79. Oh No Not My Baby	Maxine Brown	1964
80. The Last One To Be Loved	Lou Johnson	1964
81. You'll Never Get To Heaven	Dionne Warwick	1964
82. Walk on By	Dionne Warwick	1964
83. Too Many Fish in the Sea	The Marvelettes	1964
84. G.T.O.	Ronny and the Daytonas	1964
85. Things We Said Today	The Beatles	1964
86. She's Not There	The Zombies	1964
87. Off the Hook	The Rolling Stones	1964
88. Everybody Needs Somebody to Love	Solomon Burke	1964
89. I Do Love You	Billy Stewart	1965
90. Nothing Can Stop Me	Gene Chandler	1965
91. She Knows Me Too Well	The Beach Boys	1965
92. Mr. Pitiful	Otis Redding	1965
93. Little by Little	Dusty Springfield	1965
94. I Fought the Law	The Bobby Fuller Four	1965
95. The World Is Round	Rufus Thomas	1965
96. Choosey Beggar	Smokey Robinson & the Miracles	1966
97. Let's Go Away for Awhile	The Beach Boys	1966
98. Paperback Writer	The Beatles	1966
99. Pretty Flamingo	Manfred Mann	1966
100. Fried Neck Bones and Some Home Fries	Willie Bobo	1966
101. Parisian Thoroughfare	Ricardo Ray	1966
102. Bam Bam	Toots and the Maytals	1966
103. Love Makes the World Go Round	Deon Jackson	1967
104. Hypnotized	Linda Jones	1967
105. Brown Eyed Girl	Van Morrison	1967
106. Everybody Needs Love	Gladys Knight & the Pips	1967
107. Femme Fatale	The Velvet Underground	1967
108. Timer	Laura Nyro	1968
109. Soulful Strut	Young-Holt Unlimited	1968
110. We Don't Care	Vampyros Lesbos (soundtrack)	1969
111. Mister Brown	Bob Marley and the Wailers	1970
112. Went to See the Gypsy	Bob Dylan	1970
113. Til I Die	The Beach Boys	1971

114. If You Really Love Me	Stevie Wonder	1971
115. I Scare Myself	Dan Hicks & His Hot Licks	1971
116. Sweet Mountain	Spring	1971
117. Funky Nassau	The Beginning of the End	1971
118. Day Dreaming	Aretha Franklin	1972
119. Freddie's Dead	Curtis Mayfield	1972
120. Backstabbers	The O'Jays	1972
121. Trouble Man	Marvin Gaye	1973
122. My Name Is Nobody	Ennio Morricone	1973
123. The Cisco Kid	War	1973
124. The Payback	James Brown	1974
125. The Bottle	Gil Scott-Heron	1974
126. Errare Humanum Est	Jorge Ben	1974
127. Linden Arden Stole the Highlights	Van Morrison	1974
128. How Long	Ace	1975
129. Ponta de Areia	Milton Nascimento & Wayne Shorter	1975
130. Sombre Reptiles	Brian Eno	1975
131. Tribute to Spree	Lord Kitchener	1975
132. More, More, More	The Andrea True Connection	1976
133. Once You Get Started	Rufus with Chaka Khan	1976
134. Sunshower	Dr. Buzzard's Original Savannah Band	1976
135. Egyptian Reggae	Jonathan Richman & The Modern Lovers	1977
136. Warrior in Woolworths	X-Ray Spex	1977
137. Mandjou	Salif Keita & Les Ambassadeurs	1977
138. Hong Kong Garden	Siouxsie and the Banshees	1978
139. Ring My Bell	Anita Ward	1979
140. Gangsters	The Specials	1979
141. Clampdown	The Clash	1979
142. The Table Is Turning	Explainer	1979
143. Wanted Dead or Alive	The Mighty Sparrow	1979
144. Paper	Talking Heads	1979
145. Bolero	Tabou Combo	1979
146. Hands Off She's Mine	The English Beat	1980
147. I'm in Love	Evelyn "Champagne" King	1981
148. Siberian Nights	Twilight 22	1982
149. Time (Clock of the Heart)	Culture Club	1982
150. Utru Horas	Orchestra Baobab	1982

ACKNOWLEDGMENTS

Portions of this book appeared originally, in different form, in the *New York Review of Books, Tin House,* and *The Village Voice.* An earlier version of "Top Forty" was delivered as a talk at a conference of the National Poetry Foundation in Orono, Maine, in July 2000; in a shorter form, "The Rabbi's Playlist" was presented at the New Museum of Contemporary Art in New York City in March 2000; and portions of "Ambient Night at Roots Lounge" were presented at the New School University in April 2002.

I am grateful to a number of organizations who provided assistance during the writing of this book. A fellowship from the John Simon Guggenheim Memorial Foundation greatly facilitated the completion of this project. Two residencies at Yaddo provided the much appreciated opportunity to draft a significant portion of the book. Final revisions were completed during a residency at the Bellagio Study and Conference Center of the Rockefeller Foundation. A grant from the Hertog Research Fellowship Program of Columbia University provided able research assistance by Suzanne Snider. Gerald Howard and Albert Mobilio's comments on earlier drafts of the book were of tremendous help.

Much additional assistance has come from friends, colleagues, editors, and scholars too numerous to list here. I am grateful above all for the help of my family in recalling the past and in helping to see this project through in a difficult period of all our lives.

BIBLIOGRAPHY

The following books are only the most significant among many sources consulted during the writing of this work; even when not directly cited they played an important part in shaping my perceptions of the development of American and world music. Of sources unlisted here, I am most indebted to the many superb liner notes written in recent years for reissues of old recordings, among which I cannot omit mention of the material accompanying the Rhino Records box set *The Look of Love: The Music of Burt Bacharach*.

Count Basie, with Albert Murray. *Good Morning Blues*. Random House, 1985.

James Brown, with Bruce Tucker. *James Brown: The Godfather of Soul*. Macmillan, 1986.

Robert Cantwell. *When We Were Good: The Folk Revival*. Harvard University Press, 1996.

Stanley Dance. *The World of Duke Ellington*. Scribner's, 1970.

Alton Delmore. *Truth Is Stranger Than Publicity*. Country Music Foundation Press, 1977.

Susan J. Douglas. *Listening In: Radio and the American Imagination*. Times Books, 1999.

Gerald Early. *One Nation Under a Groove: Motown and American Culture*. The Ecco Press, 1995.

Evan Eisenberg. *The Recording Angel: Explorations in Phonography*. McGraw-Hill, 1987.

Mark Evans. *Soundtrack: The Music of the Movies*. Hopkinson & Blake, 1975.

John Floyd. *Sun Records: An Oral History*. Avon Books, 1998.

Gary Giddins. *Bing Crosby: A Pocketful of Dreams, The Early Years 1903–1940*. Little, Brown, 2001.

Albert Glinsky. *Theremin: Ether Music and Espionage*. University of Illinois Press, 2000.

Fred Goodman. *The Mansion on the Hill: Dylan, Young, Geffen, Springsteen, and the Head-On Collision of Rock and Commerce*. Times Books, 1997.

Tim Gracyk. *Popular American Recording Pioneers, 1895–1925*. The Haworth Press, 2000.

Peter Guralnick. *Sweet Soul Music: Rhythm and Blues and the Southern Dream of Freedom*. Harper & Row, 1986.

John Edward Hasse. *Beyond Category: The Life and Genius of Duke Ellington*. Simon & Schuster, 1993.

Dick Hebdige. *Cut 'n' Mix: Culture, Identity and Caribbean Music*. Methuen, 1987.

Dave Hickey. *Air Guitar*. Foundation for Advanced Critical Studies, 1997.

Barney Hoskyns. *Waiting for the Sun: Strange Days, Weird Scenes, and the Sound of Los Angeles*. St. Martin's Press, 1997.

Rick Kennedy and Randy McNutt. *Little Labels—Big Sound: Small Record Companies and the Rise of American Music*. Indiana University Press, 1999.

Joseph Lanza. *Elevator Music: A Surreal History of Muzak, Easy-Listening, and Other Moodsong*. Picador, 1995.

Colin Larkin. *The Virgin Encyclopedia of Fifties Music*. Virgin, 1998.

Greil Marcus. *Invisible Republic: Bob Dylan's Basement Tapes*. Henry Holt, 1997.

Greil Marcus. *Mystery Train: Images of America in Rock 'n' Roll Music*. Dutton, 1975.

Edward B. Marks, with A. J. Liebling. *They All Sang: From Tony Pastor to Rudy Vallee*. The Viking Press, 1934.

Dave McAleer, ed. *The All Music Book of Hit Singles*. Miller Freeman Books, 1994.

André Millard. *America on Record: A History of Recorded Sound*. Cambridge University Press, 1995.

James Miller. *Flowers in the Dustbin: The Rise of Rock and Roll, 1947–1977*. Simon & Schuster, 1999.

Jerrold Northrop Moore. *Sound Revolutions: A Biography of Fred Gaisberg, Founding Father of Commercial Sound Recording*. Sanctuary Publishing, 1999.

Robert Palmer. *Deep Blues*. Viking Penguin, 1981.

Richard A. Peterson. *Creating Country Music: Fabricating Authenticity*. The University of Chicago Press, 1997.

Domenic Priore. *Look! Listen! Vibrate! Smile!* Surfin' Colours Productions, 1989.

Simon Reynolds. *Generation Ecstasy: Into the World of Techno and Rave Culture*. Routledge, 1999.

John Storm Roberts. *The Latin Tinge: The Impact of Latin American Music on the United States,* 2nd edition. Oxford University Press, 1999.

Tony Scherman. *Backbeat: Earl Palmer's Story*. Smithsonian Institution Press, 1999.

Christopher Small. *Music of the Common Tongue: Survival and Celebration in African American Music*. Wesleyan University Press, 1987.

Robert W. Snyder. *The Voice of the City: Vaudeville and Popular Culture in New York*. Oxford University Press, 1989.

Jon Stebbins. *Dennis Wilson: The Real Beach Boy*. ECW Press, 1999.

David Toop. *Exotica: Fabricated Soundscapes in a Real World*. Serpent's Tail, 1999.

David Toop. *Ocean of Sound: Aether Talk, Ambient Sound and Imaginary Worlds*. Serpent's Tail, 1995.

Craig Werner. *A Change Is Gonna Come: Music, Race and the Soul of America*. Plume Books, 1999.

Joel Whitburn. *Pop Memories, 1890–1954: The History of American Popular Music*. Record Research Inc., 1986.

Timothy White. *Catch a Fire: The Life of Bob Marley,* revised edition. Henry Holt, 1989.

Timothy White. *The Nearest Far Away Place: Brian Wilson, The Beach Boys, and the Southern California Experience*. Henry Holt, 1994.

Brian Wilson, with Todd Gould. *Wouldn't It Be Nice*. HarperCollins, 1991.

bandersnatch

bandersnatch

DESMOND LOWDEN

Holt, Rinehart and Winston

NEW YORK • CHICAGO • SAN FRANCISCO

for Gill

"Beware the Jabberwock, my son!
The jaws that bite, the claws that catch!
Beware the Jubjub bird, and shun
The frumious Bandersnatch!"

Alice Through the Looking-Glass

PART

one

1

In almost a week the sprawling town of Palma shook itself free of winter and stretched between flat blue sea and sky. The hill below Bellver Castle was suddenly a soft green fold of pines, and the smart hotels of Terreno dozed under lowered eyelids of colored canvas. There were still traces of winter along the sea wall, where barelegged men sifted through wreckage on the gray mud. But above them on the Paseo Maritimo car tires howled on the melting tar, horse-drawn cabs dawdled along the pavements, and the hotel swimming pools were being mapped out by white paint. White seemed to be the color of the summer season. The line of moored pleasure boats had been painted so many times that they no longer seemed to be wooden but carved out of some dazzling white foam. And white too was the cluster of jetties that fanned out into the harbor blue midway between the Paseo Maritimo and the commercial port—jetties that formed three sides of a square around the long cement building of the Club Nautico.

Here it was another world, enclosed and gentle, where the racket of the town was replaced by more measured sounds. Varnish scrapers, creaking ropes, and the clipped messages from the loudspeaker on the yacht club roof, soft as they crossed the water. *Mr. Armstrong del yacht* Cherokee *a teléphono por favor, a teléphono por favor.* . . . It was an exclusive world, guarded from the curious by locked gates and the attendant at the entrance to the Club Nautico. A world cut off by a forest of newly varnished masts, which screened all except the town's two landmarks—Bellver Castle to the west and the cathedral to the east. And now the buttresses of the cathedral were calm and yellow in the morning haze, and the yacht basin looked exactly like its postcard.

But there was one change to the postcard. A change so enormous it altered the shape of the entire harbor. It was as if someone had built a huge white office block next to the Club Nautico. Last night one of the largest yachts in the world had berthed there, and now she over-shadowed all the other craft in the basin. *Pindar* was the name on the round stern that towered over the quay. Built on the steel hull of a cargo ship, her gleaming white walls led up to a single squat funnel. She cast a wide shadow over the club terrace, and the crowd there spoke in whispers. They said she belonged to Alexis Tzannos, one of the richest of the Greek shipowners. They said that behind the square windows of the main deck there was a swimming pool covered by a badminton court. They pointed to the two Riva speedboats and the racing yacht high up on her sunlit boat deck. And they moved along the terrace so that they could see the seaplane on her foredeck.

Across the gap of water that was the entrance to the basin, a man stood alone on the tip of the seaward jetty, staring up at the great white ship. From a distance he was tall and distinguished, in a blazer and officer's cap. But nearness showed he was older, more bulky, and somehow bruised by the bright day around. He had worn rope-soled shoes and creased trousers that were tight around his hams. His blazer was stained, and its faded crest was re-peated by the neckerchief tucked into his old khaki shirt. Silver hair, jagged and hand-cut, escaped from the band of his cap, and if his sprawling mustache had once been silver it was stained by too many cheap cigarettes, smoked

4

too short. Around the mustache his face had as many red specks as white. It showed the scars of temper, alcohol, and the discomfort of a fair-skinned man who lived in the sun. He had a nose that barmen would call expensive, small eyes that were red-streaked, burning their sockets like hot coals. They shifted their gaze away from *Pindar* now as a splintering noise from nearby made him turn to where a cable was chafing the gangplank of an American motor cruiser. "About that plank," he called out to a deck hand on the cruiser.

The man looked up, his eyes narrowing as he recognized the officer's cap. "Commander bleeding Alec Sheldon. D.S.O. D.S.C. R.N. Retired," he said. "Why don't you mind your own bleeding business?"

"If you lay hold of a fender, make it fast below the gangplank, lengthways, then that cable can rub all night without doing any harm." Sheldon's voice was British, naval, fireproof.

The man watched the cable a moment. Then saw he would have to make fast a fender, lengthways, below the gangplank. He fetched one, hesitated before kneeling at Sheldon's feet.

"Right. All squared up."

The deck hand straightened. He saw Sheldon's eyes weren't looking at him, always over his head. "Three things bloody useless aboard a boat," he said loudly. "Wheelbarrow, a thirty-foot stepladder, and a British naval officer."

"Good morning." The commander turned and marched stiffly away.

Two hundred yards away the concrete jetty made a right angle toward the shore around a water tap. A spider of colored hoses wound away to the moored yachts. There was the rasp of deck scrubbers, and the hiss of water trickling down shiny hulls to blur their reflections looping out of the scum. A tall white sail rose hesitantly into the air, drying out a winter's damp. And in its shadow a blonde girl, whose bikini was honey-brown to match the color of her skin, was standing on the gangplank of a tall two-masted schooner. Beyond her a tanned barefoot man stood on the schooner's curving deck. He had the boat's name, *Aristide*, printed across his white T-shirt, and he was part of the boat—powerful and good-looking. Softly he argued with the girl.

"Every time I see you, you look thinner," he told her. "Looks as though you could do with some hot dinners."

"I'm slimming," she said warily.

"There's food here. Plenty of food." He pointed to the gangplank between them. "If you'd like to come across . . ."

The girl ducked away from his outstretched hand. Suddenly she collided with Sheldon as he came along the quay. "I'm so sorry." She clutched at his arm to steady herself.

Sheldon pulled himself clear. He flushed as he found himself staring at her near-naked body, and was at a loss for words.

"Good morning, Captain," the barefoot man called out mockingly.

"Good morning . . . uhhh . . . Dick." Sheldon nodded at him, then marched on.

The man called Dick was now at the girl's side. "Come and have dinner aboard this evening," he murmured at her. "There's steak, champagne, and we can eat in the owner's cabin. He's not down till next week."

The girl backed away. To change the subject she stared at Sheldon's retreating figure. "Who is he?" she asked. "You called him Captain."

"If you won't eat here," Dick moved in closer, his voice low and confident, "come and have dinner ashore. I'll take you somewhere classy."

The girl still watched Sheldon nervously. "I saw him

6

standing out on the quay for a long while. He was staring at that Greek yacht. The huge one that came in last night." She remembered the boat's name. "Is he *Pindar*'s captain?"

"Him?" Dick rocked back on his heels laughing. "Alec Sheldon?"

The jetty turned a second corner where it reached the shore by the slipway. Here it broadened out into a cement yard where speedboats were beached for the winter. A group of workmen were sweating one of the boats over to the water on its wooden sledge. They paused, and sank back in its shade as Sheldon approached on his way around the harbor.

"Good morning, Captain."

"Morning," he nodded, hardly breaking step.

The workmen watched him duck into the alley behind the slipway winches. "Captain!" One of them spat carefully into the water. "He couldn't even take this speedboat out of here."

"Once he could have. He was one of the finest MTB captains in the war. Row of medals as long as your arm."

Hooding his eyes, the man saw Sheldon reappear past the red-leaded hulls on the slip. "1945 that was. This is 1968."

In the harbor corner by the Palcoa Agency there was no shade. Two fishermen sat on the warm stones outside the rope store and compared two new lengths of line, wondering if they could afford the more expensive nylon. Through the distant clatter of riveters from the slipway, Sheldon's footsteps came toward them along the quay.

"Good morning, Captain." The fisherman who'd spoken looked up awkwardly, his red neck creasing white above his humped back.

"Morning." Sheldon marched past them toward the yacht club terrace.

"How does the bastard do it?" The humpback watched him go with hopeless anger. "Eyes so bloodshot he can't see out of them, fingers brown as a board. Where does he get the money?"

"Search me. I haven't seen him with a skipper's job these past three years."

"But he spends like a millionaire." The humpback pointed with a hand that was whitened by seawater. "Galatzo Restaurant, dearest place in town, know how much he owes in there? Well, one of the waiters told me. Twenty-five thousand pesetas. Twenty-five *thousand!*"

"He owes eleven thousand at the Valdemossa. Everywhere he eats, in fact. And that's not counting the twenty thousand odd he owes the Chandlers here, for his boat."

"How does the bastard do it?" Both men watched Sheldon pause by the turquoise-blue pool on the terrace, and then go into the yacht club.

"Good morning, Captain." Luis, head barman of the Club Nautico, carefully slid the bottle of Fundador behind his back.

"Good morning." Sheldon closed the net-curtained door and came on into the long, cool room. He hesitated by a leather armchair, his eyes burning into the liquor labels all around. Then he walked past the bar to the dim corridor beyond.

Luis finished opening the Fundador before he followed the captain along the yellow stone tiles. Turning the corner he found the young attendant checking the letter rack for Sheldon.

"Nothing for you, Captain."

"Well, in that case," Sheldon glanced around nervously before darting away to the cloakroom door. "Think I'll just . . ."

"I don't get it." The attendant turned to Luis. "Every day he comes in here asking for letters. Every day there's nothing for him. Then he goes to the toilet."

"It's simple," Luis said. "That's the only thing left in this club that's free."

"But he's a member, isn't he? I mean, I should let him in?"

"He's a member all right. Fifteen years ago, he was very big here. Used to run big yachts. The rich liked him." Luis' voice was respectful. "At that time everybody liked war heroes. And he could handle a ship then."

"So what went wrong?"

Luis tipped one hand gently over his mouth. "The English disease. You know how much a bottle of wine costs in England? *Bad* wine? Hundred pesetas a bottle. For good wine you can pay anything."

The attendant whistled.

"And our commander started smacking boats against the quay, squabbling with owners, losing his crews."

"And what does he . . . ?"

Luis put out a warning hand as Sheldon reappeared. The two men followed him to the club entrance and watched him go out into the harsh sunlit world beyond. Sand and cement dust clouded the roadway, coming from the waste lot of dazzling white rubble beyond where ballast trucks crawled around pneumatic drills. Sheldon was halted by a roar of thunder as a truck tipped its load down on to a metal pontoon. Workmen in yellow oilskin trousers hauled the pontoon around to a new concrete jetty being built on the far side of the lot. Sheldon followed more slowly, making his way toward the cluster of derelict-looking craft halfway along the jetty.

"And now he's out in the cold, out in shantytown." Luis smiled sadly. "He really hates being outside the yacht basin. You saw his face as he . . ."

". . . I was asking you," the attendant said, "what he did now. I mean for a living."

"He's tried a bit of everything. One season it was

guiding bus tours, the next he was renting out villas. Only for a short time, you understand, before the police could ask him about a work permit." Luis turned away from the sunlight. "Now he's teaching at the Berlitz. But they'll catch up with him. It's only a matter of time. . . . He's finished here."

"Good morning, Captain." The woman looked up from her paintbrush, tried to hold Sheldon with her smile as he stepped up onto the dusty quay from the waste lot. Disappointed when he marched on by her, she jammed her brush savagely back into the tin of deck paint.

"Careful what you're doing," her husband pointed. "Deck paint's expensive stuff."

The deck the woman was painting was crusted with gray coats. Rust showed through from the fastenings, as it did from every bit of metal in the boat, and in the boats alongside. This was shantytown, a half-finished jetty poking out into the commercial port. Here converted war boats hung low and peeling in the water, with only their superstructures resembling their rich sisters on the Club Nautico quays—structures that were faked out of plywood and paint, deck chairs that were faded, vases of gladioli that had withered in the sun. And their crews were not the smartly uniformed professionals of the yacht club. Not crews at all—they'd be quick to mention—they owned their boats. But the boats owned them. Working ships, they stayed afloat only if they chartered. And a few seasons ago the Franco government had plugged one outflow of revenue from the country by stopping the chartering of foreign yachts out of Spanish ports. Now these boats were trapped in Palma without work. And with neither the money nor gas and oil for the trip to Tangiers, they could only sink lower in the water.

The woman straightened up from her work to watch Sheldon walk back to his boat. Five years ago she'd left Newhaven in a golden sunset, her husband at the wheel in a stiff new yachting cap, telling her about the money they were going to make in the Mediterranean. For five years she'd watched their savings disappear. For five years she'd lived in a boat where she couldn't stand upright or take a bath. Five years she'd scraped and painted, sanded and varnished. In all that time she'd never seen Sheldon so much as pick up a paintbrush to the huge Motor Torpedo Boat he lived on.

"I don't know what you see in him," her husband said.

"He's skippered damn near every boat in the yacht basin. Schooners, steam-yachts, you name it."

"And got thrown off."

"You must admit he did it very well," the woman said. "They say he told Lord Aylesham to screw himself."

"And got thrown off."

"They say he was slung out of Ibiza at gun point," the woman's eyes shone admiringly, "for making off with a village girl."

"Look!" her husband shouted. "Will you look at that old MTB over there! A hundred and fifteen feet of junk. He's never painted it, never had it out of the water. The only reason it doesn't sink is it's propped up on all the empties he's slung overboard. And he's rotting in that wreck. He and that Cantlie woman."

"They say it was the boat he commanded during the war." The woman turned her back on her husband. "That wreck, as you call it, sank a German destroyer."

2

Sheldon stopped by the boxlike stern of the MTB. She was long, twice as long as any of the craft around her. And her two colors—gray and dirty gray—cast a chill over the sunlit water. Sadly he saw once again that she was no longer an MTB, that her wartime numbers 859 had been painted over with the name *Jabberwocky*. A bad joke in keeping with the thick green weed on her waterline, the frayed ends of old ropes sucking and releasing the slime. And stripped of her guns and torpedo tubes, she sat high on the water, rolling awkwardly in the harbor swell. Sheldon walked slowly along her bare deck toward the single blockhouse, whose turrets frowned suspiciously at the rich men's yachts by the Club Nautico. Automatically his feet avoided depth charges and gun mountings that were now only pitted circles in the gray paint.

He went down the ladder to the wardroom, and the heat hit him. The Season had come around once again, and he had no ship to command. Wearily he sat on the worn cushions, watching the shafts of sunlight from the portholes slide up and down the wooden panels. The circles of light showed patches of different wood under the faded varnish, patches that covered burns and bullet holes. The dark narrow cabin and its memories crowded in on Sheldon. He pulled himself together as he heard footsteps from the galley. There were two of them now— two living on a boat built for thirty-two. "Sandy," he shouted irritably.

She stood in the galley door, short, squarish, un- remarkable except for her man's jeans and shirt. There was the usual strand of damp hair breaking loose from the bun at her neck, the usual shine on her unpowdered face. She had a short upturned nose and upturned chin. They weren't attractive, but they showed acceptance. Acceptance of her English upbringing which had required her to be a second-class man. Acceptance of the rules of rugger, and the larger game where bombs fell out of the night sky. Two bombs, 1500 miles apart, had killed her husband on a mine sweeper and her son on an evacuee train. She'd even accepted the situation when, years later, she'd put a deposit on a villa in Majorca and the building had never been finished. She'd been trapped in a cheap back-street pension by quadrupling prices and a daily six-peseta bottle of wine. Sheldon had never known whether he'd rescued her or she'd rescued him. She said very little. Her background equipped her to speak to only a few people in England, and foreigners were beyond her. Here in Palma they took her accent for criticism, her shyness for arrogance, and her jeans for lack of femininity. Sheldon knew a lot better than that, he'd stayed with her for eleven years.

Now the silence hung the length of the wardroom between them, and he felt he had to break it. "I'm not going into the Berlitz today. The class was down to three on Tuesday. I'll tell them I'm sick or something."

"Suit yourself." Her voice was low and manlike, careful in its lack of accusation.

"And if you want to know the real reason," Sheldon got up suddenly and aimed his anger away from her, "it's because I asked for an advance on next month, and they said there wasn't going to be a next month. The work permit business again." The boat rolled suddenly, and the chartroom door slid open. Sheldon saw his parallel rulers, dividers, and his row of Mediterranean Pilots. "God Almighty, what do I want with sniveling schoolkids? I've got qualifications that make all the other skippers in this port look like taxi drivers. Just two seasons' bad luck, and nobody'll give me a ship." His voice tailed away, and he leaned against the scarred varnish of the bulkhead. When he turned back to Sandy, he saw she was holding out a package of Pall Mall. "Where did you get those?" he asked in surprise.

"Barney called round this morning. He looked at the generator like you asked. I found two packs on the chart table after he'd gone."

"Barney's working. He can afford it." Sheldon lit a cigarette, inhaled with a grateful gasp. "Good chappie, best engineer in the whole damn Navy once. Wish he was still working for me."

"So does he," Sandy said. "He told me he'd come around like a shot if you found a boat."

"Just his little joke." Sheldon savored the smoke as it went down his lungs, calming him. "But Barney doesn't forget what it was like in the war. He knows I could never stand being without cigarettes. He understands that."

Sandy looked behind her to the galley. "I suppose there's no money left to buy food. After last night, I mean, in the Bar Maritimo?" She didn't say it unkindly.

"God Almighty, woman, I only went in there with twenty-five pesetas, cadged all the evening. The place was full of people returning for the season. Good for a couple of drinks."

"It doesn't really matter. I can't cook anyway. The gas butane's empty."

"God Almighty," Sheldon said.

"And the harbor master called. He said he'd come back."

"God Almighty."

"*Jabberwock* . . . oh, *Jabberwock*," the harbor master's voice came from on deck.

"God Almighty," Sheldon said. "Tell him I'm not here. Tell him somebody's offered me a job along the coast." He ran for the engine-room door but he was too late. The harbor master's face was peering down at him through one of the portholes. Swearing under his breath, Sheldon went up the ladder quickly so that he'd be standing over the man on deck. He got there first, and the harbor master was looking up at him, olive-skinned, and squat even in his expensive suit. Thick muscles reached up from his silk shirt to tauten over a heavy jaw, his tired eyes stared at Sheldon's blazer buttons. Sheldon looked over his head. They needed to be on a sloping deck to see each other.

"What can I do for you?"

"I come to tell you you must move."

"Move? Move where? We're stuck halfway out in the damn commercial port as it is."

"Move out of the harbor. There is . . ."

"*Out?*"

". . . There is a new yat, *Pindar,* come in last night. A very big yat. We have to have more space."

"Not this space, for God's sake. A half-finished jetty on the end of a pile of rubble?"

"That is the whole point," the harbor master chanced a quick look at Sheldon's face. "You don't hear why Mr. Alexis Tzannos is here? The owner of *Pindar?*"

Sheldon shook his head.

"He have come to Palma to build a new yatting marina. It start here where we are standing and go right around to the Club Nautico. That is why we build this new quay."

Amazed, Sheldon looked back down the jetty and across the vacant lot to where *Pindar*'s white hull jutted out from the yacht club. "But it'll be as big as the yacht basin itself," his mind worked quickly. "So it'll take time. You won't have to move anyone out for months."

"There is another thing. This is a big project, and to make it work Mr. Tzannos have to get himself elected on the town council. And now the council must be strict. This will be the yatting center of the world. They must enforce the regulations." The harbor master said it quickly: "The regulations say no houseboats. Only working boats allowed here."

"What about them?" Sheldon pointed to the derelict craft alongside. "Two, three houseboats. They don't cruise."

"They will have to move out too."

"My backside," Sheldon said. "You're just making an example, aren't you? Saving your own dirty skin?"

The man's head jerked up as he lost control. "No motors! You alone in the harbor have no motors! How can I say this is a working boat? And the gray paint? The gun turrets? What am I to say to Mr. Tzannos when he come down here next week? That is a preevat museum for Captain Sheldon?"

"I'll move when those other houseboats move," Sheldon tried to keep calm.

"They pay their harbor dues," the harbor master said pointedly.

"And a case of Scotch at Christmas."

"You accuse me of taking bribes?" the man shouted.

"Of course. Everybody knows about it." Sheldon got the man's angry feet going back toward the gangplank. "I'm going along the coast tomorrow, to take command of a boat. . . ."

". . . Don't make jokes, Captain. You have not had a boat in three years."

". . . To take command of a boat, as I say. So *Jabberwocky*'ll be a working ship as far as you're concerned. There'll be a case of Scotch to say it is."

Sandy was waiting for him in the wardroom. "He's said it all before," she told him. "At the start of every season."

Sheldon didn't answer. He sat in the corner where the shadows were deepest.

"Every year he's tried to move us on. Every year we stay put."

"This time it's different," his voice was unnaturally quiet. "He wants us out."

Sandy didn't understand him. She didn't understand why he spoke so softly, why he was hunched in the dark corner seat where he'd never sat before. She looked around at the wardroom's faded panels to make sure nothing else had changed.

"Out of the harbor." Sheldon moved around so she wouldn't see his face. "It's what we've never dared think about. And it's happened."

"You mean that crook of a harbor master . . . ?"

"It's not him. There's a fat Greek called Tzannos who owns a fat boat. He's bought all the land and now he's started on the sea. He doesn't want an old warship in his harbor . . . Captain Sheldon's private museum."

"He said that?"

Sheldon didn't hear her. "Good morning, Captain. Good morning, Captain," he said strangely. "Why the hell do they still call me Captain?" He knew why. Sometimes he wished he could talk to people without the aid of a megaphone. Even now his voice came out gruff and accusing. "I mean it's useless, my going along the coast. Why should it be any different to here? And we can't stay here any more. They don't want us." Suddenly he grabbed out for her hand, pleaded with her, "What do we do, Sandy? Where do we go?"

She almost recoiled in surprise. "I . . . I'd better get ready. It's my afternoon for Madame Moreno." Her face hardened to ward off her embarrassment. "I'm late already. . . . Really."

"We can't sell the boat." Clumsy, childlike, he pressed her hand. "We've tried that. Nobody wants an old warship with four bloody great Packard engines that drink up petrol. They're all small diesels nowadays. . . . And we can't let her go for scrap."

Sandy looked down at the hurt eyes, the wet mustache. Sober, she'd never seen him cry before.

"Once this was a damn fine craft. And I was all right too, dammit." He cleared his throat noisily.

"Madame Moreno will be waiting for me." Sandy freed her hand.

"Damn her. Damn you pimping after that rich old bag, pushing her wheelchair around the harbor three afternoons a week."

"She pays me. We have to eat."

"A hundred pesetas a throw. How do we eat on that?"

"It's not much. I . . ." Sandy's voice cracked. She turned away. "Why did you have to get me like this? Why don't you shout and swear like you usually do?"

"Usually . . . I'm a comic-strip ex-naval commander who can't pay for his drinks," Sheldon said slowly. "Usually I sit around on an ex-naval boat some silly bastard called *Jabberwocky* after the war."

"You could have renamed her when you bought her. You said it was bad luck."

"Bad luck?" He couldn't manage a laugh. "Look, promise me you won't bring that old bag around here this afternoon. She just treats me like some sort of bloody fairground attraction. Sits there with her hundred pesetas and won't hand it over till I've done my show."

"She likes coming around here." Sandy relaxed slightly, back on familiar ground. "It makes a nice outing for her. She's very fond of you."

Sheldon nodded unhappily. "Just so long as she doesn't get me to read that damned Jabberwocky poem again."

3

"Will you read me the Jabberwocky poem, Captain, dear?"

Sheldon stiffened, looked purposely away from the old woman, back toward her wheelchair on the quay. He felt her walking stick tap his shoulder, and he turned to face the cracked parchment of her cheeks, the shell of blue hair that closed in a tight circle around her tortoise neck. "Not just at the moment, Madame, later."

Her withered claw of a hand waved the hundred-peseta envelope like a fan, and her mouth tightened. "Well, tell me about the time you sank the German destroyer."

"You know all about that, Madame. I tell you every time you come."

"Tell me again. . . . You were hiding on this Greek island. . . . Holed up, I believe you called it, in this cave."

"Holed up," Sheldon repeated. He passed the woman's stool to the front of the bridge. Out of the corner of his eye he saw Sandy signaling urgently at him. He had to continue the ritual. "It was after the battle of Leros, November 1943. We'd taken a hell of a beating. The boat was shot to pieces . . ." he tailed off. Around him now was the same boat, the same cracked sprayshield, the same ship's wheel under his hands.

"And the ship that . . . shot you to pieces," the old woman said, "was a German destroyer. . . ." She waited for him.

"The *Burg Rostock*," Sheldon obliged her.

The woman's voice was impatient now. "You stayed

a fortnight in this cave, repairing your boat with the help of some Greeks. Then, when you were ready to leave you heard that this same destroyer, the *Burg Rostock*, was still at Leros. She'd also been damaged in the battle. . . . Go on."

"So we made for Leros again," Sheldon said mechanically. "Very slowly. Only two engines were working, and the seas were tricky. We just had the one torpedo left."

"And slowly you came into the bay at Leros where it was calmer." The woman hissed the words softly, almost to herself. "You had to be very quiet. Your men were rowing in a rubber dinghy, pulling the boat along . . . this boat." Madame Moreno gathered herself up on her stool and pointed a trembling hand out over the bows. "And there was the *Burg Rostock*, anchored in the harbor mouth, being repaired. She had no lights, but you could see her silhouetted against the lights of the town. A sitting target."

Sheldon shook his head angrily. "If you know the story so well, Madame, why d'you need me to tell it?"

The old woman smiled at him, patted her tight blue curls coquettishly. "Go on. Do the bit with the torpedo sight. Don't disappoint an old woman."

"Old bag," Sheldon muttered. He bent to the torpedo sight that was still clamped to the bridge rail.

And there square in the sights was *Pindar*.

"Fire One!" the woman shouted behind him. "Oh, he won't do it today, will he? What's the matter with him?"

"He's not feeling too well." Sandy soothed her.

"Drink, I expect," the woman's voice was tart. "Why doesn't he read the Jabberwocky poem to me? He knows it off by heart. I'm sure he does."

Sheldon did know the poem by heart. Bits of it came to his mind as he stared at the yacht through the torpedo sight. The huge white boat across the harbor, belonging to the Greek who owned both yacht and harbor. The Greek who was trying to get him out. " 'Beware the Jabberwock, my son,' " he murmured. " 'The jaws that bite, the claws that catch. Beware the Jubjub bird, and shun . . . the frumious Bandersnatch.' "

"He won't do it!" Madame Moreno's voice cracked angrily. "What about the bit where he was waiting for the torpedo to hit?"

"The Jabberwock, with eyes of flame, came whiffling through the tulgey wood, and burbled as it came." Sheldon almost saw the flash of the torpedo as it leaped over the bow and snaked toward *Pindar*.

"And that terrifying bit about the torpedo hitting. . . . Boom! . . . And then the second explosion," the woman continued. "Sheets of flame. Orange flame, he said."

"One, two. One, two. And through and through . . . the vorpal blade went snicker-snack," Sheldon muttered to himself. His eyes, straining through the sight, made *Pindar* blur and sink. It wasn't until he stood up, blinking tiredly, that he saw the Greek boat still cast its long shadow over the Club Nautico.

"He never told the whole story at all," Madame Moreno said. "He missed out all that part about repairing the damage in the cave . . . and burying the dead." Her old eyes glittered suddenly, her voice was soft and caressing. "Seven dead. One of them a young boy. Traill he said his name was. . . . He could only find an arm. He had to bury that."

For a moment Sheldon was trapped again on the bridge. The sun, flaring on the sprayshield, was a wall of fire. The wood was splintering and burning all around him. . . . He pressed his hands to his temples, waited until the dazzling light had subsided. And once again he saw the port of Palma drowsing sleepily in the late afternoon sun.

Madame Moreno waved the money envelope coyly before she handed it over to Sandy. She'd had her hundred pesetas' worth.

4

Alone now on the bridge, Sheldon watched the pale line of sunlight shiver reluctantly before sliding past the row of moored boats into the water. In little over a minute the sun had slipped below Bellver Castle on its hill until the entire harbor was a pool of shadow, and only the buttresses of the cathedral could catch its rays, slim arches rising up into the fading burnish of the sky. The racket of the commercial port was stilled, the lamps not yet lit, and the last of the daylight lingered out over the far arm of the bay, bringing red tears to the hundred eyes of Ca'n Pastilla. . . . Sheldon loved this place. The thought of leaving it was beyond his understanding.

Once again he tried to face up to the harbor master's ultimatum. The only weapon he had was the hundred pesetas in his hand. He hid it in one of the bottom pigeonholes of the locker, Sandy wouldn't think of looking there. She'd given him the envelope before wheeling Madame Moreno back to her hotel, and she'd told him to buy bread, cheese, and sobrasada. But there was no point in throwing the money away on food. Things were serious, more serious than they'd ever been. His career at the Berlitz was obviously ended, and he had to break out somewhere new—or somewhere old. The idea of going along the coast tomorrow was beginning to fix itself in his mind. Of course there wouldn't be a boat that needed a skipper, and anyway the thought of a skipper's job scared the hell out of him after three years ashore. But he had to break out, if only by getting on a bus and taking a look.

. . . Something else Sandy had said—they were out of gas. He left the bridge to fix it.

The empty gas-butane cylinder was on the foredeck. He unscrewed it from its pipe and dragged it aft toward the gangplank. Then he stopped. Someone was watching him from the shadows of the quay, a blonde girl in a honey-brown bikini. Sheldon remembered bumping into her in the yacht basin this morning. Now there was something strange about her, and as he looked more closely he saw that she was trembling. He wondered why a girl wore a bathing costume at this hour of night. "What's the matter?" he asked her.

"Cold," she replied through chattering teeth. "Landlady threw me out, kept my things."

"And you haven't any money?"

The girl stooped to the quayside in a sudden graceful movement. She emptied her handbag onto the cement blocks. Sheldon saw lipsticks, empty bottles of sun oil, very little else.

He looked at her steadily, then decided he could trust her. ". . . Keep watch a second, would you? Sing out if anyone comes."

His rope-soled shoes were silent on the next-door boat's deck as he carried the gas butane toward his neighbor's gas supply. He found a half-empty cylinder, disconnected it, and left *Jabberwocky*'s empty one in its place. Then he returned to the MTB with the stolen cylinder, connected it to the pipe outside the chartroom. Guiltily he turned back to the gangplank to find the girl was smiling at him, a strange, slow smile. "I'm making some tea," he called out to her, then wondered why he'd invited her on board.

She preceded him down the ladder to the wardroom. He found a torch and saw how clean and golden were her limbs. She was too thin, and it showed mostly in her face, but there was a strange faunlike quality about her as she trembled with cold. Sheldon didn't often bother to look at the girls around the port who pouted at everything in trousers—sticky-bun women he called them—but this one was very different. He lit the galley stove, watched her as she warmed herself at the flare. The soft lemon curl of her hair fell away from a finely modeled face. Her eyes were huge as she looked at the dark cluttered galley around her.

He cleared his throat nervously. "Tea," he said. "Indian or China?"

"Whatever, . . ." she shrugged in reply.

He crossed to the open porthole with the teapot. The squeal of fenders brought the next boat near. He reached through, opened the porthole of the other boat, removed one of the tea caddies, beyond. ". . . And one for the pot." He replaced the caddy, closed both portholes. The girl was watching him with that same slow smile. "Sorry about the lights," he told her. "The generator doesn't work without petrol."

She cradled a steaming mug of tea in her hands, and the torchlight made her very close. Sheldon went back ten years to the successful seasons. There'd been women then, cool and beautiful women, and always the surprise. They'd told him it was his mustache, his manners, even his aloofness, and he'd held them each for a few minutes. Sandy he needed when minutes became hours, months, serious. And this girl? Again Sheldon wondered why he'd asked her on board. She had the *marque* of those other beauties, the symmetry, the rhythm of movement, the sudden searching look. But there was more to this girl— the smooth oval of her face crumpled as she rubbed her eyelid with careless knuckles. She was like a child who'd overheard only yesterday that she was beautiful. And she took a child's delight, not in herself, but in the things around her. At the moment she was looking beyond the circle of torchlight to the shadows around the wardroom door. "It's such a huge ship," she said. "And strange. What is it?"

In answer he led her down the dark passage that ran the length of the boat. The torch beam narrowed and flared, glinted on planks that sweated in the heat. She wanted to see everything, and it was through her fresh young eyes, shining in the torchlight, that Sheldon saw the boat again—not *Jabberwocky* who'd been weighing on his shoulders since the harbor master's visit—but MTB859 as she'd been in the tense dark nights of the war . . . the shadowy cave of the engine room, its rows of pipes that led to the four Packards, the bilges sighing gently underfoot. The narrow cabins amidships—Captain's Cabin, and the bunks for Chief and Swain—with their smell of damp ticking, the faintest musk of fag ash. Then the wide fo'c's'le where the bunks were stepped up on the curving bow, with hammock hooks overhead, and pin pricks of forgotten Blighty girls.

This girl was alive and warm. She kept in the circle of torchlight, stroked each part of the ship as she came to it, and Sheldon felt as though she were stroking him. She winced when she felt the holes of German 20 mm. shells, cried out on the bridge as one of the few remaining signal flags crumbled to her touch. She felt the weals of cocoa mugs on the chartroom table, and back in the wardroom she pulled down one of the cots, felt in the shadows behind, and found a polished brass tube. Sheldon couldn't speak for a moment, then he told her it was a ruler, a brass ruler he hadn't seen for over twenty years. Her long slim fingers stroked the metal, and the captain drew back out of the torchlight, remembering the young boy who'd owned the ruler.

"You must be very proud to own a ship like this," she said. "Especially as you took her through the war."

"I am. Yes, I am, dammit," Sheldon replied gruffly.

"She's not like the other boats I've been on. She's not

all brassy. And she sits lower in the water as though she's really used to the sea. . . ." The girl's arm carved a graceful arc in the torchlight. ". . . The front end higher than the back. There's something fast and urgent about her."

Sheldon clenched his fists gratefully. "You're right," he said.

"Who's right?" Sandy's voice came from the darkness behind them.

The girl wheeled around at the noise. "I'm sorry. . . ."

"You needn't be. I'm not his wife." Sandy kept back in the shadows, but Sheldon knew the look on her face. A look he hadn't seen in a long time.

"She helped me get the gas butane," he shrugged uneasily. "I made some tea."

"She could wear a few more clothes," Sandy said acidly.

"Her landlady threw her out onto the street, kept her suitcase."

"And she can't find anywhere else to go? In Palma? A girl like that?"

"Nowhere I want to go." The girl's eyes flashed angrily.

Sandy laughed. "Crews been getting at you, have they? I know none of the owners are down yet." She shone the torch full on the girl's face. "What's your name?"

"Claire."

"Well, Claire," Sandy looked hard at her, then suddenly seemed satisfied. "Blonde's his favorite color. Silverblonde, he likes it in an anis glass. A few years ago I wouldn't have trusted him with a young girl, but now . . ."

"Dammit, woman."

Sandy grinned at him. "I suppose you didn't have time for the shopping?" She read his face and turned back to Claire. "He can't stand shopping. So we have to eat out again. . . . You're meant to be out on the streets. Have you eaten today?"

"Yes," Claire said. "I'm not hungry."

Sandy saw the lie on the girl's face and approved of it. "It's going to be difficult. Three of us eating out on a hundred pesetas."

"Difficult?" Sheldon said sarcastically. "Wouldn't even cover the cover charge around here."

"So?" Claire asked them.

"So we eat out," Sandy told her. "We've always eaten out, all our lives."

Sheldon led the way to the chartroom, and spread a large-scale map of Palma out under the torchlight.

"What are those crosses you've marked in?" Claire asked him.

"Restaurants," Sheldon said. "Restaurants we can't go into again."

Sandy straightened up from the map. "There don't seem to be any left, Alec. Unless Claire here knows of a place we haven't heard of."

Claire traced through the streets with her finger. "I was staying at a small pension up on the hill here. There was a tiny *bodega* on the corner."

"Mind being thrown out of it?" Sheldon asked.

5

It was night as they left the boat. The dark water reflected the harbor lights, juggling balls of fire downward in an endless chain. Fenders creaked gently along the quay, somewhere a radio played. Sheldon followed the two women around the corner of the commercial port to the Paseo de Sagrera. He knew they were approaching the Bar Maritimo, where loud English voices were arguing about the Budget. But he didn't look around toward the clink of glasses. He told himself maybe they'd be lucky up in the *bodega* on the hill. Maybe they'd get a bottle of wine, maybe a glass of anis and a bottle of wine.

"Drink, Captain?"

He turned to see Dick, the *Aristide*'s skipper, grinning at him, bare feet propped on a café table. Sheldon hesitated a second, then nodded. "Very kind of you."

"Think nothing of it," Dick signaled for more chairs at the crowded table.

They sat down. Sheldon nervous, tapping the table, waiting for the glass of anis to be placed in front of him, the water jug that would change the clear liquid into milky-white. The drinks arrived, and Sheldon's hand tapped its way over to his glass.

"Skin off your nose."

"Skin off your nose." Dick copied his accent exactly.

The thick cold liquid hit Sheldon, suddenly changed to fire. His eyes watered, and he stroked the frosted surface of the glass.

"Here's to a good season," Dick continued. "Spanish crew you can kick around. And seasick owners who want to stay in harbor." Dick's eyes were bloodshot, dangerous. "You've got a boat this season, I take it?"

"No," Sheldon replied warily.

"Never mind. There's still time." Dick leaned toward him, his mouth cruel, "One thing I will say about you, Sheldon, you are damned British about it. Damned British about everything. I mean you don't care who the hell you drink with, long as they're paying."

Sheldon swallowed the rest of his glass at a gulp, stood up. "Thanks for the drink." he said.

"Sit down. Have another." Dick shouted for the waiter.

Sheldon looked guiltily around the table. It was only then he saw that the sullen drunk faces of the other seamen were staring not at him, but at Claire. Wet-lipped they watched as she crossed her legs nervously, and her borrowed oilskin rose up to reveal her thighs. The men sniggered behind hands that itched at her near-nakedness among the winking neons of night. Dick's red eyes swung around to the girl's body, and Sheldon saw his anger had been directed at her all the time.

Sandy stood up. "We're going out to dinner. It's getting late."

"That's it, is it?" Dick suddenly lost control. "I asked you out to dinner this morning, remember?" he shouted in Claire's face.

She turned away to follow Sheldon and Sandy out of the café.

"Don't you queen it over me, my girl!" Dick shouted after her. "Don't you come the old queen! You're no different from any other bleeding yacht whore!"

They walked silently on under dark creaking palms. Sheldon unhappily watching Claire's face, pale in the street lights. She avoided his eyes and stared dully down at the pavement. He wondered how they could start the evening off again. And as they neared the end of the road he turned toward the shaded lights of the Galatzo Restaurant. "Look," he said suddenly. "They've got a new waiter over there, doesn't know us from Adam." He glanced at his watch. "And it's eight-thirty. Rafael will be having his dinner upstairs. Shall we give it a try?"

"They do an awfully good meal there," Sandy was hesitant, looking for signs of life on Claire's face.

But the girl was pale and tense as they walked across to the colored lights on the far pavement. She was impressed neither by the stiff white napery nor by the waiter who came soft-footed to take their order. She didn't smile when Sandy suggested the cold table because they were in such a frightful hurry. And she agreed to eat what they ate—lobster, cold Scotch beef, and salad. "A bottle of Pouilly-Fuissé for the lobster," Sheldon looked down the wine list. "And two bottles of Château Duhart-Milon '52 for the beef." His hands tapped the table in expectation. "Marvelous to drink French wine again. That Spanish stuff tastes like shellac after a while."

His hands were still, and his face was brick-red by the time the waiter opened the second claret bottle. The two other bottles were empty, and the plates of beef had been cleared away. Sheldon had had a good meal, the wines near perfect, but his contentment was spoiled by the sight of Claire's tight mouth, a straight line out of keeping with her smooth marble face. She'd said nothing through two courses, and he wanted to get her to talk. But the wine wouldn't give him the right words, only made his voice slurred. "I'm sorry about Dick," he said. "Back at the café."

"Sticks and stones," Claire shrugged coldly, and rummaged in her bag for a compact. Her mouth was hard and she painted it harder, stiffened her hair with a comb. The mirror gave her a face that was new to Sheldon. "Whore," she almost managed the word calmly. "I've been called it before."

Sheldon and Sandy could find no reply.

Playing for time, Claire reached for the half-empty pack of Pall Mall on the table. She took a cigarette, tapped it, lit it, and blew out a trumpet of smoke. The adult mechanism brought her a small calm voice. "I just object to men doing all the choosing, always have. Like they feel they can paw you around just because they open a car door for you." She picked a shred of tobacco from her tongue. "Some men go for blondes, some for brunettes. . . . I just happen to go for men with high cheekbones. And it's amazing how many of them have yachts in the Mediterranean." She looked defiantly at Sheldon. "You're not going to give me the Billy Graham bit, are you?"

Sheldon flushed. He looked at her hard, and the

words that came out of his mouth surprised him even more than they did Sandy. "I don't know who you are, young lady, what you've done. But I'd say you've got style." He recovered himself slightly. "And you're sitting with two people who've got style. Two people who haven't paid for a meal in years. So drink up, it's free."

She drank quickly, and then drank again when he refilled her glass. All at once the color of the claret was reflected in her face, as though her pores had been waiting to relax all this time. "Style." She waved an arm over toward the harbor. "I mean you must admit all this is one hell of an improvement over a room in Bayswater."

"Absolutely," Sheldon grinned. "Abso-bloody-lutely."

And then they were all grinning, leaning close together over the wreckage of the meal.

"None of us down here can afford to have any self-respect," Sandy said. "I mean, we're all of us leaning on the idle rich, the easy life." She pointed at Sheldon. "Like everyone else here, he only goes to sea four months of the year. Idle the rest of the time while the idle rich are making enough money to keep him."

"Don't lie for me, dammit, woman!" Sheldon's voice was suddenly loud as well as slurred. "I've been idle three damn seasons now. And you want to know why? Because a different class of people come down here now. Bloody washing-machine salesmen, they're the people who own boats nowadays. And I'm damned if I'll take any lip from them!"

At the sound of his raised voice, the waiter appeared in the doorway. "Brandy!" Sheldon shouted at him, past caring. The man nodded and went away. "In the old days," Sheldon continued angrily, "there was a good class of people who kept their boats down here. People who wanted them run the proper way. Didn't mind if you helped yourself to some of their drink. Glad to have you at their table. Now we're down to bloody spivs. Count every damn penny. Just you make so much as one damn mistake and that's it." He clicked his fingers, suddenly frowned past them to the doorway. Rafael, the Galatzo's proprietor, stared back at him.

"Señoras." He didn't forget a polite nod toward the ladies. But when he turned to Sheldon, he could barely make himself understood. "Captain, I told you if I ever saw you in here again, I would call the police."

"Steady on." Sheldon blinked at him. He was helped out by the waiter returning with brandy and glasses. The man poured the captain a generous glassful. Sandy and Claire refused politely. Rafael's hands clenched. He beckoned the waiter back into the restaurant.

"Delicious brandy." Sheldon looked around quickly to check that they were unobserved, then slid the bottle under his blazer and hitched it into his belt at the back.

Rafael reappeared, waving the bill. "Lobster! Two bottles of Duhart-Milon!" He shouted, "Can you pay?"

"Sit down a moment. Want to talk about it."

"You can't pay."

"Look at it this way. Delicious meal you gave us. We can't give you money. Haven't got any money. Can't give the meal back. All in here." Sheldon tapped his stomach. "Terrible thing."

Claire giggled.

Rafael swung around. "Señorita, it is past a joke. The bill here is for two thousand one hundred and eighty pesetas, excluding service."

"Daylight robbery." Sheldon clicked his tongue.

"And this Sheldon," Rafael continued, "already owes me twenty-five thousand and something pesetas. About a hundred and fifty English pounds.

Claire started laughing. Sheldon thumped the table in applause.

"What are you going to do?" Sandy, suddenly sober, was watching Rafael carefully. "Go to the police?"

"Leave him. Leave him alone." Sheldon got up.

"Every time we come he says he'll go to the police. Not the way to build up customers." He staggered away past the colored lights.

Rafael went after him, the bill held high in his clenched fist.

Sheldon wheeled. "You dare strike me?"

"No, I don't strike you." Rafael's voice was low, nearly controlled. "Nor do I go to the police. Tomorrow I go to see some people, restaurant owners, shopkeepers, then the harbor master. None of them likes you, Captain." He tapped the bill. "So we put our names together on a piece of paper and we take it to the mayor. The mayor doesn't like you at all. He has many troubles now that Mr. Tzannos is on the council. He has to think of the town's good name."

"Who the *hell* d'you think you are, you bloody Spaniard!" Sheldon roared suddenly. "I fought a war for people like you! While you kept out of it! On the bloody sidelines! Except for that dress rehearsal you gave the Luftwaffe in Guernica!"

Rafael came toward him then.

Sandy led him away.

"Roo-oo-oo-ool Breetanya!" Claire sang as they lurched around the harbor. "Breetanya rools thee waves. . . . Libber-libber-libber . . . *Breetons* nevah-nevah-nevah. . . ."

She was no longer singing, and Sheldon was standing barefoot in the wardroom, alone. In the torch beam a cot was pulled down. . . . All the cots pulled down. Barney, Mitch, Turton, with fags cupped in their hands, their tired eyes looking at him. So bloody tired, their eyes . . . Sheldon put the brandy bottle down, and they disappeared.

The fact remained. In the torch beam a cot was pulled down. Traill's cot. Why had she chosen Traill's? And Traill's brass ruler on the floor. Why had she been able to find it after twenty-five years? Sheldon stooped to pick it up.

Suddenly he was kneeling. The ruler cold against his cheek, he looked up. "God-bastard-God," his voice was white and flabby. "I tried to keep them all alive. But one thing I really tried. I tried to keep the bastard boy. . . . Who killed him? Who left me just an arm?"

Trembling, he hauled himself up onto Traill's cold bunk, and grabbed the damp mattress to his face. Slowly his breathing got calmer, more regular. Slowly the torch grew dimmer.

6

"*Jabberwock* . . . oh, *Jabberwock*!" The voice gradually became real through Sheldon's nightmare. The harbor master's footsteps were real enough on the deck above, and morning light filtered through the curtained porthole. Sheldon kept quite still, heard the man mutter in angry Spanish before going back toward the quay. The captain sat up and bumped his head. He was surprised to find himself on the bare wardroom cot. Then he saw the dead torch and the half-empty brandy bottle, and he remembered.

The harbor master's voice now came from farther along the quay, shouting at another boat. Sheldon left the wardroom, tiptoed through the galley to his cabin. Quickly he shaved and put on a clean shirt and Royal Thames tie. His best blazer and flannels were in a plastic bag, and he put them on, checked in the mirror that they were still quite passable. He found his briefcase and an old copy of *The Times*, and paused for a moment to make sure that Sandy was still asleep in her cabin. There was also the unfamiliar breathing of the girl—Claire—from the fo'c's'le. He waited a moment longer to calm his liquor-hammering head, then he went up on deck.

Keeping low, he climbed to the bridge and got the hundred peseta envelope from the locker. Immediately he felt bad about it. Sandy had earned it, and now she'd have no money till Madame Moreno's next visit tomorrow. But if Sheldon didn't go along the coast to look for a job there'd be no tomorrow. It was a gamble, one he'd always taken. . . . Running surprisingly fast, he went down *Jabberwocky*'s deck to the quay. Out of the corner of his eye he saw the harbor master's back turned as he argued with a boat owner, and then Sheldon reached the cover of the fence that bordered the vacant lot.

He got on a bus in the Via Roma. The driver gave him just sixty-seven pesetas change. Sheldon found a seat at the rear, cursed as the bus moved off and a strip of sunlight found him. His head throbbed and his hands shook. How much had he drunk last night? What was it Rafael had said? He looked back at the Galatzo Restaurant as they turned on to the Paseo Maritimo, and saw the tables piled up in front of shuttered windows. As far as Rafael was concerned it was still last night. He still had time. . . . But had he? Passing the car-park of the Club Nautico, he saw a black Rolls-Royce glide to a halt. The owners were arriving, the season had begun.

His ticket said San Telmo, but he got off at Puerto Andraitx. Something he saw through the bus window made him run for the folding doors. They hissed shut behind him, the bus engaged gear, and Sheldon was left alone in a white dust cloud, thinning to cover the melting tar. The heat was as sudden as the rasp of cicadas. The corniche road was deserted, a wet ribbon clinging to the pine-covered slopes. Below him the pines became almond trees, standing out from yellow maize. And lower still the stone walls of the villas, thick with oleander. Far beneath, the villas gathered into the tiled roofs of the town, its single jetty dividing shallow green water from the deeper blue of the bay.

He crossed the road and stared down at the tiny harbor. There was the boat that had made him leave the bus on some blind instinct. She was a neat eighty-footer, badly moored, her anchor dropped too short. Probably she'd been left in a hurry by a delivery crew. His instinct got stronger. The boat was new, English-built by the look of her, with a metal hull ending in a canoe stern. There was a wide square bridge, and behind it a dummy funnel. Suddenly his instinct was certain. She'd just made the trip out from England. There were black oil stains around her exhausts, and unlike the other yachts her paint work was dull, crusted with salt. "Perfect," Sheldon muttered. "Could be just perfect." He went down the road to the town.

For more than an hour he waited in the dusty main square, waited and watched. At the far end of the quay he saw the Mercedes sports car parked below the boat's canoe stern. He saw the owner—a small, frail-looking man—have coffee served on the shaded afterdeck. The boy who brought the tray wore dirty shorts and a tee shirt. Sheldon waited, but saw no other crew on board. By the time, he was certain it was midday. The quiet of the small harbor was strange after the racket of Palma. The sun was directly above the steep walls of the bay, and the sea beyond the jetty molten silver. The few yachts scarcely stirred in the heat as Sheldon walked out along the quayside.

He stopped by a small sailing yacht. American by its flag, and by the man aboard her in bulging Bermuda shorts. "Siesta. . . ." The man gave a belch. ". . . No disturb, huh?" Flushed and sleepy, he stood up from the ruins of a large lunch and went below. A young seaman in clean white uniform was servile until the American disappeared, then he helped himself to a glass of champagne.

Sheldon coughed loudly in disapproval, then he held his hand out, palm upward. Scowling, the boy filled a second glass and brought it across the gangplank.

"Thank you." The captain sipped gratefully. "That boat at the end? The one with the canoe stern?"

"*Kielhafen.*" The boy shrugged. "German name. English boat."

"That her owner on the afterdeck?"

"Right. He came down two days ago. . . . New boat. Wouldn't think it to look at her, would you?"

"He hasn't got a crew?" Sheldon asked offhandedly.

"Far as I know there's only the Spanish kid aboard. He hasn't got a cook, or why would he eat ashore?"

"All his meals ashore? Lunch?"

"Yeah. He goes around one. Uses Ramon's."

"Thank you." Sheldon handed the empty glass back.

Outside Ramon's Restaurant, the steep rutted street was deserted. Inside there was only Ramon dozing under the *Baleares.* Moving very quietly, Sheldon closed the umbrellas over all except two of the outside tables. Then he carefully stacked canvas chairs in a pile until there were only four left, all standing at the same shaded table. He sat on one of them, opened his briefcase, and took out the old copy of *The Times.* Occasionally he glanced away to the harbor.

He hadn't long to wait. First he heard the sound of distant heels, clicking in perfect time. Then he saw a dark figure, alternately four and twenty feet high in the heat haze, coming along the quay. Sheldon busied himself with the Deaths column of *The Times,* listened as the footsteps came right up to the restaurant, then paused in embarrassment.

"*Entschuldigen. . . .*"

Out of the corner of his eye Sheldon saw a hand

reach out politely to take a chair. Bloody Kraut, he thought. "Help yourself," he said.

"Thank you." The man pulled a chair along to the next table and sat down. "Singular absence of chairs," he said, roundly and perfectly as a BBC announcer. His voice was confident, belying his small build and nervous movements. He was fortyish, with a thin face and thin mouth. Dressed casually as only the very rich can dress casually. A faint aura of aftershave reached Sheldon as the man rubbed his chin, then smiled. "You are English, you read *The Times*."

Sheldon nodded, and concealed the paper's date.

"I have just bought an English yacht. . . . Thorneycroft. . . . They tell me they are the best."

"We like to think so." Sheldon didn't look up from his paper.

Disappointed, the man took off his glasses, pinched the white marks at the bridge of his nose. Suddenly his face was smaller and more vulnerable. Sheldon decided he knew exactly how to handle him.

"Ramon!" He leaped up past the startled German. "Ramon!" he bellowed again through the restaurant door.

An answering shout came from inside. Then Ramon appeared, shading his eyes. "Oh, it's you, Captain," he said.

"Serve this gentleman." Sheldon pointed to the yacht owner. Glad Ramon had remembered him, had made his rank clear.

The German ordered cheese, salad, and a small carafe of wine. Nervously he asked Sheldon to join him in a glass.

"Never drink in the middle of the day." He turned to the restaurant owner. "Just a coffee, Ramon."

"You must allow me," the German said.

"Couldn't possibly." Sheldon went back to his table, resumed his search of the Deaths column.

Marriages, and Ramon came out with the coffee.

Births, and the German could restrain his impatience no longer. "Excuse me, you are a captain?"

"Commander. RN. The name's Sheldon."

"Knaeber." The German held out his hand gratefully. "D'you live here? The man seemed to know you."

"Brought yachts in here more times than I care to remember," Sheldon said. "Few years ago, that was."

"And do you still captain . . . yachts?"

"Can't give it up, much as I'd like to. Been in America for the past three years, running the *Grigora*. Know her?"

"Of course." The man lied. "Tell me . . . d'you have a boat at the moment?"

"On my way to pick one up, actually. Huge old steam yacht." Sheldon wondered if he was going too far. "In the Canaries."

"Oh." Knaeber was disappointed. His attention was distracted as Ramon came out with his lunch, but after a few mouthfuls he leaned toward Sheldon and spoke again. "I've just bought the *Kielhafen*." He pointed back to the harbor. "My wife persuaded me. I've never done any yachting before."

"Really."

"She was brought out here last week by a delivery crew. Now there is no one aboard. Except for young Carlos. He's Spanish."

Sheldon got up from the table. "Good chappies, the Spanish. Just got to kick them around a bit."

"Wait a minute, Captain." Knaeber got the words out in a rush. "My wife and children come down here next week. I'm just here for a couple of days to find a crew. But I've been lazy. So unusual to have no telephones. Tomorrow I have to return to Düsseldorf. . . . About a crew? Should I go to the agents in Palma?"

"Bunch of crooks, the lot of them." Sheldon left two coins under his coffee saucer. "They'll come up with any old taxi driver who's out of work."

"What should I do then?"

"Word of mouth. Much the best thing."

"Could you . . . er . . . recommend anyone, Captain?"

"Don't know," Sheldon said carelessly. "Bit late in the day. Most of the boats are crewed up."

"Maybe if you saw the ship. . . ." Knaeber got up from his unfinished meal. ". . . You'd know who to recommend. She's a beautiful little yacht. I'm very proud of her."

And she was a beautiful little yacht. Sheldon saw it as soon as he stood on the new white planks. The metal bulwarks of the canoe stern were fitted with a long curving settee of tan leather. And there was a new powerboat in the center of the deck, with skis and lines made ready. Folding doors led into a small deck saloon with metal Venetian blinds along two sides, a bar and a television set taking up the third. Beyond there was a dining saloon with antique chairs and table, Georgian candlesticks. Below the bridge was the galley and the tiny captain's cabin. Newly carpeted stairs led down to the passengers' cabins, each with a bath, fitted oak, and air conditioning. There was the smell of varnish and new paint, the smell of a great deal of money. Sheldon opened the soundproof door that led to the engine room. He looked at the two brand-new diesels. "GMs," he said.

Knaeber nodded. "You know about these engines?"

"I'm not an engineer. But I know enough to start them."

"Would you like to?" Knaeber asked suddenly.

"What d'you mean?" Sheldon seemed irritated.

"I've never sailed in her." The man took a nervous step toward one of the engines. "I thought maybe if you had enough time . . . we could take a little trip together."

Sheldon glanced at his watch. "I said I'd call in on

someone along the coast. I'm only visiting the island. My plane leaves at seven."

"It was just an idea," Knaeber said.

"Why not?" Sheldon's face softened. "I've got a couple of hours."

Like an excited schoolboy, Knaeber followed Sheldon's orders. He got the gangplank aboard and singled the ropes ashore, doing twice as much work as the young Spaniard Carlos. Then Sheldon went below and started the generator. It took him five minutes to get his trembling hands to the controls of the engines. He hadn't taken a boat out of harbor in three years, and in the years before that he'd never done it with less than four gins inside him. He got hold of himself, and pressed each starter in turn. Clouds of blue smoke rose from the waterline as he climbed to the bridge. He squared his naval cap firmly on his head, signaled Knaeber on the foredeck below to start the anchor winch. "Aye aye, Captain," the man said self-consciously.

The anchor came home easily. Sheldon put both motors to Slow Ahead, kept his hands below the level of the sprayshield so Knaeber wouldn't see them tremble. He'd got them under control by the time the German joined him on the bridge, and they were clear of the harbor with motors at Half Ahead. There was scarcely a ripple, scarcely a breeze as the whining motors drove them over the velvety sea. "Give them time to warm up," Sheldon said. "Any fool can open the throttles wide, twiddle the wheel. He doesn't realize he's dealing with expensive machinery."

Then Knaeber took the wheel, unable to keep the proud grin from his mouth. He braced his feet apart as though there were a heavy swell. His eyes swept the horizon firmly, always coming back to Sheldon's naval cap. The captain knew he was going to buy himself a yachting cap at the first opportunity. Following instructions, the

German eased the throttles open to Full Ahead, steering well away from the arm of the bay where Sheldon said there were rocks.

"You know this coast well?" he asked.

"Haven't seen it in a long time. I stopped off today mainly for sentimental reasons."

"You like it here, then." Knaeber suddenly looked at him narrowly. "This boat in the Canaries? Have you signed a contract?"

"Never do before I see a boat," Sheldon said curtly.

"You've seen this one. And I think you like her."

Sheldon grunted.

"Would you consider . . . ?"

"I've got a plane ticket to the Canaries. What's more, I'm used to big boats. Captain's steward, white gloves, that sort of thing."

"A small boat is easier to handle. There'd be less strain."

"You'd want to go off to Corsica, places like that. Deep-water trips in a boat this size aren't my idea of pleasure."

"Only around the Baleares. We've got the children to consider."

"Children." Sheldon shrugged it was out of the question.

"They're very quiet. Really very quiet."

Making a wide loop, they turned back toward Puerto Andraitx. Sheldon looked at the steep shoulders of the bay, the pink stucco walls of the villas with their oleander, the bone-white rocks where sea met shore with scarcely a ripple. "Most beautiful coast in the world," he said with conviction.

"Why leave it?" Knaeber came to a rapid decision. "The job's yours, Captain, if you want it."

"Never met me before in your life."

"You handle the boat well. And I pride myself on

being a good judge of character. In business one has to be.... D'you want the job?"

"You tempt me, really tempt me. Maybe we could talk about it." Sheldon still sounded doubtful. "At least you can find out all about me. I've got my papers, for the people in the Canaries.... Usual bits of pomposity."

The usual bits of pomposity, as Sheldon called them, were in fact very impressive. Back in harbor, they were laid out on the bar in the deck saloon. They showed the captain's war record, his successful yacht commands after he left the Navy. A few dates were changed to cover the later seasons. Nothing for the past three years. "I tore up the one the Americans gave me," Sheldon said. "Too many damn superlatives." Knaeber nodded, then suddenly businesslike, he insisted the captain sign a six-month contract, to be terminated by either side.

Alone in the darkness of the captain's cabin, Sheldon let his hands tremble as they pleased. He sat on the narrow bunk and told himself he'd done it, he'd done it. Down below he could hear Knaeber moving about in his stateroom, packing for Düsseldorf. The German had left him with three checks. The first to cover a month of the highest salary Sheldon had ever asked. He needed it, all of it, to keep things quiet in Palma—three years' back harbor dues, a case of Scotch for the harbor master, and something on account to keep Rafael happy.

The second check was to hire a crew. Sheldon worked it out—Sandy as cook, Barney as engineer, and the Spanish boy could stay on as deck hand steward. The last check was the important one, and went with a supply list—two cases of good wine, two cases of Scotch, two cases of gin. Make that three cases of gin—he'd pay for the third out of his own pocket. Gordon's gin and lime juice. He licked his lips. Anis was a thing of the past.

Armed with the supply list, he went ashore. The sun

was a squashed red grape on the dark hull above the bay. Long shadows streaked the quay as he drew level with the small American sailing yacht where he'd started out at midday.

"Freshen it up a little, and gimme some more ice." The man in Bermuda shorts sprawled on his foredeck and shouted back to the young steward in the cockpit. Unobserved, the boy gulped greedily at the Bourbon bottle before refilling the man's glass.

"My dear boy, what d'you think you're doing?" Sheldon spoke sharply. "Is that your liquor? Did you pay for it?"

7

Sheldon's head throbbed. He opened his eyes to darkness. The hands of his watch said four-thirty, but the captain's cabin of the *Kielhafen* had no windows and he didn't know if it was day or night. Then he remembered finishing the bottle of wine at lunch. He must have slept two hours. A cool afternoon breeze came into the cabin as he opened the door, and he paused, listening. "Carlos!" he shouted. The sudden scrape of footsteps came from the bridge above.

Carlos' face was red, his eyes swollen. Sheldon glared at him as he climbed to the bridge. "You've been sleeping, Carlos, in the sun."

"No, Captain. I varnish the rail. Like you say."

Stiff with congealed varnish, the brush was stuck to the tin lid.

"Hasn't been touched for hours. You've been sleeping. Well?"

Carlos kept quite still.

"Sleeping on duty?" Sheldon shouted, clutching his head in pain. "Right, if we can't make things work any other way, we'll try the Navy way. Tomorrow you'll report to me every hour on the hour. Even if it's siesta time and I'm asleep. Understood?"

"Yes, Captain."

"And if that doesn't work, the day after you'll report to me at every half-hour. That way we'll both be in a bloody bad temper and we'll get some discipline around here."

"Yes, Captain." The boy peeled the stiff brush from the tin lid.

"Won't be any good now." Sheldon grabbed the brush and threw it over the side. "Never let your brush get in that state. Can't do a smooth clean job with it. Got another one?"

The boy produced another brush. Sheldon felt the bristles expertly, then crossed to the bridge rail. "Rubbed it down properly, like I showed you?"

"Yes, Captain."

Sheldon tested the smoothness of the rail. "Now just a little varnish on the brush, not too much, like this. . . . Then working quickly from left to right like this, always in the same direction." His voice softened, taking a pride in the moving brush. "Never going over the same bit twice. No streaks, no bubbles, a smooth job. Understand?"

"Yes, Captain."

"Carry on then." The captain handed the brush over, watched the boy for a moment before stepping down to the shade of the side deck. He felt in his pocket for the unusual luxury of an English cigarette, lit one, and strolled aft to the deck saloon. Automatically he crossed to the bar, stiffened as he saw the two empty bottles from last night. "Carlos!" he bellowed.

The boy came running.

"What's your first job in the morning?"

"Raise the ship's ensign at sunrise, Captain."

"And your second job?"

"Take away the empty bottles you and the engineer drank in the bar."

"The bottles *who* drank?"

"Captain?"

"The bottles *visitors* drank in the bar," Sheldon roared, clutching his head. "We don't want Mr. Knaeber to see the bottles *visitors* drank, do we?"

"No, Captain."

"Take them away." Sheldon handed him the first sticky bottle, found a ring mark underneath it on the woodwork. "And this shelf's filthy. Wipe it down and polish it. Get a bucket, water, and some polish. Cloth and duster."

"What about the varnishing, Captain?"

"Finish the varnishing first."

"Twenty-to-five now, Captain."

"That's Communism, Carlos. I don't like Communism. You'll just have to work late."

Sullenly the Spanish boy turned away.

"Carlos," the captain called him back. "In a day or two Mr. Knaeber is coming down with his family. Cook will issue you with a white tee shirt with the name *Kielhafen* written across the back. You will wear it before, during, and after the passengers' meals. You will wear it when the ship enters and leaves harbor. At all other times you will wear working clothes. Your white shoes, however, will be worn at all times."

Carlos kept quite still. Sheldon dismissed him.

Three aspirins and a mug of tea were waiting for him inside the open galley window. Sheldon swallowed them gratefully. "Crew had their tea?" he asked Sandy.

She turned from the stove, wiped a strand of damp hair from her forehead. "Sixteen hundred hours. On the dot, as you ordered."

Sheldon looked at her sharply. "You want to argue as well?"

"I heard you shouting at Carlos." She shrugged. "The whole harbor did."

"The chappie's bone idle, sleeps half the day. . . ." He broke off, stared at the box of empty bottles by the fridge. ". . . And like any other Spaniard he can't stay away from the vino. Look at that, dammit, there must be more than a dozen empties, and we've only been aboard four days."

"Carlos only drinks the rough stuff," Sandy said pointedly. "I'd hardly let him loose on those bottles."

"Well, somebody's been let loose on it."

Sandy left her saucepans, came across to the window, and looked at him steadily. "Don't you think you'd better ease up a bit?"

"Barney's drunk his share," Sheldon said guiltily.

"And there are six empty gin bottles. I threw them away this morning. A whole case."

"My case," Sheldon said. "Knaeber's stuff is locked away in the dining saloon."

"Knaeber'll be down tomorrow."

"I can restock ashore. Dammit, I can afford it, he pays me enough." He rubbed his hand over his forehead. "Just a celebration, that's all. Haven't had it so good in a long while. I'll be all right when he comes. . . . And while we're on the subject of Knaeber, can you get out a white shirt for Carlos? And one for Barney? Shoes as well?"

Sandy grinned suddenly. "Barney's agreed to wear white shoes?"

"What d'you mean?"

"I know you've been ashore a long time, but you can't have forgotten those rows you used to have with Barney, over things like white shoes."

"Barney understands the way I run a ship."

"I sometimes wonder."

Sheldon turned away from the galley window,

leaned on the rail of the side deck. Shadows were reaching out from the far side of the bay to the boats on the dusty quay. A weak sun was shredding the topmost trees on the far hill, and the sweet scent of pine came on the breeze that foretold evening. "You can't go through an entire war in the Navy," Sheldon said slowly, "without understanding its amateur theatricals. They all have a purpose, the flag-waving, the drilling, the shouting. Just a great big confidence trick, really, to trick the captain out with confidence, and trick it away from the crew. About the only thing to be said in its favor is it works. And Barney understands that."

But he was remembering things about Barney as he walked aft along the narrow side deck. Reaching the corner of the deck saloon, he suddenly had to fight back his temper once again. The engineer was sprawled on the tan-leather settee, his stubby arms and legs hunched around a comic book. Grease stains from his body were staining the new seat. Sheldon ducked back into shadow. He'd rowed with the others and he didn't want to row with Barney, rows with Barney tended to be serious. The man gave the impression of being the calmest, laziest person alive, but Sheldon knew different. He knew all about the boredom that was the occupational disease of ships' engineers. Their job was to sit back and wait for things to go wrong. And Barney was Scots, he liked to sit back a long time, and liked things to go wrong in a big way. He had sudden attacks of vicious marrow rage, when he lost his will to walk and talk. He moved again only when his fags ran out, they were his only conscience.

Now Sheldon held on to his anger as he walked toward the bench seat. "You know I don't like you lying around where people can see you, Chief."

Barney smiled up at him. "When the passengers come down, Skipper, I'll look as though I'm doing something."

"And I'll see that you do." Sheldon cleared his throat. "This isn't a holiday camp."

The engineer chalked up a win. "The word's got round—" his smile broadened "—that it's white shoes."

"It is."

"When the passengers come down," Barney repeated.

"All right, and get yourself a shave." The captain tried to treat it lightly. "That's an order."

Unshaven, Barney's face was prickly brown, right up to the flat bald crown of his head. Only his wide nose and forehead were free of hair, and they were deeply lined, tanned the color of old leather. Like a lot of other Northerners who spent their time sitting in the sun, Barney had an old cracked face on a strangely young and smooth body. Now he moved slightly, and his cigarette ash fell on a chair cushion. Sheldon managed to keep the edge out of his voice. "All squared up in the engine room, I suppose?"

"Clean as a whistle. It's all brand-new, for Christ's sake."

"And the bath tap I asked you to fix?"

"Fixed." Barney stretched lazily, watched the irritation grow on Sheldon's face. "Come off it, Skipper. Save the bull shit for the Spanish lad. You and I, we're grown men."

"There has to be discipline. It's just . . ." Sheldon tailed off. He suddenly remembered he'd never had words for Barney, remembered arguments with him that had always stopped at this point. Now Sheldon forced himself to push it a stage further. "Chief, there was a time when you liked the way I ran a ship, wasn't there?"

The engineer rolled up his comic book in surprise. "Back in the war, you mean? It was all right then, there was a call for it. All of us aboard had more medals than the other lads. And we were alive, for Christ's sake, we owed you that. You used to do things with a ship nobody else had the guts to. It was fine."

"And nowadays?" Sheldon walked to the rail, stared out at the lengthening shadows on the quayside. "It isn't fine?"

"Well, all the lads in Palma gave up working for you, didn't they?" The engineer shifted uncomfortably. "They wouldn't put up with your way."

"Why do you put up with it, Barney?" Sheldon wondered if he could say it. "Why . . . d'you always come with me? Every boat I've ever had?"

There was silence in the growing darkness. Sheldon saw Barney at the age of twenty-two, ex-trawlerman, signing aboard MTB 859 as a stoker. Barney who was boats. Then Barney who was engines, who'd learned more about Packards in two years than the Chief Mechanician had in his life. Barney who'd taken over when the Chief was killed, and had begun to hate. Hating the way the engines were abused, hating the Germans who were the cause of it. Barney's hatred had been the heart of the ship. Sheldon had only tempered it with cunning, and collected the medals.

"Skipper—" the voice came at last from the bench seat "—you don't have to worry about lads like me. I'm strictly second-wave material, down in the engine room. Nobody ever gave me a cabin to myself. . . . Look, I never had your sort of education, all hockey matches and cucumber sandwiches, and I can't say what I mean. But, honestly, I got a hell of a kick out of the war. People were always shaking me by the hand for being a shit. And sometimes I get a bit of the same kick nowadays when I'm around with you. The bloody nutty things you do."

Sheldon turned in amazement, saw Barney's face was serious.

"And I still stick around because I know that one of these days you're going to do something really nutty. And I want to be there to see it."

"Nutty?" Sheldon could attach no meaning to the word. "Nutty?"

At dinner the captain drank a great deal. Red-faced, he sat behind the Georgian candlesticks in the dining saloon, and ordered Carlos to open a third bottle of Felanitz wine.

"Alec," Sandy pleaded with him. "We don't need another. There's only the peaches to come."

"I like my peaches in red wine," he said stubbornly. "Soaked in red wine, with a little sugar on top."

"Why not use the cooking stuff?"

Sheldon ignored her, pointed his finger at the sideboard. Carlos fetched the new bottle of wine and got a corkscrew from his pocket.

"Is it at room temperature? How long's it been standing?"

"More than an hour, Captain."

"That's good." Sheldon tasted it. Then he eyed Carlos' uniform up and down, examined his cotton gloves. "You're doing all right. Now bring the peaches."

Carlos brought the bowl, served them each in turn, and went back to his position by the door.

The captain tipped wine over his peaches, a little sugar, then he started to eat. Suddenly he jerked upright. "Finger bowls!" he shouted. "Where the bloody hell are the finger bowls?"

"Finger bowls." Barney grinned at him. "The good life."

"Dammit, Chief, I've got to teach the chappie to do it properly. He's got to learn."

Carlos went quickly out of the dining saloon. Then suddenly there were heavier footsteps on the side deck, and a great figure was blocking the doorway. "Navy!" he bellowed at Sheldon.

8

"Pierre?" Sheldon blinked in disbelief. *"Pierre!"*

The huge tanned man nodded and came on into the saloon. He started laughing softly, then louder, rising on the balls of his feet. "Barney . . . Sandy. . . ." He hugged them each in turn.

"Where the hell've you come from?" Sheldon was picked up and kissed on both cheeks. "You're meant to be in Greece."

Pierre put him down. "Good to see you again, Navy. Long time. . . ."

"Five years, must be." Sheldon looked him over. "You're fatter. Wouldn't fit into a submarine now."

"That was over twenty years ago." Pierre grinned. "I wouldn't go down in one of those sardine tins now if you paid me all the money in the world."

"No, times have changed," Sheldon said reluctantly. "You're looking fatter," he repeated.

"Richer," Pierre said, and it was true. His tan was the color of old gold. From his suède boots, his blue shantung uniform, his carefully trimmed black hair, Pierre exuded success. And the eyes that flashed under thick brows hadn't known worry in a long time. "I'll show you."

He led them out onto the side deck and pointed across to the shiny Monaco cruiser moored alongside. She'd just come in, and the sea dew glittered on her chrome. Cabin lights showed cream-leather seats and steel fittings inside. "I own her," Pierre told them proudly.

"She's yours? A Monaco?" Sheldon whistled. "How did you do it? In Greece?"

"Five good charter seasons. Very good seasons."

"And chartering's legal there." Sheldon couldn't keep the bitterness out of his voice. "But how come you're back this way?"

"I got tired of the Aegean, too crowded. So I arranged charter parties for the whole season in Piraeus, quite legally, and told the passengers they'd have to pick the boat up here in Spain."

"Don't your passengers decide where they want to go?"

"They go where I tell them." Pierre smiled easily. "To Palma to look for Captain Sheldon, and when he's not there, on to Andraitx. We have a good relationship." He took them to where three people were waiting on the afterdeck. The first, a thin creased man with a glass in his hand, was swaying gently against the speedboat. "Mr. Petersen from Oslo," Pierre introduced him. "Too much money, too little sense, and a fantastic thirst for whisky."

Petersen drained his glass. "Visky time!" he said.

"His knowledge of English is very limited." Pierre led Sheldon on to a middle-aged woman, plump, the halter of her sunsuit purposely revealing an ample bosom. "Mrs. Petersen . . . Ulla . . . drunken old cow." Pierre pinched her cheek fondly. "She also speaks very little English."

"Shouldn't talk like that in front of passengers." Sheldon frowned. Then he saw that the third person was Claire.

"The little girl you know." Pierre pulled her gently forward. "We found her on your boat in Palma, dying of hunger."

Sheldon seemed disappointed as he stared at the girl's marble beauty. "I thought you said men with high cheekbones," he said, pointing at Petersen's flat face.

"Pierre took me on as cook," Claire whispered. "So I eat. And he promised to keep those two loaded all the time."

"The Navy doesn't approve," Pierre cut across her, laughing. "He doesn't approve of the way I run a boat."

"Just don't know how you do it," Sheldon said curtly. "Run around the Med, exactly where you please, and get paid for it. That cruiser must have cost a small fortune."

"Got a system." Pierre winked. "I only take on charterers I like. I fill the boat up with liquor, point her out to sea, and put her on automatic pilot. Then I play Happy Families." He looked from Claire to Petersen. "There's a little girl in a bikini for Father. A randy old captain for Mother." He hugged Ulla to him. "The mate gets Daughter, and the deck hand gets Grannie. . . . I haven't got the whole family with me this trip."

"You've got enough." Sheldon frowned again. "And I suppose you all want to help yourself to my drink?"

"Visky time!" Petersen brightened up.

"Whisky, is it?" Sheldon got the key ring from his pocket.

"Had you better start on the Scotch?" Sandy asked quickly. "It's Knaeber's, remember."

"One bottle won't do any harm." Finding the right key, he started away down the side deck. "Carlos! Glasses, water, and ice."

"And salute the Navy when it kicks you around, dammit," Pierre shouted as the boy appeared.

Like some old-time movie director in his shantung uniform and suede boots, Pierre directed the party scene. He grouped them all around the bar in the deck saloon, took over the bottle of whisky that Sheldon brought, and kept filling up glasses. He hefted the Scotch easily, the neck hanging low from his huge fingers, as though the bottle were part of him. He refilled Ulla's tumbler and she switched on her small transistor radio, tried to dance him away. Pierre shrugged himself free, poured another huge tumblerful for Petersen and propped him up against his wife. The two Norwegians danced sadly, cheek to cheek only because they were sipping over each other's shoulder. As Pierre returned to the group at the bar, they danced after him, revolving slowly so that he could refill their glasses as they came around. A film director with a dancing-bear act on his hands, the Frenchman fended them off while he talked to Sheldon.

"Skin off your nose. Great to know the horrible British Navy's still afloat."

"Don't be rude about the Navy. It got you out of enough trouble in your time."

Pierre winked. "Any time I saw you coming. Gloohglah, I went down to periscope depth."

"Periscope depth?" Claire asked.

"This man was crazy, crazy during the war," Pierre told her. "Treated his crew like dirt, treated his superiors like dirt. He got himself an MTB to command, even though he was RN, Royal Navy. . . . Most of the people on small boats were RNVR, they wore dirty old sweaters. But him, he was Captain, Navy."

"I don't understand." Claire said. "When was all this?"

"Forty-three, must have been. Ask the Navy here."

But Sheldon was silent. Hunched behind the bar, he suddenly seemed very drunk.

"I'll show you." Pierre drew a rough map in the puddles on the bar counter. "There's Beirut, Alex., and Cyprus, where the British were. And here, up in Greece, was where they wanted to be. You see, the Germans and Italians were occupying most of the Greek islands at that time, and the Greeks didn't like them one little bit. So Sheldon talked his way into a special job with this MTB. He used to cruise up among the islands with a crowd of gangsters, stirring up trouble for the Germans. . . . These gangsters were Greek fishermen mostly. Only they didn't have fishing nets on their caïques, but Bren guns. They were called the SBS. Special Boat Squadron."

"That man Spanakis," Sheldon said slowly. "Bravest man I ever met in my life."

55

"But how were you mixed up in all this?" Claire asked Pierre.

"Free French." Pierre stiffened slightly.

"What he means is," Sheldon said, "he was one of the only damn Froggies who didn't scuttle his ship. Too damn drunk to find the plug hole."

"Why should he want to scuttle his ship?"

"God Almighty!" Sheldon blinked at her. "When were you born?"

"1945."

"God Almighty, reserved occupation!"

"Visky time!" Petersen pushed his tumbler at Pierre, was disappointed by the few remaining drops in the bottle.

"Whisky pigs," Pierre said quietly. "Drink out of a bucket, both of them."

"Doesn't matter." Sheldon got off his stool unsteadily. "Get another bottle."

" 'Nother bottle, yes." Petersen grinned at him. "Where is 'nother bottle, please?"

"In the dining saloon."

Petersen bowed, and went away through the folding doors.

"Was that wise, Alec?" Behind her flushed cheeks, Sandy was worried.

"It's all locked away." Sheldon fumbled for the key chain. "In the cocktail cabinet."

"And it's locked away," she insisted, "because it's Knaeber's."

"This Knaeber you keep worrying about, he's your owner?" Pierre got an answering nod from Sandy. "Well, don't worry about a thing. I've got cases of Scotch next door. I'll send around a few bottles in the morning. . . . Six, no seven of us drinking." He swept an arm around the saloon.

"Seven of us?" Sheldon suddenly stared at the golden liquid in his glass. "How long've I been drinking Scotch, dammit?"

"I poured you two, maybe three." Pierre shrugged.

"Gin and lime's my drink. Thought there was something wrong." Scotch on gin made Sheldon thud into the folding doors as he left the saloon, made him stagger against the wall going up the side deck. When he reached the door of the dining saloon, he stopped in amazement. Petersen was lying on the long table, his empty glass propped on his stomach.

"Good-by," the man said, getting up.

"Good-by," Sheldon's voice was hoarse. He crossed to the cocktail cabinet, unlocked it, and tried to keep Petersen from seeing the crate of whisky inside.

"Von, two, sree, four, fife." The Norwegian leaned past him and counted the bottles.

"Five," the captain repeated, taking one of them from the crate. Then he closed the lid of the cabinet, put the key in the lock.

"Elephant," Petersen said, pointing past him.

Sheldon turned, expecting to see an elephant. Too late, he turned back in time to see the Norwegian throwing the key ring out of the window. Breathing heavily, Sheldon reopened the cabinet, looked at the crate of bottles, then at Petersen's grinning face reflected in the mirror shelves. Slowly the captain worked it out. The whisky had to be moved to safety. So he took all five bottles with him, in their crate. He paused a moment in the doorway and looked back. Petersen was now kneeling by the cabinet, his eye to the keyhole, trying to see if the light went out when he closed the lid. He couldn't be sure, and it worried him. "World's gone mad," Sheldon said.

He lurched away down the side deck with the whisky, and found his path blocked by a dancing couple. " 'Scuse me," Sheldon said politely. Then he saw it was Carlos dancing with Ulla. "Carlos!" he shouted. "Paragraph Twenty-four, Ship's Regulations. 'Crew not to engage conversation with passengers. If addressed crew to break off, answer politely, hands to sides. No account to *lean* on passengers.' "

Carlos drew back, his eyes staring at Ulla's huge red bosom.

"The hell you doing, then? World's gone mad. Here! take one of these and serve the passengers." Sheldon couldn't be sure, but he thought he saw Carlos sway as he reached out for the whisky bottle. Passing the two of them, the captain took the crate into the deck saloon and put it on the bar. The din from Ulla's transistor on the afterdeck seemed to bother him, so he returned to the folding doors and closed them. Automatically he lowered the metal blinds as well. If he hadn't, he'd have seen Ulla and Carlos go and sit on the two front seats of the speedboat, both of them sucking at their Scotch bottle as though it were milk.

Around the bar in the deck saloon, the party scene was in slow motion, and the movie director's talent seemed to have deserted him. There were dark stains on the front of Pierre's blue uniform, and a flush high up on his tanned cheeks. Sheldon sat next to him, his mouth open in an endless yawn. Sandy's face was unnaturally cloudy, her eyes unnaturally bright. Barney was hunched over an open bottle, playing with the tinfoil. Only Claire's luminous beauty seemed unaffected by the liquor. She moved quicker than any of the others, and the whisky in her glass was pale in color.

"Paragraph Twenty-four, Ship's Regulations." Pierre spoke at last, slow and sarcastic. "What's Paragraph Twenty-five, for Christ's sake?"

" 'At all times, crew to obtain captain's opinion when in doubt.' " Sheldon didn't look around, and his voice was very slurred.

The folding doors opened suddenly, Carlos staggered in. ". . . Captain?"

". . . Crew to obtain captain's opinion over matters of seamanship. . . .' "

". . . Captain?" Carlos cut across him. "Mrs. Petersen wants me to . . ."

". . . *Don't interrupt when I'm talking!*" Sheldon shouted. "Do what Mrs. Petersen wants! Look after the passengers!"

Carlos went out, closing the door behind him.

" 'To obtain captain's opinion over matters of seamanship, and the entire running of the ship.' " Sheldon nodded slowly at Pierre. "Paragraph Twenty-five."

"And they gave this man a medal." Pierre winked at Claire. "For sinking a German destroyer. Would you believe it? No proof, of course."

"Was proof," Sheldon said. "Sank the bloody destroyer."

"There was this sea battle at Leros, went on for days," Pierre explained. "The last anyone sees of Navy here is his boat's on fire and he's sinking. . . . Then he turns up after a month and claims he's been hiding in some cave on a deserted Greek island. What's more, he claims he sunk this destroyer on the way back home."

"Course there was a bloody cave!" Sheldon shouted. "That man Spanakis towed me there. He used it as a base for his caïques. Used to keep petrol and stores there. Isn't that right, Barn? . . ."

The sudden high-pitched scream of a motor drowned his voice, grew higher, angrier. Then it was abruptly put out of its agony by a deafening crash from the quay.

"The hell's that?" Sheldon got to his feet, stunned.

"Johnson engine," Barney told him. "Speedboat."

His face gray, Sheldon walked unsteadily over to the folding doors and opened them. Out on the afterdeck he saw the speedboat was no longer in position, its davits trailed their ropes down over the ship's side. Sheldon crossed to the rail, saw the splintered wreckage of the boat where it had reversed at full speed into the quay. Petrol flowed from the shattered engine, lodged against the stone steps. Standing above the wreck was Mrs. Petersen, her clothes hanging wetly to her as she tapped the quay with her foot. "This wall," she said. "In the water."

Sheldon gripped the rail weakly, looking around for Carlos. Suddenly he saw headlights approaching along the quay. Then a car—a Mercedes sports car—with Knaeber waving cheerily at him from the driver's seat. Sheldon turned away, retreated to the deck saloon. "Carlos!" he shouted.

A car door slammed. "Captain!" Knaeber's voice was high-pitched, near hysterical. "Captain, is that *our* speedboat?"

Sheldon didn't turn around. "Carlos!" he shouted again.

"That *is* our speedboat!" Knaeber walked quickly up the gangplank. "What is the meaning of all this, Captain? Who are all these people?"

Sheldon waved the introductions tiredly, "Pierre, Barney, Sandy, Claire . . . Mr. Knaeber."

"I *don't want names!*" Knaeber swung the captain around. "What are they *doing* here?"

"Terrible thing." Sheldon didn't look up to the man's face. "You weren't meant to be here till tomorrow."

"I came early, to talk about your job." Knaeber looked around dazedly, unable to fit words to the scene. "Naturally I made a few inquiries about you."

"Gentleman keeps his word," Sheldon said wildly. "Gentleman says he's coming tomorrow, he comes tomorrow."

"I came to tell you that I knew all about your past record." Knaeber's voice was louder. "But that you handled the boat well, and you could stay on. . . . Now." He shrugged, tight-lipped.

"Not a gentleman," Sheldon insisted.

"And you are a gentleman, I take it?" Knaeber shouted.

The captain nodded.

Knaeber paced up and down. His voice was just

under control again, an octave lower. "English gentlemen, *du lieber,* education of a gun dog, morals of a corporal, philosophy of a tennis referee."

"Umpire," Sheldon said.

"*Umpire* then!" Knaeber screamed. "Well, I don't want you, English gentleman. I don't want any part of you on my ship!"

"You bastard Hun!" Sheldon brushed Sandy's arm aside. "He and I—" he pointed at Pierre "—spent five years of our lives sweeping bastards like you off the seas!"

Knaeber turned slowly, walked away into shadow. He had his back to them, and his knuckles were white as he gripped the rail. When he faced them again he was calm. Slowly he walked through the folding doors and inspected the crate and the open whisky bottles on the bar. "You drink all my drink," he said sadly. "You wreck my speedboat."

Pierre signaled Claire it was time to leave.

"Carlos!" Sheldon bellowed once again.

Footsteps came toward them down the side deck, footsteps that were strange, slow, and clattering. Carlos appeared. Dripping wet, he slid toward them on a pair of water skis. There was a paintbrush and a pot of varnish in his hand.

Sheldon seemed relieved to see him. "Where've you been?"

"Varnishing the rail, Captain."

"That's good." Sheldon stood firm as Carlos came toward him.

"Just a little varnish," the boy purred, loading his brush. "Not too much. Working left to right, always the same direction." He varnished the captain's hand and arm. "No streaks, no bubbles, smooth clean job."

Sheldon inspected his arm. "Smooth clean job," he agreed. "Now will you show Mr. Knaeber down to his cabin?"

"Will you please *all* leave my ship?" Knaeber shouted from the bar.

"Where's Petersen?" Pierre whispered to Claire.

Petersen's glass they found on the table in the dining saloon. The mirror shelves of the cocktail cabinet were laid out on the carpet, but of the man himself there was no sign. Then they saw the lid of the cabinet open and close gently of its own accord. "On-off, on-off." Petersen's voice came from inside. Suddenly the lid opened fully, and the Norwegian appeared. "The light off when you close," he told them triumphantly. He stepped out of the cabinet, cracking each of the mirror shelves in turn.

"I'll sue you. I'll sue you," Knaeber whispered hoarsely to Sheldon. "The speedboat cost seven hundred English pounds. Now this."

Sheldon nodded, then went away to the galley.

When he returned, dragging a crate of gin and lime behind him, the afterdeck was deserted. Knaeber was sitting alone on a bar stool in the saloon. He jerked upright as he saw Sheldon. "No, you stay here, Captain. You clean up the mess, then you leave."

Sheldon nodded, and dragged the gin and lime on toward the gangplank.

"Stealing, is it?" Knaeber's voice followed him. "Stealing the ship's stores now?"

Sheldon straightened. "A gentleman never steals. Just takes what's due to him . . . in lieu of salary." He reached the stern and hauled the liquor up onto the gangplank. Pausing for breath, he gripped the rail and looked around. For a moment he was oddly impressive. This had been his command and he'd lost it.

"Visky time!" A familiar voice came from the cruiser next door.

Sheldon dragged the crate down the gangplank and went along the quay toward the party.

9

"D'you want me to go over and talk to Knaeber again?" Pierre walked toward him. "Hey, are you asleep?"

"Not asleep," Sheldon said.

"You were sitting like that when I left you two hours ago. Only difference now is the Scotch bottle's empty."

"Not asleep," Sheldon repeated. Suddenly cold, he hunched his shoulders and looked around the dew-covered cockpit of the Monaco cruiser. He was surprised to see the outlines of the boat visible in the gray light, and the sky beyond silhouetting the hills above the town. "What time is it?"

"Six-thirty." Pierre shivered and zipped his parka up to his neck. "Look, d'you want me to go over and see Knaeber again? There's a light on in his cabin."

"Is there?" Sheldon said carelessly.

"I went over to him before, remember," Pierre said. "I told him it was my fault, making you drink Scotch on gin, taking those crazy Norwegians on board. I told him the Petersens would pay for the damage."

"What did he say to that?"

Pierre looked down at him unhappily. "He said you called him a bastard Hun."

"Did I really say that?"

"Navy—" Pierre shook him gently "—I'm only trying to help. Knaeber means trouble."

"Does he?" Sheldon said flatly. "Then I should leave him alone."

Beneath their feet the deck suddenly throbbed to the bark of a generator.

"Well, can I give you a lift anywhere?" Pierre asked sadly. "We're moving off shortly."

"Where you going?"

"Back to Palma."

"Very kind of you," Sheldon said gruffly.

"Sandy and Barney are down below, sleeping in the saloon. I don't know where the Spanish boy is."

"Don't care," Sheldon said. "He should've been on watch, not fooling around with the speedboat. None of this need've happened."

Pierre was troubled as he looked at Sheldon. The captain was hunched on the cockpit seat, his head sunk low on his chest. He looked as though he were never going to move again. The growing dawn light showed his face as a livid skull beneath his mustache, his eyes sunk so deep they were invisible. But his voice worried Pierre most of all. Low, distant, it seemed to have given up hope. "Is there anything I can get you?" the Frenchman asked.

" 'Nother bottle of whisky."

"Are you sure? Wouldn't you . . . ?"

" 'Nother bottle of whisky."

Pierre got the bottle and handed it to him.

Sheldon sipped slowly as the two French crewmen got the boat ready for sea. The nylon lines were unfastened from the quay, the anchor winch whined, and the chain clanked in steadily over the bow. Then the anchor itself came home, and the cruiser's twin diesels bellowed around the harbor. Sheldon sipped on, watching the dark walls of the bay slide past, and the bow wave peel back the mirror surface of the water. All at once they were out in sunlight, dipping through the lazy silver folds of the sea. Each minute the land grew taller. Pink villas glowed in the steamy breath of pines. Above them, darker hills rose up into the morning air. The final backdrop was the mountain of El Esclop, as bare and white as its cloud. . . . Sheldon coughed, a long gray stain on the morning. He put down the Scotch bottle and looked back at the shadowy cave of Puerto Andraitx, the single lighted port-hole that marked the *Kielhafen*.

"I hope he doesn't know about the Owners' Association." Pierre was looking back too as the cruiser idled around the point.

"Owners' what?"

"Association. Tzannos' trade union for yacht owners," Pierre told him. "I was in Palma yesterday, heard all the talk."

Sheldon still looked blank.

"Christ, even you must know the yacht basin in Palma's too full. There just aren't enough ticketed skippers to go around, and there've been a hell of a lot of complaints about seamanship. So Tzannos is doing something about it."

"Tzannos? Tzannos?" Sheldon was bewildered. "Everyone talks about Tzannos. You, Rafael, the harbor master in Palma."

Pierre paused with his hand on the throttles. "I spent four years in Piraeus. I've seen what Tzannos can do. Charter work had a lousy name there. The usual rackets. Leaky old fishing boats, skippers who didn't know north from south, and yacht agents who kept quiet and took twenty-five per cent. . . . That was before Tzannos started his Owners' Association there. He got up a blacklist of lousy boats and skippers, and pinned it on the yacht club wall. Those boats and skippers don't work any more."

"Let's forget Tzannos, for Christ's sake."

Pierre shrugged. He pushed the throttles forward and the engines rose to a high-pitched whine. The cruiser came smoothly out of the water, thudding now as it found sudden hillocks in the glass-smooth sea. "Twenty knots," Pierre shouted. "Want to take her?"

Sheldon shook his head. The blare of power sickened him, as did the Frenchman's clean blue uniform, and his newly shaved face that glowed in the sunlight. He looked around, and found they were heading almost away from the sun. "This isn't the way to Palma."

"I know it isn't. We're meeting people for breakfast first." Pierre started to whistle, endlessly and without tune.

He was still whistling when twin islands loomed out of the haze ahead. Their pines and wet bracken hung between white sea and white sky. Their rocks bounced back the noise of the cruiser's engines as she slowed. Between the islands there was a channel where a small motor yacht was anchored.

Sheldon looked closely at the boat. "She's flying a French courtesy flag," he said. "She's come from France."

"Has she?" Pierre spoke offhandedly as he busied himself with the controls. The boom of the motors ceased abruptly, the anchor splashed over the bow, and the chain rattled out, slowing as the cruiser lost way. Then there was just the slap of their dying wake against the rocks on either side, and the hum of cicadas from the bracken. Suddenly the calm was broken by the sound of voices echoing across the water. On the far yacht, a man and a woman appeared. They waved, before climbing down into a white fiber glass dinghy.

Sheldon didn't want anything to do with the visitors. He took his bottle of Scotch on to the cruiser's foredeck and drank himself a small breakfast, staring down at the anchor chain curving down into the shadows below. Behind him he could hear the loud "good mornings" from the cockpit, the clink of coffee cups. Then, somebody who wanted something stronger, the familiar shout of "Visky time!" Sheldon didn't turn around. He didn't want to see new faces, and didn't need to see the faces from last night —Sandy, pale and accusing, the Petersens, stiff from their nightly hell, Claire, fresh and unharmed. Barney. . . .

"Captain?" Barney's voice was soft at his elbow.

Sheldon turned around, saw Barney was strangely excited as he pointed down to the water. Then the captain saw what he was pointing at. . . . Below the cruiser's curving hull, out of sight of the breakfast party, a seaman was straddling two dinghies. Pierre's dinghy, and the one the visitors had arrived in. They were both made of white fiber glass, were identical apart from the parent ships' names painted on their center thwarts. Furtively the seaman unscrewed these thwarts and exchanged them.

The captain sipped his whisky thoughtfully. He was still thoughtful, four drinks later, when the breakfast party broke up, and the visitors went back in the wrong dinghy.

"Dope?" Sheldon spoke quietly. He and Pierre were now alone in the cockpit, and once again the cruiser was thudding over open sea. The sun was high overhead, and the sun bathers on the foredeck—Sandy, Claire, and Barney —were as stiff as dead bodies. Sheldon sweated angrily. The only breeze came from the boat's motion through the water. The only waves were astern, curling with thick white fingers around the fiber glass dinghy. "Dope is it?" He repeated.

Pierre heard him but he didn't turn from the wheel. He was whistling endlessly and without tune.

Sheldon was forced to continue. "You swap dinghies with a French boat. You go along the coast and swap dinghies with a Spanish boat. You have a chain of yachts going from the Middle East to wherever."

Pierre stopped whistling. For a moment his face was anxious, then he turned to Sheldon with a confiding smile. "Clever, isn't it?" he admitted. "Each yacht has a crowd of drunken charterers on board, all above suspicion. Each yacht can make twenty-five knots, so it only hangs on to the dirty dinghy for a short time. And the dirty dinghy stays out at sea. We all go into harbor clean." He winked down at the captain. "All that stuff you read about—fast gunboats, searchlights—it's a thing of the past. You see, the authorities don't bother much with charter yachts. They can go where they like."

Sheldon put down his Scotch bottle. He felt sick. "I wondered how you'd made enough to buy this boat. Nobody makes that out of chartering. . . . What d'you carry? Dope?"

"I don't know. I never ask," Pierre said easily.

"Must be dope." Sheldon's lip curled angrily. "The buoyancy chamber on a dinghy wouldn't take anything larger."

"I never ask."

"That's what the traffic is nowadays, so they tell me."

"I never ask!" Pierre shouted.

"You disgust the hell out of me."

"Oh, don't play the boy scout with me." Pierre's face was bright red behind his tan. "You did enough runs out of Algeciras in your time."

"After the war," Sheldon nodded. "Everyone was doing it. But I never touched dope."

"They all say that," the Frenchman said sarcastically. "Get it from the movies."

"You're scum!"

"Hey?" Sandy's voice came from the foredeck.

Pierre waved at her to lie down again. His hands trembled as they changed course. The cruiser was close inshore now, and smooth sandstone cliffs stood over them, yellow and unreal against the startling blue of the sky. Other yachts droned past, each with its row of dead bodies on the foredeck, its dinghy streamed on a long line astern. "You want to watch who you're calling names," Pierre said quietly. "You know who I've got working for me?"

Sheldon didn't answer. "Spanakis. The Greek you keep on talking about," Pierre said. "Your fine fisherman friend from the war."

"Spanakis?"

"He used to call himself a fisherman." Pierre turned and fingered the side of his nose so that Sheldon got the message. "Even during the war he pinched more stuff from the Allies than anyone else."

"The man's not here to defend himself. You're just . . ."

"He took you to his cave." Pierre shrugged. "That one time after the battle of Leros. . . . You must have seen the stuff he had piled in there."

Sheldon drew back, suddenly remembering.

"Spanakis repaired the motors on your MTB. Sweet Jesus, you couldn't even get Packard spares in Alex. at that time."

"No. . . ." Sheldon was bothered by something he couldn't put a finger on. ". . . You know about the cave, then?"

Pierre nodded. "Spanakis still uses it." He hesitated a moment. "All right, *we* still use it. . . . And, all right, it *is* dope. . . . I know that because I run Spanakis and the whole damn operation." There was a sudden flicker of excitement in Pierre's eyes. "And it's very big. We've got the whole Eastern Med buttoned up, and we're moving westward. There's a whole damn Navy working for me. Some of my old submarine crew. D'you remember Roche? Laborde?"

"Good seamen, both of them." Sheldon felt sick again. "Why the hell are you telling me all this?"

"Because you sat there looking like a damn priest. And because I wanted to show you there were other people who hadn't settled down since the war. Some of your own crew, even."

"Just give me one."

"Turton."

Sheldon nodded unhappily. "Yes, I know."

"Turton's been in prison three times. The war taught him how to use sonar. Now he specializes in burglar alarms."

"You can't blame the war for that."

"No, I'd blame you, Navy." Pierre went on quickly. "Then there's Mitch, your cook. Five cases of fraud in three years."

The captain hissed his surprise.

"He had a lot of names, Mitch. There was a lot you didn't know about him."

"Pastry cook at the Savoy." Sheldon tried to remember the man's face. "Quiet, not much in the way of guts."

"Mitch was soft as his bloody pastry," Pierre said angrily. "And you had to make him stand out on the foredeck behind a bloody Bofors gun."

"The chappie was a damn fine gunner by the time I'd finished with him."

"Alcoholic by the time you'd finished with him."

"Everyone was drinking then." Sheldon's voice trembled. "They were bad days."

"Worse days for Mitch now," Pierre told him. "You know where his drinking's got him? Not to mention his prison record?"

Sheldon was uneasy. "I haven't kept in touch."

"Mitch is living at Dunari," Pierre said it softly.

"The colony?" Sheldon had a strange taste in his mouth. "Queer colony on the Italian coast that's run by Corelli? King of the pansy boys?"

The Frenchman nodded. "Mitch is cooking for them."

"But he isn't queer, dammit?"

"No, he isn't. He's just a good cook, and they happen to worship his cooking. Corelli gives him as much booze as he can stand, and lets him have the run of his dirty books."

"Can't he get away?"

"They let him out. A month's holiday every year. Mitch always goes back after a week."

"Why are you muckraking about with all these people?" Sheldon shouted suddenly.

"You asked me to. Asked me who'd gone wrong." Pierre kept calm. "And there's someone else."

"Who?"

"You, Navy."

"How dare you!"

"You're the biggest con man in Majorca. I heard all about you in Palma. The boats you smashed, the money you owe. I don't know how you got away with it. Anyone else'd be put inside."

"Inside? Just two seasons bad . . ." His voice was drowned by the roar of marine engines. Then he saw the large Vosper motor yacht surging by in the opposite direction. He clutched the rail as the cruiser thumped across its wake.

Pierre hung on to the kicking wheel. "So watch out who you're calling names. We're all crooks." He nodded back at the other boat, dwindling astern. "You show me a yacht owner and I'll show you a crook, or the son of a crook."

Sheldon didn't reply.

"That man—" Pierre singled out the pale man on the far shaded deck "—got a piece of the NATO contracts for early-warning stations. Only the station he built went a year over contract, and nearly forty per cent over budget. Suddenly he's got a yacht."

"How can you possibly know that?"

"I've got a copy of the Yacht Register, I read the papers, and I've got friends who know things."

Sheldon didn't know whether to believe him. He was suspicious of Pierre's every move now.

At lunch he noticed how Pierre kept filling up glasses, and then suggested that everyone sleep through the heat of the day. As soon as they'd all gone below, the Frenchman started up his endless whistling, and changed course out to sea. Sheldon was alone with him in the cockpit, running through a procession of names in his mind—Spanakis, Turton, Mitch, Pierre, himself—over and over again. But they were meaningless—meaningless as the sea that was flat and coppery under the afternoon sun, the steady drone of the engines, and the monotonous thudding of the hull. Time passed, not in minutes and hours, but in the shrinking gold column of the whisky bottle.

Then the motors slowed, and Pierre was looking worriedly around the horizon. His crewman came on deck, coiling a heaving line in his hand. Beyond him Sheldon suddenly saw the small motor yacht ahead, with a white fiber glass dinghy bouncing in its wake. Pierre slowed and came around on a parallel course. Heaving lines snaked out across the water from each boat, and the dinghies crossed over from wake to wake, attached to the lines. Not a word was spoken through the whole operation. Then Pierre spun the wheel for home, and abruptly stopped whistling. Relaxed now, he rode the boat's movement easily, grinning at Sheldon.

The sun was suddenly behind them, lurching toward evening. The sandstone cliffs loomed up again, but now they were ocher, cooling in the sky. And below them, standing out tall from the velvet sea, was a huge white ship.

"*Pindar*," Pierre said. "Going back to Palma after her engine trials."

They closed on the long trough of her wake, which was as large as a liner's. The cruiser pitched wildly, and a shout from below brought Claire up to the cockpit. She stared up at *Pindar* in amazement, looking at the twin rows of portholes in the towering hull, the gleaming brasswork of the decks high above. She searched for some time before finding the man who sat up on the bridge walk, wrapped in a blanket. Claire shouted and waved, but her voice was lost in the slow pounding of huge diesels. The man sat quite still, staring straight ahead, apparently the only passenger on the great ship.

"Tzannos." Pierre pointed him out to Sheldon.

"One of the biggest yacht owners in the world," the captain said tiredly. "Does that make him one of the biggest crooks?"

"No, it doesn't," Pierre said. "Rich Greeks are the exceptions to my rule. Onassis, Niarchos, Livanos, and Tzannos, they're a race apart. So rich they don't have to be crooked. They couldn't print it any faster than they make it."

"And how did Tzannos make it?" Sheldon asked.

"Like a couple of other people in 1945, Tzannos realized there were a lot of ships around that nobody would want after the war. He bought the ones he could convert, and suddenly he had a fleet."

Claire seemed bored by their talk. She went away to the foredeck and stood out in the spray on the cruiser's bow, calmly showing her body off in its ribbon-thin bikini. Swaying gracefully on long legs, she was like some slim golden figurehead rising out of the white waves. Suddenly she got what she wanted—an audience on *Pindar*. Two men in blazers and flannels appeared from a doorway on the main deck. They looked down at her dispassionately.

"Binoculars," Pierre called down to the cruiser's saloon.

In a moment Barney came up with a pair. He handed them over.

Pierre focused on the two men high above him. "Kavelaris and Marotta. Two of Tzannos' millionaire friends. They're cruising around the Greek islands with him in August."

"And are they crooks?" Sheldon insisted.

Pierre looked at him strangely. "They both made their money out of the war," he said. "Marotta, the Italian, out of munitions . . . Kavelaris, he's Greek, but not up with the rich Greeks . . . had a nice little line in war surplus. He couldn't miss exactly. Both the British and the Germans left enough stuff on his doorstep." He put down the binoculars. "But for the war, none of them would be where they are today. . . . I don't know if you'd call them crooks."

Sheldon looked down at the deck beneath his feet. For a moment he swore he could see a charred body lying on smoking planks. Then it disappeared. "I'd call them crooks," he said.

"Well, three of the biggest crooks in the world are cruising the Aegean in a month's time," Pierre said. "Strange. . . ." He stared at *Pindar* for a long time.

"What's strange?" Barney asked him.

"It's only been done once before," Pierre replied mysteriously.

"What has?"

"Eight years ago," the Frenchman explained, "a group of extremely rich American businessmen went cruising in the Caribbean. They were never heard of again."

"What d'you mean?" Barney asked. "Their boat sank or something?"

"Or something. The police discovered afterward that every member of the crew had a criminal record."

"So?"

"Kidnap. . . . Only they didn't get the ransom money because they asked too much." Thoughtfully, Pierre turned back to face *Pindar*. "It'd be difficult to ask too much for those three. They're among the richest men in the world, and they all go cruising on the same ship in August. Crazy, just because their yacht's as big as a cargo ship they think they're quite safe."

"They're safe," Barney told him.

But Pierre was excited. "Look at it this way. When those millionaires are ashore they're scared as hell of kidnapers. Spend their time behind bloody great walls, burglar alarms, security men. But afloat, they've only got maybe twenty crew to protect them, and a couple of bodyguards. Nothing else."

"They've got radio."

"So you disable their radio and you've got them, if they're far enough away from land. I mean, they're not royalty. They won't have a destroyer standing by or anything."

"Disable their radio and you've got them?" Barney repeated. He looked at Pierre strangely. "You're not serious about this, are you?"

"Of course not." Pierre winked. "But maybe it's time for the British Navy to send one of its famous gunboats."

Sheldon had been staring at *Pindar* for some time. He didn't react.

"I said maybe it's time for the . . ."

". . . I heard you," the captain said. "What the hell d'you mean?"

"Well, you're in a lot of trouble. You'll need money." He pointed to the huge ship that had fallen back astern. "There's plenty of money waiting there for the right person."

"Meaning me?"

"You own a gunboat." Pierre smiled at him. "All your old crew have got criminal records. Why not sign them on again?"

"Criminal records?" It was Barney's turn to look startled.

"What he means," Sheldon said angrily, "is that Mitch and Turton have got into trouble. Two of my old crew."

"Three," Pierre said.

"What he means," the captain repeated, "is that he thinks I'm a crook too."

"I'll go along with that." To Sheldon's amazement, Barney's face was perfectly serious. "And the straight-and-narrow's done sod-all for me." The engineer looked at them in turn. "So we do it?"

"You're joking, Chief."

"Of course he's joking." Pierre tried to laugh it off.

Barney stared hard at Sheldon. "I'm not joking," he said slowly.

The tension was broken by Claire coming back from the foredeck, her body wet with spray. She pointed over their heads. "*Pindar*'s stopped," she said. "They're lowering a boat."

The three men turned back to the Greek yacht. They heard the sudden bellow of powerful engines, saw the twin curtains of spray gauzed by the setting sun. Then the Riva speedboat thumped past them, cutting a broad white arrow out of the sea.

"That's the man from last night," Claire said. "Sitting on the back seat."

"Knaeber." Pierre nodded. "And he's with Tzannos."

"Where are they going?" she asked.

"Back to Palma." Pierre looked unhappily at Sheldon.

It was evening when they reached Palma. The Club Nautico was the last strip of yellow sunlight in the yacht basin. A crowd was waiting on the terrace above the wide gap of water that was *Pindar*'s berth, and they sauntered along to watch Pierre reverse his cruiser in nearby. They helped tie the nylon ropes to the bollards, and they smiled as Petersen, suddenly flushed and healthy from his day at sea, found a Scotch bottle, and shouted "Visky time!"

Sheldon backed away from the party, leaned tiredly on the stern rail, his face blotched and ill. He looked around at the growing shadows of the harbor, and seemed afraid. Sandy touched his arm and he recoiled from her, wanting her sympathy no more than he'd wanted her anger earlier in the day.

"Pierre wants to know what you're going to do," she said gently.

"Go back to *Jabberwocky*, I suppose. What else?"

"Shall I get the dinghy around?" Pierre asked as he came up to them.

"You and your damn fiber glass dinghy."

Pierre hissed him quiet. He got Barney to pick up Sheldon's crate of liquor, then he and Sandy helped the captain over the gangplank to the quay. They had to half-carry him past the curious faces on the yacht club terrace and around the corner to the road. He hung between them, a sick old man, not looking up as they crossed the rubble of the vacant lot and approached the long gray hull of the MTB. The two men got Sheldon up onto the deck, then the crate of gin and lime after him. Sudden footsteps made them all turn around. The harbor master was coming down from *Jabberwocky*'s bridge, a sheaf of papers in his hand.

10

"I know you won't believe me, Captain, but I am sorry." He looked down at Sheldon. "I have here a letter from Mr. Tzannos. He is in my office at this moment. Mr. Knaeber is with him, very angry."

Sheldon was sitting awkwardly on the deck. The harbor master helped him to his feet and gave him a piece of paper.

"Captain," Sheldon read flatly. "Since you seem to be more suited to running a gunboat than a yacht, . . ." He trailed off and slumped wearily against a stanchion. ". . . you read it." He handed the letter back.

The harbor master knew it by heart. He only referred to the words occasionally, and his voice was gruff and embarrassed. "He say you are not fit to run a yat. You always have plenty of troubles. Mr. Knaeber is no at all the first owner to be troubled by you, but he will be the last. Mr. Tzannos has many influences around the Mediterranean. He will see to it personally that you never work on a yat again."

"All this?" Sheldon was bewildered. "Because one damn speedboat was smashed?"

"That was only the latest. Mr. Tzannos, he hear about some of your other troubles, with other yats."

"Wonder who told him," Sheldon said tiredly.

"He don't have to look very far." The man showed a trace of anger.

"Doesn't matter."

The harbor master continued with the letter. "Mr. Tzannos have instructed Mr. Knaeber to sue you, Captain. He have also instructed his lawyers to contact the other yat owners you have troubled. They will take you to court. The properties of the yat owners must be safe . . . safe." He peered at the word closely.

". . . Guarded," Sheldon said. He looked across the water at the sunlight sliding up the far forest of masts.

The harbor master cleared his throat unhappily. "Now we come to my side of the business."

"Your side?" Sheldon asked in disbelief. "Haven't you said enough?"

"The money you owe the people here." The man sorted through his papers.

"The Galatzo, the Valdemossa, the Chandlers, and my office personally. A great deal of money. More than a thousand English pounds." He paused, then pointed up to the bridge behind him. A square of white paper was nailed to the MTB's mast. "I am truly sorry, Captain. I do not like to arrest a ship."

"You've done *what?*" Anger was spreading slowly down from Sheldon's eyes to his body. Unsteadily he stood up.

"We do this so that you will not leave the harbor before the proceedings next week in court. Also . . . ," he spoke quickly now in the face of Sheldon's growing anger, ". . . the port authority can now do what they like with *Jabberwocky*. Sell her. That way some of the people in the town will be paid."

"*Sell her?* You've gone off your bloody head!"

The harbor master colored. "Everyone you shout at. And you treat them like servants. Now it is finished. The people in the town will be paid. My men look around *Jabberwocky* this afternoon and they say she will fetch maybe eight, maybe nine hundred pounds."

"Eight or nine hundred pounds?" Sheldon roared. "It's daylight bloody robbery! I'm warning you!"

"And I warn you, Captain! The people here get no money from you. All they get is fairy stories about what a great man you were in the war. But for me you are no a great man. Here in Palma you have sunk more ships than you ever sink in the war!"

"Get off my ship!" Sheldon bellowed.

"Soon she is no longer your ship." The man retreated toward the gangplank.

Suddenly Sheldon's anger overcame the liquor in his system. He staggered up to the bridge and tore the piece of paper from the mast.

"Makes no difference, Captain," the harbor master shouted from the stern. "Your ship stays arrested. . . . And another thing," he pointed to the wooden crate on the deck beside him. "You think you can bribe me with whisky? Here it is, returned to you with thanks." He crossed the gangplank to the quay.

Sheldon went back to the others on the twilit deck. "Can he really do that?" he asked. "Arrest the ship?"

Pierre nodded.

"But eight or nine hundred pounds? It's daylight robbery."

Pierre looked around doubtfully. "I don't know, Navy. She seems in a pretty bad state. When did you last have her out of the water?"

"Ten, maybe eleven years."

"She'll be rotted to pieces."

"Dammit, she's copper-sheathed! D'you take me for a complete moron?" Trembling, Sheldon stooped to pick up a boathook from the deck. Painfully he leaned out over the side and scraped at the weed on the waterline. They saw the gleam of copper underneath. "The people I bought her from spent a fortune on her," he continued. "Went broke before they were halfway through converting her. Nobody told them about the thieving Spanish boat yards. By the time the hull was sheathed, they hadn't the money to go on. They were stuck with a boat that was all engines and petrol tanks. White elephant. I got her dirt cheap."

Pierre nodded in surprise. "What about the engines? Now, I mean?"

Sheldon led them down the wardroom ladder and over to a watertight door. The sour heat of the engine room hit them as he reached through the door and found a torch. Its beam trembled in his hand, showing the four silent engines and their sweating pipes. Then the light moved on to four full oil drums by the bulkhead. "Tell him, Chief."

Barney crossed over to the drums. "Everything that could rust we stripped down, labeled, and stored in here. One oil bath for each engine. And over here are the steering lines and prop-shaft bearings."

Pierre was impressed. "You mean you can get the engines working again, Barney?"

"Reckon so. I'd need some spares, of course."

"And the boat's frame?" Pierre's hand went to the bulkhead. "Is that sound?"

"Probably one or two things need looking at by now. And maybe a couple of ripe planks above the sheathing. That sort of thing."

"She'd have to be surveyed." Pierre felt the diagonal planking. "Out of the water."

"Of course," Sheldon cut across, his voice trembling. "But she's worth a lot more than nine hundred quid, isn't she?"

"A great deal more, I'd say." Pierre was thoughtful.

There was a moment's silence in the dark engine room. Gradually the torch beam in Sheldon's hand became steady. "Right," he said suddenly.

"Right, what?"

"You've got a week to get these engines running again, Chief. Can it be done . . . ?"

". . . A week?" Pierre interrupted him. "What the hell are you talking about?"

"A week's all I've got before those crooked bastards come to sell up the ship." Sheldon's anger boomed through the engine room. "But she won't be here. I'm taking her out of the harbor."

"Taking her out?" Sandy looked at him in amazement, tried to see his face behind the flare of the torch.

"You heard me."

"And what about that piece of paper on the mast?" Pierre asked. "The boat's been arrested, remember?"

"I'm taking her out."

"Navy," Pierre tried reasoning with him. "Look at those engines over there. Even if Barney can get them going in a week, they'll need money."

"How much, Chief?"

"Two-thirty . . . two-sixty . . ." Barney muttered. "I could get the whole lot going for around three hundred quid."

"And where the hell are you going to find that?" Pierre asked.

"Borrow it," Sheldon said quickly. "You said you had two villas in Greece, more money than you could spend."

Pierre stood quite still. "I don't like being told what to do with my money," he said at last. "Even three hundred quid."

Sheldon's arms fell to his sides, and the torch now pointed downward. He faced Pierre over a cone of white light, and he seemed taller, surer of himself. "We'll call it five thousand," he said curtly. "To cover the cost of putting her straight."

"Five grand?" Pierre gasped. "You're out of your mind."

"Just a business proposition," Sheldon told him. "Spend five thousand on the boat and she's worth twenty-five. You won't lose on the deal."

"But we've tried to sell her, Alec," Sandy broke in. "Nobody wanted her."

"Pierre's got some rather special friends in the Middle East," the captain said. "One or two of them would pay a lot of money for a big boat that could do thirty knots. Aren't I right, Pierre?"

"Maybe. Just maybe."

"And she'll do thirty knots," Sheldon continued. "Once we've stripped the copper off her, and got rid of her wartrim."

"Thirty knots?" Pierre shook his head angrily. "This is crazy talk. Navy, you really expect me to lend you five grand?"

Slowly Sheldon raised the torch until it shone full in the Frenchman's face. "I don't expect . . . I know," he said coldly. "I'll ask you nicely later."

Sweat broke out on Pierre's forehead. "You mean the dinghy, don't you?"

Sheldon nodded.

"What dinghy? What is all this?" Sandy asked.

Pierre didn't answer. He stared hard at Sheldon, his eyes narrowed against the torchlight. "You'd really try and screw me? Your friend?"

"I'll do *any* damn thing!" Sheldon shouted in his face. "To get this boat out of here!"

"I'm beginning to believe you."

"Right, that's settled." Sheldon lowered the torch and walked away.

They followed him up to the bridge and found him standing squarely behind the ship's wheel, muttering to himself as he stared out at the yacht basin. Twilight had given way to night. The lights of the Club Nautico were a long chain on the far side of the water. Then, way out beyond the quays, a light moved—a town of lights—and *Pindar* steamed slowly in through the port entrance. Sheldon stopped muttering and hissed in his breath sharply.

Pierre tried to get his attention back. "Look, Navy," he said angrily. "Just say you manage to get *Jabberwocky* out of here, well, she's going to be the hottest thing in the Med. Who're you going to get to do all the work on her?"

"Holve," Sheldon said absently. "He still runs a crooked shipyard in Sardinia, doesn't he?" He watched *Pindar* drift silently over toward the yacht basin.

"Yes, he does," Pierre was taken aback. "He's worked for me. But Holve's a crook. He only deals with crooks. And maybe it's got home to you at last that you're a crook. So why not take the easy way out and join our organization? You'd be rich in a month."

"What organization? What *is* all this?" Sandy asked.

"Doesn't matter," Sheldon told her. "I won't go with him. Don't like the work." His voice was strange. He seemed hypnotized by *Pindar* as she drifted on. Nearer and nearer she came, her lit decks growing wider until they seemed to fill the harbor. Suddenly the chunter of her huge engines shook the water as she maneuvered to drop anchor. On her foredeck seamen were waiting by the winch. High up on the bridge, dim faces waited by the wheel and telegraph. And on her blazing boat deck, passengers waited to sip once again at their cocktails. Slowly the huge yacht swung around directly in front of the MTB. One man's power and wealth towered over Sheldon. "If I'm a crook," he said, "he made me a crook."

"And he'll put you behind bars," Pierre told him. "You can't fight Tzannos."

"Can't I?" Momentarily Sheldon bent down to the torpedo sight on the bridge rail. "Can't I just?" His voice rose. "More suited to a gunboat, am I, Mr. Tzannos? And maybe you're right at that. Maybe it's time I went back to gunboats!"

Pierre felt a sudden chill as he looked from *Pindar* to Sheldon. "If you mean what we were talking about this afternoon . . . ?" he began uneasily.

"I do. That's exactly what I mean."

"You're not serious?" Pierre couldn't be sure.

"Dead serious." The captain stiffened, and his face was red and mottled in the light from the Greek ship. "We'll bloody well do it!" he shouted suddenly.

A low chuckle came from behind him. "And I'm with you, Skipper." Barney's voice was strangely excited. "You just signed on an engineer."

"What *is* this?" Sandy was getting hysterical. "What were you talking about this afternoon?"

"Navy wants to attack that ship . . ." Pierre told her simply, pointing out at *Pindar*. ". . . With this one." His hand fell back to the MTB's wheel.

"Attack . . . *Pindar?*" Sandy was stunned. "Why, Alec, why?"

"Because the three people on that yacht are the only buggers I know who won the war!" Sheldon roared. "They made a bloody pile out of it! While I was murdering for them! Watching my friends being murdered. And now what do they say? Good-by, we don't want you any more. But we'll take your ship."

"Come off it, Navy." Pierre pulled him around gently. "You can't blame Tzannos for what's happened to you, I mean you personally, over the past few years." He clapped a playboy hand on his shoulder. "It's not Tzannos eating into you, it's the liquor. Well, isn't it? You're rotten with it, Navy. Been soaking yourself in it for twenty-four hours."

"Drunk, am I?" Sheldon pulled himself away angrily.

"Drunk," Pierre nodded. "Look. . . ." He pointed at the case of liquor they'd brought around the harbor. ". . . And look." He pointed back to the harbor master's whisky by the gangplank.

"Right," Sheldon said. He left the bridge.

They saw him again, a moment later, staggering to the foredeck with the whisky. He put it down next to the other liquor crate. Breathing heavily, he took the bottles out and arranged gin and whisky in a row. He kept back two bottles, walked unsteadily away with them in his hands. Then he turned, swore loudly, and hurled the first bottle at the row on deck. Over half the bottles smashed. Sheldon swung his arm again and the skittles game was over. Broken glass and liquor covered the deck. "Not a drop! Not a single bloody drop until this is all over!" He shouted up at them on the bridge. "That'll show you how damn serious I am." Slowly he turned around to face *Pindar*, a blaze of lights hanging in the darkness. " 'Beware the Jabberwock, my son!' " he roared across the water. " 'The jaws that bite, the claws that catch! Beware the Jubjub bird, and shun . . . the frumious Bandersnatch!' "

Suddenly *Pindar* gave an answering roar. Her anchor thundered out from her hawsepipe and carved a white hole in the black harbor. The huge links of her chain shuddered out, tautened as they slowed the great ship's progress back toward the far quay. Then the roar came again, softer, as more chain was let out. And again, softer still, and *Pindar* slid back among the lights of the Club Nautico.

On the MTB's bridge, Pierre looked at Sandy. "Banderstock?" he asked her. "He's gone off his head at last."

"It's a poem," she told him, and now she was crying. "A poem he hates."

Pierre looked at her strangely. Then he went down to the foredeck and the reek of alcohol. Broken glass crunched under his feet as he picked his way through the liquor trails to the crate where Sheldon was sitting. The captain was trembling and exhausted, staring down at the deck. Pierre put an arm around him. "This Banderstock," he said. "It's not real."

"Bandersnatch," Sheldon corrected him. Amazingly his voice was calm and conversational. "It's just a silly name. Like the names they had for those other Naval Operations in the war . . . Overlord, Neptune."

"Naval Operations?"

"That's right." Sheldon looked up at him, and his eyes were clear. "Attacking *Pindar* seems like a crazy idea until you think of it as a Naval Operation. Then it couldn't be simpler."

Pierre stared at him blankly.

"Start with this ship." Sheldon pointed down at the deck. "An ex-D-type MTB . . . And she's still all there, if you forget her torpedo tubes. . . . So you refit her as an MGB, a gunboat. And you get back her old crew . . . Mitch, Turton, they've got nothing to lose. Barney said he'd join me."

"That's just four," Pierre told him angrily. "You can't run this ship with only four people."

"There are others . . . ex-seamen. You said you had a whole Navy working for you, remember?"

"Working for *me*."

86

"I was thinking of Spanakis, really," Sheldon continued calmly. "That cave of his on that small Greek island. How many people know about it?"

"Not more than thirty of us," Pierre said. "We use it for storing stuff. It's part of our operation."

Sheldon nodded. He picked up the stump of a broken bottle, and drew with it on the littered deck. "Now the interesting thing is that the cave . . . the cave no one knows about . . . is down here, just off the Dodecanese. . . . And *Pindar*—" he pointed back across the harbor "—when she's cruising, always calls in at the Dodecanese Islands. Because Tzannos was born at Leros. . . . Now after Leros, *Pindar* makes for Crete or Rhodes. Either way she has to pass close to Spanakis' cave. And that's where we'll be waiting for her."

Pierre spread his hands in anger and turned away.

"Don't you see? The cave is the perfect place to lie up and train a crew? And it's very lonely water around there. No other ships close at hand, and what's *Pindar* got to protect her? Only her radio. . . . So we sneak up on her at night. One shot, even from a Bofors gun, would blow away her radio truck. Then we've got them, three millionaires. And we take them back to the cave and wait for the ransom. . . . Don't you see? It all falls into place."

"Navy, this is crazy talk."

"Don't forget, I know the Aegean like the back of my hand. I fought a war there."

"And who the hell's going to finance you to fight another war there? You think I am? How much d'you think it'd cost, for Christ's sake?"

"Thirty thousand, top," Sheldon told him evenly.

"Nobody but nobody can blackmail me for thirty grand." Pierre started walking away.

Sheldon went after him, his mind working fast. "I said it was a business proposition, and it still is. . . . You pay for the refit, and for setting the whole thing up. While I plan the operation. . . ."

"Oh, great!"

"When I've made my plans," Sheldon went on. "If I can't convince you it'll work, then you can take the boat and sell her. We'll scrub the whole thing."

Pierre stopped by the chartroom windows. He wheeled around on Sheldon suddenly. "But I'd lose a bundle! I'm not going to get thirty grand for this boat. Well, am I?"

"You'll get more than thirty grand for a *gunboat,* in full working order," Sheldon told him. "You know as well as I do, there are plenty of countries in the Middle East that would pay three or four times the right price for an MTB. . . . Because none of the naval powers will sell to them."

Pierre hesitated.

"I was good in the war," Sheldon continued quickly. "Give me a month off liquor and I'll be good again. . . . Maybe when I've worked out the operation in detail, you'll like the sound of it. . . . And you'll stand to gain a great deal."

"How much?"

"A million pounds," Sheldon said, "minus your expenses."

Again Pierre hesitated. Then he started whistling, endlessly and without tune.

11

Sheldon's stomach heaved as the acid cocktail hit him. His right hand trembled around the glass of lime juice, vinegar, and sugar—the old cure. His left hand grabbed out for the ship's wheel, held on while he fought to keep the liquid down. The spasm passed. He exchanged the cocktail for the water jug, gulped at it greedily, and felt his sour, leathery tubes sizzle as the water sluiced among them. He coughed, a long, rasping, foul-tasting five seconds. Then he told himself the worst days were over. He was drying out.

The wheel spokes turned under his hand. He could feel the stiff pull of the steering lines, and the rudders moving for the first time in years. He reached over to the engine-room telegraph, its gentle clang was echoed a moment later by a much dimmer clang from the engine room below. Sheldon felt the hairs prickle on the back of his neck. It wasn't until he looked up that his fear returned. The fear that had haunted him since dawn.

From where he stood on the MTB's bridge, he could see the slate-gray sea beyond the harbor-wall, and the straight-ruled storm waves coming from the black horizon. Below the dark metal of the clouds, he could see white dots swirling like handfuls of confetti—gulls that were crossing the shore line to escape the storm. They came low and fast over the lifting spray of the quays, circled the yacht basin, crying out the bad news. A fine rain began to fall, blurring the harbor water, and suddenly the boats no longer seemed to be floating, but rolling on a dull gray floor. Masts lurched together, and rigging moaned in the wind. Sheldon tried to tell himself he'd left harbor in worse weather during the war. But he knew he never had.

Footsteps came along the deck behind him. Then Pierre climbed up onto the bridge, seeming strangely small in the rain. "You're not going out in this?" His face was grim.

"The seven days are up. They'll be coming for me at ten." Sheldon tried to make his voice sound calm. "Is the harbor master around yet?"

"He's still in bed."

"Then he hasn't heard anything?"

"Sure he's *heard*." Pierre turned and pointed at the four people waiting in the rain by *Jabberwocky's* gangplank. "And they've heard. . . . Heard the machinery coming on board, heard the engines being tested. They just don't *believe* you're going out in weather like this. Sweet Jesus, it's been forecast long enough. No boat's been out of here in two days. And the barometer has fallen five-tenths."

"Six," Sheldon said. "I just looked."

Pierre turned away hopelessly. "And Sandy?" he said at last. "Does she still say she's going with you?"

"Only as far as Holve's Yard. She'll have to leave before we start. . . ."

". . . Navy." Pierre swung him around to face the rain that hid the sea. "You're not going to make it to Holve's Yard, you won't even make the shelter of Cala Veya. You can't see the cliffs, can you? And they're only a couple of miles away."

"That's one good thing," Sheldon said uneasily. "Nobody'll come after us."

Pierre left him in disgust. "I'll go and see if I can talk Sandy out of it."

Sheldon went down to the engine room. A new smell hit him as he opened the door—white metal, engines, and hot oil. There were four new light bulbs, each blazing down on a gleaming supercharged Packard. Around the motors were piles of swarf, tools, and waste. But the center gangway, where Barney was standing, was clear. The engineer sweated with a ring spanner, and his movements were slow with fatigue. When he looked up the shadows under his eyes were suddenly no longer due to the light overhead but part of his face.

"Just about there, Skipper."

Sheldon didn't answer. Nervously he picked up a spark plug, and it trembled in his hands. He turned away so that Barney wouldn't see. An uneasy silence hung between the two men. Then, from across the harbor, the cathedral clock struck seven, followed a moment later by the clocks of the town hall and the church in the old quarter. Sheldon had heard their differing versions of the hour for the past fifteen years, and now he couldn't believe he was hearing them for the last time. Suddenly he couldn't believe in any of the events of the past few days. He faced Barney once again. "Why? . . ." He began.

"Why what, Skipper?"

"Why all this? I mean, why've you gone without sleep for forty-eight hours?"

"Sleep," the engineer said flatly. "Haven't had a good night's sleep since the war."

Sheldon stared at him, hypnotized by the strange dull purpose behind the man's fatigue.

"About time we were moving, Skipper." Barney's voice was hard. He watched the spark plug tremble in the captain's hands.

Sheldon put it down. He hid his hands behind his back and squared his shoulders. "I'll ring down when I want you, Chief," he said curtly. Then he marched out of the engine room.

Out on deck, he saw that the crowd waiting by *Jabberwocky*'s gangplank had swelled from four to fourteen. Deciding he'd better put on a show for them, he went and found an empty Gordon's bottle, and filled it with water. Then he took up position at the top of the wardroom ladder and waited for Pierre to come up from below.

"Navy, she won't listen to reason." The man's head and shoulders appeared, then the rest of his body. "Sandy says she's going with you whatever the . . ."

Sheldon didn't let him finish. Suddenly he swung the Gordon's bottle past the man's head.

Pierre ducked. "What is this?" he hissed angrily.

"Try to tell me what to do with my damn ship?" Sheldon roared for the benefit of the people on the quayside. "I'll see you in hell first!"

"What are you doing, for Christ's sake?" The

Frenchman ducked again as Sheldon swung the bottle at him a second time. He side-stepped around the captain and backed away toward the gangplank.

"Taking my damn boat out! That's what I'm doing!" Sheldon went after him. He reached the stern, and kicked the gangplank down into the water just as Pierre scrambled ashore. Then he put the Gordon's bottle down on deck, and began unfastening the gray matted ropes from their bitts.

"You can't take her out. There's a bloody great storm out there," a voice shouted from the quayside. "Tell him, someone."

Sheldon straightened with the stiff old rope in his hands. Suddenly he flung it at the faces on the quay. "Scared of a bit of weather, are you?" he bellowed. "Call yourselves seamen? Bloody taxi drivers, the lot of you!"

The crowd swung back as the heavy rope snaked out toward them. A moment later it was followed by the second warp, and *Jabberwocky*'s stern swung clear of the jetty. Sheldon picked up the gin bottle again, sucked water from it greedily. He swayed as he looked at the faces over the widening gap of water. "And tell the damn harbor master, next time he arrests a boat to take the engines out of her first!" He hurled the bottle so that it smashed against the quayside.

Catcalls came from the onlookers as Sheldon lowered the Blue Ensign from the stern pole, and lurched away with it to the bridge. More catcalls as he raised it to the yardarm. Then he reached out for the engine-room telegraph, rang down "Stand By Engines," and went for'ard to deal with the anchor. The winch on the foredeck was slimy with rain. Sheldon released the brake, and the links roared out in a cloud of rust. Then the shackle he'd unfastened earlier down in the chain locker winged its way out over the deck, clattered through the fair-lead, and plopped into the water. The MTB's bow lifted and swung free. Nothing held them to the harbor any longer. They had already left.

Unable to rid himself of the Naval Custom, the captain lowered the Anchor Jack on the bow flagpole, and took it aft with him to the bridge. There were no more catcalls from the crowd on the quayside. Sheldon looked around to the Club Nautico and was surprised to find binoculars were being trained on him from every yacht in the basin. His hand trembled on the telegraph as it rang up "Slow Ahead." He heard with satisfaction the cracked puny sound that came up from the waterline. They were leaving harbor on only four cylinders of one engine, to give the impression they couldn't get through the waiting storm, but only he and Barney knew that. The horrible splutter of the exhaust gradually edged them out past the yacht club.

Turning the wheel to port, Sheldon automatically pressed the siren button. The sound whopped up into the still air. Then a second whistle blared suddenly from one of the jetties, and the captain saw Dick grinning at him from the *Aristide*. Then a third whistle, another, another, until the whole yacht basin was a huge wedge of sound, throbbing, lifting Sheldon's hand to his head in a naval salute, bringing sudden hot tears to his eyes. He steered out to the harbor entrance and he gave them their satisfaction, standing rigidly at attention. His eyes dim, he was hearing another harbor full of sound on a rainy morning. The same boat was heading for open water in a column of other Dogboats, MLs, and two escorting trawlers. MTB 859 was new and dazzle-painted, her crew drawn up on the foredecks by the huge deck tanks that were to take them to the war in the Med.

He didn't see the lighthouse as they passed, didn't remember ringing up Half Ahead as the bows dug into the first long gray wave. He was looking back at the two great landmarks of Bellver Castle and the cathedral, listening to the wail of whistle gradually falling away between them. Then a shrill whistle close at hand jerked him around to the engine-room tube. Barney's angry voice asking when, for God's sake, when, he could switch on the other three engines. Sheldon felt the bows slide down to meet a wave, felt the useless power of the one screw as they were sucked up into the mound of water. But they were too close inshore. They had to reach the safety of the wall of rain, coming toward them from the sea.

Sandy clambered up onto the bridge beside him. The MTB was yawing and rolling, her one propeller alternately plowing and racing as it drove them on desperately slowly. Then, thankfully, the rain closed around them. Sheldon gave the order to change over, and heard the healthy roar of eighteen good cylinders, metal sharpening its teeth against metal. Immediately the boat gathered herself, punched her way into the next wave, rode out over the top, singing in the spray. Sheldon whistled up Barney.

"Done a grand job, Chief."

"Yes and no," Barney shouted back. "We held her too long on four pots. It'll take a bit of time to sort her out."

"How long?"

"Ten, fifteen minutes."

"No more." Sheldon's voice suddenly rose as a gust of wind battered against the bridge. "I can't give you any more."

And the wind came again, a second burst which thundered around the boat, parted the rain to show the black storm center was suddenly on their beam. Sheldon caught a glimpse of Sandy's frightened face, then he saw the two straight lines of storm waves, reaching out for them, curling copper-green and black. Too late he spun the wheel. The ship lurched sideways into darkness, swung. They were down in the green underbelly of the sea, then up in the exploding gray of the sky. And then again they went skidding down black water, hard as rock.

This time the boat was soft and whimpering, burrowing down into the black. Sheldon swore, his voice was snatched away by salt water. Snarling at the huge glove of the sea that slapped his face again and again, he hung on to the wheel, hauled it around to starboard. Slowly, slowly, the ship came around, and the captain saw the sky he'd never expected to see again. The black lines of storm waves were now ahead. He hauled Sandy over to the wheel. "Keep her there," he shouted.

Down below in the wardroom, he worked with a sledge hammer, smashing tables, lockers, cots, and floor boards. Once he stopped, certain the hammer was useless. All around him the ship was shaking herself to pieces. Then he worked on, splintering the woodwork in a growing fury. When his arms were aching he put down the hammer, and carried the first load of wreckage to the deck.

And he saw they were going backward, keeping pace with the curling waves. On a lee shore, he suddenly remembered. Swearing, he hauled himself up to the bridge. Sandy was hunched below the sprayshield, her body kicking around the wheel. Then she was outlined in fire— lightning unzipped the darkness all around her. Sheldon froze as he saw how close the storm had come, its rain as solid as sea. He grabbed up the voice tube.

"Engines, damn you! Give me more power!"

"One minute, Skipper."

"Make it one minute! Or by Christ we'll all be at the bottom!"

He fell down the wardroom ladder. Black spray lashed at the portholes as he gathered up armfuls of debris, pushed them out on to the shrieking deck. Timbers, mattresses, old oilskins, gas masks, the Jabberwocky poem, skidded around on the wet planks. Then Sheldon's hand closed on Traill's brass ruler. He looked down at it a moment, and decided to keep it back. As he stroked the cool metal, the engines suddenly roared out—a scream of joy he hadn't heard since the war. Screaming himself now, Sheldon went up on deck and kicked heap after heap of debris over the side. The waves to leeward were strangely calm, and the snake of wreckage clung to the ship.

He ran for the bridge. Through the wall of rain, lightning showed two, three, *no, four* black lines. And they went down into the first wave with engines screaming. Then suddenly it was calm, a strange black calm, and Sandy's face was close to his under the sea. The note of the engines dipped sharply, stuttered—and won. The propellers dug a hole up through the water, up to the buffeting sky. Then they were staring down at the second wave, the motors screaming again. And Sheldon screamed louder, for the pure joy of it. . . . This they could beat. Not the storm center. But this they could beat.

They made the lee of Cala Veya before the storm center got to them. The sea was black, polished by ragged cloths. But the waves were no longer so sharp, no longer scarring the MTB's hull and making her groan aloud. Sheldon needed Halt Speed to keep them in calmer water. And it was dark, dark through day and night for all he knew—exhaustion took time and danger away. When finally he straightened, he found the roar of wind was only in his ears. He found the boat was closing up on the cliffs, and he could see pines bent double above the spray. Slowly he throttled back, slowly they fell farther and farther away from the cliffs, testing the sea until it was theirs. Then he rang down for Full Speed and squared his cap on his head, once again going to war.

PART

two

12

DEATH OF BRITISH WAR HERO. EX-MTB WRECKAGE WASHED ASHORE said the small headline in the airmail edition of the *Daily Telegraph*. There was a tribute from a fellow officer, a mention of the Special Boat Squadron and the sinking of the *Burg Rostock*. Nothing to say Sheldon had ever survived the war.

Claire looked down at the old wartime photo in the paper, and she felt sad. Sheldon's face had been different then, his cheeks smooth and pale above the mustache—a kind man whose nerve ends were all crushed up into the deep shadows below his eyes. Claire remembered the coarse mottled face she'd last seen, and wondered if Sheldon had ever stood a chance. She took the *Telegraph* with her to the stern of Pierre's cruiser. Steam was rising from the puddles on the yacht club terrace, the boats along the quay were no longer surging against their ropes, and out over the sea weak shafts of sunlight were trying to pierce the haze. But there were dark clouds rumbling on metal bearings at every horizon. The storm was circling —Sheldon's storm. And Claire was sad, because she seemed to be the only one who knew about it.

She was angry too as she faced Pierre, sprawling in his deck chair. She could see what had attracted her about the man, what had made her come aboard the boat, stay aboard for the Petersens' cruise, and sleep with Pierre in his cabin below. It was the way the Frenchman always seemed to be carrying a Scotch bottle, low down in his huge hand, the way he took his own party with him everywhere he went. Now the sight of the whisky in his hand made her turn away in disgust. Pierre had mourned Sheldon for just two days. Then he'd got a telegram from somewhere called Holve's Yard with news about a boat he was interested in, and suddenly he'd started throwing parties that stretched halfway along the quay.

"Claire," he called out to her. "What's the matter?"

She went toward him, and he saw the newspaper in her hand.

"Poor Navy." He shrugged. "Suddenly he is a great man. Everyone makes little speeches about him. Even the harbor master. Nobody mentions why he had to sail out of here."

"It's all wrong."

"Maybe. But nobody wants to speak ill of the dead."

"It's all *wrong*."

"You want me to cry?" he asked gently. "Everything in this life has to come to an end." He reached out for the whisky bottle, frowned as he saw it was empty. "Everything. Even bottles of Scotch."

She was about to reply when a car horn blared from along the quayside.

Pierre turned around and waved at the driver. "And at last," he breathed a sigh of relief, "the Petersens have come to an end. That beautiful, beautiful taxi is going to take them away to the airport."

The Norwegians were led up on deck in an alcoholic stupor. Obediently they followed their suitcases along the quay, and slumped in the rear seats of the taxi. "Visky time." Petersen's voice was hoarse, barely audible. He and Ulla waited, staring down at trembling hands, as the tray of whisky was brought from the boat. Two glasses were filled and emptied without pleasure or pain. Then Petersen gave out shy handshakes through the window, and the taxi pulled away.

Claire found a roll of bank notes screwed up in her palm. The top one had an Oslo phone number scrawled on it, and suddenly she was angry again.

"Don't be upset." Pierre winked at her. "For a small amount, yes. But a big pile like that has to be a present."

Claire watched the smile break out over his tanned cheekbones. And she was even angrier as she saw what that smile could still do to her. "Let's make it a bigger pile, shall we?" The words were out before she could stop them. "You took me on as cook, remember? Well, now I'm signing off."

For a moment Pierre was hurt. Then he handed over the large tip Petersen had given him. "It doesn't mean anything," he said softly. "And you're more than welcome to stay aboard. I don't want you to leave."

"I know." Claire turned and walked away along the quay.

The black limousine made no sound as it passed her. Almost without thinking she classified it as a Mercedes 600—the car that was number three on her charts. Then she saw it draw up below *Pindar*'s huge white stern, and heard the chauffeur blow the horn three times. Two seamen came down the steep metal gangplank with a matching set of suitcases. They put them in the trunk and went back on board *Pindar*. So the millionaires were leaving too. Claire stopped. The hum of a liner filled the air around her. She looked up at the dazzling white walls, the long shaded decks, the P & O calm it took a hundred hidden men to achieve. Then she found that she was being watched. High up on the ship, outlined by the boat deck's blue awning, a man was looking down at her. A squat, powerful man, middle-aged, wearing a light gray suit. He leaned forward, and his teeth gleamed in the sun as he smiled at her.

She walked through *Pindar*'s shadow that stretched right across the quay. Returning to the sunlight once again, she glanced up at the blue awning, and saw that the man had crossed the boat deck to watch her from the near side of the ship. Claire paused, noted that the small yacht moored alongside was unoccupied, its cockpit covered by a lashed tarpaulin. She hesitated a moment longer, then ran onto the small yacht, lay face-downward on the warm planks of the foredeck, and undid the top strap of her bikini. The weak sun was gentle on her body as she stretched lazily, listening to the blood thumping through her temples. Then the rhythm speeded up, became a sharper sound, no longer in her head. Surprised, she opened her eyes and looked up at *Pindar*. The man was now directly above her on the boat deck, tapping the rail with his signet ring to get her attention. "Café de los Plataneros," he whispered down to her, "twenty minutes."

"Plataneros . . . plane trees." She remembered the Spanish word as the taxi dropped her in a small square high up in the town's old quarter. The trees lined the square in dusty rows, their leaves rustling like tinfoil against the close storm clouds. To her right she saw the café which bore their name. The man's name she knew even before he stood up to introduce himself.

"Dimitri Kavelaris." He waved her to a chair.

"Claire." She wished she could see his eyes behind the dark glasses.

"Just Claire?"

"Just Claire," she said.

"Well, Just Claire, I'm sorry the rendezvous couldn't be more exclusive, but there are one or two photographers along the Paseo Maritimo." He signaled the waiter. "Coffee?"

She studied him covertly as he ordered. At ground level Kavelaris was a disappointment. He was shorter than she was, a fat man who'd lost weight, judging by the way he sucked in his stomach. His pouchy cheeks were shaved nearly white, and what there was of his hair was heavily greased. But there was something attractive about the man—the way he sat so still. Kavelaris was taut and controlled. It was his hour for the chase, and everything was computed and channeled for that end. Without moving he got the time from his chunky wrist watch, and Claire felt she had two minutes to get the job as his secretary.

"No time for flowery words, I'm afraid. My plane leaves at two o'clock." His voice was calm, his Levantine accent soft and liquid. "All I can offer you is some information, which I hope will be of interest. D'you know St. Tropez?"

She nodded.

"Well, tonight a young man will be dancing in a club called Palmyr in St. Tropez. You could maybe go and have a look at him, maybe talk to him." His smile was gentle and ironic. "He could maybe fall in love with you, and ask you to cruise on *Pindar* in August."

"You don't waste time, do you?"

"No."

The waiter came with the coffee. Claire turned away to face the square and its planc trees. In the middle of the trees was a small cement roller-skating rink. Children and beginners hugged the rail at the rink's edge, while out in the center a man in the startling blue uniform of a professional carved his way grimly through the laughing couples like a dreadnought. Claire watched him squeal to a halt, swearing, behind a fallen child, and she waited for Kavelaris to speak again.

"A golden girl smiled at me this morning." His voice was soft. "She also smiled at me a week ago, from the deck of a motor cruiser out in the bay."

"She smiled at you?" Claire turned back to him, again wishing she could see his eyes.

"No, I don't flatter myself. She was smiling at something beautiful, a great white yacht. And she had the right to smile, because she is a golden girl. . . . There's something special about the dolce vita, the dolce *dolce* vita, that makes it easy for golden girls to get on great white yachts."

"Depends who with."

"I told you I don't flatter myself. I've been married for twenty-three years now and I think of myself as a spectator only. But I like to see the young enjoying themselves."

"Oh sure."

"This young man I mentioned earlier, who'll be dancing in St. Tropez tonight." Kavelaris continued smoothly. "His name is Michaeli Tzannos, Alexis' son. He's a quiet boy, a little lost away from Greece. And he has no steady girl friend at the moment. I think you'll make a great impression on Michaeli."

"Bloody nerve."

"I think we understand each other. Perhaps it might amuse you to talk to a millionaire's son. And you could introduce yourself easily enough. You could say you'd met him before, at the Madelons' party in Cap Ferrat. I don't know what happened that night, but young Michaeli got very drunk for the first time in his life."

"But St. Tropez? It's miles away."

"Airplanes, airplanes." Kavelaris opened a small diary. "Palma to Nice. KLM. Here we are . . . KLM keeps back a complimentary trade seat under the name of Clio. C-L-I-O. If you feel like using it."

"And you really think I will?"

"Not at all sure about it, not at all. You underestimate me, Just Claire. I'm flying off to Milano at two o'clock, and I'm just trying to give fate a little nudge." He finished his coffee, felt in his pocket for change. "Maybe your curiosity will take you to St. Tropez, it brought you here. Maybe you'll like Michaeli. He's really very charming. . . . Unlike my own son, Lakis." He frowned at some memory that hurt. "Thank God he's away in the States, racing his sports cars. He won't be joining us on the cruise this year. He's sulking about the marriage I arranged for him with Giulia Marotta . . . a fat girl." His smile returned. "Now you must excuse me. If you want a taxi, there's a stand just around the corner. I hope we meet again." He stood up, bowed politely, and walked away through the tables.

13

She told herself she left Palma to escape Sheldon's storm. But it followed her more than four hundred miles, and the Riviera was no different from Majorca. By the time she reached St. Tropez it was evening, night was piled up black and heavy over the roof tops. Then a sudden rainstorm sowed golden grass knee-high under the street lamps. Water chuckled down narrow alleys, and the thick stucco walls of the town sagged toward the harbor in their center. The townspeople—who seemed to be naked and under thirty-five by law—cowered in doorways, scared of wetting their bathing suits. A sudden flash of lightning was followed by a huge explosion, and the lights of the town went out. The harbor became a fairground, surrounded by dark streets, its generators whirring on, its mast lights swinging like some mad big dipper. On one of the yachts a man and a woman were dancing with champagne glasses. Above their heads a canvas awning caught the downpour and filled, bulging slowly downward like a stranded whale. Then it burst with a gunshot. The dancers vanished under a waterfall, but they danced on, sipping the rain from glasses, their wet clothes plastering them together. The woman's cigarette was now a strange gray square of paper, clinging to her chin.

Claire sheltered in the doorway of a harborside boutique. Behind her in the shop she noticed a woman lighting candles among the glass floats and fishing nets that made up the décor. Claire hesitated, purse in hand. Then she went in through the doorway to the warm woman smell of expensive sweat and scent. And it was only at that moment she decided she was going to meet Michaeli Tzannos in Palmyr. For a millionaire's son she'd need a whore's uniform, judging by the swinging trapeze artists she'd seen in the streets. She felt through the racks of clothes, and by the time the shop lights had come on again, she'd chosen a white leather pants suit, tight hipsters and a tiny jacket. In the mirror she admired her stomach, olive-brown against the thin white belt. The suit cost her a small fortune, and left only a few notes in her purse.

The rain stopped and the evening parade started again. For people wanting to be seen, the circuit was about a mile. From Sènèquier's and the fashionable quayside cafés, up past the fish market and a cobbled street of boutiques. A sharp right turn past the old fishing port, now loud with transistors and people who felt they couldn't sprawl on the pavements of their home towns. Then up the hill past the discothèques, and back down a street with stone arches to the harbor. For some time Claire was part of the bright tapeworm that wound through the town's dark innards. Then she left the procession up on the hill, and went on alone to Palmyr.

The driveway at the top of the hill was crowded with Italian sports cars, parked haphazardly. They seemed to wink and leer at Claire in the flickering light of colored bulbs. Up here the wind was suddenly noticeable, and the music from Palmyr—a rickety Provençal tune—reached her only in disjointed phrases. She went past the wet outside tables and leaned against one of the stone arches that pierced the dance cellar. She watched the man turning the handle of the mechanical piano, stripped to the waist. She watched the shadows of the dancers leap around the stone walls and pillars. The dancers themselves twitched awkwardly, grafting the twentieth-century St. Vitus' dance on to the forgotten village tune. . . . Clever of Kavelaris, she thought, to suggest a place where a girl could come alone.

Michaeli Tzannos she noticed in a corner, and recognized his type. He had heavy blue jowls around lips overripened by the Mediterranean sun. He appeared older than his twenty years, but his eyes weren't old. They blinked in childlike amazement behind his glasses as he tried to force his body to twitch. The green cashmere shirt and tailored Levis couldn't disguise his clumsy peasant frame, his close roots with the tune but not the dance. A young man caught between two worlds. . . . The sheltered upbringing in Greece, where marriage was a contract and not an experiment. And the European world of nipped taste buds, screaming leisure hours. . . . Claire noticed that the women around him weren't women but girls. Their lives had been finished at finishing school, and their bodies were plump and golden with the bloom of the very best. Until they moved, then their bloom was the bloom of sugar, and their bodies merely custom-built. . . . Claire walked across the cellar floor. The leather suit was right. Kavelaris was right. She had no competition.

A tanned young man asked her to dance, and she led him gradually over toward the millionaire's son. Michaeli looked around, was held by the smile of recognition on her face, then by the smooth leather of her thighs as they itched apart in her dance. His eyes became troubled, his tongue flicked nervously around his lips. The music stopped, and Kavelaris' dialogue crossed the gap between them. When the mechanical piano started again it was the easiest thing in the world to lead Michaeli away. The slow rhythm of her body gradually tamed his jerky movements, and she danced away from him slightly, easing his gaze down, enjoying playing the whore. His eyes were locked and unhappy as the technicolor woman who had invaded his private cinema screen closed up on him once again. His face and neck were hot as she looped an arm around him, smiling gently to take the fear from his eyes. They danced close, and she felt disappointed as his body began to tremble. Then he was standing back from her, no longer dancing. The crowd behind him had suddenly frozen into a half-circle. She turned to follow their gaze, didn't need to hear the name.

"Lakis!"

"Lakis Kavelaris!"

"You're in the States. Motor racing. What happened?"

"Crashed in practice." Lakis smiled. "Wrote the car off. So I came back."

Now Claire could see what the elder Kavelaris' eyes had looked like behind his dark glasses—small, mean, and too close together. His son had the same dark Levantine face and nose, the same hard lines around his mouth. But Lakis was taller, and more urgent. Alone among the people around him, he had none of the chubbiness of the rich, and he moved arrogantly. Claire watched his hand leave the girl he'd come in with, and reach out toward her in formal introduction. Nervously she glanced at her watch.

She glanced at it again, no more than twelve minutes later, as she slid into the sand-suède lap of the Maserati Mistral parked outside, and laid her head back on the head rest. The wind whipped the trees and colored bulbs above her, whipped Lakis' coarse hair away from his head as he pressed the starter. The engine screamed all around her. The back of the seat slapped her forward as they roared away. A pain, a physical pain. All she could think of, over and over again, was her mother's silly childhood song: "Oh me oh my, ain't that perfection?"

She was so certain she was going to die out there on

the road. The headlights fingered every blunt instrument they could find to kill her with. Walls, trees, then crooked rocks, as the road spun crazily through the hills. Belly-down through the screaming wind, the car howled, crackled from twin phlegmy exhausts, squealed in sudden sharp pain as it dug its claws into the road. Lakis didn't look at her, his face was calm and cruel in the glow of the dash light. Claire closed her eyes.

Silence, and she looked up to find they were running across soft silvery sand. Pamplonne, and the beach deserted, their wheel tracks spinning out behind were the only signs that they were actually touching the ghostly shore. Lakis parked directly under the moon, and turned to her. Claire shied away from his hard hands. Then suddenly stiffened in horror as she saw the woman smiling over his shoulder, her lips gleaming as she darted forward to strike. Lakis turned too, and grinned as he pulled her around to see: *Ambre Solaire* said the life-size cutout, clattering against the stake that held her to the beach. Claire shivered. Lakis covered her. Still she shivered, finding no warmth in him. There was just the moon. And the steady rhythm of the cardboard woman as she beat against her stake. Claire started to cry.

14

Two nights later the storm had passed. The cafés of St. Tropez were again shadowy villages of chatter. And the quay was crowded with night strollers, weaving in and out of the parked cars. At the end of the quay there was a clear space between two cars—a Maserati Mistral and a Porsche Spider. Guarding this space was a white-uniformed seaman with the word *Pindar* across his shoulders. *Pindar* herself was out in the bay, a blaze of light suspended in the blackness. Then the seaman stiffened, and the night walkers pointed out to the ship as they saw small figures run down the Mediterranean ladder to the speedboat moored below. The movement of people along the quay suddenly ceased, and a crowd gathered around the clear space.

Sitting behind the wheel of the Maserati, Lakis turned to whisper to Claire beside him.

"I can't come," she replied angrily. "You know I can't. Your father got me into all this. I told you."

"My father," his lips curled in a sneer. "Out of his Swiss clinic in June, and randy as a goat all summer. Look, I fight with him over women all the time. And I always win. I've only got to remind him of that sordid little business down in Portofino last year."

"If you think I'm going to cruise with you and him on the same boat you're out of your mind."

"*Pindar's* big," Lakis told her. "My father'll be up on the upper deck with all the other museum pieces. We'll be below. . . . And you must have got the picture by now. He and dear Mama are shit scared of Uncle Alexis. They'll have to behave themselves this trip. There's the business merger they're going to discuss. Kavelaris-Tzannos-Marotta."

"Marotta," Claire repeated tiredly. "There's Marotta's daughter Giulia." She pointed to the pudgy girl who stood next to the seaman on the quay. "You're meant to be marrying her, aren't you? Part of the business merger?"

"That little cow picks her nose."

"And you'll have to watch her all through the cruise. And hold her hand. I mean, how can I go with you?"

"Sometimes," Lakis smiled at her, "my father gets good ideas. He said you should go with Michaeli. So go with Michaeli."

"I'm too much for him," Claire insisted. "I really think he's scared of me."

"More scared of me." Lakis got out of the driving seat, and overcasual for the benefit of the crowd, made his way over to the open Porsche. Michaeli Tzannos was behind the wheel, his face sullen, as was the face of the girl beside him. Lakis bent over the car's cockpit, smiling. He talked to Michaeli in a low pleasant voice, and the crowd murmured the name Tzannos, the name Kavelaris.

In the shadow of the dashboard, Lakis reached out for Michaeli's hand. He grabbed it and held on while he opened the car door very slightly. Then he pushed Michaeli's fingers into the catch and closed the door again. He leaned his full weight against it, and still he smiled. The crowd turned away to the waterfront as *Pindar*'s speedboat swung toward the quay. In the shadows Lakis' forearm was braced against the car door and Michaeli's head was bowed in pain. Suddenly he gasped and nodded. Lakis opened the door. Gently he pulled Michaeli out of the car and led him across to Claire.

The Riva speedboat chuckled by the quay, held by the waiting seaman. He saluted Michaeli and Claire, helped the girl down onto the cushions. They were followed by the plump Giulia. Lakis paused a moment on the quayside and waved back at the girl sitting alone in the Porsche. Her mouth was a thin line, no different from the sullen faces of the crowd around her. Then Lakis dropped lightly into the speedboat.

The motor bellowed, the boat climbed on top of the water, crushing black waves into white. To Claire it was all a dream, as warm spray dashed her face and the fairy-tale castle that was *Pindar* rose from its own reflection to greet her. The speedboat bumped against the Mediterranean ladder and she was climbing up past yellow portholes in a great white wall. She arrived on a vast deck, pale in the moonlight. An officer saluted her, then talked in low Greek to Michaeli behind her. She went over and leaned on the rail.

The moon, which had been hidden from sight in St. Tropez, now shone low over the coast, shone from them alone, frosting the sea in its path. Music filled the great deck, soft muted trumpets, coming from nowhere. Not a tremor disturbed the awning above, shading them from the night dew. Not a tremor on the faces of the two stewards, standing one on each side of a silver punch bowl. Claire felt for a cigarette, and one of them moved. His starched white arm ended in a flame. He lit her cigarette, bowed, and stood at attention once again.

Lakis grinned at her, led her over to the punch bowl. The Venetian goblet he gave her was heavy with strawberries. Not floating, she found as she raised the glass, because she was sipping pure moonlight. Then she was dancing with Lakis, and Michaeli and Giulia were dancing nearby. It wasn't real. Claire was somewhere high up, watching the two small couples on the huge silver deck, and the white-coated statues around them. The lights of the coast weren't real either, just accessories to the silver deck.

Lakis stiffened suddenly, then pushed her toward Michaeli. Their hands fell to their sides and they turned toward the white-haired man coming out on deck. Alexis Tzannos was smaller than she'd imagined. His calm face and gentle mane of hair belying the harshness of his newspaper pictures.

"Giulia . . . Lakis. . . ." He nodded at them, then turned his attention to Claire. "And who is this young lady, Michaeli? I don't believe we've met."

"Claire," Michaeli told his father.

Alexis smiled at her. "Are you French?" he asked.

"English."

He nodded. His gaze was frank and approving. Then he turned back to Michaeli. "I see you've been idling your time away profitably while we've been hard at work. How was the university?"

"The same."

"Did they teach you anything this year?"

"I did quite well in the exams."

"I saw." Alexis nodded. "And I was very pleased." He turned back to include the others. "I'm sorry the rest of us aren't out here to dance with you. We find the evening air a little chilly."

He produced four embossed cards from his pocket, handed one to each of them. "I look forward to seeing you all on the fourteenth of August." His smile singled out Claire. "At Piraeus. We'll be away for a month. I hope you can spare us all that time."

Claire nodded.

15

A dead British war hero sat smoking a cigarette on the bridge of an ex-MTB. The deck was rock-steady beneath his feet. The ship had been on the boatyard cradle for two weeks now, but still Sheldon couldn't get used to the idea of being on dry land. Nor could he get used to the changes all around him. The whole ship had been stripped of its gray paint, red-leaded, and then painted in blue-and-white dazzle stripes. The bridge where he was standing had been brought forward over the chartroom roof, and the chartroom itself was smaller and squarer. The twin machine-gun turrets on either side had been removed, and now, as Sheldon watched, Holve's yardmen bolted the second of two long-range fuel tanks to the deck.

And the captain himself had changed. Dressed in a white naval uniform and cap without insignia, he looked younger and firmer. His mustache was combed, and his eyes were steady as he looked down past the yardmen and the work lights to the shadowy floor of the boathouse far below. The huge dark shed echoed to the ring of hammers and the burr of saws. Outside it was morning, the sun was climbing over the brown hills of Sardinia, and the cicadas beginning their daily chorus. But here inside the locked doors it had been night for two weeks. Men had been working around the clock to Sheldon's orders—working well—and he should have been happy. But he wasn't. There was still one change to go before *Jabberwocky* became a gunboat. Sandy was waiting to leave, sitting in his cabin below. Sheldon stubbed out his cigarette, nerved himself to go down and say good-by to her.

Slowly he went down the ladder. What had once been the wardroom was now a narrow gray corridor with doors on either side. He opened one of them, and the smell of new paint hit him. The small cabin was littered with charts, papers, and lists. In one corner was a small bunk, and on it, huddled defensively against the harsh gray walls, was Sandy. Her hair was cut short, and she was dressed in a man's shirt and tie, man's gray suit and white shoes. She toyed nervously with the panama hat in her hands.

"I'm afraid it's time," Sheldon said uneasily. "Turton will be here at midday."

She didn't answer.

"Will you be there to meet me at Selini in September?" he asked. "When this is all over?"

She shrugged.

"If it's the man's clothes?" Sheldon had to break the silence. "The phony passport? . . ."

"That's the only sensible part of the whole damn thing," she said. "I'll get through all right. It's all this." She pointed at the new-painted cabin around her. "The work you've done on the ship. The new superstructure, the deck tanks. They all cost a hell of a lot of money. And that was the money Pierre cabled you when he heard about the survey. . . . Don't you see? You could have stopped there. The money could have got us a small house somewhere. We could have lived quietly for a while."

"No more than a couple of months. And it would have been the same old business," he told her. "I mean, this is going to be real money, like winning the football pools. We won't have to worry for the rest of our lives."

"But you've never worried." She got up angrily. "You're a drinking man, you've never had any money. It doesn't mean anything to you. You just put everything down to bad luck."

"This'll be good luck," Sheldon said quickly. "It's going to work."

"Alec, it's just plain crazy." She tried to get through to him for the last time. "You've done crazy things in the past, criminal things, even. But afterward they were funny. . . . And I helped you because I felt maybe we were owed some of the things we lost in the war."

"We still are, dammit." Sheldon sorted absently through the papers on his table. "I know it all sounds crazy, but it's working. We're well under budget, and we've damn near found a crew. . . . You see, as a Naval Operation it's a piece of cake. Surprise, everything on our . . ." He broke off suddenly. She was close behind him, taking her cheap suitcase with her to the door.

It only needed an Italian suit and a panama hat to change Sandy into a man. She looked up at him, and her face was bewildered, stripped of its reasons. A moment longer she waited, but he couldn't bring himself to touch her thin arm in the man's jacket. Then he was too late. She went quietly away through the shadows.

Sheldon was ashamed to admit it, but he felt easier after she'd gone. He hummed softly to himself as he stood on the foredeck, watching the yardmen tighten the last bolts of the large deck tank. Then the hammering was drowned by the huge grating noise of the boathouse door. A shaft of sunlight split the darkness in two as Sheldon went to the rail.

"Captain?" A man looked up at him from the doorway. "There's an Englishman here to see you."

"Thank you." Sheldon climbed down the ladder on the shipyard cradle and made his way through the piles of timber and damp shavings to the door.

Outside in the sunlight, a small pale man was waiting by the wire fence. He stiffened, raised his hand in an automatic salute as the captain approached.

"Turton." Sheldon returned the salute, glad that twenty-five years hadn't taken the habit of naval discipline away from the Radar Rating. Nor had they changed him. Perhaps he was smaller, his shoulders more rounded, perhaps the veins that quivered on either side of his domed forehead were more pronounced. Turton stood nervously to attention, his hands twisting his trouser seams. Large hands, tools, that had to be doing something. Turton was all hands, his body merely following them to the next job. "Good to see you. Were you surprised to get my cable?"

"I was more surprised when somebody showed me that bit in the *Telegraph*, Sir." Turton's face was expressionless, his eyes staring over Sheldon's shoulder. "You couldn't die that way."

"What way?"

"At sea, in a bit of a wind. I remember when we were blown eighty miles west of Cyprus. We had the chart table, everything, over the side for sea anchors."

Sheldon nodded. "But you understood my cable?"

"Orders, Sir. Operational orders. Going back to war."

"They don't call it war nowadays, don't hand out any medals. The wrong side of the fence. That bother you?"

Turton didn't answer.

"Understand," Sheldon pointed behind him. "There's a ship in that boathouse back there, and she's fitted out for a certain job. Once you go in through that door, you stay in. I have to be sure."

"I got the message," Turton said. "And I'm here, reporting for duty."

"There's no one . . . who wants to know where you are?"

"I did my time, came out five weeks ago. You know that, Sir."

"Not what I meant." Sheldon said curtly. "There's no one employing you, who might want to keep in touch?"

"With my record?" Turton laughed. A shovel rattling into a pile of coke. "Sort of job I get offered nowadays, like there's this flat in Maida Vale where the owner's away in the Canaries for three months. That sort of employer doesn't keep in touch."

"No ties?" Sheldon insisted. "Family ties, I mean?"

"She left," Turton said slowly. "Last time I went inside. I don't blame her or anything."

"I'm sorry."

"You needn't be. She's grateful to you, and so am I. . . . The money you sent. The Christmas cards."

"Wish I could've kept it up, really do. Times have been bad."

"Bad," Turton repeated.

Sheldon clenched his hands behind his back, moved in until he was looking down at Turton's pale, glistening forehead. "This job is big, very big. If we're caught they'll put us away for a long time. There'll be no going back to England for a few years."

Turton's small white body seemed to shrink in the sunlight. Through the wire fence, the spiky Mediterranean undergrowth shrilled at his alien figure.

"Well?"

The man's mouth moved, but the words it wanted to frame wouldn't fit the situation.

"Go ahead."

"How much money, Sir? That's all I need to know."

"Fifty thousand pounds in it for you. Small used notes." Immediately Sheldon saw it was too much. Turton became wary, and the spell of the officer's uniform was broken. The captain rose on the balls of his feet, his voice was louder. "This is a Naval Operation, Turton. Striking force is one MTB. Object, to disable and take command of another ship."

The Radar Rating stiffened once again to attention, but he didn't speak.

Sheldon spoke more gently. "Peacetime, isn't it, Turton? We can't go around killing people nowadays."

"That's right, Captain."

"There'll be no killing. I can promise you that, quite categorically. Not for any sentimental reasons, we've both killed in the past, just that we know it's always the wrong people who get killed. Any more questions?"

"No, Sir."

"Right." Sheldon knew he'd won. He looked at Turton's crumpled suit, his small kit bag, and saw that the man had been waiting for officers to speak all his life. Naval officers, police inspectors, magistrates, anyone with the right tone of authority. "There's only one way to carry out this operation. The Navy way. Once you come aboard, you're back in the Navy, understood?"

"Aye aye, Sir." Turton's face was serious. "I tried to join up again. They wouldn't have me."

"This way." Sheldon led him along the wire fence to the boathouse. The corrugated-iron door creaked back on its runners. "What d'you make of that?" The captain pointed up to the huge dazzle-painted hull that towered above them on its cradle.

"PT boat." Turton's eyes blinked at the darkness. "American PT boat. Where did you get hold of her?"

"Look again."

"But she's wood-planked. And below the waterline she's wrong. . . . The chine." Turton looked along the hull in surprise. "And it's a dummy bow. You've filled in the torpedo grooves."

"You won't see the difference once she's in the water."

"It's a Dog Boat! It's the old 859, by Christ!"

"It is."

"Why's she done up like a Yankee?"

"The old 859 is on the bottom. You read the papers," Sheldon told him. "We had to choose a disguise that worked, and this was the obvious one. There are plenty of ex-American PT boats in the Med. The Greek Navy bought a lot after the war, so did the Italians."

Turton crossed to the shadow of the hull, ran his hands lovingly along the diagonal planks.

"There's work to do." Sheldon started up the ladder.

On deck, Turton stood in the glare of the work lights and looked at the new long superstructure behind the bridge. He went toward it and whistled in surprise as he saw a row of flush-fitting doors behind the blue-and-white dazzle paint. He opened one of the doors and found a small cell, no more than four feet wide, six feet deep. "This whole thing's a cell block, Skipper. You running a slaver?"

Sheldon frowned, motioned him on up to the bridge.

But Turton didn't notice. His large hands fussed down to the bolts that secured the superstructure to the deck. "And why's it only bolted on?"

"Turton!" Sheldon glared down at him. "We sail tomorrow night. The operation's planned for five weeks' time. And there's a hell of a lot to do. . . . What you do is carry out orders."

"Captain." Turton nodded.

"Right, through here." Sheldon led the way down the bridge ladder. "We've fitted you out with a radar room."

"Beautiful." Turton's hands itched as he passed the captain. He stroked the control panel. "Beautiful job. With a range of about eighty miles."

"You're familiar with the type?"

"Yes."

"Well, your first job is to get the set operational. The scanner's been fitted, but there's some wiring to do."

"I'll have this baby singing in twenty-four hours," Turton crooned happily. "It'll be a real pleasure after the junk I've been working with."

"Thirty-six hours, maximum," Sheldon said. "This radar'll be our only defensive weapon at sea. We've got to keep clear of all other shipping." He signaled Turton to follow him through to the next gray-painted compartment, the chartroom. "Your second job is more difficult. It concerns the Aegean." The captain found a chart on the littered table, and unrolled it. "We're basing ourselves down here, in a cave you may remember."

"You mean the one that Greek guy took us to? After that brawl at Leros?" Turton's eyes widened in surprise.

"Spanakis."

"That was a hell of a long time ago."

"It was," Sheldon agreed. "Now, as you can see, the cave's in the eastern Cyclades, over two hundred and fifty miles from Piraeus. And there's a certain yacht leaving Piraeus in three weeks' time that we're interested in." He traced a curving line on the chart. "If she runs true to form, she'll be cruising up around here—Skyros, Limnos, and Lesbos in the first week. Then coming slowly down through the Dodecanese toward us in the second, to be down within striking distance at the end of August. . . . But you see we can't be sure of her course. We have to track her all the way, can't lose her. . . . Can it be done?"

"Radar's no good. Out of range." Turton looked at the chart thoughtfully. "Except maybe if you lessened the distance, ran some patrols out toward her."

"We can't do that. Number one, petrol." Sheldon

counted on his fingers. "Number two, risk of being spotted. Number three, radar might give us the wrong ship. There are plenty of ships her size in those waters, island boats, tourist cruises, and so on. We've got to be certain."

"So it'll have to be radio. DF." Turton said.

"Fair enough. Can you set up a tracking station in the time? Three weeks?"

"Two stations. We'd need two receivers to get a fix." Turton frowned slightly. "It could be done, always providing I got hold of the gear I wanted."

"Anything you need," Sheldon said. "We've got the biggest black market in the Med working for us."

"And there'd have to be somebody operating the second receiver."

"That's no problem." Sheldon returned to the chart. "Now once you're set up, are you sure you can track the ship we want? It seems a hell of a distance."

"Nothing to it, as long as she transmits regularly."

"Sends out more messages than the *Titanic*." Sheldon reached for a small tape recorder, switched it on. There came the metallic raindrops of a high-speed signal, two-tone. "We got this when she came around from St. Tropez."

"FSK" Again Turton was surprised. "That means Telex."

"Does that make it more difficult?"

"Easier. Much, much easier," Turton said. "There aren't going to be any other boats with Telex up in that part of the world. Precious few stations neither. We could get a fix with two bent pins." He wheeled around suddenly as footsteps came down the ladder behind Sheldon.

Barney came into the radar room. He looked tired, dirty, and he left a grease mark on the bulkhead as he leaned against it. Barney hadn't seen Turton since the war, and he nodded now as though they'd last spoken at lunch time. Then he turned to Sheldon. "They're bringing the petrol around tomorrow morning. The deck tanks'll give us fifteen hundred gallons extra. More than enough to pick up Mitch and get to the cave without refueling."

"Thank you, Chief. What time do they . . . ?"

"Captain," Turton cut across him worriedly. His pale face sweated in the heat, and his eyes darted around for a way of escape. "You said a yacht."

"What's that, Turton?"

"You said this ship we were after was a yacht." Turton spoke quickly. "There aren't many yachts in the world equipped with Telex."

"I know that."

"Well, I don't know about planning an operation, Captain. I leave all that to you."

"Quite right." Sheldon tried to slow him down.

"What I do know about is planning a job. I never got nicked for half the jobs I pulled. Why? Because I always kept them small."

"So?"

Turton pointed out through the ship's side. "All those people out there. It takes quite a few to fit out a boat like this."

"The man who runs this yard is called Holve," Sheldon told him patiently. "Not many people know his name. He doesn't know anyone's name at all. He pays his men a lot of money, and he gets what he pays for."

"That may be."

"Anything else, Turton?" Sheldon asked dangerously.

"Mitch," the man said.

"What about Mitch?"

"He's not reliable. Never was. His drinking and that."

"Mitch never let me down," Sheldon said. "And he's a damn fine gunner."

"*Gunner?*"

"We're mounting a Bofors gun on the foredeck." Barney grinned crookedly. "Big bang."

16

There was the soft blue glow of the hooded compass. The velvet night unbroken ahead, split by their straight white wake astern. And the faint flicker of summer lightning behind the clouds on the horizon, like a burglar's torch through curtains on the far side of a deserted ballroom. The MTB's engines, which had settled to a steady roar when they'd left Holve's Yard, were now almost unnoticeable nine hours later. The sea was calm, creaking gently apart around the hull, and Sheldon felt content. The ship was a taut compact weapon beneath his hands, blacked out, safe from enemy eyes. She was moving slowly to conserve fuel, but she was moving steadily eastward across the Mediterranean.

He turned toward the faint green light that came from the radar room below. Turton, he knew, was hunched in front of the small screen, following the finger of light that was probing the darkness for eighty miles around. Different in the old days, Sheldon thought, the temperamental little boxes that could reach no farther than fifteen miles around the ship, and then were useless anywhere near mountains or high ground. . . . But they weren't to know that on the trip out from England. It was the first time some of them had seen a radar aerial, and it was their protection. Sheldon had never known a wardroom so relaxed. Faces came back to him, and the sudden strange glimpses of private lives that had come out in the cold night watches. Traill telling about the whore he'd picked up in Gibraltar. She'd shown him her British passport, and still he hadn't been able to do it. . . .

"Skipper." Turton was suddenly at his elbow. "Three miles away now. We're dead on course."

Then Sheldon got the first smell of land. The sweet scent of pines and damp earth. Once again he got the pleasure of a landfall after a sea voyage that scoured his nostrils, cleared his brain. Suddenly his pleasure vanished as he remembered the land was Dunari. He handed the wheel to Turton. "Keep her there."

He went down the ladder and saw Barney was already dressed in commando kit, blacking his face and hands from a tin. Sheldon crossed to his cabin and closed the door. He hoped Barney wouldn't come in and see the effort it cost him to get thick woolen socks over his shoes. Then he pulled on a long blue sweater and a balaclava. He was about to join Barney at the blacking tin, when he remembered his gun. He got the .38 service revolver from a locker, and loaded it.

Back on the bridge, he waited for the hiss of waves on rocks before he cut the motors. Through night glasses, he could see the surf, luminous under a moonless sky. Dunari was a small promontory, less than a mile long. It was thickly wooded with tall bent pine trees, whose swaying branches closed around the lights of a villa. Below the house, a path led down to a tiny harbor where a cabin cruiser was moored. Nothing could be more peaceful. Sheldon felt far from peaceful as he stared long and hard at the cruiser, finding no light, no sign of life aboard her. He took a deep breath to calm himself, unlooped the glasses from his neck, and left them with Turton on the bridge. Then he walked quickly aft to join Barney in the rubber dinghy.

He and Barney each took a paddle, and the dinghy flapped over waves that were suddenly much larger. Then the surf was near and loud, and they were lurching into breakers. Gravel crunched under their feet as they beached the dinghy, hid it among rocks. Keeping to the shadows, Sheldon led the way around to the harbor, and pulled his revolver from his belt. The two of them waited in the undergrowth by the path, staring at the cabin cruiser. then Sheldon nodded, and Barney darted away toward the boat. His dark figure showed once, briefly, as he dropped into the cockpit. There was a long silence before he returned, his smile visible only in his white teeth and eyes. He held out two rotor arms for Sheldon to see, and threw them away into the bushes. The captain led the way up the path toward the house.

Pine needles crunched softly beneath their feet as they climbed the slight rise. The wind swayed the branches overhead, brought sudden bursts of clashing music from the villa above. Music that grew louder, built to a weird climax as they pushed their way through a row of young cypresses to reach the corner of the building, ablaze with light. They paused in amazement. Wild, anguished shadows, human only in their shape, danced across thin window blinds. There was a roll of thunder, rain water chuckled in the gutters. Sheldon looked up and saw the night was still clear and starry bright. He heard a sudden scream, glass smashing as a shrub hurtled out through a window to land in the spiky shadows of oleanders. Through the torn blind, raindrops spilled out into the clear night. The storm was only in the room, the steady drumming of rain, the moaning wind coming from inside. The shadows on the blind slowed to a dull fumbling dance, an endless chain of reeling figures.

Sheldon shivered. Turning, he led the way across spongy grass to the back of the building. The music got fainter, the shadows deeper as they passed unlit windows. Suddenly the captain stopped, pointed to a column of smoke rising from a chimney. "Kitchen," he said. "He must be there."

They broke in through a window, crossed a dark room. Sheldon eased open a door to a narrow hallway, backed suddenly as footsteps approached. His arm fell to his side, the door stayed open, as he caught sight of the figure lurching up the hallway. Moaning horribly as he came, naked apart from a gory sheepskin around his shoulders, the man staggered past them with his pain. The stench of the recently slaughtered animal filled the passage behind him. Trembling, Sheldon pressed the cool steel of the revolver against his forehead. He saw pictures on the walls around him, pictures of minute anatomical detail living and dissected. Then he heard a low laugh from behind him, turned to see Barney sitting on a broad metal chair, fitting himself into wrist straps, a metal skullcap.

It was a little while before the captain could move. And when he moved, it was away from the man-made storm at the far end of the passage. Silent no longer, but sick, he hurled open doors as he came to them. The kitchen he found halfway down a second passage. Pots bubbled on a huge range, vegetables and a kitchen knife lay abandoned on a long scrubbed table. Then he found Mitch. The cook was lying in a pool of liquor and vomit under the table. His face was hardly recognizable, swollen into a flaccid mask, a dull putty color. Barney ripped off the man's stained T-shirt, and slung him over his shoulder. They left by the first door they could find.

Past the lawn, the oleander, the cypresses they ran, not stopping until they reached the path under the pine trees. Gasping for breath, Barney slid Mitch's limp body to the ground, and leaned up against a tree trunk. He felt something soft brush across his face. A man's white foot. "Jesus!" he gasped.

"Yes?" The voice came from above.

They whipped around. There on the tree, tied to a crossbar on the trunk, was a man. His body inert, his weight supported by lashed wrists and a small platform under one heel. He looked down at them calmly, proudly.

Sheldon raised his gun.

"Not today," the man said. "Friday."

The revolver fell to Sheldon's side. "Let's get out of here!" he shouted.

With Mitch slung between them, they reached the shore and the dinghy. The cook made no sound as they paddled out to the MTB, didn't stir as they swung him up on deck, then made for the open sea. He only jerked awake as the third bucket of sea water slapped his body. He saw Sheldon, and got to his feet in fear. Running to the gun mount on the foredeck, he groped wildly for the Bofors that wasn't there. "I wasn't asleep, Skipper," he whispered. "Wasn't asleep on duty."

"You've been asleep for over twenty years," Sheldon said softly.

17

Again the soft blue glow from the hooded compass. But now it paled insignificantly beneath the brilliant canopy of stars that seemed to stretch even below the horizon. Diamonds, polished by the soft wind that ruffled the inky waters of the Aegean. Three days and nights at sea had scoured the smell of Dunari from Sheldon's nose. The only reminder of the island was Mitch, strapped to his bunk below, whimpering at the four-hourly infusions of soup, bread, and ever-more-watered wine. The nightmare had been carried away by more than seven hundred sea miles, empty, blinding days and gentle nights that had ushered them southeast toward the islands of Greece.

Sheldon had a strange feeling he was returning home. He'd always thought of the Aegean as his corner of the world—a sanctuary where the floor, the walls, and even the ceiling closed in on him. Mountains rising out of hard blue water. The sky, glazed by the sun into a brittle shell by day, trellised by stars into a peaceful cage by night. There had been very bad times, the shrieking Stuka attacks at dawn and dusk. There had been gray-black days, terrible days, in the deep-water channels between the islands. But the captain remembered only the calm days, threading his way through sea, mountains, and sky, as though walking through familiar corridors of some vast childhood home.

He looked again at the distant mountains of Crete on the horizon, ghostly blue as they shouldered their way out of the dark sea. He remembered approaching them in the war, the lights and cigarettes on the beach, a fairground just waiting for the E-Boat patrol. The usual bloody chaos onshore, then the Cretan *andartes* coming out in the dinghy—barefoot—custom demanded they leave their boots behind. . . . Now Sheldon looked out at the dark water between him and the mountains, searching for the fishing fleet, the caïque Turton had told him was twelve miles nearer than the rest. There were no lights ahead, and the captain didn't expect any. It wasn't like Spanakis to bother with navigation lights in war or peacetime.

"Only half a mile away now, Skipper. See anything?" Turton's voice came up from the radar room.

"Not yet," Sheldon squared his cap. He was dressed in tropical whites to give the lie they were a Greek naval vessel on patrol. There were also fake numbers on the ship's side, and Sheldon hoped they were the right ones. Suddenly he saw the bowl of light dancing on the water ahead, growing bigger. Through glasses he watched the caïque's high bow swing round to reveal working lights on the afterdeck. "Turton?" he called.

The man clattered up onto the bridge, also dressed in whites.

"Take over, would you?" Sheldon took off his cap, handed it to the Rating. "Spanakis'd spot me a mile away." He checked that the Greek flag was flying free from the yardarm, plainly visible. Then he ducked into the shadows, trained his glasses on the fishing boat. He could see the twin otter boards hanging from their davits, the net being winched home in short bursts of the panting motor. "Take her in slowly alongside. It's quite safe, they've got their trawl aboard."

As they got nearer, he saw the fishermen turn from the trawl and point out toward them. Spanakis' short figure appeared from the work house, hailed them in Greek.

"It's working," Sheldon said softly. "Keep going."

Two naked bulbs swung above the caïque's curved deck, cast weirdly moving shadows on the men's faces. They left their oozing net on the hatch cover, and leaned against the bulwark, staring out at the naval boat. A pall of thick blue smoke hung over them, coming from the tiny galley shaped like a sentry box. Again Spanakis hailed them in Greek.

"Stop engines," Sheldon whispered. "Bring her around."

There was sudden silence as the two boats drifted toward each other. Sheldon heard the slap of water as the hulls came together, then the roar of the pressure stove from the fishing boat's galley. Spanakis stood with his head cocked in surprise, one hand shielding his eyes as he stared out into the darkness.

"Spanakis," Sheldon called softly, standing up into the light.

"*Oh Anglos eenay*," Spanakis said in surprise. "*Kapitane . . . Kapitane Shel-don!*" The laugh of approval rattled deep in his throat. He removed his cigarette holder, spat over the side. Then he grabbed one of the MTB's stanchions and held the two boats together. "*Ella. . . .* Come on board."

Sheldon crossed the scarred bulwark to the slippery deck, littered with flapping fish, boxes, and weed. Suddenly he was in Greece. The smell of burning oil, *marides*, and sharp tobacco. Then the acrid whiff of garlic and diesel oil as Spanakis pulled him close. The rasp of the Greek's stubbled chin, the brush of his mustache, and the trawler skipper was holding him at arm's length, searching for cracks in the Shel-don he remembered. The captain stared back in the light of the swinging bulbs. Twenty years, a hundred years, could not change a whisker of the Cretan fisherman. His fine black hair, thinning at the crown. His tanned cracked face, old with work and sweat, young with a child's brown eyes, and the perfect teeth under the thick mustache. The sweater and trousers looked as though they'd been slept in every night since the war, they fitted Spanakis' paunchy body like a worn glove.

"I think it is the Greek Navy boat coming around from Suda Bay, going to Agia Galini." The phlegm crackled in his throat as he laughed again. "Then I see your strange numbers. Where is your boat? Eight-five-nine?"

Sheldon pointed to the MTB.

Spanakis' eyes widened in astonishment. "That is eight-five-nine?"

"With a few things done to her."

"*Oraio prarma*," Spanakis chuckled. "*Oh Gallos*, Pierre, tell me to expect you tonight. But in a British Navy boat." He shrugged. "Come. We must talk."

"What about the ship?" Sheldon pointed at the MTB.

"If you trick me, you trick everybody," Spanakis replied. "You have the radar? You can tell if the real Navy boat come."

Sheldon called across to Turton to lay off a little way in the darkness, then he followed Spanakis around to the narrow tilting stern. The Greek opened a tiny door behind the wheelhouse, led the way down to a cabin no larger than a cupboard. He motioned Sheldon to sit on the unmade bunk, and got a bottle of clear liquid from a locker. Grinning, he filled two glasses to the brim, and handed one to the captain.

Sheldon, nervous at the sight of liquor, felt for his cigarettes.

Spanakis frowned angrily, put down the glasses. "*Oichi, apo 'tho.*" He offered a crumpled packet of Papastratos Fives, and made Sheldon put his own cigarettes away. He took a light from the captain, then again offered the glass of clear liquor. "*Raki. . . .*" His Cretan accent made the word ratchi. "You like it too much during the war. . . . *Ee sigia. Ya mas.*" He clinked Sheldon's glass, and downed his drink at a gulp.

"*Ee sigia.*" Sheldon's hands trembled as he wet his lips with the fiery liquor. The strong grape alcohol coursed around his mouth, and his stomach heaved. Still trembling, he put the glass down.

Spanakis eyed him curiously. "You have a *provlima,* a problem, with the drink?"

Sheldon nodded.

"Is better not to take." Disappointed, Spanakis refilled his own glass.

A young galley boy, his face rimed with grease, his forelock singed short from bending over a pressure stove, came in with a plate of spitting gold *marides.* Sheldon took one of the small fish gratefully, crunched it between his teeth. He'd forgotten how good fresh-caught *marides* were. The tang of the sea and fresh oil, the indefinable sharp taste of night. "Delicious," he said.

"Good, yes, but no enough." Spanakis sent the galley boy away for more. "No enough in the sea today. One night's fishing. Maybe five, maybe six boxes. That's all."

"Times are bad?" Sheldon asked.

"Bad for the *marides.*" Spanakis winked "But good for the other fishes. The fishes that come already in boxes, from Alessandria, Taranto."

"Pierre told me," Sheldon said. "He told me you would help."

"I hear something from Pierre. So I come to meet you." Spanakis suddenly became serious. "He say something about the cave."

Sheldon nodded. "Did he say anything else? Why we want to use it?"

"A little." Spanakis' face was wary.

"The cave's still as it was then?" Sheldon asked. "Nobody knows about it?"

"Only I," the Greek told him. "And I use it, for my boxes from Alessandria, And for petrol, gas and oil, like in the war."

Sheldon saw why he was so reluctant. "You have other places?" he asked.

"Of course. But the cave is big. In there I keep my big boxes. Nylon shirts? . . . Crazy, you think, to carry nylon shirts. But they are a little extra."

"But you have other places?" Sheldon insisted. "You could keep the boxes somewhere else? I'll only want to use the cave for a month at the most."

"If you use it," Spanakis was hurt, "I cannot put my boxes back there. It's true, isn't it?"

"Yes," Sheldon admitted. "But I'll pay you for the boxes, and a lot more beside. Pierre told you there was a lot of money involved?"

"He send me many messages in the past few weeks. He ask me to find you all the things you need for your little war. And this I have done. . . ." He paused, not looking at Sheldon. "But I get one more message from Pierre. He say it is my my choice only, if I give you the cave or no. He say your plan is maybe very good. He say I like your plan maybe very much. . . . So you tell me about it. Then I give you my answer."

Slowly, Sheldon went over the operation, and his voice got more and more nervous. He told himself it was the strange motion of the caïque, that reared up on every seventh wave and slammed the locker door behind the Greek. He told himself it was the smell of *marides*, cigarette smoke, unwashed bodies. The steering cables that rattled through the bulkhead above his head. The monotonous procession of engine, winch, and silence, that marked every sweep.

But as he talked, he knew the real reason for his unease, remembering what he'd known about Spanakis in the past. The Cretan who'd worked in British merchant ships for seven years, who'd captained one of his father's coastal freighters at the age of twenty-four. Then the entire fleet sunk, and the father killed by the Germans in the war. And Spanakis the son, who'd waged a one-man war against the Germans long before Sheldon's MTB had come on the scene. Spanakis, whose love for his country had been a wet brown blade. . . . And as Sheldon got to the point of Operation Bandersnatch, he realized he was asking this man to help him kidnap two of his compatriots.

At the mention of Tzannos and Kavelaris, Spanakis stiffened. Then his eyes shone like a delighted child's. Sheldon got to the ransom amount, and the Greek roared with laughter, slammed his glass down on the locker top. "*Endax.* . . ." He said. "Okay. The plan is good. *Extra prima.* And I work with you, Captain. I let you have the cave." He gathered up his reefer jacket and led the way out on deck.

Amazed, Sheldon leaned against the low bulwarks and felt the sea piling past. Spanakis had gone to talk to the man in the wheelhouse, his face lit by the green glow of the instruments as he slipped another cigarette in his holder. Sheldon wondered why he'd never thought about the Greek's nationality before tonight, and wondered why he'd said he'd work with him. He gave it up and turned to watch the galley boy sitting on the trawl winches, a hand on each of the two cables to feel if they snagged an obstruction far below. The other fishermen were hunched on the hatch cover, tiredly sorting fish into boxes. . . . Three boxes. The fishing was bad, as Spanakis had said.

Suddenly the Cretan skipper shouted from the wheelhouse. The boy jumped off the winches, grabbed up a scarred stick, and handed another to one of the men. The beat of the engine slowed, was drowned abruptly by the whining of the winch. The cables snickered wetly as they were fed on to their drums by the man and boy with the sticks. The caïque swung around, hissing against the dark waves, and a deafening thud from astern told Sheldon the otter boards had come up from the water to smack against their davits. There was a tense silence as the ship drifted, rolling sluggishly. Then the tail rope of the trawl was passed under the cables to the capstan. Brief bursts of the motor winched the net too easily on to the foredeck. The fishermen paused unhappily before attacking the quivering bag. Their tired eyes told them there was no more than half a boxful of *marides* inside.

"And you are surprised I am happy to take the money from these millionaires?" Sheldon turned to see Spanakis by his side. "I see your face as you tell me the plan. You think Spanakis will not harm his countrymen?"

Sheldon nodded.

"Countrymen, *pau!*" The Greek spat over the side. "They live in Italy, they keep their money in Switzerland. They visit Greece just one time a year, and they throw ten-drachma pieces from their shiny cars." He was almost ashamed as he continued. "Shel-don, my country is the third biggest maritime nation of the world, and we built no ships here until three years ago. And then just little ships, in a little yard at Skaramanga. . . . Tzannos and Kavelaris, they buy their ships from Japan. And why? Because they are Greek, and they do not want to throw money away on other Greeks." He paused for breath.

"Poor country, this is a poor country. We are told it all the time." He clutched Sheldon's arm. "We have no much industry—three, maybe four factory, and then they are German, or Dutch, or American. So the money leave the country, and the young people leave the country. There is no work for them here." He pointed at the weed in the open trawl bag. "I tell you Shel-don, I do more good for my country with my little boxes than these millionaires. Young people, they stay with me. They have a good suit for Sunday, they marry, they have families . . . here . . . they don't go to Germany. . . . That is why I help you get these millionaires' money." His fingers fanned delicately in the Greek gesture of stealing. "And what money."

"Right." Sheldon stretched stiffly. "When do we start?"

"Pierre, he give me definite instructions," Spanakis told him. "You are to take your MTB along the northwest coast of Crete, and hide it in a small bay. You have the camouflage nets?"

"Yes." Sheldon was bewildered. "But why near here? Where it's risky?"

"Because Pierre want you to come with me to pick up the equipment, and check it is all there."

"Is that really necessary?"

"Pierre say it is. And he is my boss." Spanakis led Sheldon toward the green glow of the wheelhouse, and the grimy chart spread out in front of the wheel. "He say you are to hide your ship here," he pointed. "And then, when I finish the night's fishing, I pick you up and take you into Canea with the other trawlers. Pierre say that everything must go on as normal. There must be no suspicion."

"And all the equipment's waiting for us in Canea?" Sheldon asked. "You managed everything? Radio equipment, automatic rifles, ammunition, Bofors gun?"

"Everything is waiting in a large truck, outside the town."

"And the men I asked for? Roche and Laborde? And the other two?"

"They are waiting also, ready to join the Navy."

Sheldon nodded, then asked suddenly: "Where the hell d'you find a Bofors gun?"

Spanakis stroked his mustache, grinned. "Difficult," he said. "But no impossible."

18

The line of caïques rocked gently against the quay of the inner harbor at Canea. Below faded blue topsides, their brilliant red hulls cast dazzling reflections down on the water. Trawls hung from mastheads, drying in the sun. Throughout the morning the nets had sprawled on the hot cobbles of the quay, fishermen straddling them, their fingers darting between the tears in the mesh and the spindles of twine in their hair. Now the men had returned to their boats, faces surly with fatigue. A pot of thick stew, made from unsalable fish, was placed on each hatch cover, together with loaves of bread and wicker bottles of wine. The men ate in silence, throwing scraps overboard to the waiting shoals of tiny harbor fish.

Aboard Spanakis' boat, hidden under a canvas awning, Sheldon watched the crew shovel food in their mouths with the weary haste of the poor. He himself hadn't touched the bowl of soup at his side. It wasn't hunger eating into him, but a growing sense of frustration at the slowness of the Greeks all around. Things had moved very slowly since he'd met Spanakis out at sea. He'd known they would, and he'd managed to keep himself in check. But he'd been on the caïque now for thirty-two hours, and he cursed Pierre who'd insisted he check the arrangements in Canea. This was the second day he'd spent staring at the Cretan fishing port, not to mention a night out at sea trawling. And during that time nothing —absolutely nothing—had happened.

It was now nearly midday, Thursday, August 10— four days before *Pindar* sailed. The MTB couldn't possibly get to the cave before dawn tomorrow at the earliest. Worse, the truckload of equipment that should have been ready for them yesterday was still waiting somewhere on the outskirts of the town. Spanakis wouldn't allow the stuff on board until he'd settled the price. Worse still, the MTB's crew were hanging about with time on their hands. Time to become individuals, undisciplined, friends.

Sheldon widened a split in the canvas awning and looked toward the café tables on the quay. Looked at the Greeks who wouldn't be hurried, the Greek in particular who had a Bofors gun for sale. Medium height, middle-aged, a middle-class Levantine businessman, carefully shaking out his smooth cuffs as he talked. Sheldon knew he wouldn't be able to pick out the face from twenty others in a week's time. The man was still arguing slowly and softly with Spanakis. The coffee cups on the table no colder than they'd been half an hour ago. Sheldon wondered if they'd ever strike a bargain.

He looked past the café tables and the wooden derricks that lined the quay, on to where the loose-axled wine carts rattled around the half-ruined mosque. The drivers stood upright, flicking their whips to clear the road ahead. Around the outer harbor were the houses of two forgotten empires—Turkish and Venetian—tottering together. At the port entrance, the old Venetian lighthouse seemed like a crudely painted water color in the haze, threatening to topple into the water at any moment.

The tourist attractions Sheldon noted without interest. He'd been staring at the same view for too long. The dark alleys leading up from the harbor to the town. The roofs thinning out among dark green olive groves above. And the olives giving way to the huge shoulders of the White Mountains, gray crags of rock, black shadows of pine, changing places as the overhanging clouds remapped them every second. The only sight which pleased the captain was the wisp of smoke curling steadily eastward from the rusty factory chimney. He wasn't allowing for a change of wind or weather in August.

"Too much he want. Still twenty-five thousand drachs, too much." Spanakis was suddenly leaning into the shade of the tarpaulin, clicking his tongue.

"Twenty-five-thou. . . . That's over three hundred pounds." Sheldon looked up angrily. "Can you get him down?"

"Maybe." Spanakis turned back toward the man at the distant café table. "Maybe if I offer him dollars, he take my price."

"Dollars? You mean in cash?"

The Greek nodded. "We are a big organization."

"If you're so big, why the hell don't you pay him what he wants and have done with it?"

Spanakis flushed. "You think I don't know why you're here in Canea? To watch over me? To watch over the money for Pierre?"

"All the same to me, I assure you," Sheldon said carelessly. "Three hundred quid here or there."

"To me, no. And to Pierre, no. He is a businessman." The Greek held one hand out toward Sheldon, and wrote imaginary figures on his palm. "The ransom money is for two million sterling. You get one million, Shel-don, because it is your idea and you take the risks. . . . Pierre also get a million. But out of that he has to pay the boat, the gun, the crew, and me. Now, I am a businessman too. I know to keep my expense down. Then Pierre, he is pleased with me, and there is more of the million for me. You understand, I use this," he tapped his head.

Sheldon nodded tiredly.

"Maybe he take dollars," Spanakis repeated. He went back to the quay.

Sheldon peered through the rip in the awning, saw

Spanakis sit down once again at the café table. The old soft argument was repeated, gesture for gesture. No conclusion seemed to have been reached when suddenly both men got up and walked away. Sheldon turned back to the deck of the fishing boat. The only movement was the galley boy slowly collecting the dirty tin plates and mugs, rinsing them in a bucket of seawater. The shadows under his eyes were huge violet flags, and his face was thick with grease under the singed forelock. Around him the fishermen sprawled in any shade they could find, guarding their heads and groins from the day.

Over an hour late by Sheldon's watch, Spanakis returned.

"Well?"

"You are angry, *Kapitane?*"

"You've been a hell of a time."

"I work for you. I use my head," the Greek said stiffly. "I fix the price in dollars. I get much information. I remember one thing you maybe forget."

"Such as?"

"Insulin."

"Insulin? What the hell are you talking about?"

"You think only of guns and radios. You think nothing of the millionaires. One of them, Marotta, is sick."

"Sick?" Sheldon was alarmed. "You mean seriously?"

"Sick now seven, eight years. Sick all the time." Spanakis got a small metal case out of his pocket, opened it to show a row of ampoules. "He stick one of these in his arm before every meal." He pressed an imaginary hypodermic.

"Thank you for that news item." Sheldon spoke softly.

"Three for every day." Spanakis pointed at the ampoules. "Enough for twenty days."

The captain took the case. "And what's the latest bulletin on the millionaires?"

"The old ones, they are at the villa of Tzannos at Vouliagmeni, on the coast near Athens. The young ones are still in Italy. My friend tells me that Giulia Marotta, the daughter, is like this with Kavelaris' son." He rubbed his two forefingers together. "He tell me that young Michaeli Tzannos bring a girl too."

"Any idea who?"

"My friend doesn't know," Spanakis admitted. "She is no Greek. Maybe Michaeli know her from the university in Paris."

"We've got room for her, whoever she is," Sheldon said. "*Pindar's* only carrying her eighteen crew, as usual?"

"And one doctor."

"Hope we don't need him. What about security men?"

"Four."

"Armed?"

"They have pistols. And pens that beep-beep-beep," Spanakis shrugged, not understanding the pens, just passing the message on.

"Same sort of thing thay have in hospitals. Won't be much use against a Bofors gun."

"Four, nineteen, ten," Spanakis added it up. "Thirty-three persons. Is too much."

"We've allowed for thirty-five. . . . Any other news? Your friend know where *Pindar*'ll be cruising?"

"He think the same as last year. They come down to Rhodes at the end of the second week."

"Perfect. Well within range. Now we've just got to get that bloody equipment on board."

"We can no bring the truck before night."

"Why the hell not?" Sheldon looked angrily at the fishermen sleeping on deck. Then on to the silent quayside, the idle derricks, the cart drivers stretched out on café chairs, the horses stirring in their shafts only to rummage in the corners of their nose bags. "Usual bloody caper. Everybody's asleep."

"We can no do anything before tonight," Spanakis insisted patiently. "You want me to load my boat with a Bofors gun now? You want me to take you around to your MTB? Want me to pilot you to the island, all in broad daylight?"

Sheldon shrugged tiredly.

"Night will come when it's ready," Spanakis told him.

Night did come. And Spanakis' caïque stayed by the quayside while the rest of the fishing fleet put-puted across the harbor to scatter out over the dusky sea. The Greek skipper had a pair of diesel injectors in his hand, and had told anyone who was interested that he'd got engine trouble. Now he waited, staring through the growing shadows at the habor police office. The night watch was sitting inside, his back to the harbor, a two-hundred-drachma bonus in his pocket. Spanakis hesitated a moment longer, then flashed a torch briefly at the dark warehouses beyond the café. Headlights answered him, a motor started up, and a large truck lumbered over the cobblestones to the derrick at the caïque's stern. Four men lowered the tailboard from inside.

Sheldon recognized Roche and Laborde, two of Pierre's wartime crew, but he didn't greet them. Quickly, they and the two other men eased crates down over the tailboard, and carried them across the gangplank. Finally the Bofors gun, a much larger crate that needed the derrick to swing it on deck. The boat bounced slightly under the sudden weight. Sheldon looked at the stenciled inscription: HANDS ACROSS THE SEA, he read. Then the American flag with two clasped hands below. The initials C.A.R.E. . . . The legend AGRICULTURAL IMPLEMENTS. IOANNINA. NORTHWEST GREECE.

Spanakis quickly covered the crate with a tarpaulin. "Nobody ask questions about such boxes," he said. "Only the people of Ioannina."

19

Night, and the heavily laden caïque lay far behind the MTB. Ahead there was daylight, and the island they were making for. The false dawn made the distant shoreline flat, merging hills with cloud, leaving only the lower slopes to fact. The sky, a firm ice blue, suddenly edged a smear of startling red into the cloud. The neutral sea waited to reflect any color it could believe. Then hills emerged shyly as the red smear diffused into a thinner, more credible sunrise. Beyond the land, a distant chain of other islands stood out from the sea. The shadows around them soft in the morning haze.

Sheldon was irritated by the beauty of it all. The island was much larger than he remembered, and so was the breathtaking size of the dawn, the calm water that linked the islands in some vast mysterious plan. All that had stayed in his mind was the dark dripping cave, and the tense days of waiting.

Spanakis, the pilot, turned toward him. "The last time we come to the cave much slower. You remember, I pull you with a rope? Away from the battle of Leros?"

The captain grunted.

"And what a mess your boat was in then." Shaking his head sadly, the Greek stroked the new varnish of the bridge rail. "All where we are standing was gone. Torn out, and dragging over the side. The 859, she was only half a ship, black and burning."

"You'd be burning if you'd had a German destroyer pumping shells into you for twenty minutes."

"The *Burg Rostock*." Spanakis nodded. "A big ship.

And you try to attack her with a torpedo boat."

"It was one God awful mess." Sheldon's tired brain tried to work its way back to November 1943. "Maybe it was the third night of the attack. I don't remember."

"The second."

"Doesn't matter. Anyway, it was the night the German invasion force arrived from Piraeus. The night some genius at Allied Command, safe in his bomb shelter, decided Leros had to be held. . . . There were just too many damn ships around."

"I know. And I keep clear." Spanakis' face was harsh in the gray dawn light. "I was coming from the harbor with refugees."

"It was near the harbor," Sheldon agreed. "We were out on patrol. And we came across these Siebel ferries close inshore."

"The German landing boats?"

"Landing craft. They were too damn shallow for torpedoes. Only way to sink 'em was to run close alongside and drop depth charges. We did just that. . . ." He paused suddenly, then his voice was soft. "I take the blame. I was looking astern to check the Siebel had sunk. And we were moving fast. . . . When I turned around, there was this destroyer close ahead. Just for a second I thought she was the *Echo*, the British ship. Then it was too late."

"I saw you. We all saw you. . . ." Spanakis looked away. "Like a huge fire on the water. And the searchlight on you. Then the shells, the tracer bullets, green and red. You were stopped."

"Our stern was blown off," Sheldon said curtly. "Wing engines gone, rudders gone. Controls and radio gone. The bridge was just a bloody great hole in the deck. . . . It killed two men stopping those engines, and the rest of the stokers were vomiting their guts out because of the methyl-bromide fumes. . . ." His hands trembled on the ship's wheel. "Sixteen left alive out of thirty-one. And that damn German searchlight still on us, the shells coming like ten-ton trucks. So we got away in the Carley raft."

"I watch you from the darkness," Spanakis said gently. "Still keeping near your 859. Then I see the searchlight go out, the shells stop. The German destroyer go away. . . . And the 859, she is still burning, but not so much. And I see you paddle your raft back to your ship, and get back on board her. With the flames all around the petrol tanks, just waiting to go boom."

"Didn't fancy rowing a Carley raft back to Cyprus," Sheldon said. "I reckoned we might get the fire out, get an engine started maybe."

Spanakis nodded his approval. He watched the island approach, the line of the hills becoming hard through the fading mist. "And I helped you put the fire out, and I tow you back here, very slowly, very sadly." He hesitated a moment, then turned back to the captain. "One thing I never understand about you, Shel-don. When you reach the cave, you only have half a ship, half a crew. . . . And two weeks later you go back to Leros and sink the *Burg Rostock*. Because you have one torpedo left. But why do you go?"

"I don't know." *He did know. Because when they'd climbed back on the MTB from the raft, only Sheldon had seen the body on the torpedo tube. The one tube that was unharmed in the stink of cordite and burnt wood. And the body lying near the firing bottle—the blackened body saying Cunjeezer, Cunjeezer, over and over again. Traill's voice, Traill's eyes, but no eyelids in the charred black face. Sheldon wanted morphine, wanted a vein in the stiff arm. But the vein was dry. The ship rolled, there was a tiny crunch, and Traill had gone. Sheldon held only an arm. And he stared down at the torpedo.*

"*Kapitane!*" Spanakis shouted suddenly.

Startled, Sheldon saw the island coming toward them fast. He spun the wheel, the boat heeled around, and they were running along the blue shadow of the shore, the sunrise above and missing them. The noise of the engines came back sharp as gunfire. Sheldon throttled back, but there was no one to hear within fifty miles. No birds, no lizards on the dark rocks, carved into a thousand knuckles by the sea. Nothing lived, nothing grew beyond the few patches of furze, the stunted bushes on the slopes. No fresh smell of land, just the dry breath of rocks, dust, and rotting driftwood. The hill rose more steeply now, square slabs of rock stood up, black against the growing sunlight. Tombstones marking out the dead land. . . .

And this was Traill's burial place, this lonely island out on the sea. There were seven graves on the far side of the hill, one of them a smaller grave. . . . Not that he'd liked Traill. He wasn't officer material, not what the lower decks would call a pig. He'd been tired the whole time because he spent long hours on deck, staring at sunsets, islands, and mountains. Traill got Homer and Aeschylus in his parcels, not cake. And once, early in the morning, Sheldon had found him in a Cairo bar, the girls creased and yawning, the waiters waiting by the door. Traill was at the phonograph, playing Mozart from an old faded album. He'd looked up suddenly, and it was the only time Sheldon had ever seen him angry. . . . If he had had any one feeling about Traill, it was that he would probably have voted for him.

There were cliffs now, rising up to his right. Sheldon forced himself back to the present. It was no longer 1943, he was no longer twenty-five. He could no longer take a boat a couple of hundred sea miles and still feel fit. Sleep he needed desperately, but there was no time for sleep. Trying out his body, he found a tiny knot of life below his spine. He focused it painfully on the western tip of the island, where the cliffs were highest.

"If you want, I take her in through the channel," Spanakis spoke to him gently, leaning across the wheel. "It is difficult, a boat of this size, and it's many years since you are here."

But Sheldon gripped the spokes firmly. "Got to do it

sometime. You just sing out where I go wrong."

He stopped engines. The boat drifted silently into the deeper shadows below the cliffs. From this distance he could see the wall wasn't solid, but carved into limestone pillars, squared roughly off, with dark vertical cracks where seams of softer rock had been eroded. Sheldon stared for a long time at the cliffs, but couldn't see what he was looking for. Then Spanakis pointed out the larger crack between two pillars, where the water was clear of scum.

Sheldon shouted for Turton to go on to the foredeck with a boat hook. Then he reached out for the throttle levers and found his hand was trembling. The telegraph clanged, a short burst on wing motors drove them in fast—too fast—toward the channel. Sheldon spun the wheel. The rock pillars closed in on them, wet and black, smelling of salt. On the foredeck, Turton was tense behind his boat hook. Then the whole boat lifted on a back surge as the channel curved, and abruptly they were through to softer light.

A pool opened out around them. To their right were the limestone cliffs, a sheer wall, casting a straight shadow down on the water. These cliffs fell gradually as they went inland, and then crumbled into the line of the hill that was the highest point on the island. The upper slopes were in sunlight, bald and pink where they met the wind. The lower slopes curved down to form the left side of the pool, and they were gray, a strangely luminous shale. The shore was soft, pounded to a fine dust by the winters that had poured in through the channel. But now the water was calm and transparent. And the boat seemed to shiver as it drifted on the landlocked harbor.

Spanakis pointed to the far corner of the pool, over to where the cliffs jutted into the hillside. "You take her in there. But slow."

Sheldon saw what he meant. The water around them was even shallower than he'd remembered. He leaned over the bridge rail and shouted down to Turton. "Give us some marks. I'll want the depths in feet, and keep 'em coming as quick as you can."

The man nodded, and picked up a coiled lead line. He swung it over the side. "Twenty-five." He shouted back.

The captain gripped the engine-room telegraph. Its clang echoed suddenly around the walls of the bay, followed by the mutter of one engine, cut off as abruptly as it had begun. The MTB started slowly forward.

"Sixteen."

The water was quite clear, and they seemed to be rushing over a green meadow, the grasses parting at their approach.

"Twelve!" Turton's head jerked up anxiously.

Sheldon rang down, Slow Astern. He could see rocks on the bottom, smooth and round like speckled eggs. Then larger rocks ahead, breaking the surface. His hand hovered over Half Astern.

"Six!"

And then the propellers bit. Sheldon stopped engines, saw with relief the shock wave leave the ship and go on toward the shore alone. It curled over soft gravel, and fell back with a thin coating of white dust.

"And now," Spanakis said, "you turn her around."

Slowly, Navy fashion, with short bursts of the engines, Sheldon worked the ship around until they were facing the way they'd come. The limestone cliffs were now to their left, and they could see that where the cliff edged into the hillside there was a jagged rock fault. At the bottom it widened to form the entrance to a cave.

"You remember it, Captain?" Spanakis grinned at him.

"Now I do. But I'm damned if I could have found it without your help."

"You can only see it from here, the shallow water. That is why nobody know about it." Still smiling, the

Greek went down to the foredeck. He got Sheldon to edge the bows in toward the cave mouth, then he reached over the side with a boat hook and hauled up a dripping fisherman's float from the shadows. Attached to the float was a nylon rope, stained red where it led on into the dark sandstone walls of a tunnel.

With Turton's help, Spanakis hauled the rope the length of the ship so that it went back into the water through the stern fair leads. They took a couple of turns around the winch on the foredeck, and started the motor. Suddenly darkness closed around them as the red rope snaked steadily back over the deck to the cave mouth. All that was left of the day was a glow of milky blue in the water astern. And then that disappeared.

Sheldon switched on work lights and the bridge searchlight. They showed smooth red walls, convex on the left, concave on the right, rising to a point high above and to the left. It was as if they were floating between two skins of some vast sandstone dome. The captain shivered as cool air and spray fanned his face. And the winch droned on, dragging them farther and farther into the earth.

Then the channel widened. The searchlight showed a long tall cave ahead, its walls rising sheer from the water. The nylon rope was now taut on the surface, and it was pulling them steadily over to a small concrete jetty, where crates were stacked under a large metal sheerlegs. There was a slight graunch as the ship bumped against the jetty. Then Spanakis jumped ashore with a line.

Sheldon waited on the bridge while faces—tired, weirdly downcast faces—gathered below him on the foredeck. Barney, Turton, and Spanakis, their arms hanging limply to their sides.

"You've done very well," Sheldon told them. "Very well indeed. A long sea trip, short-handed. . . . And now the real work begins. But we've got at least fifteen hours before the caïque gets here. So I suggest you all take a watch below."

The two Englishmen turned away without a word, but Spanakis came up to the bridge. "And you, Captain? You are tired?"

Sheldon ignored him. "Work to do. . . ." He turned to the huge metal tripod on the jetty. "That sheerlegs. Forgot to ask you about that. Will it take four tons?"

"More. Eight *tonnès.*" Then Spanakis was suddenly anxious. "You must rest, Shel-don. I see you when we approach the island. You were very tired."

"Don't keep saying that." Sheldon squeezed the bridge of his nose, tried to keep the exhaustion from reaching his brain. Slowly his ears, which had been deafened by six hours of roaring Packards, heard the steady boom of the waterfall from the inner cave. "That water through there, is it still fresh?"

Spanakis nodded.

The captain reached out for the searchlight. He shone it past the jetty to where the channel curved around an outcrop of jet-black rock, black because it dripped with water. And beyond it, apparently without end, there were moving swirls of mist that turned the searchlight beam into a tunnel of rainbows. "There's room for us to anchor in the inner cave?" Sheldon asked. "I mean, we could take your mooring rope on?"

"Of course." Spanakis looked surprised. "But you have the jetty here."

"And we'll anchor around by the spring," Sheldon said flatly. "Unless you've made any changes there?"

"No. But why not leave the boat here? Where there is already a place?"

Sheldon was too tired to argue. He swung the light beam back to the jetty and to the crates that were piled behind Spanakis. "Those boxes? You'll move them when your boat gets here? . . . And there are more things I'll want on the second trip. . . ." He paused, his voice seemed to come from very far away—a bad connection. "Things like carnival masks. Half a ton of kapok."

Spanakis looked at him worriedly. "You sleep," he said. "I don't tell the others. And I wake you before them, when the caïque gets here with the gun."

20

The remains of the huge wooden crate lay on the concrete jetty, but now the American flag and clasped hands were split apart. Sheldon turned around to face the Bofors gun which was now mounted on the foredeck. Its long flared barrel gleamed dully, and its ring sight jutting out from the top of the shield like some misplaced ski pole. Around the gun the deck was long and bare, now that the long-range fuel tanks had been removed. The whole MTB sat differently on the water, sloping up from its low stern to its pointed bow, looking lean and powerful.

He left the jetty and crossed the gangplank. Up on the bridge, he removed the waterproof covers from the two machine guns, mounted one on each side of the wheel. Then he switched on the masthead lamp, and suddenly the blue-and-white painted ship leaped out of the darkness all around him. It was almost 7:30 A.M. by his watch. He waited for the minute hand to come around, then he crossed to the ship's bell and rang it three times. Three bells, time for the morning inspection to begin. Dark figures in Navy blue assembled on the foredeck with rifles. They seemed gaunt and menacing in the harsh downlighting.

Sheldon watched them from the bridge—three

Greeks, two Frenchmen, and the three Englishmen who were the only remaining members of his old crew. They stood in a crooked line, holding their rifles carelessly. The captain swallowed his anger. Five days ago, when they'd first faced him on the deck, he'd seen that parades and bull were useless—they were only in it for the money. So he'd kept the drill to a minimum, and only in areas where they could still smell money—rifle drill, weapon training, and rehearsing the operation itself. They were now disciplined, but only because they were exhausted. Sheldon, and five days of endless night, had seen to that.

Spanakis, his second-in-command, came up and saluted Sheldon as he reached the deck. The two men went slowly along the line, inspecting the SLR rifles. Sheldon took Barney's rifle first, broke it, and eased the working parts back past the stock. He raised it to the light and saw that the barrel gleamed like a core of silver. Barney was grinning at him. That meant he'd got Mitch to clean his rifle again. Sheldon didn't mind—the more troubles heaped on Mitch the better.

The cook's gun was trembling. And his two bellies trembled, one above and one below his belt. There were lines of exhaustion starting from his eyes, spreading out over his bald creased forehead, and down to his flabby blue cheeks. Mitch's eyes were lifeless, turned inward, looking for strength that wasn't there. In five days the man had lost fourteen pounds, in five more days he'd either be dead or useful. Sheldon took his rifle, saw it was as clean as any in the small arms school. He took a slow deep breath. "Bloody filthy! Didn't you learn anything yesterday? What the by-Jesus d'you think this is? A rifle, or a Dago's prick? Bring it to me cleaned at oh-nine-hundred hours. And report for the heavy-duty party."

He moved on to Turton. The Radar Rating's mind was elsewhere. His gun hadn't been touched, but Sheldon left him alone. The man had troubles enough with the radio equipment. It had turned out to be Greek black-market stuff, most of it dating from the last war, some of it useless. Turton was having to cut a lot of corners, and more important, waste a lot of time. Time was precious. The DF tracking station was nowhere near completed, and *Pindar* had sailed from Piraeus four days ago.

He reached the two Frenchmen who'd been submariners with Pierre during the war. Roche, the smaller of the two, was deeply tanned. He was in his late forties, but prided himself on his good shape. Sheldon knew he had a big villa on Rhodes, and a Greek wife who asked no questions. What was more important, he had four kids. The captain gave them a present: "Two-hundred-dollar bonus for you, Roche. That was good work you did, diving for that cable we lost overboard. We'd have been in a hell of a hole without it." There was a flicker of gratitude on Roche's face, before the anger returned. But anger was good, Sheldon thought. Anger was something positive, something to focus on. Anger took their minds away from the unreality of what he was doing to them. A bond of hate. Far better than the shocked disbelief of yesterday when he'd made them double around the island in full kit, then form up and double around again. Yesterday he'd lost a day's work, but he'd got the beginnings of a crew.

Turning to Laborde, he saw a muscle flicker on the man's cheek. The Frenchman was remembering yesterday too, when he'd refused to run around the island the second time—until Sheldon had put a .38 bullet past him. And Laborde understood bullets. Scarred and nervous, he'd been a mercenary in three countries since the war. He was also a crack shot, a talent Pierre had found no use for. Sheldon handed the rifle back, fascinated by the way Laborde's fingers gently stroked the butt. He knew the man had fired all the guns before making his choice. Laborde preferred war in dirty combat gear, but he preferred war.

At the end of the line were the two Greeks. They were both young, fresh from national service in the Greek

Navy. The captain left them to Spanakis, and watched their faces set sulkily as they were pulled around. He's only included these in the crew for show. Nine was a much better number than seven to take on thirty-three. On the day, Sheldon would make sure their rifles were loaded with blanks.

He walked away from the men, turned and faced them. Steeling himself, he looked each of them squarely in the face. Barney and Turton he was sure of. Roche and Laborde, thrown off their balance by anger, were beginning to be malleable. The two Greeks would follow Spanakis' orders, and that only left Mitch—the trembling sacklike Mitch—the only one without an anchor. He needed time and special care.

"Orders. August eighteenth," Sheldon said. "Turton, you carry on with the DF receivers. Roche and Laborde, make up a firing detail. Chief, you're in charge of the heavy-duty party through to the inner cave. When I give the order, Move, fall out. . . . Right, MOVE!" Footsteps clattered away on deck, then Sheldon was standing alone. There was silence apart from the dripping of the cave walls. And the foredeck was pale and white, as though moonlit, apart from the long shadow of the gun.

The radar room smelled of the long hours Turton had put in. Stripped to the waist, the man was doubled up awkwardly around a radio chassis. He was sweating and angry, glancing repeatedly between his soldering iron and the circuit he was working from. "Effing-bastard Greeks," he muttered. Then he looked up and saw Sheldon standing in the doorway. Deliberately he made no effort to control his language. "Effing-bastard war surplus. It's meant to be effing-bastard war-surplus stuff, untouched."

"When will you be through, Turton?" Sheldon asked coldly.

"Oh, yeah," the man said sourly. "Tomorrow, like always, Skipper," he added finally.

"It has to be tomorrow. There's a boat sailing around the Aegean where she pleases. We've just got to keep tabs on her."

"Well, look at that." Turton pointed to a crate with a smoking soldering iron. "R.11.55. Receiver. . . . Still in its box. None of the seals broken. . . . So tell me how the effing-bastard Greeks get their effing-bastard hands inside and sod the whole thing up?"

"You've worked long hours. Much longer than the rest of us, and I'm grateful. . . . But you have to find a way around. The whole show depends on it."

Turton scowled, and turned back to his circuit. Sheldon wondered about it for a moment, then decided to leave the man alone. As he left the radar room, he told himself that Turton would have to be watched. It wasn't just the insubordination, that didn't matter too much in private. It was the effing-bastard Greeks. . . . Turton was the only Englishman in the crew who wasn't expatriate. And Sheldon knew all about the English working-class hatred of Wogs, Krauts, and Spicks. That would have to be watched.

He took his oilskin on deck and went aft to join Spanakis in the rubber dinghy. The Seagull motor fired, and its echo was deafening in the confined space. Spanakis took the helm, steered the dinghy out over the dark water while the lights of the MTB and the concrete jetty faded astern. Then they were level with the outcrop of wet black rock, and suddenly found themselves enveloped by blackness and thick clinging mist. The Greek kept the throttle hard open, sure of the channel even without a light. All at once the motor lost its sharp echo and they were through to the inner cave.

Facing them now across a pool of blurred water were two dim lights. Lights that flickered far apart in the swirling mist, showing the size of the cave—maybe 250 yards across. There was the steady roar of a waterfall, the torrent of fresh water that over the years had carved a narrow chimney into a vast domed cavern. High above the two men now, the roof was dimpled into smaller domes, smooth and dripping with spray. Spanakis steered for the nearer light, where the noise of the water seemed to be louder. Then the mist parted, and they could see the waterfall, a dazzling column of silver in a narrow cleft, the spray below it falling in whirls and rainbows around a hooded floodlight. Near the light stood two men, wearing oilskins. One of them had a rifle in his hands, and suddenly he raised it as a target leaped up into the light beam. Flame spat from the muzzle of the SLR. The crackle of automatic gunfire echoed around the cave walls.

Sheldon and Spanakis beached the dinghy, then walked up over the wet sand to the two men by the light. The man who had fired was Roche, and standing behind him with a pair of binoculars was Laborde. Sheldon borrowed the glasses for a moment and focused them on the target. He saw that the black silhouette figure had been clipped by two shots out of the five. Angrily he turned on Roche. "Why the hell d'you think I bothered to get targets made that had a white surround five times as big as the silhouette figure?"

Roche stared back at him sullenly.

"Well?"

"Because you want us to miss the figure and hit the surround."

"Too damn right I do. I want you to *miss!* I want you to be able to put a bullet over a man's left shoulder in your sleep." He handed over the binoculars. "See for yourself. You killed that poor swine."

Roche shrugged.

"Doesn't that mean anything to you? You'd be up on a murder charge. You'd have us all up on a murder charge." Sheldon saw his words had their effect. "Right. Go and relieve the Greek chappie in the target butts. . . . Now, Laborde, let's see what you can do."

Laborde slapped a fresh magazine into his gun,

stood waiting calmly while his compatriot disappeared into the butts. The target vanished suddenly. Then almost immediately it leaped up again in a different place. Before it came to rest, Laborde had fired a burst of four. Sheldon watched in amazement—he hadn't even seen the rifle come up. Turning back to the target, he saw a small group of holes above the silhouette figure's shoulder. Four holes, he counted them. "Finest shooting I've ever seen in my life," he said with conviction. "Two-inch group, must be. No one's going to top that today."

Laborde turned away carelessly.

"Which means you've won yourself another hundred-dollar bonus. Fifth day in a row. Finest shooting I've ever seen in my life," he repeated.

Laborde glared at him coldly. But Sheldon knew he was right to rub it in, knew that no one in the world could resist being praised for something he was born with—beauty, speed, or a steady hand. The captain walked back to the rubber dinghy with Spanakis, and he told himself he could rely on Laborde. The man now had a reputation to live up to.

The outboard pushed them steadily through swirling mist, past dripping rock formations that got lighter as they neared the second floodlight. It stood on a narrow beach on the far side of the cave. Here the sound of the waterfall was covered by the throb of a small generator, which—like the floodlight—was wrapped in plastic against the falling spray. Silhouetted by the light were three men in oilskins. They were working slowly, sawing up timber and laying it out in a rectangle on the beach. One of them—Barney—looked up as Sheldon approached.

"How's it going, Chief?"

"Well. . . ." Barney pointed over to Mitch, who was swaying dangerously under a heavy beam of four-by-four. "Maybe that one's had enough of heavy-duty parties by now."

Sheldon swung around to watch the cook's slow, uneven progress up the beach. The man had to stop with each pace because his feet were sucked down into the wet sand. He was trembling, and as he got nearer they could hear his breathing was a shallow whistle for air. The captain hesitated for a moment, then he turned back to Barney. "Otherwise you're up to schedule?" he asked.

"More or less. We had to dig the main posts in pretty deep. It's bleeding soft." Barney dug a half-moon in the sand with his heel. It filled with water. "But we're just about ready to start building the platform itself."

"And how long d'you . . . ?" Sheldon didn't finish. He heard a low bubbling moan from nearby. When he looked around for Mitch, all he could see was the beam of timber lying on the beach. They pulled it clear and found the man was lying face down, half-buried in the sand. They rolled him over and saw his mouth and nostrils, and the front of his body, were caked with mud. By the time they'd cleaned him up, Mitch's face was still a dirty gray color, and it had nothing to do with the mud.

Sheldon was suddenly shocked by his own callousness as he looked down at Mitch's imprint in the beach— a shallow grave—slowly filling with water. "Come back to the ship," he said gently.

He got Mitch into the rubber dinghy and took him back to the outer cave. It took some time to heave the cook's flabby body up on deck. Then Sheldon sat him in the shadow of the Bofors gun and gave him a cigarette. For a moment he wondered about giving the man something to drink, and finally he went and fetched him a tot from the rum locker. Mitch sipped with no apparent pleasure. His eyes were streaked and dull, and his eyelashes were pricked out by mud.

"Two weeks ago you were just a sponge full of liquor," Sheldon spoke quietly. "Nobody would have given you a year to live. Nobody would have given a monkey's."

Mitch didn't look at him.

"You're dried out now. In a month you'll be able to say no to a drink." The captain continued: "In a month you'll have twenty-five thousand pounds in your pocket. We'll get you to somewhere quiet. You can start all over again."

Mitch was dead still—dead. He couldn't be reached by words, or fags, or tots of rum.

"Don't you see? You're finished with that damn queer's paradise. You've broken away from Dunari."

At the mention of the island, Mitch suddenly smiled, wetly, for home.

Sheldon backed away, hissing his amazement. He didn't understand Mitch any more, didn't understand anything about men in peacetime any more. He spelled out his power over the cook, and suddenly knew it was blackmail. "You can go where you bloody well like! But until we're through here, you'll work for us! And by Christ you'd better pull yourself together by the time we start on sea maneuvers tonight."

The moon shone down on the open sea, spreading wide rivers of silver between the dark shadows of the waves. The MTB rolled as it drifted, and on its landward side the rocky cliffs of the island rose up toward the oily stars. Sheldon leaned over the bridge sprayshield. Below him on the foredeck, the seamen's faces were white, upturned in the moonlight. "Right, pay attention. This is going to be an attack. I want you to treat it as the real thing. . . . We've got a United Nations crew aboard, and I've explained I'm not going to give you the old orders, Crash Start, and so on. The attack is divided into nine parts, and I'm going to give you the orders One to Nine. You all know what they mean?" The men nodded. "Action stations," Sheldon said.

The faces disappeared, became dark heads jerking away to take up their positions. Mitch in the Bofors seat, Turton at the shell rack by his side, Barney and one of the

Greeks down in the engine room, the other Greek on the afterdeck with Roche, standing above the round life raft that bobbed in the water. And Laborde leaning casually against the foredeck rail, cradling his rifle in his hands.

Spanakis was with Sheldon on the bridge, standing by a loaded machine gun. Both men waited until they heard a brief whistle from the engine-room tube. Barney was in position. Sheldon uncapped the tube.

"*One!*" He shouted suddenly, his hand jerking the engine-room telegraph. The motors woke with a bellow. Water boiled under the stern, and they were roaring toward the coast—the target on the cliffs—lights that pricked out *Pindar's* rough size and shape. Carefully, Sheldon watched Mitch on the Bofors seat. He waited for the gun barrel to slow, waited for Mitch to choose his own moment. Then he saw Mitch's hand jab at the button.

Flame belched from the barrel. *Blomp-Blomp.* Twin gouts of white smoke. The huge explosions tilted the deck.

"*Two!*" Sheldon jerked back the telegraph, saw two shell cases spin away, smoking, as they bounced on the deck. Mitch was apparently satisfied, and he signaled. . . . Turton jumped clear to the foredeck, grabbed up his rifle. . . . Beyond him Laborde waited with his rifle half-raised. . . . There were footsteps as the Greek clattered up from the engine room, stood on guard. . . . Roche and the second Greek waited on the afterdeck, covering the shore. All of them waited for *Three.*

Three didn't come. Sheldon spun the wheel away from the coast, glared angrily at the dust plumes on the cliff, a full eighty yards away from the target light that was the size and height of *Pindar's* radio bridge. "Right, we're going again," he said quietly. Then he lost control.

"Filthy bloody drunken sod!" He ran down from the bridge, grabbed Mitch out of the Bofors seat, and worked the controls until the barrel pointed low over the side. "We stay up nights while you play golf with your blasted cannon!" He hauled Mitch around to the end of the barrel, signaled Laborde and Turton to hold him there with his stomach across the muzzle. "No bloody courts-martial on this trip!" Sheldon went back to the firing button, his thumb covered it. "No bloody Admiralty to tell me what to do!"

Mitch came alive suddenly at the end of the barrel. All at once his eyes were white with fear as he believed Sheldon.

21

Through night glasses, the captain watched the helicopter hover over the moonlit plateau above the cliffs. Then it fell, bouncing slightly on the hard rocky surface of the island. It came to rest, its rotors slumping wearily. A rating—Sheldon was glad he thought of the small white figure as a rating, not Turton—went forward and helped Pierre down from the cockpit. The two men hurried away from the moonlight, down to the dark shadows of the bay below. Then Sheldon heard the whine of the outboard, and a moment later saw the life raft bouncing out toward him on the black waves. The captain left the bridge, went aft to where Roche was waiting, standing at ease, his rifle jutting out from his hand.

Detail, thought Sheldon, it's the detail that impresses. And he waited until the precise moment that Pierre's tanned face reached the MTB's shadow before he uttered a low word of command to Roche. The Frenchman jerked to attention as Pierre put one foot on deck. The smile on the yacht skipper's face froze as his compatriot stared straight through him from behind the rifle barrel. Pierre then stuck out his hand to Sheldon and was greeted with a cold naval salute. The captain ushered him for'ard along the deck, sensing that Pierre was impressed by the silent service, impressed even more by the quietly throbbing ship, where not a light showed under the baleful eye of the moon.

Sheldon took Pierre up to the bridge, then leaned out over the sprayshield with his back to the Frenchman. Without a word of command, Turton ran to the foredeck and winched the anchor home. The MTB shook herself free, and rolled in the low waves. Turton returned to his position by the Bofors gun, Mitch was motionless in the seat above him. There was a brief whistle from the engine-room tube, and Sheldon turned back to the wheel. He addressed a few curt words to Pierre. The first the Frenchman had heard since he'd come on board.

"See that cliff over there, with the lights?" Sheldon pointed. "That's the target, roughly the length and size of *Pindar*."

Pierre nodded.

"And you see the topmost light? That's where *Pindar*'s radio bridge will be." Sheldon paused for a second, then he uncapped the voice tube.

"*One!*" he shouted, at the same time jerking at the engine-room telegraph. The bellowing engines pushed them forward. Sheldon kept his eyes on Mitch. Waited, waited, until he saw the hand reach out . . . jab at the button.

Blomp-Blomp. The flame and the white smoke. The deck tilting.

"*Two!*" The clang of the telegraph as Sheldon jerked it back. Then the boat came around slightly, and footsteps sounded on the deck. . . . Turton going away from the Bofors, the Greek coming up from the engine room.

"*Three!*" They lost way under the cliffs and the target lights. Sheldon snapped on the bridge searchlight, its beam came to rest on the rock wall, and the Bofors barrel followed it.

"The Bofors is now pointing at the millionaires," Sheldon said. "I do my bit of shouting. Get them to heave-to. Get the crew separated from the passengers."

Pierre looked at Spanakis who was behind the starboard machine gun. He looked down to Mitch, tense behind the Bofors sight. Then on to Laborde and Turton on the foredeck, with their rifles leveled at the cliff.

"*Four!*" Again the clatter of footsteps as Laborde and Turton ran aft. They joined Roche and the two Greeks on the stern. Then the five men disappeared over the side into the life raft. The outboard roared into life, and the large rubber circle flapped away over the dark water, carrying the dark figures over to the lights on the cliff face.

"How do they get up *Pindar?*" Pierre asked.

"Grappling hook."

"Bit risky, isn't it? All those people waiting on deck?"

"With a searchlight blinding them? Two machine guns pinning them down?" Sheldon pointed out Barney, who'd come up to the bridge and taken up position behind the port machine gun. "Not to mention a bloody great Bofors muzzle. And they've seen what damage that can do with a high-explosive shell." He swung the searchlight up the cliff face. The light that marked the position of *Pindar's* radio bridge had gone. In its place there was a gaping hole in the rock, and a lingering dust cloud.

Pierre was still silent, half an hour later, as Sheldon edged the MTB slowly toward the dark cliffs that marked the entrance to the pool.

"How the hell d'you find your way in, Navy? At night?"

"Show him, Turton."

The Radar Rating came between them on the bridge. In his hands he held a small metal box that hummed slightly. He pressed one of the switches on the box and immediately a pair of white lights showed up on the cliffs ahead.

"Radio-controlled," Sheldon said. "Leading lights." Slowly he lined one light up above the other, then went in through the dark channel between the limestone pillars.

There were two more sets of leading lights that Turton switched on and off with his transmitter. Then they were in the cave mouth, and Roche held a torch out over the bows while Laborde picked up the fisherman's float. The red nylon rope came through the fair-leads to the winch, and Sheldon could relax. They droned through the sloping sandstone walls and on into the wider channel. As they passed the concrete jetty with its sheerlegs, Pierre looked at the captain in surprise.

"Why don't you moor there?" he asked.

Sheldon didn't answer for a moment. He waited until they'd rounded the outcrop of wet black rock, and were through to the dark spray, the booming waterfall of the inner cave. "We need the noise," he said. "To stop the millionaires hearing anything they shouldn't."

Below them on the foredeck, seamen got the mooring cables on board and made fast. Then the whole crew gathered by the Bofors gun, and looked up to the bridge.

"Well done. First-class job. Do it like that on the night and we're in the money," Sheldon told them. "There's a tot of rum waiting for you in the galley. Chicken supper . . . dismiss."

The faces disappeared. The two men on the bridge heard the rattle of chairs and tables from the afterdeck, then low tired voices. Absently, Pierre toyed with the bridge searchlight. Its beam moved around the dripping walls of the cave and came to rest on the large wooden platform that Barney and the heavy-duty party had constructed on the narrow beach.

"What's that for?" Pierre asked.

"Tell you later," Sheldon said. "Meanwhile I'll show you how we spent the rest of your money." He led Pierre down from the bridge and stopped by the Bofors gun.

Pierre felt the still-warm barrel. "You surprised me about Mitch," he said.

"Surprised myself. Maybe the rum ration helped in the end."

"And the rest of the crew as well. You've done a lot with them in one week. I'm very impressed."

"Just the Navy way." Sheldon smiled. Then he led Pierre on past the gun to where a companion ladder jutted out from the deck. "Now we come to Millionaires' Row. It's got two entrances in case of trouble. One here, and one farther for'ard." He pointed to another companion-way up in the bow.

Pierre followed him down the ladder and came to a narrow corridor with a row of locked doors on each side. There were barred lights set into the bulkheads, but otherwise nothing else to break up the surface of the gray-painted walls. The reek of new paint filled every corner of the hot, confined space, and as Pierre looked in through a spy hole in one of the doors, he saw more gray paint, and an even more confined space. The cell beyond was tiny, almost half of it taken up by a narrow bunk, and there was no porthole.

"A dozen cells like this one," Sheldon told him. "At the moment *Pindar* has ten passengers, but she may take on more. Or else we might want to berth her doctor down here with the millionaires."

"They're not going to like that." Pierre looked once again through the spy hole. "Not going to like that at all."

"Just what I'm hoping." Sheldon replied. "And they're not going to break out either. The walls are made up of two layers of fiber glass with steel mesh in the middle."

Pierre nodded slowly.

Sheldon turned back to the ladder. "We have to go

back the way we came. This part of the ship's completely self-contained, for security reasons."

They went back on deck and stopped in the shadow of the long dazzle-painted superstructure behind the bridge. "Two reasons for this," Sheldon said. "One, it changes the shape of the whole ship, makes us look like a PT boat. And two—" he unlocked one of the doors that fitted flush against the smooth wall "—it's a cell block for *Pindar*'s crew. There are twenty-four cells. They haven't got walls between them, but bars. . . . Aluminum bars for lightness."

Pierre went inside the cell and snapped on his lighter. He found a six-foot bunk to his right, and a clear space no more than a yard wide where he was standing. "Jesus, it's small, Navy."

"There's enough room to stand or lie down," the captain said defensively.

"Just like a bloody monkey house." Pierre looked through the alloy bars at the cells on either side.

"And it'll smell like one too, after those Greek seamen have been inside for a fortnight."

"You're not going to keep them in here?" Pierre was incredulous. "The whole time?"

"No option. We'll exercise them twice a day. Otherwise we've got to keep them locked up. If the whole twenty-three of them got together, we'd be in a lot of trouble."

Pierre shook his head in amazement and followed Sheldon up to the bridge once again.

The captain led him down the ladder to the radar room, then showed him his own cabin with the bunk and chart table. "We'll come back here in a second, to go over the operation in detail. But first I'll show you the rest of the ship." Sheldon walked down the gray corridor, opening each door as he came to it. "Galley . . . armory . . . forward mess deck, with bunks for Roche, Laborde, and the Chief." He stopped by a metal watertight door, on the far side of which a generator throbbed gently. "Engine room. We've spent quite a bit of your money in there. Want to check on it?"

"I trust you."

"And beyond that there's the tiller flat, where we've slung four hammocks. Mitch, Turton, and the two Greek chappies mess there."

Pierre nodded slowly. His huge body seemed to fill the narrow corridor, and his shantung uniform intruded strangely on the harsh gray paint work. "Now," he straightened suddenly, "let's hear what it's all about."

Returning to his cabin, Sheldon picked up a handful of folders from the chart table. He opened the first one. "*Pindar*. One of the largest yachts afloat. With ten passengers." He showed Pierre a sheaf of enlargements. "Spanakis' boys have been taking some photos for us. . . . First we have Alexis Tzannos. He's had one duodenal ulcer and eats a special diet. Otherwise he's healthy for a man of sixty-three. His son, Michaeli. No problems about him. . . . Then a woman called Marilena, Alexis' girl friend. She's an artist, and also a vegetarian. . . ."

"How're you going to handle all these diets?" Pierre cut across him.

"We'll have *Pindar*'s cooks. They'll take care of their passengers and crew. And we've got a hell of a lot of provisions stacked away." Sheldon turned on to the next photo. "Now Marotta, the Italian. He happens to be diabetic, but we've got a month's supply of his injections on ice, and half a chemist's shop thrown in. And of course there's *Pindar*'s doctor to look after him. . . ." He flipped through the next two pictures quickly. "Marotta's wife, Laura. She likes pastries, which she won't get. Then there's daughter Giulia who could do with some slimming."

Pierre wrinkled his nose at the girl's photo and turned on to the next.

"Dimitri Kavelaris," Sheldon continued, "who eats, drinks, and screws anything. Healthy. . . . His wife, Maria. No peculiarities as far as we know. And their son, Lakis, sportsman and loudmouth. Maybe he's going to be our troublemaker."

"And the last one?" Pierre pointed to a blurred photograph of a girl swimming. Only her head was visible, and she wore a bathing cap.

"That's Michaeli Tzannos' girl friend," Sheldon told him. "She's English, apparently. Her name's Harding, but that's all we know."

Pierre looked down at the photo for a moment, then shrugged and dropped it on the table.

"Now we come to the next folder." Sheldon opened it. "*Pindar*'s crew. There are four security men, all with side arms, all very experienced."

"How are you going to handle them?"

"Well," Sheldon replied. "They'll be quick. They'll put their bosses on the deck, and they'll cover them with automatic pistols." He grinned suddenly. "But that's not going to be one hell of a lot of use when there's a Bofors staring them in the face. They'll get the message. . . . I mean, they're not trained to fight a Navy. . . . Shoulder holsters, bleeper pens, that's their line."

Pierre nodded.

"Nineteen crew." The captain turned the pages. "That includes personal maids, seaplane pilot, and doctor. Thirty-three in all."

"A lot."

"We'll just have to keep our distance while we sort them out." Sheldon closed the file. "And we will sort them out."

Pierre was sweating in the small stuffy cabin. He unzipped his windbreaker and rolled up his sleeves. "Tell me," he said.

Sheldon showed him the second file. It was labeled *Operation Bandersnatch*, and inside it had lists, timings, and diagrams. The captain also produced a small-scale chart of the Aegean, and unrolled it. There were crosses penciled on it, with dates and times beside them. They formed a zigzag course which started at Piraeus, went to the islands of Andros, Skyros, and Lesbos, and then curved away to the open sea. The last cross had today's date penciled next to it, and showed that *Pindar* was coming south toward the Dodecanese.

"How did you get these fixes?" Pierre asked.

"Turton has a DF receiver up on the hill here. He's also in contact with a Greek chappie who's operating a second receiver up in the mountains of Leros. Ironic, really," Sheldon shrugged. "Tzannos was born on Leros."

"And *Pindar*'s bound to call there, for that very reason." Pierre examined the chart. "Which brings him pretty close."

"Even closer, once he's left the island." Sheldon traced two courses with his finger. "He'll make for Crete or Rhodes, we're told. Either way, he'll have to pass within twenty-five miles to the east of this cave."

"So?" Pierre stretched stiffly. "Let's hear about the attack."

"*Pindar* has Telex," the captain told him. "But even so she only transmits twice a day for security reasons. She comes on the air at oh-nine-hundred hours and again at twenty-one-hundred hours, every day the same, like clockwork. Transmissions last for thirty minutes. . . . And we attack at night, just after twenty-one-thirty, to give us cover of darkness, and to give us over eleven hours before the next transmission's due. . . ." He pointed down at the chart. "We wait until we're sure she's heading toward us, then we leave here and lie in wait for her. . . . By this time she'll be close enough for us to track her on our radar screen. And we go through the attack procedure you saw just now out at sea."

"Yes, I saw all that," Pierre said quickly, "and I think it'll work. But *Pindar*'s a large ship. How d'you know there won't be heads poking out of portholes all over the place? You can't cover them all."

Sheldon found a sheet of paper and handed it to him. "Spanakis has got a lot of friends watching this cruise, from harbors, from fishing boats. . . . And this is *Pindar's* evening program. It never varies."

"Twenty-one-hundred hours. Crew's evening meal," Pierre read. "Table set for twelve down on the foredeck."

"Which leaves seven crew in other parts of the ship."

"Twenty-one-fifteen . . . Passengers' cocktails on the boat deck," Pierre continued. "Always four crew present. . . . Captain, First and Second Officers, and Doctor. The security men are there, of course, and the officers hand around drinks." He looked up from the sheet of paper and smiled. "Very democratic."

"So at twenty-one-thirty we're ready to attack." Sheldon rummaged around and produced a large photograph of *Pindar*. "And at that time there'll be twelve crew down here on the foredeck. . . . Eighteen people, including passengers, officers, and security men, up here on the boat deck. Two men for'ard on the bridge. And finally, the Telex operator, who'll be still in the radio bridge, aft of the funnel."

"What happens to the Tclex operator?"

"We'll be listening in to him. When he stops transmitting, we'll give him ten minutes to clear up any messages, and get down to his supper waiting for him on the foredeck. Then we attack at twenty-one-forty, to be precise." Sheldon showed the distance between the radio bridge and main bridge on the photograph of *Pindar*. "There's a clear forty feet. We don't have to hurt anybody. That's why we didn't want anything larger than a high explosive Bofors shell."

"And if Mitch handles that gun like he did tonight . . ." Pierre left the sentence unfinished. "But after the attack? After what I saw out in the bay?"

Sheldon told him. Then he opened a third folder and told him about the ransom.

Pierre's grin got wider and wider, his gold teeth picked up the light. "It'll work," he said finally. "It'll just work."

"There's one little thing," Sheldon asked nervously. "According to my plan, it's Spanakis who takes delivery of the ransom money. How far d'you trust him?"

Pierre flushed suddenly. "Spanakis is okay," he said.

"But two million quid?"

"He couldn't spend it in Greece. He'd have to get out. And Spanakis would never leave his country. . . . Sweet Jesus!" Pierre turned on him angrily, "you know about Spanakis."

"I don't know about two million quid, in small used notes."

The Frenchman's voice was suddenly quiet. "We only have a couple of rules in our organization. And they about cover this." His eyes warned Sheldon off. "Spanakis knows what would happen to him. He knows I'm the only one with international money. I'd come after him wherever he went. . . . You trust me, don't you?"

"Yes, I do." The captain changed the subject. "But tell me, how did you get here tonight? Without arousing any suspicion?"

"Food poisoning." Pierre told him.

"Food poisoning?"

"That's right. You see, my Monaco cruiser's got a crowd of charterers on board at the moment. And we're anchored at Syracuse." He grinned suddenly. "I forgot to warn them about eating *moules* in the harbor cafés. . . . And strangely enough we went and ate *moules* in the harbor cafés. Lots of *moules*. The passengers are all being sick in their cabins, and they think I'm the same way. But I took a quick trip to cure me. And I'll be back on board before they get up from their bunks." He looked at his watch suddenly. "Have to be moving soon. Which means that now I've got to make the big decision—whether I let you go ahead with your crazy scheme or not. . . . Because it's my money I'm risking."

Sheldon waited tensely. He didn't speak, because he saw Pierre was thinking hard. This was the moment he'd been afraid of all along.

Finally the Frenchman stood up and started pacing. He could only take two steps before he met the bulkhead, and he turned to face Sheldon in the narrow cabin, trapped into a decision. "I have to look at it like a businessman," he said slowly. "I give a man . . . call it sixty thousand pounds in cash, credit, and good will, to plan an operation. I have this boat—" he tapped the chart table "—in exchange. And I know I can get nearly fifty-five grand for her, fitted out as she is like a gunboat. . . . But that loses me five grand, and maybe I can't afford it."

Sheldon relaxed slightly.

"But as a businessman I can't afford to lose the whole deal," Pierre continued. "And the gamble is fifty-five grand against a million. Call it eight-hundred-and-fifty-thousand profit, free of tax, when I've paid wages. . . . So the answer is, what do I think of Op-er-at-ion Ban-der-snatch?" He rolled the syllables off his tongue. Then he turned away and riffled through the folders on the table.

Sheldon waited, and suddenly he didn't want the silence to end.

"Well, I think it's very good." All at once Pierre's voice was brisk and cheerful in the corner. "And there's something else I think. There's only one good thing to be said for British Naval Officers, and that is . . . they win wars." He turned and came over to Sheldon, smiling at him. "It's on."

22

The captain still couldn't get over the feeling of relief that had been with him since Pierre's visit. He was almost lightheaded as he left the rubber dinghy at the cave mouth and started climbing the hillside that rose up above the pool. He kept to the rocky outcrops, away from the loose shale where he'd leave footprints, and as he climbed higher he was surprised to find it was evening. Back in the cave, he reflected, there was no evening—nor morning, nor afternoon, just one long dark night, lit by the masthead lamp, punctuated by mealtimes. But here outside, the sun went down at about eight o'clock. And sunrise and sunset were about the only two things that happened to this mound of rock out on the ocean.

He reached the shoulder of the hill and paused for breath. From this height he could still see the last traces of day—tiny rocks that glowed with a faint red heat on the horizon. But the nearer islands had long shadows, and the sea between them was ruffled by the tiny feathers of sudden breezes. The water was dull, the color of beaten brass, and the rocks were set in it like old faded jewels. Sheldon turned away from the view, and climbed on toward the sky line. At last he saw the group of rounded boulders, and heard the metallic squeal of the radio signal that came from among them.

Panting now, he reached the boulders, and saw the trench behind them half-covered by a ground sheet. Poking up from the trench there was the strange sight of a DF loop, a metal ring, about a foot in diameter. Below it, in the shadows, Turton was squatting, surrounded by his boxes. There was a 12-volt battery, a whirring convertor, a tape recorder, and finally the radio receiver with its colored knobs. He watched as Turton adjusted the knobs, then swung the DF loop slightly until the signal was loud and steady. A two-tone signal, chirping at high speed, like a pair of mechanical birds in a cage.

"That's *Pindar*," Turton told him.

"How d'you know?"

In answer, the radar rating switched off the tape recorder and rewound the spools until he came to silent tape. "I told you *Pindar* transmitted Telex," he said. "Which makes it easier for us in one way. You see, Telex is an FSK system . . . Frequency Shift Key . . . and it comes too fast to be identified by ear." He pointed down at the recorder. "So I doctored that to run at high speed too. It's what's known as stretching the tape."

"You've lost me."

"It's simple enough." Turton found the beginning of *Pindar*'s message and pulled that part of the tape clear from the machine. "All we want to be sure about is that the message starts with *Pindar*'s call sign. Then we know it's her." He found a tiny silver bottle with a brush set in the inside of the screwcap. "This stuff's colloidal iron. If I paint it on tape, I can see the mods, see the signal, in fact." He did so, and Sheldon saw silver marks on the tape, where the paint stuck.

"Now all I've got to do . . ." Turton continued, ". . . is to check this call sign with the one you got when she came from St. Tropez." He got a small roll of tape from an envelope, saw that the two sets of silver marks matched up. "And that's *Pindar*," he said.

Pindar's message shrilled on, but Turton ignored it. He turned to a war-surplus transmitter and tapped at the Morse key. Then he waited a short while, and tapped at the key again. "Effing-bastard Greeks." His voice was suddenly hard. "This effing-bastard Greek on Leros."

"The chappie with the second receiver?"

The radar rating nodded. "I have to get through to him before I can get a fix on *Pindar*." He scowled. "Every effing night I have to hand the whole thing to him on a plate. Give him the frequency and practically give him the bearing. Three hands that bastard's got on Leros. None of 'em any effing good."

It was some time before the coded bearing came through from Leros. Turton noted it down next to his own bearing, and handed the sheet of paper to Sheldon. Without having to go back to his rulers and charts, the captain could see that *Pindar* was making her way out toward them. So tomorrow night it was. August 27. . . . He looked down to the calm sea. Somewhere out there a white ship was steaming over the dark sea, it's evening transmission nearly over. Its Telex operator thinking of his supper down on the foredeck. And on the boat deck there'd be the gentle clink of cocktail glasses and the sound of laughter. Tomorrow the party would be better. They'd raise the roof.

PART

three

23

Claire stopped suddenly, surprised to find how far she'd climbed. Below her now she could see the whole pattern of the archaeological site, the roofless corridors and chambers the guide had whispered about. And the millionaires seemed tiny and insignificant as they threaded their way through the maze. For the hundredth time Claire told herself they wouldn't dare harm her, wouldn't dare to cause her any real physical harm. She wondered if she'd been exaggerating the menace of the past few days. To calm herself, she sat in the shadow of a rock and closed her eyes. She tried to think it out, tried to get back to the peace of the first few days of the cruise.

It had been like the crisp touch of a new dress, but drawn out to cover every second of that first week. . . . The smart crowded harbor at Tourkolimano. The speedboat taking her out to the great white ship in the bay of Phaleron. The small craft wheeling around. Then the wide smooth deck that had carried her away, had opened the arms of islands. Tiny harbors, where waiters had moved the cruising party's tables slightly away from the other customers in the restaurants. Where peasant fingers had pointed in amazement at Claire's slacks and painted toenails, where thick blue smoke from charcoal grills hung overhead like a cloud. . . . And the larger, more fashionable harbors, where the poster-painted houses had surrendered to harsh European voices, harsh European music, and harsh European whisky.

The second week had begun as a slow beautiful dream. Alexis Tzannos had pointed his white ship at long-forgotten islands, immune to the tramping feet of steamers and the disease of the discothèque. He'd said he wanted the peace his own private steamer could bring him, and the time for business talks with Marotta and Kavelaris. Claire had been lulled into forgetfulness by the sudden pockets of scented breeze that ushered new islands over the horizon, by their umber shadows at evening, and the sky hardening into crystals with the passing of the sun. She'd heard a new story, seen new ghosts at each archeological dig they'd visited. But she'd forgotten the ghosts that stalked *Pindar*'s shaded decks, forgotten why she'd been brought on the cruise.

Now the dream had become a nightmare. For the past few days *Pindar* had stayed out in the open sea, and Claire had been trapped on the ship, trapped by the strange silent maneuvers of the boat-deck. She didn't understand any of the other people on the deck, didn't understand what they were trying to do to her. And she had no help from beyond the ship's rails. The few islands they called at seemed to be deserted. She'd seen no more than ten outsiders since they'd left civilization. And she herself was an outsider. That had been made very plain to her. The beauty had turned sour. The islands had become rocks.

Rocks. She suddenly heard them rattling away down the slope below her. That could mean one thing. Lakis must have seen her from the beach where he was supposed to be swimming with Giulia. And he was climbing furtively up toward her.

Reluctantly Claire opened her eyes. She looked down to where the bare shoulders of the bay became bone-white rocks warding off the waves, and again the unreality of the situation came back to her—the feeling that she was being chased across some weird planet. Out on the blue sliding water, *Pindar* seemed like a spaceship, resting on the copper-blue velvet of some strange sea. Its astronauts were down in the archaeological site, inspecting the polished stones of some previous century when there'd been life. . . . And one of the astronauts was climbing up toward her now, the outsider, the ripe spacewoman from the silent planet. In the bad space movie, she'd take off his helmet, and he'd be amazed to breathe air. More amazed by her beauty, he'd lower her to the ground for the fade-out.

In real life there was no fade-out. Lakis, panting from his climb, gripped her roughly. She felt the shale dig into her back. Not a word was spoken.

As soon as he'd finished he looked away from her, down down toward the party of people in the ruins below. He ducked down suddenly, and his face was angry. Claire looked over his shoulder and saw the woman in the lilac bathing suit staring up at her from the beach.

"Did she see us?" Dirty and used, she sank back to the ground. "Your mother?" she added disgustedly.

Lakis shrugged, and turned away to recover his breath.

"What the hell gives?" Claire didn't know where to begin. . . . The mother on the beach, the son hiding in the rocks, the strange bay, all conspired to make questions meaningless. "I mean two weeks ago you were a big boy driving your sportscar. Now suddenly you're scared of Mummy."

"Not scared of her."

"Look at you," she said angrily. "Look at us. Like two animals in a ditch."

"I've told you before." His voice was sullen. "It's just the marriage she's arranging with Giulia Marotta. She wants to keep me away from you."

"But you're not a child. Can't you say no?"

"You don't understand the way we do things."

"That's right." Claire looked around helplessly at the hot fetid rocks which hemmed her in on every side.

"It's only been like this for the past few days, while we've been out in the middle of nowhere. We can't get away from any of them. It'll be different when we get to Rhodes."

"Very different," she said quietly. "I might just jump ship."

He looked at her anxiously. "You wouldn't do that?"

"What's to keep me, for Christ's sake? I only have one rule about people. I only go with them if they're fun. And right at this moment *Pindar*'s about as much fun as a concentration camp."

"Has my father been bothering you?" he asked suddenly.

Claire felt sick. "Apart from booking a double room in every port we've made. Apart from leaving marks on my body trying to drag me off to that room. . . . No, he hasn't bothered me since that brawl you had with him."

"Well then?"

"Giulia Marotta, your future fiancée," she told him wearily. "She's making life pretty poisonous. She must have heard us together in your cabin. And she hasn't kept that exactly quiet."

"She has told one or two stories."

"Then there's your mother. She gives me the creeps. Always staring at me the whole time, and never answering when I talk to her. . . . Then there's that steward she paid to spy on us."

"That's nothing new for her."

"It's new for me. Having to meet up with a grown man behind a rock."

Lakis flushed. "But she hasn't actually harmed you or anything."

"Not if you forget that cup of coffee that nearly went over me." Claire shivered. "Or the time I found myself water skiing straight at a cliff when she was driving the speedboat."

"Accidents." Lakis was alarmed. "You can't blame her for those."

"Oh, sure. Don't you remember what she said she'd do? If she ever caught us together again?"

He paled suddenly as he peered furtively around the rock to the beach below. "She's seen us. Staring right up here at us."

Claire sat quite still. This time she didn't bother to look over his shoulder. Because now she knew she was scared of the woman in the lilac bathing suit.

24

Maria Kavelaris was still staring at her two hours later when *Pindar* had sailed. She sat in the lounge at the end of the boat deck, where Monets and Pissarros glowed on the shadowy walls, and she seemed to glow too. From this distance she was a striking blonde woman in her lilac outfit. Her body was overoiled, bulging out of the outfit at shoulder and thigh, and she could have been voluptuous if she'd allowed her mouth and eyes to play. But now, as always when they were fixed on Claire, they were hard with distaste. Her hair was beginning to show its dark roots, as was her face—a dark peasant scowl for Claire's benefit.

Uneasily, Claire turned back to the sunlight. The boat deck throbbed gently to the sound of distant engines. Overhead the blue awning rumbled on its wires, forming a tent of shadow that seemed to be suspended between burning sea and burning sky. Astern the white petals of propeller marks pushed back in a straight line to the horizon. And around this straight line were rocks, blinding in the midday heat, rising out of the water. Just rocks, and when one passed, another took its place. To Claire it was like steaming around some vast disused quarry. None of it was real. Least of all, the game she was playing with the three children of the millionaires. They were playing Monopoly for real money.

Giulia, her bikini hanging drably on her plump body, shook the dice. "Seven," she said. "Two, three, four, five, six." Her voice faded away as she saw where she'd landed on the board.

"Mayfair, with one hotel." Claire checked her property card. "Two thousand pounds. I mean drachmas."

Giulia scowled, turned away to her portable record player on the deck beside her.

"Not that goddamn record again," Lakis said savagely. "I'll throw it over the side."

"Don't you like it?" Giulia asked with the arm poised.

"The first hundred and fifty times I didn't mind it," Lakis replied. "I promise," he added warningly, "it'll go over the side."

She put the arm down and pretended to examine the record.

"Well, are you playing?" Lakis scowled at her. "Two thousand drachmas you owe her." He pointed at Claire.

"Can't pay." Giulia childishly scattered her mortgaged properties over the board, breaking up the rows of wooden houses. "That's the end of the game, then."

"Anyone else want to go on?" Claire asked.

"Not much point. You'll win in the end." Michaeli looked at his small row of properties. "You've got Mayfair and all along that line. Here." He handed her the rest of his money.

Claire tried to refuse, but he made her take it. Then

Lakis threw in his pile as well, and that really surprised her. Lakis was usually a very bad loser. Suddenly Claire remembered the angry conversation he'd had with his mother when they'd returned on board. Maybe Lakis had lost more than money.

As if to bear this out, Dimitri Kavelaris suddenly appeared and walked toward her over the deck. He was freshly shaven, his belly was sucked in, and he seemed as taut and controlled as when he'd first met her in the café at Palma. Leaning down, he put his hand on her shoulder —something he hadn't dared do since they'd been on *Pindar*. He smiled at her confidently as he watched her stuff her winnings in her purse. "Who won?" he asked unnecessarily. "I'll take on the winner at table tennis."

"Not right now." Claire tried to refuse. "It's too hot."

"Come on." He leaned over her and gripped her arm. "Somebody's got to help me keep my weight down. And the rest of the Jet Set seem bored to tears."

Claire felt herself being hauled to her feet. There was a limit to how hard she could struggle in front of the others, and she followed Kavelaris dumbly toward the stern rail. He led her down the steps to the afterdeck. The wake, which fanned out toward the horizon, showed hardly a fleck of foam, as though there were no life left in the sea. And there was no life left in Claire. Tiredly she avoided Kavelaris' hand as he ushered her through the gymnasium door. But she couldn't ignore the hand that strayed over her body while he showed her how to hold a table-tennis bat, how to stand away from the table. Flushing angrily, she ducked out of his grasp, ran to the far end of the gymnasium, and told him to serve. He was an expert player, delighted to show off his skill. Crouching warily behind his gnarled forearm, he took a game off her without conceding a point. She managed to avoid him as they changed ends. Grinning, he said he was going to give her a chance.

She soon saw what he meant. Now his smashing returns missed the table, but they weren't inaccurate. Stung repeatedly on her breasts, thighs, and belly by the buzzing white ball, Claire began to lose her temper. Then she saw to her surprise that his lightning smashes weren't sadistic. His smile was charming and polite, and there was nothing sensual about his face. It was just his way of touching her body at long range, turning his skill at table tennis into sexual prowess. Twisting and weaving, she still couldn't avoid the stinging ball. Still he smiled, still he insisted that they continue the game.

Ten-all. And Claire was now trying to lose her serves, now trying to win. Anything to finish the game off quickly. But Kavelaris outsmarted her at every point. Fifteen-all. Stung once again on the inside of her thigh, Claire's mind went past surprise, temper, to the borders of lunacy. The sheer unreality of what was happening came across to her. . . . A huge, shadowy, air-conditioned gymnasium was floating on the sea. Through the wide windows there were yellow rocks drifting past on velvet water. And at one end of a green ping-pong table, a politely smiling man was batting balls at a girl in a gold bikini, as hard as the muscles in his forearm would allow. . . . Searching for some frame to the strange picture, Claire realized it was as mad and orderly as a Salvador Dali canvas.

Then there was an extra face painted in to the corner of the picture: Maria Kavelaris' face suddenly appeared at one of the windows. A face that snarled in hatred as she saw another of her husband's successful smashes. Kavelaris turned around, and his wife disappeared. Claire took the chance to put down her bat. The game, she said, was over.

Going out through the gymnasium doors, she suddenly saw that one of the deck chairs was sprawled crookedly against the ship's rail. She clutched the door handle to steady herself.

"What's the matter?" Kavelaris panted.

"My purse." Claire felt herself flushing again. "It was on the chair. With all my winnings."

"Maybe the wind," Kavelaris said uneasily.

"I only put it there when we came in. There's been no wind."

He nodded slowly. "And how much did you win at Monopoly?"

"About fourteen thousand drachs."

"Nearly one hundred and ninety pounds." His face was worried as he worked it out. Then all at once he smiled and moved toward her. "We'll have to find some way to refund you the money."

Claire burst into tears. She started running.

And the nightmare returned. She was running through this vast deserted ship—deserted because it was siesta time. Kavelaris was padding along behind her, falling back, slower than she was. Then suddenly appearing ahead of her, around corners, or at the top of stairways. There was nowhere she could find safety—their footsteps kicked up dust from carpet after carpet. There was no one to help her—the bridge ladder and engine-room door were both locked—the crew sleeping guiltily in the sun. Claire ran on through nightmarish surroundings. She passed paintings she knew only as postcards, passed ikons, Victorian telephones, a Hammond organ, and a bar shaped like a Crusader tent. Suddenly she came out to blue sky. There were sea and rocks far below her, and she saw she was on the upper deck. She ran quickly aft, trying to reach the boat deck and Lakis. Then she realized she'd chosen the wrong side of the ship. Her way was blocked by the elevator housing, a smooth white block she couldn't climb. Turning, she found that Kavelaris was coming along the deck behind her.

"Are you young people bored?" It wasn't Kavelaris speaking, and for a moment Claire was mystified. Until she saw that she was standing by the window of Tzannos' stateroom. And it was his calm voice coming out to her.

"Bored?" She tried to say it evenly. Kavelaris had stopped, thirty feet away down the sunlit deck. Deliberately Claire went toward the window and looked into the shadowy stateroom. Tzannos was sitting in an armchair halfway across the room, his back toward her. She could see his mane of white hair, his long flecked hands that were joined in prayer, touching the bridge of his nose.

"I feel I must apologize for the monotonous scenery," he said softly. "We've been out in the wilderness for four days now."

"Is it really four days?" Claire tried to open the window farther, but the slats of the metal blind prevented her. Warily, she looked around at Kavelaris. Twenty feet, and two windows away, he was sizing her up.

"And I'm sorry we couldn't stay at Leros," Tzannos continued. "But it never works. The people expect me to drive around handing out money, and they hate it."

Kavelaris was nearer on the side deck. He chanced a quick look through one of the windows at Tzannos. Then he came on slowly, uncertain of Claire.

"Really they hate me." The voice coming through the window was tired and gentle, like a schoolmaster's. Claire pressed herself close to the open gap, caught the smell of Tzannos' cigar smoke, and a hint of the hair oil he used. "The people of Leros say I own half the ships in the world. And they say I don't build any. Neither is true."

Claire saw that Kavelaris was now only ten feet away, coming at a crouch as he passed a window, his belly hanging between his knees. . . . She told herself she had to stay by the window, she had to stay by the window, it was her only protection. But it was a nightmare, and she could do nothing she wanted to. The sight of Kavelaris' belly, wet with sweat, made her back away toward the elevator housing. He grinned suddenly, and came closer.

"I build small ships because the yard at Skaramanga

is small. I buy my large ships where the price is best."
Tzannos' voice droned on from the stateroom. "There are
over eight million people in Greece, over eight million
trade unions. And forgetting all about politics, just talking
about the economic situation. . . . The key to the whole
thing isn't industry, it's getting people back to the land."

Kavelaris still came on at a crouch although he'd
passed the last window of the stateroom. His eyes squinted
up at her in the sunlight, wondering about his luck. Claire
backed away until she reached the elevator housing.

"There have to be new ideas. . . . Tobacco and cotton. Those are the areas where Greece could be strong,"
Tzannos continued. "But you can't get Greeks together.
Try and get four of them to share a tractor, and they
scream about collectives, call you a Communist."

The voice was muffled now. Claire had retreated
until a corner of the elevator housing now hid Tzannos'
window from view. And there was no way around to the
boat deck—unless she tried the ship's rail. It was dangerous. There was a gap where the rail itself merged into the
lift shaft. And the sea was hard and creamy, forty feet
below her. . . . Kavelaris was very close. Claire swung
herself over the rail. . . . She came to the gap, and could
go no farther. This was the end of the nightmare. She'd
wake up . . . .

"Methods are two thousand years old on the land."
Tzannos' words were fainter, blurred by the wind. Claire
tried to imagine herself back by the window, tried to smell
the cigar smoke once again, and forget her body on the
sunlit deck. "In Crete last year, half the sultana crop was
ruined by rain. That meant a lot of people were ruined
too. Crete could feed a third of Greece. She doesn't even
support herself."

Hanging on to the outside of the ship's rail, Claire
couldn't defend herself. She knew Kavelaris was kneeling
beside her, could feel his sweat, and his wet mouth. . . .
But what could she say? Mr. Tzannos, your partner has

his hands under my bikini? . . . If she shouted, Kavelaris would have time to get away before Tzannos came to the window. . . . A scream built up in her throat.

Then suddenly the hands were gone. She heard Kavelaris pad away, heard a door closing quietly. And gradually she understood why—there were footsteps approaching from the far end of the upper deck. Around the corner of the radio bridge came Marilena—Tzannos' girl friend—and a steward carrying her easel and paints.

"*Na to theesis etho.*" Marilena showed the man where to leave the easel. Then she dismissed him, and put on her paint-smeared smock. Suddenly she looked around and saw Claire. Her eyes showed no surprise at finding a girl in a gold bikini clinging to the outside of the ship's rail. They just became hard and thoughtful.

Claire wondered if the woman had heard Kavelaris leaving. She was a little afraid of this dried-up gypsy of a woman, who missed nothing that happened on board. But she needed to be near her for protection, and so she slowly made her way back along the rail until she could climb over onto the deck. Hiding her trembling hands behind her back, she walked toward Marilena.

The older woman had turned around to her painting. Her clawlike hand dabbed quickly at the canvas with a cloth soaked in paint, trying to reproduce the rocks that rose up on the far side of the breeze-ruffled water. Rocks that were slipping by the rail, escaping from her, and Marilena painted faster. She was like her picture—taut, angry, barely controlled. Chunky bracelets jangled on her wrist as she smeared more paint on her cloth. The smock around the palette was spattered with livid colors. And beneath the kerchief, her eyes burned as she spat out her breath angrily.

Claire watched the canvas quiver in a growing frenzy, appalled by the fury of the woman's hawklike face. But she stayed next to her, watching the tortured progress of the painting. And as she stayed, she felt strangely relieved, felt that some of her own pain had been taken away from her. This woman's strange problem was so different from her own.

Suddenly the stateroom door opened behind her, and Tzannos came out on deck. Dressed in a white linen suit, white shirt, white shoes, it was as if he were trying to camouflage himself against the walls of his ship. He was the only person on board who kept religiously out of the sun, and his mottled face and hands had got steadily paler throughout the cruise. A thin, shy man, he stood first on one foot, then on the other.

"I've just been apologizing to—" he waved an arm at Claire "—for cruising in such uninteresting waters."

"Most beautiful coast in the world. This is the real Greece," Marilena spat once again. The cloth in her hand skidded across the canvas, and destroyed the rock pile she'd built. "But impossible, quite impossible to paint it." Then something about the line of her angry erasure seemed to please her. She began stabbing rocks on top of it once again. "Any fool can paint rocks. Rocks and sea. But how in God's name d'you paint light? How d'you make anyone reach for their dark glasses when they look at your painting?"

Tzannos laughed. He put one arm around her, and got a smear of paint on his suit for his pains.

Marilena worked on. Claire felt she had to break the silence. "When do we get to Rhodes? I heard we were going to Rhodes," she added weakly.

"Not before tomorrow night," Tzannos told her. "We're calling somewhere this evening." He seemed to be sizing her up carefully. "I haven't told anyone about it. In fact, I'm a little ashamed of my secret in front of all these sophisticated people."

"What secret?" Marilena snorted angrily. Then she took up another handful of rocks.

"There is a small island, shaped like a nose." Tzannos decided he could tell them. "It's called Miti, the Greek word for nose. And there's nothing on this island apart from a tiny church, no more than two meters high." He glanced at Claire. "D'you understand?"

She shook her head.

"Sometimes you see small churches on deserted rocky islands. It means people were shipwrecked there." He shrugged. "And in the storm and the waves, these people promise God that they'll build a church on the island if they're saved. . . . They are saved, and they build a church. A very small one. Either because they aren't rich, or, in the case of my father, because he never built large churches when the sea was calm."

Claire smiled.

"Now only we three and the captain know where we're going tonight." Tzannos put his finger to his lips. "And we'll keep it our little secret."

"What for?" Marilena grunted.

"Because the captain seems to be very worried about sailing through such lonely seas. He seems to think something could happen to us." The millionaire smiled and pointed around to the empty horizon. "I ask you, what could possibly happen to us?"

25

Green baize table.
Names that are written in silver on ebony
plaques.
Cut glasses of whisky.
Cigars come from Cuba and nobody asks.
Old necks in new collars.

> One more than usual. He's new and he's
>   scared he looks wrong.
> Special occasion.
> They hand him some whisky.
> They hand him the key to the Executive's
>   john.
> Arthur Bunny has ar-RIVED . . .
> Her-hive got the key of the door.
> Ner-never been sixty-one before.

Only eighteen times before, eighteen times in the past
hour, Claire had counted them. She watched as Giulia's
English beat record ground to a halt, watched as Giulia
replaced the pick-up arm at the start of the record. Nobody tried to stop her, even Lakis had stopped complain-
ing. The tune had been playing for so long that no one
could hear it any more.

> One more than usual. He's new and he's
>   scared he looks wrong.
> Special occasion.
> They hand him some whisky.
> They hand him the key to the Executive's
>   john.

August 27, August 27. Claire found herself repeating the date over and over to herself in time to the tune.
Would the day never end? And now Tzannos had said
that they wouldn't reach Rhodes till the day after tomorrow—August 29. That made another thirty-six hours
she'd have to endure. Suddenly she decided she'd definitely leave the ship at Rhodes. She'd make her way to the
post office, and there'd be a telegram: COME HOME AT
ONCE, PET, ALL IS FORGIVEN, CHARLIE CLORE. . . . But
Claire couldn't make herself laugh any more. And there
was nothing around her to laugh at.

> Green baize table.
> Names that are written in silver on ebony
>   plaques.

Cut glasses of whisky.
Cigars come from Cuba and nobody asks.

August 27, and it was nearly a quarter to nine. Almost time to get changed for the evening cocktail. Claire shivered slightly—a bikini wasn't enough protection at this late hour. But she hadn't dared to leave the boat deck since that episode with Kavelaris. Here, in the public eye, was the only place on the whole ship where she felt safe. Beyond the rail, the few squat rocks were cooling in the water, hardly seeming to move past. The sun moved quicker as it lipped over the horizon, changing the shape of the rocks while it slid up and over them, causing the upper slopes to blink down in yellow surprise at the grape-colored sea all around them. It should have been beautiful.

Arthur Bunny has ar-RIVED . . .
Her-hive got the key of the door.
Ner-never been sixty-one before.

Then suddenly the record ended, and Giulia made no effort to start it up again. The silence was suddenly deafening. The blue awning rumbled steadily overhead, and a barrel of ash fell from Tzannos' cigar with a crash. There was no other movement on the long twilit deck. Far away, by the stern rail, Tzannos and the two other millionaires were sitting absolutely still, their lips unmoving as they muttered about money—or about her, Claire suddenly realized with a start. All three men were now staring at her while they whispered together.

Nearer at hand, between the long shadows of the speedboat and the racing yacht, sat the women. Again, they all seemed to be staring at her. Marilena pretending to inspect a corner of her painting, Laura Marotta looking up suddenly from her knitting, and Maria Kavelaris staring quite blatantly, with nothing to occupy her hands.

Shifting uncomfortably, Claire turned around to the millionaires' children, grouped by the record player.

Maybe their attention had been caught as she'd moved, or maybe they'd been looking at her all the time. . . . Claire tried to hold on to her fear, told herself she was imagining it all. But the facts remained—everyone on the boat deck had been speaking Greek since the early afternoon—and all the English magazines had disappeared from the rack in the lounge.

Still nobody moved. The shadowy deck was like some strange mortuary, with its bodies laid out on their separate slabs, and watched over by white-coated morticians—the two stewards, standing by the lounge doors. And Claire was lying alone in the center of the deck, like some diseased corpse, waiting for dissection. . . . She forced herself to stay calm, forced herself to plan out the moves ahead. The next danger area was the pre-cocktail period, when the decks would be deserted, and everybody would be in their cabins changing. Claire decided she'd wait on the boat deck until the rest of them had gone. Nothing could happen to her here, in full view of the stewards who'd be preparing the cocktails. And she wouldn't go down to her own cabin to change until five past nine. That would minimize the risk.

All at once the evening routine began. Soft-footed, the Telex operator walked the length of the deck over to the millionaires by the stern rail. He saluted, and got the last messages for the evening transmission. As he walked back past Claire, the three women got up from their chairs and followed him toward the lounge. Then Lakis got up stiffly, and led Giulia and Michaeli after their parents. That just left the men at the far end of the deck. Claire turned toward them and watched—fascinated—as Marotta pulled out the tail of his silk shirt, and speared himself unemotionally in the rump with a hypodermic. He did this before every meal. Why couldn't he do it in the privacy of his cabin? Claire didn't look up as the three millionaires walked by her, whispering to each other in Greek.

Then she was alone on the twilit deck. There was just the clink of glasses from the lounge, as the stewards polished them and laid them out. And suddenly a new sound—the chatter of Telex keys from the radio bridge above. Claire stayed where she was for a moment, then she got up, unable to stop herself. She had to see this link with the outside world. In an Athens office, a machine was printing the words being tapped out here. In Athens people were laughing, talking about football teams, phoning up girls. Claire crept toward the bridge ladder.

Too late, she realized she was passing the millionaires' cabins. Kavelaris ran out and grabbed her as she got her first foot on the ladder. His smile was scented and confident. He stuffed a sheaf of bank notes in her bikini top. "This'll make up for your Monopoly winnings." Then he clamped his other hand across her mouth as she struggled. She bit it. He grinned and held on. There was only one thing to do. She did it with her knee. Kavelaris doubled up, and she ran past him.

Down below on the main stairway, Lakis was waiting for her. What really made her mad was the transistor radio in his hand. It was the same radio he'd used to drown their voices and movements during the first nights of the cruise. Crazily, Claire reached out for the radio and smashed it against the banister rail. Lakis drew back in amazement, and let her walk on down the carpeted corridor, past the doors with the porpoise handles.

And now the whole bloody family. Claire was stopped in her tracks by Maria Kavelaris. The woman was suddenly glowing and beautiful. Her hair was arranged so that it was perfectly blonde and smooth, and she was dressed in a cool silk shift. But it was her face that amazed Claire most of all. The eyes and the lips were moist and voluptuous, and they pleaded with her. A gloved hand was laid on Claire's bare shoulder as she tried to walk past. And Maria Kavelaris was trembling, wordless, trying to hold Claire with her smile. Then she backed down. A steward—the steward who took bribes—came past them both with a wet bath towel. Claire ran on to her cabin.

She locked the door, and leaned against it, no longer understanding anything. Was the woman a dyke? Had that been the trouble all along? Claire gave it up. The orchid walls, the ikon over her bedside table gave her no answer. She went through to the marbled bathroom and turned on one of the porpoise taps. Then she turned it off again. She didn't feel like cocktails tonight, she felt like going to bed.

Between the sheets, her foot dug into a cold pulpy mess. Before she could even scream, slimy grabbing arms had wound around her legs. Then she saw the octopus, fully two feet long, writhing on the bed. There were two tentacles wrapped tightly around her shin. . . . Not to faint. . . . She stared at the gray suckers, watched as more of them reached out for her. They blurred. . . . Not to faint. . . . And suddenly she was touching it. She tore the tentacles from her leg, jumped clear. She forced herself to wind the sheets up into an oozing, kicking bundle, throw it in the closet, and slam the door. With her reeking hand clenched over her mouth, she ran for the basin.

She washed herself three times, and her shoulders were still heaving, the smell still on her hands. Tears streamed down unchecked as she remembered Maria Kavelaris' smile, the gloved hand trying to keep her out of her cabin, and the steward with the wet bath towel. . . . Her brain was no longer her own. Mechanically it noted the dull thuds from the closet door, the laughing voices from the boat deck, and the faint clicking of the Telex keys from the bridge.

26

In the gray radar room, *Pindar*'s Telex transmission got steadily louder. Turton faded down the volume and swung his chair around to the radar screen. He watched the moving pencil of light print a larger star almost on top of the last, right by the screen's center. "She's coming straight for us." He turned to Sheldon in amazement.

"Why the hell's she want to come in so close? A boat that size? With rocks all around her?" The captain looked down at the chart in his hands. "Clearly marked. They even call the biggest rock an island, give it a name . . . Miti."

"And there's nothing on this island?" Turton asked. "I mean, nothing that would bring her this way?"

"Nothing. Completely deserted. There's just one of those tiny churches. You know the things?" Anxiously, Sheldon went over the facts again: "That's why we chose this spot to lie up and wait for her. Dammit, we've had her on our radar screen five hours now. She's kept to a steady course, the right course, one that would take her by us in the deep water to the north. So we anchored to the south of this island, where we'd be hidden. . . . And we can't be spotted by her radar because of the shoals all around. That's right, isn't it?"

Turton nodded.

"It seemed all right on paper," the captain continued. "She steams past us just before twenty-one-hundred-thirty. We keep low until her Telex transmission ends, then we attack. Closing speed of eighteen knots, and we can reach her in three minutes. . . . How much longer's she got on the air?" he added quickly.

"I make it about six minutes."

"Damn. She'll be well past us. That makes it much more risky."

"Skipper!" Turton's voice was suddenly hoarse. "She's changed course again. She's making straight for the north coast of the island. She's slowing down!"

Sheldon found he was trembling as he compared the dots on the radar screen with the contours of the chart. Then he crumpled up the roll of paper and threw it away. "She's in the bloody channel, making straight for the bay. There's only one thing she can do now, anchor on the far side of the island!"

Turton watched him uneasily. The burble of high-speed Morse from *Pindar* got louder.

All at once Sheldon leaned past him and faded the volume down. "Keep that damn thing quiet. Keep it through the phones," he snapped. "And go and get the crew assembled on the foredeck. Tell them I want absolute silence."

Turton got up from his chair.

"Then come back here and keep radio watch. Tell me the moment they finish transmitting." Sheldon made for the door. "This is it."

In his cabin, the captain tried to keep his hands under control. But they still trembled as he picked up the rubber carnival mask from his bunk. Attached to the mask was a crude hat made out of folded newspaper—a child's version of a pirate hat. He took them with him as he made his way slowly up to the bridge. Then he leaned over the sprayshield to see the crew waiting for him below. All of them had masks and paper hats in their hands, all of them wore blue Navy issue that merged into the thickening night.

"Pay attention," Sheldon whispered down to them.

"Change of plan. *Pindar* is anchoring on the far side of the island." He pointed around to the near coast line, the shoulder of rock that was now cloaked in twilight. "And that makes it one hell of a lot easier for us, except that we're too close to go in under power. They'll hear us, and they'll be waiting for us. . . . So I want all of you over the side in the life raft with paddles. You'll take a line from the ship, and you'll tow her around that point there." The men turned toward the rocky promontory, where a hole in the clouds caught a strange freak sunset from the long-departed sun.

"The operation itself I'm not worried about," Sheldon continued. "But I want to run over the standing orders concerning the millionaires once again. Millionaires are no ordinary people, or they wouldn't have got where they are. They're extra-ordinary. But the Navy has a way of getting cooperation out of extra-ordinary people. Firstly it takes them away from everything they've ever known. Secondly it disciplines them. This is called basic training. . . ." He paused suddenly. There was something eerie about the freak sunset and the unusual layer of low cloud above him. The whole sky seemed to be sagging toward the hole of light in the west, where *Pindar* was coming from.

"Basic training for millionaires." He got a low ripple of laughter from the men below. "Is only slightly different. We have to take them away from everything they're used to. . . . Their money, their power, their sense of importance. . . . And we have to discipline them through fear. Real fear. Fear that they could die at any moment. Now I've told you all this before. I want no violence, but the threat of violence. Menace." He held his carnival mask and hat up into the fading light. "You've all got these. They'll make you look bloody horrible, and sound bloody horrible, thanks to the scrambler mikes that'll fit over your mouths. But I want you to talk as little as possible. I want you to move slowly, and think before moving.

. . . That's all." He stared over the men's heads. The hook of yellow glare in the west faded to a dirty gray. Inexorably night, and the operation, had begun.

Then they all heard it. The slow tramp of engines from the far side of the promontory.

The sound grew louder, vibrating through the sea and slapping at the rocks. Sheldon's hands shook uncontrollably as he saw the faint flicker of light outlining the far tip of the island. Then the flicker became a white glow, moving steadily up the rocky slope until it silhouetted the church on the summit—the strange squat church that was no bigger than a dog kennel. Suddenly the throbbing engines stopped. There was a long tense pause. Broken abruptly by the thunder of an anchor chain and a brief burst astern on one engine. Then silence.

Turton came up from the radar room. He whispered that the Telex transmission had finished. Sheldon nodded, and told the man to join the rest of the crew in the life raft. He watched them all go over the side into the raft: Turton, Barney, Mitch, Spanakis, Roche, Laborde, the two Greeks. And in his mind's eye, he saw Sandy and Pierre, a thousand miles apart, waiting tensely for news.

Then he heard the gentle swish of paddles from the life raft, and he was suddenly calm. His hands stopped trembling, and he forgot the names of ships and men. . . . Because it was the same. It was the *Burg Rostock* all over again. . . . *The men in Navy blue, paddling steadily as they pulled the MTB through the water. The rocky promontory coming slowly toward them through the darkness. And around the promontory, the lights that outlined the* Burg Rostock, *anchored off Leros harbor—a sitting target for the one torpedo they had left to fire.*

27

Green baize table.
Names that are written in silver on ebony
plaques.

The sound echoed strangely around the rocky walls of the
bay. There was no moon to break through the dark
clouds, and the shape of the island was indistinct except
where it caught the lights of the ship. And *Pindar* seemed
like two ships, the real one standing on top of its own
reflection in the smooth black water.

Arthur Bunny has ar-RIVED . . .
Her-hive got the key of the door.
Ner-never been sixty-one before.

The beat record came to an end on the boat deck. And
then there were just soft footsteps, laughter, and strange
half-sentences crossing the still night air. The people on
the deck were beautiful in their evening dress. Jewels and
white shirt fronts caught the light. And nobody bothered
to look around as the Telex operator left the radio bridge,
went down two flights of steps to the main deck.

He paused by two seamen who were lowering the
Mediterranean ladder over the side. They fitted the
chromium uprights, and the white cord that linked them,
then they went with the Telex operator along to the foredeck, where a long table was laid for supper. A buzzer
sounded, and deck hands, greasers, stewards, filtered
slowly out of the fo'c's'le hatch. In little groups they
leaned against the rail, cigarettes in their cupped hands,

talking down at the dark water. Their voices were louder and cruder than the gentle conversation from the boat deck. Suddenly they turned as a cook appeared with a steaming soup tureen. Cigarettes flew over the ship's side like fireflies, fizzling out in the water as the men moved toward the table.

Out in the darkness the MTB was gray and silent. Men in dark blue swarmed quickly on board her from the life raft bobbing at her side. Then the raft was fastened to a line at the stern, and the men took up their positions. They put on masks, and on top of these they put on hats made of folded newspaper. There was one difference about the man behind the ship's wheel. The pirate captain had a small red light set into the peak of his hat. Suddenly he shouted, a huge metallic bleat that shattered the night: "*One!*"

Water boiled under the stern, and the engines bellowed. The gray ship raced toward the blaze of light that was *Pindar*. High up on her boat deck, faces whipped around in surprise.

Blomp-Blomp. The faces vanished in a cloud of black smoke. Smoke that quickly enveloped the upper part of the huge ship followed by a shower of sparks, raining down into the water as the MTB approached.

"*Two!*" The engines roared again, and the MTB spun around as it slowed. Shadowy pirate figures raced along her decks, took up their positions with rifles raised.

"*Three!*" The pirate captain snapped on a searchlight. Its beam pierced through the smoke, found debris knifing down through tattered awnings, found speedboat covers ablaze, found a group of frightened people in evening dress running from the flames.

"*Stand quite still!*"

But there was panic on the boat deck. Passengers and stewards milled around, trying to escape the beam of the searchlight. Security men chased after them, hurling them to the deck.

"*Fire!*" Every small arm on the MTB opened up. A hail of bullets ripped the awnings above *Pindar*'s boat deck and foredeck to shreds. Crew and passengers, far apart on the great white ship, dropped down and stayed down.

"*Stop firing!*" And then there was just the echo of gunfire, rattling around the walls of the bay. The pirate captain waited until he could be heard. "Security men! Stand up when I say! . . . *Stand up!*"

Nobody moved.

"Guns." The captain's voice was softer.

Blomp. At this range the smoke from the Bofors was one with the smoke of *Pindar*'s afterdeck. Curling away, thick and acrid, it revealed part of the white stern as a claw of twisted metal. *Pindar* was *Pindar* no longer. Under the gleaming paint, the buckled plates were those of any other wounded ship. And on the boat deck, the millionaries were crouched in fear—millionaires no longer.

"*Stand up!*"

Sheepishly, the four security men stood up into the searchlight beam and raised their hands.

"That's better." The pirate captain clicked on a second searchlight and trained it on the long supper table on *Pindar*'s foredeck. "I want the crew also to stand up, hands above their heads. . . . *Stand up!*"

Chairs grated back on the foredeck. The row of frightened men stood up from their meal, blinking in the bright light.

"*Pindar.*" The strange metal voice now seemed calmer. "There is a forty-millimeter gun trained on you. There are also two machine guns and five automatic rifles. So keep quite still."

They kept quite still.

"*Four!*" There was sudden activity on the MTB. Men ran aft to the rubber life raft moored below the stern. Its outboard motor fired at the second pull, and then it bumped away through the debris on the water, over to *Pindar's* Mediterranean ladder. Seven men in all, but each with the same weirdly grinning face, they ran up to the wreckage of the boat deck. The last two men carried a long clanking chain between them. They clipped one end of it to an awning strut, and the other end to a second strut about forty feet away. Hanging down from the chain's center were pairs of open handcuffs. Using their rifle butts, the pirates edged the security men over to four of the handcuffs.

The gunmen had their wrists chained above their heads, and their guns removed. Then it was a simple matter to get the millionaires on their feet. Terrified, with their shirt fronts and faces blackened by the embers on deck, they were handcuffed in a line. Meekly the stewards and officers followed them, until every member of the cocktail party was hanging from the chain, swaying in the smoke that still billowed down from the burning radio bridge.

"*Five!*" The macabre pirate figures came down from the boat deck and ran the length of *Pindar* with another clanking chain. This they fastened to two struts of the foredeck awning, and then went along the row of uniformed crew, handcuffing their wrists in turn. Only one man resisted. A rifle butt slapped him forward over the supper table. He was hauled back, with soup stains down his front, and manacled in line with the others. Finally the whole crew was chained together, and one of the pirates went down the row, counting heads.

It was a strange sight. The huge Greek yacht was still gleaming and unmarked below the main deck. But her white stern was torn apart, and her boat deck was on fire. Flames flickered up from the blue covers of the speedboats and the racing yacht, their smoke joining that of the shattered radio bridge above. Then there were the two rows of chained figures, each held in the cold white grip of a searchlight on their separate decks.

Suddenly, at the forward end of the boat deck, one of the lounge doors opened. And a blonde-haired girl appeared.

"*Godalmighty!*" The strange shout came from the bridge of the MTB.

28

Sheldon was stunned. . . . Claire Harding. Claire *Harding*. He'd never known her second name. And here she was, walking calmly out through the doors as though she were looking for her cigarettes. Then she stopped, seeing the smoke and the chained figures. . . . It was easy enough to catch her. Two pirates raced up from the main deck and handcuffed her next to the millionaires.

"*Six!*" The captain heard himself give the order, but he no longer knew what it meant. And he couldn't work out what the girl meant, here, in this place, at this time. He watched as she came over the water toward him in the life raft, sitting with *Pindar's* passengers in a sullen chained circle. She was the last to be hauled on board the MTB and as she saw the weird pirate figures reach out for her with their rifles, she fainted.

Past understanding, past belief, Sheldon followed Spanakis down the ladder to the cell block they'd called Millionaires' Row. Revolver in hand, he waited with the Greek in the narrow corridor, listening to the handcuffs being unshackled from the chain on the deck above. They came down one by one. To each, Sheldon said the same: "*Strip!*" His microphone blaring the word into a horrible obscenity. Hating the sight of their paunchy bodies, he pushed them into their cells with his pistol, and pointed to the prison clothes on each bunk. Finally the millionaires were nothing more than a pile of clothing in the corridor, and there was just the one cell that was still empty.

She came down the ladder slowly, swinging back in fear as she saw the two armed men. Sheldon lowered his pistol, and motioned her past him to the cell. But Spanakis wanted his oats. His eyes glinting behind the leering rubber mask, he screamed at her to strip. Suddenly Sheldon lost control. With one hand he hauled the Greek off and flung him to the ground. With the other, he pushed Claire into her cell and slammed the door. Then, without a word, he led the way on deck.

Someone must have given the order, "*Seven.*" Because *Pindar's* crew were now crossing the MTB's deck in a slow, fumbling chain. Seven pirates, with rifles at the ready, lined them in front of their cell block. Still handcuffed, they were made to step back into their cells one by one. The chain that linked them passed through wide cutouts in each door. . . . But Sheldon saw none of it, the operation went on like clockwork without him. All he could see was a young girl's face split open in terror, and a leering pirate mask bending over her.

When his reason returned, he was standing alone on the bridge, and there was a strange rhythmic chant in his ears. Then he realized it came from the cell block, a building roar of fury, and the steady beat of chains flailing at metal doors. Rising to a crescendo, the voices were echoed back by the walls of the bay, and by *Pindar's* towering hull. The yacht was more distant now, and pointing straight at the MTB which had drifted away and around. There was a faint haze of smoke and sparks over her funnel, but from the bows the Greek ship seemed to be undamaged. And on her foredeck, dark figures were moving quickly under yellow work lights, lowering the seaplane over the side on its hoist. As the plane bounced on the water, more dark figures approached it in the life raft. They made fast a line and towed it across to the MTB's stern.

Sheldon went aft, and the noise from the cell block was deafening. He watched the two masked figures in the life raft as they attached a long storm warp—thick cable and supple Manila—to the seaplane's floats. Then they brought the warp through the MTB's stern fair-leads, and fastened it to the bitts on deck. Satisfied with the work, the captain sent the two men down to the engine room, and swung himself up on the bridge once again. Anxiously he looked across at *Pindar,* and saw the two distant figures muttering over the controls of her anchor winch. One was Barney, by his size, the other Turton. Suddenly they straightened. Steam hissed from the winch, and the great links of her chain clanked steadily up through the hawsepipe.

There was silence from the cell block as the huge anchor grated into position. The sound rang right around the bay. Through glasses, Sheldon watched the ship, saw Spanakis—a small, strange figure—alone in *Pindar's* vast wheelhouse. Barney was down below in the engine room. He'd assured Sheldon he could start any engine in the world. And apparently he could, because suddenly the sound of a compressor stuttered out across the water. The air bottles that turned over *Pindar's* giant diesels were now filling up.

It took five minutes by Sheldon's watch, but it seemed like thirty. Then the compressor stopped, and the wheezing tread of one engine replaced it. Slowly the huge ship came past the MTB, and she showed her shell scars once again. The sparks from her awnings and smoldering boats were no more than shooting stars as she headed out into the night. Sheldon rang down Slow Ahead, and followed in her wake.

They were out in the open sea now, rolling in deep water. The millionaires had returned to the foredeck and were drawn up by the Bofors gun, guarded by four masked men with rifles. But they weren't looking at the masked men, they were staring dully out across the water. Hate, shock, and disbelief flitted across their faces as they watched their ship—one of the largest yachts in the world—slowly settle in the water. Torn metal scarred the radio bridge and stern, the boat deck was charred and black, but the power of the great white ship was still evident. Lights blazed from every window and porthole. Deck chairs, cocktail shakers, and glasses were still where they'd been left. The table in the dining saloon shone with silver that would never be touched again. And on the crew's supper table, the soup was cold, untasted.

Curtains flapped out of the square windows as the ship sank faster. Carpets bulged, and chairs ran crazily downhill. Monets and Pissarros swung around, then fell into the water. And the water reached the main deck, then the boat deck, and could rise no farther—the rails were hanging on to the surface. Until a sudden bellow of pain slid the whole ship forward and downward into the black sea. Incredibly, they could still see the slots of light diving into the darkness below. Then no more, as every cabin light went out. A vast explosion welled up from the depths, built a mountain of white water on the surface, rumbling, falling back upon itself. Then suddenly the sea was bare. And night closed in on the few remaining bits of wreckage.

Sheldon felt sick. He was glad that *Pindar*'s captain hadn't been on deck to see his ship go down. But the exhibition had its point. The millionaires, their ladies, and their children had shrunk to the size of gaunt convicts, clutching their coarse uniforms to them in sudden chill.

29

Moving slowly under its heavy load, the MTB returned to its hide-out on the island. Reaching the outer cave, it prepared to shed half its load onto the concrete jetty. A searchlight snapped on from the bridge. And in its beam, masked men lowered the heavy block and tackle that hung down from the metal sheerlegs. This tackle they swung over to the MTB and fastened to a large ring set into the roof of the superstructure. The bolts securing the structure to the deck were each unscrewed in turn, and then the whole thing was hoisted and swung over to the jetty. There were screams of fear from the prisoners inside as their cell block came to rest in a cloud of cement dust.

Some time later, the MTB picked up her moorings in the inner cave. The boom of the waterfall echoed around the ship as the stage was set. Now there was a large expanse of clear deck behind the bridge, and on it a table was erected, and covered with a black cloth. The pirate captain—still recognizable by the small red light in his paper hat—watched as documents and a small tape recorder were placed on the table. Then he climbed up to the bridge and switched on the two searchlights. One he beamed down onto the deck, throwing a harsh white circle around the table. The second he swung up to the dripping cave roof so that its beam was at right angles to the first, forming a weird letter L of light, picking up eerie rainbows in the spray. Satisfied, he turned to the masked men waiting for him on deck. Four of them held strait jackets in their hands.

"Only three." The captain held up three fingers.

"Keep one back. The girl stays below in her cell."

The men nodded and turned away. Picking up their rifles, they went around to the foredeck, and disappeared down the ladder to Millionaires' Row. He waited in the falling spray, standing stiffly in the apex of the dazzling letter L.

The three millionaires and their women were led aft in a faltering line. Chained together, they glanced nervously at the sinister figures who guarded them. But they looked no farther—the darkness, the booming spray, and the strangely angled lights were beyond their understanding. They didn't resist as their chain was clipped to the ship's rails.

Up on the bridge the pirate captain was visible only as a glowing red light. He waited with his back toward them. Then suddenly he turned. *Right! Pay attention!*

The weird metal voice echoed away around the cave. Then it was answered by slow gentle tones from the deck. "You may scare the others, Captain, but not me." Alexis Tzannos stared down at his hands, as though trying to focus on something familiar. His calm face made the prison uniform look like a well-cut business suit. "Before you go too far, it may be as well to remember that you will all be caught by morning."

"By nine-thirty in the morning? To be precise?"

Tzannos nodded. "When there is no morning transmission from *Pindar*, the entire Mediterranean will be searched."

"They could look for a hundred years and never find us here." The pirate captain looked around at the darkness. "But just to put your mind at rest. . . ." He pointed down to the masked man waiting by the table in the searchlight's beam. The man bent over and clicked on the tape recorder.

There came the high-pitched squeal of a radio signal —two-tone. The message was very short.

"You see, there will be a morning transmission from

Pindar. A Telex transmission with your call sign." The captain continued. "And it will say . . . Hold Market Reports. Tzannos returning Athens eleven-hundred hours.

"Tzannos returning?" The man pointed to his own chest in amazement.

"That's right. We brought your seaplane with us. And you will fly back to Athens in it tomorrow morning. Only you will go. Everyone else stays here."

Suddenly Alexis Tzannos got the message. He jerked his head back in fear, and as if for the first time he saw the bare spotlit deck, the masks grinning at him behind rifle barrels, and the searchlight beams with their rainbows in the spray. Then he looked up to the bridge. "How much?" He asked.

"Six hundred and sixty-six thousand, six hundred and sixty-six pounds, thirteen shillings and fourpence. From each of you." Like a weighing machine the robot voice blared out the millionaires' weight, their worth. "Two million sterling in all. Small used notes. Any nationality."

There was a gasp from the chained figures. Then the line surged forward as Kavelaris struggled, bellowing in Greek. Eight automatic rifles swung to cover him, eight safety catches clicked. Kavelaris, his face ashen, gradually calmed. "Not a chance," he said.

Marotta shook his head feebly.

"It's too much," Tzannos whispered.

On the bridge, the red glow that marked the captain's hat nodded gently. Then it moved over to one of the searchlights. Slowly the beam swung across the roof of the cave until it came to rest on a small beach at the water's edge.

The millionaires turned around. Against the far wall they saw the gallows, dripping in the spray, and the rows of bodies. Sixteen men and four women were hanged from two long beams. They wore strait jackets, their hoods twisted around broken necks. Below the jackets, white uniform trousers and rope-soled shoes swung slowly in midair.

"Twenty dead. Your crew." The mechanical voice continued calmly. "The seaplane pilot, cook, and doctor are still alive. . . ." The captain paused. ". . . You'll see there are three more nooses. For your children."

The millionaires spun back to face the deck. And then they saw a second chain gang being led toward them. A smaller chain, with three figures, all wearing strait jackets. The first one came into the light and revealed Michaeli Tzannos' face beneath the hood. Suddenly the cave was filled with the sick anger of the men, and the low moans of the women.

"*Silence!*" The captain blared down at them. "It's quite simple. It takes two minutes for your children to cross the water to that gallows and be hanged. You have two minutes to make up your minds. *Move!*"

Michaeli Tzannos was pushed down into the life raft below the ship's rail. The two other figures jerked after him.

"Two-thirds of a million sterling?" Marotta's voice was a howl of pain. "It's quite impossible!"

"Two minutes."

"In *cash*, Captain?"

"You know nothing about these things!"

"If we said we'd pay, we'd be lying!"

"One minute, fifty seconds." The captain spoke calmly, watching the life raft move slowly across the water to the spotlit gallows.

"We'd be *lying!*"

"Tzannos runs the Merchant Bank of Greece," the voice answered them from the bridge. "Kavelaris runs the Union Bank of Greece. Marotta has one of the largest chains of banks in Italy. Among you, you control over four hundred branches. There must be five thousand in cash in each of those."

"Just take the money?" Tzannos shouted. "Rob our own banks? What about the police?"

"There are five thousand policemen in Athens. Tzannos alone employs over eight thousand people in Athens. He can find a way. . . ." The captain paused. ". . . Just one minute left."

The life raft had now reached the searchlight's beam. The three hooded figures were dragged over wet sand toward the gallows. Then the men in Navy blue hauled them up onto the platform, their grinning masks showing no effort. Above them the rows of bodies quivered as they got the children under three empty nooses.

"I'll pay!" It was Marotta's voice.

"Yes," Tzannos echoed him.

"*Hold on!*" The captain shouted across to the beach. Then he turned back to the millionaires on deck. "In front of you there is a table. On it there are letters of authority for the three of you to sign. Tzannos will take them to Athens with him. You will sign them? Now?"

White-faced, Tzannos and Marotta nodded.

But Kavelaris kept quite still. "You wouldn't dare," he said, and then he grinned. "Anyway, I wouldn't give a damn if you did."

"*Abraham!*" The captain suddenly lost control. "Who would kill his own son Isaac!" He leaned over the bridge-rail, screaming. "God rules Abraham, not Isaac, must die!"

It took four men to get Kavelaris down into the life raft. He lurched overboard on the way to the beach, and they towed him sobbing through the water. He was still sobbing when they got his head into a noose. But suddenly he was sobbing, *yes.*

30

Tzannos was now alone with the pirate captain on the spotlit deck. On the black-covered table between them there were three signed letters of authority.

"And you're sure these are enough to guarantee the money?" The strange metal voice was quieter, almost conversational.

"The money, yes," the millionaire replied.

"The money and nothing else. No search planes, no policemen when the ransom is delivered."

"As far as my organization is concerned, I can guarantee secrecy," Tzannos said stiffly. "But I can't answer for the Greek government or police, once the news of my return to Athens gets out."

"Of course it will get out. There'll be radio reports, news bulletins. And we'll be listening to them. We'll hear something like this. . . . Alexis Tzannos returns halfway through cruise to arrange massive merger. No holiday for millionaires, he says."

"Halfway through the cruise?" Tzannos eyed him savagely. "You sank *Pindar*, remember?"

"Only the people in this cave realize that. To the rest of the world, *Pindar* is cruising up the lonely Turkish coast. Lonely coast. No one will see her, understand?"

"What do you mean?"

"Simply this. There has been no kidnaping. Nothing at all has happened. So how could the police find out about the two-million ransom?"

"The transmissions," Tzannos said. "You're forgetting about the Telex transmissions."

"They all go through your office. Only your own people will know they've stopped. And remember, Tzannos, we have an extremely large organization. If so much as one whisper of this kidnaping leaves your office," the captain traced a circle on the black cover of the table, "eight people will die. Eight more. It makes no difference."

The millionaire took a step back. "And they die if the money isn't delivered within one week?"

The captain nodded.

"Two million pounds, in small notes. It'll hardly fit into a suitcase. How d'you think I'm going to collect it together without anyone noticing?"

"Put it in oil drums, tomato cans. You own a lot of businesses. You'll think of something." The bloated voice got suddenly louder. "Understand this. Only half the money is to be in Greek notes. The rest in any currency, dollars for choice. No consecutive numbers, no marked notes, no magnetic dyes. It'll all be checked very thoroughly before your family and friends are freed."

Tzannos looked straight into the captain's eyes. "I can guarantee it," he said. "You have my word that everything will be done as you say. I have no other choice. . . ." He seemed to grow taller. "But you'll never live to spend a . . ."

"Dismiss," the captain said tiredly.

But the Greek stood where he was. "You'll never live to spend a penny of it. Because of what happened here tonight." He pointed across the water to the gallows.

The captain turned away, and beckoned at the masked seaman waiting in the shadows to take Tzannos down to his cell. Alone on the deck, he listened to the footsteps fading away. Then he shouted across to the two men standing below the gallows platform, told them to cut the bodies down. Each corpse fell to the planks below with a tiny thud, like a pillow dropped from the same height. The last one was wet through, and split open as it fell, showing that the trousers and strait jacket were stuffed with kapok.

Slowly the pirate captain stripped away his mask. Beneath the sneering rubber face, his own was small and soft with disgust. Sweat hung over his cheeks and brow like a film, and his mustache was dark and wet. . . . Sheldon was suddenly sick of his carnival as he looked at the kapok-filled dummies. He told himself *Pindar's* crew were safe, locked up in their cells in the outer cave. He told himself the same trick had been used on German prisoners in the war, far away in the Cairo suburb of Maadi. He tried to tell himself it didn't matter any more now than it did then.

Footsteps came toward him along the deck. Spanakis looked strangely plump and harmless without his mask. "*Kapitane,*" he spread his arms wide, "I think now I . . ."

Sheldon cut him short. "We're leaving in thirty minutes, with Tzannos and the plane. You'll stay here with five men, I'll need Barney and Turton out at sea."

"What about the other millionaires?" the Greek asked.

"It's much too risky to take them outside with us. Keep them here in this cave, away from their crew. Keep them on the gallows platform. Two men with them always."

"How long will you be away?"

"A couple of hours. We'll have to steam around in circles for a bit, to fool the seaplane pilot. Otherwise he'll know the cave isn't far from where he takes off. . . . But we'll come straight back of course, at full speed."

"So call it four hours altogether?"

Sheldon nodded. "And you know the instructions if we don't return," he said curtly. "We don't know what's going to happen outside."

31

But there was no danger in the velvet dawn. Calm and unreal, it was like any other morning. Sheldon took off his mask as they left the shadow of the island, glanced at the seaplane riding in the wake. He stopped engines, and lost ten minutes while he found the correct towing position. Then he made Barney open the throttles gradually, until he discovered the plane could take almost any speed. Trailing far back on the storm warp, the twin floats climbed the smooth glass wale that bulged astern of the MTB. Sheldon kept the pounding boat at a steady twenty-five knots, wondered if he could make up sufficient time to get Tzannos air-borne before 0900, the time *Pindar's* next transmission was due. . . . Because what Tzannos hadn't worked out was that a tape recorder might be able to play back a Telex message, but it could never transmit one in a thousand years.

The sun climbed in the sky, the breeze freshened, and Sheldon had to slacken speed. At 0830 he was still five miles from the position he'd picked for the seaplane's take-off. Swearing to himself, he stopped engines and glared around at the horizon, expecting a spotter plane at any moment. But still the sea was empty. The MTB gradually lost way, and the seaplane swung around to scrape against the ship's side. Sheldon heard footsteps coming up from below, and he put his mask on once again.

Alexis Tzannos, freshly shaved, and dressed once again in his soft, expensive suit, came out on deck. Slowly, almost pleasurably, he looked around at the sea. It was smoothly dented as far as the eye could see, as though some giant copper beater were at work over the horizon. Then a shadow fell across the millionaire. The pirate captain's grinning mask brought back the fear of last night, and Tzannos walked quickly aft to where the seaplane's wing protruded over the deck. The pilot was waiting in the cockpit, with a bulky sealed envelope strapped to one knee. Tzannos went past the other two masked men on deck, and climbed up to his seat beside the pilot unaided. He didn't look around as the seaplane was pushed clear of the ship.

Spinning slightly, it drifted slowly away. Then it bounced on larger waves as it left the lee of the hull. Ailerons and tail fin waggled in turn, as if trying to halt the plane's awkward motion. Suddenly twin puffs of smoke came from the exhausts, a second later the roar of the engine. The propeller vanished, caught its own momentum, spinning backward, then faded once again to the faintest blur. And the plane started forward over the sea.

The three masked men didn't move. They watched the seaplane's floats smack ever more gently against the waves, until they hung dripping over the water, and there was no reason for the cloud of spray behind. They watched the wings change from silver to black as they crossed the horizon, watched them hesitate before settling on a course, and dwindle to the faintest speck in the sky. Only then did the three men move off at a run—the captain up to the bridge, and the other two men below.

The motors fired, and rose to a shattering scream. The hull slammed at the waves, faster and faster, until it was leaping over them, touching the surface only at sudden intervals. The scream of the engines could rise no higher, and still it rose. Sheldon's mask was suddenly jerked away by the wind, and the mask beneath it was just as strange. Hard, wet, and haunted, he held the boat to the water.

There were footsteps behind him. Turton appeared at his side, hanging on to the kicking sprayshield. "It's all over, Skipper!" he shouted through the gale. "You've done it!"

Sheldon didn't turn around from the wheel. He'd heard those words before. . . . He remembered they'd left him alone on the way back, alone with his mug of cocoa and the dawn. Post-Operational Blues they'd called it— the standard complaint of MTB commanders. . . . But he'd had a conscience then—the Report Sheet. Now there was no Report Sheet. No one to pass the buck to. And no Operational Orders for tonight, the building tension that would come to take away his sickness.

"Relax, Skipper! It's all finished with!"

"Get back on radar watch, Turton!" Sheldon snapped at him. "Anything on the screen?"

"Something. Maybe a freighter, by its speed." Turton's voice was softer. "But it's twelve miles away. Quite safe."

"Well, get down there and watch it! And tell me the moment you see anything! *Any* damn thing!"

Turton nodded unhappily, and went below.

Sheldon held on to the jerking spokes of the wheel. . . . There was one thing he could see, right in front of his nose. And it wouldn't show up on the radar screen. . . . Claire Harding's face, as she'd looked up at him from the foredeck last night. Had she recognized him? Could she recognize the boat? And if she did, what the hell was he to do about it?

He swung his head from side to side, trying to shake her face out of his brain, and listening all the time for more footsteps behind him. Because there was one person he was even more afraid of than the girl. And that was Barney. Barney was the only member of the crew who'd seen Claire before. But there was a chance the engineer wouldn't remember her. He'd only known her for less than twenty-four hours of his life, and he'd been drunk that first evening long ago in Puerto and hungover for the most of the next day. . . . But if he did remember her?

Sheldon refused to think about it. Because Barney was hard, the hardest man he'd ever met. And now Barney was on the run, and he'd know exactly what to do about anyone who threatened his safety.

Thankfully, Sheldon found he was left alone for the rest of the trip. And as they returned to the island, he saw that the hill and the cliffs below were dark with sand, kicked up by the wind. Sand that hung out over the choppy water like a veil. The captain shivered as he throttled back. For the first time in over two months, all he wanted was a drink.

32

It was the third day of waiting. The third day Sheldon had stayed in his cabin and stared at the rum locker on the bulkhead. He'd been forced to go out in the mornings and evenings, to inspect the cell blocks and the guard posts. But the rest of the time he'd sat here on his bunk, listening to the boom of the waterfall, and looking at the rum locker. For the hundredth time he told himself he had to stay sober. If he got drunk, the Daily Report Sheets, the Rosters, and even the ransom plan waiting to go into operation in Athens, would seem as remote and unreal as a Disney cartoon. . . . But if he got drunk, he would no longer have to think about Claire Harding.

Because in those three days, nothing had happened. The girl had eaten her meals, taken her exercise periods, without saying a word. And Barney too, when he'd spoken to Sheldon, had concerned himself only with generators and gas cylinders, never once mentioning the girl. The silence and the tension were beginning to eat away at

Sheldon's reason. There were still four days of waiting in front of him, and he had to stay in control. Turning his back on the rum locker, he picked up the report sheet and forced himself to concentrate on it.

Millionaires' Row. . . . The doctor said Marotta was comfortable, and his wife had again stayed with him last night. . . . Kavelaris was still in a strait jacket, force-fed. The children, even Lakis Kavelaris, were giving no trouble. . . . And there was no remark under Claire Harding's name.

The crew's cell block in the outer cave. . . . Complaints about the usual things, the cold, the cold food, thin sleeping bags, lack of space, lack of exercise. And something new—the growing stink from the water below the concrete jetty. Sheldon smiled to himself. That acted two ways—*Pindar*'s crew no longer tried to swim for it. The first two days they'd tried swimming, even though they were still chained together, and they'd nearly drowned two men. They'd also made a lot of trouble for the two guards Sheldon had left with them on the jetty. So he'd removed the guards. It was as simple as that. Escape was impossible from the outer cave—the sandstone walls were sheer and smooth, and the channel's depth went right off the echo sounder's gauge. The crew's cell block was now self-contained, with two cooks and a tin opener. The life raft visited them twice a day with hot soup, otherwise they were left alone.

Even so, the pirate crew were shorthanded. They were having to work long hours, and by now they were exhausted. Sheldon turned to the Duty Roster, found its news wasn't exactly encouraging. . . . By night Turton had to keep a twelve-hour watch at the radio receiver out on the hill. And they also needed another man out there by day to look for spotter planes. At all times there had to be one man guarding Millionaires' Row, and another supervising the exercise periods on the MTB's deck. Then at mealtimes there had to be one man watching the food being prepared, and two men distributing it. It wasn't easy, guarding thirty-one people with seven. And now there were only seven crew left, since Spanakis had gone.

Sheldon thought about the Greek. He'd probably be in Athens by now, making the last arrangements for collecting the ransom. That particular two-million-pound transaction was due to come about in four days' time. Once again the captain went over the whole operation in his mind, and tried to see what could go wrong. . . .

It would take place at 9 P.M. on Friday, in the crowded Plaka area of Athens. There'd be Tzannos, waiting in the back of a closed van parked outside the Vrachou Taverna, with £2 million by his side. There'd be two tourists in carnival masks, who'd get into the front of the van. The millionaire would catch no more than a glimpse of the gas pistol before he passed out. Then the van would drive away through narrow streets, down Adrianou to Eolou, traveling slowly, unbothered by pursuit. At the corner of Eolou and Ermou there'd be a traffic jam—easy to arrange in the evening rush hour. Surrounded by snarling traffic, Tzannos and the four suitcases would be bundled quickly out of the van, down a dark alley, through a house and garden, to a back street behind Monastiraki. There'd be a large refrigerated Berliet truck parked in the street. Inside it, there'd be Pierre's accountants, to check whether the money was marked.

The Berliet would leave Athens slowly on the Sounion road. Tzannos remaining unconscious while the money was cleared, counted, and stuffed in a large waterproof sack. Past Sounion the road would become rougher, and clear of traffic. There'd be a hairpin bend on a cliff top overlooking a beach. Here the Berliet would stop for the driver to check his tires. While he was doing this, the waterproof sack would be dropped down onto the beach. Below in the darkness there'd be a trawl net spread out on the sand. And half a mile out at sea, Spanakis would start up the winch on his caïque. The net and the money would vanish into the water. Spanakis had orders to sail his fishing boat back to Crete, and dump the money if he was stopped. Dump it, anyway, on a six-fathom shelf off the North of Crete, with three good bearings on the coastline.

Sheldon decided it was foolproof. The point was that Tzannos wouldn't be released, nor the All Clear sent, until the money was well out to sea. And that was in four nights' time. . . . The captain found he was staring at the rum locker once again. He told himself he had to get out of his cabin. Putting on his microphone and mask, he picked up the swagger stick he needed nowadays to keep his hands still. At the door he hesitated, and then went back to check the exercise roster, to make sure that Claire Harding wasn't walking around on the deck above him. But it wasn't her. The footsteps he could hear were those of Giulia Marotta.

The first thing he saw from the bridge was the masthead-light, dim in the shifting spray. The second thing he saw was Claire Harding, trudging around and around in a heavy oilskin. They'd changed the Roster. And Sheldon drew back . . . but he was too late. She stopped suddenly and stared up at him, stared right at the swagger stick in his hands. And then she gasped. . . . Sheldon saw why. Because the stick he carried about with him was a brass ruler. Traill's brass ruler. And she'd been the one who'd found it, long ago in Palma.

Behind Claire, a tall masked man with a rifle was watching her closely. Suddenly his fingers started snapping together, quicker and quicker, as his mind chased after something. Then he ran over to the girl and spun her around. His grinning pirate mask bent closely over her, and it began to nod. "It's you, Sweetheart," Barney blared out. "I've got your face at last."

33

It was the fifth day of waiting, and still Barney hadn't done anything. He hadn't said a word to Sheldon, nor to anyone else. And the captain had finally given up. He'd decided to get drunk.

His chance had come this morning. Mitch had said he was sick, and then proved it. Sheldon had taken over his duties—which meant plane-watching out on the hill. He'd filled his water bottle with rum, and told himself he'd have six hours out of the cave, away from the others. One hour to drink the rum, and five hours to sober up.

Now he was finishing the bottle. And it was having a strange effect on him. He told himself it was because he hadn't drunk anything in a long time. But he didn't feel drunk. He felt younger and younger, happier and happier. And then he couldn't think about it any more. Because he was part of the whole thing. Part of the warmth of the rum and the sunlight, part of the bare hill where he sat, and the pool below with its limestone pillars and gray dust bowl. Then he was even part of the sea—the blue floor that was maybe a yard wide, maybe a thousand miles wide as he blinked at it happily. . . . And he was happy, very very happy. Gently he started laughing.

Because the humor of the situation had entirely escaped him up to now. There he was—Captain Navy—sitting on a rock in the middle of nowhere, and guarding it. What's more, he had a perfect right to guard it. Because the rock was his. He'd made the dents in it. Over there on the far side of the hill, for example, there were seven graves. One of them just an itsy-bitsy grave, a hole with an arm in it. And that arm had once used a brass ruler. Which had been lost for twenty years, and then found by a girl called Claire. She'd given it back to Sheldon. . . . He looked down at the ruler in his hands. It was the baton in the relay race. Traill had started the race, had passed it on to Claire to give to him. And it meant something. . . . Traill was telling him, through the trembling, faunlike girl, that it was time to stop. . . . Naughty, naughty Captain Navy.

Sheldon laughed, louder and louder. The puny sound made no impression on the rocky island or the sea. This pleased him even more, and he went on laughing.

Then there was a new sound—the clatter of falling rocks. Barney's squat figure suddenly appeared on the path below. He came up toward the captain, his face red from the climb. All at once, he was suspicious, and he bent quickly over Sheldon to smell his breath. "You've been drinking," he panted. "Are you too drunk to listen to me?"

Sheldon shook his head.

The engineer took some time to recover his breath. He sat on the next rock to the captain, and when he spoke again, his words were quick and angry. "Look, I'm not saying you aren't the best. You were, and you still are . . . I'm just saying there are some things people like me have got over people like you."

Sheldon didn't understand any of it, but he nodded in agreement.

"Take me," Barney continued. "You made me Chief Engineer back in the war, but I've always been what you'd call lower-deck material. Backbone of the sodding British Navy, carrying out orders, sometimes the foulest stinking orders. Maybe you'd say that was . . . no imagination, no responsibility. But you haven't lived in a fo'c's'le."

"Fo'c's'le." The captain nodded again. He'd learned long ago to repeat people's last words when he was drunk. It made them go on talking.

"Like anyone else, people down in the fo'c's'le remember good times, bad times, and the times when not a goddamn person was up to it," Barney continued, slower now. "But what you don't know is that the people down there can understand that, and they don't bear grudges. . . . That's because they don't have to keep on looking up words like responsibility and imagination in the Encyclopaedia bloody Britannica. They can face facts, that's all."

Sheldon giggled suddenly. He hadn't meant to, but Barney's mouth looked so funny, opening and closing. He supposed everyone's did. He supposed dogs must spend all their time laughing.

"I'm talking about Claire," Barney said suddenly.

Claire. That was an important word. That was a word he had to hang on to.

"Claire Harding," Barney repeated. "I'll do it."

"Do what?" Sheldon asked, a full second later.

"Get rid of her." The engineer shrugged.

The captain tried to speak, but Barney cut across him. "I know what you're going to say. Maybe we can buy her off, or maybe we can take her with us. . . . But don't you see? They'd have a *lead*! And that's the bloody brilliance of this whole operation, *your* operation! There's no lead for them to follow." He paused for a moment. "I know you're not understanding much of this, but it helps to get it out. . . . Look at the facts. Nobody'll even hear about the kidnaping until we've got clear with the money. The boat that did the job's supposed to have sunk two months ago. You and I are dead. Pierre's in the clear. All Spanakis' boys come from the same village in Crete, and they've got mouths tighter'n a debutante's arse. . . . It's just too good to think of bloody silly stunts like letting the girl go free."

Sheldon had turned away, and suddenly he was shivering in the warm sunlight. He didn't understand Barney's torrent of words, but he understood the man's tone, and the look on his face.

"Funny, I've never bothered about money before." The engineer was talking to himself now. "And then I was forty-seven. That's too old to go on fiddling fuel bills on evaporation, or waiting for the fat man to fall asleep in his deck chair before nicking his Scotch. And I never could get away with nicking his girl. . . . Don't forget, I spent fifteen years crewing fat men's yachts in Majorca, and I was thirty-two when I started. But maybe it didn't affect you like that." He got up suddenly, and looked past the cliffs to the sea. "Then there was this chance to be the fat man. Me the fat man. Like I can open the paper and have my horoscope tell me I'm going to screw Miss World tonight. . . . But first, there's this other bird to take care of."

There was a long pause. "Bird?" Sheldon whispered.

"Bird . . . bird . . . *bird!*" Barney shouted angrily.

"Jubjub bird!" Sheldon couldn't help it. He started screaming with laughter again. "The . . . bit . . . I . . . left . . . out! Beware . . . the . . . Jubjub . . . bird!"

Then Barney came at him, and swung him around by his shoulder. "One more thing," he hissed. "I'm taking over command until we get away from here."

34

It was the evening of the sixth day, and Barney had taken over. He'd kept Sheldon locked in his cabin since noon yesterday, and he'd told the rest of the crew the captain was sick. So he was—sick with anger. Because the whole thing now worked so neatly against him. The booming waterfall in the cave drowned his shouts for help, and just like the millionaires, he was a prisoner on the ship.

The first thing he'd done was to throw the bottles of rum through the porthole. The second thing he'd done was look for his revolver. But it was missing. Barney must have taken it. And that really bothered Sheldon, along with a lot of other things. He'd had plenty of time to think about Barney in the past thirty hours. He now saw that the engineer had been the one real driving force behind the operation all along—just as he'd been in the war. Barney had been the first person to endorse the idea in the first place, the first person to translate Sheldon's ideas into fact, and the person who'd come up with the more macabre ideas—the cell blocks, and the phony gallows he'd remembered from Cairo days. Sheldon wasn't trying to pass the buck, it was his responsibility, all of it. . . . Except for what was going to happen this evening.

And it was going to happen in the next few hours. Because tomorrow night—when and if the All-Clear signal came—there'd be no time to bother about Claire. Barney would have to take care of the girl now. And he was going to do it—Sheldon knew—because he'd planned the thing systematically, right down to removing the pistol. The captain only had one weapon left—a pair of nail scissors he was using to carve out the lock on the door. It was slow work.

Suddenly he stopped. Crossing to his bunk, he stood on it and pressed his ear to the deck planks above. He heard the slow footsteps of the evening exercise period—Lakis Kavelaris guarded by Mitch, according to the roster. And then Sheldon heard a second set of footsteps, going aft. Barney's footsteps, and the bump of the life raft against the ship's side as the engineer towed it to the stern. A pause while he made the line fast to the rail. And a moment later, the footsteps coming back, getting louder until they creaked the planks over the captain's head. He heard them scrape around by the ladder that led down to

Millionaires' Row. And then silence, apart from the booming spray.

Feverishly Sheldon put on his mask. Pressing himself once again up against the planks, he heard the first light step the girl took on deck. And then the captain threw himself across the width of his cabin at the locked door. Three times he battered against it, and the wood began to splinter where he'd worked with the scissors. He tensed himself for the fourth attempt, when suddenly a rifle clattered to the deck above his head. Sheldon rushed the door again. The lock tore away from the wood, and he was running for the bridge ladder.

Keeping low, he spotted his revolver in a flag locker and grabbed it up. Then he looked down to the afterdeck, and saw a lot of things had happened. Mitch was lying unconscious on the deck. Lakis Kavelaris was standing with his back toward the bridge, with Mitch's SLR in his hands. The rifle was pointing straight at Barney's back. And Barney was standing in the shadows of the stern, with Claire at his side.

"Drop it!" Lakis shouted. "Drop the rifle!"

Barney lowered his arms, but kept hold of the gun.

"Get away from him!" Lakis shouted again. "*Claire!*"

She ran away across the deck.

Lakis raised his rifle. But he didn't shoot. Instead the barrel began to shake.

From the bridge, Sheldon could see he was looking desperately down at the gun, trying to find the safety catch.

Then he saw something else. He saw Barney's rifle slowly swing around to cover Lakis, saw the muscles of Barney's shoulder tense as he got ready to fire.

Unable to stop himself, Sheldon fired two shots at Barney's back. Snap shots, pulling the trigger through each time.

The sound of the pistol echoed around the cave.

Then Barney slowly crumpled and fell around his rifle.

"Drop that bastard gun!" Sheldon screamed at Lakis.

The boy did so, trembling with fear. . . . Then suddenly he glanced around at Barney, and he began to run.

Sheldon was too late. He saw the whole thing as if in slow motion. . . . Barney's rifle barrel coming up once again. . . . Lakis running, trying to make for the shelter of the bridge. . . . Barney firing. . . . The tiny wooden butterflies leaping alive below Sheldon. . . . Butterflies that got nearer and nearer Lakis' back. . . . And then the boy falling, trying to shake off the pain.

This time the roar of the automatic weapon blasted around the walls. When it subsided, Sheldon went slowly down to the deck. Claire passed him, making for the safety of Millionaires' Row. And then the captain was standing alone in the spray, midway between two corpses. Barney seemed to be unmarked, his mask grinning up into the light. Lakis' face and arms were dead white, but his body was pumping blood out on the deck and over the side.

Sheldon stared down at the gleaming red stain, and he suddenly realized that the last body he'd seen lying on this spot had been black. There'd been a torpedo tube here then, and a charred body lying across it, saying Cunjeezer, Cunjeezer, over and over again.

35

Nothing mattered any more. Not Kavelaris' face when he told him his son had been shot in self-defense. Not Turton coming in the life raft with the news that the ransom had been delivered a day early, not the crew moving quickly as they got the MTB ready for sea. . . . Then one thing did matter. Sheldon saw it as he lined them up on deck and saw their relaxed faces. He was their captain, and he had to look after their safety. There was just one last thing he had to find out before they left the cave. And he sent them all off duty for a two-hour watch below.

For the first seventy minutes of that two hours, he stood alone on the bridge, hunched under the masthead light and the falling spray. He stared down at the dark stain on the deck below him. Then he went slowly down to Claire's cell and unlocked the door. She cowered back against the bulkhead when she saw him, and he had to take off his mask to calm her. "I want you to come with me," he told her gently, "I won't harm you."

She got into an oilskin and followed him up the ladder. Both of them walked carefully around the stain on the wet planks, and over the afterdeck to the life raft moored at the stern. He followed her down into the raft and cast off, letting it drift away. Gradually the lights of the ship vanished in the spray, and they were both sitting in darkness. Sheldon waited until he could no longer see the girl's face, or any part of her. Then it was easy to speak.

"It all went wrong," he said hoarsely, "the whole damn thing. You saw it on the deck back there."

She didn't answer.

"And I don't know what the hell to do with you. We can't take you with us. There'd be someone for them to trace. The only one. They'd find you next month, next year. . . . Then they'd find us."

There was still no reply, just the cold mist pressing close around him in the dark.

"I want to know where you stand," Sheldon said. "I have to know. For my crew's sake."

A small desolate voice answered him at last. "I won't give you away."

The captain paused, not believing her. "A boy was killed," he said deliberately. "Maybe your boy friend. One of *Pindar*'s passengers."

"You tried to stop him being killed. Tried as hard as anyone could."

Sheldon shivered. He hunched himself lower down into the raft. "The fact remains, a boy was killed. Which makes it murder."

"Which could make me an accessory to murder, if I linked my name with yours!" She suddenly shouted at him. "Christ, haven't you worked it out? Don't you know about these damn Greeks? . . . Well, I do! If I say one word about you, they'll reckon I was in it!"

Only one small part of Sheldon felt relieved. The rest of him was still an aching void, as cold and dark as the cave around him. "But maybe if you felt strongly enough about this . . . particular murder, you'd feel you had to do something about it. And take your chances."

"I didn't recognize that crewman of yours who got killed. And his death didn't affect me at all." She spoke very coldly and calmly. "But I knew Lakis very well. And his death didn't affect me at all."

Sheldon was shocked by the hatred in her voice. Hadn't she understood what had happened back there on the deck, what had started the shooting? . . . That Barney was taking her off in the life raft to kill her?

And that Lakis had realized this, and tried to save her?

"I told you I knew all about these damn Greeks," she continued wearily. "They gave me one hell of a bad time on board *Pindar*. And I mean one hell of a bad time. . . . And now, if there's anything I can do to get me away from those spooky people. . . . Keep my mouth shut, lie to the police, *any* damn thing . . . well, I'll do it."

"But they'll ask you a lot of questions. There'll be newspapermen. It may go on for some time."

"And I can go on for some time. Just so long as I get a shot of those millionaires. She paused suddenly. "Look at it this way. All in all, you could say I had a pretty lousy season. And I'm only in it for deck chairs, and sun, and nice people. . . . Well, this season I've only met three nice people. And I met them back in Palma."

"Three people?" Sheldon asked after a pause.

"You and Sandy. You took me in, fed me, gave me money, let me stay. No questions asked. And that counts a lot in my book." She moved slightly, and her voice was nearer in the darkness, her breath warm on his face. "Then there was Pierre. He was really good to me, something quite special. . . . And it turns out now that I left him for no reason at all."

Sheldon thought about it for a long time. Then he took the gamble. "If it makes any difference," he said, "Pierre's in this. He's half and I'm half."

"It makes a difference," she replied slowly. "You don't have to worry about me."

The captain started paddling the raft back to the ship.

He only saw her once again. She was standing on the concrete jetty with the rest of *Pindar*'s passengers, and her face was screwed up against the stinking water of the outer cave.

From the bridge, Sheldon signaled Laborde to push

the MTB clear. He didn't bother to tell the millionaires that their crew were still alive, in the cell block behind them. Or that the keys to their handcuffs were in a crate on the jetty, together with the parts of a radio transmitter, and a soldering iron. It didn't matter all that much, they'd find out soon enough.

Nothing mattered any more, he told himself as the MTB went through the dark channel and out into the night. Nothing, now that he was sure of Claire—not the body of Lakis Kavelaris they'd left behind them, not Barney's body, stitched into its canvas shroud on deck. And certainly not the fact that the MTB itself would soon be on the bottom of the sea with the engineer—in deep water, off the northeast tip of Crete.

PART

four

36

Claire couldn't believe it. The nightmare wasn't over. It had just got worse. Two days ago, when she'd arrived at the Greek Air Force base, she'd been questioned with the others by a police inspector. She thought her answers had satisfied him, because she'd been taken to an Athens hotel to sleep. But yesterday the inspector had questioned her again, in the Alien Police Department. Tzannos and the other millionaires had been in the next office, and they'd done a lot of whispering together in between periods of questioning. Then last night, they'd suddenly told her she'd have to sleep in the office, on a chair. And this morning she'd found that she didn't even rate an inspector's office any longer. She was now in a small windowless room, which contained just two chairs, a table, and a filing cabinet. And she'd been alone for three hours.

She started up nervously as the door opened. Tzannos came in. And he was no longer the beautiful white-haired man she knew, but the man who'd climbed on top of one of the largest piles of money in the world. He closed the door and came toward her.

"We have come up against a brick wall," he said curtly. "Twelve days ago, *Pindar* was sunk by a gunboat. And yet every gunboat of that size and shape, which could have been in the Aegean at the time, has been accounted for. The same goes for any Naval or ex-Naval

Officer who speaks English without a trace of an accent. . . . And the police have no record of any large criminal organization based in Greece."

"I'm sorry," Claire told him. "But I don't see how it concerns me."

"Oh, but it does." He clasped his hands gently in front of his face, but his eyes weren't gentle. "We think they had someone inside."

"Inside?" Suddenly she was frightened.

"We think they used Claire Harding."

"You can't be . . ."

"Claire Harding was invited to cruise on *Pindar* by my son Michaeli. But he claims to have only a very slight acquaintance with her."

"But I told them all about that yesterday," Claire's voice trembled. "Lakis forced Michaeli to . . ."

"*Forced him?*" Tzannos shouted suddenly. "*Why* d'you have to speak ill of the dead? Because Lakis is dead. And he can't disprove your lies."

"They're not lies."

He waved her to be quiet. "Let's stick to what we know. Before you even met Lakis, you were dancing with my son in a club in St. Tropez. You said you'd met him before, at the Madelons' party."

Claire waited.

"I've been in touch with the Madelons. You weren't on their guest list, and there were no gate-crashers at the party. So how could you have met Michaeli there?"

"I *told* them!" Now it was Claire's turn to shout. "Yesterday I told them about the whole bloody sordid business! About Dimitri Kavelaris!"

Tzannos turned away angrily. "I know all about Dimitri's troubles in the past. He's not a discreet man." He reached the filing cabinet, and wheeled around to face her. "But are you going to tell me he's going to lie about a thing like this? When his son's been killed?"

"He's a very small man," Claire said slowly, "and he doesn't want to appear any smaller. . . . All the confessions in the world won't bring Lakis back to life."

"It's your word against his. Against the whole Kavelaris family, in fact. . . . Marilena, who notices much more of these things than I do, tells me you caused quite a lot of trouble for the Kavelaris family on board *Pindar*. No doubt it was due to the size of your bikini."

Claire could only shake her head.

"Facts. . . ." Tzannos tapped slowly against the metal top of the filing cabinet. " . . . The way you got on to *Pindar* was very mysterious, to say the least. . . . And now it appears you haven't got a passport."

"It fell into the sea. Maria Kavelaris threw my bag into the sea, when she wanted to get rid of my Monopoly winnings."

"The Kavelaris family again!" The millionaire slammed his hand down onto the cabinet. "All we can say definitely is that you have no passport. Which turns out to be very convenient. Because when we checked the number you gave us with the British Foreign Office, we found that particular passport was issued to a girl called Claire Mansell."

Claire sat very still. "I changed my name" she said, "when I left England."

"Which would also turn out to be very convenient, if you wanted to try your hand at anything . . . shall we say, illegal. And the facts suggest that this was the case." He left the cabinet, and walked around behind her chair. "Fact. You and Marilena were the only people I told about visiting Miti. And the gunboat was waiting for us at Miti. Fact. You were the last person to leave the boat deck that evening. You could easily have signaled to the gunboat. Fact. . . . Just before the gunboat left the cave for the last time, you had a visitor. He came into your cell and spoke to you in his normal voice, therefore he wasn't wearing a mask."

Tzannos was behind her now. Suddenly his hands gripped her head, and pulled her around. "Who was that man?" he shouted in her face.

"I don't know." She willed him to believe her. "No one came and talked to me."

The millionaire released her, and walked away toward the door. "You can't lie to a Greek," he said. "A Greek or a Hungarian." Then his voice became harder, much harder. "We'll just have to arrange for you to tell us what we want to know. It won't be difficult."

Claire suddenly realized he was going to leave her. Leave her alone in the bare, windowless room. "I want to see the British Consul," she said firmly.

Tzannos just smiled at her.

"All right!" She was getting desperate now. "There are such things as newspapers. British newspapers! They'll find out you're holding me here."

He came back from the door, and unfolded a *Daily Mail* from his pocket. There was a front-page picture of a blonde girl who might have been Claire's double. She was sitting on the far side of a swimming pool. ENGLISH BLONDE ON MILLIONAIRE'S KIDNAP CRUISE RECOVERS AT THE VILLA OF . . . Tzannos refolded the paper.

"I'm a very rich man," he said quite simply. "I can find any amount of Claire Hardings for the newspapers. . . . And what makes it twice as simple is that your parents, Mr. and Mrs. Mansell of Woking, England, don't seem to care what happens to you."

"And what is . . . ?" Hot tears took her suddenly by surprise.

"Don't cry!" Tzannos snapped. "A young boy was shot, remember?"

She nodded. "And I can't help you."

"Well, I'll tell you where we're going to send you," he said. "To one of the islands the tourists never see.

People sent to these islands hardly ever return. . . . So either you talk to us, or you stay there—" his face was completely expressionless as he looked at her "—until you die."

"You can't do that. There are laws."

He shrugged, and went out of the door.

37

She was marching down this road on the edge of the settlement. She recognized it as the road she'd seen from the police boat this afternoon. Now it was evening, and the tall cypresses to her right were casting long shadows over the gray rocky shore. The evening was very still, apart from the twin columns of women marching around Claire. And it was very quiet, apart from their moaning song, and the shuffling sound of the rags wrapped around their feet.

Claire didn't believe in any of it—not in the penal settlement, laid out in squares between the mountains and the sea, nor in the guards, who walked at the roadside, with whistles in their mouths, and not at all in the marching women. Because they were like skeletons, their heads no more than skulls, with tight gray skin and lank hair. And their brown shifts were stained with sweat, flapping around their ankles. . . . But she had to believe in it. All of it. Because she herself was wearing one of the shifts. She could feel it against her skin, and she breathed through her mouth to avoid its smell.

The road was straight, and came to an end by a large square building, shaded by a eucalyptus tree. One of the guards blew her whistle, and the columns of women squatted where they were and relieved themselves. Then the whistle blew again, and Claire found herself jostled in through a doorway. She was in a huge dark hall with a row of brick ovens in its center. The light from these ovens flickered out past piles of stacked cordwood. Just for a moment, Claire thought this was the end of the line.

But it wasn't. An old woman with a harelip took her away into the shadows. She placed her at one end of a trolley, which was wooden, and stained a deep nut-brown. The whistle blew again, and Claire followed the trolley over to a large pit in the corner, where women were working with shovels. Knee-deep in a strange brown mush, they dug to a steady rhythm, filling up long wooden trays with the mush. The harelipped woman showed Claire how the trays fitted onto the trolley, and got her to help load it up. They were very heavy, and the old woman took more than her share of the weight. The strange mush in the trays stained Claire's hands and arms a sticky brown, and its smell was sharp and sweet like new wine.

When the trolley was loaded, Claire helped push it toward the roaring ovens. Flames licked out of the metal grates, and the heat scorched the side of her body. The woman showed her how to wrap the hem of her shift around her hands to protect them. Then she lifted one end of a tray, and nodded at Claire to lift the other. They had to put the trays in metal racks in the oven. The topmost rack they left till last, and Claire couldn't make it. At the second attempt she could make it, with a pain that knifed her back.

Then they went back to the pit, and the whole routine was repeated. The pain in Claire's back got worse, and then it just got to be a number . . . the sixth, the twelfth, the eighteenth tray. . . . Until it got to be the hundred-and-fifty-sixth tray. And then the whistle blew again.

The women gathered together in the shadowy corner by the pit, muttering in low tired voices. Claire stayed where she was by the trolley. She couldn't move, now that she no longer had to. And now that she no longer had to resist, she gave way. She cried as she'd never heard herself cry before—a thin moaning wail—like the women's song out on the road. Then she felt a gentle touch on her shoulder. The harelipped woman was stooping over her with a plate of bread and oil. Slowly the woman's hand kneaded a piece of bread into a brown sticky ball. She put it carefully into Claire's mouth.

Claire spat it out. And suddenly she was screaming. She ran toward the guards at the doorway, and she screamed the two words of Greek she knew best—Alexis Tzannos.

38

She woke up in a hospital room. It was clean and white, and the roar of city traffic came through the windows. Tzannos was watching her anxiously from a chair by the bed. He took a deep breath and then leaned forward.

"Just tell me the name," he whispered. "The name of the man you know."

She was silent for a long time. Until his face hardened once again, and she saw it was hopeless. "Sheldon," she said slowly. "Commander Sheldon."

"Who?"

"You had him thrown out of Palma."

Suddenly he seemed to remember. "That madman. It fits . . . anyone else?"

She thought of Pierre, his brown hand curled around a bottle of Scotch. "No," she said.

"It doesn't matter. We'll find them." He got up and went to the door.

"Whitey!" she said, stopping him in his tracks. "If you get hold of Sheldon, you're going to find out I had nothing to do with him. I knew him slightly in Majorca, and later I recognized something about him." She made herself sit up. "And you're also going to find out everything else I told you was true. And then you're going to need every bloody lawyer you've ever heard of. And a hell of a lot of money to keep me quiet."

Tzannos blinked at her in surprise.

39

In the shadow of the monastery the land had been blessed by God, water, and workmen—in the days when God had more servants. Now there were only a few small vines, shorn of their grapes, swinging wildly in the late autumn wind. There were marrows too, and beans, and patches of sparse white stubble between the olive trees. The stone threshing circle still bore traces of straw and chaff, but its work was finished for another year. Below it the land was barren—gray rocks, brown shale, and gorse, falling steeply away on every side. The monastery of Selinus stood on a ridge, close underneath the sky. Its stone walls were gray- or honey-colored, according to the clouds that raced past its bell tower. Up here there was always wind, bringing dust up from the bare valley below. Dust which gritted the wine in Sheldon's mouth—monastery wine— old and dark and musty. He saw the bottle in his hand was nearly empty, and he went back around the corner to refill it.

At the entrance to the courtyard there was a narrow archway where tire marks ended and footmarks began.

Through the arch, the courtyard was rocky and uneven, with grasses clutching at the slightest hint of soil. Sheldon went in toward the sound of the bell, tolling at every stronger gust of wind. Around him, on four sides, there were high walls and narrow windows. Once there'd been more than fifty monks here, but now the yard was just a funnel for the wind. Dust and straw whirled around in a perpetual spiral, old newspapers slid along the walls. Overhead the sky raced past the roof, but on the ground Sheldon moved more slowly, sipping and staggering his way around the chapel. Its whitewash still bore the scars of German machine guns. They'd been no respecters of churches, and they'd been right in this case—throughout the war the monks had operated a transmitter, hidden down in the crypt with their icons.

There were now only two faces Sheldon remembered from the war, and only four monks left in the entire monastery. Machine guns had cut down sixteen. Others had left, never to return. Just four monks and their women, and a villager or two to work the land. Sheldon emptied his bottle sadly, and lurched up the cracked stone steps to the balcony. It was whitewashed, and ran around three sides of the courtyard. Two of its sides had empty cells, with broken doors and shutters banging in the wind. But the doors on the third side were painted, and the captain hesitated as he passed them. Then he went up the steps to the bell tower.

Up here the bell was no louder, its tolling was carried away by the screeching wind. Wind, which in August —Sheldon remembered—could bring the sand of the Sahara ninety miles over the sea. Now it was October, and it smelled only of the bitter thyme of Crete. Cloud shadows raced across the valley, rippling the few bent grasses that had been sickled by the summer. Sheldon turned around to his left. From the tower he could see the whole northeast tip of Crete. On three sides, the tiny pores of the sea stretched away to the sky. And on the fourth—the western side—the mountains were black under ruffs of cloud. There were just two tiny fingers of silver, separating the low mountains from the higher ranges beyond. Sunlight that picked out the two tourist attractions far away along the coast—Sitia and the Minos Beach at Agios Nikolaos were living up to their brochures. . . . The captain turned the full circle. He'd come up here to check that the monastery road was empty. It was empty.

He went down the steps to his cell. It was dark and musty like the monastery wine, and its walls and mattress were damp. There was a table, a chair, and a bed in the gloom. And on the table, a demijohn of wine. Sheldon refilled his bottle, and caught sight of his face in the shaving mirror. Shaving mirror. Since he'd removed his mustache his face had been small and strange, undistinguished apart from its dark wine color. His chin seemed weak and pointed, his mouth tired, with lines that made it tireder. It was a face that dated from before the war. A face Shirley had known. . . . Sheldon grabbed hold of himself viciously. He didn't want to think about Shirley.

A strip of sunlight widened over the cell floor and made him turn. Sandy was standing in the doorway behind him. Every time she saw him now she seemed bewildered. She'd never known him without a mustache, and some intuition told her to be jealous now he'd shaved.

She held a Greek newspaper out toward him. Folded inside it was a sheet of handwritten paper. "Pappa Grigoris has done the translation," she said.

Sheldon read the spidery writing: A new policeman in charge of the kidnap case. Tzannos and his son recovering in Bermuda. English blonde on her way back home. "It's all over," he said. "They've let her go back to England."

Suddenly there were shouts from the balcony behind Sandy. . . ."Effing-bastard Greeks. . . ." And then Pappa Grigoris' voice, just as angry.

"It isn't all over." Sandy beckoned him to the door.

"You just act as though it was. Sit there drinking all the time, talking to yourself."

He saw she was angry, and he put down his wineglass. Going past her to the balcony, he could still hear Turton's voice swearing at the monk, but couldn't see either of them. There was just Mitch, sitting at the far end of the row of banging doors. The cook lay on two chairs, wedged into a corner. His face was completely white, almost like a baby's face, all its lines softened by the raki bottle balanced on his stomach. Then a cloud shadow raced along the balcony and reached him. As if this was his cue, Mitch tipped up the bottle and drank.

Sandy pointed at him. "Your crew," she said.

"No longer my crew. I can't order him around now."

"But he's drunk, all the time. Don't you see you've got to get him off the bottle? Don't you see you've got to stop drinking in front of him?"

"There's nothing else to do. Well, is there?" Guiltily, Sheldon glanced back to his cell. His wineglass was on the table where he'd left it.

Then the sound of arguing voices got louder. Turton and Pappa Grigoris came up the steps to the balcony. Turton was thin and burnt up, and while he shouted at the monk in the stovepipe hat, he kept his distance from him. Sheldon knew why. Even from where he stood, he could smell Pappa Grigoris' dirty white robe and matted beard. The two men were still arguing as they went on up to the bell tower.

"Turton's the one that really bothers me." Sandy leaned toward him, whispering now. "He won't eat anything, just swears at the Greeks all the time. Can't you see how he's changed in a month? With nothing to occupy him?"

Sheldon grunted, and looked away. The sun had returned, and brought back the glow of honey to the courtyard.

"Well, he's got something to occupy him now,"

Sandy continued. "Yesterday I saw an old rusty shotgun in his cell. This morning it was cleaned up. And there was a box of cartridges beside it."

"Oh?" Sheldon felt another cloud shadow pass over. He saw it go the length of the balcony, bringing out gray brush strokes in the whitewashed walls. When it reached Mitch, the man took another quick sip from his raki bottle. The cloud shadow was his cue to drink. The captain could only admire his ingenuity. Needing another drink himself, he went back into his cell.

Sandy came after him. "I've kept out of this whole thing," she said. "It's none of my business."

"That's right." Sheldon refilled his glass. "It isn't."

"But you've got to be careful. You've got to watch those two. They've been cooped up here a month, less than a hundred miles away from where you sank *Pindar*." Her voice rose suddenly. "For God's sake, Alec, you had the boat. You had the whole damn Mediterranean to choose from."

"And the police are looking around the whole damn Mediterranean," Sheldon told her. "Not here."

40

At midday, a dust cloud suddenly appeared below them in the plain. Through glasses, Sheldon saw it was a new American Ford—one of the police cars from Heraklion. But it was still at least a mile away, and they had time to get down to the chapel in the courtyard. Behind the altar, Pappa Grigoris and two monks raised one of the flagstones. There were steps beneath it, leading down into darkness. Sandy led the way down with a torch, followed by Mitch, who seemed to be sleepwalking, his raki bottle pressed against his soft chin. Sheldon went next, carrying the demijohn of wine. And finally Turton with his shotgun, an old hammer twelve bore.

The flagstone was lowered, and then they could hear nothing. Not a hoot from the police car, not a footstep, not the sound of a voice. The four of them faced each other in the torch beam, and around them gold icons gleamed on the walls. There was so much gold it looked cheap, like handouts for a whiter-than-white campaign. Turton examined them in turn, he was the only one who seemed nervous. He listened with his head on one side, and then suddenly ran up the steps to the flagstone. Again he listened, but heard nothing. He came back to the group in the torchlight, and sat down with his gun across his knees. He looked at his watch. They'd been down there two minutes.

Then they'd been down there three hours. The torch was a faint yellow circle, and the icons just a tiny glow on the walls. Mitch lay full length on the cold stone floor, his raki bottle propped on his stomach. In his mind he must have felt another cloud shadow pass, because he sucked at the bottle neck. Next to him, Turton was breaking and closing the shotgun on his knees. He was out of cigarettes, and nearly out of control. Sheldon sat on a packing case, stroking the wicker cover of his wine bottle. And Sandy still held the torch. It flickered suddenly, and she switched it out.

"How long does it take to search an effing monastery, for Christ's sake?" Turton's voice echoed around them in the darkness.

"They've come a long way," Sheldon told him. "The monks have to give them a meal. It's their rule."

"Goat cheese and bloody oil. . . . Effing-bastard Greeks. How d'you know they haven't shopped us? How d'you know they haven't walled us up here on purpose? I mean you don't even speak their effing language."

"I was down here for three days in the war." Sheldon took a sip of wine. "Three days, and I got out."

"And I've never had to rely on effing foreigners before. Look, we can't even shift that effing stone!" he shouted suddenly.

"Steady on."

"Well, how d'you know they aren't on to us?"

"You've seen the newspapers," Sheldon said.

"Newspapers?"

"We're safe as long as everything stays normal. It's nearly the end of the yachting season. In a day or two Pierre'll bring his boat back from France. Nothing unusual in that. He picks me up on his way back to his villa at Rhodes. We go along the coast a little way and pick up the money. Couldn't be simpler."

"Like the police turning up here where we're meant to be safe?" Turton's shotgun snapped shut suddenly. His footsteps felt their way through the darkness toward Sheldon. "You keep Mitch stoned all the time. But I've got ears. I've heard you talking about this girl."

The captain let the silence last too long. "What girl?"

"That blonde who was on *Pindar*. What is it about her?"

"Nothing."

"What is it about her?" Turton's voice was loud as he shouted right into Sheldon's face.

"I knew her name . . . Claire, that's all." The captain replied slowly. "She used to be Pierre's girl once, a long time ago. There's nothing to connect her with us."

"Did she know you? Did she recognize you?"

"No."

"No, like the police turning up here," Turton said. "No connection."

"No," Sheldon said.

There were slow footsteps in the darkness. Then Turton's voice came from a different place. "Maybe it's time to get away," he said.

Sandy switched on the torch to find him.

The Radar Rating stood just beyond its flickering glow, with the shotgun held low in his hands. "I said maybe it's time to get away."

"Thought you didn't trust foreigners, Turton," Sheldon said curtly. "That's Crete out there. Mountains. How d'you think you're going to manage?"

"You can get me away. You said you had an escape route."

"After we've picked up the money. Everything stays normal until then."

Turton moved back into the faint circle of light. Suddenly he grabbed the torch from Sandy and swung it around onto Mitch. "What do you say?"

Mitch started trembling, a quivering pile of clothes on the floor, his baby face sucking the raki bottle dry.

Turton bent over him. "The police are here. Understand?"

"Police?" Mitch's voice hummed the word strangely across the bottle top.

"What are you going to do?" Turton insisted. "Get away from the police? Or stay here and wait for the money?"

Mitch tried to get up, but couldn't. "I never wanted no money," he sounded as if he were crying. "Just wanted to go back to Dunari."

"God help us," Turton said disgustedly. He pointed from Mitch to the captain. "I got a drunk on one side of me, a drunk on the other. So what the hell do I do?"

Sheldon saw Sandy signaling at him urgently from the shadows. He put down his wine bottle and waited until he'd found the right voice of authority. "Nobody leaves here!" he bellowed suddenly. "Nobody at all, until we've got the money! Is that understood?"

There was a sudden black stain on Mitch's trouser leg, the stink of urine.

Turton jerked away from him. Savagely he shook the

torch until its beam was stronger. Then he shone it full on Sheldon's face. "All right," he said at last. "If we get out of here and find the police gone, then I'll stay on with you. Understand. . . ." He leaned right over the captain. ". . . There isn't much in it. But when Mitch's sober, he keeps house for a bunch of nine bobs. And when you're sober, you're a bleeding Naval Commander." He switched off the torch and sat down.

Naval Commander. The words hung in the darkness.

In 1938 he'd been an employee of a fire-extinguisher firm, and a weekend sailor. Munich had changed all that. He'd joined the Navy early enough to have a good chance of promotion. And it wasn't until twelve years later, when he returned home, that he discovered he was a Naval Commander. He was shocked to find he had a mustache, a loud upper-class voice, and a sudden vicious temper. Shocked to find he was used to larger rooms and better food. Shirley had changed too. Someone else's wife, she was short of breath and had rough hands that pushed obstacles away, no longer tried to soften them. The children were frightened as he tripped over their fairy tales.

Then there was one evening he'd remember for the rest of his life. He came home early, and found a chain on the front door. He stood quite still, counted the pints of Bass he'd drunk and rang the bell. There were screams from the front room where his daughter was being toweled in front of the gas fire. Screams which got louder and louder as they came out into the hall and up the stairs. Sheldon realized his daughter hadn't said good night to him in a month. Once he'd smelled her hair and she'd clawed him. Now he stood outside the front door for more than an hour, and the tears from upstairs got no calmer. There was a letter in Sheldon's pocket—from Palma. Barney writing to say that MTB 859 was up for sale in the harbor. A few good seasons' chartering would pay for her. How did he feel? Sheldon worked out how he felt. Then he called himself a rotten stinking fucking bastard, and walked away from the chained front door.

Suddenly there was a noise the captain couldn't place. Then he realized it came from the stone flagstone, and a shaft of light was shining down into the crypt. The first person up the steps was Turton, and he had his loaded shotgun under his arm. He went past the monks in the chapel and out into the sudden sunlight. Running across to the archway, he saw the police car's dust cloud far below him in the valley. But he didn't put down his gun until he'd searched every room in the monastery.

Then it was evening, and Sheldon was surprised by the look on Turton's face. The man led him up to the bell tower and pointed out over the plain. The captain couldn't see anything in the long purple shadows, or on the far hills where villages still caught the light, like pigeon droppings on rocky ledges. Turton pointed again, and pushed a pair of binoculars into his hands. Then Sheldon saw the tiny figure lurching away through the shadows with a raki bottle. Mitch was nearly a third of the way toward the first village.

"You'll have to bring him back," Sheldon said slowly. "Take the van."

Two hours later, the old Opel returned in the darkness. Its headlights swung around to the arch of the courtyard, and lurched up and down as the brakes squealed. Shielding his eyes, Sheldon went past the lights, and saw that Turton was sitting behind the wheel, with his hands crossed inside his jacket. On the seat beside him there were two used cartridges, and there was a wet stain on the stock of the shotgun.

"Two. . . . I had to finish him off with the second." Turton didn't look up. His voice was a low scared whisper. "Accident. It was just an accident." He drew his hands out of his jacket, they were stiff with dry blood. "An old hammer gun, and he had to grab it. . . . I had to finish him off with the second."

41

In the dim refectory, Turton sat with his back to the pressure lamp. He'd washed his hands four times, but he still hid them under the lapels of his jacket. At the center of the long scrubbed table, Sandy sat alone. And at the far end, Sheldon whispered to Pappa Grigoris. The old monk got up, and laid a hand on the captain's shoulder before leaving. Sheldon finished the wine in his glass, and nodded at Sandy to follow him through the door to the kitchen.

He led her away through the shadows, over to the sink. There was dust on the wooden drain board, and the whole kitchen smelled unused, smelled of old washed wood and grease. There was no dignity in the squalid room, and no dignity in the woman who followed him. Sheldon was only sorry it had to come at night, when the wine was singing in his ears. Sorry he couldn't fit a good-by onto his leaden face.

"The man's come. I have to leave now," he said at last. "I'm meeting Pierre tomorrow night."

She didn't speak, didn't look up at him.

Quickly he loosened his trousers and shirt, then handed Sandy a thick money belt. There was no dignity in what he was doing to her. "Pierre didn't get all he paid for. I kept some of it back."

Sandy seemed dazed as she buckled the money belt below her sweater. "Why do I need it?"

"I don't want you to leave with Turton, that's all. I've worked you out a new route. Trust only Pappa Grigoris and whom he tells you to trust. He'll get you out tomorrow night."

"But why?" Sandy tried to get him to look at her. "Why change things?"

"Just Turton." Sheldon broke off suddenly as he heard footsteps coming up the stairs to the kitchen—slow, tired footsteps. "I'll meet you in Capetown in eight days' time," he added.

Now the footsteps creaked on the kitchen's wooden floor, and a huge old woman came toward them at the sink. Carrying a tin bowl, she came slowly, pausing, and gasping for breath. She wore a mountainous robe and cowl, once black, but now old and faded green. And her face seemed to be blue, with slack folds corded by veins. She stopped once again, sucking in air, and measuring the last two steps to the sink.

Sandy drew Sheldon out of her way. "You will be there, Alec? In Capetown?"

But Sheldon didn't hear her. He watched the old woman get to the sink. She leaned her body, then the bowl, on the stone coping, and waited to get her strength. Suddenly she raised the bowl over the coping, and it grated on the sink's rough stone. The captain stared at the blue-veined face. He knew that the woman wouldn't have her burden long, and he thought he knew what she was thinking—that the sound the bowl made on the stone sink was the same sound it would always make—placed there by any hand.

42

The sun beat down on Sheldon's head. And the wind up here on the ridge was thick with stinging dust, bringing him no relief. The ridge was very high—there were eagles below him—their huge shadows floating across the rocky screes. And still the guide's donkey climbed up toward the white-hot dome of the sky. Sheldon no longer knew whether he was awake or asleep. There was just this ridge, a curve of cracked red shale, swaying around in space. Then there was a different motion—they seemed to be going down. And the wind was stronger, its dust re-opening the wounds on Sheldon's face. He'd fallen many times. And the guide had been forced to rope him to his wooden saddle, and take away his demijohn of wine.

Rough hands suddenly held a water bottle to his lips. The water was warm, and tasted of metal. Then the man held the bottle upside down and showed that it was empty. He was an old man with a black cloth wound around his white hair. His face was stubbled gray and sweatless, and he'd drunk none of the water since they'd started out last night. Nor were there any traces of sweat on his faded shirt or baggy Cretan *vraches*, which ended just above his knees. His knees were bare and scarred, and the boots below them were made of pale *suède*, covered with the dust of the mountain.

Sheldon nodded his thanks. The man went back to his animal and slowly pushed himself up into the saddle with a stick. The stick smacked on the donkey's rump, the bridle of Sheldon's donkey jerked, and its hoofs stumbled on down the track. The man in front rode sidesaddle, slouched away from Sheldon and the wind. One foot hung nearly to the ground, the other was hooked forward against his creaking boat-shaped saddle. The captain's head sank lower. Now he could see only the animal's hindquarters, the crupper jerking the tail from left to right. And now he could see only the shadows on the ground. The donkey's shadow and the man's, sliding down over the rocks ahead of him.

When he awoke, he found himself in shadow. He saw they were going down a steep dry gully, with stones rattling away from the animals' hoofs. The gully looped on downward, getting darker and strangely chill. Then suddenly the shadows were green. There was the sound of rushing water, and branches overhead—branches of carob trees. They shaded a cleft in the mountain. And perched in this cleft, there was a tiny meadow, a square of luminous green. Its border was perfectly straight, and below it a small rock face dropped to a second flat meadow. Sheldon didn't believe his eyes. It was like a child's painting—the two square steps of green, and right in the center of the lower step, surrounded by a waterfall, was a white church.

The guide untied him from his donkey, and helped him over steppingstones toward the church. Then Sheldon saw the two square meadows were pools—man-made—damned with stones and mortar. Their green was moss and weed, clinging to the surface. And the church was on a concrete island in the lower pool. Between it and the cliff face there was a pile of mossy rocks, splashed by the waterfall from the upper meadow. Sheldon fell into the curtain of gleaming water. Its icy cold hit him like a sword, first his head and then his body. For the first time in his life he slaked his thirst.

The guide stooped, and delicately cupped his hand in the pool. He drank just once, and then he pointed back to the donkeys. But Sheldon stayed where he was on the moss-covered rocks, he didn't want to go on. Mist from the waterfall jeweled the branches above him. Sunlight and shadow fought over the flat green meadow, dappling the white church roof. The guide beckoned once again, beckoned Sheldon on down the mountain to Pierre and two million quid. And slowly Sheldon ducked back into the waterfall. Slowly the cold cut through to the core of his brain, cut back through thirty years, through the skins they'd piled onto a man called Sheldon.

The officer's voice. . . . There was the class thing that Barney had hated so much. The terrible understated language of the playing field they'd used as a defense against war. . . . Sheldon had adopted it very quickly, like the rest of them. His first raid had been with commandoes. The men who'd fought hand-to-hand with Germans in pajamas. Panting, like schoolkids at a dormitory feast, until the long-handled knives went in.

Then there was the temper. . . . That had begun at Alex., because of the crazy spares situation, the dangers of refueling from 44-gallon drums in the heat, and the constantly repeated signal—REGRET NO AIRCRAFT COVER AVAILABLE. Other MTB's had three enemies—the sea, mechanical failure, and the Axis. Sheldon had made bloody sure that 859 was only up against the Axis.

And the madness? . . . Because that's what it was, Operation Bandersnatch. For a long time people had been calling him mad, and he hadn't believed them. When had that begun?

Its roots had lain in silence. He'd never been able to talk about the war to anyone, never been able to unload it and relax. Until the madness had come out into the open —that night he'd heard his daughter screaming, and the door had been chained. Because after that he'd been able to talk. In bars, with bearded men, the war had come out strangely, a lie. They'd had to make it better than the gray world beyond the bar door. And suddenly, in a flood of booming words, Sheldon was at his least articulate. He needed the oily meniscus of drink and half-truths to cover up his disgust and failure. The war had become another thing, and he'd become another thing—a bar commander.

"*If you had it all to do over again, would you do it any different?*"

"*Aye, Wilfred, I would.*"

"*Don't give 'im the moony, Barney.*"

But he was going to give him the money. He was going to give him two million quid.

43

There was something wrong. Pierre wasn't whistling. Calm and neat in his shantung uniform, he sat behind the chromium wheel. The deep shadows under his eyes had come from bringing the cruiser singlehanded to Crete. He waited now until they were well clear of the shore, then he switched on the cockpit light. "Aren't you drinking?" he asked Sheldon in surprise.

"Given it up," the captain replied.

"Oh? I heard you were hitting it pretty hard at the monastery. And I heard something else from Pappa Grigoris."

Sheldon waited.

"That girl, Claire," Pierre said slowly. "From what Grigoris heard, she must have recognized you."

"She did." Sheldon's voice was as flat as the Frenchman's. "But she said she'd keep quiet. She hated the millionaires' guts. . . . And apparently she thought a lot of you."

"I thought a lot of her." Pierre looked straight ahead

through the windscreen. "But it just depends on what they think of her in Athens. You can't trust the newspapers."

"No," the captain said, "you can't."

"Well, I haven't heard a whisper about her anywhere, and we have to pick up that money now," Pierre shrugged. "It's lying on a six-fathom shelf, and the winter storms are coming on."

Sheldon left him, and went to sit on a cockpit seat. It smelled of leather, and the scent of summer women. This was the second night he'd stayed awake, and he couldn't believe in any of it. The cruiser was thudding flatly over the sea. But it wasn't sea. The twin walls of spray seemed solid in the cockpit light, and it was just as if they were ripping through a bolt of black-and-white-sided cloth.

In the dawn, Pierre throttled back, cursing the haze and the low cloud. He'd been forced to navigate by dead reckoning, and his face was drawn and angry as he looked out at the sea—slow-moving piles of quicksilver, which came at them through the mist.

"Give it half an hour," he said. "I'll go below and change."

Gradually the haze lifted from the water. Sheldon began to make out the two long gray islands on the beam, and the long strip of land ahead. Then he realized the land was Crete, shorn of its mountains by the cloud.

Pierre came on deck in a wet-suit, carrying a mask and air tanks. He glanced around at the horizon, and signaled Sheldon to start the engines.

For maybe twenty minutes, Sheldon juggled the cruiser in the straits between the islands, following Pierre's commands. The Frenchman lined them up between the two near rocky points, working all the time toward a cross bearing he got from the coast of Crete.

"That'll do." He went to the anchor winch on the foredeck, and nodded as the chain went out. "Six fathoms."

They swung on the anchor. Around them it was a flat calm, the water slow and treacly, bursting its bubbles under the cruiser's hull. A few shreds of haze still clung to the coast line, and then the cloud rolled back up the mountain, leaving the land gray and black below. Suddenly a dot drew clear of the sky line, moved along below the cloud. They heard the drone of an airplane engine.

Pierre followed the plane with glasses. It came no nearer, but kept above the shore, turning in lazy loops. Its wings flashed silver as it crossed a sudden path of sunlight in the clouds. "Yank." Pierre put the glasses down. "From the air base at Heraklion. Training flight."

He came back to the cockpit, and squatted on the wet planks. He tested the air tanks, and then Sheldon helped him clip them on.

Suddenly the roar of the plane was loud. They saw it coming low over the water, its silver reflection darting out like a tongue. The scream of its engine fell all around them as it passed. A two-seat trainer, with two men looking down. Then there was a strange plop. They saw a small plume of water a hundred yards away. And then a yellow stain, widening in a circle around the cruiser.

Pierre kept quite still. And when he spoke, his voice was almost conversational. "Dye marker. On target." Quickly he pulled on his underwater flippers, and reached for his mask. "There's two million pounds down there. And maybe half an hour before anyone can reach us." He went to the side, and lowered himself into the water.

Then they heard the plane again, its engine rising as it tipped up on one wing. A dark figure dropped from the rear cockpit. A parachute opened, came down slowly to the flat sea. They saw the figure was a frogman, with air tanks, before he hit the water.

And still Pierre's voice was conversational. "Using their brains. They're out of pistol range." Clinging to the cruiser's side, he looked up at Sheldon calmly. "There's a compressed-air gun under the bunk in my cabin. Get it, will you. And bring the Lüger for yourself."

Sheldon fetched them both. When he got back, Pierre's face was hidden by his mask and mouthpiece. He reached up for the harpoon gun, gripped it, and fell back into the sea. He turned over slowly and then his black shadow disappeared. There was just his footprints in the water, and a chain of bubbles moving slowly through the yellow sea that now surrounded the cruiser.

Sheldon still had the heavy Lüger in his hand. Its case was as large as a shotgun's, old buffed leather with a Gothic monogram. He unbuckled it, and unwrapped the long-barreled 9 mm. pistol from its oiled silk. Then he found the light metal Sten butt, and screwed it to the handle. The magazine was a foot-long curve of black tin that stuck out from the handle like a sickle when he'd fitted it. He cocked the gun and turned around. Suddenly he saw the second chain of bubbles coming through the yellow water toward the cruiser's stern.

Slowly they moved around the boat, an endless chain popping on the yellow surface. Then they stopped, quite close to the other bubbles by the anchor. The two chains circled warily, then closed. Suddenly a huge explosion welled up, a shriek-for-life breath, as a bottle was wrenched open far below. It tore a hole in the sea, hissed back in yellow spray. There was still one chain of bubbles left, and it got stronger, louder. . . . Then a black figure jerked up onto the surface. Pierre lay quite still with arms outstretched. The sea around him was empty.

Sheldon went to the foredeck, and started the anchor winch. He saw the five-fathom mark on the chain, then the three, two. . . . The motor raced, but the chain would come no farther. He looked over the bow, and saw the dripping rubber sack attached to the chain. The sack that contained £2 million. Then he looked around behind him—a weird sight. There was a black figure lying crookedly in its own red stain. Around the red, there was a wider yellow circle that held a white cruiser in its grasp. And beyond that, the sea was slow and gray. Sheldon threw the Lüger into the water. Then he reached down with a knife, and cut the waterproof sack away from the chain. He watched it sink beneath the surface.

The plane was a steady drone, almost a mile away. Sheldon was suddenly surprised to see the width of the morning. The haze had gone, and the sun was trying to break through thin white cloud. Then he saw what the plane was doing. Standing out from the coast of Crete, there were two gray warships. Destroyers, pencil-thin, with heavy bow waves. Sheldon watched in admiration for a moment. Then he pressed the starter.

A blinding gap between the clouds was turning the sea to metal. The chase was useless. The destroyers had one-and-a-half times the Monaco's speed. Their bow waves slackened slightly as they took up stations on each quarter, correct firing stations. Suddenly the sun was low between them, sullen in the winter sky. There was something of a stained-glass window in the scene. Gray sea, gray ships, hard against the light, their steady bow waves silver. Sheldon thought they were a moving sight.

"Heave-to. Stop Engines. Heave-to," the metal voice crackled, then came again across the water. "We will send a boarding party."

Sheldon turned back to the wheel. His hands stayed on the spokes, and left the throttles alone.

A sudden crack from behind him, a whistling noise he remembered, then a column of white water, far ahead over the bow.

"Heave-to. Stop Engines. Heave-to."

He turned back to the warships, a loud hailer in his hand. His voice was exactly as he wanted it: "Target's speed, eighteen knots." He glanced at the cruiser's compass. "Target's course, oh-seven-four . . . target's range. . . ." He measured the distance to the two destroyers. ". . . Eight hundred yards . . . fire as you bear.

The ones that whistled were the ones that missed. They all whistled, and the columns of water got nearer, closer together. One very near, the spray thundered on the windshield, the wheel spun in his hands. Then a crack. A shell that didn't whistle. Sheldon started the salute.